THE
SIXTEENTH-CENTURY ITALIAN
SCHOOLS

NATIONAL GALLERY CATALOGUES

THE
SIXTEENTH-CENTURY
ITALIAN SCHOOLS

BY

CECIL GOULD

The first series of major catalogues of the various Schools of Painting in the National Gallery Collection was launched in 1945. The series is now being extensively revised and the initial volumes of the second series, *The Dutch School* and *The Early Italian Schools*, are in preparation.

Meanwhile five of the original text volumes have been reprinted. Each has been reissued without alteration to the text, but a list of paintings in the relevant school acquired since the publication of the last edition is added as an appendix. For further details about these paintings the reader is referred to the *Illustrated General Catalogue* (2nd edition, 1987) and successive volumes of the *National Gallery Report*.

NATIONAL GALLERY CATALOGUES
First series reprints

The Earlier Italian Schools by Martin Davies
The Sixteenth-Century Italian Schools by Cecil Gould
The Seventeenth and Eighteenth Century Italian Schools
    by Michael Levey
The Flemish School 1600–1900 by Gregory Martin
The Early Netherlandish School by Martin Davies

National Gallery Publications
The National Gallery
London

Published by order of the Trustees

© The National Gallery 1975
Reprinted 1987

Note: this catalogue was first published in 1975 to combine the separate editions of *The Sixteenth-Century Venetian School* (1959) and *The Sixteenth-Century Italian Schools excluding the Venetian* (1962), both by Cecil Gould.

ISBN 0 947645 22 5

Printed and bound in Great Britain by
William Clowes Limited, Beccles and London

Cover
Titian, *Portrait of a Man* (detail)

NOTE

THE PRESENT CATALOGUE combines the separate editions of 1959 (the sixteenth-century Venetian School) and 1962 (the sixteenth-century Italian Schools, excluding the Venetian). It includes the few, but important, pictures of those schools which have been added to the collection since then, and it endeavours to take account of the relevant research which has been published during the same period. As anyone will know who has tried to revise earlier work of this kind, the new material does not always take kindly to the format of the old. A few entries have had to be re-written. In certain others some stitching may be apparent, though it is hoped not obtrusive. My debt to the colleagues and friends who helped me with the earlier editions, and whose names are mentioned in them, naturally remains unchanged. Since then Lady Dorothy Lygon of Christie's has clarified, but not published, a number of obscure early nineteenth-century provenances, of which I have had the benefit.

The references to the 1937 edition of the *Illustrations* have been retained, as many libraries must still possess copies. Reproductions of nearly all the pictures in question will also be found in the folio volume published in 1964 (*Sixteenth-Century Italian Schools*) and of all of them in the *Illustrated General Catalogue* (1973).

CECIL GOULD

This volume is one of a series produced under the editorship of the Director to replace the catalogue of 1929.

EXPLANATIONS

ABBREVIATIONS: As certain books and institutions are repeatedly referred to an abbreviated form is normally used, as follows:

Abbreviation	*Fuller Title*
Bartsch	Adam Bartsch: *Le Peintre Graveur*, 1803–
Berenson: *Lists* (with date)	Bernhard Berenson: *North Italian Painters of the Renaissance*, 1907. *The Florentine Painters of the Renaissance* (3rd ed., 1909). *The Central Italian Painters of the Renaissance* (2nd ed., 1909). *Italian Pictures of the Renaissance*, 1932. *Pitture Italiane del Rinascimento*, 1936. *Venetian School*, 1957. *Florentine School*, 1963. *Central Italian and North Italian Schools*, 1968.
Berenson (in the context of drawings)	*The Drawings of the Florentine Painters*, 1903 and 1938.
B.I.	British Institution.
Buchanan: *Memoirs*	W. Buchanan: *Memoirs of Painting*, 1824.
Fischel	Oskar Fischel: *Raphaels Zeichnungen*, 1913–. Also monograph (in English), 1948.
Hill	G. F. Hill: *A Corpus of Italian Medals of the Renaissance*, 1930.
Litta	(Conte Pompeo) Litta: *Famiglie Celebri di Italia*, 1819–
Lugt	F. Lugt: *Répertoire des catalogues de Vente*, 1938–
Morelli: *Munich and Dresden*	Giovanni Morelli: *Italian Painters, The Galleries of Munich and Dresden*, 1893.
Parker	K. T. Parker: *Catalogue of the Collection of Drawings in the Ashmolean Museum*, vol. II, Italian Schools, 1956.
Popham/Wilde	A. E. Popham and Johannes Wilde: *The Italian Drawings of the XV and XVI Centuries at Windsor Castle*, 1949.

Abbreviation	*Fuller Title*
Prussian *Jahrbuch*	*Jahrbuch der (Königlich) Preuszischen Kunstsammlungen*, Berlin.
R.A.	*Royal Academy.*
Redford	George Redford: *Art Sales*, 1888.
Ridolfi	*Le Maraviglie dell' Arte*, by Carlo Ridolfi, edited by Detlev, Freiherr von Hadeln, 1914–24.
Thieme-Becker	U. Thieme and F. Becker: *Allgemeines Lexikon der bildenden Künstler . . .*, 1907–
Vasari	*Le Vite de' più Eccellenti Pittori Scultori ed Architettori*, by Giorgio Vasari, edited by Gaetano Milanesi, 1878–
Venturi	Adolfo Venturi: *Storia dell' Arte Italiana*, 1901–
Vienna *Jahrbuch*	*Jahrbuch der Kunsthistorischen Sammlungen (des Allerhöchsten Kaiserhauses)*, Vienna.
Waagen	Dr Waagen: *Treasures of Art in Great Britain*, 1854. *Galleries and Cabinets of Art in Great Britain*, 1857.

ATTRIBUTIONS: No claim to completeness is made in listing the suggestions that may at one time or another have been published, but an attempt has been made to quote or discuss those for which serious evidence has been brought forward.

CONDITION: All pictures are on canvas and have been lined unless the contrary is stated. The brief notes on this subject which are included in the catalogue have no claim to be a comprehensive report on the picture's condition as this would normally require several pages to itself. They are meant rather to indicate (since this may not always be evident in normal Gallery lighting at a given time) which areas in each picture seem in a sufficiently reliable state to support art historical deductions. In the event of subsequent cleaning the notes may require modification.

DRAWINGS: In general only published drawings have been taken into account.

MEASUREMENTS: Unless the contrary is stated the dimensions given refer to the area of the original painted surface now visible—i.e. exclusive of bindings. In some cases the word 'circa' is used, since the two sides are often not of precisely the same dimensions, nor the top and the bottom.

Alessandro ALLORI
born 1535, died 1607

Florentine school. Brought up from an early age by the painter, Bronzino, whose pupil he became and whose name he subsequently took. Borghini (*Il Riposo*, 1584, pp. 623–4) says he went to Rome at the age of nineteen. He returned to Florence in 1560 and remained there, in the service of the Medici, for the rest of his life, actively engaged as portraitist, frescoist, religious painter and designer of tapestries. He was the father of the painter, Cristofano Allori.

Ascribed to Alessandro ALLORI

670 A KNIGHT OF S. STEFANO

Panel, 82½ × 47¾ (2·095 × 1·212).

Somewhat darkened at present, but condition appears fair for a picture of its size and age.

Variously catalogued as Pontormo,[1] Bronzino,[2] Bronzino School,[3] Salviati[4] and Jacopo da Empoli.[5] The attribution to Alessandro Allori has apparently not been suggested before. The combination displayed, however, of a Bronzinesque technique with a post-Bronzinesque type of portraiture would accord with Alessandro's practice, and there is some similarity of type between no. 670 and the full length, life size portrait of Francesco Datini at Prato (Palazzo Communale) attributed to him. Furthermore, the *trompe-l'œil* grisaille painting (or sculpture group) of the legs of a female and a child behind the sitter is similar to those in the background of Allori's *Cleopatra's Feast*,[6] while one of the *putti* in the foreground of that work resembles the one supporting the table in no. 670. Borghini (1584)[7] says 'infiniti sono i ritratti dipinti da Alessandro per Principi, Signori e gentilliuomini'. Few of these are now identifiable, but one, signed and dated 1580, appeared at auction in 1971.[8]

The military Order of S. Stefano was founded by Cosimo I de' Medici in 1561 and had its headquarters at Pisa.[9]

PROVENANCE: Presented by G. F. Watts, R.A., 1861.

REPRODUCTION: *Illustrations, Italian Schools*, 1927, p. 70.

REFERENCES: (1) Under which attribution presented. Catalogued as such in the editions of 1862–3. (2) In the catalogues of 1864–1906. (3) In the catalogues of 1911–29. (4) Note by J. P. Richter in the Gallery archives. (5) Suggestion by E. K. Waterhouse in the Gallery archives. (6) Florence, Palazzo Vecchio,

Studiolo of Francesco I; reproduced, after a fashion, in Venturi; *Storia . . .*, IX, VI, fig. 54. (7) *Riposo*, p. 628. (8) W. van Gelder sale, Sotheby's, 14th May, 1971 (18). *I Ricordi di Alessandro Allori* (ed. Supino, 1908) do not seem to contain an entry corresponding with no. 670 but only cover the years 1579–83. (9) Alessandro da Morrona: *Pisa Illustrata . . .*, III, 1793, p. 2.

BACCHIACCA
1495–1557

Florentine School. The date of his birth is sometimes given as 1494. But as it fell on 1st March of that year by Florentine reckoning (in which the New Year fell on 25th March) the correct date by modern reckoning is 1495.

The family name was Verdi (or Verde): his name was Francesco d'Ubertino, known as Bacchiacca. Vasari says he was a pupil of Perugino and a friend of Andrea del Sarto, who helped him. Vasari praises his small figures and his designs for tapestries. Among his existing works mentioned by Vasari are nos. 1218 and 1219 below and the predella (now in the Uffizi) from an altarpiece by Sogliani in S. Lorenzo, Florence. His style seems to some extent a throw-back to that of the *quattrocento*.

1218   THE HISTORY OF JOSEPH. I

Panel, $14\frac{1}{4} \times 56$ ($0 \cdot 36 \times 1 \cdot 42$).
Very good condition.

Three scenes are combined. On the left, Joseph's brethren (of whom the boy Benjamin, dressed throughout in blue, is on the extreme left) are shown bearing presents for Joseph from Jacob. In the centre they present the gifts to Joseph who stands in the doorway of a polygonal building. On the right the brethren are seen departing, with Benjamin on an ass in the middle. The text is Genesis xliii, 15 and xliv, 3.[1]

DRAWINGS: (1) Portion of cartoon (showing the group around Benjamin on the ass, right in no. 1218). Pricked for transfer. Christ Church, Oxford (B 28), Berenson 185. (2) Red chalk study for man (with a staff) standing to the left of the right hand column in no. 1218. Albertina S.R. 190, Berenson 189.

For commentary and Provenance see no. 1219 below.

REFERENCE: (1) In *Reale Galleria di Firenze* (series 1, vol. II, 1824, pp. 27–8) the subject is given as the brethren departing with gifts from Joseph to Jacob and orders to bring him to Egypt (i.e. Genesis xlv, 23). This cannot be correct as the brethren on the right of no. 1218 are clearly leaving Joseph and are carrying only corn, not presents.

1219   THE HISTORY OF JOSEPH.   II

Panel, $14\frac{1}{4} \times 55\frac{3}{4}$ ($0 \cdot 36 \times 1 \cdot 41$).
A few small losses of paint due to past flaking. General condition perhaps slightly inferior to that of no. 1218, but still good.

Two episodes in one. On the left the brethren are being brought back
to Joseph, with Benjamin, in whose sack Joseph's cup has been discovered, a prisoner. On the right they throw themselves on Joseph's
mercy (Genesis xliv, 13 and 14).

The two figures on the right appear to derive from two in the same
position in no. 1032 in this Gallery (*Agony in the Garden*, attr. Lo
Spagna) which is itself a *pastiche* of Perugino.

DRAWINGS: (1) Cartoon (in two halves) for entire picture. Pricked for transfer.
Louvre (1966 and 1967)[1] Berenson 186 and 187. (2) Study for Joseph. Uffizi
(350 F), Berenson 181. (3) Study for left hand figure of right hand group.
Albertina (S.R. 191), Berenson 189.

ENGRAVING: By C. Rancini in Rosini's *Storia della Pittura Italiana*, epoca
terza (1845), pl. CXXXIII.

This and no. 1218 are clearly from a *cassone* or *spalliera* in the famous
room decorated for Pier Francesco Borgherini (see entry for no. 1131,
Pontormo). The most specific (as regards nos. 1218–19) of Vasari's
references is in his biography of Aristotile da San Gallo (Milanesi
edition, vol. VI, p. 455): *Nella camera di Pier Francesco Borgherini, della
quale si è già tante volte fatto menzione, fece il Bacchiacca, in compagnia
degli altri, molte figurine ne' cassoni e nelle spalliere, che alla maniera sono
conosciute, come differenti dall' altre.* Four smaller pictures by Bacchiacca
(Rome, Borghese Gallery nos. 425, 427, 440, 442) are intimately
associated with nos. 1218 and 1219, in style and iconography alike, and
two of them, at least, must have decorated the same *cassone* or *cassoni*.

PROVENANCE: Pier Francesco Borgherini, then passed to the Gaddi collection
and thence, from the Marchesa Vittoria Pitti Gaddi, to her daughter, Signora
Luisa Nerli of Siena.[2] Sold to the Rev. John Sanford in 1834.[3] Exh. B.I., 1839
(2, 5) and 1848 (50, 54) lent Sanford. Mentioned by Waagen, 1857,[4] as in Lord
Methuen's collection (to whom they had passed by inheritance) who exhibited
them, R.A., 1877 (170, 176) and from whom purchased, Walker Fund, 1886.

REPRODUCTION: *Illustrations, Italian Schools*, 1937, p. 15.

REFERENCES: (1) Reproduced by Venturi, *Storia* . . ., vol. IX (I), figs. 349 and
350. (2) This information from *Reale Galleria di Firenze Illustrata* series 1, vol.
II (1824), p. 27. A translation is printed in the *Catalogue Raisonné* (1847) of the
collection of the Rev. John Sanford (p. 30). (3) Date from an account book of
Sanford's in the Barber Institute of Fine Arts, Birmingham University. Footnote 2 above gives them as still in the possession of Signora Nerli in 1824. They
are mentioned as belonging to Sanford in a letter of 1837 from George Augustus
Wallis, 'Professor of the first class of Painting of the Imperial and Royal
Academy of Florence' to a friend (MS. copy in the Gallery archives). They
are lots 6 and 7 in the Sanford sale, 1838, presumably bought in. (4) *Galleries
and Cabinets* . . ., pp. 397 f.

Ascribed to BACCHIACCA

1304 MARCUS CURTIUS

Panel, painted area 10 × 7⅝ (0·254 × 0·194).

Some fairly discreet retouching; but in general well preserved.
Pentimento in the hero's leg.

The horse's harness and trappings and the ornamentation of the armour are in gold paint.

Although acquired as early as 1860, not catalogued until the 1891 edition, having been on loan in the interval. Then and in succeeding editions as 'Umbrian School'. The identification with Marcus Curtius has always been queried but seems probably correct to the present writer.

This attribution to Bacchiacca was first made by Frizzoni[1] and has received substantial support.[2] Frizzoni based it on comparison with similarly rearing horses in Bacchiacca panels in the Uffizi. Resemblance to a drawing of Mucius Scaevola in the British Museum has also been pointed out.[3] Though Bacchiacca might indeed have been the author of no. 1304 the present writer is not entirely convinced that he was.

PROVENANCE: Conceivably identical with an entry in the 1627 Mantua inventory[4]: *piccolo con Quinto Curcio a cavallo che salta nella voragine*. Acquired with E. Beaucousin collection, Paris 1860. On loan to South Kensington Museum, 1862–89.

REPRODUCTION: *Illustrations, Italian Schools*, 1937, p. 369.

REFERENCES: (1) *Archivio Storico dell'Arte* 1895, pp. 103–5. (2) E.g. from Jacobsen (*Repertorium für Kunstwissenschaft*, 1901, p. 370), Berenson (*Lists* 1932 and 1936) and McComb (*Art Bulletin* VIII, 1925–6, p. 157). (3) Cf. Berenson, *Florentine Drawings* 2nd edition, fig. 932. Also from F. Abbate in *Paragone*, November 1965, p. 33 and pl. 20 (as 'Horatius ?'). (4) Note by E. K. Waterhouse in the Gallery archives.

Federico BAROCCIO
1535(?)–1612

He was from Urbino. Bellori (1672) says he was born in 1528.[1] This may be derived from Baglione (1642) who says that Baroccio was eighty-four when he died in 1612.[2] It was stated by Lazzari (1801),[3] confirmed by A. Venturi[4] and denied by H. Olsen[5] that the register of Baroccio's death also gives his age at the time as eighty-four. The diary of Francesco Maria II della Rovere and an epigraph by Bernardino Baldi, on the other hand, constitute contemporary evidence and both give 1535.[6] During the years 1560–63 Baroccio was in Rome. Bellori says he had also been there on a previous occasion. He had returned before 1567 and apart from visits to Perugia, Arezzo and Florence remianed at Urbino for the rest of his life, assailed, according to Bellori, by chronic ill health.

Bellori says Baroccio was a pupil of Battista Franco and then of his uncle, Bartolommeo Genga. It is not difficult to understand that the young Baroccio, as Bellori says, should have wished to emulate his great fellow-Urbinate, Raphael. But it is more difficult to account for the fact that Raphael's art left a less lasting mark on him than that of Correggio, and most difficult of all to trace how his influence was transmitted. Bellori says it was merely through drawings. Certainly there is no record of a visit by Baroccio to Parma, Modena, Reggio or Mantua, where Correggio's best work was then located.

Most of Baroccio's œuvre consists of oil paintings of religious subject. There are also some portraits. He had a considerable number of followers and was probably the most important Italian painter outside Venice around the third quarter of the sixteenth century.

REFERENCES: (1) *Le Vite de' Pittori Scultori et Architetti Moderni*, p. 171. (2) *Le Vite de' Pittori, Scultori ed Architetti*, p. 134. (3) *Delle Chiese di Urbino* p. 29. (4) *Storia* . . . IX, VII, p. 879. (5) *Federico Barocci*, 1955, p. 18, n. 1. (6) Olsen, *loc. cit.*

29 MADONNA AND CHILD WITH S. JOSEPH AND THE INFANT BAPTIST ('LA MADONNA DEL GATTO')

$44\frac{3}{8} \times 36\frac{1}{2}$ (1·127 × 0·927).

In the mid nineteenth century extensive cracking caused some concern and led, in 1855, to relining.[1] Traces of the cracking are still visible but on the whole the paint is well preserved. Some damage above and below the Madonna's left eye; also the draperies below her left knee (next to the hanging part of the table cloth). These, to judge from engravings and old photographs, have been incorrectly restored. Many *pentimenti*, notably in the Madonna's right hand, S. Joseph's left, the Christ Child's cheeks and the Baptist's legs. Cornelis Cort's engraving of this design is dated 1577 which is therefore the *terminus ad quem*. Cleaned, 1951.

Bellori describes this design as follows[2]:

> *Per questo Signore* [i.e. Conte Antonio Brancaleoni] *dipinse vo altro scherzo, la vergine sedente in una camera col Bambino in seno à qui addita un Gatto, che si lancia ad una Rondinella tenuta da San Giouannino legata in alto col filo, e dietro si appoggia San Giuseppe con la mano ad un tauolino, e si fà auanti per vedere.*

Bellori's specification that the scene takes place 'in una camera' more or less rules out the version from the Corsini palace, Rome, which has a landscape background. No. 29 and a version at Chantilly are almost identical and the history of neither is complete. No. 29 is first recorded at Perugia (Orsini, 1784).[3] Bellori's picture was for Conte Antonio Brancaleoni who had a castle at Piobbico (some thirty-five miles north of Perugia).[4] Though there would thus be no difficulty in assuming identity between no. 29 and the picture mentioned by Bellori no means of establishing it has yet been found.[5] Nevertheless, no. 29 is clearly for the most part autograph Baroccio. In this connection the various *pentimenti* may be noted—in particular that of the big finger of the Madonna's right hand, which was originally considerably nearer the outstretched index finger. Judging from comparable *pentimenti* in one of the preliminary sketches (see DRAWINGS below) this feature was a source of prolonged difficulty to the painter. The fact that no such *pentimenti* are apparent in the Chantilly picture would appear to tip the scale decisively in favour of no. 29's being the original and the Chantilly version a repetition.

VERSIONS: Chantilly, Musée Condé and Rome, Galleria Nazionale (from Palazzo Corsini) (these two discussed above). Many old copies exist—e.g. in the Ambrosiana, Milan, Galleria Estense, Modena, Ascoli Piceno Pinacoteca and elsewhere.[6]

DRAWINGS: Filippo di Pietro: *Disegni Sconosciuti . . . di Federico Baroccio negli Uffizi*, 1913, pp. 26–34. Two drawings reproduced (Uffizi 11635 and 11593) containing sketches for the Madonna's right hand (*pentimenti* in the fingers) and for S. Giovannino's right arm. The author also mentions another sheet (Uffizi 11583) likewise for the Virgin's right hand and said to be almost identical with Uffizi 11593. Two studies at Windsor for the Virgin's head (Popham and Wilde 94 and 95). H. Olsen (*Federico Barocci*, 1955, p. 124) catalogues many other drawings but does not reproduce them.

ENGRAVINGS: By C. Cort (1577) (in reverse) and by N. Lauwers. Also, in *The British Gallery of Pictures*, by A. Cardon (book dated 1818 but this engraving dated 1810).

PROVENANCE: Palazzo Cesarei, Perugia, 1784.[3] Offered to Irvine in Italy in 1805 and later acquired by Buchanan.[7] Brought to England in 1807[8] and already owned in that year by the Rev. W. Holwell Carr, since he lent it then to the British Institution 'for the use of the students in the School of Painting'.[9] Exh. B.I., 1821 (81) (lent Carr). Bequeathed by the Rev. W. Holwell Carr, 1831.

REPRODUCTION: *Illustrations, Italian Schools*, 1937, p. 18.

REFERENCES: (1) Notes in the Minutes of the Gallery Board meetings at the time. The Samuel Rogers sale catalogue (fifth day, 2nd May, 1856, lot 621) says, à propos another version of the design: 'It was lent to Palmaroni for some months to assist him when repairing Mr Carr's picture of the same subject, now in the National Gallery'. (2) *Le Vite de' Pittori, Scultori et Architetti Moderni*, 1672, p. 193 (3) *Guida . . . per . . . Perugia*, pp. 242–3. (4) The version of the *Rest on the Flight* which was, according to Bellori, also painted for Conte Antonio is now in the church of S. Stefano at Piobbico (Olsen: *Federico Barocci*, 1955, p. 121). (5) The Chantilly picture when compared with no. 29 appears somewhat truncated particularly on the left side. It also shows a different pattern on the floor. (6) Olsen (*op. cit.*, p. 124) lists further copies. (7) Buchanan: *Memoirs*, II, p. 166. (8) *The British Gallery of Pictures* (letter press connecting with Cardon's engraving). This specifies that it was from the Palazzo Cesarei. (9) Thomas Smith: *Recollections of the British Institution*, 1860, p. 40.

After BAROCCIO

29A MADONNA AND CHILD WITH S. JOSEPH AND THE INFANT BAPTIST ('LA MADONNA DEL GATTO')

$11\frac{1}{2} \times 9\frac{1}{8}$ (0·293 × 0·232).
Black and red chalk drawing. Squared. On paper.
Reduced scale copy of no. 29.

REPRODUCTION: Negative in the Gallery's possession.

PROVENANCE: Bequeathed by Miss Ada C. Lance, 1954.

Fra BARTOLOMMEO
1472(?)–1517

Florentine School. His name was Bartolommeo (or Baccio) di Paolo (or Pagholo) del Fattorino, known as Baccio della Porta, from the house (at the Porta a San Piero Gattolini, Florence) where he lived at an early period of his life. The evidence for the date of his birth is conflicting. A baptismal entry, discovered by Knapp,[1] gives it as 28th March, 1472, but Bartolommeo's father, in his *catasto* declaration of 1480 (according to Milanesi 1481)[2] states his age as six. But mistakes of this kind are not unknown in Renaissance *catasto* declarations and if, as seems likely, the baptismal entry concerns the right person, its authority must be final.

Pupil according to Vasari, of Cosimo Rosselli. During the 'nineties of the fifteenth century he came under the influence of the preaching of Savonarola and in 1500 entered the monastery of San Domenico at Prato as a novice, taking his vows the following year and returning to Florence as Fra Bartolommeo di San Marco. His activity as a painter was thus interrupted but was started again in 1504 and continued for the rest of his life. At different periods he ran a joint studio with Mariotto Albertinelli. In the spring and early summer of 1508 he was in Venice, and later, according to Vasari, he visited Rome.

REFERENCES: **(1)** Fritz Knapp: *Fra Bartolommeo della Porta* (1903), pp. 8–9. **(2)** Milanesi's edition of Vasari, vol. IV, p. 206.

3914 THE VIRGIN ADORING THE CHILD, WITH S. JOSEPH

Wood, $54\frac{1}{4} \times 41\frac{1}{4}$ ($1 \cdot 38 \times 1 \cdot 05$). Probably slightly cut on the right.[1]

General condition appears fairly good; the noticeable repaint is mainly along the cracks in the flesh areas. The ground shows through in places in S. Joseph's flesh. *Pentimenti* in Joseph's right sleeve and along most of the upper outline of the Child's body, particularly His left arm. Slight indications of preliminary drawing for two small figures in the background, to the left of, and slightly below, the finished woman and child. Cleaned, 1967–8.

In the background, right, the Infant S. John.

Two similar pictures are known—in the collection of the Marchese Carlo Visconti Venosta, Rome[2] and in the Borghese Gallery, Rome (no. 2).[3] Both incorporate the most characteristic motive of no. 3914—the Madonna crossing her hands on her breast—but differ in some other respects. The Borghese picture appears to have been executed by Albertinelli, but on Fra Bartolommeo's design, as the Child is almost identical with that in no. 3914 and the Madonna very similar. If, as seems likely, Albertinelli made use, in his picture, of Fra Bartolommeo's cartoon for no. 3914,[4] he seems to have adhered to it in some respects more closely than Fra Bartolommeo himself, since the Child's left arm in the Borghese picture appears to follow the original rather than the altered form of that in no. 3914. The Borghese picture is dated 1511 and

in the circumstances it seems likely that no. 3914 would have been somewhat earlier.

COPIES: Apparently an old copy in the possession, in 1930, of the Rev. J.
Shine of Dublin,[5] later acquired by the National Gallery of Ireland. Another was
lot 42 in the Wegg sale, Brussels, 11th May, 1925.

DRAWINGS: Louvre (Berenson, *Drawings*, no. 502). Sketch perhaps connected
with no. 3914, but with the Infant S. John playing with the Christ Child in the
foreground. Uffizi (Berenson, *Drawings*, no. 285). Study of the Infant S. John
very similar to that in the background of no. 3914. Formerly private collection,
Milan, head of a man. Perhaps connected with S. Joseph in no. 3914.[6] Formerly
Wilton, Earl of Pembroke (sold Sotheby's, July 1917, no. 400). According to
Berenson (*Drawings*, no. 1837) a copy by Fra Paolino of no. 3914. Other drawings doubtfully connected with no. 3914 are catalogued in Hans von der
Gabelentz: *Fra Bartolommeo und die Florentiner Renaissance*, 1922, I, p. 151
and II, p. 178.

ENGRAVING: By Engelhart in Forster's *British Gallery of Engravings*. The first
part of this book appeared in 1807, but this particular engraving is dated 1812.[7]

PROVENANCE: Purchased by Sir Richard Colt Hoare, probably in Italy at the
end of the eighteenth century.[8] Exh. R.A. 1870 (135), lent by Sir Henry Hoare.
Lot 57 in Sir Henry Hoare sale, Christie's, 2nd June, 1883, bought Lesser.
Bought 1885 by Ludwig Mond, having in the meantime belonged to Sir J.C.
Robinson.[9] Exh. R.A. 1891 (101), New Gallery 1893–4 (239) lent Ludwig
Mond. Mond Bequest 1924.

REPRODUCTION: *Illustrations, Italian Schools*, 1937, p. 19.

REFERENCES: (1) The engraving in Forster's *British Gallery of Engravings*
(1812) suggests that the cutting may have taken place since then. (2) The
cartoon for this picture is in the Uffizi (Berenson, *Drawings*, no. 315). Picture
and cartoon reproduced by A. Venturi (*Storia*, IX, I, pp. 283–4). (3) No. 310,
p. 157, in the catalogue (by A. Venturi) of 1893. (4) Berenson (*Lists*, 1936)
states positively that a cartoon by Fra Bartolommeo was used. (5) Photograph in
the Gallery archives. This picture was published as the original by Knapp
(*Pantheon*, 1930, p. 37). (6) Published by Frizzoni, *Rassegna d'Arte*. 1911, pp.
43–8, where the reproduction of the drawing is mis-labelled as belonging to
Mond. (7) Forster identifies no. 3914 with a picture described by Giovanni
Cinelli (*Le Bellezze dela Citta di Firenze*, 1677, p. 565) in the house of the Abbate
Francesco and Angelo Doni: *Una Madonna con S. Giuseppe, Giesù, e S. Gio:
di Fra Bartolommeo, bellissima dipinta nel* 1516. This description in fact probably
refers to the Palazzo Barberini picture (see entry for no. 1694) which, unlike
no. 3914, includes S. John among the principal figures and bears the date 1516.
(8) Mentioned in the latter's description of Stourhead in vol. 1 (1822) of his
History of Modern Wiltshire. His initials against it show that it was one of his
own purchases. Also mentioned on p. 276 of vol. XV (part II) of Britton's
Beauties of England and Wales (1814). (9) Information in J.P. Richter's catalogue
of the Mond collection.

Ascribed to FRA BARTOLOMMEO

1694 THE MADONNA AND CHILD WITH S. JOHN

Canvas transferred from wood. 34¾ × 28 (0·88 × 0·71).

Fairly extensive local damage, perhaps occasioned by the transfer to
canvas. Some modelling seems missing from various flesh areas and the

under-drawing is visible in S. John's right foot. *Pentimento* in Madonna's right hand.

Its present condition makes it difficult to attempt a decision whether it is autograph or a studio production. The fact that there are two signed variants (Corsini, and formerly Cook collection—see VERSIONS below) both with extra figures indicates that Fra Bartolommeo experimented with this particular design and therefore a third autograph version would not be inconceivable. The fact that there is a *pentimento* in the Madonna's right hand in no. 1694 and that this hand is different in the Cook version, constitutes, if anything, evidence on the credit side of no. 1694. The town in the background is virtually a repetition of that in Fra Bartolommeo's 'Vision of St Bernard' (Florence, Accademia).

The motive of the two holy children embracing derives from a design by Leonardo of which there is a studio sketch copy at Windsor (no. 12,564) and numerous (mainly Flemish) painted variants (e.g. Chatsworth, Naples, etc.).[1]

VERSIONS: A somewhat superior version (signed and dated 1516 and with the addition of S. Elizabeth) was in the Cook collection, Richmond, another (with S. Elizabeth and S. Joseph) is in the Pitti. A version or copy with the Madonna and the two children alone belonged, in 1931, to Gunnar Kassman of Stockholm.[2] A related composition with S. Elizabeth and S. Joseph belonged, apparently in the mid nineteenth century, to Giuseppe Volpini of Florence.[3] Another with the same figures but differently arranged is in the National Gallery of Art, Washington attributed to Fra Bartolommeo and Fra Paolino. A version in reverse (signed and dated 1516, with S. Joseph) is in the Galleria Nazionale, Rome (Barberini) and a copy of it at the Musée Fabre, Montpellier.

DRAWINGS: Uffizi (Berenson, *Drawings*, nos. 1775 and 1787). Two drawings attributed by Berenson to Fra Paolino after the Corsini and Cook versions respectively.

PROVENANCE: Purchased, Lewis Fund, 1900, from Cavaliere Nicola Landolfi, Rome, through Conte Cozza Luzi. The former stated that the picture had been bought by a member of his family around 1820 from the collection of the Duke of Lucca.[4]

REPRODUCTION: *Illustrations, Italian Schools*, 1937, p. 19.

REFERENCES: (1) Cf. Glück in *Pantheon*, 1928, p. 502. (2) Photograph in the Gallery archives. (3) Engraving and description in the Gallery library. (4) Letter in the Gallery archives.

BARTOLOMMEO VENETO
active 1502, still active 1546

A shadowy figure, not mentioned by Vasari or Ridolfi. His usual form of signature on pictures is 'Bartolommeo' (various spellings), 'Venetus' or 'de Venetia' but the earliest example (1502) is in the unique form 'Bortolamio mezo venizian e mezo cremonexe' (picture formerly in the Donà dalle Rose collection).[1] A 'Bartolomeo da Venezia, pittore', mentioned several times in contemporary documents as engaged, between 1505 and 1508, on decorative and other work in the apartments of Lucrezia Borgia and elsewhere at Ferrara,[2] is usually identified with the author of the signed pictures already referred to. Nevertheless there is a possibility of confusion, since another painter by the name of Bartolomeo da Venezia had been active at Ferrara since at least 1473 and is described as son of 'fu Filippo, cittadino ferrarese'.[3] Some measure of confirmation, however, of the traditional view—that the Bartolommeo Veneto of the signed pictures was active for a time at Ferrara early in the sixteenth century—may perhaps be provided by the Ferrarese element in the costume of no. 2507 below.[4]

Periods in Bergamo and also in Milan have likewise been postulated in respect of the artist of the signed pictures, but though these would not be impossible there is no firm evidence in their favour. The signed works of 1502-6 are religious pictures which are little more than pastiches of Giovanni Bellini. Thereafter Bartolommeo seems to have specialized in fashionable portraiture of which a number of signed examples survive. Of these, one in the Rosebery collection bears the date 1530, and this year was hitherto the last definite date in his career. But since it has been established that the same date formerly read on no. 287 of this Gallery should in fact be read as 1546 his active career must henceforth be extended accordingly.

REFERENCES: (1) Inscription and date noted by the present writer (anon-sale, Sotheby's, 9th December, 1959, 59). The name was misread and the date inaccurately given as 1503 by André De Hevesy (*Art Quarterly*, vol. II, 1939, p. 233), where the picture was also erroneously said to be in the Museo Correr. (2) Documents published by A. Venturi: *Archivio Storico dell' Arte*, vol. VII, 1894, pp. 297-8. (3) L. N. Cittadella: *Notizie Relative a Ferrara*, 1864, pp. 579 and 596, and *Documenti ed Illustrazioni risguardanti la Storia Artistica Ferrarese*, 1868, p. 146. (4) See also: Giacomo Bargellesi: *Bartolomeo Veneto. Il Ritratto della Beata Beatrice Estense e Lucrezia Borgia*, 1943, *passim*.

287 PORTRAIT OF LUDOVICO MARTINENGO

Panel, $41\frac{1}{2} \times 28$ (1.055×0.71).

The face and right hand somewhat retouched. The most conspicuous areas of the dress—the sleeve projecting from the coat and the three rows of satin on the latter—are well preserved. The red of the coat, the waistcoat and, to a lesser extent, the dark background to the left of the curtain are very worn and retouched.

The *cartellino* has suffered damage in a number of places. Original letters remaining are as follows:

– V (only lower half of letter remains) D O (right half) V I | – V M (left half) | M (left half) A (upper half) R T (upper half) | A (left half) T A – – S | S V Æ | A N – – | B – – T O L – (probably small o above the line) M | V (left half) – N (right half) E T V S | F A C I E B A T | M.D.XXX | X V I I (or Z) V N

This had been restored to read as follows:

LVDOVI | CVM | MARTI | –TATIS | SVÆ | ANN– | BARTOL– M|
VENETVS | FACIEBAT | M.D XXX | XVI I (or Z) VN

The fact that the picture came from the Martinengo family is a fairly reliable indication that the fragmentary letters remaining of the sitter's name originally spelt Ludovico Martinengo. Enough, likewise, remains of the signature to leave no doubt of its having been that of Bartolommeo Veneto. The date has hitherto been read as 1530, 16th June, but the sitter's costume (which clearly marks the height of fashion) would absolutely exclude so early a date.[1] There can thus be no reasonable doubt that the date is really 1546, June—with which date the costume accords well. The space available to be occupied by the *cartellino* evidently dictated a narrow format for the latter in which there was no room for all the letters MDXXXXVI on the same line. As explained in the biographical notes on Bartolommeo Veneto this new reading extends the period of his working career by sixteen years.

The suggestion made in the National Gallery Report of 1856, that the sitter is wearing the dress of the *Compagnia della Calza* is untenable, since he is not shown wearing the distinguishing badge.[2] Even without the remains of the signature no. 287 would be immediately recognisable as a characteristic work of Bartolommeo Veneto. The motive, in particular, of the curtain looped over a rod is also found in the Dresden *Salome* and in a female portrait formerly in the Contini Bonacossi collection.

PROVENANCE: Purchased in Venice, 1855, from the representatives of Conte Girolamo Michiel Pisani, heir of Conte Girolamo Martinengo.

REPRODUCTION: *Illustrations, Italian Schools*, 1937, p. 377.

REFERENCES: (1) Notes by Stella Mary Pearce in the Gallery archives. The distinguishing features of the fashion as shown include the small hat and the short coat. These features recur in the costume of the smart young men in Niccolò dell' Abate's frescoes of 1547–51 in the university at Bologna where the costume in general is closely comparable with that in no. 287. Many other parallels among dated pictures could also be quoted. Research by Dr. Camillo Boselli, kindly communicated by Professor Creighton Gilbert, reveals two men called Ludovico Martinengo, born respectively in 1506 and 1509. Either of these would have looked, in 1546, older than the sitter of no. 287, which may therefore represent an unrecorded member of the family, or, just possibly, be a posthumous portrait. (2) A reference was made to the illustration facing p. 50 of Cesare Vecellio's *Habiti Antichi et Moderni* (1589), but such resemblance as there is is purely superficial.

2507 PORTRAIT OF A LADY

Panel, 22 × 17¼ (0·55 × 0·44).

Thin, and retouched in many places. A biggish patch of repaint, in particular, on her left shoulder.

The beads worn by the lady are ornamented with the emblems of the Passion. One of them is inscribed SAP.

The somewhat unsatisfactory appearance of the picture is probably due in great part to the messy remains of old varnish and engrained dirt. Datable to the early years of the sixteenth century from the costume, which bears a strong resemblance to some in frescoes in

Palazzo Costabili, Ferrara.[1] A Ferrarese origin seems therefore probable. A certain divergence, which no. 2507 seems to show, from Bartolommeo Veneto's normal style in portraiture could be explicable on the grounds of its being a relatively early work.

VERSION: Rouen, copy on canvas, 0·49 × 0·38.[2]

PROVENANCE: From the collection of Conte Alessandro Castellani.[3] Salting Bequest, 1910.

REPRODUCTION: *Illustrations, Italian Schools*, 1937, p. 378.

REFERENCES: (1) Reproduced in A. Venturi: *Storia* . . ., VII, III, pl. 849–55, particularly pl. 850. (2) Letter in the Gallery achives from the Director of the Rouen museums. (3) Salting MS. in the Gallery archives.

JACOPO BASSANO
active *c.* 1535, died 1592

His name was Jacopo dal Ponte, called Jacopo Bassano from his home city of that name. His father, Francesco I, was also a painter. A census of 1561 gives his age as 45; another, of 1589, as 70.[1] Ridolfi says he was born in 1510[2] and Borghini that 'hoggi' he was 66 years old.[3] There is no reliable guide to which, if any, of these four birth dates (1510, 1516, 1519 and *c.* 1518) is correct. Of his earlier works, Verci mentions a picture as dated 1531, but it is no longer identifiable; also a further painting which he says was dated 1534.[4] The latter work—*Flight into Egypt* (Bassano, Museo Civico, from the church of S. Girolamo)—is not dated now. The earliest surviving approximately datable paintings are, in fact, three oblong religious pictures from the Sala dell' Udienza of the Palazzo Pretorio, Bassano. In one of these—*Shadrach, Meshach and Abednego in the Fiery Furnace*—the Navagier arms are displayed, and since Luca Navagier was *Podestà* of Bassano from October, 1534 to February, 1536[5] it can be deduced that the pictures were probably commissioned during that period.

In addition to training which he would have received from his father Jacopo probably had some in Venice where, in 1535, he was given a patent for an invention.[6] Ridolfi says that according to one version he was a pupil of Bonifazio for a short time. Early paintings such as the three already mentioned would bear this out, as showing marked influence of Bonifazio. The influence of Lotto is also strong. Nevertheless, even in his early work Jacopo shows an individual style which at this period was rustic in character and relatively primitive. Later his art was refined by the influence of engravings after Raphael and, more particularly, by that of Parmigianino's etchings.

Despite the scarcity of dated pictures it is certain that Jacopo's art continued to evolve until an unusually late period of his life. Though a letter of 1581 from Jacopo's son, Francesco Bassano, was formerly interpreted to mean that Jacopo had virtually retired by that date, recent research has established the likelihood that he continued to paint a certain amount himself until the end, or nearly, of his lifetime.[7] The later style, though extremely original, in outlook, design and technique alike, was able to be canalised into the work of Jacopo's sons, whose activities both as collaborators during their father's old age and later as plagiarists have contributed to obscuring his achievement.

Both Vasari[8] and Borghini,[9] each of whom was writing within Jacopo's life-time, draw attention to his excellence as a painter of animals.

REFERENCES: (1) For both documents see *Bollettino del Museo Civico di Bassano*, II (1905), pp. 67 and 104, note. (2) Ridolfi/Hadeln, I (1914), p. 385. (3) *Il Riposo*, 1584, p. 563. (4) Giambatista Verci: *Notizie . . . della Città di Bassano*, 1775, p. 86 and 79. (5) Ridolfi/Hadeln, *op. cit.*, p. 388, note 8. (6) W. Arslan: *I Bassano*, 1931, p. 46. (7) See A. Ballarin (*Chirurgia Bassanesca*) and W. R. Rearick (*Jacopo Bassano's Last Paintings: The Baptism of Christ*) in *Arte Veneta*, 1966 and 1967 respectively. (8) Ed. Milanesi, VII, p. 455. (9) *Loc. cit.*

228 THE PURIFICATION OF THE TEMPLE

$62\frac{1}{2} \times 104\frac{1}{2}$ ($1 \cdot 587 \times 2 \cdot 65$).

In general in very fair condition.

The youth, top right, was probably an after-thought. His right arm is painted on top of the pillar which he holds and his head on top of the moulding over the door. Good condition apart from some wearing. Cleaned 1962.

The figures left and right appear truncated: some cutting is probable.

Probably an autograph work of Jacopo Bassano dating from the last decade of his life, in the 1580's.[1] Closely related to another version of the subject, of more upright format, known in several replicas, e.g. Lille (signed Leandro), formerly Sambon collection (signed Francesco), Doria, Prado (no. 27) Vienna and elsewhere. The prototype of this latter composition may date from before no. 228,[2] and a third type (Prado no. 28) is likely to be earlier still.

The money-changer seated on the right at the table has been thought to be a portrait of Titian. While the context would conform with his widespread reputation for avarice, the likeness is in fact non-committal and is a facial type which occurs frequently in Jacopo's late works.[3]

VERSIONS: See above. Several pictures of this subject are recorded in the inventory of Jacopo's pictures made after his death.[4] Distant derivatives are in the Museo Correr, Venice and Palazzo Spada, Rome.[5] Pictures of this description recorded in the collection of the Earl of Arundel,[6] in Palazzo Raggi, Genoa,[7] the Lansdowne sale, 2nd day, 20th March, 1806 (26) and the James Cooke sale, 2nd day, 27th February, 1813 (42).

PROVENANCE: Presented, 1853, by Philip L. Hinds. At a sale (Christie's, 11th June, 1870) of pictures belonging to the latter, two (nos. 81 and 96) are specified as from the collection of the Earl of Shaftesbury and are thus identifiable with lots 37 and 56 in the Earl of Shaftesbury's sale, Christie's, 15th May, 1852. The fact that both pictures were bought at the Shaftesbury sale by Hickman, who also bought lot 48[8] ('Giacomo Bassano. Christ driving the money changers from the Temple. *A grand gallery picture*'), is a good indication that the latter was identical with no. 228. Stated in the National Gallery catalogue of 1859 to have been 'brought to England by Mr A. Wilson in 1806' and therefore perhaps identifiable with lot 22, Andrew Wilson sale (by Peter Coxe), 6th May, 1807, in the catalogue of which stated to have been bought at Leghorn.

REPRODUCTION: *Illustrations, Italian Schools*, 1937, p. 23.

REFERENCES: (1) This has become clearer since the re-reading of a date—1585 —on the *Susannah* (Nîmes) which is very similar in handling, and bears Jacopo's initials. Previously (W. Arslan, *passim*) Gerolamo had been suggested. (2) See A. Ballarin in *Arte Veneta*, XX, 1966, p. 112. (3) Examples are the most prominent member of the congregation in the *Paul Preaching* (Marostica), the bearers at Christ's head in the *Entombment* and *Deposition* (Padua, S. Maria in Vanzo and Lansdowne collection) and several figures in the *Gloria* (Bassano, Museo Civico). (4) See Giambatista Verci: *Notizie Intorno . . . alle Opere . . . della Città di Bassano*, 1775, pp. 92–100, nos, 34, 96 and 187. (5) The Palazzo Spada picture was, in 1957, hanging in the private rooms on the *piano nobile* and not in the Gallery. It does not figure in F. Zeri's catalogue of the latter. (6) Mentioned by Ridolfi (Ridolfi/Hadeln I, p. 399) and figuring in the 1655 Arundel inventory (Mary F. S. Hervey: *Thomas Howard, Earl of Arundel*, 1921, p. 475). (7) Ratti's guide to Genoa of 1780, p. 236. (8) Marked copy of the sale catalogue in the Gallery library.

277 THE GOOD SAMARITAN

$40 \times 31\frac{1}{4}$ ($1 \cdot 015 \times 0 \cdot 794$).
Probably cut down on all four sides.

The sky damaged in many places by flaking. Other flaking damages elsewhere, but less extensive. Cleaned, 1968.

The priest and the Levite are shown in the middle distance, left. In the background, the city of Bassano.

Attributed by Waagen to Francesco Bassano.[1] Otherwise the attribution to Jacopo has been general and is acceptable as a middle-period work.

VERSIONS: Two pictures, variants of each other rather than of no. 277 and both apparently earlier than it—Hampton Court (ex-coll. Charles I—oblong) and Rome, Capitoline (upright)[2]—show a different moment in the story; the Samaritan is not carrying the man to his ass but binding his wounds. Derivatives of these pictures are at Vienna (no. 283 and in the 1907 catalogue) and Berlin (no. 314 in the 1931 catalogue). A picture of this subject is listed on pp. 116–17 of the 1734 catalogue of the collection of Cardinal Tommaso Ruffo at Ferrara. In 1965 (*Burlington Magazine*, CVII, p. 606 and *Arte Veneta*, XIX p. 65) attention was drawn to an unfinished version recently discovered at Prague. A later copy, larger than no. 277 and with a groom added, is at Chatsworth.

DRAWING: London, Courtauld Institute (Witt Collection). No. 2235. Black chalk sketch of the two main figures and the ass. Oblong format, extensively retouched.

ENGRAVING: No. 277 (or a hypothetical identical replica) engraved as no. 34 in P. Monaco: *Raccolta di Cento e Dodeci Quadri . . .*, Venice, 1772.

PROVENANCE: No. 54 in the sale (18th May, 1821) of pictures in the estate of the Dowager Marchioness of Thomond, niece and heiress of Sir Joshua Reynolds. Therefore identifiable with lot 36 in the Reynolds sale of 9th May, 1798 and with lot 48 in the Reynolds sale of 17th March, 1795 (catalogue dated 8th March, 1794)—presumably bought in on both occasions. On the strength of the engraving in Monaco's *Raccolta* (see ENGRAVING above) almost certainly identical with the picture in the Pisani collection in the eighteenth century.[3] Bought at the Thomond sale by 'Mr Rogers' (Henry Rogers)[4] by whom exhibited, B.I., 1823 (142).[5] Henry Rogers apparently bequeathed his pictures to his brother, Samuel Rogers, at whose sale (3rd May, 1856) purchased (lot 709).

REPRODUCTION: *Illustrations, Italian Schools*, 1937, p. 23.

REFERENCES: (1) *Treasures* . . ., vol. II, p. 77. (2) Reproduced by W. Arslan: *Contributo a Jacopo Bassano* in *Pinacoteca*, 1928–9, pp. 194–6. (3) Therefore, as pointed out by Hadeln (Ridolfi/Hadeln, vol. I, p. 395, note 6), not identical with Ridolfi's mention of the 'Samaritano . . . tra le cose . . . che passarono in Inghilterra'. (4) The name is printed in one copy of the catalogue in the National Gallery library and written in another. (5) The name is specified as 'Henry Rogers' in the exhibition catalogue.

After JACOPO BASSANO

2148 THE DEPARTURE OF ABRAHAM

$33\frac{1}{2} \times 46\frac{1}{2}$ (0·85 × 1·19).

Much damaged near the edges. Paint in centre seems in good state. Cleaned, 1971.

In the 1929 catalogue ('withdrawn from exhibition') as 'School of Jacopo Bassano'.

Studio version of a Bassanesque design of which the original (signed by both Jacopo and Francesco) is at Berlin. Two others are at Vienna.[1] Another (attributed to Leandro and closer to no. 2148 in design than to the Vienna pictures) was lot 4, Lord Clinton sale, Sotheby's 19th July, 1950. Another is at Hatfield.

VERSIONS: See above. Others are recorded in the Palazzo Camuccini at Cantalupo in Sabina and (formerly) in the Vom Rath collection, Amsterdam.

PROVENANCE: Bought with the Galvagna collection (Venice) 1855. Said to have been earlier in Casa Savorgnan.[2] On loan to Dublin, 1857 to *c.* 1926. Not catalogued until 1915.

REPRODUCTION: Negative in the possession of the Gallery.

REFERENCES: (1) One reproduced by W. Arslan: *I Bassano*, 1931, pl. LXVI. They figure as nos. 266 and 325 in the catalogue of 1907, attr. Francesco Bassano. A third comparable picture at Vienna is no. 294 in the 1907 catalogue. None of these pictures is included in the catalogue of 1938. (2) National Gallery Report, 1856.

LEANDRO BASSANO

1557–1622

Leandro dal Ponte. The third of Jacopo Bassano's sons to reach maturity.[1]

Ridolfi[2] says he stayed with his father in Bassano after his elder brother, Francesco, settled in Venice. He himself seems to have settled in Venice by 1588[3] and he completed a number of Francesco's pictures after the latter's premature death in 1592.[4] His active and successful career included work at the Doge's Palace, but Ridolfi stresses that his fame rested chiefly on his skill as portraitist and that it was this which procured him a knighthood from the Doge, Marin Grimano.[5] There-after the word 'eques' after his signature is normally added.

In his subject-pictures Leandro's point of departure was the late work of his father; in portraiture, probably Tintoretto.

REFERENCES: (1) For dates of birth and death cf. Hadeln (Ridolfi/Hadeln, II, pp. 167–71) and W. Arslan: *I Bassano* (1931, pp. 247–73). (2) Ridolfi/Hadeln, II (1924), p. 165. (3) Ridolfi says that it was on Francesco's death that Leandro removed to Venice. But Hadeln (*op. cit.*, p. 166, note 2) produces evidence for the earlier date. (4) Ridolfi/Hadeln, I, p. 409, and II, p. 166. (5) Ridolfi, *op. cit.*, p. 166.

60 THE TOWER OF BABEL

$53\frac{3}{4} \times 74\frac{1}{2}$ ($1 \cdot 39 \times 1 \cdot 892$).

Signed, on the block of stone bottom left, LEANDER A PONTE BASS. The last letters are indistinct.

Good condition.

In earlier editions of the catalogue as 'School of Leandro', but the signature, which has not been recorded hitherto, seems genuine, and the style of the picture characteristic of Leandro. Some of the costumes are apparently intended to be oriental.[1] That of the horseman, left, seems contemporary and suggests a dating soon after 1600.[2]

VERSION: Prague, square format (photograph in the Gallery archives). If this was the version engraved in the *Theatrum Pictorium* (see below), it has since been considerably truncated on the right and slightly on the left. Another (said to be signed) is in the Berkshire Museum, Pittsfield, Mass. Another was in the Brass collection, Venice.

ENGRAVING: The design, but not necessarily this version, engraved in the *Theatrum Pictorium* of Teniers (pl. 154).

PROVENANCE: Bequeathed by Lt.-Col. Ollney, 1837. On loan to Dublin, 1862 to *c.* 1926.

REPRODUCTION: *Illustrations, Italian Schools*, 1937, p. 24.

REFERENCES: (1) There was some tradition for this in representations of the Tower of Babel. Examples are Giusto de' Menabuoi, Padua, Baptistery (pl. 76 in Sergio Bettini's monograph, 1944), Benozzo Gozzoli, Pisa, Campo Santo; also Martin van Valckenborch, Dresden (no. 832 in 1902 catalogue). The writer is grateful to Stella Mary Pearce for drawing his attention to these examples. This would perhaps constitute some evidence against the identification of the subject as the *Building of Solomon's Temple*—proposed for the Prague version. (2) Notes by Stella Mary Pearce in the Gallery archives.

Style of LEANDRO BASSANO

2149 PORTRAIT OF A MAN

$25\frac{1}{2} \times 21$ ($0 \cdot 647 \times 0 \cdot 533$).

Inscribed: HIC SATVS EST | CVLTOR PHÆB– | ORPH– | GRATVS PRINC– | PROMPTVS IN |

Somewhat rubbed. To judge from the truncated form of the inscription, evidently cut on the right. The inscription (more easily legible in an infra-red photograph than to the naked eye and not hitherto recorded) may be part of a couplet with reference to the sitter.

In the 1929 catalogue as 'School of Leandro Bassano'.

An inferior example of a type of portraiture associated with Leandro Bassano.

PROVENANCE: Purchased with the Galvagna collection (Venice), 1855. On loan to Dublin, 1857 to *c.* 1926. Not catalogued until 1915.

REPRODUCTION: *Illustrations, Italian Schools*, 1937, p. 24.

Follower of the BASSANO

1858 ADORATION OF THE SHEPHERDS

$25\frac{1}{4} \times 35\frac{1}{2}$ (0·645 × 0·901).

Some wearing, particularly in the back of the foreground shepherd. Otherwise in good state.

A later derivative, perhaps via Leandro, of a design by Jacopo of which the best version is probably that in the Galleria Nazionale, Rome. Others in the Reinhart collection (Winterthur), in the Accademia, Venice, at Nancy (no. 16), and in the collection of Viscount Allendale.

In the 1929 catalogue ('withdrawn from exhibition') as 'School of Jacopo Bassano'.

PROVENANCE: Bequeathed by Sir John May, 1847, but apparently never exhibited.

REPRODUCTION: Negative in the Gallery's possession.

DOMENICO BECCAFUMI
1486(?)–1551

Sienese school. Vasari says he was called Mecherino, that he took the name Beccafumi from an early patron and that he died at the age of sixty-five. There is documentary evidence that Beccafumi died in 1551, from which it would follow that he was born in 1486 if Vasari is right about his age at death. But as Vasari says his death occurred in 1549[1] this may not be the case.

There are a number of documented paintings from the year 1513 onwards.[2] Before that Beccafumi had paid a visit to Rome. Thereafter he was active at Siena for the rest of his life with the exception of a visit to Genoa and Pisa. In 1517 he started work on designs for the marble pavement of Siena cathedral which occupied him off and on for most of the rest of his life.

REFERENCES: (1) Vasari/Milanesi, V, 654. (2) For some discussion of the early Beccafumi see D. Sanminiatelli in the *Burlington Magazine*, XCIX, 1957, pp. 401 ff.

1430 AN UNIDENTIFIED SCENE

Panel, $29\frac{1}{8} \times 54\frac{1}{4}$ (0·74 × 1·378).

Most of the draperies of the female figures seem fairly well preserved. Other areas have worn thin, particularly the shadowed portions of the main loggia. The youth painted on the steps under the throne is now partly transparent. Cleaned, 1972.

The shape and size suggest that it was painted as part of a piece of furniture or of the panelling of a room.

Esther and Ahasuerus and the *Queen of Sheba and Solomon* have been variously suggested for the title, but the lack of the trappings of royalty would militate against both identifications, while the absence, in particular, of a sceptre in the case of the enthroned figure would seem fatal to the former. Perhaps the recognizably Roman buildings in the background[1] indicate a scene from Roman history, such as the story of Virginia.[2]

Comparable with the *Birth of the Virgin* (Siena, Pinacoteca) and more particularly with its predella (Earl of Oxford and Asquith)[3] which are vouched for as Beccafumi's by Vasari[4] and said to date from 1543.[5]

VERSION: Lot 57, Sir Philip Burne-Jones sale, Sotheby's, 8th December, 1926—*Beccafumi. The Story of Esther. Canvas*, 31 × 58.[6]

PROVENANCE: Perhaps in the Medici collections at Rome in the seventeenth century.[7] Perhaps lot 1065, Northwick sale, 11th day, August 11th, 1859—*Domenico Beccafume [sic] A Landscape, with numerous figures. In the centre, a Hall, in which a Court appears to be assembled, probably intended to represent the subject of Esther and Ahasuerus* (bought by A. and J. Abrahams). No. 1430 was bought by George Salting in 1889[8] from F. de Tivoli.[9] Presented by George Salting, 1894.

REPRODUCTION: *Illustrations, Italian Schools*, 1937, p. 26.

REFERENCES: (1) E.g. Colosseum, Arch of Constantine, Castel S. Angelo etc. No attempt at accuracy seems to have been made in portraying these buildings while the others are more fantastic still. (2) Oral suggestion by Michael Levey. Rinaldo de Liphart Rathshoff (*Rivista d'Arte*, 1935, pp. 48 ff.) attempts to identify some drawings in the Beccafumi sketch book as the story of Esther, and mentions no. 1430 in this context. The former proposition is questionable while any relation to the drawings to no. 1430 seems excluded. The writer is also wrong in referring to no. 1430 as having belonged to Duveen. (3) Exh. R.A., 1960 (112, 113, 116). (4) Vasari/Milanesi V, 651. (5) M. Gibellino-Krasceninnicowa: *Il Beccafumi*, 1933, p. 156, quoting a MS by E. Romagnoli in the Biblioteca Comunale at Siena. D. Sanminiatelli (*Domenico Beccafumi*, 1967, p. 93) proposes instead a dating in the 1520's. (6) A note in the Gallery copy of the catalogue says 'like Nat. Gall. picture'. (7) Sanminiatelli (*op. cit.*, p. 196) publishes part of an inventory of 1670 (*tavola . . . entrovi un Culiseo con figure alto br.* 1½ *e lungo br.* 3 *mano del Micherino . . .*). (8) Salting papers in the Gallery archives. (9) Letter from F. de Tivoli in the Gallery archives.

6368 TANAQUIL

Panel, painted area $36\frac{1}{4} \times 21$ (0·92 × 0·53).

Inscribed: .SVM TANAQVIL BINOS FECI QVE PROVIDA REGES PRIMA VIRVM SERVVM [F]OEMINA [D][E][I]NDE M[E]VM

Damage from blistering in a number of isolated spots, and in a short vertical strip along much of the length of the skirt on the spectator's left of the knotted material. Cleaned 1965 and on that occasion transferred from panel on to canvas and Sundeala board with wax resin.

For Provenance and Commentary see no. 6369.

6369 MARCIA

Panel, $36\frac{1}{4} \times 21$ (0.92×0.53).

Inscribed: .ME CATO COGNOVIT VIR MOX HORTENSIVS ALTER. DEINDE CATONIS EGO MARTIA NVPTA FVI.

Generally good condition. Some blistering in the past, and some retouching, notably in the sky round the figure's head. But better condition than no. 6368. Cleaned 1965.

Nos. 6368 and 6369 are recorded together since the nineteenth century. Another picture of approximately the same size, representing Cornelia, the daughter of Scipio Africanus and mother of the Gracchi, is in the private apartments of the Doria palace in Rome, and was clearly part of the same series.[1] The theme was evidently remarkable women of Antiquity. Tanaquil was the wife of Lucomo whom she persuaded to emigrate from Tarquinii to Rome, where he was subsequently elected king with the title Tarquinius Priscus. After his assassination Tanaquil secured the succession for Servius Tullius. The destiny of Marcia was still more curious. She was the wife of Cato, who ceded her to his friend, Hortensius, with the consent of all concerned. After Hortensius' death she returned to Cato.

The costumes and hair styles in both pictures accord best with a dating between about 1522 and about 1525.[2] The colouring is comparable with that of several of the scenes on the ceiling of the Sala del Concistoro in the Palazzo Comunale at Siena, commissioned of Beccafumi in 1529. The Beccafumi attribution, which is unassailable, for nos. 6368 and 6369 seems first to have been published by Borenius in his catalogue of the Northwick pictures (1921).

PROVENANCE: Charles O'Neil sale, Foster's, London, 6th July, 1833, 65 and 66 (as Andrea del Sarto). Bought then or soon after by Lord Northwick. Northwick catalogue of 1864, nos. 58 and 64, as Sarto. Northwick catalogue, 1921 (by Borenius) nos. 7 and 8 as Beccafumi. Acquired 1965 by application of the Finance Act, 1956.

REPRODUCTION: Report of the National Gallery, 1965–6 (published 1967). Facing p. 17.

REFERENCES: (1) Reproduced Venturi: *Storia* . . ., IX, V, p. 451, pl. 251. A further picture—of Penelope—is in the Seminario Patriarcale at Venice and may be another from the series. Two more, in the Victoria and Albert Museum, claimed by Borenius in his Northwick catalogue to belong, clearly do not. (2) Notes by Stella Mary Pearce (Mrs Eric Newton) in the Gallery archives. D. Sanminiatelli (*Domenico Beccafumi*, 1967, p. 85) associates nos. 6368 and 6369 together with the Doria and Venice pictures and three others of different format with a commission of about 1519 for Francesco Petrucci.

BERNARDINO DA ASOLA
recorded 1526

Maistro D. Bernardin da Asola de Bressana is recorded as collaborating with his father, *maistro Zuanne*, on a pair of double-sided organ doors (now in the Museo Correr, Venice) for S. Michele in Isola, Venice in a document of 6th April, 1526. The father, Giovanni, died in 1531.

The arguments, and further references, for ascribing to Bernardino the following four pictures are put in some detail in a forthcoming (1974) article by the present writer in *Arte Veneta*.

REFERENCE: (1) L. Seguso: *Bianca Visconti e Francesco Sforza . . .*, 1878. Also G. Ludwig: Prussian *Jahrbuch*, 1905, supplement, pp. 112 ff.

Ascribed to BERNARDINO DA ASOLA

41 DEATH OF S. PETER MARTYR

$40\frac{1}{4} \times 57$ (1·015 × 1·448).

Much worn, and retouched in many parts—particularly in the clouds (including the *putti*). The following passages in fair condition: centre soldier's pink breeches and hose (*pentimenti* in his legs), most of the lower part of the saint's white robe, the tree (right centre) and figures on either side of its trunk. Cleaned, 1972.

As Giorgione in the collection of Queen Christina and in the National Gallery catalogues up to and including the edition of 1887. Attributed to Cariani from 1888 to 1959. Called by Crowe and Cavalcaselle 'a Titianesque composition adapted by a Venetian or Ferrarese artist of a modern time'.[1] The pinkish tone of no. 41 is a feature common in authentic works of Cariani, but a considerable element of doubt concerning his authorship must remain, owing to the lack of other parallels of this kind. The costume accords best with a dating in the 1540's, but the arrangement and the format is traditional, and harks back less to Titian's great altarpiece of this subject than to an earlier type, represented by no. 812 of this Gallery.[2] No. 41 has fairly strong affinities with no. 930 of this Gallery which, in its turn, is linked with nos. 1377 and 2907 and with various pictures of disputed attribution in other places. No. 41 seems to the present writer to be probably by the same hand as no. 930, and therefore probably by the same hand as the other pictures associated with the latter, namely Bernardino da Asola.

PROVENANCE: No. 267 in the 1689 inventory of Queen Christina's collection and no. 162 in the 1721 inventory.[3] Thence Orléans—pp. 168–9 in the 1727 catalogue. Presumably no. 44 in the sale (Bryan's, 14th February, 1800) of the remaining part of the Orléans collection (consistently as Giorgione).[4] Bequeathed by the Rev. Holwell Carr, 1831. Exh: Stockholm (Queen Christina) 1966 (1165).

REPRODUCTION: *Illustrations, Italian Schools*, 1937, p. 82.

REFERENCES: (1) *North Italian Painters*, III, p. 54. (2) Baldass (Vienna *Jahrbuch* 1929, pp. 97–8) suggests a derivation from an altarpiece of the same subject at Alzano Maggiore, attr. Lotto. The connection is not apparent to the present writer. F. Heinemann (*Giovanni Bellini e i Belliniani*, 1962, I. p. 71 and fig. 606) proposed an unacceptable attribution to Romanino (with query). (3) Both printed (pp. LXXXVI and CIII) in Olof Granberg: *La Galerie de Tableaux de la Reine Christine de Suède*, 1897. (4) For the intermediary history of the Orléans collection see entries for nos. 270 or 1326.

930 'THE GARDEN OF LOVE'

$87 \times 58\frac{3}{8}$ $(2 \cdot 2 \times 1 \cdot 49)$.[1]

Much worn and retouched. Cleaned 1955.

As 'Venetian School, XV–XVI century' in the 1929 catalogue, where also the name Girolamo Muziano is improbably suggested. Until 1915 as 'School of Giorgione'. Cariani has also been mentioned.[2] As 'Brescian School' in the 1962 catalogue.

The buildings and other features of the background are noticeably similar to those in no. 2907 of this Gallery in which the main figures (Madonna and Child) are copied from Titian. If, as is likely, the painter of no. 930 had no Titianesque or other superior prototype for the figures it would not be difficult to imagine him the same as the executant of no. 2907, provided that due allowance were made for the difference of scale and condition. The latter picture seems to the present writer to be one of a group of pictures by the same hand as each other (others are a *S. Jerome* in the Rijksmuseum and a *Holy Family* from the Chillingworth sale, 1922). There is also a further group of three pictures, all *Adorations of the Shepherds* and all derived from Titian, one of which is no. 1377 of this Gallery. Of this group it is noticeable that in no. 1377 two doves are shown which are similar to those in the present picture (930). This may be an indication that the same hand was responsible for both groups as well as for no. 930. For this latter Berenson tentatively suggested Giovanni da Asola.[3] But this painter died in 1531 whereas the costumes in no. 930 are appreciably later—around 1540:[3] they also appear to be regional to the Brescia area.[4] Giovanni's son, Bernardino, is more likely.[5]

PROVENANCE: Wynn Ellis Bequest, 1876.

REPRODUCTION: *Illustrations, Italian Schools*, 1937, p. 373.

REFERENCES: (1) Possibly transferred from panel. (2) W. Schmidt in *Repertorium für Kunstwissenschaft*. XXXI, 1908, p. 117. (3) Oral communication and 1957 *Lists*. (4) Notes by Stella Mary Pearce in the Gallery archives. (5) For Giovanni and Bernardino da Asola cf. G. Ludwig in the Prussian *Jahrbuch*, vol. XXVI (1905), *Beiheft*, p. 114 and G. Fiocco in *Bollettino d'Arte*, anno V, 1925–6, pp. 193–205.

1377 ADORATION OF THE SHEPHERDS

Original canvas measures *ca.* $41\frac{1}{4} \times 63\frac{1}{4}$ $(1 \cdot 05 \times 1 \cdot 606)$.

Strips added at the top and bottom were removed in 1973, when the picture was cleaned. Infra-red photographs reveal a seated dog behind the shepherds and an alternative placing of the background figures farther left.

Worn thin in many places and also damaged by past flaking. Cleaned 1973.

Bequeathed as by Savoldo, and catalogued as such until the edition of 1912 when it first appeared as 'Venetian School, XV–XVI century'.

In the 1959 catalogue as 'Venetian School, Sixteenth Century'. No. 1377 is one of a group of three pictures of the same subject, all pastiches of Titian[1] and all evidently by the same hand. The second is at Kansas City (ex-Leuchtenberg).[2] The third, said to have been in the Heseltine collection, was exported to the U.S.A. in 1961.[3] It seems likely to the present writer that the artist concerned was also responsible for nos. 41, 930 and 2907 of the National Gallery and for the further pictures associated with those. The three *Adorations* appear to derive from another picture of the same subject in the Duomo at Asola, datable 1516–18, itself a pastiche of Titian but attributable to Giovanni da Asola.[4] In the present writer's view, this painting is by a different hand from the rest, and this would at least be no argument *against* the hypothesis that the others, including no. 1377, are by Giovanni's son, Bernardino da Asola.[5]

PROVENANCE: From Manfrin collection, Venice.[6] Lot 745, G. A. F. Cavendish-Bentinck sale, Christie's, 5th day, 13th July, 1891, as Savoldo, bought Sir William Gregory, by whom bequeathed, 1892.

REPRODUCTION: *Sixteenth-Century Italian Schools*, Plates, 1964, p. 237.

REFERENCES: (1) A remote ancestor, through the Asola picture (for which see later), is probably no. 4 (Titian) of this Gallery. A number of other derivations from Titian could be traced without difficulty. (2) Reproduced Herbert Cook, *Burlington Magazine*, vol. II. (1903), p. 85. (3) Photograph in the Gallery archives. (4) Reproduced and discussed by G. Fiocco, *Bollettino d'Arte*, anno V, 1925–6, pp. 193–205. (5) An attribution to Calisto da Lodi was suggested by E. Jacobsen (*Repertorium für Kunstwissenschaft*, vol. XXIV, 1901, p. 368). G. Ludwig (Prussian *Jahrbuch*, vol. XXVI, 1905, *Beiheft* p. 114) suggested an attribution to Giovanni da Asola, which was adopted by Berenson (*Lists*, 1936 and 1957) in respect of no. 1377, the Kansas picture and also the one in the Duomo at Asola (in the 1957 edition adding 'with Bernardino' in the case of no. 1377). The Kansas picture was attributed by Fiocco to Francesco Vecellio (*Arte Veneta*, IX, 1955, p. 76). M. G. A. Trenti (*Arte Antica e Moderna*, 1964, pp. 404 ff.) reverts to 'Giovanni da Asola (?)' in respect of the Kansas picture and no. 2907. Stella Mary Pearce, in notes in the Gallery archives on the costumes, favours a dating not earlier than 1525 and very possibly later than 1530 for no. 1377. She also points out various irrational features in the Virgin's costume which would be explicable if it derived from another painting. (6) Label on the back. Probably no. 428 in the 1856 Manfrin catalogue ('Adorazione dei Pastori. Girolamo Savoldo. Tela, larghezza 1.61, altezza 1.17'), and no. 104 in the 1872 Manfrin catalogue. Sir W. Gregory's account of his purchase of the picture is printed in *An Autobiography*, ed. Lady Gregory, 1894, pp. 398–9.

2907 MADONNA AND CHILD

Panel, $30\frac{1}{2} \times 40\frac{1}{2}$ (0·775 × 1·029).

Worn thin in places, particularly in the sky; condition otherwise fair.

The group of the Madonna and Child seems to be based on a

Titianesque design of which the original may be the damaged fresco lunette in the Doge's Palace.[1] This was an influential design; it is reproduced not only in no. 2907 but also, in its essentials, in the central group in the Jacopo Bassano *Flight into Egypt* (Bassano, Museo Civico). The detail of the child kicking with one leg was even more widely borrowed: it occurs repeatedly in pictures by Romanino[2] and Savoldo[3] among others.

The attribution of no. 2907 has been much disputed. As 'Brescian School' in the 1962 catalogue. It passed under a Giorgione attribution in the nineteenth century and entered the Gallery as 'School of Titian'. An attribution to Romanino was first made by Sir Charles Eastlake but was not published until many years later by Sir C. Holmes[4]. Other suggestions have included Dosso Dossi,[5] Cariani,[6] School of Jacopo Bassano[7] and Bernardino da Asola.[8] Since it seems clear that the executant was not responsible for the design of the main group the clue to his identity must lie primarily in the landscape and in the colouring and technique. The type of landscape recurs very precisely in two further pictures—a *S. Jerome* in the Rijksmuseum (ex-Otto Lanz) and a *Holy Family* formerly in the Chillingworth collection.[9] All three pictures show similar ducks on a pond and similar dark trees and mountains. In addition, the Chillingworth picture includes a peasant carrying bundles suspended from a pole on his shoulders, as on the left of no. 2907, while the Amsterdam picture has an armed man on horseback almost exactly like the one on the right of no. 2907. The Amsterdam picture has been attributed to Dosso Dossi[10] and to Romanino[11]: its blueish tone is close to that of no. 2907, and the technique also is similar to the extent of a tendency to drag the brush sluggishly through thick paint. These features are not characteristic of Romanino, or Cariani or Dossi. The Chillingworth picture has not been available to the present writer for inspection but from the photographs published it seems certain that it is of the same group and by the same hand as the other two pictures. This group suggests an eclectic painter. The background in all three is Romaninesque; the figures in the Chillingworth picture show Titianesque as well as Romaninesque elements while those in no. 2907 seem a straight borrowing from Titian. Berenson attributed the Chillingworth picture to Bernardino da Asola,[12] to whom Fiocco and Arslan had already attributed no. 2907. As a minor Brescian who is recorded as active in Venice in the '20's of the sixteenth century[13] he fulfils the conditions better than any of the other painters so far suggested.

PROVENANCE: Exh. R.A., 1873[14] (177) (lent Contessa Cotterell)[15] (as Giorgione), no. 96, Christie's 10th May, 1873, offered for sale by order of the Court of Chancery (passed).[16] In the possession by 1883 of Lady Lindsay,[17] by whom exh. R.A., 1888 (141, as Giorgione) and by whom bequeathed, 1912.[18]

REPRODUCTION: *Illustrations, Italian Schools*, 1937, p. 311.

REFERENCES: (1) Reproduced Suida: *Tiziano*, 1933, pl. LXXXV (a). This is mentioned as Titian's by Vasari (VII/439) but nevertheless attributed to Francesco Vecellio by W. Arslan (*I Bassano*, 1931, p. 56). It is presumably this painting which Van Dyck sketched (repr. Cust: *Sketch-book . . . at Chatsworth*,

1902, pl. III). (2) E.g. no. 297 of this Gallery, in the Brera Madonna and in the altarpiece formerly at Berlin. (3) E.g. in the Hampton Court, Turin and Brescia *Nativities* (the Hampton Court picture dated 1527). (4) *Burlington Magazine*, vol. 43 (1923), p. 253. The author quoted Sir Claude Phillips as agreeing with the Romanino attribution. (5) Originally published by Otto Lanz (*Burlington Magazine*, vol. 43 (1923) p., 184). Subsequently supported by R. Longhi (*Precisioni nelle Gallerie Italiane, I, R. Galleria Borghese*, in *Vita Artistica* anno II, 1927, pp. 32–3; also published in book form, 1928, pp. 110–12). (6) Berenson, *Lists*, various editions (with query). (7) K. T. Parker in *Burlington Magazine*, Vol. 44, 1924, pp. 202–7. (8) Wart Arslan: *I Bassano*, 1931, pp. 56, 62 and 345. Attribution there stated to have been made originally by G. Fiocco orally. See also Felton Gibbons: *Dosso and Battista Dossi*, 1968, p. 255, containing further attributional references. (9) Lot 89 in the Rudolf Chillingworth sale, Lucerne, 5th September, 1922, repr. in the sale catalogue. (10) Lanz, *loc. cit.* (11) Holmes *loc. cit.* In this letter Holmes associates the Chillingworth picture with no. 2907 and with the Amsterdam *S. Jerome*. In a later letter (*Burlington Magazine*, vol. 44, 1924, p. 260) Holmes quoted Nicodemi as agreeing with the Romanino attribution for no. 2907 and as regarding it as 'painted in 1512 during his residence in Padua. One of the churches in that city is introduced into the background'. In Nicodemi's monograph on Romanino (1925) he appears to uphold the Romanino attribution for no. 2907 (p. 198, no no. given). (12) *Lists* 1957 (under 'Giovanni and Bernardino da Asola'). (13) For Bernardino da Asola cf. G. Ludwig in the Prussian *Jahrbuch*, vol. XXVI (1905), Beiheft, pp. 112–17 and G. Fiocco in *Bollettino d'Arte*, 1925–6, vol. I, pp. 193–203. (14) Not 1872, as earlier editions of the catalogue have it. (15) So the exhibition catalogue. A label formerly on the back of no. 2907 gave G. F. Watts as the owner. Watts had been a friend of Cotterell and was presumably acting on behalf of his widow. (16) Note in the copy of the sale catalogue in the Gallery library. (17) Label on the back. (18) Not 1913, as earlier editions of the catalogue have it.

BONIFAZIO di Pitati
1487–1553

A Veronese who settled at Venice. The confusion which long persisted concerning him started with G. Moschini[1] (who postulated two painters of this name), was aggravated by Bernasconi[2] (who produced a third) and culminated with Morelli[3] (who divided the existing Bonifazian *œuvre* stylistically into three groups and called them Bonifazio I, II and III). The ground was then cleared by G. Ludwig,[4] who showed from archival research that the Pitati family had been established at Verona since the fourteenth century but that only one of them was a painter, that the second painter called Bonifazio bore the surname Pasini and that the third was a phantom. The unequal quality of many of the existing pictures in a Bonifazian style was explained by Ludwig's discovery of documents which showed that Bonifazio kept an abnormally large studio.

Ludwig produced indications which suggested that Bonifazio's father moved in 1505 from Verona to Venice, but the first record of the painter at Venice is of 1528, while the earliest dated picture by Bonifazio which survives is of 1530 (Venice, Accademia no. 61: *Christ enthroned with Saints*). In addition a number of surviving paintings are reasonably associated with him, notably a large series of (partly documented) decorations dating from 1530 onwards, painted for the Palazzo Camerlenghi at Venice and now dispersed.

If, as is probable, pictures such as no. 1202 of this Gallery are in fact early works of Bonifazio it would be an indication that his earliest work was modelled on Palma. But in default of further firm evidence as much must remain obscure in the career of the one as in that of the other.

REFERENCES: (1) *Guida per la Città di Venezia*, 1815. (2) *Studj sopra la storia . . . della scuola pittorica Veronese*, 1864. (3) *Munich and Dresden*, 1893. (4) Prussian *Jahrbuch*, vols. XXII and XXIII.

1202 MADONNA AND CHILD, WITH SS. JAMES THE GREATER, JEROME, INFANT JOHN THE BAPTIST AND CATHERINE OF ALEXANDRIA

Panel, painted surface $28\frac{3}{4} \times 46$ (0·73 × 1·168).

Good condition.

S. James has thrown his pilgrim's hat (decorated with his shell and cross and with Veronica's veil) over his shoulders.[1] S. Jerome, next him, is without his lion but identifiable by his scarlet robes.[2] The coat of arms above the door in the background appears indecipherable. There are also traces of cabalistic characters on the wall below it to the right.

This type of *Santa Conversazione* is pre-eminently associated with Palma Vecchio to whom, indeed, no. 1202 was long ascribed.[3] Nevertheless the handling is coarser than Palma's and more summary, and the picture, with others of similar kind, is generally attributed to a relatively early (and still Palmesque) phase of Bonifazio's career.[4]

VERSION: Venice, Accademia (no. 275), where catalogued as a copy.

PROVENANCE: From the Terzi[5] and Andreossi collections at Bergamo. Purchased, 1886, from the heirs of Enrico Andreossi, Walker Fund.

REPRODUCTION: *Illustrations, Italian Schools*, 1955, p. 45.

REFERENCES: (1) He is shown wearing a similar hat in a painting reproduced by Kaftal: *Iconography of the Saints in Tuscan Painting* (1952), fig. 595. (2) It is possible that the lion shown attacking a sheep in the background (to the consternation of the—presumably hireling—shepherds) is meant to be S. Jerome's which has got out of hand. (3) E.g. by the former owner and by Crowe and Cavalcaselle (*Painting in North Italy*, III, 1912, pp. 367-8). Morelli (*Munich and Dresden*, 1893, p. 41) first put forward the Bonifazio attribution. This has found almost general favour since, but cf. Venturi's whim of including no. 1202 under both Jacopo and Antonio Palma (*Storia*, IX, III, pp. 436 and 1059), in the former reference as 'Andreossi coll., Milan'. (4) Notes by Stella Mary Pearce in the Gallery archives on the costumes in no. 1202 favour a dating around 1529-32. (5) Information from Crowe and Cavalcaselle, *loc. cit.* Morelli (*loc. cit.*) mentions that no. 1202 was exhibited at Bergamo as Palma.

Studio of BONIFAZIO

2145 A HUNTSMAN

$46 \times 25\frac{1}{2}$ (1·169 × 0·648).

Fair condition.

In the Galvagna collection, Venice, as Giorgione. Lent to Dublin
from 1857 to 1926 and not catalogued until 1915 ('School of Giorgione').
In the 1920 edition as 'Venetian School'. As Bonifazio in the edition
of 1929, and this attribution supported by Berenson[1] and by Westphal.[2]
In point of fact no. 2145 would seem a routine production of Bonifazio's
large studio. Westphal[3] suggests it was one of a series of Labours of the
Months (cf. nos. 3109 and 3110 of this Gallery).

PROVENANCE: Collection Baron Galvagna, Venice, with which purchased,
1855.[4] Said to have been in Casa Savorgnan.[5]

REPRODUCTION: *Illustrations, Italian Schools*, 1937, p. 46.

REFERENCES: (1) *Lists*, 1932, 1936 and 1957. (2) *Bonifazio Veronese*, 1931,
pp. 54–5. (3) *Loc. cit.* (4) Noted by Mündler (note book in the Gallery archives)
in October, 1855 in Baron Galvagna's possession. (5) National Gallery Report,
1856.

Style of BONIFAZIO

3109   THE LABOURS OF THE MONTHS—JANUARY TO
JUNE

Canvas, mounted on wood. Each painting *c.* $5\frac{1}{4} \times 4$ (0·133 × 0·102).
Apparently in good condition for the most part.

1. An old man asleep by a stove.
2. A youth asleep on a rampart.
3. Pig-killing.
4. A falconer with hounds.
5. A man cutting corn.
6. Ploughing.

For commentary see no. 3110.

3110   THE LABOURS OF THE MONTHS—JULY TO
DECEMBER

Canvas, mounted on wood. Each painting *c.* $5\frac{1}{4} \times 4$ (0·133 × 0·102).
Apparently in good condition for the most part.

1. Threshing.
2. Squeezing grapes.
3. Coopering wine-casks.
4. Pointing vine-poles.
5. Making vine-trellises.
6. Vine dressing.

The Labours of the Months was a subject which had been extremely
common in mediaeval art and which became popular again in a somewhat altered form around the middle of the sixteenth century in northern
Italy, particularly with the Bassano and their followers. The present
set (nos. 3109 and 3110) has been attributed to Bonifazio since Layard's
time.[1] There is some generic resemblance to works such as no. 2145
of this gallery which is acceptable as a product of Bonifazio's studio,

but the erratic draughtsmanship of nos. 3109 and 3110 presupposes an even more distant connection with the master.

PROVENANCE: Bought, 1888, by Sir A. H. Layard from Marini.[2] Layard Bequest, 1916.

REPRODUCTION: *Illustrations, Italian Schools*, 1937, pp. 47–8.

REFERENCES: (1) Admitted as Bonifazio by Berenson (1897) and Hadeln (article in Thieme–Becker). An oral communication from P. Toesca (October, 1930) favoured Andrea Schiavone. D. Westphal (*Bonifazio Veronese*, 1931, p. 97) says 'die Bilder gehören gewiss dem Kreise des Bonifazio an'. (2) British Museum (Add. MS. 38950, r 62, Layard to Gregory).

3536 MADONNA AND CHILD WITH SS. JOHN THE BAPTIST, ELIZABETH AND CATHERINE OF ALEXANDRIA

$28\frac{3}{4} \times 47$ (0·73 × 1·194).

Fair state. Some damage due to flaking.

Traces of scribbled characters, probably always devoid of meaning, on the pier behind S. Catherine.[1]

Probably as Bonifazio when in the Manfrin collection, thereafter ascribed to Palma Vecchio until entering the Gallery. As Bonifazio in the 1929 catalogue.

The type of the figures, particularly that of S. Catherine, is much closer to that of acceptable Bonifazio's than to Palma. But the poverty of the execution militates against assuming his active participation, while the tameness of the design suggests rather a pastiche of Bonifazian motives put together by a follower.[2] The costumes accord best with a dating in the early 1530's.[3]

PROVENANCE: From the Manfrin collection, Venice (label on the back).[4] In the collection of the Earl of Dudley by 1868 when exh. by him at Leeds (label on the back).[5] Exh. R.A., 1871 (335) ('Palma Vecchio'), by Lord Dudley. Dudley sale, 25th June, 1892 (probably lot 72).[6] Exh. New Gallery ('Venetian Art'), 1894–5 (92) ('Palma Vecchio'), lent by Wickham Flower. No. 54 in the latter's sale, 17th December, 1904 ('Palma Vecchio') as ex-Manfrin and ex-Dudley,[7] where bought Colnaghi by whom sold to Alfred A. de Pass. Presented by the latter, 1920.

REPRODUCTION: *Illustrations, Italian Schools*, 1937, p. 47.

REFERENCES: (1) Cf. similar characters on no. 1202. (2) The S. Catherine in no. 3536, as already indicated, is of a usual Bonifazian type, comparable with several figures in the Brera *Finding of Moses* and to some extent with the same saint in no. 1202 of this Gallery. The infant S. John in no. 3536 is almost a repetition of the same figure in the *Santa Conversazione* in the Gardner Museum, Boston. Berenson (*Lists*, 1936 and 1957) gives no. 3536 to Bonifazio 'in great part'. (3) Notes in the Gallery archives by Stella Mary Pearce who points out that the costumes alone in no. 3536 suggest a different hand from no. 1202; also, that while S. Catherine's costume is consistent with the fashion of the early 1530's, that of the Virgin and S. Elizabeth is unusually archaic, which seems to support the theory of a pastiche. (4) Probably no. 417 in the Manfrin catalogue of 1856—'Bonifazio, Madonna, Bambino e Santi, tela, larghezza 1.22, altezza 0.77'. The latter picture no longer figures in the 1872 Manfrin catalogue. (5) Could be any of nos. 2912 ('Bonifazio'), 2913 ('Bonifazio') or 2916 ('Palma Vecchio') in the exhibition catalogue. (6) Lots 72 and

73 are given in the sale catalogue as of identical dimensions, both as 'Palma Vecchio' and both as 'exh. R.A., 1871' and as 'ex-coll. Alexander Barker, 1874'. There therefore seems to be some confusion. If no. 3536 was the property of Lord Dudley in 1868, 1871 and 1892 it is most unlikely to have been in the Barker collection in 1874. The latter date was that of the Barker sale, in which no. 3536 certainly did not figure. Barker, however, had bought pictures from the Manfrin collection, and a *'Holy Family* by Palma Vecchio', listed in the National Gallery Board minutes of 9th June, 1856 as one of the pictures recently sold from the Manfrin collection could be no. 3536 and could have been bought by Barker. (7) Also as ex-Alexander Barker, 1874, evidently copying the Dudley sale catalogue.

After BONIFAZIO

3106   DIVES AND LAZARUS

Panel, $18\frac{1}{2} \times 33\frac{1}{3}$ (0·47 × 0·845).
Much damaged, and disfigured by engrained dirt.

The textual source is Luke xvi, 19 ff: *There was a certain rich man which was clothed in purple and fine linen, and fared sumptuously every day: And there was a certain beggar named Lazarus, which was laid at his gate, full of sores, And desiring to be fed with the crumbs which fell from the rich man's table; moreover the dogs came and licked his sores.*

A MS. note by Layard[1] says that the following information was on the back of no. 3106 before it was cradled; *Di mano di Bonifatio— Originale et modelo del quadro famoso delle Nozze del Ricco Epulone in Casa Giustinian a Stae per cui il Zanetti vuolse pagar doppie di Spagna No. mille e cinquecento a Marco.*

There is no indication of the date when this notice was written, but it may be deduced from the reference to Zanetti that it could not have been earlier than the eighteenth century, and therefore too late to be of any documentary value for the origin of the picture. The same objection applies to a further MS. note by Layard quoting a letter written to him in 1868 by Rawdon Brown. According to this, a former owner, Signor Vason of Venice, had deduced that no. 3106, like the large picture in the Accademia at Venice, had been painted for the Giustiniani family. Even if this was the case it would still not prove that no. 3106 was a study for the big picture and not a copy after it. The main differences between the two are as follows:

1. No. 3106 shows more space at the right and at the base than the Accademia picture and less on the left hand side. This could be explained by assuming that no. 3106 had been cut on the left and the Accademia picture at the base and on the right.

2. Several features in the middle distance of the Accademia picture are omitted in no. 3106, viz. the shield or banner on the wall behind the falconer (left centre), the figures under the arch in the central perspective and those on the extreme right (running up to the horse).

3. Details of the foreground group are simplified in no. 3106, viz. the unpatterned tablecloth, the lack of a bowl on it, the plain right sock

of the negro page, centre (in the Accademia picture he has a striped one) and the details of the rich man's hat and lapels. The second and third of these differences (as well as the fact that the dog in no. 3106 who licks Lazarus is only lightly outlined) would be by no means incompatible with a copy on so greatly reduced a scale. A further difference, arising from the fact that Lazarus is nearer to the pillar in the Accademia picture than in no. 3106, on the other hand, would be more natural in a study than a copy. The present condition of no. 3106 precludes a confident verdict, but the apparent feebleness of the execution seems to the present writer to be the deciding factor in favour of the theory of a copy.[2]

PROVENANCE: Purchased by Sir A. H. Layard. February, 1868, from Vason, Venice. According to a note already quoted from Rawdon Brown (which cannot be confirmed) no. 3106 was among property which passed from a branch of the Giustiniani family to the Donà family and was presented by Marina Donà (who had married Piero Grimani in 1796) to Vason about 1845. Exh. South Kensington, 1869 (no. 29, lent Layard). Layard Bequest, 1916.

REPRODUCTION: Westphal: *Bonifazio Veronese*, 1931, pl. 17.

REFERENCES: (1) In the Gallery archives. (2) No. 3106 is considered an autograph study by Westphal (*op. cit.*, pp. 47–8).

PARIS BORDON

1500–1571

The notice of his death is dated 19th January, 1571 (1570 in the then Venetian style), and gives his age as 70. As the entry of his baptism is dated 5th July, 1500 the latter is the year of his birth. He was from Treviso but spent most of his life at Venice where he was living by 1518. Vasari, who is probably reliable, mentions, *inter alia*, visits by Bordon to Vicenza and Milan and apparently also to Augsburg.[1] He also speaks of a journey to France made in 1538 at the instance of 'Re Francesco'. If the date is correct, the king would be François I. But a local Trevisan tradition, started by Orlandi (Abecedario) and reported by Federici,[2] gives the date as 1559 which was during the short reign of François II, and this seems, on the whole, the more probable.

Vasari says that Bordon was apprenticed for a time to Titian and that he then set himself to follow the manner of Giorgione. While both these statements are probable, insufficient of Bordon's early work has been identified to permit of an analysis of his development. Probably his earliest acceptable work is an altarpiece from Crema (now Lovere, Accademia Tadini). This is mentioned as Bordon's by the Anonimo Morelliano and incorporates, according to Vasari, a portrait of Giulio Manfron who was killed in 1526. It probably dates from shortly before then.[3] There are enough signed works to define Bordon's strongly individual style, but as hardly any are dated and as he seems to have evolved very little the chronology of his *œuvre* is uncertain.

REFERENCES: (1) Vasari seems to imply (Milanesi ed., vol. VII, p. 464) that Bordon actually worked at Augsburg, rather than merely sending pictures there (as he is reported to have done in the case of Flanders and for the King of Poland) but the wording is less unequivocal than in the case of the visits to Vicenza, Milan or France. A portrait in the Louvre, signed by Bordon and dated 1540, includes the word 'Augusta' in the inscription and was most probably painted at Augsburg. But the possibility would remain that it was painted at Venice though of an Augsburg resident. Cf. also G. Canova in *Arte Veneta*, 1961, p. 77. (2) Domenico Maria Federici: *Memorie Trevigiane*, vol. II (1803), pp. 41–2. Bailo and Biscaro: *Paris Bordon* (1900), pp. 41–4, discuss the problem of the French journey in full. (3) Bailo and Biscaro, *op. cit.*, pp. 45–6 and 132–3.

637   DAPHNIS AND CHLOE

$53\frac{1}{3} \times 47\frac{1}{2}$ (1·359 × 1·206).

Flesh and hair in good condition. In Chloe's dress, the foliage behind her, the tree trunks on the right and elsewhere a good deal of wearing is apparent, probably caused by pressure at the time of lining.

The source of the Daphnis and Chloe story is the Greek pastoral romance of Longus.

The attribution of no. 637 to Bordon is acceptable, probably somewhat earlier than no. 674.[1] The *Jupiter and Io*, signed by Bordon (Göteborg, Konstmuseum) is of approximately the same size as no. 637 and may therefore have been intended as a companion piece to it.

VERSION: Vienna, Kunsthistorisches Museum (no. 253 in the catalogue of 1907; not in the 1928 or 1938 catalogues). The design is given an oblong format. The female figure holds a bow and arrows instead of the reed pipes. Called 'Venus and Adonis'.[2] A third version (Dubrovnik)[3] is of the same format as no. 637 but with the bow and arrows as in the Vienna picture, though arranged differently.

PROVENANCE: Purchased with the Beaucousin collection, Paris, 1860.

REPRODUCTION: *Illustrations, Italian Schools*, 1937, p. 50.

REFERENCES: (1) In notes (in the Gallery archives) on the hair styles shown in no. 637 Stella Mary Pearce favours a dating around 1540. (2) No. 637 is said to have been called 'Mars and Venus' when in the Beaucousin collection. (3) Photograph in the Gallery archives.

674   PORTRAIT OF A YOUNG WOMAN

$42 \times 33\frac{3}{4}$ (1·067 × 0·857).

These dimensions include strips *c.* 3″ wide at the top of the picture, *c.* 2″ wide at the sides and *c.* 1″ wide at the base which are later additions.[1] As the strip on the left hand side of the picture includes part of the lady's right sleeve it is probable that the picture had been cut down at some stage before the additions were made.

The hair and nearly all of the dress in good condition, the face and hands fair. The area of flesh within the pearl necklace a good deal retouched.

Inscribed: . ÆTATIS. SVÆ | ANN. XVIIII.

In earlier editions of the National Gallery catalogue it is said to be

signed PARIS .B.O., but only faint indications of some of these letters
are now visible. Nevertheless no doubt can be entertained regarding
the attribution.

Hitherto called 'A Lady of the Brignole Family, Genoa'. As there is
no coat of arms or inscription to the effect such a title was presumably
that used by the former owner, the Duca di Cardinale. There is otherwise no evidence in its favour.[2] Another suggestion—made by Bailo
and Biscaro[3]—that no. 674 is identical with the picture of a '*donna
lascivissima*' painted by Bordon, according to Vasari,[4] for Ottaviano
Grimaldi of Genoa, seems questionable, since Ridolfi refers to what is
clearly the same picture as a '*Venere ignuda*'.[5] The costume of no. 674—
which is fashionable—suggests a dating in the late 1540's or early
1550's.[6] This dating is also applicable to the costume of a young man
in a portrait by Bordon in the Uffizi (no. 292). The sitter rests his right
hand on the table containing his helmet and lance, together with a floral
crown and ring. In the top right hand corner there is a view of steps
and columns similar to that shown in the top left corner of no. 674, but
with a female figure (greeting an *amorino*) instead of the young man.
The complementary arrangement of the arms in the two pictures and
of the direction of the eyes would also support a theory that the two
were painted as pendants—very possibly on the occasion of a betrothal.[7]
While this seems possible to the present writer it cannot be finally
established on the basis of identity of size owing to the changes under-
gone by no. 674 in this respect.

PROVENANCE: Said to have come from Genoa (letter from Sir Charles
Eastlake, quoted in reference 1). Purchased in Naples from the Duca di
Cardinale, 1861.

REPRODUCTION: *Illustrations, Italian Schools*, 1937, p. 50.

REFERENCES: (1) Writing from Naples on 20th September, 1861, Sir Charles
Eastlake, the Director of the National Gallery, says (letter in the Gallery
archives): 'I have purchased here a portrait of a lady by Paris Bordone—about
half length, but enlarged. It came originally from Genoa, where it was the
fashion to increase the size of pictures. It will be a question when it reaches
England how far to cut it down. I think the original boundary, at least above,
would be too close to the head.' Evidently for that reason nothing was done.
(2) In the Brignole-Sale catalogue of 1813 a similar picture is listed (no. 97—
Ritratto di Signora con abito ricamato, di Paris Bordone) but this was probably
the one still in Palazzo Rosso, since attributed to Parrasio Micheli (N.I.42).
(3) *Paris Bordon*, 1900, pp. 128–9. The authors also claim that the sitter of
no. 674 is identical with that of a Bordon portrait at Vienna (no. 231). As she
is there shown décolletée this is used to support their theory. In point of fact
Bordon's female portraits often tend to approximate to a type—for example,
a third portrait (Vienna no. 248) shows a lady similar to both the other two.
In the present instance identity of the sitters cannot necessarily be assumed.
(4) Vasari/Milanesi, vol. VII, p. 465. (5) Ridolfi/Hadeln, vol. 1, p. 233. If, as is
possible, Ridolfi was merely paraphrasing Vasari, this argument has less force.
(6) Notes in the Gallery archives by Stella Mary Pearce. The derivation of the
staircase in the background from Serlio, Book 2 suggests 1545 as *terminus post
quem* (cf. C. Gould, Warburg Journal XXV, 1962, p. 61). (7) A third portrait by
Bordon—of a bearded man (Genoa, Palazzo Rosso)—also has a similar
architectural background, the small figures in this case being apparently a lady

distributing alms to a beggar. The design of this picture would preclude its having been intended as pendant to no. 674. Since the costume seems somewhat later than that in the National Gallery or Uffizi pictures it might in theory represent the sitter of the latter some years later, but there is no positive evidence in favour of this.

1845 CHRIST AS THE LIGHT OF THE WORLD
$35\frac{1}{4} \times 28\frac{3}{4}$ (0·908 × 0·73).
Good condition.
Traces of signature, centre of base of pilaster, top left: O[?]PARIDIS. bor-on-.[1]
Inscribed on the scroll: EGO. .SVM. LVX. MVD(I) (*Ego sum lux mundi; qui sequitur me non ambulat in tenebris, sed habebit lumen vitae,* John. VIII, 12).
A comparable picture at The Hague (Mauritshuis no. 310) is signed PARIS. BD O. and there are various early references to pictures of this subject by Bordon.[2] Even irrespective of the remains of the signature on no. 1845 the style and handling alike are eminently acceptable as Bordon's.

VERSIONS: See above. A fairly close replica is at S. Benedetto Po.[3] A variant, with the right hand lowered, is in the Ravenna museum. A similar composition to the latter has been revealed by X-rays under Bordon's portrait of Jerome Crofft (Louvre), which is dated 1540.[4] A copy of no. 1845 in the Accademia, Venice (no. 307: no. 121 in S. Moschini Marconi's catalogue) (1962) has been attributed to Rocco Marconi.[5]

PROVENANCE: Presented, c. 1829, to Dr Henry Greenwood by a member of the Sicilian embassy in London who stated that it had been painted as the altarpiece of a private chapel of his family and had never been out of their possession.[6] Passed by inheritance to Dr. Greenwood's daughter, Mrs. Mary A. Wood, by whom presented, 1901, through her brother, the Rev. G. Greenwood.

REPRODUCTION: *Illustrations, Italian Schools,* 1937, p. 51.

REFERENCES: (1) More clearly visible in an infra-red photograph than to the naked eye. The form of Bordon's signature on his pictures varies, the most common being O. PARIDIS BORDONI (BORDONVS, BORDONO, etc.). (2) See Bailo and Biscaro: *Della Vita e delle Opere di Paris Bordon* (1900), p. 110, no. 1. A picture of similar design at Ravenna (Istituto di Belle Arti, ex-coll. Rasi) attributed to Bordon by Bailo and Biscaro (*op. cit.,* pp. 146–7) is doubtfully his work (see Andrea Moschetti in *L'Arte,* 1901, pp. 280 ff.). (3) Reproduced in *Inventario degli Oggetti d'Arte d'Italia,* VI, p. 148. (4) Published by S. Béguin: *Bulletin du Laboratoire du Musée du Louvre,* 1964, no. 9. (5) E.g. by F. Heinemann: *Giovanni Bellini e i Belliniani,* 1962, p. 120, no. S. 205. (6) Document in the Gallery archives.

3122 CHRIST BAPTISING S. JOHN MARTYR, DUKE OF ALEXANDRIA
Painted area $24\frac{1}{4} \times 26\frac{3}{4}$ (0·615 × 0·68).
The original turn-over of the canvas is preserved at the base and at both sides.
Thinly painted and probably somewhat rubbed in places, but the paint on the whole seems in fair condition.

Traces of *pentimenti* in Christ's right foot. Above the latter are some marks which may have been an inscription. If so, it is unlikely to be original.

In Layard's MS. catalogue[1] as 'Christ . . . baptising a Doge in Prison' and published as such by Sir Charles Holmes[2] and in the National Gallery Catalogue of 1920. The title was changed in the 1925 catalogue from 'baptising' to 'anointing'—presumably on the assumption that the kneeling figure was a Doge of Venice who would therefore be in no need of baptism. Nevertheless the action seems to be baptism and not anointing (which in any case would be surprising in prison) and in consequence the ducal cap (*corno*) shown on the ground would indicate a potentate with a ducal title but not a Doge of Venice. In point of fact no. 3122 corresponds so closely with a picture described by Ridolfi (in the biography of Paris Bordon, under the heading 'Venetia') that identity can be assumed[3]: *Due piccioli quadretti sono in oltre appresso la Signora Gradenica Gradenico, Monaca in San Daniele . . . nell' altro è San Giovanni Duca di Alessandria nella prigione battezzato dal Salvatore, e vi sono due Angeli con sciugatoi in mano.* The church of San Daniele held the body of S. John Martyr, Duke of Alexandria (Alexandretta), which had arrived at Venice in 1214 from Constantinople. He was said to have been miraculously baptised by Christ in prison, but his cult was local and unofficial as his legend had been taken over from that of S. Procopius of Caesarea.[4]

The attribution of no. 3122 to Bordon seems not to have been questioned and is acceptable.

PROVENANCE: In the mid-seventeenth century in the possession of Gradenica Gradenico, S. Daniele, Venice (see above). Bought by Sir A. H. Layard from 'Signor Marcato'.[5] Layard Bequest, 1916.

REPRODUCTION: *Illustrations, Italian Schools*, 1937, p. 51.

REFERENCES: (1) No. 75 —with the Layard papers in the Gallery archives. (2) *Burlington Magazine*, vol. XXXII (1918), p. 107. (3) Ridolfi/Hadeln, I, p. 234. (4) The present writer's grateful thanks are due to Miss Rosalie B. Green, Director of the Index of Christian Art at Princeton, who drew his attention to this. Further references are the *Acta Sanctorum*, May, vol. IV, p. 304, 19th May; also G. B. Tomaselli: *Memorie spettanti alla Vita di S. Giovanni Martire Duca d'Alessandria ed alla Traslazione del suo Corpo che si venera nella chiesa delle Canonichesse lateranensi di San Daniele di Venezia*, 1776, and *Leggenda di S. Zuane martire . . .*, 1543. The present writer has not been able to consult a copy of the last-mentioned work. (5) Layard MSS. Giordana Canova (*Paris Bordon*, 1964, p. 81) gives pre-Layard ownership as 'Casa Cappello a S. Polo, Venice', but this was Layard's own address.

Imitator of BORDON

2097 A YOUNG WOMAN WITH CARNATIONS

$38\frac{1}{2} \times 29\frac{1}{4}$ (0·978 × 0·743).

Some retouching in the face (notably the eye-lids and eye-brows) and in the sitter's left arm.

Hitherto as 'School of Bordon', but the technique and costume alike are unacceptable as of the sixteenth century. Probably a deliberate and not very skilful imitation of Bordon dating from the seventeenth or eighteenth century.[1]

PROVENANCE: From the John Samuel collection (no. 23 in the catalogue of 1895), which passed to the Misses Cohen, by whom exh., New Gallery, 1894–5 (207). Bequeathed by the Misses Cohen, 1906.

REPRODUCTION: *Illustrations, Italian Schools*, 1937, p. 52.

REFERENCES: (1) Stella Mary Pearce, in a note on the costume in the Gallery archives, is inclined to prefer a dating in the eighteenth century to one in the seventeenth. The technique, however, could well be that of the seventeenth.

ANDREA (active 1506–25) and RAFFAELLO
(active 1506, died 1545) DEL BRESCIANINO

Sienese school. Andrea di Giovannantonio di Tommaso Piccinelli da Brescia, called Andrea del Brescianino is recorded at Siena between 1506 and 1524 and at Florence in 1525. His brother Raffaello, also first recorded at Siena in 1506, is mentioned by Vasari as having a studio at Florence in 1527–9, where he died in 1545.[1] An altarpiece of the *Baptism* (Siena, Muso dell' Opera del Duomo) is the only surviving work by either brother which is documented. It is stated in 1524 to be already in position.[1] The document, however, specifies it as the work of both brothers. Furthermore, the earliest printed account of the Brescianino— Isidoro Ugurgieri Azzolini: *Le Pompe Sanesi*, vol. II, 1649, p. 348— attributes to the two brothers conjointly two further altarpieces which still survive at Siena. These are the *Madonna and Child with Saints* from Monte Oliveto di Porta Tufa (now in the Accademia) and the high altar of SS. Pietro e Paolo (*Coronation of the Virgin*, still in position). These three paintings are the nucleus round which a number of others, including no. 4028 can be grouped stylistically. The fact that modern scholarship has elected to attribute all of them to Andrea and to overlook Raffaello may be noted without further comment.

REFERENCES: (1) For documentation see G. Milanesi: *Documenti per la Storia dell' Arte Senese*, vol. III, 1856, pp. 31–3. Also Vasari/Milanesi, VII, 9 and notes.

ANDREA and/or RAFFAELLO DEL BRESCIANINO

4028 MADONNA AND CHILD WITH SS. PAUL AND CATH-
ERINE OF SIENA AND THE INFANT BAPTIST

Panel, $28\frac{1}{4} \times 21\frac{1}{8}$ ($0\cdot718 \times 0\cdot536$).

Much of the paint is very thin. Made up in places, but general condition quite good for a picture of this type on panel.

Characteristic of the group of pictures called 'Brescianino' (see biographical notes above) and evidently a popular and therefore repeated design. At least two versions are known which substitute S. Sebastian for S. Paul[1] as well as other variants.[2]

VERSIONS: See above.

PROVENANCE: Claude Phillips bequest, 1924.

REPRODUCTION: *Illustrations, Italian Schools*, 1937, p. 67.

REFERENCES: (1) One in the John G. Johnson collection, Philadelphia, the other in a private collection at Leghorn in 1935. (2) Berenson, in the John G. Johnson catalogue, vol. 1 (1913, p. 61) refers to a Madonna then in the collection of Baron Chiaramonte Bordonaro, Palermo (described in his 1932 *Lists* as 'Madonna with Infant John and two Youthful Saints') and a S. Catherine in the Lanckoronski collection.

BRONZINO
1503–1572

Florentine School. His name was Agnolo di Cosimo. The date of his birth is from a baptismal entry published (by A. Furno) in 1902. Attempts have been made to prove that his surname was Allori and (by Milanesi) that it was Tori. But there seems little or no evidence in favour of either, the first, in particular, being in all probability merely a confusion. Allori was the name of Bronzino's favourite pupil in the house of whose family he was living at the time of his death. His usual signature on documents was 'Il Bronzino' and on one occasion (Gaye: *Carteggio*, III, p. 116) he specifically refers to himself as 'Agnolo di Cosimo, detto il Bronzino'.

Nearly all his life was spent in Florence. There are numerous authentic pictures of different kinds but his fame has depended primarily on his portraits. Bronzino also made designs for tapestries and wrote verse.

According to Vasari Bronzino was successively the pupil of Raffaellino del Garbo and of Pontormo. He was for some years the intimate and assistant of the latter whose work was the conditioning factor in the formation of his style.

651 AN ALLEGORY OF VENUS AND CUPID

Panel, $57\frac{1}{2} \times 45\frac{3}{4}$ ($1 \cdot 46 \times 1 \cdot 16$).

Good condition in general. A certain amount of local retouching, particularly along the vertical join of the wood about a quarter of the picture's width from the left-hand side. Cleaned in 1958, when later additions, such as some drapery between Venus' legs and a spray of leaves which partly obscured Cupid's buttocks, were removed.[1]

An unusually large number of *pentimenti* are visible. Bronzino seems to have had second, and sometimes even third, thoughts about all the major outlines in the picture. In addition to those visible to the naked eye X-ray photographs reveal further changes, some of them of major importance. Cupid's arrow, for instance, as held by Venus in her right hand, appears to have been an afterthought. Originally Venus' right arm bent back more acutely from the elbow and her right hand caressed Cupid's curls. The upper part of her arm and her right hand then assumed their present form, but Time's fingers were first shown extended, linked with Venus'. The arrow was only added when the clenching of Time's fist left a space between his hand and Venus', whose outstretched fingers would otherwise no longer have fulfilled any purpose. The figure of Jealousy was originally lower down, and a series of curves in the region of Cupid's buttocks are most plausibly identified with experiments in placing them. At the (spectator's) left-hand lower corner what seems to have been a mask, like those visible on the right, occupied the area now filled by the toes of Cupid's right foot. Between Venus' left arm and the left leg of the *putto* on the spectator's right of her what is apparently the outline of a buttock, and therefore, from its position, presumably Venus', is also visible on the X-ray photographs.

Known as 'Venus, Cupid, Folly and Time' since it entered the Gallery but there seems to be no old authority for this style which in itself is not entirely satisfactory. There is no authentic key to the allegory. Of the characters portrayed, Cupid is easily recognizable by his wings and his quiver, Venus from her relation to him and Time from his hour-glass. Four figures remain: top left, a woman (?), who may be wearing a mask, holds the blue curtain with both hands; underneath, one of indeterminate sex tears its hair with both hands. On the right, a naked boy holds roses with both hands and wears an anklet of bells. He has trodden on thorns, one of which has pierced his right foot. Behind him, a figure with the head of a girl, the hind quarters of a furry animal and the tail of a scaly one holds a honeycomb in one hand and the sting at the extremity of her tail in the other. A pair of white doves are shown in the lower left corner, Venus holds a golden ball in her left hand, and a pair of masks, apparently male and female, lie on the ground, bottom right.

Vasari—if this is the picture he speaks of (see below)—mentions figures of Pleasure and Jest ('piacere' and 'giuoco') as being on one side and Fraud and Jealousy on the other. Jest or Folly in some form is very likely conveyed by the naked boy with the roses, and Jealousy by the hair-tearing figure on the left. The crouching figure on the right, and the one at the top left, remain. Two different identifications of them have been suggested in recent years. Erwin Panofsky called them Deceit and Truth,[2] Michael Levey, Pleasure and Fraud respectively.[3] Panofsky went on to interpret the allegory as signifying that Time reveals sensual pleasure as leading to jealousy and despair. For Levey it is the disarming of Cupid by Venus. He derives the thematic inspiration from Michelangelo's Venus and Cupid (executed by Pontormo) and the pose of Venus from that of the Virgin in Michelangelo's Doni tondo. This interpretation would accord better than Panofsky's with Vasari's description: *Fece un quadro di singolare bellezza, che fu mandato in Francia al re Francesco; dentro al quale era una Venere ignuda con*

Cupido che la baciava, ed il Piacere de un lato e il Giuoco con altri Amori, e dall' altro la Fraude, la Gelosia, ed altre passioni d'amore.[4]

As the pedigree of no. 651 is not complete it cannot be taken as certain that this is the picture Vasari meant, and it may be noted that he says nothing of the figure of Time, but does speak of non-existent 'other Cupids' (*altri Amori*). If, nevertheless, as he says, the picture had already gone to France such inaccuracy might be explicable, and a better explanation than that he was referring to a different picture. The picture described by Vasari, whether or not identical with no. 651, seems not to have remained for long in the French royal collection, since it is not included in the lists of important pictures at Fontainebleau by Cassiano dal Pozzo (1625) or the Père Dan (1642) nor does it figure in the *Inventaire Générale* of 1709. While there is possible supporting evidence that no. 651 came from France[5] there is no certain knowledge of its movements earlier than the mid-eighteenth century. A further difficulty in the way of the identification is that Francis I died in 1547, and although the hair-style of Venus in no. 651 accords well with the fashions of the first half of the 1540's that of Deceit looks later by about a decade.[6]

Another picture by Bronzino of similar theme but less complicated design and iconography is in the Gallery at Budapest.

VERSIONS: A copy was given by the 2nd Earl Spencer after the Battle of Camperdown (1797) to Admiral Duncan who later specified that it was to be given 'to that young rascal Jack Tufton'[7] This picture may be the one engraved in 1813 by W. P. Sherlock as in the possession of 'Mr Complin'[8] Perhaps the same picture again was bought by Dr. G. C. Duncan *c.* 1895 from Dr. Abercrombie and sold by the former at Robinson's, 9th January, 1936 (131). This picture passed to Sir Ronald Graham, after whose sale (Sotheby's, 6th April, 1949, lot 150) it was bought by Signor Scaretti of Rome. A smaller picture, stated to be of the same design,[9] was in the H. A. J. Munro sale, Christie's, 1st June, 1878 (78) (Primaticcio) and another is listed by Mireur in an anonymous sale, Paris, 1893.[10] The naked *putto* of no. 651 is incorporated into a drawing of different subject inscribed Primaticcio (Louvre: reproduced in *L'Œil*, January, 1955). A kind of pastiche, by G. C. Procaccini, engraved as *tavola IV* in Zancon's *Galleria Inedita . . . Milanesi* (1812).

PROVENANCE: Bought with the Beaucousin collection, Paris, 1860. Almost certainly the picture included in a list of mortgaged pictures at Althorp in 1742 ('Venus, Cupid, Jealousy, Deceit etc. by Angelo Bronzino 4. 8¾-3·9')[11] Apparently sold privately by Christie's for Lord Spencer, July, 1847, to Emery.[12]

REPRODUCTION: *Illustrations, Italian Schools*, 1937, p. 68.

REFERENCES: (1) These additions, made when the paint crackle had already partly formed, do not figure in the Scaretti copy nor in the Sherlock engraving of a copy (see below under 'Versions'). (2) *Studies in Iconology* (1939). See also Hubertus Lossow: *Das Werk des Künstlers*, vol. 1, 1939. In his second edition (1962), pp. 86 ff, Panofsky recorded an alternative identification of his 'Truth' figure with 'Night'. (3) *Sacred and Profane Significance in two paintings by Bronzino* in *Studies . . . Presented to Anthony Blunt*, 1967, pp. 30 ff. (4) Milanesi edition, vol. VII, pp. 598–9. Sir Kenneth Clark (*The Nude*, 1956, p. 128) derives the Venus in no. 651 from Michelangelo's *Pietà* (Florence, Duomo). Wölfflin (*Die Klassische Kunst*, 1924 ed., p. 195) had already compared the two works. Though no. 651 was pretty certainly the earlier of the two it should be possible to trace the roots of both in the Doni tondo (see above). (5) The Hon. John Spencer who apparently owned no. 651 in 1742 also owned a Leda (now no. 1868 of this Gallery) which, according to the Sir Joshua Reynolds sale catalogue, came from the French Royal Collection (see entry for no. 1868). (6) Notes by Stella Mary Pearce in the Gallery archives. (7) Letter from Dr. G. C. Duncan in the Gallery archives. (8) Impression in the British Museum. (9) By Scharf in his copy of the sale catalogue now in the National Portrait Gallery library. (10) *Dictionnaire des Ventes d'Art*, vol. I, p. 28. (11) Document at Althorp discovered by the present Earl Spencer to whom the compiler's thanks are due. (12) Documents in the Gallery archives. There is no means of verifying that the Beaucousin and Althorp pictures were definitely the same though there can hardly be any reasonable doubt, as such is stated to be the case in the National Gallery catalogue of 1861. Beaucousin was in full buying spate in the 1850's.

1323 PORTRAIT OF PIERO DE' MEDICI ('THE GOUTY')

Panel, 23 × 17¾ (0·58 × 0·45).
The face considerably rubbed and retouched. Cleaned, 1958.

The subject (1416–69) was the son of Cosimo ('Pater Patriae') and father of Lorenzo the Magnificent. Some of the details of the costume correspond closely with those in a bust by Mino de Fiesole (Florence, Bargello) on which it is presumably based.[1]

The attribution to Bronzino himself appears to be justifiable. Although the quality seems hardly up to his highest standard a partial explanation may be the difficulty of producing a satisfactory posthumous portrait.

VERSION: Florence, Museo Mediceo (exh. Mostra Medicea, Florence, 1939, p. 90 of 2nd edition of catalogue, no. 15).

PROVENANCE: Exh. Leeds, 1868 (125) (where stated to have been in the collection of Conte Galli Tasse (Tassi), Florence) and R.A., 1872 (71), lent on both occasions by Sir W. R. Drake, by whom bequeathed, 1891.

REPRODUCTION: *Illustrations, Italian Schools*, 1937, p. 68.

REFERENCE: (1) Mario Salmi (*Bollettino d'Arte, anno XXXIX*, 1954, pp. 36–42) postulates in addition an hypothetical Castagno painting as source.

5280 MADONNA AND CHILD WITH S. JOHN THE BAPTIST AND S. ANNE OR S. ELIZABETH

Panel, 40 × 32 (1·01 × 0·81).
Considerably damaged and extensively retouched. The hair of S. John (together with the face of the female saint on the right) is one of the few important areas which seem to give some idea of what must have been the original surface quality. *Pentimento* down most of the (spectator's) left side of the Christ Child's body. Probably in other areas too, but the quantity of repaint present makes this point difficult to establish.

Sir Claude Phillips in 1914 read the remains of a signature (in the lower left corner) as B · ONZO FL · · ETINO, and said he considered the foundation of it genuine but that it had been 'refreshed'.[1] The picture seems to have been restored since that date and probably some of the 'refreshment' removed on that occasion. The surviving letters which seem original are (upper line) · N Z · (lower line) F · · · E(?)T I N. There are also traces of the original outline of other letters.

The child whose head and shoulders are seen towards the bottom of the picture is identifiable as S. John the Baptist by his hair shirt and by the baptismal bowl in his left hand. The Christ Child has evidently taken from him the reed cross.

McComb[2] claims that this is one of the *Holy Family*'s recorded by Vasari[3] as having been painted by Bronzino for Bartolommeo Panciatichi, but there is no external evidence for this.[4]

DRAWING: Michael Jaffé (private communication) draws attention to a related one at Frankfurt, attr. Rubens.

VERSIONS: Parma, Museum (without the female saint on the right). Another (with signature) was lot 90, Mrs. N. Martins sale, Christie's, 20th March, 1964.

PROVENANCE: W. A. L. Fletcher sale, Christie's, 15th May, 1914 (105) (as Perino del Vaga)[5] where bought Carfax and then sold to Sir George Faudel-Phillips on the advice of Sir Claude Phillips.[6] Exh. Olympia 1928 (X3, lent Sir Lionel Faudel-Phillips). Bequeathed by Sir Lionel Faudel-Phillips, 1941.

REPRODUCTION: 16-century Italian School, plates, 1964, p. 34.

REFERENCES: (1) Article in the *Burlington Magazine*, vol. 26 (1914–15), p. 3. (2) Arthur McComb: *Agnolo Bronzino* (1928) pp. 10–11. (3) Vasari/Milanesi vol. VII, p. 595. (4) The Bronzino *Holy Family* in the Uffizi was presumably one of these since the flag in the background shows the Panciatichi arms. This picture is slightly larger than no. 5280. In *Studies in Renaissance and Baroque Art presented to Anthony Blunt* . . . 1967, pp. 30 ff, Michael Levey examined the religious symbolism of no. 5280 and traced a thematic connection with the Uffizi picture. (5) The Fletcher collection was formed, apparently early in the nineteenth century, by John Bolton who bequeathed it to the Rev. Thomas Staniforth. It later belonged to Annabella, Lady Boughey. Waagen (*Galleries and Cabinets of Art in Great Britain*, 1857, pp. 426–8) mentions pictures in the Staniforth collection but not this one. (6) Cf. article by the latter already referred to.

Studio of BRONZINO

704 PORTRAIT OF COSIMO I DE' MEDICI, GRAND-DUKE OF TUSCANY

Panel, $8\frac{3}{8} \times 6\frac{3}{4}$ (0·214 × 0·172).

Very good state on the whole. A certain number of local retouchings, mostly small.

The sitter united the two branches of the Medici family and was the founder of the Grand-Duchy of Tuscany.

The quality of no. 704 is hardly high enough to warrant an attribution to Bronzino himself, but of the several extant versions (see below) none seems entirely acceptable as Bronzino's original.

VERSIONS: Turin, Rome (Borghese), Florence (Pitti) Vienna. Also lot 101, Sedelmeyer sale, Paris, 1907, and lot 3, anonymous sale, Christie's 20th March, 1959 (said to be identical picture). There are even more numerous Bronzinesque replicas of the portrait of Cosimo in armour.

PROVENANCE: From the collection of the Maréchal de Luxembourg.[1] Said to have been bought in Paris, August 1815, by Count Joseph von Rechberg and sold, a month later, to Prince von Oettingen-Wallerstein.[2] No. 28 in the lithograph catalogue, of 1826(?), of the latter collection, as Antonio Moro: same number and attribution in MS. catalogue of 1827 (in the Alte Pinakothek, Munich).[3] The collection was ultimately bought by the Prince Consort who kept it at Kensington Palace. No. 20 in Waagen's catalogue (made in 1854 but published in his *Galleries and Cabinets of Art . . .*, 1857). Exh. Manchester, 1857 (192). Presented by Queen Victoria in fulfilment of the wishes of the Prince Consort, 1863.

REPRODUCTION: *Illustrations, Italian Schools*, 1937, p. 69.

REFERENCES: (1) Old label on the back. (2) A certain amount of information about the circumstances of this transaction emerges from an article by Dr. Georg Grupp: *Fürst Ludwig von Oettingen-Wallerstein als Museumsgründer* (in *Jahrbuch des Historischen Vereins für Nördlingen und Umgebung*, vol. VI 1917, pp. 73–109, see particularly pp. 99 and 100). From this it appears that Oettingen-Wallerstein had already been negotiating with Rechberg for the sale of the latter's collection and when, in 1815, Rechberg (who was a general) was sent to Paris in connection with the renewed campaign against Napoleon, he availed himself of his presence there to continue his activities as collector and as agent for Oettingen-Wallerstein. (3) Also no. 85 in an undated catalogue (datable 1848 through a reference in the *Tübinger Kunstblatt* of that year, p. 256). Oettingen-Wallerstein had at that time sent the collection to England and was offering it for sale.

Follower of BRONZINO

2085 PORTRAIT OF A LADY

Panel, $23\frac{1}{8} \times 19\frac{1}{8}$ (0·58 × 0·48).

Very fair condition. Cleaned 1953. The cleaning revealed that the face had been entirely repainted, changing, notably, the position and direction of the eyes. Formerly catalogued as 'School of Bronzino' and called 'Bianca Capello'. This identification of the sitter is fanciful. Since the cleaning the technique of the face is seen to be closer to Bronzino than before, but the period of the costume—late 1570's or early 1580's[1] —would indicate a late follower.

PROVENANCE: From the John Samuel collection, bequeathed by the Misses Cohen, 1906. An article by M. H. Spielmann in *The Connoisseur* (vol. 17, 1907, pp. 229–34) states that it was in Lord Farnham's collection 'which was dispersed by auction in Dublin in 1827' and that it may be identifiable with one 'which came under the hammer at Christie's in 1859, and was purchased for only £24'. The latter may be a confused reference to a portrait catalogued as by Bronzino and representing 'Bianca Capella, Grand Duchess of Tuscany' which was lot 1013 in the tenth day's sale (10th August, 1859) of the Northwick collection, conducted by Phillips. This picture fetched £24 3s. on that occasion but as no further details or dimensions are given in the sale catalogue there is no means of establishing whether or not it was identical with no. 2085.[2]

REPRODUCTION: *Illustrations, Italian Schools*, 1937, p. 69 (before cleaning).

REFERENCES: (1) Notes in the Gallery archives by Stella Mary Pearce. The lace collar seems earlier to have been painted in a closed position across the chest. (2) In the priced copy of the sale catalogue in the library of the National Gallery the buyer's name is given as 'J. Cheetham, Esq., M.P.' while Redford (*Art Sales*, II, 1888, p. 221) gives it as 'Rowbotham'.

Giovanni Busi, called CARIANI
active 1509, still alive 1547

The christian name is often given in the dialect form Zaninus or Zuane in contemporary documents. His family was from the Bergamo area. He himself adds the word 'Bergomeus' to his signature on several occasions, but he is first recorded in Venice, and subsequent documentary references confirm his residence there over a period of years.

Only three surviving pictures by Cariani are signed and dated—a group portrait of 1519 (Roncalli collection, Bergamo), an altarpiece of 1520 of the Resurrection (Milan, Brera, ex-Gerli collection) and a Madonna and Child with Donor, also of 1520 (Bergamo, Accademia Carrara). A signed portrait of an old man (Vienna, published by Baldass, Vienna *Jahrbuch*, 1929, p. 108) is datable from an inscription 1536–40. Two signed but undated male portraits (Bergamo and Ottawa Galleries) are similar in style to the 1519 group portrait and with them may be associated a group of further portraits (including no. 2494 of this Gallery) some of which are not signed but which are obviously by the same hand. Cariani's style, indeed, as it was around the year 1520, is easily recognizable from these few works. The chief influences seem to be Titian and Palma Vecchio, but the touch is much coarser and the colours tend to approximate towards pink. The fact that the dated works only define Cariani's style at isolated periods in what was apparently a long career and that he seems to have been something of a chameleon has caused the utmost confusion in attempting to define his *œuvre*.

For the documents concerning Cariani's career see G. Ludwig in Prussian *Jahrbuch*, vol. XXIV, 1903, *Beiheft*, pp. 33–41, and vol. XXVI, 1905, *Beiheft*, p. 153.

2494   A MEMBER OF THE ALBANI FAMILY
  $42\frac{3}{4} \times 32\frac{3}{4}$ (1·06 × 0·8).

The robe and most of the face in good condition. Retouching covers old slits in the canvas in the landscape and in the beard. The identification of the sitter's family is due to the presence of the Albani arms on another version of the picture, in Casa Suardi, Bergamo.[1] The handling of no. 2494 is clearly the same as that of several signed portraits by Cariani and its authenticity need therefore not be questioned.

The identity and status of the sitter is more conjectural. Morelli referred to him as Francesco Albani but gave no evidence.[2] The costume also is not certainly identifiable.[3]

VERSION: Bergamo, Casa Suardi (see above).

PROVENANCE: Said to have been in the Noli collection, Bergamo, then Luigi Albano in the same town.[4] Before 1883 in the possession of George Salting,[5] by whom exh., New Gallery, 1894–5 (144) and Glasgow International Exhibition, 1901.[6] Lent National Gallery, 1902. Salting Bequest, 1910.

REPRODUCTION: *Illustrations, Italian Schools*, 1937, p. 83.

REFERENCES: (1) The proportions of the Suardi picture are slightly different from those of no. 2494—there is more space at either side (permitting, on the sitter's right, on the parapet behind the table, the inclusion of a coat of arms) and slightly more at the top. Otherwise the two versions are almost identical. While it is not possible to decide on visual evidence whether or not no. 2494 has been cut it is unlikely that this was the case since in the Suardi picture the coat of arms immediately adjoins the sleeve (which indeed slightly breaks the outline of the shield). It may therefore perhaps be deduced that no. 2494 was painted first, that the sitter objected to the non-inclusion of his arms and that as there was no room for them the Suardi replica was made. (2) *Munich and Dresden*, English edition, 1893, p. 25. (3) Notes by Stella Mary Pearce in the Gallery archives. The costume would accord best with a dating around 1520. (4) Crowe and Cavalcaselle, *North Italian Painters*, III, p. 453. (5) Salting MSS. in the Gallery archives. (6) Page 106 (no number) in the catalogue of the Fine Art Section.

1203 MADONNA AND CHILD WITH SS. JOSEPH, LUCY, ANOTHER FEMALE SAINT AND A YOUTHFUL DONOR

$33\frac{3}{4} \times 46\frac{1}{2}$ (0·85 × 1·18).
Extensively damaged and repainted.

The arrangement, and to some extent also the types, are comparable with those in a similar picture, formerly in the Frizzoni collection, Bergamo.[1] The latter is a signed work of Cariani. The coarseness of the execution of no. 1203 is marked, even for Cariani, but some, at least, of this effect may be due to the fact that the picture is, apparently, unfinished.[2] For the rest, the attribution to Cariani seems justifiable.

For some reason unspecified the female saint on the left was identified in earlier editions of the National Gallery catalogue as S. Barbara, while the one in front of her was called the Magdalen. The identity of the former with S. Lucy can hardly be doubted but the other figure has no attribute and may merely be a portrait of the donatrix (presumably mother of the boy on the right) to whom a nimbus has been added.

PROVENANCE: Enrico Andreossi, Milan, from whose heirs purchased (Walker fund), 1886.

REPRODUCTION: *Illustrations, Italian Schools*, 1937, p. 83.

REFERENCES: (1) Earlier still in the possession of Sir Charles Eastlake and exchanged by him for a Tura (now no. 772 of this Gallery). The story of the exchange is given by Gustavo Frizzoni: *Arte Italiana del Rinascimento*, 1891, p. 281, and by Morelli: *Munich and Dresden*, English edition (1893), p. 23. It should be noted that the exchange affected Eastlake's private collection and not, as far as he was concerned, the National Gallery. (2) The amount of repaint present makes it difficult to pronounce with absolute confidence on this point, though it seems probable to the present writer. It might also account for some of the peculiarities of the costume—e.g. the very inorganic appearance of the clothes worn by the kneeling female saint in the centre.

No. 41 (Ascribed to CARIANI) *see*
Ascribed to BERNARDINO DA ASOLA

2495 MADONNA AND CHILD (*LA VIERGE AUX LAURIERS*)

Canvas, transferred from panel,[1] $35\frac{1}{2} \times 28\frac{1}{2}$ (0·9 × 0·72).

A great deal of local repaint. The important areas most affected are the Madonna's eyes and the whole of the outline of her face on the far side, together with the dark inside of the veil adjoining it. Also most of her left hand. Repaint also in the Child's body, particularly in the lower part of His right leg; but His head, in spite of some disturbance in the outline of the forehead, is better preserved than the Madonna's.

Catalogued as Cariani since its entry into the Gallery except in the editions of 1925 and 1929, when it appears as Bonifazio. In the Leuchtenberg gallery as Giorgione. Attributed by Crowe and Cavalcaselle to Moretto.[2] The Cariani attribution—the least improbable of those suggested—was first made by Herbert Cook[3] and was supported by Borenius[4] and by Berenson.[5] Attributed to Palma Vecchio by Suida.[6]

The case, put in the greatest detail by Berenson, for attributing no. 2495 to Cariani as an early work turns on its resemblance to a *Madonna and Child with SS. Elizabeth and the Infant Baptist* in the Galleria Nazionale, Rome. This is not a documented Cariani but is acceptable to the present writer as his work. It is more evolved in style than no. 2495. Some reserve should be retained in view of the fact that the most primitive in style of the Cariani's acceptable to the present writer—*Madonna and Child with Saints*, no. 156 of the Venice Accademia —has little in common with no. 2495.

The date (1514) on the present frame appears to be modern and is presumably a guess at the date of origin of the picture.

PROVENANCE: In 1828 already in the Leuchtenberg gallery, Munich.[7] Bought by Salting, by whom lent, 1903. Salting Bequest, 1910.

REPRODUCTION: *Illustrations, Italian Schools*, 1937, p. 46.

REFERENCES: (1) 'in three pieces' (1929 catalogue). (2) *Painting in North Italy*, III (1912 ed.), p. 305. (3) *Burlington Magazine*, II (1903), p. 78. (4) In Crowe and Cavalcaselle, *loc cit*. (5) Notably in *Arte Veneta*, 1954, p. 150; reprinted in *Essays in Appreciation*, 1958, pp. 111–15. (6) In *Belvedere*, XII (1934–7), p. 87. (7) No. 56 in the Leuchtenberg catalogue of that year. No. 7 (with line engraving) in Passavant's catalogue of 1851. Before 1871, when Crowe and Cavalcaselle's *History of Painting in North Italy* was first published, the Leuchtenberg collection had been moved to St Petersburg.

VINCENZO CATENA
active 1506, died 1531

The earliest dated reference to him is of 1st June, 1506 in an inscription on the back of Giorgione's *Laura* portrait (Vienna). This refers to Giorgione as being a partner of Catena's. With the exception of a possible visit to Rome in the year of his death there is no documentary evidence of his presence outside Venice, and Crowe and Cavalcaselle, in particular, have long ago been shown wrong in identifying him with a certain Trevisan painter called Vincenzo dalle Destre.

Some half dozen religious pictures are signed by Catena, but none of them is dated. They are in an idiom ultimately dependent on

Giovanni Bellini before his final period and thus are entirely *quattrocento* in style. The key picture for Catena's later development is a signed portrait of a man (Vienna) which shows a more evolved style, mid-way between the *quattrocento* and the High Renaissance. Round this painting and an altarpiece of the Martyrdom of St Christina at S. Maria Mater Domini, Venice (dated 1520 on the frame and vouched for as Catena's by an early, but not contemporary, source) may be grouped a number of others, including nos. 234 and 694 of this Gallery, once attributed to Palma, but more probably late works of Catena.

In his monograph (1954) Giles Robertson points to the text of Catena's wills as constituting evidence that painting was not his only source of income and to contemporary correspondence as proving that he moved in the same Humanist circles as Marc Antonio Michiel, Bembo and others. In consequence he would have appeared something of a mandarin among the professional painters, and Giorgione may well have chosen to associate himself with him for that reason.

234   A WARRIOR ADORING THE INFANT CHRIST AND THE VIRGIN

Canvas,[1] $61\frac{1}{8} \times 103\frac{3}{4}$ ($1 \cdot 55 \times 2 \cdot 63$).

Much worn and extensively retouched. In particular the face of the page, together with the cloud behind, seems largely modern.[2] General appearance of other areas probably less altered by retouching.

First catalogued (in 1854) after entering the Gallery as 'attributed to Giorgione' but altered in Wornum's catalogue of the same year to 'School of Giovanni Bellini' as which it remained until the edition of 1898 when it appeared under the Catena attribution originally put forward by Crowe and Cavalcaselle (1871),[3] and supported by Morelli and Berenson among others. As Catena in subsequent editions except those of 1925 and 1929 when it underwent its Palma Vecchio phase. The case for Catena's authorship, with which the present writer is in agreement, is best put by Giles Robertson.[4] The fact that no. 234 is appreciably more evolved in style than Catena's *Martyrdom of St Christina* which is dated (on the frame) 1520 would involve a dating between then and Catena's death in 1531.

The iconographic problems in this picture arise from the fact that the warrior's armour and doublet are European, but the enamelled trappings of his horse, his belt and curved dagger hanging underneath, as well as the silk of his head-gear, appear to be of Islamic design.[5] His features, too, seem non-European, though some of this effect may be due to retouching. The question therefore arises whether the warrior is a European affecting some measure of Eastern accoutrement or whether he is a Saracen convert wearing European armour. On the whole the present writer inclines to the latter hypothesis, from which it would follow that no. 234 might well have been painted to commemorate a conversion—probably one that had caused considerable stir. A case of this kind occurred after the capture by the Turks of the Venetian colony of Modone in the Peloponnese in 1500. On this occasion a certain Bernardino Mocenigo was captured with two of his sisters who subsequently married two Turkish officers. All five eventually returned to Venice where the two Turks were baptised in 1515 by the Patriarch, Antonio Contarini, receiving the christian names Pier Giovanni and Giovanni Piero respectively. On the 13th May, 1522, the Doge Antonio Grimani made provision for the two converts in Cephalonia. The fact that no. 234 probably dates, as already indicated, from some time after the year 1520 and that the Turks in the Mocenigo story are specified as being warriors would provide a possible link, though not a sufficiently strong one to be classed as more than conjecture.[6]

A similar quail to those on the left also occurs in no. 694 (Catena) of this Gallery, in the entry for which picture another example is cited (cf. also bird in foreground of picture attributed D. Caprioli, reproduced Berenson, *Venetian Painters* 1957, II, pl. 902).

PROVENANCE: From the Standish collection. Subsequently, in 1841, with Italian dealers in Florence and Rome. Sold by Baldeschi to Woodburn,[7] at whose sale in 1853, purchased for the National Gallery.[8]

REPRODUCTION: *Illustrations, Italian Schools*, 1937, p. 236.

REFERENCES: (1) Certain parts of the craquelure suggest that the picture may originally have been painted on panel and transferred to canvas at an early date. It is not, however, possible to pronounce with certainty on this point. (2) Crowe and Cavalcaselle (*Painting in North Italy*, 1871, vol. 1, p. 255, note 2) mention the page as 'blackened and spoiled'. (3) *Loc. cit.* (4) *Catena*, 1954, p. 68 and elsewhere. (5) Notes in the Gallery archives from various authorities on these subjects. See also O. M. Dalton in *Proceedings of the Society of Antiquaries*, 2nd series, vol. XXI, pp. 376–80 and 383, and Sir James Mann in *Archaeologia*, vol. LXXXIII, 1930, p. 301. The silk of the warrior's cap, which is not a proper turban, is said to be North African. (6) The sources for this anecdote are Litta: *Famiglie Celebri*, XII, Mocenigo di Venezia, Tavola XIX and Sanudo's diary (entries for 7th January and 22nd February, 1515) (the present writer's attention was kindly drawn to the Sanudo reference by Stella Mary Pearce). According to Sanudo, provision was already made for the converts at Cephalonia or Zante at the time of baptism in 1515. The Doge's letter of 13th May, 1522 to this effect is mentioned by Litta but not by Sanudo. Mrs. Jameson (*Legends of the Madonna*, 1879 ed., p. 108) says the soldier is supposed to be Duccio Constanzo of Treviso. (7) All this information in a record dating from 1853 in the Gallery archives. (8) Lot 80, 1st day (24th June) as Giorgione.

694 S. JEROME IN HIS STUDY

$29\frac{7}{8} \times 38\frac{3}{4}$ (0·75 × 0·98)[1]

The paint has worn thin and a great deal of retouching is apparent. But it is mostly local and though widespread does not involve any whole feature.

Purchased as Giovanni Bellini, but attributed to Catena as early as 1871 (Crowe and Cavalcaselle).[2] The alternative attribution to Palma[3] (under whose name no. 694 appears in the National Gallery catalogues of 1925 and 1929) is now generally discredited.[4]

The iconography of this picture is unusual in several respects. The colours of S. Jerome's robes—bright pink and blue—are abnormal and the blue cardinal's hat particularly so. If this is not merely a whim of the painter or of whoever commissioned the picture it may be meant as an indication of S. Jerome's penitence.[5] Alternatively, Moroni mentions a tradition that newly elected cardinals, on their way to receive their red hats, wore for the occasion hats of the same '*pontificale*' shape which were green if they were bishops and blueish or lilac ('*pavonazzo*') if they were not.[6] S. Jerome, though normally depicted as a cardinal, was not a bishop.

A similar bird to that on the left of no. 694 also occurs in Catena's *Holy Family* at Dresden and in no. 234 ('*Warrior adoring Christ and the Virgin*') of this Gallery. Also, *inter alia*, in no. 1418 (Antonello) of this Gallery. The fantastic building in the background of no. 694 recurs in the same position in the Dresden *Holy Family*.

In his will of 1518 Catena bequeathed to Giovanni Battista Egnazio '*unum aliud telarium sancti Hieronymi ab heremo*', but this in itself hardly constitutes sufficient evidence to presuppose a connection with no. 694.[7]

VERSION: Frankfurt-am-Main, Staedel Institute. Replica adapted to smaller format, thereby cutting out the floor in the foreground and some of the area to the left of the desk, including the stool and the lion. S. Jerome's hat apparently red. A water-colour copy was lot 82, Christie's, 24th October, 1960.

PROVENANCE: Manfrin collection, Venice (no. 406, as Giovanni Bellini, in the 1856 catalogue), from which (with nos. 695 and 696) purchased, 1862.[8]

REPRODUCTION: *Illustrations, Italian Schools*, 1937, p. 265.

REFERENCES: (1) A strip about ½″ wide running along the bottom of the original canvas has been painted over at some later date with dark paint. (2) *Painting in North Italy*, vol. 1, p. 256. (3) Holmes and Collins Baker in *Burlington Magazine*, vol. 42 (1923), pp. 230 and 239. (4) Giles Robertson: *Catena* (1954), pp. 61–3, gives the best summary of the Catena/Palma problem and demonstrates the impossibility of the Palma attribution in the present instance. (5) A blue cardinal's robe (but not a blue hat) occurs in no. 4759 (Sassetta) of this Gallery, in connection with which Martin Davies (*The Earlier Italian Schools*, catalogue, 1951, p. 395, note 6) pointed out that cardinals wear violet for mourning or penitence. Giles Robertson, *loc. cit.*, suggested that the sitter in Catena's portrait of a man at Vienna might also be the patron of no. 694 as he wears the same combination of colours. In a miniature in the British Museum (MS. Add. 38126, f. 227ᵛ) S. Jerome is shown with a blue hat and also a blue gown. (6) Moroni: *Dizionario Storico-Ecclesiastico*, 1859, vol. IX, p. 183, and vol. XCVI, p. 230. In the latter reference he says '*cappelli pontificali verdi se vescovi o paonazzi se semplici prelati*'. Elsewhere (vol. LV, p. 142) Moroni quotes the definition of a '*prelato*' given at the Council of Toul (859) as '*chiunque presiede ad una comunità religiosa*'. Notes by Stella Mary Pearce on the subject, and on the exact colour indicated by the word '*pavonazzo*', are in the Gallery archives. (7) See Robertson, *op. cit.*, p. 7. (8) Seen in the Manfrin collection by Mündler in 1858 and attributed by him to Lotto (MS. in the Gallery archives).

1121   PORTRAIT OF A YOUNG MAN

Panel, painted area 12 × 9¼ (0·3 × 0·23).[1]

Some obvious small retouchings, mostly in the face and in the clouds, but in general well preserved. *Pentimento* in the spectator's left side of the face.

In the Hamilton Palace collection as Leonardo da Vinci. Catalogued after entering the National Gallery as 'Venetian School, 15th century'. Other suggestions have been Cima,[2] Basaiti[3] and Bissolo.[4] The attribution to Catena, first made in 1897 by Berenson,[5] has been pretty generally accepted since and seems justifiable. Giles Robertson[6] pointed out that it depends primarily on the resemblance of type between no. 1121 and the donor portrait in the signed pictures by Catena of the *Sacra Conversazione* type at Liverpool and in the Pospisil (ex-Melchett) collection, though both of these are profiles.

VERSION: The 1929 catalogue mentions a picture at Isola Bella (a photograph is Alinari, no. 14,492). Berenson (*Lists*, 1957) as perhaps Pietro degli Ingannati. Any resemblance this picture may bear to no. 1121 is likely to be fortuitous.

PROVENANCE: Hamilton Palace (lot 344, as Leonardo, in sale of 24th June, 1882, when purchased).[7]

REPRODUCTION: *Illustrations, Italian Schools*, 1937, p. 93.

REFERENCES: (1) The panel has been cut at the top but not on the other three sides. (2) Collins Baker (with reserve) in the *Burlington Magazine*, vol. 42 (1923), pp. 239 ff. (3) *Notes on the National Gallery* (reprinted from *The Guardian*) by Sir Walter Armstrong, 1887, p. 24. (4) Jacobsen (with reserve) in *Repertorium für Kunstwissenschaft*, 1901, p. 372. (5) *Venetian Painters* (3rd edition). (6) Giles Robertson: *Catena* (1954), p. 46. (7) Robertson (*op. cit.*) suggests tentatively an identification with an entry in an inventory of 1643 of the Duke of Hamilton's pictures. He is, however, mistaken in assuming that no. 1121 might have been cut at the bottom. Despite the present cradling it is still possible to see that the priming ends short of the present edge and therefore that there has been no cutting along it. Robertson points out that, contrary to what is stated in the National Gallery catalogue of 1924 and 1929, no. 1121 is not identical with the picture described by Waagen at Hamilton Palace as Girolamo da Santa Croce (Waagen—*Treasures of Art* . . ., III, p. 300—says that the latter picture had a landscape background). There seems no warrant for the statement in the 1929 catalogue that no. 1121 was 'purchased as by Giovanni Bellini'. It appeared as Leonardo in the Hamilton sale catalogue and as 'Venetian School, 15th century' in the next edition of the National Gallery catalogue (1883).

5751 PORTRAIT OF THE DOGE, ANDREA GRITTI

$38\frac{1}{4} \times 31\frac{1}{4}$ (0·97 × 0·79).

The face, neck and beard much abraded and extensively repainted. The hands rather less so. Parts of the robe and nearly all the cap well preserved. *Pentimenti* in the outline of the latter. The identity of the sitter can be vouched for by comparison with contemporary inscribed medals—e.g. Hill, *Corpus* 456.

A votive-picture by Titian of the Doge Andrea Gritti kneeling before the Madonna and Child was painted in 1531 and destroyed in the Doge's Palace fire of 1574. Hadeln[1] demonstrated convincingly that it is reproduced in a surviving wood-cut except that in the latter the Doge Francesco Donato is substituted for Andrea Gritti. The substitution (presumably in honour of the then reigning Doge) would have involved no more than the head, since a drawing by Titian on the back of a study for S. Bernardino in the same picture shows the same pose as in the wood-cut—kneeling in profile.[2] This wood-cut was evidently the source used by Tintoretto when painting the existing replacement to the Gritti votive-picture (in the Sala del Collegio of the Doge's Palace) which follows the general arrangement of Titian's picture as shown in the wood-cut. Since the Doge's features in the wood-cut were not those of Gritti, however, he would have had to take another model, and in fact his model was almost certainly no. 5751, with which his representation corresponds exactly, even to the handkerchief in the clenched left hand and the unusual gesture (for a votive-picture) of the right.[3]

No. 5751 was generally attributed to Titian (even being cited as a perfect example of Titian's 'finish' by Burne-Jones in the libel action brought against Ruskin by Whistler in 1878)[4] until identified as Catena by Wilde in 1931.[5] The Catena attribution was subsequently upheld by Robertson.[6] Inasmuch as Andrea Gritti (1455–1538) did not become Doge until 1523 the Titian attribution is impossible, since by that time Titian was painting more broadly (cf., for example, no. 1944 of this Gallery which is certainly earlier than the year 1523 but already more evolved in style than no. 5751). Despite the bad condition of the face and hands, the type of pose, system of folds in the draperies and the handling of the embroidery (cf. the warrior's cap in no. 234 of this Gallery) seem to the present writer fully to justify the Catena attribution.[7] The picture must therefore be a late work—between Gritti's election in 1523 and Catena's death in 1531.

The linen head-cloth ('rensa') just visible projecting from under the cap should have a string hanging down in order to tie under the chin. Presumably it had one once, but the area where it would be is now largely repaint.[8]

The device on the ring worn by the sitter apparently represents the Doge kneeling (on the right) to St Mark (left) whose banner is vertical in the centre. This device was normal on contemporary Venetian coins.[9]

VERSIONS: 1. Tintoretto, Doge's Palace, Sala del Collegio (see above). 2. Formerly Cambridge, Fitzwilliam Museum (ex-Holford) (sold Sotheby's 25th February, 1959, lot 149, and 11th May, 1960, lot 154, both times as 'J. Tintoretto'. Now in Bob Jones University as Titian). Inferior old replica.

PROVENANCE: Noted by Otto Mündler, 31st October, 1855, in 'Palazzo Contarini' (from the context, Palazzo Contarini del Zaffo) Venice: 'By Titian the portrait of Doge Agostino Barbarigo [sic], profil'.[10] Collection of Dr. Gilbert Elliott, Dean of Bristol, who exhibited it, as Titian, B.I., 1863 (53). Bought from him by Ruskin, shortly before 2nd September, 1864.[11] Lent by Ruskin (as Titian) to R.A., 1870 (57). Hung for many years in Ruskin's house, Brantwood, Coniston.[12] Passed with the house to Ruskin's cousin, Mrs Arthur Severn. Bought by Langton Douglas by whom sold to Otto Gutekunst, 1917.[13] Exh. Olympia, 1928 (X57) (as Titian, lent Mrs. Gutekunst). Presented by Mrs. Gutekunst in memory of her husband, 1947.

REPRODUCTION: Photographs available from National Gallery negatives. Also reproduced by Giles Robertson: Catena (1954), pl. 45.

REFERENCES: (1) Prussian *Jahrbuch*, vol. XXXIV (1913), pp. 234–8. (2) For this reason alone Hadeln's subsequent attempt (*Pantheon*, 1930, p. 489) to identify no. 5751 as an actual fragment of Titian's votive-picture is untenable. Ruskin had already advanced the same view (*Works*, Library Edition, vol. XXIV, p. 184). (3) Of the other three Tintoretto votive-pictures in the Sala del Collegio only one (that of Francesco Donato) shows the Doge in the old-fashioned praying attitude. In the other two (Alvise Mocenigo and Nicola da Ponte) the Doge is shown with arms outstretched. This is a conventional gesture of wonderment, essentially different from the gesture in the Gritti votive-picture. (4) Some of Burne-Jones' evidence in this connection is printed in Whistler's *The Gentle Art of Making Enemies*, 1890, p. 16. (5) J. Wilde in the Prussian *Jahrbuch*, vol. LII (1931), p. 96. (6) Giles Robertson: *Catena* (1954), p. 69. (7) Robertson, *op. cit.*, convincingly relates no. 5751 stylistically to other late works of Catena. Tietze (*Tizian*, 1936, Textband, p. 135) mentions an oral attribution (by Fiocco, subsequently published in his monograph, 1939, pp. 135–6) to Pordenone which he wisely ignores. His own suggestion that no. 5751 is after Tintoretto's picture rather than the source of it is best treated in the same fashion. Berenson (*Lists*, 1957) assumes that in no. 5751 Titian was copying Catena. (8) This contention is supported by the fact that such a string occurs in Tintoretto's version already mentioned. (9) This is made clear by comparing a macro-photograph of the ring with representations of the same device on coins of Andrea Gritti or Giovanni Dandolo (reproduced on pp. 46 and 47 of the *Guida Illustrata del Museo Civico Correr*, 1909). (10) Mündler's notes in the Gallery archives. A portrait 'by Titian' of 'Duke Grettie' was in Charles I's collection, but was larger than no. 5751 (4′ 4″ × 3′ 4″) and showed him 'with his right-hand holding his robes' (Bathoe's catalogue, 1757, p. 105, no. 5). (11) Letter of that date to Rawdon Brown published in Ruskin's *Works*, Library Edition, vol. XXIV, p. 184. (12) Where seen by Sydney Cockerell as Ruskin's guest (letter in the Gallery archives). (13) Information supplied by Messrs P. and D. Colnaghi from Gutekunst's records.

Ascribed to CATENA

3540 MADONNA AND CHILD WITH THE INFANT S. JOHN THE BAPTIST

Panel, $28\frac{1}{2} \times 22\frac{1}{2}$ (0·72 × 0·57).

Much damaged, particularly down the centre, where repeated flaking and worm holes have led to extensive repainting. A good deal of repainting in other areas. The only parts in reasonably good condition are the area of the Madonna's mantle (which is painted over a red underpaint) on the spectator's right and S. John's green tunic.

In the 1929 catalogue as Catena. Its status was affected by the publication, in 1957, by Cornelius Müller Hofstede of an X-ray photograph of the Giorgione self-portrait at Brunswick.[1] This revealed part of a composition of a Madonna and Child underneath the self-portrait. It was truncated like the portrait, but showed clearly the most unusual and original feature of the design of no. 3540 and the other versions, namely the attitude of the Child, who supports Himself by holding on to the Madonna's neck with His left hand while turning His head in the opposite direction. Müller Hofstede argued convincingly that the Brunswick portrait was the work of Giorgione and not a copy as had been alleged, and went on to claim that the Madonna underneath was in essentials of Giorgione's invention, that it was the model for the various versions, including no. 3540, painted by Catena and his followers and that it could be dated around the year 1506 when Giorgione and Catena were in partnership. The fact of this partnership—which is documented by the inscription on the back of the Giorgione portrait called 'Laura' at Vienna—would admit of the possibility that Giorgione painted the Brunswick portrait over a Madonna not by himself but by Catena. Though Müller Hofstede may well be correct in arguing that the essential novelty in the design of no. 3540 and the other variants— the motive of the Child's left arm—is probably due to Giorgione, the germ of the other elements in the Madonna and Child group is already present in an earlier work undoubtedly by Catena—Virgin and Child with Saints and a Donor (Liverpool). Some collaboration between Giorgione and Catena in the evolution of the design of no. 3540 is therefore possible, as Müller Hofstede admits (*op. cit.*, p. 25).

As regards the execution, a version at Posen, including in addition S. Zacharias and a female saint, is generally considered superior to no. 3540 and attributed to Catena himself. A somewhat inferior variant, with an adult S. John the Baptist, a female saint and two donors, is in the Galleria Estense at Modena, attributed to a follower of Catena. Of the several versions without flanking saints no. 3540 is the best and the possibility is not to be excluded that the execution may be Catena's own, but the bad condition of most of it, together with the evident popularity of the design, precludes a dogmatic judgement.[2]

VERSIONS (see also above): Basel, Museum (Bachofen-Burckhardt Stiftung) (attributed Bissolo) and Florence, Museo Bardini.[3] Another as part of a polyptych in church of S. Niccolo, Giappona, near Ragusa.

DRAWING: Vienna, Albertina. Red chalk drawing closely corresponding with no. 3540. Robertson (*op. cit.*) calls it a student's copy.

PROVENANCE: Acquired from Colnaghi by Alfred de Pass, by whom presented 1920.

REPRODUCTION: *Illustrations, Italian Schools*, 1937, p. 92.

REFERENCES: (1) Cornelius Müller Hofstede: *Untersuchungen über Giorgiones Selbstbildnis in Braunschweig* in *Mitteilungen des kunsthistorischen Institutes in Florenz*, October, 1957, pp. 13–34. (2) Berenson (*Three Essays in Method*, p. 122) suggested that the design may have originated in Giovanni Bellini, but Müller Hofstede's arguments (*loc. cit.*) render this unlikely. In Berenson's *Lists* (1957), no. 3540 appears as Catena. Giles Robertson (*Vincenzo Catena*, 1954, p. 79) opposes the attribution of no. 3540 to Catena himself on the grounds that the warm flesh tones and the quality of the modelling are not quite Catena's. It could be answered that much of the pink tone of the Child's body may be due to retouching and for the same reason it is difficult to judge what the quality of the modelling originally was. (3) The Mansueti at Venice (mentioned by Berenson, *loc. cit.*) is only indirectly connected and contains other figures. Other variants with flanking saints are too numerous to specify.

CORREGGIO
active 1514, died 1534

His name was Antonio Allegri, known as Correggio from the town, in the Emilia, of his birth. Vasari says that when he died, in 1534, he was aged about forty, which would date his birth around 1494. The fact that he entered into a contract on 30th August, 1514 (the earliest surviving documentary evidence of his activity as a painter) 'cum consensu eius patris presentis et consensum dantis' can be variously interpreted to mean that he was over or under twenty-five years of age at the time, according to which of the local statutes was applicable.[1] There is fairly good evidence that he was a pupil of the Modenese painter, Francesco Bianchi Ferrari, who died in 1510,[2] but the chief formative influences were Mantegna and Costa who were successive court painters at Mantua. Later on, Correggio evidently reacted to certain aspects of the art of Leonardo da Vinci, and finally, to some extent, to that of Giulio Romano.

Active in maturity mainly in Correggio and Parma. Vasari, who tended to claim artistic dependence on Michelangelo in respect of as many contemporaries as possible, laments the fact that Correggio was never able to go to Rome.[3] Ortensio Landi, whose book was published two years later (1552), also states that he did not go there.[4] Both these testimonies, being of early date (only sixteen and eighteen years respectively after Correggio's death, Landi's made from personal knowledge of the artist's home town and Vasari's made against his own interests as historian) are of weight. Nevertheless a number of writers claim a Rome visit.[5]

Correggio's significance as a major High Renaissance master and as the chief precursor within that period of the Baroque system of decoration has been copiously discussed. The literature up to 1934 is tabulated in S. de Vito Battaglia's *Correggio Bibliografia*, published in that year. Of the pictures in the section of the present catalogue which follows it may be noted that several pedigrees are curiously interrelated. Two of them, nos. 10 and 23, were in Spain, in different collections, in the eighteenth century. Early in the nineteenth the former passed to Murat's collection at Naples where it joined a third, no. 15.

REFERENCES: (1) See A. E. Popham: *Correggio's Drawings* (1957), p. XV. (2) Venturi: *Storia* . . . IX, II, pp. 457-9. (3) 1550 ed., vol. 2, p. 582. (4) 'Sette libri di cathalogi a' varie cose appartenenti', 1552. (5) Most recently Popham, *op. cit. passim*. Fischel (*Raphael*, I, 1948, p. 323) adduces the influence which he sees of certain Roman works of Raphael on Correggio in support of a visit by the latter to Rome 'about 1518'.

10 MERCURY INSTRUCTING CUPID BEFORE VENUS ('The School of Love').

$61\frac{1}{4} \times 36$ $(1\cdot55 \times 0\cdot915)$.

Evidently cut down, probably on all four sides, and at a relatively early date since the measurements given in the 1639 catalogue of Charles I's collection are almost identical with the picture's present dimensions.[1] Cleaned 1969-70.

Condition very unequal. The best-preserved passage in the figures is Cupid's head, wings and part of his chest, which are in fair state. Most

of the upper part of Mercury's body (including his head) is somewhat
rubbed and repainted, and there are numerous worn and retouched areas
elsewhere, particularly in the shadows of the flesh. Among other areas of
repaint and damage is one to the left of Venus' right foot where in Peter
Oliver's miniature copy, the Massias copy, De Jode's engraving and Jan
de Bisschop's drawing (see below) a quiver and arrows emerge from
behind Venus' leg. During the restoration of 1969–70 parts of the quiver
and arrows were uncovered. *Pentimenti* in Venus' right ankle and left
foot. Mercury's blue drapery appears at an earlier stage to have extended
across (and not, as now, under) his left fore-arm, and (judging from
X-ray photographs) to have covered the upper part of his left thigh. It
also swept downwards from under his right eye, covering his right
shoulder. In addition, the X-ray photographs show that his face was
originally painted almost full face. X-rays also reveal earlier positions of
Venus' and Mercury's faces and a different arrangement of Cupid's
legs.

The title 'School of Love' dates at least from the eighteenth century.
Correggio's so-called 'Antiope' (Louvre) was in the same collection,
namely the Gonzaga, as no. 10 as early as 1627,[2] while earlier still, in
1607, two pictures seeming to answer to the descriptions of these, but
perhaps old copies (see PROVENANCE below) were recorded in the
Granvella collection.[3] Even at this date the dimensions of the 'Vénus
dormante avec un Cupido et un Satyre' (i.e. the 'Antiope') are given as
somewhat larger than those of the 'Vénus avec Mercure', as is the case
with the Louvre picture and no. 10.[4] Despite this, and despite the fact
that the Louvre picture seems to reflect a more evolved phase of Correggio's art than does no. 10, the association of the two designs from so
early a period suggests that they may originally have been intended as
pendants, and with this the two subjects would accord well.

Analogies have recently been indicated with a bronze relief of the
education of Eros and Anteros and with a description of reliefs flanking
a door in the *Hypnerotomachia Poliphili*, first published in 1499.
Neither work corresponds with Correggio's picture in every detail, but
both are close enough to show that all three probably derive from the
same source. Whatever may be the precise theme in either case, some
version of the contrast between sensual love (the Louvre picture) and a
more sublimated form of love (no. 10) would emerge clearly from such a
juxtaposition. In Van der Doort's inventory of Charles I's collection
copies of the two pictures are already referred to as *Venerie Mundano* and
Venerie Coeleste.[5]

The existence of a study for the Christ in the *Agony in the Garden*
(Apsley House) on the *verso* of a sketch for the Cupid in no. 10 (see
DRAWINGS below) would normally indicate a similar date of origin for
the two paintings. This date is likely to be around the end of the time
when Correggio was decorating S. Giovanni Evangelista, where he
worked from 1520 to the beginning of 1524. A drawing in the British
Museum for one of the S. Giovanni pendentives (Popham 18) has, on
the *verso*, a sketch associable with the Anteros theme, one aspect of

which is probably illustrated in no. 10 (see Verheyen, quoted in reference 5 above).

VERSIONS: The most famous copy passed successively through the Queen Christina, Odescalchi, Orléans, Willett and Erard collections and was apparently lot 18 in the Comte de Franqueville sale, Paris, 31st May–2nd June, 1920. What claimed to be it was in the Queen Christina exhibition, Stockholm, 1966, no. 1168, lent by the Duc d'Ursel. It was engraved by Villain, 1786. Also in the Queen Christina and Orléans collections was a variant of no. 10, attributed to Titian (engraved in the *Galerie du Palais Royal*, vol. 2, no. 11 of Titian), later with A. L. Nicholson, London (reproduced by Suida: *Tiziano*, 1933, pl. CXIX) and now Kress Collection, El Paso, Texas. Another was at Sans Souci, Potsdam (no. 26, larger than no. 10—1·75 × 1·17). Others were a version formerly in the collection of Baron Massias, Paris[6] and at Ham House and Chenonceaux. Miniature copies at Windsor (signed by Peter Oliver and dated 1634) at Burghley House and at Sibiu (larger than no. 10). A copy of Cupid alone was no. 1098 in the 1900 edition of the catalogue of the Aeltere Pinakothek, Munich. Various other copies of no. 10, of uncertain date, could be listed.

DRAWINGS: British Museum (1862-10-11-200) (Popham, *op. cit.*, no. 79 *verso*). Study in red chalk for the Cupid. Another drawing in the British Museum (1900-8-24-119) (Popham, *op. cit.*, no. A71) is a copy from the Cupid in the painting. There is also a drawing in the Uffizi (reproduced Ricci, 1930, pl. CCXLVI b), showing Mercury's head in its present position and, apparently, also his drapery as it now appears. This is also probably a copy from the painting (Popham, *op. cit.*, no. A26 as 'perhaps by Girolamo da Carpi'). There is a wash-drawing copy of no. 10 by Jan de Bisschop (Ashmolean, Oxford, no. 111*) which may have been made from a copy or from de Jode's engraving.

ENGRAVING: By Arnold de Jode, dated 1667, 'Londini'.[7]

PROVENANCE: Recorded in the inventory of 1627 of the Gonzaga collection at Mantua.[8] Though it cannot be proved that it was not identical with one of the two pictures already mentioned as in the 1607 Granvella inventory it seems more likely that it was not and that the latter were copies for the following reasons. No. 10 is undoubtedly an original by Correggio, it was at Mantua in 1627 and Correggio seems to have worked for the Mantuan court during his life time. It is therefore more reasonable to assume that it was painted for Mantua and that it stayed there than that it was painted for someone else and reached Mantua between 1607 and 1627. Equally difficult would be the hypothesis that though painted for Mantua it got into the Granvella collection at some time later in the sixteenth century and then came back to Mantua between 1607 and 1627. Purchased for Charles I in 1628 and recorded at Whitehall in van der Doort's inventory of 1639.[9] Valued at £800 in the Commonwealth inventory of 1649 and sold for that sum, 23rd October, 1651 to 'Mr Baggley'.[10] Recorded by Richard Symonds in 1651–2 in the hands of 'the King's Glassier' who was offering it for sale.[11] Purchased, 1653–4, by the Spanish ambassador in London, Alonso de Cárdenas, acting on behalf of the Conde-Duque de Olivares.[12] When, in 1688, the daughter of Olivares' heir, Gaspar, married the 10th Duke of Alba she brought to that house the Carpio and Olivares titles and estates, including no. 10 which was seen in the possession of the Duke of Alba by Mengs, c. 1770, and by Swinburne (book published in 1779).[13] During the litigation between the heirs of the Duchess of Alba, who died in 1802, and the 7th Duke of Berwick and Liria (who then inherited the Alba estates and titles) no. 10 was sold by order of Charles IV of Spain to his favourite, Emmanuel Godoy, 'Prince of the Peace'.[14] It figures in the MS. inventory (dated 1st January, 1808) of the latter's collection. After Godoy's arrest in March 1808 his collection was put up for sale in the same year, but on the morning of the day appointed Joachim Murat, then military commandant of Madrid, secured for himself some of the finest pictures including no. 10, which he afterwards took with him to Naples.[15] Taken from Naples, apparently on the night of 20th May, 1815[16] to Vienna by Caroline Murat who sold it there, with no. 15, to Baron Stewart, later 3rd Marquess of Londonderry,[17] from whom both were purchased, 1834.

REPRODUCTION: *Illustrations, Italian Schools*, 1937, p. 102.

REFERENCES: (1) The dimensions are omitted by Vertue but are specified as 5′ 1″ × 3′ 0″ in the van der Doort MS. (Ashmole 1514). (2) See PROVENANCE and reference no. 8. (3) Auguste Castan: *Monographie du Palais Granvella à Besançon* in *Mémoires de la Société d'Emulation du Doubs*, IV series, 2nd vol., 1866, published 1867, p. 126 (à propos the Granvella inventory of 1607): *Une Vénus dormante avec un Cupido et un Satyre, faitz du Correggio, 6 piedz d'haulteur et quattre de largeur* . . . 155 and on the same page *Une Vénus avec Mercure, du Corregio, d'haulteur de 5 piedz et neufz polces, large de 3 piedz 9 polces, fait sur toille* . . . no. 156. (4) The truncation of Mercury's left knee in no. 10 suggests, irrespective of other considerations, that it has been cut down on the right. Peter Oliver's miniature copy (see VERSIONS below) in fact shows this area untruncated and is dated 1634. However, as already stated no. 10 was already its present size as early as 1639 and Charles I, who had owned it since 1628, is most unlikely to have permitted it to be cut. As the dimensions of the Granvella picture of 1607 were also smaller than those of the 'Antiope' it seems at least possible, whatever the status of the Granvella pictures, that the truncation of no. 10 had occurred before Peter Oliver made his copy and that in it he was merely indulging in copyists' licence. (5) See Myron Laskin: *Art Bulletin* 1965, pp. 543–4. Panofsky, in a letter in the Gallery archives, draws particular attention to the fact that in no. 10 Venus is shown winged. This is highly unusual in Italy though not uncommon in the North (Heinrich Kohlhaussen— *Minnekästchen im Mittelalter*, 1928, p. 41—cites various fifteenth-century Northern representations of winged Venuses in the sense of 'Frau Minne'). According to Ficino the 'Venus Urania' even corresponds with Christian *Caritas*. For the subject, see also L. Soth (*Art Bulletin*, 1964, pp. 539 ff. and 1965, p. 544), E. Verheyen (*Gazette des Beaux-Arts* 6th period, 1965, vol. 65, pp. 321 ff. and *Art Bulletin*, 1965, pp. 542–3) and the present writer (*Burlington Magazine*, 1964, p. 420). Verheyen postulates a connection with a sculpture of Mercury teaching Cupid to read, which is recorded in Isabella d'Este's possession, but of which nothing else is known. (6) A line engraving of this picture is published in C.P. Landon's catalogue (1815) of the Massias collection. (7) The engraving is inscribed as done from the original. As de Jode was born as late as 1638 and no. 10 had been in Spain since 1654 this statement raises difficulties and there would remain a possibility that the engraving was in fact made from a copy. Peter Oliver's miniature copy of 1634 seems never to have left England but when compared with de Jode's engraving does not seem adequate as sole source. Robin Gibson (*Burlington Magazine*, January, 1972, p. 31) publishes a contemporary mezzotint of Nell Gwyn after the Venus in no. 10. (8) Printed by Carlo d'Arco: *Delle Arti . . . di Mantova . . .*, 1857, vol. II, p. 154, and by Alessandro Luzio: *La Galleria dei Gonzaga venduta all' Inghilterra nel 1627–28*, 1913, p. 92. (9) The substance of van der Doort's entry is given by Vertue: *A Catalogue and Description of King Charles the First's Capital Collection . . .*, printed for W. Bathoe, 1757, pp. 106–7. See also O. Millar's edition (Walpole Society, 1960). No. 10 is also noted at Whitehall by Sandrart: *Lebenslauf und Werke Joachims von Sandrart*, ed. A. R. Peltzer, 1925, p. 24. (10) Public Record Office L.R.2, 124 f., 194, no. 20 and British Museum, Harley 4898, p. 282. (11) Symond's diary, British Museum, Egerton MSS., no. 1636. (12) H. Léonardon: *Une Dépêche Diplomatique relative à des Tableaux acquis en Angleterre pour Philippe IV* in *Bulletin Hispanique*, 1900, pp. 25–34, also the Duchess of Alba: *Documentos escogidos del Archivo de la casa Alba*, Madrid, 1891. From these works it emerges that Olivares intended to present no. 10 to Philip IV but kept it for himself when doubts regarding its authenticity were expressed by Velázquez and by Angelo Nardi. (13) Henry Swinburne: *Travels through Spain*, 1779, p. 353. There is also the following contemporary reference in an anonymous and unpublished diary, in 1949 in the possession of Mr. John Hanbury Martin: *Madrid, 1st May, 1772 . . . went . . . to see the Duke of Alba's a fine and elegantly furnished House there is either an Original or Copy of the famous picture of Mercury reaching Cupid to read.* The author of the diary may have been John Skipp (1742–1811). Also A. Conca: *Descrizione Odeporica della Spagna*, I, 1793, p. 235 (as in the Alba Palace). (14) A. M. De Barcia: Catalogue of the Alba Collection, 1911, pp. 260–1. (15) W. Buchanan: *Memoirs of Painting*, II, 1824, p. 227. (16) See note 12 to no. 15 in the present catalogue. (17) See note 13 to no. 15 in the present catalogue.

15   ECCE HOMO

Poplar, $39\frac{1}{4} \times 31\frac{1}{2}$ (0·99 × 0·80).
Excellent condition. Cleaned, 1967–8.

Pentimento in the Virgin's face, the lower portion of which was originally covered by the blue mantle in a line continuing to the left that which now constitutes the portion of the drapery on the far side of her face. Christ's pink mantle likewise originally covered considerably more of His flesh including most of His left breast. His hands also were originally in different positions. In addition, X-ray photographs reveal another face close to the Virgin's and only slightly above it—as the mouth is open probably an earlier version of the Virgin's. None of these differences appears in Agostino Carracci's engraving of 1587 (which shows the picture in its present state except for narrow strips added to the bottom and to the right of the picture) and their fundamental character is a good indication, irrespective of the type and quality of the handling, that no. 15 is Correggio's original, and not an early copy as has been claimed.[1] Probably painted in the later 1520's.[2]

The unbiblical inclusion of the Virgin Mary in this scene is apparently an innovation.[3] The turbaned Pilate derives from the same subject in Dürer's *Engraved Passion*.[3a]

VERSIONS: Of the many old copies the most famous is the picture recorded in the Salviati collection at Florence which was later in the Robert Udny sale (19th May, 1804) and later still, it was claimed, in the Villa Dusmet sale, Rome, 1955. This picture is discussed in detail under PROVENANCE below. Other old copies are no. 96 of this Gallery, in the Parma Gallery, the Galleria Estense at Modena, the Palazzo Communale at Rimini (according to Ricci, 1896, p. 226), the Palazzo dei Conservatori, Rome (marked '220' on the frame), at Northwick Park (no. 22 in Borenius' catalogue, 1921) and in the Hamilton Palace sale, 1st July, 1822, lot 705. A small head of Christ, vaguely connected with no. 15, is at Firle (ex-Panshanger).[4] Numerous other copies of uncertain date could be mentioned. A distant derivative by Sigismondo Coccapani was exhibited Florence (Pitti): *Caravaggio e i Caravaggeschi*; 1970 (63).

DRAWINGS: Popham (*Correggio's Drawings*, 1957) cites two connected drawings (his no. A144, p. 198); he does not accept the first as autograph; the second has disappeared.

ENGRAVING: Agostino Carracci, 1587 (Bartsch XVIII, 20).

PROVENANCE: No. 188 in the 1783 catalogue of the Colonna Gallery, Rome. Before then its history is confused owing to conflicting accounts by the early writers. Agostino Carracci's engraving of 1587, which corresponds closely with no. 15, contains the inscribed information that the painting from which the engraving was taken was then in the Prati collection, Parma. Scannelli (1657) mentions such a picture as still in the Prati possession.[5] A second version, apparently of the same design, is first mentioned in 1591 as belonging to Francesco and Lorenzo Salviati in Florence.[6] During the eighteenth and nineteenth centuries the Prati and Salviati pictures are constantly confused. The most probable chain of events is that recorded by Pungileoni[7] who quotes statements to the effect that the Prati picture had been sold to the Colonna between 1675 and 1680, the Prati family retaining a copy which later passed to the Dalla Rosa or Bajardi families with other Prati possessions. An alternative theory current in eighteenth-century Rome maintained that the Colonna picture was a copy, the original having been taken to France,[8] while a third held that it was the Salviati picture and not the Prati one which had been acquired by the Colonna.[9] It is certain that the Colonna picture was not a copy, since it is demonstrably identical with no. 15 in which the X-ray evidence would preclude such a possibility, while the third theory is incompatible with a statement in the Udny sale catalogue of 1802 to the effect that the version in that collection had been in the possession of the Salviati family at Florence until it was taken to London.[10]

Sold by the Colonna to Alexander Day and by him, in 1802, to Ferdinand IV of Naples.[11] Taken from Naples by Madame Murat when she fled on the night of 20th May, 1815 to Vienna[12] where sold by her about 1822[13] to Lord Stewart, later 3rd Marquess of Londonderry, from whom purchased, 1834.

REPRODUCTION: *Illustrations, Italian Schools*, 1937, p. 103.

REFERENCES: (1) E.g. by Louis Viardot: *Les Musées . . . d'Angleterre*, Paris, 1843, p. 231 or Julius Meyer: *Correggio*, 1871, pp. 357–62. In the latter work no. 15 is catalogued among the doubtful works. (2) Earlier writers have suggested differing dates of origin. Meyer (*op. cit.*, p. 150) and Waagen (*Treasures of Art in Great Britain*, I. 1854, p. 327) agree with Pungileoni (*Memorie Istoriche di Antonio Allegri . . .*, I, 1817, pp. 111 and 118) in assigning it to 1520. Ricci (*Correggio*, 1896, p. 226) suggests 1521 and in his later book (1930) *c.* 1525 (p. 169). Gronau (*Correggio* in the *Klassiker der Kunst* series, 1907, p. 121) *c.* 1526–8. (3) Cf. Mrs. Jameson: *The History of Our Lord*, 4th ed., 1881, II, p. 98. (3a) See the present writer in the *Gazette des Beaux-Arts*, February, 1970, p. 109. (4) A version of the head and shoulders of Christ, certified as Correggio by A. Venturi and G. Fiocco, was reported in 1958. Another (with the rope round His neck) is in the Ambrosiana, Milan. An Ecce Homo, attributed to Correggio, figures in the 1627 inventory of the Mantua gallery where it is described as '*N.S. Ecce Homo mezza figura di mano del Correggio*' (cf. Carlo d'Arco: *Degli Arti . . . di Mantova*, 1857, p. 160), but such a description is inadequate to establish whether the design was the same as that of the Prati and Salviati versions. (5) Francesco Scannelli: *Il Microcosmo della Pittura*, 1657, pp. 78 and 281–2. (6) Francesco Bocchi: *Le Bellezze della Citta di Fiorenza*, 1591, p. 187. Cf. also Scannelli, *op. cit.*, p. 284. Meyer, op. cit., p. 359, quotes the will (1668) of Duke Giacomo Salviati which includes a description of the picture. (7) Pungileoni, *op. cit.*, 1, pp. 118–21, and II, pp. 162–5. (8) Perhaps for this reason Ramdohr (*Ueber Mahlerei und Bildhauerarbeit in Rom*, II, 1787, p. 85) goes out of his way to express his belief in the authenticity of the Colonna picture. Cf. also Mengs: *Opere*, 1787, p. 187. C. G. Ratti (*Notizie . . . intorno la vita . . . del . . . pittore . . . Correggio*, 1781, pp. 116–17) also seems to accept the Colonna picture as identical with the Prati one. The source of the doubts was presumably the rumour, probably long current but published first by Tiraboschi (*Biblioteca Modenese*, VI, 1786, pp. 283–4) according to which the Prati original (not the copy) passed with the Prati possessions to the Dalla Rosa family and that the Marchese Pier Luigi Dalla Rosa sent it by request to Louis XIV who kept it, returning only a copy. In point of fact the only Ecce Homo attributed to Correggio which figures in the inventories of the French royal collections from 1683 to 1754 is demonstrably not the Prati picture. It is recorded in the inventory of 1706, Bailly's inventory of 1709–10 (Correggio no. 9) and Lépicié's catalogue of 1754 (Correggio no. 4) and is also described by d'Argenville in 1745

(*Abrégé* . . ., I, 1745, p. 211). Christ was shown seated on a drapery and had a reed between His hands. Bailly and Lépicié also give dimensions which show that this picture was very small. **(9)** Advanced by Coppi (*Notizie di un Quadro del Correggio, lette nell'Accademia Romana di Archeologia*, Rome, 1845, note 54) and accepted by Meyer (*op. cit.*, p. 359). It was based on a story to the effect that the Salviati picture passed to the Colonna together with a Leda attributed to Correggio about 1718 as a result of a Colonna/Salviati marriage (as was in fact the case with a picture now in this Gallery—no. 32, ascribed to Damiano Mazza), **(10)** Cf. Redford, I, p. 91. The 1802 Udny catalogue completes the cycle of confusion by stating that the picture in question had entered the Salviati collection, about 1660, from the Prati. The same mistake is perpetrated in the catalogue of the Udny sale of 19th May, 1804 (94) to the extent of associating the picture with Agostino Carracci's engraving. This constitutes confirmation that the Salviati picture was a close replica of the Prati one. **(11)** On the back of no. 15 is the seal of the Venuti family, the seal (monogram) of Carlo Ramette and the following old label:'*No. 114 Quadro in tavola denotante un Cristo avanti Pilato, mezze fig.ª al vero, del Correggio. Esisteva nella Galleria Colonna. Comprato dl* (*sic*) *Cav. Venuti per S.M. Il Re di Napoli dal Sig. Alessandro Dey* (*sic*) *in Roma l'anno 1802.* (*signed*) *Cav: Domenico Venuti*'. No. 15 also figures as no. 114 in Tommaso Conca's inventory (of 29th November, 1803) of pictures acquired by Venuti (printed in *Le Gallerie Nazionali Italiene*, V, 1902, p. 315—the article in question contains further material relevant to the history of no. 15. This is sufficient to disprove the statement made in the National Gallery catalogue of 1838 and succeeding editions to the effect that no. 15 was bought from the Colonna by Sir Simon Clarke, who being unable to remove it from Italy, sold it to Murat. A picture described as an 'Ecce Homo' by Correggio sent in 1806 from the gallery of Francavilla to Palermo is too small to have been no. 15 (no. 18 in the inventory printed on p. 321 in *Le Gallerie Nazionali Italiene*, V.). A certain amount of confusion regarding the agents active at the time of the Colonna sales may be assumed to explain a MS. note in a copy of the Colonna Catalogue belonging to E. K. Waterhouse which says of the *Ecce Homo:* '*venduto a Giov. de Rossi e da questo al Re di Napoli*'. Meyer (*op. cit.*, p. 359) also mentions Rossi. **(12)** Marcel Dupont: *Carolina Bonaparte*, n.d. (1937), p. 246. In Stanislao Morelli's *La Pittura Comparata*, 1816, p. 71, no. 15 is stated to be still at Capo di Monte, but this is presumably due to a publication time lag or perhaps to ignorance. **(13)** The issue of the *Tübinger Kunstblatt* which reports this transaction is dated 28th April, 1823. But on the back of no. 15 (and of no. 10) is the seal of Lord Stewart who succeeded to the Marquessate in August, 1822 and who resigned his embassy to Vienna at the end of that year, in consequence of which the *Kunstblatt* notice is presumably retrospective. The same issue of the *Kunstblatt* seems to imply (wrongly) that, like no. 10, no. 15 had belonged to the Duke of Alba. This account is followed by J.D. Passavant (*Die Christliche Kunst in Spanien*, 1853, p. 152). It may be noted that J. J. Angerstein had tried to buy nos. 10 and 15 but without success (see D. E. Williams: *The Life and Correspondence of Sir Thomas Lawrence*, II, 1831 pp. 169–71 and 273–6).

23 THE MADONNA OF THE BASKET

Panel, $13\frac{1}{4} \times 9\frac{7}{8}$ (0·33 × 0·25).
In general very well preserved.[1] Cleaned, 1967–8.
In the background S. Joseph is seen at work.[2]

Close in style to the *Pietà* of *ca.*1524 (Parma gallery, from S. Giovanni Evangelista). Always accepted as the original of a design which was engraved within the sixteenth century and of which numerous painted copies were made. Such fame in so small a picture as no. 23, together with the fact that some of the replicas are larger, might in theory give cause for doubting this assumption. Nevertheless, no other version has yet been produced which appears so convincingly autograph, while if Correggio's original *had* been larger it would have been uncharacteristic of him to paint a smaller replica of it himself.

Probably identical with a picture described by Vasari in his life of Girolamo da Carpi as '*di mano del Correggio, nel quale la Nostra Donna mette una camiscia indosso a Cristo fanciulletto*'.[4] He says that this picture belonged to the Cavaliere Boiardo in Parma and that Girolamo da Carpi copied not only it but also a Parmigianino in the Certosa di Pavia. Bottari, in his edition of Vasari (1760),[5] claims a twofold confusion on Vasari's part, alleging that the Baiardo (not Boiardo) picture was the Parmigianino Cupid, now at Vienna, and that it was the Correggio which had been at the Certosa di Pavia. He added that the latter picture was in his day in Spain and that it had been engraved by Francesco Aquila. No. 23 (or a hypothetical identical replica) was indeed engraved by Francesco Aquila (see ENGRAVINGS below) and was in fact in Spain from at least the mid-seventeenth century to the beginning of the nineteenth. But in view of its boudoir size it would be surprising had it ever been in the Certosa di Pavia. Moreover an alternative identification of Vasari's picture was advanced by Pungileoni[6] who claimed that it was not the Baiardo one (which he confirmed had been in Spain) but another, now known only from engravings and copies.[7] In it, in addition to the motive of the Madonna putting a shirt on the Child, S. Joseph was offering the latter some cherries (a feature of which Vasari made no mention).[8] Nevertheless the recent publication (Popham's *Drawings of Parmigianino*, 1971, p. 264) of a Baiardo inventory of ca. 1561 includes (no. 11) what is almost certainly the present picture.

VERSIONS: Girolamo da Carpi's version, mentioned by Vasari, might in theory be identical with one of the many existing old copies. One was engraved in the Stroganoff Gallery, 1807 (13). Of these, mention may be made of those in the galleries of Dresden (no. 156 in the 1908 catalogue), Dulwich (no. 246 in the 1914 catalogue), the Prado and one which passed through the Orléans,[9] Bridgewater, Stafford and Ellesmere collections and in 1950 was the property of Mrs. Hewer of Bristol. These are all of approximately the same size as no. 23. Larger versions are in the Hunterian collection of Glasgow University, in the Ambrosiana at Milan and in the collection of the Duke of Buccleuch at Drumlanrig. Another was in the collection of Lord Radstock (no. 54 in the second day's sale, 13th May, 1826) This was given as $35\frac{1}{2} \times 24\frac{1}{4}$ and though Redford (II, p. 226) says it passed to the Northwick collection a version which claimed to be ex-Northwick (successively Alan Fenwick sale, Christie's, 21st July, 1950, lot 30, and anonymous sale, Sotheby's, 28th February, 1951, lot 96) was not identical with it, being of the same size as no. 23.[10] Another is at Detroit (Institute). A version from the Colloredo family was the subject of a short manuscript published by Carlo Marin in 1830.

DRAWING: Popham (*op. cit.*, pp. 193–4, no. A119) lists one at the Albertina, Vienna which he considers a seventeenth century pastiche.

ENGRAVINGS: Diana Mantuana (Rome, 1577) and Francesco Aquila (dedicated to G. P. Bellori, 1691). For further engravings cf. Julius Meyer: *Correggio*, 1871, p. 482.

PROVENANCE: Baiardi, Parma (see above). 1666 inventory of the Alcázar, Madrid and then in subsequent royal inventories up to that of 1789.[11] Next recorded in

1813 among pictures which Wallis was bringing from Spain to Buchanan in England. In Buchanan's list of that year stated to have come from 'The first collection at Madrid'.[12] Exactly how or in what circumstances it left the Spanish royal collection is not known, and contrary to what is generally stated it is unlikely that it was ever in Godoy's possession.[13] Nevertheless, the fact that Wallis was able to acquire it must be attributed to the upheavals consequent on the Peninsular War. Buchanan and Wallis having failed to find a buyer in England, the picture was taken back to the continent and by 1820 was in the possession of M. Lapeyrière at Paris.[14] No. 16 in the sale of the latter's posses-sions, Paris, 19th April, 1825, where bought by the elder Nieuwenhuys, from whose son purchased, June, 1825.[15]

REPRODUCTION: *Illustrations, Italian Schools*, 1937, p. 104.

REFERENCES: (1) Julius Meyer (*Correggio*, 1871, p. 327) and following him Corrado Ricci (*Correggio*, 1896, p. 181 and 1930, p. 167) say the picture was overcleaned when in Godoy's possession. In fact it is highly unlikely that it ever belonged to Godoy. For a suggested explanation of this anomaly see note 13. (2) A. E. Popham (*Correggio's Drawings*, 1957, p. 17 n. 2) sees 'Düreresque inspiration' in the background. (3) Waagen (*Treasures of Art in Great Britain*, I 1854, p. 330) assigns it to 'the later period of Correggio'. Meyer (*op. cit.*, p. 326) suggested 1520 tentatively, Gronau (*Correggio* in the *Klassiker der Kunst* series, 1907, pp. 85 and 162) about 1522 and Ricci 1519–20 (1896, p. 396) and about 1523–4 (1930, p. 167). The present writer agrees with Gronau in relating no. 23 stylistically to the Parma *Deposition* which is assumed to have formed part of the work which Correggio did at S. Giovanni Evangelista, Parma, 1520–4 (for the latter work cf. Popham, *op. cit.*, chapter 4 *passim*). (4) Vasari/Milanesi VI, p. 477. The motive of the Madonna putting a shirt on the Child occurs also in Jacopo della Quercia's sculptured group in the centre of the principal lunette of the façade of S. Petronio, Bologna—which may in fact be stylistically relevant to no. 23. (5) Vol. 3, note (at the end of the volume) to p. 12. (6) *Memorie Istoriche di Antonio Allegri detto Il Correggio*, I (1817), pp. 111–12, II (1818), p. 155 (but giving a false reference to p. 206 of vol. 1 instead of pp. 111–12), III (1821), pp. 141, 145, 151. (7) An engraving is reproduced on p. 181 of Ricci's monograph (English edition) of 1896. (8) The original of this picture had belonged, according to Tiraboschi (*Biblioteca Modenese*, VI (1786), 285–6) to the Ab. Carlo Bianconi who, at the time of publication of Tiraboschi's book, still possessed a sketch for it (still owned by the Bianconi family in 1854—No. 2 in their catalogue of that year). Pungileoni (*loc. cit.*) further confuses the matter by referring at some length to a picture owned by Padre Resta at the end of the seventeenth century which may either have been a copy of no. 23 or the Bianconi picture or a copy of the latter. (9) Page 59 of the Orléans catalogue of 1727 by Du Bois de Saint Gelais. (10) Redford, II, p. 225, also wrongly identifies a version at the Panné sale, Christie's, 29th March, 1819, lot 63 with no. 23. (11) These inventories which are preserved in the Royal Palace at Madrid are unpublished. The relevant entries are as follows: 1666 'no. 641 (old numeration) *media vara de alta y un pie de ancho de una Nra. Sra. del mismo Corezo en 3,000 dus*'. 1686 inventory (under heading '*Passillo que llaman de la Madona*'—no inventory number) '*otra de media vara de alto, de una tercia de ancho, de una Nuestra Señora con el Niño original de mano del Corezo*'. 1700 inventory (under heading '*Passillo de la Madona* (old numeration) 42') '*Item, otra de media vara de alto y una tercia de ancho; de una Nuestra Sēnora con el Niño: original del mano del mismo Corezo, tasada en mil y quinientos doblones*'. A *media vara* is about 16½ inches and a *pie* or *tercia vara* about 11 inches. The inventories of 1772 and 1789 repeat the measurements of '½ vara' high and '⅓ vara' wide. The fact that no. 23 does not figure in the inventory of 1636 might be thought to indicate that it was among the important Italian paintings bought by Velázquez during his visit to Italy in 1648–51 but no positive evidence on this point has come to light. Furthermore, there is at least a possibility that no. 23 was the picture seen by Jusepe Martinez (who died in 1682) in the possession of a certain Conde de San

Clemente at Saragossa. The following passage is from his *Discursos Practicables*, datable around 1675, published by F. J. Sánchez Cantón in vol. 3 of *Fuentes Literarias* (1934), p. 28: *En esta ciudad de Zaragosa se halla un cuadrito, en poder del Sr. Conde de San Clemente, de una tabla de roble de grandeza de poco más o menos de una tercia, pintada una imagen de Nuestra Señora que muda la camisa al Niño Jesus y en lejos San José trabajando su oficio.* It is to be noted that no. 23 is on poplar, not on oak, and in consequence it may not have been identical with the Saragossa picture. No. 23 was seen in Madrid by Mengs who published descriptions of it (Mengs: *Opere*, 1787, pp. 190 and 312). No. 23 was also described by Antonio Conca (*Descrizione Odeporica della Spagna*, vol. 1, 1793, pp. 128, 129) in the Madrid palace. **(12)** W. Buchanan: *Memoirs of Painting*, vol. 2, 1824, pp. 225 ff., 243, 246–7. **(13)** In the National Gallery catalogue of 1838 and in almost all subsequent works on the subject no. 23 is stated to have been given by Charles IV of Spain to Emanuel Godoy, the 'Prince of the Peace' (1767–1851). This seems very doubtful. There is no mention of Godoy in any of the (fairly circumstantial) accounts of the picture's pedigree which were published between Mengs' and the 1838 catalogue—viz. Buchanan (*op. cit.*), George Yeates (letter of 19th January, 1814, to Thomas Penrice, published with the latter's correspondence), the Lapeyrière sale catalogue of 1825, Passavant (*Kunstreise durch England und Belgien*, 1833, p. 11), Nieuwenhuys (*Review of the Lives and Works of some of the most Eminent Painters*, 1834, p. 48), Ottley's National Gallery Catalogues of 1832 and 1835 or the *Tübinger Kunstblatt* of 17th May, 1836. Above all, the MS. inventory of Godoy's collection dated 1st January, 1808 (only two and a half months before his arrest) contains no mention of any picture corresponding with no. 23. The explanation of the error seems to be that the compiler of the 1838 National Gallery catalogue confused the history of nos. 10 and 23, stating that the former passed from the Alba collection direct to that of Murat (whereas in fact it belonged to Godoy in between) and including Godoy's collection in the pedigree of no. 23. Waagen (*loc. cit.*) in following this account says 'unhappily this gem, presented by Charles IV to the Prince of the Peace, has been injured in some parts by cleaning' and Meyer (*loc. cit*) embroidering this story, says that the picture suffered through cleaning *while* it was in Godoy's possession. Meyer's version was swallowed by Ricci (both editions). The resulting gap in the pedigree of no. 23 is awkward but there seems no doubt that it really is the picture described by Mengs and recorded in the Spanish royal inventories, since Mengs gives a detailed description and accepts it as autograph, while the inventory dimensions tally well enough. It is significant too that the valuations in the inventories (quoted in reference 11) are exceptionally high for so small a picture. **(14)** Cf. C. J. Nieuwenhuys: *A Review of the Lives and Works of some of the most Eminent Painters*, 1834, p. 48. Also Buchanan, *loc. cit.*, and *Le Cabinet de l'Amateur*, 1, 1842, p. 528. **(15)** Nieuwenhuys, *loc. cit.* On the back of no. 23 is a seal which is also found on the following other pictures in the National Gallery: Cuyp 823, Heyden 866, Hobbema 831 and 833, van de Velde 871. Of these, all but Cuyp 823 and Hobbema 833 are known to have been at one time in the possession of a Nieuwenhuys.

2512 THE MAGDALEN

Painted area approx. 15 × 12 (0·381 × 0·305).

General condition quite good. Flesh somewhat rubbed in parts. The darks of the drapery and of the landscape appear to have 'sunk' a little. There is a *pentimento* in her left ankle. Some disturbance visible above her right breast—apparently at an earlier stage more of this area was covered by falling hair. This would be evidence against Longhi's suggestion (*Paragone*, 1958) that the picture is a copy.

Other versions cited by Ricci in the Chigi-Saracini coll. (Siena),

'Rome, Bologna, Parma, Milan and elsewhere'.[1] The design of no. 2512 is acceptably Correggesque and on the balance of evidence it seems to the compiler to be the original and an autograph work. Of modern writers it is accepted as such by Ricci[2] and by Berenson.[3]

COPIES: See above. A small line drawing at Mannheim (no. 1731). Further copies in the Uffizi and the Prado.

PROVENANCE: A Magdalen attributed to Correggio and measuring about 1·027 × 0·77 m. is recorded in the collection of the Duke of Savoy at Turin in 1631[4] and Vertue describes a version 18″ high by 15″ broad in Charles I's collection in which the Magdalen is 'standing and leaning, being a little intire figure, which has been too much washed'.[5] But it is doubtful whether either of these entries is relevant to no. 2512. Both sets of dimensions are too large and it seems that no. 2512 has not been cut down, since round the painted area there is an unprimed strip, about a quarter of an inch wide, of what appears to be the original canvas.

Apparently no. 25 in the Ravaisson-Mollien sale, Paris (Hôtel Drouot) 23rd November, 1903, bought by Christian de Marinitsch.[6] Next recorded in England, in 1907, in the possession of George Salting (by whom lent to B.F.A.C. exhibition, 1907 (32)). Although on the strength of a reproduction in colour of lot no. 25 in the Ravaisson-Mollien sale catalogue there can be little or no doubt that no. 2512 is identical with that picture, its history during the intermediate period of four years is not satisfactorily accounted for. On the one hand it is stated by Herbert Cook that the picture came to England from Italy in 1907 and was then purchased by Salting.[7] On the other, a picture of the Virgin and Child with two Angels (now National Gallery, no. 2608, (?) after 'Campin') which had also been bought by Christian de Marinitsch at the Ravaisson-Mollien sale had entered Salting's collection by 1904.

Salting Bequest, 1910.

REPRODUCTION: *Illustration, Italian Schools*, 1937, p. 103.

REFERENCES: (1) Corrado Ricci: *Correggio* (1930, pp. 156–7). (2) *Op. cit.* (3) Bernard Berenson: *Pitture Italiane del Rinascimento*, Milan, (1936), p. 132. (4) G. Campori: *Raccolta di cataloghi ed inventarii inediti*, Modena, 1870, p. 76. Ricci (*op. cit.*, p. 156) gives the dimensions wrongly. It is specified in Campori that the unit of measurement is the *Piede Liprando* which is larger than an English foot. (5) George Vertue: *A Catalogue and Description of King Charles the First's Capital Collection . . .*, London, 1757, p. 125. (6) Letter in the Gallery archives. (7) Article in *L'Arte* 1908, p. 57.

3920 HEAD OF AN ANGEL

Fresco. Irregular shape. Greatest dimensions 14 × 14 (0·356 × 0·365). Much damaged.

For commentary and provenance see no. 3921.

3921 HEADS OF TWO ANGELS

Fresco. Irregular shape. Greatest dimensions 17½ × 24 (0·445 × 0·61). Much damaged.

Fragments of the decoration painted by Correggio (payment recorded in 1522) in the apse of the church of S. Giovanni Evangelista, Parma and destroyed in 1587 when the choir was enlarged. The central figures (Coronation of the Virgin) are in the Parma gallery. Other surviving fragments are no. 4067 of this Gallery and other angel heads at Glasgow (no. 124 in the 1935 catalogue), Boston, Mass., Museum of Fine Arts (Charles P. Kling Fund 56.263) and in the Lechi collection, Brescia (nos. 12 and 13 in the 1824 catalogue, nos. 8 and 9 in the 1852 catalogue; still in the Lechi collection in 1951). The copy painted in the new apse by Cesare Aretusi (reproduced by Ricci, 1930, plate CXXVII) still survives and on its evidence and that of several partial copies it is possible to relate the fragments to the whole. No. 3920 is the head of the angel reclining at the feet of S. John the Evangelist (to the spectator's left of the Virgin): the two angels whose heads survive as no. 3921 were behind S. John the Evangelist (to the spectator's left of him). They also occur in the copy of part of the apse decoration which is no. 7 of this Gallery.

PROVENANCE: Almost certainly two of the fragments stated in the *Mercurio Errante*[1] and by Vasi,[2] Mengs,[3] and Tiraboschi[4] to have been in the Palazzo Rondanini, Rome in the second half of the eighteenth century. Mentioned by S. Woodburn (letter and lithograph in the Gallery archives) as being for sale in Rome (owner unspecified) in 1844. Mentioned by Waagen (1854)[5] as belonging to Lord Ward in England, who exhibited them in the Egyptian Hall, London[6] and lent them to the Manchester exhibition in 1857 (nos. 403 and 404). Lord Ward was created Earl of Dudley in 1860 and lent them to the R.A. exhibition of 1871 (nos. 382 and 424). At the Dudley sale, 25th June, 1892 they were bought by Richter for Mond. Ludwig Mond bequest, 1924. Cf. also provenance of no. 4067.

REPRODUCTION: *Illustrations, Italian Schools*, 1937, p. 106.

REFERENCES: (1) 1760, p. 84. (2) French edition (*Itinéraire instructif de Rome*) 1797, p. 37. (3) *Opere*, 1787, p. 173. (4) *Biblioteca Modenese*, vol. VI, (1786), p. 261. (5) *Treasures of Art in Great Britain*, vol. II, p. 233. (6) See *The Athenaeum*, 1851, pp. 722–3 and 1855, pp. 816–17.

4067   HEAD OF AN ANGEL

Fresco, apparently completely repainted in oil. Original (irregularly shaped) fresco portion set into square form, $14\frac{1}{2} \times 13$ (0·369 × 0·33).

Recognizable from Aretusi's copy (see no. 3921) as the angel who held the crozier on the spectator's left of the Virgin in the S. Giovanni Evangelista apse fresco.

PROVENANCE: Certainly one of the fragments from the Palazzo Rondanini (see no. 3921). Purchased about 1841 by G. Croker Fox in Rome from the Marchese O. P. del Bufalo, who stated that it had come into his family with two other fragments (possibly nos. 3920 and 3921) from Zacchia Rondanini.[1] Exhibited R.A. 1882 (207) by G. Croker Fox. Anon. sale, Christie's, 5th July, 1920 (85), bought in. G. Croker Fox sale, Sotheby's, 25th February, 1925 (58), bought in. Purchased from Captain Croker Fox by Sir Robert Witt by whom presented, 1925.

REPRODUCTION: *Illustrations, Italian Schools*, 1937, p. 107.

REFERENCES: (1) Letter in the Gallery archives.

4255   CHRIST TAKING LEAVE OF HIS MOTHER

$34\frac{1}{8} \times 30\frac{1}{8}$ (0·87 × 0·77).
The paint is worn and thin in places. Cleaned, 1971.

The subject, which does not figure in any of the four Gospels, is rare in Italian Renaissance painting. X-ray photographs show that fundamental alterations were made by Correggio during the course of work on the picture. Thus Christ seems originally to have been conceived standing, not kneeling, and at one stage there was a third Mary between S. John and the Virgin—features which suggest that Correggio was acquainted with Dürer's wood-cut of this subject in *Das Marienleben*.[1]

On grounds of style an early work—probably somewhat earlier than the earliest surviving documented painting of Correggio (the altarpiece of the Madonna and Child with S. Francis, no. 150 of the Dresden Gallery, painted 1514–15).

PROVENANCE: Probably identical with the picture mentioned in 1786 (with a detailed iconographic and stylistic description) by Tiraboschi, who states that his informant was the Abate Carlo Bianconi.[2] The picture is stated to belong to 'a certain Signor Rossi' in Milan. Tiraboschi's description was reproduced almost verbatim by Fiorillo in 1801.[3] Pungileoni[4] says that in his day the picture was in the possession, at Milan, of 'Signor D. Antonio Rossi, one of the heirs of the Rossi mentioned by Bianconi'. He adds that a certain Signor Jesi, writing to him in 1815 from Milan, complained that the picture had been so drastically restored that the grain of the canvas was visible even from some distance. In view of the fact that, later in the nineteenth century, there is a gap of some twenty years in the picture's pedigree, this information on the condition of the Rossi picture increases the probability that it is no. 4255. Tiraboschi's reference to Biaconi is also quoted in Lanzi.[5] What was presumably the same picture was seen in Milan on 1st December, 1856, by Mündler in the possession of an unspecified lady.[6] No. 4255 was discovered by Dr. J. P. Richter about 1879 in the possession (at Brixton) of Professor Vitale de Tivoli. The latter stated that he had acquired it from the widow of Professor Parlatore in Florence.[7] Professor Parlatore, who died in 1877, had married, in 1860, a certain Eugenia Crippa of Milan,[7] and it may have been in this way that the picture entered into his possession. It was purchased, soon after 1882, by Fairfax Murray, who took it back to Florence[8] and later sold it to R. H. Benson. Purchased from the latter by Sir Joseph (later Lord) Duveen, who presented it, 1927. Exhibited B.F.A.C., 1894 (50); R.A., 1896 (131); Grafton Galls., 1909–10 (72); Manchester, 1927 (30).

VERSION: A Correggesque picture of the same subject was in the Farrer collection in 1901. What may be the same was with Steinmeyer, Lucerne, in 1924.

REPRODUCTION: *Illustrations, Italian Schools*, 1937, p. 105.

REFERENCES: (1) Cecil Gould: 'A Probable Adaptation by Correggio of Dürer's Iconography' in *The Burlington Magazine*, October, 1948. (2) Girolamo Tiraboschi: *Biblioteca Modenese . . .*, Modena, 1781–6, vol. VI (1786), p. 287. (3) J. D. Fiorillo: *Geschichte der zeichnenden Künste. I. Geschichte der Mahlerey*, Göttingen, 1798–1808, vol. II (1801), p. 306. (4) Luigi Pungileoni: *Memorie Istoriche di Antonio Allegri detto Il Correggio*, Parma, 1817–21, vol. III (1821), p. 155. (5) Luigi Lanzi: *Storia Pittorica della Italia*, 4th ed., Florence 1822, vol. IV, p. 59. (6) The diaries of Otto Mündler, travelling agent for the National Gallery in the early years of Sir Charles Eastlake's tenure as Director, are in the Gallery archives. (7) Letter in the Gallery archives. (8) See *Italienische Malerei der Renaissance im Briefwechsel von Giovanni Morelli und Jean Paul Richter*, 1876–1891, 1960, pp. 74, 99, 360, 387–8, 465.

After CORREGGIO

7 GROUP OF HEADS

Canvas, $54 \times 42\frac{1}{4}$ ($1 \cdot 372 \times 1 \cdot 073$).
Somewhat damaged. Cleaned, 1966.

37 GROUP OF HEADS

Canvas, $54 \times 41\frac{3}{4}$ ($1 \cdot 372 \times 1 \cdot 06$).[1]
Somewhat damaged. Cleaned, 1966.

Copies of the clusters of heads at the lower extremities of Correggio's destroyed fresco in the apse of S. Giovani Evangelista, Parma, No. 7 is the group on the spectator's left in that work; no. 37 on his right (see no. 3921). The theory, advanced in earlier editions of the National Gallery catalogue, that these copies are the work of Annibale Carracci is possible, but at least incapable of proof. The facts are as follows. Annibale, in a letter to his cousin Ludovico, written from Parma on 28th April, 1580,[2] indicates that he is engaged on copying 'heads' by Correggio from the 'cupola'. The 'cupola' in question might be that of either the cathedral or S. Giovanni Evangelista, but, as it stands, is less likely to refer to the apse vault of the latter church. Bellori (1672),[3] and following him Baldinucci,[4] says that in his day there were various copies in the Palazzo Farnese, Rome, by Annibale of portions of Correggio's destroyed apse fresco at S. Giovanni Evangelista. Ruta (1752)[5] and Tiraboschi (1786)[6] state that the copies in the Palazzo Farnese, Rome subsequently passed to Naples where, in fact, they still are. Malvasia (1678)[7] says that Agostino and Annibale Carracci were commissioned to copy the apse fresco shortly before its destruction in 1587 in order to facilitate Aretusi's work of painting the replica on the new vault.

It emerges from the above that Annibale was probably copying frescoes at Parma by Correggio both in 1580 and about 1586 (in which year the decision was taken to demolish the apse)[8] and it is possible that he thus executed two different sets of copies of the apse fresco. In fact two sets attributed to him survive—at Naples and at Parma. Ricci,[9] giving the origin of the latter set, says that two of them did not join the others when they passed from the collection of the Counts Baiardi to that of Antonio Rosazza and thence to the Parma Gallery. It is open to doubt, however, whether nos. 7 and 37 could be the two in question since they cover roughly the same area of the fresco as two now at Parma. Stylistic comparison with authenticated works by Annibale is equally inconclusive since the artist's own style is rarely apparent on copies made by him of other painters' works, and in this case there is the added complication that a work in fresco has here been copied in oil. To sum up: there is no certainty that nos. 7 and 37 are not early copies of two of the Parma copies and no certainty even that the latter are by Annibale Carracci.

PROVENANCE: Collections of Queen Christina of Sweden, Duke of Bracciano, Orléans (page 58 in the 1727 catalogue). Bought by J. J. Angerstein on the dispersal of the Orléans collection at the end of the eighteenth century. Purchased with Angerstein collection, 1824. Exh.: Stockholm (Queen Christina), 1966 (1169).

REPRODUCTIONS: *Illustrations, Italian Schools*, 1937, p. 108.

REFERENCES: (1) Dimensions given in earlier editions of the catalogue in respect of those pictures are incorrect. (2) Published by Malvasia: *Felsina Pittrice*, vol. I (1678), p. 366 and by Bottari: *Raccolta di Lettere . . .*, 1822, vol. I, p. 123. (3) *Vite . . .*, 1672, p. 23. (4) *Notizie . . .*, 1846 ed. vol. 3, p. 332. (5) *Guida . . . di Parma.* p. 58. (6) *Biblioteca Modenese*, vol. VI, p. 306. (7) *Felsina Pittrice*, vol. I, p. 334. (8) Meyer, *op. cit.*, p. 301, note 2. (9) 1930, p. 165.

76 THE AGONY IN THE GARDEN

Poplar, $15 \times 16\frac{1}{2}$ (0·38 × 0·42).
Good condition.

Purchased as an original but clearly inferior to the picture at Apsley House of which it must be considered a close and old copy. In view of datable changes in the original no. 76 was probably painted between 1640 and the mid 'fifties of the seventeenth century.[1] It is stated in the Angerstein catalogue (1823) that no. 76 'was brought to this country from Turin, in the early part of the French Revolution'—probably an allusion to a statement in the catalogue of the Novellara sale (Christie's, 3rd March, 1804) where a *Passion of our Saviour*, attributed to Correggio, is stated to have come from the ducal villa of Novellara 'in the neighbourhood of Modena' and to have been 'purchased from the French during the late troubles in Italy'. It is stated further that the picture in question bore, on the back, 'the seal of the Academy of Parma'—which no. 76 in fact does. But even assuming the two pictures to be identical its earlier history is obscure owing to the presence of various old copies of the Apsley House picture recorded as early as the sixteenth and seventeenth centuries.[2]

PROVENANCE: Purchased with the Angerstein collection, 1824.

REPRODUCTION: *Illustrations, Italian Schools*, 1937, p. 107.

REFERENCES: (1) See Cecil Gould: *A Correggio Discovery: Burlington Magazine*, May, 1950. (2) Meyer, *Correggio*, 1871, pp. 333–6 and Evelyn, Duchess of Wellington: Apsley House catalogue, 1901, vol. I, pp. 162–170, gives the best account of the evidence relating to the various versions. A 'Christ in the Garden, by Corregio [sic], from the Aldobrandini Cabinet at Rome' was no. 11 in an undated catalogue of pictures belonging to Alexander Day, shown in London at the Egyptian Hall, Piccadilly, early in the nineteenth century.

96 ECCE HOMO

Canvas, $39\frac{1}{2} \times 31$ (1·003 × 0·788). Cleaned, 1968.
An old copy of the original in this Gallery (see no. 15).

PROVENANCE: Bequeathed (as by Ludovico Carracci) by the Rev. William Holwell Carr, 1831.[1] Lent to Edinburgh, 1871 to 1932.

REPRODUCTION: *Illustrations, Italian Schools*, 1937, p. 109.

REFERENCE: (1) Perhaps no. 94 in the Robert Udny sale, 18th May, 1804 (see PROVENANCE in the entry for no. 15).

Lorenzo COSTA
1459/60–1535

Ferrarese School. The approximate year of his birth is deducible from the register of his death (at Mantua) which took place on the 5th March, 1535 and in which he is described as '*de età de anni 75*'. Vasari's statement that he studied in Florence cannot be checked and is probably wrong. A S. Sebastian, at Dresden, signed by Costa in Hebrew characters, is so entirely in Tura's manner as to suggest that it was substantially the latter's work,[1] finished and signed by Costa. In Costa's earliest surviving dated work (the Madonna of 1488 in S. Giacomo Maggiore, Bologna) the influence of Ercole Roberti is clear.

Costa had probably settled at Bologna by 1483 and spent most of his time there (with short visits to Ferrara in 1499 and to Rome in 1503) until 1506. By the spring of 1507 he was installed at Mantua as court painter to the Gonzaga (in succession to Mantegna, who had died in 1506). He seems to have lived at Mantua until his death.

REFERENCE: (1) Berenson: *Lists* (1936) and elsewhere. Longhi (*Officina Ferrarese* (1934), p. 85) assumes a deliberate imitation by Costa of Tura.

629 ALTARPIECE: THE VIRGIN AND CHILD WITH SS. PETER, PHILIP, JOHN THE EVANGELIST and JOHN THE BAPTIST

Five separate panels, transferred to canvas in 1848 by Maillard at Antwerp.[1] Centre $66 \times 28\frac{3}{4}$ ($1\cdot67 \times 0\cdot729$) (arched top). Large side panels $43\frac{1}{4} \times 22\frac{1}{2}$ ($1\cdot098 \times 0\cdot57$). Small side panels $21\frac{1}{4} \times 22\frac{1}{2}$ ($0\cdot551 \times 0\cdot57$).

Signed (on the lintel beneath the Madonna's throne):

LAVRENTIVS·COSTA·F·1505

The three main panels seem in fair condition for transferred pictures. The two smaller panels have obviously suffered somewhat, perhaps before the transfer as well as during it. Cleaned, 1972.

The grisaille panels on the throne appear to represent (left) the Presentation in the Temple and (right) the Marriage of the Virgin. A panel of the Dead Christ supported by two angels was recorded by Crespi in 1770 as surmounting the altarpiece.[2] This may have become separated from the rest soon afterwards since it is not included in Calvi's description (1780) of the altarpiece which was then in the Hercolani collection, Bologna.[3] This type of polyptych, of which the chief characteristic is that the central panel is higher than the wings, was not uncommon in the Ferrarese School—two distinguished examples are Tura's Roverella altarpiece and Cossa's Griffoni altarpiece of which the centres are nos. 772 and 597 respectively of this Gallery (see relevant entries in *The Earlier Italian Schools*, by Martin Davies). For the remaining constituents of such polyptychs, nevertheless, there was no uniformity. The Roverella altar was apparently crowned with the Pietà lunette now in the Louvre which is the width of the whole polyptych. A

Dead Christ supported by two angels, formerly in the Benson collection, which might have formed the top of no. 629, is only of the width of the centre.[4] It would also be possible that no. 629 once had a predella, though none of the earlier authorities refers to one.

DRAWINGS: Albertina, Vienna. Two bistre drawings for the two S. John's. These drawings, which show some minor differences from the paintings, are attributed to Costa himself.[5]

PROVENANCE: First published in 1770 by Crespi[2] who says '*serviva di sportello all' altar maggiore dell' oratorio di S. Pietro in Vinculis in Faenza (ora ad altr' uso convertito)*' (the oratory of S. Pietro in Vincoli at Faenza had been transferred in 1760 to the Cathedral).[6] A polyptych of this type on wood would be an unusual '*sportello*' and it may be noted that Crespi's description is not quite exact—he speaks of S. Peter and S. John the Evangelist as oblong panels and S. John the Baptist and S. Jerome [sic] as half-lengths *under* the other two. Nevertheless he quotes the signature correctly and was certainly attempting to describe no. 629. It had, in fact, been acquired for the Hercolani collection in 1766 or 1765 (Oretti MS., B 384, f. 9 v, Archiginnasio, Bologna, also later MS. in same volume). Discussed, when in the Hercolani collection, Bologna, by Calvi in 1780[3] and specified, in a foot-note to Baruffaldi's life of Costa (1844),[7] as having been sold to Rome in 1837. The purchaser on this occasion was C. Wigram at whose sale (1848) bought by Van Cuyck, who had it transferred to canvas.[1] Bought from Van Cuyck by Frédéric Reiset, 16th April, 1859,[1] from whom purchased, 1859.

REPRODUCTION: *Illustrations, Italian Schools*, 1937, p. 109.

REFERENCES: (1) Letter from Sir Charles Eastlake in the Gallery archives. The entry (dating from the time of purchase) in the MS. catalogue (also in the Gallery archives) refers in two places to the transfer, of which the date was written as 1847 in both cases and only corrected to 1848 in one. (2) Letter from Luigi Crespi to Innocenzo Ansaldi, published in Bottari and Ticozzi: *Raccolta di Lettere*, vol. 7 (1822), p. 101. (3) J. A. Calvi: *Versi e Prose sopra una Serie di Eccellenti Pitture poss luta dal Signor Marchese Filippo Hercolani . . .*, 1780, p. 10. (4) No. 58 in the (privately printed) catalogue of the Benson collection (1914). The dimensions are given as 22 × 28½. The picture is oblong, not a lunette, and is reproduced in Venturi: *Storia . . .*, vol. VII, part III, p. 781. (5) See Stix and Spitzmüller: Albertina catalogue, vol. VI (1941), nos. 5 and 6 (with reproductions). (6) See Antonio Montanari: *Faenza, Guida Storica* (1882), p. 145. Calvi (*op. cit.*) refers to the oratory as 'delle Grazie' which apparently became its name after the move. (7) Vol. 1, p. 120.

2083   PORTRAIT OF BATTISTA FIERA

Panel, 20¼ × 15¼ (0·514 × 0·387).

Condition in general very good. Some retouching round the eyelids and in the shadows of the chin. The inscription on the parapet gravely damaged (see below).

The evidence for the identification of the sitter is as follows:

1. On the back is written

BATT̃A. FIERA. MEDIC. MAÑVA

This was evidently put there to record the inscription on the parapet when it became difficult to read. Infra-red photographs show enough traces of letters on the parapet to leave little or no doubt that this is the case, and the most clearly legible word—Mantua—is abbreviated in the same way as on the back (i.e. N and T run together).

2. No. 2083 appears to have been the basis of an indifferent engraving which was published in the 1649 edition (Padua) of Fiera's *Coena*. . . . The features and pose correspond exactly, though the setting is different.

Battista Fiera, who was a poet and a writer on medicine, was a Mantuan but Costa was not certainly resident there before 1507. In that year Fiera was aged 38 and his apparent age in no. 2083 suggests that the portrait may have been taken within a few years from that date. The attribution of no. 2083 to Costa is generally accepted and seems certainly right.

DRAWING: Boymans Museum, Rotterdam (ex-Koenigs and Dalhousie collections, exh. Ferrara, 1933–4, 243 and Amsterdam, 1934, 538). Black chalk, 0·319 × 0·24.

PROVENANCE: Exported from Milan between 1814 and 1848.[1] John Samuel collection before 1894. Exh. B.F.A.C., 1894 (15) (lent by the Misses Cohen). Bequeathed with other pictures by the Misses Cohen as the John Samuel Bequest, 1906.

REPRODUCTION: *Illustrations, Italian Schools*, 1937, p. 111.

REFERENCES: (1) A seal of the *Accademia di Milano* on the back bears the words '*Per l'esportaz* . . .' and the Austrian eagles with the initials F.I. From 1814–15 Lombardy and Venetia were part of the Austrian empire. The initials F.I. would be applicable to Francis I (†1835) or to Ferdinand I (abdicated 1848).

2486   A CONCERT

Panel, painted area 37½ × 29¾ (0·95 × 0·75).

General condition good. Some damage (among other places) along the lady's nose and the adjoining area of cheek. *Pentimento* on the outline of the face of the central figure. The black loop worn by the lady was originally lower, and farther to the right.

An old inscription on the back reads: *Scuola Ferrarese Capo d'opera di Ercole Grandi*. Hitherto catalogued as Roberti, but clearly an early work of Costa, close in style to the Bentivoglio altarpiece (S. Giacomo Maggiore, Bologna) which is dated 1488. The gesture of the man on the right of no. 2486, who clutches at his person with his right hand, is repeated almost literally in the figure on the right of the Bologna picture (the hand itself is noticeably small in both cases).[1]

In an article in *Emporium* (September, 1931) it is claimed that the chief instrument in no. 2486 is a Ferrarese rebec.

PROVENANCE: Probably the picture described (as Ercole Grandi) in the Hercolani collection, Bologna in 1780[2] which had passed to the Pasini collection, Rome by 1844.[3] Bought by Salting in 1877 who stated that it had belonged to Otto Mündler (†1870).[4] Exh. B.F.A.C., 1894 (14) (as Roberti: lent Salting).[5] Lent by Salting to the National Gallery from 1903. Salting Bequest, 1910.

REPRODUCTION: *Illustrations, Italian Schools*, 1937, p. 307.

REFERENCES: (1) Herbert Cook (*Burlington Magazine*, vol. XXVII (1915), p. 103) while seeing a resemblance between the lady in no. 2486 and 'one of the daughters' in the Bentivoglio altar nevertheless attributes the National Gallery picture to Baldassare d'Este. He draws the conclusion that the singers are members of the Bentivoglio family. (2) By J. A. Calvi. No. 32 in his *Versi e Prose*. . . . The same picture is mentioned in the 1782 edition (p. 286) and 1792 edition (p. 314) of Malvasia's *Pitture . . . di Bologna* (nothing in previous editions). (3) Boschini's note to Baruffaldi, I, p. 144: '*Signor Pasini in Roma . . . già in Bologna nella galleria Hercolani*'. Boschini describes the picture as '*conservatissima*' and suggests that the central figure is a portrait of the artist. (4) Salting's notebooks in the Gallery archives. A letter (also in the Gallery archives) from Eastlake to Wornum (dated 11th May, 1863) may indicate that Mündler was already the owner at that date . . . 'Mündler's Van Eyck will not do, nor his Ercole Grandi (which I had seen before)'. (5) In the introduction (by R. H. Benson) to the exhibition catalogue Frizzoni and Harck are quoted as already attributing it to Costa.

3105 **THE NATIVITY**

Panel, painted area $20\frac{5}{8} \times 14\frac{3}{4}$ (0·523 × 0·372).

Good condition in general. Many of the fingers seem to have been coarsely outlined at a later date.

On the back the letters C.G.B.C. branded (for Costabili collection), also a Costabili label and the number 92.

Nine choirs of music-making angels on each side. Two larger angels, centre, blowing trumpets, herald the arrival of a further group of angels bearing instruments of the Passion.

Hitherto catalogued as 'ascribed to Costa', and although Berenson calls it 'Costa in part'[1] the execution seems homogeneous and must be substantially the work of one hand. Inasmuch as the stylistic peculiarities which it shows—chiefly the elongation of the figures which taper to very small feet—can be precisely paralleled in a predella of the Epiphany in the Brera which is a signed work and constituted an undertaking of some importance,[2] it would seem unreasonable to doubt that that hand is Costa's own. Such, indeed, is the view of Longhi.[3] The Brera predella is dated 1499, to which period no. 3105 also should therefore, in all probability, be assigned.

PROVENANCE: Costabili collection, Ferrara (no. 57 in the 1838 catalogue). Purchased from the Marchese Costabili by Layard, 1866.[4] Exh. South Kensington, 1869 (45). Layard Bequest, 1916.

REPRODUCTION: *Illustrations, Italian Schools*, 1937, p. 111.

REFERENCES: (1) Lists, 1936. (2) It was the predella to Francia's altarpiece of the Nativity (Bologna). (3) *Officina Ferrarese*, 1934, p. 99. Other opinions have been Morelli's—'*di L. Costa . . . una perla da gabinetto*' (in the MS. catalogue of the Layard collection in the Gallery archives)—and Adolfo Venturi's—'*lavoro debolissimo di seguace*' (*Storia . . .*, VII, III, p. 820). (4) Layard MS. catalogue.

Follower of COSTA

3103 THE STORY OF MOSES (THE ISRAELITES GATHERING MANNA)
3104 THE STORY OF MOSES (THE DANCE OF MIRIAM)

Tempera (?), on linen, each 47×31 (1·18 × 0·78).

Both now darkened, and retouched in parts (particularly in some of the faces), but in general well preserved for pictures of this type. On the back of each stretcher the letters C.G.B.C. (for Costabili) branded. Also Costabili paper labels with the numbers 17 (Manna) and 19 (Miriam).

The text for 3103 is Exodus xvi, 14–36; for 3104 Exodus xv, 20–21. In the nineteenth century[1] (and by Berenson)[2] attributed to Ercole Grandi: by A. Venturi to Costa[3] and by Longhi to Boccaccino.[4] The costumes shown accord most easily with a date around 1504–8,[5] and the pictures seem to have come from Mantua (see PROVENANCE), where Costa settled in 1506–7. Nevertheless, it can be excluded that he was involved in their execution. By the Mantuan period of his career his personal mannerisms had fully developed, and included attenuation of the figures (with feet very small in proportion to the heads) and draperies breaking and complicating the outlines wherever possible. In nos. 3103 and 3104 the proportions of the figures are normal and the outlines noticeably simplified. The problem of identifying the hand responsible for the execution is aggravated by the fact that both pictures are, to some extent, *pastiches* of earlier works of art—no. 3103 of Roberti's picture in this Gallery (no. 1217) and no. 3104 of Mantegna's *Parnassus* (Louvre). Longhi's suggestion of Boccaccino has something to commend it but is not entirely convincing. On the strength of some general resemblance in lay-out to Costa's Mantuan allegories (Louvre), together with the undistinguished nature of the execution of nos. 3103 and 3104, the proposed attribution to a follower of Costa would seem the most prudent.

Nos. 3103 and 3104 are very possibly to be identified with two from a set of eight Old Testament scenes at Mantua in the seventeenth century, attributed to Costa—'*Otto pezzi di quadri con l'opera del testamento vecchio di mano del Costa vecchio*' ('*Inventario degli oggetti d'arte posseduti da Carlo II. duca di Mantova, compilato al 10 di novembre del 1665*').[6] Eight such pictures, certainly including nos. 3103 and 3104, were in the Costabili collection, Ferrara (as Ercole Grandi), 1838 (nos. 71–78).[7] Of the other six, four were later in the Visconti-Venosta collection, Rome,[8] one is in the Accademia Carrara at Bergamo (no. 560) and the last has disappeared.[9]

PROVENANCE: Perhaps Mantua, 1665 (see above). Costabili collection, Ferrara, by 1838, from which purchased, apparently by Layard on behalf of his brother-in-law, Sir Ivor Guest (later 1st Baron Wimborne).[10] Re-acquired by Layard from Sir Ivor Guest in exchange for a Romanino altarpiece (*Marriage of the Virgin*) and exh. by him at South Kensington 1869 (25 and 26).[10] Layard Bequest, 1916.

REPRODUCTION: *Illustrations, Italian Schools*, 1937, p. 112.

REFERENCES: (1) E.g., Costabili catalogue (1838), Crowe and Cavalcaselle: *History of Painting in North Italy* (1871), vol. 1, p. 552, Morelli: *Munich and Dresden* (1893), p. 138. (2) *Lists*, 1936. (3) *Storia . . .*, VII, III, pp. 807–10. (4) *Officina Ferrarese*, 1934, pp. 119–20. Also by A. Puerari: *Boccaccino*, 1957, p. 82. (5) Notes by Stella Mary Pearce in the Gallery archives. (6) Carlo D'Arco: *Delle Arti . . . di Mantova*, vol II (1857), p. 182. (7) See Costabili catalogue of that year. Also Boschini's footnote to Baruffaldi: *Vite de' Pittori* . . . *Ferraresi*, vol. I (1844), p. 143. **(8)** See Venturi, *loc. cit.* **(9)** Morelli (*loc. cit.*) says 'now in England'. **(10)** Layard papers in the Gallery archives.

COSTA and (?) MAINERI

1119 ALTARPIECE: THE VIRGIN AND CHILD ENTHRONED BETWEEN (?) S. WILLIAM OF AQUITAINE AND S. JOHN THE BAPTIST ('LA PALA STROZZI')

Panel, $97\frac{1}{4} \times 64\frac{1}{2}$ ($2 \cdot 47 \times 1 \cdot 63$).[1]

In general very well preserved for a picture of its size and age. Damaged in the lower corners where new wood has been inserted at each side, extending several inches upwards and towards the centre. The surface has been repainted correspondingly in these parts but it all represents flooring, with the exception of the lower half of the Baptist's left foot. A band of repaint, a quarter to a half inch wide (covering a join in the wood), extends about thirty inches upwards from the toes of (?) S. William's right foot.

The male saint in armour has been usually identified as S. William: alternatively as S. Louis or S. Vitus.[2] A similarly youthful figure in armour is identified as S. William of Aquitaine in Guercino's altarpiece at Bologna and in no. 671 (Garofalo) of this Gallery. Nevertheless there were eleven Saints William and their lives are confused.[3]

The lower row of scenes, in colour and in monochrome, along the base of the throne, represent (right to left) the Nativity, Presentation, Massacre of the Innocents, Flight into Egypt and Christ among the Doctors. In the row immediately above is the Fall of Man (centre) flanked by circular medallions (? of prophets). In the spandrels of the arch are (left) the Angel of the Annunciation and (right) the Virgin Annuntiate. The scene to the right of the arch represents the Sacrifice of Isaac, that on the left has been variously interpreted as Esther before Ahasuerus and the Judgment of Solomon.[4] The latter seems the more probable.

Recorded in 1621 in the Oratorio della Concezione (called S. Maria della Scala) at Ferrara. Recent research by Maurizio Calvesi (*Bollettino d'Arte*, 1958, pp. 141 ff. and 309 ff.) has shown that in the years 1497–1500 the oratory had been moved to a new site in the upper part of a building adjoining the church of S. Francesco. No. 1119 would have been ordered on this occasion, together with a series of frescoes attributable to Baldassare d'Este, Boccaccio Boccaccino and others. These were later concealed by portable pictures and partly destroyed, but fragments of them were revealed in 1957. No. 1119 was the main element in the composite altar. The early accounts are not entirely in agreement in all points regarding it but the most detailed, namely the 1772 inventory quoted by Calvesi specifies, in addition to two painted terracotta figures of later date, three '*quadretti incassati in detta Ancona*' representing the Pietà, Crucifixion and Resurrection. The first of the latter was evidently the lunette now in the Massari Zavaglia collection, Ferrara.[5]

No. 1119 was attributed in the eighteenth century to Francia, in the mid-nineteenth to Costa and, from Morelli's time, normally to 'Ercole Grandi' (a largely hypothetical painter—see entry for no. 3102: Ferrarese School).

The problems connected with this picture may be summarized as follows:

1. The main figures, for the most part, are recognizably in the style of Costa, but the small reliefs and painted scenes are unlike any phase of his work and must be by another artist.

2. X-ray photographs show that the main figures (with the exception of (?) S. William's armour and his left hand) were originally somewhat different.[6]

The question therefore arises: who painted the small scenes, and was it he, or Costa, or a third artist, who was responsible for the underpaint of the main figures?

Two authoritative recent commentators propose different solutions. Philip Pouncey[7] concludes that no. 1119 was started by G. F. Maineri who finished it, with the exception of the top paint on the Madonna, the Child, the Baptist and (?) S. William's head and right hand, that Costa was thereupon called in to finish these parts and that he altered them somewhat in the process. Roberto Longhi[8] suggests that it was Costa who started the altarpiece, between 1492 and 1496, and that only the underpaint of the Madonna and of the Child were executed at that stage. There was then an interruption, but shortly before the end of the decade Costa resumed work by repainting his own figure of the Madonna and adding that of (?) S. William. Costa thereupon abandoned the work for good, thereby causing a second interruption (during which time the Child was only an underpaint and the Baptist and the background non-existent). The altarpiece was finally finished when, about 1510, an unknown Ferrarese hand painted the Child, the Baptist and the background.

Of these two hypotheses it may be pointed out that Longhi's dating for the start of the work would accord ill with the dates as now known for the move of the oratory to its new site. Longhi's refusal, furthermore, to recognize the hand of Costa in the visible painting of the Child and the Baptist is hard to justify. The figure of the Baptist does not, as Longhi claims, necessarily presuppose knowledge of the same saint in Raphael's *Ansidei Madonna* (no. 1171 of this Gallery). In fact such elements as these two figures have in common are derivable in each case from a Peruginesque source,[9] and the appearance of the Baptist in no. 1119 is not essentially different from figures in other works by Costa, such as the *Assumption* in S. Martino Maggiore, Bologna. As to the Child, it is true that his pose is uncharacteristic of Costa, but this can be explained by the fact that His outlines follow the underpaint in essentials (this is the best indication that over- and underpaint are by different hands). As pointed out by Pouncey, He derives from Mantegna, and closely resembles the *putto* (likewise Mantegnesque) on the left of the throne in an altar-piece in the Metropolitan Museum, New York. The attribution of this work to Maineri (which was subsequently supported by Longhi)[10] is the crux of Pouncey's case. The picture shows close parallels, of lay-out and detail, with no. 1119 and even employs the same type of base for the figures—a striped marble floor which ends, disclosing the vertical section, just this side of the main figures. In addition, the painted gold mosaic backgrounds, the grisaille figures and some of the architectural ornaments are almost identical with similar features in no. 1119. Unlike the signed works of Maineri the New York picture is on a large scale (in fact somewhat larger than no. 1119). If the attribution to Maineri, which seems plausible stylistically,[11] were proved, Pouncey's thesis in its entirety could be considered established. As it is, it seems the most likely, and the following external factors may be considered in the same context. The brothers Carlo and Camillo Strozzi of Ferrara had commissioned an altarpiece of Maineri which had to be ready by Christmas, 1498. It was not in fact finished when Maineri was summoned to Mantua in November of that year. Maineri is not recorded again at Ferrara until 1502, but Costa was there in 1499. The main figures in no. 1119 in their present state would accord well with Costa's style at that period, while the date of this episode accords admirably with the date of the oratory's move.

VERSION: Ferrara, Pinacoteca, attributed to Bononi (Calvesi, *op. cit.*, p. 316).

PROVENANCE: First recorded, by Guarini, in 1621, over the high altar in the Oratorio della Concezione attached to the church of S. Francesco, Ferrara.[12] Removed, probably in 1772, to the Ospizio degli Esposti and then to the adjoining church of S. Cristoforo, Ferrara,[13] whence bought, 1859, by the Marchese Massimiliano Strozzi,[14] from whom purchased, 1882 (through W. B. Spence).

REPRODUCTION: *Illustrations, Italian Schools*, 1937, p. 163.

REFERENCES: (1) Roberto Lenghi (*Ampliamento nell' Officina Ferrarese*, 1940, pp. 25–7) puts forward an elaborate hypothesis to account for the difference in width (as given by him) between no. 1119 and its lunette (Ferrara, Massari Zavaglia collection). They are in fact of approximately the same width, though the 1929 National Gallery catalogue gives the width of no. 1119 incorrectly. It is possible that the sides of no. 1119 may have been trimmed a little, but a substantial cut may be excluded. Not only is the lunette of the same width: the figure of Isaac in the *Sacrifice* on the right of no. 1119 at the top shows an unfinished strip on the extreme right where the underpaint has not been covered by the red top paint. Evidently this area was intended to be covered by the frame, as in fact it is. (2) Identified as S. William in the undated MS. by Carlo Brisighella, who died in 1710. This MS. is in the *Biblioteca Comunale dell'Archiginnasio*, Bologna (B. 175) and is entitled *Descrizione delle pitture e sculture che adornano le Chiese et Oratorj della città di Ferrara*. G. A. Scalabrini (*Memorie Istoriche delle Chiese di Ferrara*, 1773, p. 195) makes a confused statement (*la SSma Vergine in trono, e li Santi Giovanni, e Vito, ed altro armato*) which may explain Boschini's note to Baruffaldi (*Vite de' Pittori ... Ferraresi*, 1844, 1, p. 121)—*sul piano S. Giovanni Battista e S. Guglielmo, o secondo altri S. Vito, tutto armato d'acciajo dal capo in fuori*. The 1772 inventory (*Bollettino d'Arte*, 1958, p. 314) has S. Louis. (3) Kaftal: *Iconography of the Saints in Tuscan Painting*, 1952, p. 1032. (4) As Esther (with a query) by Pouncey (*Burlington*

Magazine, 1937, vol 70, p. 162, footnote 21). As Solomon by Longhi (*op. cit.*, p. 26). (**5**) Laderchi. *Pittura Ferrarese*, 1856, p. 50, says that in his day the lunette belonged to Signor Saroli. (**6**) Philip Pouncey (*loc. cit.*) analyses the X-rays in great detail. (**7**) Pouncey, *loc. cit.* (**8**) Longhi, *loc. cit.* This was in effect a rejoinder to Pouncey's article. Longhi had earlier (*Officina Ferrarese*, 1934, pp. 121–3) proposed a different solution which he recanted in view of Pouncey's publication of the X-ray photographs. (**9**) Particularly as regards the upturned eyes of both figures. (**10**) *Ampliamenti* . . ., p. 19 (footnote). (**11**) At the Metropolitan Museum the picture is currently attributed to Pellegrino Munari. (**12**) Marc Antonio Guarini: *Compendio Historico . . . di Ferrara*, 1621, p. 275. The description is too short to establish the identity of the picture without further evidence. Nevertheless this is provided by the more detailed descriptions given in Brisighella's MS. (see Pouncey, *loc. cit.*) and by Scalabrini (*loc. cit.*) of the picture over the high altar. (**13**) In Scalabrini (*loc. cit.*) which was published in 1773, no. 1119 and other pictures are described as still in the Oratory. Nevertheless this may well be accounted for by delay in printing the book, since in Laderchi's *Pittura Ferrarese*, 1856 (p. 50) it is related how in 1772 the revenues of the Oratory were diverted to the Ospedale degli Esposti, and the pictures sold to the Englishman, John Udny, with the exception of no. 1119 which remained for a long time in a corridor of the hospital and was later set up in the adjoining church of S. Cristoforo. Already mentioned by Citadella (*Catalogo Istorico de' Pittori e Scultori Ferraresi . . .*, vol. IV, 1783, p. 326) as belonging to the Oratory but housed in the hospital. (**14**) Extract (in the Gallery archives) from the *Gazzetta di Ferrara*, 5th April, 1859. It seems that Strozzi bought the picture to prevent its sale to the National Gallery who were in fact negotiating for it at the time. It is also mentioned, as a desirable acquisition for the National Gallery, in the diary (in the Gallery archives) of the travelling agent, Otto Mündler (23rd August, 1856).

DOSSO Dossi
active 1512, died 1542

Ferrarese School. His name was Giovanni di Luteri. The family apparently came from Trent, but the name Dosso seems to derive from that of a place in the neighbourhood of Mantua. The double form—Dosso Dossi—was not used before the eighteenth century. Vasari says that Dosso was almost coeval with Ariosto, who was born in 1474. Nevertheless there is no evidence in support of the year 1479, given by Boschini in his commentary on Baruffaldi (1844) and generally followed since. First recorded in 1512, when he was paid for a picture at Mantua. Then active (from 1514 to his death) at Ferrara in the service of successive dukes, Alfonso and Ercole d'Este.

Dosso painted mythologies, portraits and decorative frescoes as well as religious pictures. Above all he was important as a pioneer of landscape, in which he shows the influence of the Giorgionesque. Some Raphaelesque influence is also probable. Caution should in general be exercised with regard to paintings in a Dossesque style, since Dosso's brother, Battista, is known to have collaborated with him, and although Dosso seems to have been the dominant (and also the elder) of the two there is as yet insufficient evidence to identify either the share of each in the joint works or, in some cases, the style of Battista when working alone. It may be noted that in 1520 Battista is recorded in

Rome, apparently in the studio of Raphael, with whom Dosso had been in correspondence. Though it has not been demonstrated that Dosso also had been in Rome this would remain a possibility.[1]

REFERENCE: (1) In this connection cf: Henriette Mendelsohn: *Das Werk der Dossi*, 1914, pp. 10–11.

1234 A MAN EMBRACING A WOMAN

Panel. The central piece of wood measures $20\frac{1}{4} \times 28\frac{7}{8}$. Round this four narrow triangles of wood have been added, making up a rectangle $21\frac{1}{2} \times 29\frac{5}{8}$ (0.53×0.75). These additions are certainly very old and almost certainly the painter's own. They have the effect not merely of enlarging the panel but also of canting its axis somewhat.

Some obvious damages in the sky, in the lady's wreath and in her right eyebrow. No other important damage is apparent through the present discoloured varnish.

Hitherto catalogued as *A Muse inspiring a Court Poet*, but the lady's expression would seem more appropriate to a Maenad than to a Muse. However her wreath (from which the man appears to have taken the sprig which he wears behind his left ear) is of summer-flowering jasmine (*jasminum officinale*)[1] whereas the approved head-gear for Maenads was ivy, oak or fir.[2]

Though the execution has sometimes been questioned as Dosso's this has more generally been upheld[3] and seems justifiable in the main, although Mendelsohn suspects studio assistance in the pattern on the lady's sleeve which imperfectly follows the form of the shoulder underneath.[4] The parapet in the foreground and the clouds behind would clearly indicate that no. 1234 was intended probably as part of a series, for the decoration of a room.[5] Five similar pictures by Dosso (though from a different series from no. 1234) are in the Modena Gallery.

VERSION: An apparently similar picture, attr. Dosso Dossi, is in the Jacquemart-André Museum, Abbaye de Châalis (523). A comparable picture (of a youth with a basket of flowers) is in the Fondazione Roberto Longhi at Florence.

PROVENANCE: Said to be from the Palazzo Borghese, Rome.[6] Bought, 1828, from a Mr. King by T. B. Bulkeley Owen, No. 198 in the latter's sale, Christie's, 30th April, 1868. John Heugh sale, Christie's, 11th May, 1878 (276). Anonymous (with Roupell) sale, Christie's, 25th June, 1887 (123), bt. C. Fairfax Murray (in all three sales specified as ex-Palazzo Borghese, King and Bulkeley Owen and described as *Fiametta and Boccaccio* by Giorgione). Bought from C. Fairfax Murray, 1887, Clarke Fund.

REPRODUCTION: *Illustrations, Italian Schools*, 1937, p. 125.

REFERENCES: (1) Letter from Wilfrid Blunt in the Gallery archives. (2) *The Oxford Classical Dictionary* (1949), p. 528. (3) E.g. by Berenson, *Lists*, 1936. (4) Henriette Mendelsohn: *Das Werk der Dossi* (1914), pp. 95, 96. The authoress also draws attention to the man's mutton-chop whiskers which were very unusual in the Renaissance. (5) The alterations in the dimensions of the panel and in its axis would be compatible with the assumption that the picture was designed to be let into the wall of a room as part of a scheme of decoration.

There is also a diagonal incision on the back of the panel as if it were intended to fit over a strut. (6) In the Bulkeley Owen catalogue, 1868. No picture answering to this description occurs in the description of pictures at the Palazzo Borghese given by Randohr (*Ueber Mahlerei und Bildhauerarbeit* . . ., vol. 1, 1787) but it is possible that the Bulkeley Owen catalogue is confusing no. 1234 with a picture described by Ramdohr (*op. cit.*, pp. 294–5) as of a man and woman embracing, with a reference to Gavin Hamilton's *Schola Italica* and to the fact that the latter attributes the picture to Giorgione (under whose name no. 1234 passed in the nineteenth century). The engraving in the latter work, however, shows a different picture.

3924   THE ADORATION OF THE KINGS

Panel, $33\frac{1}{2} \times 42\frac{1}{2}$ (0·84 × 1·07).

Somewhat damaged by cracking in the wood and some of the paint rather worn, but on the whole in good condition. The outline of the head of the young king standing on the right is 'worried' and was probably originally somewhat larger. Cleaned, 1974.

The large circular heavenly body is referred to by Richter[1] as a 'portent', but it is possible that Dosso merely intended it as a romantic representation of the moon.

The relative freedom of the handling would suggest that it is rather a late work—and as such it has generally been regarded. Nevertheless the chronology of Dosso Dossi is difficult or impossible to establish with precision.

PROVENANCE: Sir William W. Knighton, at whose sale, Christie's, 23rd May, 1885 (524) (as Giorgione) bought by Richter.[2] Mond collection 1888. Exh. B.F.A.C., 1894 (63) (lent Mond). Mond Bequest, 1924.

REPRODUCTION: *Illustrations, Italian Schools*, 1937, p. 127.

REFERENCES: (1) In the Mond catalogue. (2) *Op. cit.*, vol. II (1910), p. viii. Richter here refers to the picture's having been in a London sale, '1886', where bought Richter. This is presumably a confusion with the Knighton sale of the previous year. Previously, no. 3924 may have been identical with a picture bought from the Sampieri collection at Bologna by Gavin Hamilton, and offered by him to the Earl of Upper Ossory in a letter of 27th September, 1769 (communicated by E. K. Waterhouse) 'The Re Magi . . . as . . . by Giorgione, but I rather think it is of Dossi of Ferrara'. (Letter in the National Library of Ireland, MSS.)

4032   PIETÀ

Panel, $14\frac{3}{8} \times 12$ (0·36 × 0·3).

Good condition. A little worn in places.

Formerly considered an early work.[1]

PROVENANCE: Said to have been for more than a century in the family of Baron Bernard de Rothem, 'who brought it from Hungary.'[2] Bought by Sir Claude Phillips at an auction in London about 1905[3]; bequeathed by him, 1924.

REPRODUCTION: *Illustrations, Italian Schools*, 1937, p. 126.

REFERENCES: (1) E.g. by Berenson (*Lists*, 1936). Longhi (*Officina Ferrarese*, p. 137) says at earliest in second decade of the sixteenth century, perhaps later. (2) Label on the back, probably cut from the sale catalogue at which Phillips bought it. It should be noted that Phillips, and following him Mendelsohn (*Das Werk der Dossi*, 1914, p. 39) mis-reads the label and says the picture had belonged to the Rothem family for three hundred years. Also on the back are several seals, one with the Imperial eagle and the legend 'Dogana di Milano'. (3) See Claude Phillips in *The Art Journal*, 1906, p. 353 and in the *Burlington Magazine*, vol. 27, p. 133. Phillips does not specify the auctioneer and search among Christie's catalogues at the relevant date has failed to identify the picture.

5279 A BACCHANAL

$55\frac{1}{2} \times 66\frac{1}{4}$ ($1\cdot409 \times 1\cdot682$).
Much damaged and extensively repainted.

Datable by the costumes *ca.* 1512–16,[1] and, partly for that reason, sometimes thought to be identical with a bacchanal by Dosso which was part of the series, to which Bellini and Titian also contributed, painted for the Studiolo of Alfonso d'Este at Ferrara (see no. 35. Titian). These pictures were confiscated by Cardinal Pietro Aldobrandini in 1598 and taken to the Rome area. Nevertheless, the Aldobrandini inventories published since the first edition of the present catalogue include a Dosso which is evidently the one in question but of which the description does not correspond either with no. 5279 or with an alternative existing candidate (now in Castel S. Angelo, Rome).[2] The picture in the inventories included a Vulcan and a figure asleep.[3] The Vulcan (and, in another inventory, a reference to armour) (*armature*) would seem to connect with Vasari's reference to scenes from the story of Aeneas and of Mars, Venus and Vulcan, painted by Dosso for Ferrara.[4] But it would also seem to exclude the possibility that no. 5279 is the picture in question. Despite this, and despite the damaged state, the attribution to Dosso need not be doubted, but the textual source of the subject would now be debatable.[5]

PROVENANCE: Very possibly lot 116 in the Sir Thomas Lawrence sale, 15th May, 1830 ('Giorgione . . . A Bacchanalian Festival; an extensive composition, with fine landscape background . . . 66 × 56' bought Gilmore). Douglas Guest collection.[6] Marquess of Breadalbane sale, 5th June, 1886 (lot 52—as Giorgione) where bought in. Major the Hon. Thomas George Breadalbane Morgan-Grenville-Gavin sale, 6th July, 1917 (lot 51, bought Martin).[7] Bequeathed by Sir Lionel Faudel-Phillips, 1941.

REPRODUCTION: Negatives in the possession of the Gallery. Also J. Walker, *op. cit.* fig. 20.

REFERENCES: (1) Notes by Stella Mary Pearce, who points out that some of the most conspicuous features in the foreground, particularly the lady in the striped dress in the centre, seem to have been altered to accord with the fashions of around 1530. (2) *Palatino*, 1964, p. 162, no. 154 (1603 inventory) and 153 (inventory before 1665). Also *Arte Antica e Moderna*, 1963, p. 73, no. 299 (1682 inventory). (3) 'Una figura dorme' (inventory before 1665). Paola Della Pergola's reading of the 1682 inventory is 'una figura donna' which does not make sense and is presumably a mistake. (4) Vasari/Milanesi VII, 433. In another place (VI, 474) Vasari speaks of a *baccanaria d'uomini* which would suit no. 5279 better. (5) P. Dreyer (*Pantheon*, 1965, pp. 22 ff.) denies the attribution. (6) According to catalogues of the Breadalbane and Morgan-Grenville-Gavin sales. (7) Extract from this catalogue affixed to the back of the stretcher.

FERRARESE School

73 THE CONVERSION OF S. PAUL

Panel, $22\frac{7}{8} \times 27\frac{1}{2}$ (0·581 × 0·698).

A little worn, and unevenly cleaned in the past, but basic condition of the paint seems quite good.

Catalogued as Ercole di Ferrara ('Ercole Grandi') until 1915. As Battista Dossi in the 1920–9 editions. In 1903 A. Venturi[1] linked it with a *Purification of the Temple* in the Doria Gallery (signed with the initials IA) and ascribed both to a follower of Dosso Dossi. Previously (1900)[2] he had linked the Doria picture with another of the same subject (Louvre, no. 1388) and attributed both to a follower, probably Flemish of Dosso and Mazzolino. The landscape background of no. 73 is obviously of a Dossesque type—perhaps specifically of the kind associated with Battista rather than with Dosso (cf. the landscape in the Modena *Adoration of the Shepherds*, no. 179, together with the Almighty in that work with the Christ in no. 73; also the landscape in the Dresden *Justice*). But the figures have an archaic appearance and when it is borne in mind that the kneeling man holding his shield over his head (bottom right corner) is a motive found in Piero della Francesca it seems possible that no. 73, though certainly by some painter in the Dosso circle, is partly based on an earlier work.[3]

PROVENANCE: In the Rev. Holwell Carr's will (1828) ('no. 26, Ercole di Ferrara') as from the Aldobrandini collection and therefore identifiable with the 'Garofalo: Conversion of S. Paul' from the Villa Aldobrandini imported by Alexander Day and exhibited by him for sale in London, 1800–01.[4] Therefore perhaps no. 23 in Cardinal Pietro Aldobrandini's inventory of 1603.[5] The Rev. W. Holwell Carr Bequest, 1831.

REPRODUCTION: *Illustrations, Italian Schools*, 1937, p. 125.

REFERENCES: (1) In *L'Arte*, 1903, p. 141. (2) *La Galleria Crespi in Milano*, p. 50. The further literature on the Doria picture is tabulated and discussed by E. Sestieri in his catalogue (1942) of the Doria Gallery, pp. 152–3 ('N. 220— Incognito Fiammingo—Sec. XVI'). (3) The corresponding figure by Piero occurs left centre in the fresco of *Heraclius' Victory over Chosroes* (Arezzo, S. Francesco). It may be indicated that the motive in question is more appropriate to a battle scene than to a Conversion of Paul and that this in itself could be read as an indication of some derivation of no. 73 from another work. A further National Gallery picture—no. 1062—may also be based on Piero's lost frescoes at Ferrara (see the entry in *The Earlier Italian Schools* by Martin Davies; also J. Lauts: *Zu Piero dei Franceschis verlorenen Fresken in Ferrara* in *Zeitschrift für Kunstgeschichte*, X, 1941, pp. 67 ff. As regards the dating of no. 73 Stella Mary Pearce favours the period 1538–48 on the evidence of the costumes. In this connection it may be noted that the saddle-cloth of the white horse in the centre is covered with fleur-de-lis. (4) Buchanan, *Memoirs . . .*, II (1824), p. 6. Conceivably identical with 'Una . . . Conversione di San Paolo di mano del Mazzolino', no. 7 in the *Inventario . . . di . . . la Duchessa d'Urbino . . . 1592* (published by Paola Della Pergola, *Arte Antica e Moderna*, 1959, pp. 342 ff.). (5) Printed in *Palatino* Jan.–March 1964, p. 16. The same picture figured in Olimpia Aldobrandini's inventory (pre-1665). But there was also a big *Conversion of Paul* in the Aldobrandini collection in the seventeenth century, attributed to Salviati.

3102 THE VIRGIN AND CHILD, WITH SS. DOMINIC AND CATHERINE OF SIENA

Panel, $18\frac{1}{4} \times 13\frac{3}{4}$ (0·463 × 0·348).
Condition in general good.
Hitherto catalogued as Garofalo.

The throne is decorated with numerous reliefs in rectangular frames, most of which are too small to permit of certain identification. The chained monkey derives from one in an engraving by Dürer (Bartsch 42) in which, as in no. 3102, the Child has a bird on a string. In no. 3102 the bird is a goldfinch and in both works the conjunction of the two creatures may well be intended to constitute the same symbolic antithesis—the soul, as represented by the bird, a voluntary captive of Christ, while the baser instincts, represented by the monkey, are forcibly subdued by His example.[1] Dürer's engraving is undated and is assigned by Panofsky[2] to the period around 1498. Whoever the author of no. 3102 the partial derivation from Dürer appears certain, and if the period suggested by Panofsky for the latter's engraving is correct it would constitute no objection to the attribution of no. 3102 to the young Garofalo (who is not certainly recorded as a painter before the year 1506). The case for Garofalo's authorship was put by Venturi[3] and has been supported by Longhi.[4] It may be correct, but there is at present insufficient evidence to define Garofalo's early style with any confidence. On the other hand there were minor Ferrarese painters, such as Domenico Panetti, whose style appears comparable with that of no. 3102. The latter was attributed throughout the nineteenth century to 'Ercole Grandi'—a painter at that time confused with Ercole Roberti—and by Berenson (with a query)[5] to the real Ercole Grandi—an historical, but entirely undefined, personality. In the circumstances it hardly seems possible to settle the attribution.

PROVENANCE: From the Costabili collection, Ferrara (1838 cat. no. 83)[6] whence bought by Layard, 1866 (MS. cat., in the Gallery archives, no. 44). Exh. Leeds, 1868 (84) and South Kensington, 1869 (43). Layard Bequest, 1916.

REPRODUCTION: *Illustrations, Italian Schools*, 1937, p. 150.

REFERENCES: (1) See H. W. Janson: *Apes and Ape Lore* (1952), p. 151. Also H. Friedemann: *The Symbolic Goldfinch* (1946). (2) E. Panofsky: *Albrecht Dürer*, vol. 2 (1945), p. 23. (3) *Storia . . .*, IX, IV, 1, p. 289. (4) *Officina Ferrarese* (1934), p. 130—he gives a general blessing to Venturi's reconstruction of the early Garofalo. (5) Successive editions of the *Lists*. (6) On the back is the Costabili brand and another—a cross in a circle with the letters SRDS, one in each segment—also a Costabili paper label with the number 98.

FLORENTINE School

650 PORTRAIT OF A LADY

$44\frac{1}{2} \times 31\frac{1}{2}$ (1·12 × 0·8).
The green curtain seems in fair condition. Most of the rest of the surface is worn, with repaint stippled liberally.

Bought (and originally catalogued) as Bronzino. In later editions of
the National Gallery catalogued as Alessandro Allori. The costume
accords best with a dating in the late 1550's or early 1560's[1] but the
style does not seem specific to any identifiable painter.

PROVENANCE: Probably the picture noted by Waagen (1854) in the possession
of Lord Shrewsbury.[2] It is true that Waagen's description is extremely vague
('Cristoforo Allori.—A female portrait; to the knees. Very animated; the
colouring excellent') but the description in the catalogue of Lord Shrewsbury's
sale at Alton Towers (8th July, 1857) of what is apparently the same picture
would fit no. 650 more precisely,[3] and exactly at this time Edmund Beaucousin,
from whom no. 650 was ultimately bought, was adding to his collection.
Purchased in Paris with the Beaucousin collection, 1860.

REPRODUCTION: *Illustrations, Italian Schools*, 1937, p. 7.

REFERENCES: (1) Notes by Stella Mary Pearce. (2) Waagen: *Treasures of Art
in Great Britain*, vol. III, 383. (3) Lot 234 (as Bronzino): 'A noble Venetian
lady, in a rich black dress and white collar, pearl necklace and cross; a green
drapery suspended behind'. Bought at the sale by the dealer Nieuwenhuys.

932　A KNIGHT OF S. JOHN
　　Panel, 38⅛ × 30 (0·968 × 0·762).
　　Much darkened. The paint is rubbed and thin in most areas and also
made up. The relative lack of individualisation in the features gives an
impression that the picture was never entirely finished but this is probably a false impression, due to damage.
　　Previously as 'Italian School, XVI century'.
　　The scale is life size or perhaps slightly larger; the artist evidently
some sub-Sarto painter in the Florentine tradition immediately before
the Mannerist phase. Owing to the picture's damaged and darkened
state no more precise attribution seems justifiable. The costume accords
best with a dating around 1520.[1]
　　The cross worn by the sitter at the waist could also be worn round the
neck.[2] See also no. 1035 (Franciabigio) for another portrait of a knight of
S. John. The Order was expelled from Rhodes in 1522–3 and established
itself at Malta in 1530.

PROVENANCE: Lot 81, as Sebastiano del Piombo, in the Louis Philippe sale,
London, 6th May, 1853, where bought Pearce. Wynn Ellis Bequest, 1876.

REPRODUCTION: *Illustrations, Italian Schools*, 1937, p. 176.

REFERENCES: (1) Notes by Stella Mary Pearce. A verbal attribution to Rosso
Fiorentino has been made by F. Zeri. (2) Information from the Curator of the
Order of S. John in London. (3) Marked copy of the sale catalogue in the Gallery
library.

6375　MADONNA　AND　CHILD　WITH　THE　INFANT
　　　BAPTIST
　　Panel, 32 × 23 (0·81 × 0·58).
　　The paint has worn thin in places, but in general very well preserved.

The thumb of the Madonna's left hand seems originally to have extended higher up—almost to the Child's lower lip. Her right eyebrow once joined the nose at a point lower than it does now. Cleaned 1966. The number—383—painted in light paint at the lower right corner is of the same type as the figures visible on nos. 168 (Raphael: S. Catherine), 213 (Raphael: An Allegory), 20 (ascribed to Girolamo da Carpi: Double Portrait) and 1194 (after drawing by Michelangelo: Purification of the Temple). All these pictures were in the Borghese collection, and these numbers refer to the inventory of 1693. The present picture, no. 6375, appears in the 1693 Borghese inventory as follows:

> ... un quadro di quattro palmi in circa in tavola, la Madonna, il Bambino e S. Giovanni del No. 383 ... d'Andrea del Sarto.[1]

The attribution to Sarto is now untenable. An attribution to Pontormo —datable by the costume to the early 1520's[2]—would be more likely,[3] though not entirely convincing. It should also be borne in mind that at this period the young Bronzino was living with Pontormo and, according to Vasari, was painting indistinguishably from him.[4] An earlier attribution of no. 6375 to Sodoma is recorded in a label and an inscription on the back of the panel. Recently the Chicago version was ascribed to Maso da San Friano.[5]

VERSION: Chicago, Art Institute.

PROVENANCE: Borghese collection, Rome. Presumably sold at the time when many others were, during the Napoleonic upheaval, since recorded early in the nineteenth century in the Camuccini collection, with which purchased by the 4th Duke of Northumberland, 1856.[6] Lent by the Duke of Northumberland to an exhibition entitled 'Noble Patronage' (University of Newcastle upon Tyne, November–December, 1963, no. 56). Exhibited at the Hazlitt Gallery, London, 1966, from which purchased in that year, after a licence to export to Berlin had been rejected.

REPRODUCTION: Illustrated General Catalogue, 1973, p. 569.

REFERENCES: (1) Published by Paola Della Pergola, Arte Antica e Moderna, 30, 1965, p. 204. (2) Opinion from Stella Mary Pearce (Mrs Eric Newton). (3) The Madonna seems to the present writer to be modelled in all probability from the same figure—evidently a youth—whom Pontormo used for the bearer kneeling in the foreground of his Deposition (Florence, S. Felicita). The least Pontormesque feature of no. 6375 is the head of the Christ Child. The present picture was ascribed to Pontormo in the National Gallery Report of 1965–6 and (tentatively) in the Illustrated General Catalogue (1973). (4) Vasari/Milanesi, VII, p. 593: Costui [Bronzino] essendo stati molti anni col Puntormo, come s'è detto, prese tanto quella maniera, ed in guisa immitò l'opera di colui, che elle sono state molte volte tolte l'une per l'altre, così furono per un pezzo somiglianti. (5) Kurt W. Forster in Museum Studies 7 (Chicago), 1972, pp. 35 ff. (6) Alnwick and Camuccini provenance communicated by the Hazlitt Gallery at the time of purchase. There are three seals on the back of the panel. It is tempting to identify the picture with a reference in Waagen (Galleries and Cabinets of Art in Great Britain, 1857, p. 467) to a 'Pontormo. The Virgin and Child. From the Borghese Collection ... quite in the style and manner of ... Sarto'. The omission of the youthful Baptist, however, suggests that this was a different picture—one which is mentioned by Crowe and Cavalcaselle (History of Painting *in Italy*, vol. VI, 1914, pp. 201, 202) as a replica of Sarto of the Madonna and Child alone then in the Baring Collection.

FLORENTINE School (?)

21 PORTRAIT OF A LADY

Panel,[1] $23\frac{1}{4} \times 19\frac{1}{8}$ (0·591 × 0·485).

The paint was worn thin and been retouched in numerous places.

In the Rev. Holwell Carr's will (1828) as Sofonisba Anguisciola or Bronzino. Catalogued as Bronzino from 1831 to 1859, as Cristofano Allori 1861–1911 and thereafter as Florentine School, sixteenth century. It belongs to a type of portraiture—like another problem picture of this Gallery, no. 649, *Portrait of a Boy*—which is vaguely Bronzinesque without being precisely attributable. In the present instance the difficulty is aggravated by the thin state to which the paint has been reduced. The costume accords best with a dating around 1540.[2]

PROVENANCE: According to the Holwell Carr papers, from the collection of the 'Duca di San Vitale, Parma'. The Rev. W. Holwell Carr Bequest, 1831.

REPRODUCTION: *Illustrations, Italian Schools*, 1937, p. 138.

REFERENCES: (1) The panel has a seal on the back with a monogram of which the main letter is B. (2) Notes by Stella Mary Pearce. She points out, however, that certain features of the costume are peculiar. Some but not all of these peculiarities may be due to the picture's dubious condition.

649 PORTRAIT OF A BOY

Panel, $50\frac{3}{4} \times 24$ (1·29 × 0·61).

Despite a number of obvious retouchings general condition good for a picture of the period.

Variously attributed in the past to Pontormo,[1] Bronzino[2] and Francesco Salviati.[3] The first two attributions can hardly be seriously considered now. The third has found some support[4] but is still unacceptable to the present writer. The touch has none of Salviati's sparkle (in particular, the hair seems tamely handled when compared with the brilliant high lights characteristic of Salviati in this respect). An attribution to Girolamo Mazzola Bedoli was made by W. Suida.[5] It depended largely on a fancied likeness of the sitter in no. 649 to that in Mazzola Bedoli's portrait of the young Alessandro Farnese with the personification of Parma (Parma). Some degree of resemblance may be admitted, but it may well be superficial or fanciful. It may also be pointed out that there is no trace in no. 649 of the Farnese fleur-de-lis. The picture in general seems to follow a vaguely Bronzinesque pattern but the handling is insufficiently individual to justify a precise attribution. The fashionable costume accords best with a date in the mid 1540's.[6]

PROVENANCE: At the time of purchase (1860) with the Edmond Beaucousin collection, Paris, stated to have been in 'the collection of the Duke of Brunswick'.

REPRODUCTION: *Illustrations, Italian Schools*, 1937, p. 317.

REFERENCES: (1) E.g. National Gallery catalogues 1861–98. (2) E.g. National Gallery catalogues 1901–11. (3) E.g. National Gallery catalogues 1912–29. (4) E.g. Berenson: *Lists* 1932 and 1936: 'Florentine Unknown, 1465–1540, probably Salviati'. (5) In *Crisopoli*, III (1935), pp. 105–13. (6) Notes in the Gallery archives by Stella Mary Pearce.

1150 A BEARDED MAN

Panel, $24\frac{7}{8} \times 19\frac{3}{4}$ (0·632 × 0·501).

Somewhat damaged by cracking.

Hitherto catalogued as ascribed to Pontormo. The painting of the black silk dress seems indeed not so far from him, but the work as a whole appears not to be specifically connected with him and is evidently due to some humbler painter.

Berenson at one time (*Lists*, 1932 and 1936) tentatively suggested Lotto.

The costume accords best with a dating around 1527–8.[1]

PROVENANCE: Purchased from C. Fairfax Murray, Florence, 1883.

REPRODUCTION: *Illustrations, Italian Schools*, 1937, p. 287.

REFERENCE: (1) Notes by Stella Mary Pearce.

1301 PORTRAIT OF SAVONAROLA

The verso has a view of his execution.

Panel, painted area each side *c.* $8\frac{3}{8} \times 6\frac{1}{2}$ (0·212 × 0·165).

The head of Savonarola on the *recto* is in fair state. The scene on the *verso* is rather more worn and retouched.

Any doubt there might be concerning the identity of the profile portrait on the *recto*—which shows a slightly different cast of feature from Fra Bartolommeo's inscribed portrait at S. Marco, Florence—is dispelled by the scene on the *verso* which clearly represents the execution of Savonarola and his two companions, Domenico da Pescia and Silvestro Maruffi. This took place on the Piazza della Signoria, Florence on 23rd May, 1498. It is difficult to decide how long after the event no. 1301 would have been painted.[1] Earlier editions of the catalogue assume it to be contemporary and list it as fifteenth-century Florentine school. It seems certainly later than this and certain scholars put it considerably later.[2] The present writer, however, inclines to see both sides as likely to date from the Pontormesque phase of Florentine painting. This would accord well with political events, since during the years 1527–30 there was a great revival of enthusiasm for Savonarola in Florence.

PROVENANCE: Given to Robert Southey on the occasion of his second marriage (1839) by Walter Savage Landor who stated that he had bought it from a member of the Tornaquinci family of Florence who had had it from the Medici. Sold by Southey's granddaughter, Miss Warter, shortly before 1890, to Dr. William Radford of Sidmouth, by whom presented, 1890.[3]

REPRODUCTION: The *verso* is pl. 25 of *Paintings and Drawings on the Backs of*

National Gallery Pictures by Martin Davies (1946). Negative of the *recto* in the Gallery's possession. *Illustrated General Catalogue*, 1973, p. 236.

REFERENCES: (1) The *Marzocco* at the angle of the Palazzo Vecchio at the time of Savonarola's execution was subsequently destroyed and this part of the building modified in other ways. It seems correct for the period in no. 1301 but this would not necessarily stop the picture's being a copy or part copy of something else. (2) E.g. Martin Davies: *Paintings and Drawings on the Backs of National Gallery Pictures*, 1946, p. x 'execution not as early as the XVI century'. (3) All this information from notes in the Gallery archives.

FRANCIABIGIO
c. 1482/3–1525

His name was Francesco di Cristofano. The approximate date of his birth is from Vasari's statement that he died at the age of forty-two. His death occurred on 24th January, 1524, which is 1525 according to modern reckoning. His father was Milanese but he himself appears always to have worked in Florence.

Vasari says he was the pupil of Albertinelli, though the latter was only eight years his senior. He collaborated with Andrea del Sarto who, with Fra Bartolommeo, was the chief formative influence on his style. His portraits, of which no. 1035 below is a fair example, are his best work. A reasonable number of authentic pictures (usually signed with a monogram), comprising both subject-pieces and portraits, survive.

1035 PORTRAIT OF A KNIGHT OF RHODES

Panel, painted surface 23¾ × 18 (0·60 × 0·45). Not cut.

Inscription on the parapet: ·TAR·VBLIA·CHI·BIEN·EIMA· At either end of this inscription is the monogram (apparently consisting of the letters F, R and C interlaced) associated with Franciabigio.

General condition fairly good.[1] Scattered areas of damage in sky, flesh and garments. Cleaned 1974.

The writing on the letter is not legible but at the end of it is what appears to be a date—1514—clearly written.

The motto ('who loves well is slow to forget') is said to be in Provençal or else in French phonetically spelt by an Italian.[2]

The white cross worn by the sitter is of the type known as a Maltese Cross and is associated with the Order of S. John. The Order was expelled from Rhodes in 1522–3 and established itself at Malta in 1530—five years after Franciabigio's death and sixteen after the date of this picture. The designation 'Knight of Rhodes' rather than 'Knight of Malta' would thus be applicable.

PROVENANCE: Bought by W. Fuller Maitland, 1863, from 'Mr. Seymour FitzGerald's collection'.[3] Exh. R.A., 1872 (127) lent by W. Fuller Maitland, from whom purchased, 1878.

REPRODUCTION: *Illustrations, Italian Schools*, 1937, p. 145.

REFERENCES: (1) Crowe and Cavalcaselle, in the nineteenth century, describe it as 'in first-rate preservation'. (2) Letters in the Gallery archives. (3) Manuscript note in the copy in the National Gallery library of the privately printed catalogue (1872) of the Fuller Maitland collection at Stansted Hall.

GAROFALO
1481(?)-1559

Ferrarese school. His name was Benvenuto Tisi. The date of his birth depends only on Vasari who may not be reliable in this case. Baruffaldi reproduces a letter dated 29th January, 1499 from (Boccaccio) Boccaccino at Cremona referring to Garofalo as to a pupil.[1] To judge by the evidence of Garofalo's style an apprenticeship to Boccaccino would have been by no means improbable, but the letter in question has not been rediscovered and is suspect, and since Boccaccino was at Ferrara in 1497–1500 Garofalo could have come in contact with him there. Vasari says Garofalo visited Rome on two occasions, but this is not confirmed. Many authentic paintings by Garofalo survive, mainly of religious subjects together with a few mythologies. The allocation of certain works as between Garofalo and L'Ortolano has long caused some confusion.

REFERENCE: (1) *Vite de' Pittori e Scultori Ferraresi*, I (1844), pp. 315–16 .

81 S. AUGUSTINE WITH THE HOLY FAMILY AND S. CATHERINE OF ALEXANDRIA ('THE VISION OF S. AUGUSTINE')

Panel, $25\frac{3}{8} \times 32\frac{1}{4}$ (0·64 × 0·81).

Rather worn in places. Cleaned, 1966.

The scene depicts S. Augustine walking on the shore when contemplating his treatise on the Trinity. He saw a child trying to empty the sea into a small hole with a spoon. On S. Augustine's indicating the impossibility of success in this project the child alluded to the greater folly of trying to comprehend the Trinity with the human mind. The subject is not uncommon (another example in this Gallery in no. 3811, F. de Nomé) but the inclusion of S. Catherine is unusual; also the figure (of S. Stephen)[1] in the background.

The vision of S. Augustine in this form occurs in the *Golden Legend* and in Petrus de Natalibus' *Catalogus Sanctorum*. It is not found among S. Augustine's own writings, but in the commentary (1764)[2] to S. Possidius' Life of S. Augustine the suggestion is made that the story may be connected with one described in a letter ostensibly from S. Augustine to Cyril, Bishop of Jerusalem. Some connection may indeed exist, though the letter in question has long been recognized as a forgery probably dating from about the same period as the *Golden Legend* (cf. in this connection, and for bibliographical references, the entry for no. 3946 (Signorelli) of this Gallery in *The Earlier Italian Schools* by Martin Davies, 2nd edition, 1961, particularly reference no. 6).

The costumes of S. Catherine and of the Virgin in no. 81 accord best with a dating around 1518.[3]

ENGRAVING: By P. W. Tomkins, 1816 (in *The British Gallery of Pictures*, 1818).

VERSION: Old copy formerly in the Wittgenstein collection, Vienna.

PROVENANCE: In the collection of Cardinal Silvio Valenti in Rome before 1749, since Panini's view of the Valenti Gallery (now at the Wadsworth Atheneum, Hartford, Conn.) is dated that year and shows it. No. 480 (*Quadro di palmi 3, once 8 per altezza, e palmi 2, once 10 per larghezza, rappresentante S. Agostino, la Madonna, coll' Angiolo in Gloria, in tavola, di Benvenuto Garofalo*) in an unpublished inventory at Mantua (*Catalogo dei quadri, tuttavia esistenti nella Galleria della ch.mem. dell'Emo Sig. Cardinale Silvio Valenti*)[4] of the Valenti collection datable between 1749 (when Panini's picture was painted) and 1763 (when much of the collection was put up for sale at Amsterdam). Mentioned as in Palazzo Corsini, Rome by Volkmann (1770).[5] Offered for sale by private treaty at 118, Pall Mall, London with pictures bought by Ottley in Rome in 1799 and 1800 (no. 29 in the undated catalogue, as from Palazzo Corsini).[6] No. 47 in the Ottley sale, Christie's, 16th May, 1801 'from the Corsini Palace', where bought by Lord Radstock.[7] Afterwards bought by Lord Kinnaird and, then (before 1816) by the Rev. Holwell Carr,[8] by whom lent B.I., 1818 (49) and by whom bequeathed, 1831.

REPRODUCTION: *Illustrations, Italian Schools*, 1937, p. 147.

REFERENCES: (1) Mrs. Jameson (*Sacred and Legendary Art*, I, 1833, p. 313) confidently identifies this figure as S. Stephen and points to S. Augustine's known interest in this saint. As he is shown here as a deacon and appears to be holding stones there is no reason to doubt the identification. (2) P. 203–246 of the 1764 edition. (3) Notes by Stella Mary Pearce in the Gallery archives. (4) The present writer is very grateful to Harald Olsen, of the Royal Museum of Fine Arts, Copenhagen, for kindly contributing the text of this entry. See also Olsen's article published in the *Kunstmuseets Årsskrift* for 1951 (published 1952). It will be noted that the measurements in the Valenti inventory indicate an upright picture. Nevertheless in Panini's painting the picture clearly appears, as it is, wider than it is high. (5) *Historisch-Kritische Nachrichten von Italien*, II, p. 610. What is probably also no. 81 is mentioned on p. 160 of vol. 2 of Ramdohr's *Ueber Mahlerei und Bildhauerarbeit in Rom.* (6) The copy in the National Gallery library (photostat) of the catalogue has the date January 1801 in MS. Ottley's name is not revealed in this catalogue. (7) Buchanan: Memoirs, II (1824), p. 29. (8) Buchanan, *loc. cit.*; Tomkins' engraving mentioning Carr as owner is dated 1816.

170 THE HOLY FAMILY WITH SS. JOHN THE BAPTIST, ELIZABETH, ZACHARIAS AND (?) FRANCIS

$23\frac{3}{4} \times 18\frac{7}{8}$ (0·603 × 0·478).[1]
Condition very fair.

VERSIONS: 1. Bayntun sale, 8/9th April, 1853 (35).
2. H. Wedewer sale, Cologne, 1899.[2]

PROVENANCE: According to Waagen[3] from the domestic chapel of the Aldobrandini family, Rome. Therefore identifiable with no. 86 in Cardinal Pietro Aldobrandini's inventory of 1603 and with the same item in the inventory before 1665 (*Palatino*, 1964, p. 159). No. 108 in the sale catalogue (7th day) of the Fonthill (Beckford) collection, 1822. This sale did not take place as the whole contents were bought by Mr. Farquhar. No. 189 in the Fonthill sale 11th October, 1823. Redford[4] gives the purchaser on this occasion as Hume. Again in Beckford's possession by 1833, however, since seen then at Bath by Passavant.[5] Purchased from Beckford, 1839, together with nos. 168 (Raphael) and 169 (Mazzolino).

REPRODUCTION: *Illustrations, Italian Schools*, 1937, p. 147.

REFERENCES: (1) The 1929 catalogue's '30¼ × 23½' is an inexplicable aberration. (2) Reproduction in the Gallery archives. (3) *Works of Art and Artists in England*, 1838, vol. III, p. 123. (4) *Art Sales*, vol. II (1888). (5) *Kunstreise . . .*, 1833, p. 151.

642 THE AGONY IN THE GARDEN
Transferred from panel to canvas, 19⅜ × 15¼ (0·49 × 0·38).
Apparently a certain amount of local damage (very likely caused during the transfer). Cleaned 1968.

PROVENANCE: Beaucousin collection, Paris, with which bought, 1860.[1]

REPRODUCTION: *Illustrations, Italian Schools*, 1937, p. 148.

REFERENCES: (1) Giuseppe Boschini (commentary on Baruffaldi's *Vite de' Pittori . . . Ferraresi*, 1844, vol. 1, p. 363) lists a Garofalo with 'Sig. co. Prosperi. Piccola tavoletta colla orazione all' orto che stava una volta ad un lato dell'altare di Lazzaro in S. Francesco'. In the Duke of Lucca sale, London, 5th June, 1841, a 'Christ in the Garden' by Garofalo figured as lot 16 and was described as 'one of the most brilliant small pictures by the master'. It is possible that one of these was identical with no. 642.

671 ALTARPIECE: MADONNA AND CHILD, WITH SS. WILLIAM OF AQUITAINE, CLARE, ANTHONY OF PADUA AND FRANCIS
Panel, originally painted area *c.* 78 × 82 (1·982 × 2·08). Cleaned 1970.
A strip about 16 inches wide, extending across the top of the picture and arched at the top (now covered by the frame) was found, during the cleaning of 1970, to contain Prussian blue, a pigment which was not discovered until the eighteenth century. This addition seems to have been in existence when Eastlake first saw the picture in 1858 and may have been added when the picture was removed from its original setting in 1832. The 1970 restoration also disclosed repainting, since removed, in the architecture in the background and on the marble floor in the foreground. Otherwise excellent condition.[1]
From the high altar of the Franciscan church of S. Guglielmo, Ferrara, where mentioned by, among others, Marc Antonio Guarini (1621),[2] Barotti (1770),[3] Scalabrini (1773)[4] and Cittadella (1782).[5]
Regarding the identification of the four saints, the youthful figure in armour on the left is easily recognizable as S. William since it was to him that the church was dedicated,[6] while the fact that the other three saints are Franciscans is understandable, since it belonged to nuns of that Order.
In his *Memorie* of Garofalo (1872) Cittadella prints documents dating the work 1517–18.[7]

VERSIONS: Formerly Bologna, S. Giuseppe a' Cappuccini.[8] Venturi (*Storia* . . ., IX, 4, p. 318) lists in the Costantini collection, Florence, a Garofalo Madonna and Saints *simile alla pala della Galleria Nazionale di Londra*.

PROVENANCE: S. Guglielmo, Ferrara, on the suppression of which, in 1832, transferred successively to the Cathedral[9] and to the Arcivescovado.[10] By 1856 in the possession of Conte Antonio Mazza[11] from whom purchased, 1860.

REPRODUCTION: *Illustrations, Italian Schools*, 1937, p. 148.

REFERENCES: (1) Giuseppe Boschini (in note to Baruffaldi's *Vite de' Pittori e Scultori Ferraresi*, vol. 1 (1844), p. 362) refers to it as a *conservatissima tavola*. For further information on the treatment of the picture in the nineteenth century see Cecil Gould: Eastlake and Molteni: The Ethics of Restoration, in *Burlington Magazine*, 1974. (2) *Compendio Historico . . . delle Chiese . . . di Ferrara*, pp. 217–18. (3) *Pitture e Scolture . . . di Ferrara*, pp. 107–8. (4) *Memorie Istoriche delle Chiese di Ferrara*, pp. 171–4. (5) *Catalogo Istorico de' Pittori e Scultori Ferraresi*, vol. 2, p. 26. (6) Cittadella (*loc. cit.*) identifies this figure with S. Jerome (Girolamo) but this is plainly a mistake for Guglielmo. The attributes and lives of the different Saints William are somewhat confused, but Scalabrini (*op. cit.*, p. 172) mentions S. William of Aquitaine, the disciple of S. Bernard, in connection with the church at Ferrara and there seems no doubt that the figure represented here is intended for him. (7) p. 59. (8) According to the National Gallery catalogue of 1861 (by Wornum) and successive editions it was by Alessandro Candi of Ferrara. The church of S. Giuseppe a' Cappuccini was severely damaged in the war of 1939–45 and the present writer saw no trace of the picture when he visited the church in 1954. (9) Mentioned there on p. 36 of F. Avventi's *Guida per Ferrara* (1838). (10) Baruffaldi, 1, p. 362. (11) Laderchi: *Pittura Ferrarese* (1856), p. 91.

1362   AN ALLEGORY OF LOVE

50 × 70 (1·27 × 1·77).
Good condition.

The subject had previously defied identification. In the Midleton sale catalogues[1] what is probably the same picture is called 'Mars and Venus with two attendants, and Cupid'. The winged boy on the left, with bow and quiver, obviously is intended as Cupid and his presence underlines the nature of the scene whose erotic character is already unequivocally indicated by the remaining four figures. But the male in the pair on the right can hardly be Mars, having no armour (there is only a bow and a quiver of arrows on the ground, right, as attribute of either in this pair) and apart from the fact that he wears a tunic and his nymph a wreath there is little to distinguish them from the other pair of lovers farther to the right.

The probable meaning of the allegory has recently been convincingly explained by Edgar Wind[2] as the growth of love illustrated by the elements *Amor* (on the left), *Pulchritudo* (the centre couple, contemplating each other's beauty) and *Voluptas* (right hand group).[3]

PROVENANCE: Bought with the Beaucousin collection, Paris, 1860.[4] Perhaps the picture in Lord Midleton's sales, 31st July, 1851 (80) (bought in) and 20th March, 1852 (214) (bought Nieuwenhuys).

REPRODUCTION: *Illustrations, Italian Schools*, 1937, p. 149.

REFERENCES: (1) See below, under *Provenance*. (2) *Pagan Mysteries in the Renaissance*, 1958, p. 126. Also, in greater detail, in a private communication. (3) This legend was inscribed on Pico della Mirandola's medal (Hill no. 998). Professor Wind points out that according to Ficino, Pico and other writers, including Bembo in Venice and Calcagnini at Ferrara, the contemplation of beauty leads to the pleasures of love, but the latter is not pure unless aroused by the former. In no. 1362 the theme is pointed by the presence of the animals: the lover must be shy as a lizard but passionate as a goat. (4) Immediately after purchase no. 1362 was lent to the National Gallery of Scotland and was not even given a number at that time. Its present number had been allotted in 1892 to Richard Brompton's portrait of Thomas, 2nd Lord Lyttleton which was one of the pictures bequeathed to the National Gallery by Marianna Augusta, Lady Hamilton which, as a result of reconsideration of the testamentary provisions, were surrendered in 1900. The present no. 1362 does not figure in editions of the National Gallery catalogue prior to that of 1929 (the inclusion of the Brompton portrait as no. 1362 in the 1925 edition is clearly an oversight: one of the Hamilton pictures—now no. 2077, Reynolds—re-entered the Gallery at a later date) and continued on loan to Edinburgh until 1932.

3118[1] S. CATHERINE OF ALEXANDRIA

Panel, $17\frac{3}{4} \times 15\frac{1}{4}$ (0.45×0.38).
Good condition.

Attributed when in the Costabili collection to Marco d'Oggiono, but already figures as Garofalo in Layard's note-book.[2] Since then the attribution to Garofalo has been fairly general with the exception of Frizzoni's suggestion of Francesco Caroto.[3] While the latter is hardly acceptable the attribution to Garofalo seems plausible.

PROVENANCE: Costabili collection, Ferrara (apparently no. 446 in the 1838 catalogue).[4] Bought by Layard, probably 1866. Exh. South Kensington, 1869 (48). Layard Bequest, 1916.

REPRODUCTION: *Illustrations, Italian Schools*, 1937, p. 150.

REFERENCES: (1) Misprinted as no. 3116 in the 1929 catalogue. (2) No. 62. In the Gallery archives. (3) *Gazette des Beaux-Arts*, 1896, II, p. 463. R. Longhi (*Paragone*, 1958) asserts Correggio and does not deign to say why. (4) Costabili brand in two places on the back. Also Costabili printed label with the number 96.

3928 A PAGAN SACRIFICE

$50\frac{1}{2} \times 73$ (1.28×1.75).[1]
The base of the altar is inscribed with the date: MDXXVI AG.[2]
Good condition.

This picture is an elaborated copy of a wood-cut illustration in the *Hypnerotomachia Poliphili*[3] which had been published at Venice twenty-seven years earlier (1499).[4] In the text of the book there is a description of a visit of the hero, Poliphilo, to the cemetery of those who have died for love's sake in which he sees a sacrifice being performed round an inscribed tombstone. Garofalo has followed the description in general very closely and in some places includes features, such as the shepherd's girdle of leaves and his tunic with the fur inside, which are specified in the text but omitted in the wood-cut. Nevertheless he himself omits the inscription (HAVE/LERIA/OMNIVM/AMANTISS/ VALE) and by transforming the tombstone thereby into an ordinary altar changes the whole meaning of the scene. What, indeed, is the significance of no. 3928 is mysterious. Saxl,[5] who showed that it is not a *Sacrifice to Ceres* (as had been supposed earlier and as it appears in the National Gallery catalogue of 1929) and that it can hardly reproduce a classical model, suggested plausibly that it may be intended merely as a representation of a pagan sacrifice in general.

PROVENANCE: Marqués de Salamanca sale, Paris, 1867 (66) in the catalogue of which stated to be from the collection of the 'Duchesse de Chincon'. Apparently bought at the Salamanca sale by Lord Dudley[6] who lent it to the Leeds exhibition of 1868 (134) and to the R.A. in 1871 (373). Earl of Dudley sale, 25th June, 1892 (64) where bought by Richter for Mond. Exh. R.A., 1895 (161). Mond Bequest, 1924.

REPRODUCTION: *Illustrations, Italian Schools*, 1937, p. 149.

REFERENCES: (1) Approximate measurements of original linen. About half an inch of the relining canvas surrounding it has been painted to conform with the original paint adjoining. (2) Presumably standing for AGOSTO. (3) This fact was first pointed out by Miss A. Cameron Taylor to J. P. Richter and published by him in the catalogue of the Mond Collection—vol. II (1910), pp. 558–67. (4) The book is actually dated (at the end) 1467. (5) F. Saxl: *A Scene from the Hypnerotomachia in a Painting by Garofalo* (*Journal of the Warburg Institute*, vol. I, 1937–8, pp. 169–71). (6) In E. K. Waterhouse's draft catalogue entry (in the Gallery archives) it is stated that the purchaser at the Salamanca sale was 'Cooke for Lord Dudley'.

GAUDENZIO FERRARI
active 1508, died 1546

At the time of his death he was said to be 'annorum circa 75', but was probably rather less. The words 'de Varali' after his name in many of the early documents indicate his home town (Varallo).[1] A cryptic passage in Lomazzo was once interpreted to mean that Gaudenzio was a pupil of Luini, but probably merely means that they were co-pupils of Stefano Scotto.[2] In any case it seems to have been Luini's style—and the particular use which he made of Leonardo's example—which reformed Gaudenzio's art from its beginnings in the manner of Borgognone and Bramantino.

Gaudenzio was very prolific, and was active over a wide area of Lombardy and Piedmont.

REFERENCES: (1) Printed by Giuseppe Colombo: *Vita ed Opere di Gaudenzio Ferrari*, 1881. (2) Lomazzo: *Trattato*, 1584, p. 421. In the index (p. 693) Gaudenzio is mentioned as a pupil of Perugino. This, and the even more startling legend that Gaudenzio was Raphael's pupil, are discussed by A. M. Brizio in *L'Arte*, XXIX, 1926, p. 104.

1465 CHRIST RISING FROM THE TOMB
Poplar,[1] 60 × 33¼ (1·524 × 0·845).
Some retouching apparent. General condition probably fairly reliable.

For Commentary and Provenance see no. 3925.

REPRODUCTION: *Illustrations, Italian Schools*, 1937, p. 133.

REFERENCE: (1) Letter in the Gallery archives from B. J. Rendle of the Forest Products Research Laboratory.

3068 THE ANNUNCIATION

Two panels, each *c.* 23 (0·584) square.[1] That of the Madonna is not painted up to the edges all round. A good deal of repaint in the angel's white robe, face and right hand. His hair, wings and red drapery in better state. The scroll round his cross inscribed:

·Ave· grã· plẽa· dns̃· tecũ.

A certain amount of retouching apparent on the Madonna panel also, but less obtrusive.

Very close in style to a set of four panels at Turin. All six pictures seem rather less developed than Gaudenzio's Arona altar which is dated 1511, and would therefore be among his earliest surviving works. The Turin panels are of the same size as each other but cannot have been arranged in a row. The one of the *Madonna and Child with S. Anne and Angels* would presumably have been flanked by the *Meeting of Joachim and Anne* and the *Expulsion of Joachim*. The fourth panel—the *Almighty* —is the only single figure of the four and would presumably have been in the centre of the upper tier, above the *Madonna*. It is at this point that no. 3068 may be reverted to, since its two panels are not only extremely close in style to the Turin ones. They are also of the same width. It is therefore suggested that they may originally have flanked the *Almighty* on the upper tier.[2] This theory, which does not seem to have been put forward before, seems plausible to the present writer, but he cannot prove it.[3]

PROVENANCE: Bought by Sir A. H. Layard from Baslini of Milan[4] before 1864.[5] Lent by Layard to South Kensington, 1869 (51). Previously the panels had belonged to 'Dottore Acerbi of Milan'.[6] Layard Bequest 1916.

REPRODUCTION: *Illustrations, Italian Schools*, 1937, p. 134.

REFERENCES: (1) Poplar, according to a letter in the Gallery archives from B. J. Rendle of the Forest Products Research Laboratory. (2) If this was so it could be objected that the omission of the dove in the panel representing the Almighty would be odd. Nevertheless, the Borgognone polyptych at S. Spirito, Bergamo (which, being dated 1508, is a contemporary work) also shows the Almighty without the dove in the uppermost tier, flanked by Gabriel and the Madonna Annuntiate. The dove is included, however, in the central pane of the main tier, underneath that of the Almighty. (3) The provenance of the Turin panels is given in the 1899 catalogue simply as 'venduti alla R. Pinacoteca dal sig. Antonio Prina; provenivano dal Novarese'. (4) Layard MSS. in the Gallery archives. (5) Letter from Morelli to Layard, 26th October, 1864 (British Museum, Add. MS. 38963, Layard Papers, vol. XXXIII). (6) G. Colombo: *Gaudenzio Ferrari*, 1881, p. 23.

3925   S. ANDREW (?)

Poplar,[1] $59\frac{1}{4} \times 33\frac{1}{4}$ (1·505 × 0·845).
Some damage. General condition fair.

The saint has hitherto been identified with S. Andrew, and may be.
But that saint's cross is more normally of X shape.

Though the two pictures are not recorded together until the mid-
nineteenth century there can be little or no doubt that nos. 1465 and
3925 were painted as part of the same altarpiece. The virtual identity
of size of panel, scale of figure and style indicate this, as does the presence
of the same—and very odd—type of mountain in the background,
looking like a rough sea seen from close to. The inferior quality of the
execution of no. 3925 indicates a greater degree of studio assistance.[2]
Both pictures seem characteristic of the later phase of Gaudenzio's
style.

Bordiga (1821)[3] says that no. 1465 was the centre panel of an ancona
from Maggianico, near Lecco. The other compartments, according to
him, consisted of SS. Peter, Paul, Ambrose, Bernard and Anthony
Abbot, together with a predella in chiaroscuro of Christ and the 12
apostles. Bordiga says that the latter belonged in his day to the Dottore
Carlo Dell' Acqua at Milan. Colombo (1881)[4] refers back to Bordiga
and says that in his day the church of S. Pietro at Maggianico still had
the panels of SS. Anthony (centre), Bonaventure and Ambrose, together
with the predella in chiaroscuro which had apparently been returned to
the church from the possession of Dottore Dell' Acqua.

It will be noticed that Bordiga appears to say nothing of no. 3925,
although it was in the Scarpa Gallery in the mid-nineteenth century
and perhaps already in his day.[5] Furthermore, only two of Bordiga's
five saints (Anthony and Ambrose) are mentioned by Colombo, though
the latter includes a third—Bonaventure—not specified by Bordiga.
Presumably the one Bordiga calls S. Bernard is the same as Colombo's
S. Bonaventure. What are presumably these three panels are still at
Maggianico—S. Anthony Abbot (centre) flanked by a saint with mitre
and crozier (presumably S. Ambrose) and one with a cardinal's hat
(apparently S. Bonaventure or perhaps S. Jerome).[6] In the foreground
of these three figures there is vegetation comparable with that in no.
3925. But if the execution of the latter picture can be considered no more
than studio that of the Maggianico panels is still farther away from the
master,[7] while the predella, which is not in chiaroscuro, seems to be in a
primitive or neo-primitive style which has nothing to do with Gaudenzio.

VERSION: The central figure in the *Risen Christ* (Turin, no. 54) signed by
Giuseppe Giovenone the Younger, seems based on no. 1465, with some modifications.[8]

PROVENANCE: Both panels, as explained above, said to have come from
Maggianico, near Lecco.[9] No. 1465 was acquired by Professor Antonio Scarpa
of Pavia certainly before 1821 (date of Bordiga's book, already quoted) and
apparently as early as 1811.[10] No. 3925 seems first recorded in 1855.[11] Antonio

Scarpa died in 1832. His heir, Giovanni Scarpa, built a gallery for the pictures at Motta di Livenza (Treviso). In the sale of the Pinacoteca Scarpa di Motta di Livenza which was held at Milan, 14th November, 1895, no. 3925 was lot 28 (where bought for Ludwig Mond) and no. 1465 lot 29 (where bought for the Gallery). No. 3925 was exh. B.F.A.C. 1898 (53) (lent Mond) and entered the Gallery with the Mond Bequest, 1924.

REPRODUCTION: *Illustrations, Italian Schools,* 1937, p. 133.

REFERENCES: (1) Letter in the Gallery archives from B. J. Rendle of the Forest Products Research Laboratory. (2) Ethel Halsey (*Gaudenzio Ferrari*, 1908, pp. 117 and 133) attributes most of the execution of no. 1465 to Giovanni Battista della Cerva, who assisted Gaudenzio at the end of his career, but, perversely, makes no such comment à propos no. 3925. A. M. Brizio (*La Pittura in Piemonte*, 1942, p. 207) also, and unjustifiably, appears to favour the execution of no. 3925 at the expense of that of no. 1465. (3) Gaudenzio Bordiga: *Gaudenzio Ferrari*, 1821, p. 44. (4) Giuseppe Colombo: *Vita ed Opere di Gaudenzio Ferrari*, 1881, p. 221. (5) While it seems unlikely that any pictures were added to the collection after Antonio Scarpa's death in 1832 there were eleven years intervening between that and publication of Bordiga's book in 1821. Alternatively Bordiga could have overlooked the picture or perhaps even have confused the identity of the saint. (6) Colombo (*loc. cit.*) refers to the church as S. Pietro, but contemporary guide books (e.g. T.C.I.) refer to it as S. Andrea. E. Halsey (*op. cit.*, p. 137) says that the church for which Gaudenzio executed the altarpiece was destroyed at the beginning of the nineteenth century. Photographs of the pictures which are still *in situ* were kindly sent to the Gallery by Signora Mazzucato. (7) Bordiga (*loc. cit.*) had said that in the panels of saints which originally flanked the Christ 'le sole teste manifestavano la maniera di Gaudenzio'. The figure of S. Ambrose at Maggianico is comparable to some extent with that on the spectator's left in Gaudenzio's polyptych in the church of S. Gaudenzio at Varallo, but is much cruder, in design and (apparently) execution alike. (8) Repr. Venturi: *Storia . . .*, IX, VII, 543. The cartoon for the picture is said to be that in the Accademia Albertina, Turin (326). This may be the origin of the cryptic statement in the 1920–29 editions of the Gallery catalogue: 'the cartoon is in the Accademia, Milan'. (9) Anna Maria Brizio (*op. cit.*, p. 207) seems to cast doubt on the provenance of no. 1465, but not of no. 3925, from Maggianico. No reason is given for this which directly conflicts with Bordiga. (10) Lepido Rocca: *Motta di Livenza e Suoi Contorni*, 1897, p. 455. (11) Mündler's diary, in the Gallery archives, under 8th November, 1855.

Ridolfo GHIRLANDAIO
1483–1561

Florentine School. Member of a family of artists of whom his father, Domenico, was the most famous. Vasari says he died in 1560 at the age of seventy-five, but Milanesi (edition of Vasari, vol. VI, p. 547) reproduces documents which disprove this. According to Vasari he was a pupil of his uncle, David, and of Fra Bartolommeo, a friend of Raphael and a student of Michelangelo's cartoon. He was also clearly influenced by Leonardo.

He always lived in Florence, ran an active studio and accepted commissions for diverse works of art such as festive decorations and pennons as well as numerous religious paintings and portraits.

1143 THE PROCESSION TO CALVARY

Panel transferred to canvas, $65\frac{1}{2} \times 63\frac{1}{2}$ (1.66×1.62).

Considerable and widespread local damage and repaint, particularly in the background, but certain areas, such as the body of the horseman in armour, are largely free of repaint and apparently well preserved.

Identifiable with the picture described by Vasari as follows[1]:

> *Nella chiesa di San Gallo fece in su una tavola Cristo che porta la croce, con buon numero di soldati; e la Madonna ed altre Marie che piangono insieme con Giovanni, mentre Veronica porge il sudario a esso Cristo, con prontezza e vivacità: la quale opera, in cui sono molte teste bellissime ritratte dal vivo, e fatte con amore, acquistò gran nome a Ridolfo. Vi è ritratto suo padre, ed alcuni garzoni che stavano seco; e, de' suoi amici, il Poggino, lo Scheggia, ed il Nunziata, che è una testa vivissima.*

The portraits mentioned by Vasari have not been identified with certainty, though at least three heads in no. 1143—second from the left (with wood over his right shoulder), immediately to the left of Christ's head (and on a level with it) and on the extreme right—are clearly portraits of specific people.

Vasari implies that the San Gallo picture was one of Ridolfo's earliest important commissions. The fact that the head of the helmeted soldier in no. 1143 (behind Christ, appearing between two arms of the cross) seems to derive from one in Leonardo's cartoon of the *Battle of Anghiari* would indicate the end of 1504 as a *terminus post quem* for dating no. 1143 as it is most unlikely that Leonardo's cartoon was finished before then.[2]

VERSIONS: Louvre, Paris and S. Spirito, Florence, attributed to Benedetto and Michele Ghirlandaio respectively. The former picture is stated also to have come from S. Spirito, as is no. 1143. The three pictures differ considerably and none is in any sense a copy of another, though less direct connections are plausible.

ENGRAVING: Plate CXXV of Giovanni Rosini's *Storia della Pittura Italiana* (1845).

PROVENANCE: Purchased, 1883, through Charles Fairfax Murray, from the heirs of the Antinori family, Florence.[3] The church of San Gallo, for which in all probability it was painted, was destroyed for strategic reasons during the siege of Florence in 1529. According to the account given by the Antinori family at the time of purchase the picture was then removed to S. Spirito and finally to the Palazzo Antinori da San Gaetano, Florence, where it remained until 1883.

REPRODUCTION: *Illustrations, Italian Schools*, 1937, p. 154.

REFERENCES: (1) Milanesi edition, vol. VI, p. 535. (2) Leonardo's own drawing for the head of the soldier in question exists and is at Budapest (reproduced by Popham: *The Drawings of Leonardo da Vinci*, 1946, pl. 198). For the dating of Leonardo's cartoon the best reference book is Beltrami: *Documenti e Memorie riguardanti la Vita e le Opere di Leonardo da Vinci* (1919). (3) Seen in Florence in 1856 and 1864 by Sir Charles Eastlake (note-book in the Gallery archives).

2491 PORTRAIT OF A MAN

Panel, $27\frac{3}{4} \times 22\frac{1}{8}$ (0·704 × 0·56).

Very well preserved in general. A little rubbed in the sky. *Pentimenti* round the outer edge of the skull cap.

Alternative candidates have been suggested as the sitter:

(1) A version of this picture without the landscape, formerly in the collection of the Earl of Darnley, was inscribed HIERONIMUS BENIVENIUS. This legend was stated to be of later date than the picture and was erased after its sale in 1925.[1] The design was engraved in 1762 by Francesco Allegrini, inscribed, not on the picture but beneath it: *Girolamo Benivieni, Fioren.ᶰᵒ Filosofo, e Poeta Illustre.* . . . The owner at that time was the Marchese Alamanno Bartolini Salimbeni, to whom the engraving was dedicated. As no. 2491 also is stated once to have belonged to the Salimbeni family, it would be possible that the engraving was from it, and not from the other version, despite the omission of the landscape in the engraving. A certain Florent de Gravier offered to the National Gallery on several occasions between 1847 and 1850 a picture (stated to bear the signature of Raphael and the date 1504) which he claimed was the one which had been engraved by Allegrini and for which he produced an unbroken pedigree from the Benivieni family. There seems no reason to exclude the possibility that this later became the Darnley picture, since the owner was apparently anxious to find a purchaser in England, and the Darnley picture, not being mentioned by Waagen, would probably have been bought by Lord Darnley later than 1850.[2]

(2) At the time when no. 2491 was purchased by Salting it was stated by the Torrigiani family that the sitter was Bernardo del Nero and that the small bridge in the background represented one on the del Nero estates. More than one Bernardo del Nero is recorded at about the time in question.[3]

The general arrangement, with a parapet and a panoramic landscape behind the sitter, probably owes something to Leonardo's *Mona Lisa* of about 1503–06. The handling is close enough to that of certain heads in no. 1143 of this Gallery and in Ridolfo's *Miracles of S. Zenobius* (Florence, Uffizi) to justify the attribution to him.

ENGRAVING: See above.

PROVENANCE: Stated to have passed by inheritance to the Florentine families of Salimbeni and Torrigiani. The arms of the latter are on the back, and from them the picture was bought, *c.* 1901, by Salting. Exh. R.A., 1902 (33). Salting bequest, 1910.

REPRODUCTION: *Illustrations, Italian Schools*, 1937, p. 153.

REFERENCES: (1) Letter in the Gallery archives. The Darnley sale was in May, 1925. The same picture came up at Christie's again (as Lorenzo di Credi) in an anonymous sale, 26th January, 1951 (100) and again, Christie's, 4th June, 1965 (102). (2) A bust inscribed as representing Girolamo Benevieni was bought in 1866 by the Louvre and soon afterwards some Italians claimed that it was a forgery, recently manufactured in Florence. The affair, which bears a striking resemblance to *die Angelegenheit Flora* of 1909–10, is documented in *Zeitschrift für bildende Kunst*, 1868, pp. 121–3. The features of the bust bear some relation to those on no. 2491, and the source of the inscription on it may have been the inscribed Darnley picture, or the engraving. **(3)** See *Istorie di Giovanni Cambi ... pubblicate ... da Fra Ildefonso di San Luigi ...*, vol. 3 (1786), p. 337 (vol. XXII of *Delizie degli Eruditi Toscani* of which the general index contains references to others of the name of Bernardo del Nero). A portrait of a Bernardo del Nero is stated (in a note in the Gallery archives) formerly to have been in the collection of Lady Henry Somerset.

Giorgio da Castelfranco, called GIORGIONE
active 1506, died 1510

The form 'Giorgione', instead of the Venetian 'Zorzi', or 'Zorzo', for 'Giorgio', seems first to be used in print by Paolo Pini (1548). It was adopted by Vasari and has been universal since.

He is referred to as 'maistro Zorzi da Castelfranco' in an inscription of 1st June, 1506 on the back of a portrait of a lady at Vienna.[1] Also, under the same name, in two documents, of August, 1507 and January, 1508, in connection with a painting for the audience chamber of the Doge's Palace at Venice, and finally (still by the same style) in two more documents, of 1508, connected with paintings on the exterior of the Fondaco dei Tedeschi, Venice. No other document certainly dating from his life time and mentioning him has survived,[2] but an exchange of letters in October and November, 1510, between Isabella d'Este (who was anxious to secure a painting by Giorgione) and Taddeo Albano, shows that he was then recently dead (of the plague). There is no reliable evidence for the date of his birth,[3] and the theory that he belonged to the noble family of Barbarella is probably no more than wishful thinking of the seventeenth century.[4] Nevertheless, it cannot be doubted that he was still a young man at the time of his death.[5] It can also be deduced with confidence that he enjoyed a considerable reputation as a painter during his life time[6] and that less than a generation after his death he was already considered one of the greatest Venetian artists.[7]

The extreme scarcity of facts concerning Giorgione's life and work, combined with the rapid growth of his legend, the degree to which he was imitated and the high market value of pictures attributable to him, has created the utmost confusion in identifying them. In fact no surviving painting can be ascribed to him with complete certainty.[8] However it cannot reasonably be doubted that the following four pictures (whose attribution has in each case a certain degree of documentary or other external support) are his work: *Portrait of a Lady* (Vienna),[9] *The Three Philosophers* (Vienna), *The Tempest* (Venice),[10] the *Castelfranco altar*.[11] Round this nucleus can be grouped a few others—pre-eminently the *Judith* (Leningrad), and the *Portrait of a Young Man* (Berlin)—which, though lacking documentary support, are yet generally accepted as Giorgione's at the present time. The major problem still in dispute centres round five pictures of high quality and more evolved style than those so far mentioned—*Venus* (Dresden),[12] *Madonna and Child with Saints* (Prado), *Judgement of Solomon* (Bankes collection, Kingston Lacy),[13] *Christ and the Adulteress* (Glasgow), *Fête Champêtre* (Louvre) These, in one view, constitute 'late Giorgione' which would then blend imperceptibly into early Titian, to whom, with the exception of the Kingston Lacy picture (for which Sebastiano is the favourite alternative candidate), the other view attributes them. Even without considering this group, however, and judging only from the other paintings already specified, it is clear that Giorgione, emerging from the orbit of Giovanni Bellini, introduced a new note, at once lyrical and fantastic, into Venetian painting which for a time had wide influence.

REFERENCES: (1) First correctly published, and discussed, by J. Wilde in the Prussian *Jahrbuch*, 1931, p. 91: *Ein unbeachtetes Werk Giorgiones.* (2) A contract of 13th February, 1508, between Giorgione and Alvise de Sesti in respect of four pictures illustrating the story of Daniel was published in 1878 and reprinted by G. M. Richter (*Giorgio da Castelfranco*, 1937, p. 303). This document has now disappeared and doubts have been cast on its authenticity. Recently (*Arte Veneta*, 1954) Philip Hendy (quoting Tietze-Conrat) attempted to bring the Glasgow so-called *Adulteress* into connection with this document. The fragmentary inscription on the back of the San Diego portrait (see reference no. 9) may be a further contemporary reference to Giorgione, but its incompleteness precludes any certainty. (3) It is Vasari who first gives a date for Giorgione's birth—1477 in his first edition (1550), 1478 in his second (1568). In addition to this discrepancy he gives the date of his death as 1511 which is demonstrably a year too late. For these reasons it would clearly be unwise to accept his literal word without confirmation, though the general sense of his information on this subject is no doubt reliable. In view of the number of people who would have remembered Giorgione and who were still alive when Vasari wrote, the latter's statement may be accepted as constituting good evidence at least that the former died young. (4) This legend was published by Ridolfi (*Maraviglie*, 1648). (5) See reference 3. (6) The contracts both for the Doge's Palace and for the Fondaco dei Tedeschi were of some importance and would only have been given to a painter whose work was well thought of. Moreover, Isabella d'Este's letter, already referred to, shows that by the time of his death Giorgione's fame had spread to Mantua and that Isabella thought him worthy of her attention. It is also significant in this connection that not even her influence could persuade the owner of the picture by Giorgione which she had asked for to part with it. (7) Baldassare Castiglione (*Il Cortegiano*, 1524) mentions Giorgione with Leonardo, Mantegna, Raphael and Michelangelo as most excellent painters. Furthermore the *Anonimo Morelliano* (see reference 10) pays particular attention to Giorgione's pictures. (8) i.e. in the sense of a painting (such as Titian's Frari *Assunta*, for example) whose history can be traced back with certainty to an unquestionably authentic document. In Giorgione's case the fragment of a fresco from the Fondaco dei Tedeschi would in fact answer to this definition. But its condition is so ruinous that it can no longer qualify as a work of art. (9) The attribution of this work depends on an inscription on the back published by J. Wilde (*loc. cit.*). This states that the picture is by Giorgione and gives a precise date and precise details. As it cannot be *proved* that the inscription is authentic and contemporary the attribution of the picture to Giorgione must stop just this side of complete certainty. Nevertheless Wilde demonstrated the overwhelming probability that the inscription is genuine and in consequence the picture must be considered the best authenticated of any still surviving. The portrait of a man (San Diego, California) known as the 'Terris Portrait' may be in a similar category to the Vienna portrait, since it is attributed to

Giorgione on the strength of an inscription on the back. But this inscription—to judge from the photograph published by Richter (*op. cit.*, p. 227)—is so damaged and so fragmentary as to afford less evidence for its being contemporary than is the case with the Vienna portrait. **(10)** The attribution of these two pictures to Giorgione depends on identifying them with two described in a MS. in the Marciana, Venice. The author is referred to as the 'Anonimo Morelliano' and is generally identified with Marcantonio Michiel, a Venetian aristocrat. He gives short descriptions of pictures he had seen. His entries in respect of paintings by Giorgione range in date from 1525 to 1532. Only one of them—the *Christ* of S. Rocco—is still in the place where he described it, but in this case his wording is ambiguous and not certainly to be interpreted as meaning he thought the picture by Giorgione. The subsequent fate of all the other pictures he mentions as by Giorgione cannot be traced with certainty beyond the seventeenth century, and as most of his descriptions are very short it is usually hazardous to identify existing pictures with them. But the subjects of the *Three Philosophers* and of the *Tempest* are so very unusual that in spite of gaps in their pedigrees (and, in the case of the *Tempest*, also of a certain oddity in the *Anonimo's* wording) it is universally assumed that they are the ones he means. Even then, naturally, the date of the *Anonimo's* notes does not render his statements first-rate documentation. Recently (*Arte Veneta*, 1954, p. 165) W. Suida has published a portrait of an armed man (Vienna) which corresponds with a description by the *Anonimo* of a picture sufficiently unusual in subject to render identification very tempting. **(11)** From a documentary point of view the attribution of this work to Giorgione is the least supported of the four, since it goes back no farther than the mid-seventeenth century (Ridolfi). Apart from Ridolfi's testimony (of little value in itself) the attribution rests on two main factors. First, the altarpiece has always been in the town from which it is known that Giorgione came. Secondly, it is both a major masterpiece and utterly different in style from that of the very few other artists of the requisite stature to have painted it. **(12)** Often (but not universally) identified with the *Anonimo's* '*Venere nuda, che dorme in uno paese cun Cupidine, fo de mano de Zorzo da Castelfranco, ma lo paese et Cupidine forono finiti da Titiano.*' The identification in this case is clearly more hypothetical and more hazardous than with the *Three Philosophers* or the *Tempest* owing to the greater common-ness of the subject. **(13)** This, as a large picture of a judicial scene, would have been suitable as the subject of Giorgione's Doge's Palace contract of 1507. If he had delivered such a picture it would doubtless have been burnt in the fire of 1574. The Kingston Lacy picture is unfinished and therefore could not have been delivered. Assuming for this reason that the Kingston Lacy picture was intended for the Doge's Palace and that it is by Giorgione, Philip Hendy (*Arte Veneta*, 1954, pp. 170–1) also points out that Vasari, in his life of Titian, says that Giorgione changed his manner of painting around the year 1507. These points must all be borne in mind, but are inconclusive in themselves that the picture is by Giorgione.

1160 ADORATION OF THE MAGI

Panel, painted area (irregular) *c.* 11¾ × *c.* 32 (0·29 × 0·81).

There have been innumerable small losses of paint, caused by flaking, over most of the area, but no substantial portion is entirely lacking in original paint. Much of the original surface quality seems still present in small areas, particularly in the well-preserved doublet and belt of the youth on the right, leaning on a staff. Cleaned, 1947.

Perhaps originally part of the predella of an altarpiece.[1] Purchased as by Giovanni Bellini. Catalogued, from the edition of 1889 on, as Giorgione, with the exception of the editions of 1925 and 1929, when it appeared as Bonifazio.[2] Other attributions have been Catena,[3] Cariani[4] and Palma.[5] The most recent cleaning (1947) has shown the virtual impossibility of any of the four last-named masters. Meanwhile there has been increasing agreement in favour of a return to the former attribution to Giorgione himself.[6] This seems to the present writer to be justified.

The costumes shown would accord most easily with a date around 1506 or 1507.[7] This is a factor in the attribution, since Catena is the only serious alternative, and even his advocates in this matter (e.g. L. Venturi: *Giorgione e il Giorgionismo*, 1913, p. 229) point out that if it were his it must be late—after 1520.

PROVENANCE: No. 23 (as Giovanni Bellini) in the printed catalogue (1822) of pictures at Leigh Court, near Bristol, in the collection of Philip John Miles. In the introduction to this catalogue it is stated that most of the Miles pictures had originally been collected by Richard Hart Davis and purchased from him privately.[8] In the Miles collection (where noted, as Giovanni Bellini, by Waagen in 1835 and 1850)[9] until 1884. Exh. R.A., 1870 (63) (as Giovanni Bellini, lent by Sir William Miles). Sir Philip Miles sale, Christie's, 28th June, 1884 (5) (as Giovanni Bellini) where purchased by Waters for the National Gallery (Clarke Bequest).

REPRODUCTION: *Illustrations, Italian Schools*, 1937, p. 45.

REFERENCES: (1) Suggested by G. M. Richter: *Giorgio da Castelfranco*, 1937, pp. 223–4. (2) First suggested by Sir Charles Holmes: *Burlington Magazine*, vol. 42 (1923), pp. 237–8. (3) By Morelli (*Munich and Dresden*, 1893, p. 205), followed by Berenson (*Lists*, 1897), and, with a query, in editions of 1932 and 1936, and by Lionello Venturi (*Giorgione e il Giorgionismo*, 1913, pp. 299–30). (4) Tancred Borenius in his edition of Crowe and Cavalcaselle: *History of Painting in North Italy*, vol. III, p. 11, note. (5) By Gamba: *Giovanni Bellini*, p. 35. More recently also by Fiocco (*Giorgione*, 1941, p. 45, no. 97). (6) The attribution to Giorgione was made by Crowe and Cavalcaselle, *op. cit.*, vol. III, pp. 10–11, and was supported by H. Cook (*Giorgione*, 1907, p. 53) and by L. Justi (*Giorgione*, 1926, vol. I, *Anhang* no. 25), also by Roberto Longhi (in *Vita Artistica*, 1927, pp. 218–19 and in *Viatico per Cinque Secoli di Pittura Veneziana*, 1946, p. 19), by Antonio Morassi (*Giorgione*, 1942, pp. 70 and 164) and by Berenson in the latest edition (1957) of his Venetian lists. The so-called 'Allendale Group' consists of the ex-Allendale *Nativity*, the ex-Benson *Holy Family* (both Washington) and no. 1160. According to Cook (*op. cit.*, p. 21) these three pictures were first assigned to an independent 'Beaumont Master' in a letter to the *Daily Telegraph* of 29th December, 1899. Cook (*op. cit.*, p. 22) admits that the three pictures were even then 'universally admitted to be by the same hand'. A dissenter from this generally held view was Berenson in *Venetian Painting in America*, 1916, p. 256, where he called no. 1160 and the ex-Benson picture Catena and the ex-Allendale *Nativity* the work of 'another artist'. All three as Giorgione in his 1957 *Lists*. (7) Notes in the Gallery archives by Stella Mary Pearce. As early as 1927 Longhi (*Vita Artistica*, pp. 218–19) had associated no. 1160 with the Vienna portrait and had suggested a date around 1505. This was before the publication of the date (1506) on the back of the Vienna portrait. (8) Redford (*Art Sales*, vol. II, 1888, p. 232) lists a Giorgione 'Offering of Magi' as bought by Woodford for £38 17s. from 'N.N' in 1803. At the Hon. C. F. Greville's sale (31st March, 1810) lot 86 was catalogued as 'Giorgione: The Adoration of the Magi, in a finely illumined landscape' and sold for £89 5s. There is no reason why these should be identical with each other, or either with no. 1160, though a possibility would remain. (9) *Works of Art and Artists in England*, vol. III (1838), p. 144, and *Treasures of Art in Great Britain*, vol. III (1854), p. 185.

6307   SUNSET LANDSCAPE WITH S. ROCH (?), S. GEORGE
AND S. ANTHONY ABBOT (IL TRAMONTO)

$28\frac{7}{8} \times 36$ (0·733 × 0·915).

Much of the bank on the right, including most of S. George's horse, and of the water underneath, are restoration, in places conjectural. Also most of the interior of the foliage of the tree on the left. Most of the rest of the picture, including the two figures in the foreground, in good condition.[1]

If, as is likely, the foreground figures are S. Roch and Gothardus (who tended the ulcer on S. Roch's thigh) the picture may have been painted to commemorate relief from the plague (against which S. Roch was normally invoked). The outbreak of 1504 in the Veneto would accord with the style of the picture.

The attribution to Giorgione is fairly general and is acceptable.

PROVENANCE: Discovered in 1933 by Giulio Lorenzetti in the Villa Garzone at Ponte Casale. This belonged at that time to the family of Donà Dalle Rose and had formerly belonged to the Michiel family, one member of which in the sixteenth century, Marcantonio, is identified with the so-called Anonimo Morelliano, whose notes are a prime early source for Giorgione.[2] Bought privately, 1933, before the Donà Dalle Rose sale, by Vitale Bloch, from whom purchased, through Messrs Colnaghi, 1961. Exh., Venice (*Giorgione e i Giorgioneschi*, 1955, 30, described as 'Londra, Collezione privata').

REPRODUCTION: 16th–century Italian Schools, plates, 1964, p. 91.

REFERENCES: (1) The picture was in a neglected condition when it was discovered in 1933. A summary restoration was immediately carried out by Vermeeren of Florence. Photographs of the picture in its unrestored state and after treatment by Vermeeren were published in the *Illustrated London News*, 4th November, 1933. A more thorough restoration, by the Roman restorer Dumler, carried out in 1934, revealed the group of S. George and the Dragon. Photographs taken after the second restoration were published by R. Longhi (*Viatico per Cinque Secoli di Pittura veneziana*, 1946) and in the catalogue of the Giorgione exhibition at Venice in 1955. A third restoration, by Arthur Lucas, after the picture was acquired by the Gallery, revealed the blue saddle cloth of S. George's horse. A diagram showing the reconstructed areas of the painting was reproduced in the National Gallery Report, January 1960–May 1962, facing p. 80. A critical essay, masquerading as a catalogue entry, written by the present writer, was printed in the catalogue of National Gallery Acquisitions, 1953–62, pp. 32 ff. The picture had previously been offered to the Trustees of the National Gallery in 1956–7. (2) G. Sangiorgi, who first published the picture (*Giornale d'Italia*, Rome, 26th October and 1st November, 1933 and in *Rassegna Italiana*, November, 1933) tried to identify it with a Giorgione of Hell, with Aeneas and Anchises noted by Michiel in possession of Taddeo Contarini in 1525. See also the Introduction, by Giulio Lorenzetti, to the sale catalogue of the Donà Dalle Rose sale, Venice, 1934.

Imitators of GIORGIONE

Taddeo Albano's letter of November, 1510 to Isabella d'Este included the information that the picture by Giorgione which she had wished to acquire was not to be had at any price. Fourteen years later Castiglione listed Giorgione among the most eminent Italian painters and the only representative of Venice, and during the rest of the sixteenth century and throughout the seventeenth there was no diminution of Giorgione's fame. In view of this situation and of the limited quantity of genuine works by Giorgione resulting from the shortness of his career, it is clear that the demand for them not only exceeded the supply at the time of his death but also that it would not have been likely to diminish with the passage of years. There would thus have been every inducement for painters to imitate his work, and the essential fantasy of much of it would have rendered the task incomparably simpler than in the case of the other short-lived giant of the sixteenth century, namely Raphael.

The imitations of Giorgione may be divided into three groups. For some years after his death his followers who were his contemporaries continued to work in a Giorgionesque vein. Some time later there were various revivals and partial revivals in which painters, probably with no fraudulent intent, attempted to reconcile forms *alla Giorgionesca* with some version of the then current idiom. A considerable body of evidence exists in respect of this activity. Niccolò Frangipane, active in the second half of the sixteenth century, put his name to at least one picture which was little more than a pastiche of Giorgione,[1] and Caravaggio himself was accused in his lifetime of reverting to Giorgionesque features. The case of Pietro della Vecchia (1605–78) whose fame rested on the skilfulness of his Giorgionesque imitations links this category with the third—that of the deliberate forgers. Whether or not Pietro's own motives were entirely dishonest there is no doubt that his pictures were mistaken for Giorgione's on occasion, as we know from Boschini[2] and Sandrart.[3] It is likely that deliberate forging of Giorgione had started long before Pietro's time—probably soon after the extinction of the living tradition before the middle of the sixteenth century—but documentation of this activity is lacking, for obvious reasons. Though the three pictures catalogued in the following section seem to the present writer to belong to this last category and to date variously from the mid-sixteenth century to some time in the seventeenth such a view of them cannot be regarded as more than hypothetical.

REFERENCES: (1) See editorial, *Burlington Magazine*, October, 1945. (2) *Le Ricche Minere della Pittura Veneziana* (1674), pp. 14–15 of *Breve Instruzione*. (3) *Teutsche Academie* . . ., ed. Peltzer (1925), p. 373.

269 A MAN IN ARMOUR

Panel, painted area $15\frac{5}{8} \times 10\frac{5}{8}$ ($0 \cdot 39 \times 0 \cdot 26$).

X-rays reveal losses extending over most of the sitter's left arm and also his features. But the most conspicuous parts of the armour seem to be well preserved.

A variant of the figure on the left in Giorgione's *Madonna and Saints* in the Duomo at Castelfranco.

In the 1929 catalogue as 'Giorgione'. Despite the claim made by

Crowe and Cavalcaselle[1] (put forward again, more recently, by Antonio Morassi)[2] that no. 269 is an original study by Giorgione for the Castelfranco altar its technique seems to the present writer to be appreciably later, very possibly of the seventeenth century. It differs from the corresponding figure at Castelfranco in not wearing a helmet and in details of the armour—e.g. the breast-plate is unornamented and in one piece and the rosette at the shoulder comprises seven sections instead of six. Of these features, the bare head and plain breast-plate recur in a fresco of a single saint by Pellegrino da S. Daniele at the church of S. Antonio at S. Daniele (Friuli)[3] and to that extent no. 269 is closer to it than to the figure in the Castelfranco altar which was doubtless the origin of both. Though the present writer is inclined to regard no. 269 as an imitation of Giorgione, the alternative possibility, that it is a copy of a lost picture by Giorgione (cf. Berenson: *Lists*, 1957) should be recorded.

The large copy, apparently of no. 269, made by Philippe de Champaigne for Cardinal Richelieu was engraved as representing Gaston de Foix, and this title has at times been applied to no. 269 also, but without justification.

VERSIONS: A large version corresponding with no. 269 rather than with the figure on the Castelfranco altar was painted by Philippe de Champaigne for Cardinal Richelieu's *Galerie des Hommes Illustres* in the Palais Cardinal (Palais Royal) and is now at Versailles. A 'Gaston de Foix by Giorgione' from the Orléans Gallery was included in the sale of Orléans pictures at Bryan's, 26th December ff, 1798 (lot 76—marked in the National Gallery copy of the catalogue as reserved for the Earl of Carlisle) and was lent later to the B.I. in 1818 (38) and 1844 (33). This was another composition, showing the figure only at half length and with a page—engraved by Besson (in *Galerie du Palais Royal*, 1808, vol. II) and described (in *Description des Tableaux du Palais Royal*, 1737, p. 167) as '*haut de sept pouces, large de six pouces*'. This picture was lent by George Howard to the Giorgione exhibition, Venice, 1955 (53). A late copy of no. 269 is in the Czartoryski Museum, Cracow. Another was lot 165, anonymous sale, Christie's, 2nd April, 1954. A picture described as 'Knight in Armour, believed to be a study for the figure of San Liberale in Altarpiece at Castel Franco' was lent by Sir H. M. Vavasour to the Fine Art and Industrial Exhibition, York, 1879 (517).

ENGRAVINGS: By M. Lasne (as Raphael: background and halo added). A further engraving, unsigned and undated, has a border consisting of small scenes from the life of Gaston de Foix with sub-titles in French.

PROVENANCE: In the possession of Benjamin West by the year 1816, when he exhibited it at the B.I. (56). An inscription in French still existing on the back[4] makes it probable that before that it was in the Prince de Conti sale (1777, no. 89—'*Le Giorgion. Le Portrait de Gaston de Foix. Bois. 14 pouces sur 10. On en connaît l'estampe par Lasne. 500 liv.*')[5] and, before that again, in the Pierre Vigné de Vigny sale, 1st April, 1773 (no. 1—'*Georges Barbarelli dit le Giorgion.—Un homme en cuirasse qui se trouve dans le tableau qui est à Castel Franco, dans le Trevisan, représentant une Sainte Vierge assise sur des nuées entre St François et la figure peinte dans ce tableau; on prétend que c'est Gaston de Foix . . . 15 pouces de haut; sur 10 pouces de large; on en trouve l'estampe gravée par l'Asne avec la marque de Raphael d'Urbin . . . 499 liv. 19*').[6] Earlier still perhaps in the collection of the first Duc de St Simon ('*le portrait de Gaston de Foix, attribué longtemps à Raphael, et probablement du Giorgione*').[7] Benjamin

West sale, 2nd day (24th June, 1820), lot 62, bought Samuel Rogers,[8] by whom bequeathed, 1855.

REPRODUCTION: *Illustrations, Italian Schools*, 1937, p. 156.

REFERENCES: (1) *History of Painting in North Italy*, vol. III (1912), p. 13. (2) *Giorgione* (1942), p. 79. (3) Reproduced in Venturi: *Storia*, IX, 3, fig. 401 (p. 611). (4) *'figure tiré d'un tableau de Giorgione, d'une Ste. Vierge assise sur des . . . St François et la presente figure qu'on pretend être Gaston de foix. Le Tableau est a Castel franco dans le Trevisan. Cette note est de Monsieur Mariette'*. (5) Catalogue in *Le Trésor de la Curiosité*, vol. 1, p. 375. (6) *Réunion des Sociétés des Beaux-Arts des Départements*, 1894, p. 634. (7) Bonnaffé: *Dictionnaire des Amateurs français au XVII siècle*, 1844, p. 282. If this French provenance during the eighteenth century is justified for no. 269 it can hardly be identical with lot 70 in an anonymous sale, 125, Pall Mall, London, 10th December ff., 1789 ('Giorgione . . . full length portrait of Gaston de Foix') since it is there said to have come from the collection 'of the late Sig. Guarienti at Venice'. (8) Priced copy of sale catalogue in the National Gallery library.

1173   HOMAGE TO A POET

Panel, $23\frac{1}{2} \times 19\frac{1}{4}$ (0·59 × 0·48).

The main area of damage is vertical, slightly to the spectator's left of the centre, where splits in the wood have brought about extensive stopping and repainting. Repaint also in the clouds and in different parts of the figures.

Hitherto catalogued as 'Studio of Giorgione'.

The subject is obscure.[1] 'The Golden Age', proposed by H. Cook[2] and incorporated in the National Gallery catalogues from 1913 to 1929, is a vague title. The wreath worn by the enthroned figure presumably indicates a poet.

A certain naïvety in the execution, particularly of the figures,[3] must preclude an attribution to Giorgione himself.[4] Clearly the work of a painter trying to emulate Giorgione, but not necessarily a member of his studio, while if the analysis of the costumes is taken into consideration—which accord best with a dating as late as about 1540[5]—the picture would emerge as a very early imitation or forgery, which is what the present writer inclines to consider it. Such an explanation might also account for the obscurity or confusion of the subject matter.

PROVENANCE: Probably identifiable with a picture listed in inventories of the Aldobrandini collection in the seventeenth century. In the 1603 inventory of Cardinal Pietro Aldobrandini's collection the latter appears as:

> *Un quadro con un poeta coronato di lauro con tre altre figure attorno con una tigre, et un pavone, di mano di Raffaelle da Urbino.*

Similar wording, but with the additional information that the picture was on panel and the height $2\frac{1}{2}$ *palmi* was given in another (undated) inventory (before 1665).[6] Probably no. 15 ('Giorgione—King David instructing a pious man in his devotions'—'from the Aldobrandini Villa') in the catalogue printed by Buchanan[7] of pictures exhibited for sale by Alexander Day in 1800–1. No. 9— '*Solomon instructing Youth* by Giorgione'—in the exhibition of pictures belonging to Alexander Day, Egyptian Hall, London, before 1833, where stated to be from the 'Aldobrandini Cabinet at Rome'.[8] No. 21 (under the same description) in the Day sale, Christie's, 21st June, 1833, where bought White.[9] No. 301 (as Raphael) in Edward White sale, Christie's, 6th April, 1872, where bought H. B(ohn).[10] No. 113, H. Bohn sale, Christie's, 19th March, 1885, where bought Lesser for the Gallery.

REPRODUCTION: *Illustrations, Italian Schools*, 1937, p. 156.

REFERENCES: (1) Andrew Pigler (*Burlington Magazine*, vol. 92, 1950, p. 135) suggested a derivation from a fifteenth-century Florentine engraving representing the 'children' of Jupiter. The arrangement is indeed similar, but this does not seem a satisfactory explanation of no. 1173, since it leaves out of account the crucial factor of the enthroned figure's wearing the poetic wreath. This latter element would in fact have been taken into account in an alternative suggestion by R. Eisler (cf. G. M. Richter: *Giorgio da Castelfranco*, 1937, p. 224) that no. 1173 represents 'the boy Plutus calling on the poet laureate with his brother, Philomelus (with the lute), and his father, Jasion (with the bowl)'. Unfortunately, Eisler's work seems never to have been published, and the bare statement quoted by Richter is insufficient to assess its validity. (2) *Giorgione*, 1907, pp. 92–3. (3) Cf., in particular, the disproportion of scale between the seated figure and the others. Furthermore, the perspective of the steps is wrong, and the child and the kneeling man are shown at right angles, not to them (as would be logical), but to the spectator, thereby revealing their profiles, rather than the more difficult *profil perdu* pose. (4) As made, among others, by H. Cook (*op. cit.*, pp. 91–3). (5) Notes by Stella Mary Pearce in the Gallery archives. See also her article on the picture in the *Bulletin of the Metropolitan Museum of Art*, August/September, 1971 which is partly in answer to a claim by Terisio Pignatti (1969) that the picture was a production of Giorgione's studio. (6) Printed in *Palatino*, January–March, 1964, p. 19. P. Della Pergola (*Arte Antica e Moderna*, 1960, pp. 432 and 442 and 1963, pp. 66 and 84) tries to identify no. 1173 with no. 102 in the 1626 inventory and no. 167 in the 1682 one, but this picture was on canvas. (7) *Memoirs*, II, p. 6. In this catalogue a distinction is normally drawn between pictures 'from the Aldobrandini Cabinet' and 'from the Aldobrandini Villa'. Since the picture shown later by Day (which is certainly identical with no. 1173) is described as from the 'Aldobrandini Cabinet' a possibility would remain that the one shown in 1800–1 ('from the Aldobrandini Villa') was a different one. (8) Undated catalogue. The copy belonging to E. K. Waterhouse is inscribed at the top 'Day's Colln'. (9) Marked copy of catalogue in the Gallery library. (10) Redford, II, p. 248.

1695   NYMPHS AND CHILDREN IN A LANDSCAPE WITH
        SHEPHERDS

Panel, painted area $18\frac{1}{3} \times 34\frac{1}{2}$ (0·465 × 0·875).

Damaged as a result of flaking in a horizontal strip across the middle and in many other places near the right hand edge. Cleaned 1957.

As 'Venetian School, 15th–16th Century' in the 1929 catalogue. Attributions have included Campagnola, Battista Dossi,[1] Cariani,[2] 'early Bordone'[3] and 'copy of early Titian'.[4] All these suggestions seem wide of the mark to the present writer who sees in no. 1695 either a copy of a lost Giorgione (cf. Berenson: *Lists*, 1957), or, more probably, a deliberate forgery of Giorgione dating from a relatively early period. It seems to be, in fact, a pastiche of Giorgionesque elements. The oval face of the recumbent nymph as well as her jewelled head-dress can be paralleled in the Hermitage *Judith*, the type of her right hand and of that of the standing nymph (with the index finger crooked) occurs in the naked woman in the *Tempest* (Venice, Accademia), which picture also offers a close prototype for the dark wispy foliage to the spectator's left of the head of the recumbent nymph in no. 1695 and above it. The head of the standing nymph in no. 1695 exactly echoes the ex-Melchett *Courtesan* and also that of the Adulteress in the Glasgow picture. Finally, the foliage in no. 1695 is too close in type (though not in quality) to that of the *Tempest* and many other Giorgionesque pictures to need stressing. These factors go beyond mere 'influence' and suggest deliberate imitation. Certain coarsely painted details in no. 1695— notably the two children—together with the other elements already indicated, suggest a date late in the sixteenth century or some time in the seventeenth.

REPRODUCTION: *Illustrations, Italian Schools*, 1937, p. 374.

PROVENANCE: Bequeathed (Mitchell Bequest), 1878, to the Victoria and Albert Museum (341–78), by whom lent, 1900.

REFERENCES: Referred to in the 1929 catalogue. (2) W. Schmidt in *Repertorium für Kunstwissenschaft*, 1908, p. 117. (3) A. Morassi (orally) in 1938. (4) Berenson, *Lists*, 1932 and 1936.

GIROLAMO DA CARPI
c. 1501–1556

Ferrarese School.

The date of his birth derives from Vasari's statement that he was fifty-five at the time of his death in 1556. Vasari is unlikely to be far wrong in this case as he mentions that he became friendly with Girolamo when they were both in Rome in 1550. Vasari specifies that Girolamo was a pupil of Garofalo at Ferrara and then set up for a time at Bologna. This was for an unspecified period in the early 1530's (the frame of Girolamo's altar in the Bolognese church of S. Martino is dated 1532). Vasari adds that Girolamo's style was modified by influence from Correggio whose works he went to Modena and Parma from Bologna to study. Vasari also mentions Raphael's *S. Cecilia* at Bologna as an influence. Dosso Dossi, Giulio Romano and Parmigianino were clearly others. Girolamo returned to Ferrara some time in the 1530's where he was patronized notably by Cardinal Ippolito d'Este who later took him to Rome and for whom he worked in a variety of capacities. In 1550 he did some architectural work for Pope Julius III at the Vatican. He died at Ferrara.

The difficulty in defining Girolamo da Carpi's *œuvre* in painting springs partly from its rarity (he only gave a limited amount of his time to it, while a good deal which Vasari lists is known to have perished) and partly from the eclecticism of his style.

Ascribed to GIROLAMO DA CARPI

20 CARDINAL IPPOLITO DE' MEDICI AND MONSIGNOR MARIO BRACCI

Panel, painted area *c.* 54½ × 44 (1·385 × 1·118). Some damage has been caused by repeated flaking, but condition basically good. Cleaned 1970.

Bottom left, the no. 4 (of the Borghese collection).

The red cap worn by the cardinal was clearly altered during painting. An X-ray photograph shows several different outlines. As the head is shown from the same angle as in Titian's portrait (in the Pitti) and as that picture shows different headgear this may indicate (since the cardinal may have had little time for sitting) that the present portrait was based on Titian's.

The legend to which the cardinal points reads (upside down):

Hyppol· · ·Vice cancell

the last letters of the first word are uncertain; the last two letters of the last word are scored through, perhaps intended as an abbreviation.

The further legend at the base of the scroll apparently reads:

M de Braccijs

The letters, of which the capitals are of fanciful form, are difficult to read. They are discussed in detail in an article by the present writer which also examines the identifications of the sitters as given above together with the evidence for the ascription to Girolamo da Carpi.[1]

Traditionally and variously attributed to Raphael, Titian and Sebastiano del Piombo. As the last-named, or ascribed to him, in earlier editions of the Gallery catalogue. During the eighteenth century the sitters were identified with 'Cardinal Borgia and Machiavelli'. When the picture was attributed to Sebastiano the figure in black was called a self-portrait. Ippolito de' Medici was appointed Vice Chancellor of the Church on 3rd July, 1532.[2] He was in Bologna for a short time at the end of that year and beginning of 1533. Monsignor Mario Bracci had been a 'chierico di Camera' on the occasion of Charles V's coronation at Bologna by Pope Clement VII in 1530.[3] The document depicted is a papal bull.

A further document signed by Mario Bracci in the same way is shown in a portrait in the Fitzwilliam Museum, Cambridge (no. 1653). On the strength of the sitter's resemblance to a head in a fresco of the Angel appearing to Zaccharias in the Oratory of S. Giovanni Decollato in Rome, by Jacopino del Conte, the Fitzwilliam portrait is ascribed to that painter. And since he appears to have signed the name 'F. De Pisia' on the document which also bears the name of Bracci the sitter of the Fitzwilliam portrait is assumed to be De Pisia. The features suggest that he is not identical with the man on the left of no. 20, and the two pictures are not very likely to be by the same hand. But what the connection may be between the sitter of the Fitzwilliam portrait and Bracci is not clear to the present writer.

VERSION: Old copy of right hand figure with N. Dhikeos, Lyon, 1965.

PROVENANCE: Mentioned as in Palazzo Borghese, Rome by Tessin[4] (1687–8), (no. 145 in the Borghese inventory of 1693—*Arte Antica e Moderna*, 1964, pp. 226 and 230), the Richardson's (1722),[5] Volkmann (1770)[6] and Ramdohr (1787)[7] among others. At some stage of the Napoleonic invasion of Italy, or as a consequence of it, it entered the possession of Alexander Day, who exhibited it in London (Royal Mews Gallery, 1816, no. 10).[8] Acquired by the Rev. Holwell Carr by 1819 when lent by him, B.I. (16). Holwell Carr Bequest, 1832.

REPRODUCTION: *Illustrations, Italian Schools*, 1937, p. 283.

REFERENCES: (1) *Burlington Magazine*, March, 1962, pp. 117–18. See also E. H. Ramsden in *Burlington Magazine*, April, 1965, pp. 185 ff. and Cecil Gould in *Saggi e Memorie di Storia dell'Arte*, 5, 1966, pp. 46 ff. Also letters from both, *Burlington Magazine*, May, 1968, p. 277. (2) *Enciclopedia Italiana*, article Medici, Ippolito de'. (3) Gaetano Giordani; edition of the chronicle of Clement VII's visit to Bologna in 1529–30 (1842), p. 55. (4) Nikodemus Tessin D.Y:S *Studieresor*, ed. Sirén, 1914, p. 171: *Im dritten zimber wahren 58 qvadri worunter der Card. Porzi wahr mit dem Machiavello zusammen vom Rafael gemahlet*. (5) *Account of . . . Pictures in Italy*, p. 183: *Cardinal Borgia and Machiavel, said to be of Raffaele, but I think 'tis rather of Titian*. (6) *Historisch-Kritische Nachrichten . . .*, vol. II, pp. 360–1: *Der Kardinal Borgia und Machiavell, auf einem Stücke von eben diesem Meister* [Raphael]. (7) *Ueber Mahlerei und Bildhauerarbeit in Rom . . .*, vol. I, pp. 289–90. He refers to the earlier Borgia/Macchiavelli identification but points out that Ippolito de' Medici's name is inscribed. He considers the seal to be that of the Piombo and therefore that the other figure is Sebastiano. (8) Note by E. K. Waterhouse.

GIROLAMO DA TREVISO
active 1524, died 1544

He is referred to in the contract for the decoration of the Saraceni chapel in S. Petronio, Bologna as 'magister Hieronimus quondam Thome de Trivisio pictor ac sculptor'.[1] One of the frescoes in the chapel in question is signed, like no. 623 of this Gallery, 'Hieronimus Trivisius'.[2] If, as seems justifiable, the wording of the S. Petronio contract be interpreted as meaning that his father's name was Tommaso it would preclude the identification of him, first proposed by Federici,[3] with a member of the family of Pennacchi, since the crucial document for that thesis, a baptismal entry of 2nd February, 1499, gives the name as 'Hieronimus Joannes filius ser petri marie de penachis'.[4] It would also eliminate any more reliable date for his birth than Vasari's statements, which in fact are contradictory. Forty-six is given as his age at death in Vasari's first edition and thirty-six in his second.

According to Vasari Girolamo worked in Treviso, Venice, Bologna, Trento and Genoa.[5] The S. Petronio frescoes, already mentioned, are documented as of 1525–6. Some sculptural work by Girolamo in the same church is documented as of 1524–5.[6] Some frescoes at Faenza are signed and dated 1533. By 1538 he was in England in the service of Henry VIII.[7] Killed at the siege of Boulogne (1544) when acting as military engineer to Henry.[8] Vasari mentions his attempt to emulate Raphael—presumably mainly by study of the *S. Cecilia* at Bologna. His art also shows elements derived from Parmigianino, the Venetians and the Ferrarese.

REFERENCES: (1) Document printed in I. B. Supino: *Sculture delle Porte di S. Petronio*, 1914, p. 104, no. 78. (2) Crowe and Cavalcaselle: *North Italian Painters*, vol. III (1912), p. 128, note 2. (3) *Memorie Trevigiane . . .*, 1813, vol. I, pp. 117, 118, 238, vol. II, pp. 9, 25. (4) Document printed by G. Biscaro

in *Archivio Storico dell' Arte*, 2nd series, 1895, p. 364, note 1. (5) Vasari/
Milanesi, V, pp. 135–9. For the work at Genoa p. 614 of the same volume
(life of Perino del Vaga). (6) Documents published by Corrado Ricci in *Arte
Nostra* (Treviso), 1910, pp. 5–7. Supino (*Nozze Treves-Artom*, 7th April, 1927)
proposed a dating of 1523 for an altarpiece at Dresden, there attributed to
Bagnacavallo. (7) Letter, dated 30th August, 1538 from Pietro Aretino to
Andrea Odoni (Aretino's *Letters*, vol. II, Paris, 1609, p. 50). Philip Pouncey
(*Girolamo da Treviso in the Service of Henry VIII* in *Burlington Magazine*,
vol. 95 (1953), pp. 208–11) suggests a connection between Girolamo's visit to
England and an earlier commission for an altar in S. Salvatore, Bologna,
which according to Malvasia was used by English students. (8) Letter of 1545
from Aretino to Sansovino (Aretino's *Letters*, vol. III, Paris, 1609, p. 158V).

623   ALTARPIECE. MADONNA AND CHILD WITH
      ANGELS, SAINTS AND A DONOR

Panel, painted area $88\frac{3}{4} \times 58$ ($2 \cdot 254 \times 1 \cdot 473$).

Splits in the wood have led to repeated flaking. Where this has not
occurred the paint is in good condition. Cleaned 1973.

Signed (on the plinth): IEROHIMVS. TREVISIVS. P̄.

The saint on the right is identifiable as S. James the Greater by his
pilgrim's staff.[1]

Despite gaps in the pedigree there can be little or no doubt of the
identity of no. 623 with the altarpiece mentioned by Vasari and other
early writers as in the church of S. Domenico at Bologna. Vasari calls
it Girolamo's best work.[2] Masini (1666)[3] specifies the chapel from
which it came as that of the Boccaferri family[4] and adds that the
chapel also contained representations in fresco of the four patron saints
of Bologna. Malvasia/Zanotti (1706) mentions only SS. Petronius and
Domenico as lateral frescoes by Girolamo.[5] No. 623 would have been
removed when the church was remodelled by Carlo Francesco Dotti in
1728–32.[6]

WOOD-CUT: Chiaroscuro by Alessandro Gandini, dated 1610 (Bartsch, XII,
p. 65), with variations, particularly in the background.

PROVENANCE: Boccaferri chapel of S. Domenico, Bologna until shortly before
1732 (see above). Said to have passed thence to a private collection at Imola
and then to have been sold abroad.[7] In England in the Solly collection by
1835.[8] Lot 40, Solly sale, 8th May, 1847, bought Lord Northwick,[9] by whom
exh. B.I., 1847 (52).[10] Northwick sale, 3rd August, 1859 (565), where purchased.

REPRODUCTION: *Illustrations, Italian Schools*, 1937, p. 160.

REFERENCES: (1) No attributes are shown for the other two saints. The
National Gallery Report of 1860 and I. B. Supino (*L'Arte nelle Chiese di
Bologna*, 1938, p. 237) identify them as SS. Joseph and Paul but take the
opposite view as to which is which. (2) Vasari/Milanesi, V, p. 137. See also
P. Lamo, *Graticola di Bologna*, 1560 (ed. of 1844, p. 21) and Scannelli, *Microcosmo*, 1657, pp. 258 f—both descriptions more detailed than Vasari's. (3)
Bologna Perlustrata, I, p. 114. (4) I. B. Supino, *loc. cit.*, identifies the donor
in no. 623 with 'Lodovico Boccadiferro'. (5) *Le Pitture . . .*, p. 241. (6) Dates
from Thieme-Becker's article on C. F. Dotti. Malvasia/Zanotti's edition of
1732 no longer mentions no. 623. (7) Schorn and Förster's edition of Vasari,
vol. III, 2nd part (1845), repeated in Milanesi's note in his edition (vol. V,
p. 137, note 3). Search in Giovanni Villa's *Guida Pittorica d'Imola* (1794,

ed. Gambetti 1925) failed to find any trace of no. 623. (8) Seen by Waagen on his first visit which took place in that year (*Works of Art and Artists in England*, II (1838), p. 191) as from S. Domenico, Bologna. Solly catalogue, n.d., no. 15. (9) Marked copy of sale catalogue in the Gallery library. (10) No. 270 in *Hours in Lord Northwick's Picture Galleries*, 1858, where the provenance is wrongly given as 'the church of St Salvatore'.

Ascribed to GIROLAMO DA TREVISO

218 THE ADORATION OF THE KINGS (AFTER BALDASSARE PERUZZI)

Panel, 56¾ × 49½ (1·442 × 1·257).

Movement in the panels has led to flaking at different times, and the present discoloured varnish makes it difficult to assess the state of the paint. It seems probable, however, that this is basically good for a picture of its age.

A painted version of the cartoon by Peruzzi which is no. 167 of this Gallery. The latter is neither punched nor squared but the individual figures are of approximately the same size in both. The larger over-all size of no. 218 is due to the greater space above the heavenly host and between the latter and the top of the arch; also to the inclusion of extra figures at the sides. As no. 167 has certainly been reduced in size at the top and at the sides (and the figures at the edges made up in places) it is possible that it originally included the latter figures. In that case, however, they could hardly have been in exactly the same relative positions. Of the two dogs, lower right in no. 218, who do not figure in no. 167, the foremost one conceals the legs of the man looking over the top of the chest, which are clearly visible in no. 167 and not appreciably retouched. Similarly, on the left of no. 167, above the horse's head on the extreme left, there is no sign of a further horse's head and of a pointing hand which occupy this area in no. 218. It should be pointed out, moreover, that Agostino Carracci's engraving of 1579 after no. 167 (see below) shows it with the sides in their present state, without the extra figures.

Vasari says that Girolamo da Treviso made a painted version of Peruzzi's cartoon of the Adoration of the Magi for Conte Giambattista Bentivoglio, who also possessed the original cartoon.[1] Both the cartoon and the painted version were recorded by Pietro Lamo in the possession of Conte Andalò Bentivoglio.[2]

Though it is stated in the Higginson catalogue that no. 218 came from the Bentivoglio family this information was clearly derived from a note in the Lapeyrière sale catalogue of 1825 of which the wording leaves no doubt that this provenance was not a continuous tradition but depended merely on the inscription on Agostino Carracci's engraving after no. 167 which gives Conte Costanzo Bentivoglio as the owner of the original.[3] Furthermore, Lanzi (*Storia Pittorica . . .*, vol. 1, 1823 ed., p. 288) mentions a story current in his day at Bologna to the effect that Girolamo's version had perished at sea. Nevertheless, stylistic factors, though slight, do seem to the present writer to point to Girolamo da Treviso (to whom no. 218 is attributed by Berenson—*Lists*, 1936). Though no. 218 is a fairly accurate copy of no. 167 it is immeasurably coarser in draughtsmanship and in physiognomical differentiation, and certain details, such as the angels supporting the Almighty, whose faces are of different types from Peruzzi's, seem to show an approximation to Girolamo da Treviso's idiom. When no. 218, moreover, is placed next to no. 623 of this Gallery (a signed work of Girolamo da Treviso) a marked similarity of colouring is also noticeable. It may also be pointed out, without being unduly stressed, that no. 218 is clearly a sixteenth-century work and that as no. 167 was in private possession at that time the number of copies taken from it might be expected to be relatively small; also that since the owner possessed in addition one painted version he would have less inducement to commission another, whether or not he permitted copies to be made for other people. In fact, only one other copy is recorded as having been made in the sixteenth century, and this was probably done in connection with Agostino Carracci's engraving. The latter is dated 1579, the former, which was on canvas and has since disappeared but which belonged in the nineteenth century to Michelangelo Gualandi, 1576. Both depart from no. 167 and no. 218 alike in that additional angels and some heads of cherubs are included in the heavenly host.[4]

VERSION: A picture formerly in the Northwick collection (no. 511 in 'Hours in Lord Northwick's Picture Galleries', 1858, no. 141 in the Northwick sale catalogue, 27th July, 1859) is referred to in editions of the National Gallery catalogue from 1915 on as a 'repetition' of no. 218. The present writer, however, has not been able to check if it was of the same design.

PROVENANCE: Probably exported from Italy at the time of the Napoleonic upheavals, since Buchanan, who was much concerned in that traffic, noted that it had once belonged to him,[5] and the preface of the 1825 Lapeyrière sale catalogue mentions it among the pictures which had become available as a result of the Revolution. Conceivably, but improbably, identical with a picture in the Truchsessian Gallery—1804 exhibition catalogue, no. 537 'The Adoration of the Magi, 1486, B. Peruzzi' and no. 222 in the sale, 29th March (3rd day), 1806 ('B. Peruzzi . . . The Adoration of the Magi, a curious specimen of that early period'). No. 41 in the Lapeyrière sale, Paris, 19th April, 1825.[6] Probably no. 112 in the Delahante sale, London (Phillips), 8–9th July, 1828.[7] Pages 220–4 of the 1841 catalogue (by Henry Artaria) of the Edmund Higginson Gallery and no. 227 in the latter's sale (where bought in), Christie's, 6th June, 1846, in both cases as from Bentivoglio, Lapeyrière and 'Mr Gray's' collections. Presented by Edmund Higginson, 1849.

REPRODUCTION: *Illustrations, Italian Schools*, 1937, p. 274.

REFERENCES: (1) Vasari/Milanesi, IV, 597 f, and V, 137. (2) *Graticola di Bologna*, 1560. Ed. of 1844, p. 35. (3) 'Ce tableau, qu'Augustin Carrache trouve digne d'exercer son burin, se voyait du temps de cet artiste dans le palais du Comte Constantin Bentivoglio, à Bologne.' (4) See publication of 1853 by Gualandi—'L'Adorazione dei Magi, Pittura del XVI Secolo'. The copy in question is there attributed to Bartolomeo Cesi, or to Cesi and Agostino Carracci in conjunction. Gualandi points out, among other things, Rosini's error in assuming that Agostino Carracci's engraving was made after the painting formerly in the Rinuccini collection, which, as can be seen from the engraving (pl. XXXVI of the *Etruria Pittrice*) was quite different. (5) MS. note in copy of the 1851 National Gallery catalogue in the Gallery library. (6) Date corrected in MS. in the National Gallery copy from 14th March. Not in the 1817 Lapeyrière sale, as stated in earlier editions of the National Gallery catalogue. (7) The sale catalogue specifies that the picture is on panel and is from 'the Palace of Constantine Bentivoglio at Bologne' therefore following the 1825 Lapeyrière catalogue). No immediate provenance is given, but these particular Delahante pictures are specified as having been collected 'during the last ten years'. The long catalogue entry makes hypothetical identifications of some of the figures in no. 218, e.g. Michélangelo and Sebastiano del Piombo 'in the centre' and 'on the right . . . the Artist . . . with his dogs by his side, and next him Pope Leo X'. The man with the dogs in no. 218 does indeed look like a self-portrait, whether of Peruzzi or Girolamo da Treviso.

GIULIO ROMANO
1499(?)–1546

The year of his birth is not certain, but 1499 has the best claim.[1] His father's name was Pippi. After he moved from Rome to Mantua Giulio signed 'Giulio Romano' (or 'Julius Romanus') and this form has been universal since. It may be noted in this context that Giulio was the only important artist of the Renaissance who was a native of Rome.

At an unspecified date Giulio entered the studio of Raphael who, according to Vasari, left him and Penni his heirs at his death in 1520. In 1524 Giulio settled in Mantua where he remained, in the service of the Gonzaga, for the rest of his life. Here he was called on, as Raphael had been at Rome, to engage in a vast programme of work of the utmost diversity—architectural, theatrical and decorative as well as pictorial. But unlike Raphael, Giulio Romano had no effective rivals. His position as Pooh Bah of the arts at the Gonzagan court was in fact comparable with that held by Charles Lebrun at Versailles a century and a half later. The volume and diversity of his output could only be achieved, as Raphael had already demonstrated, by able organization of studio assistance. Vasari specifically mentions that it was from Raphael that Giulio learned how to farm out decorative work among his pupils but yet contrive a homogeneous result.[2]

Early in Giulio's Mantuan period there seems to have been some mutual influence between him and Correggio. Later on, Giulio's style as decorator was a decisive factor in the formation of Paolo Veronese, among others; while later still, artists as dissimilar as Rubens and Poussin reacted emphatically to different aspects of his art. The fact that Giulio Romano is apparently the only Italian Renaissance artist who is mentioned by Shakespeare may be regarded as a further indication of the extent of his fame in the early seventeenth century.[3]

REFERENCES: (1) For a summary of the evidence cf. F. Hartt: *Giulio Romano* 1958, p. 3, n. 1. (2) Vasari/Milanesi V, p. 539; . . . *elle* [frescoes in the *Sala di Psiche* in the *Palazzo del Te*, Mantua] *furono dipinte con i cartoni grandi di Giulio da Benedetto da Pescia e da Rinaldo Mantovano, i quali misero in opera tutte queste storie, eccetto che il Bacco, il Sileno, ed i due putti che poppano la capra: ben è vero che l'opera fu poi quasi tutta ritocca da Giulio, onde è come fusse tutta stata fatta da lui. Il qual modo, che egli imparò da Raffaello suo precettore, è molto utile per i giovani. . . .* (3) *The Winter's Tale,* Act V, Scene 2: First Gentleman: *Are they returned to the court?* Third Gentleman: *No; the princess hearing of her mother's statue, which is in the keeping of Paulina—a piece many years in doing, and now newly performed by that rare Italian master, Julio Romano; who, had he himself eternity and could put breath into his work, would beguile Nature of her custom, so perfectly is he her ape: he so near to Hermione hath done Hermione that they say one would speak to her and stand in hope of answer: thither with all greediness of affection are they gone, and there they intend to sup.* F. Hartt (*op. cit.,* pp. 193–4, n. 1) points out that there is no record of a work of sculpture from Giulio's hand and deduces from this that Shakespeare's reference is not to him but to an obscure Bolognese sculptor, also called Giulio Romano. This seems highly improbable. Some echo, no doubt distorted by time and distance, of Giulio's fame as an artist would have reached Shakespeare who then happened to choose the one art he did *not* practise. The fact that there happened to be a sculptor of the same name would thus be coincidental and irrelevant. Since Shakespeare also speaks in *The Winter's Tale* of 'the coast of Bohemia' it would remain for some diligent scholar to draw attention to a coast line of that name believed by the Elizabethans to exist in the neighbourhood of the North West Passage. In an article in the Shakespeare-Jahrbuch of the Deutsche Shakespeare-Gesellschaft, vol. 92, 1956 (*Julio Romano im Wintermärchen*) E. Künstler piles hypothesis on hypothesis, postulating that the character of Hermione is based on that of Giovanna d'Arragona, that Shakespeare had seen the portrait of her later at Warwick Castle, that it was then attributed to Giulio Romano and that it had entered England during the reign of Mary I.

Studio of GIULIO Romano

624   THE INFANCY OF JUPITER

Panel, $41\frac{7}{8} \times 69\frac{1}{8}$ ($1 \cdot 064 \times 1 \cdot 755$).

Extensively damaged, probably mainly by flaking. The sky and distant landscape on both sides of the picture is a network of repainted passages. Many small retouchings also in the naked flesh of the four main figures and in the sheet the child lies on. The foliage much better preserved.

The nine figures in the background—variously styled the Corybantes or the Curetes according to different versions of the legend—are shown making music, the object being that the noise should distract or frighten away Jupiter's father, Saturn, who was given to devouring his offspring.

A pair of pictures at Hampton Court of the same height as no. 624 and slightly narrower—*Jupiter suckled by the Goat Amalthea* (291) and a *Birth Scene* (286)—can be traced back through the collection of Charles I to Gonzaga possession at Mantua and accord so completely in style with no. 624 as to leave little or no doubt that they were intended as companions to it. Despite gaps in its pedigree no. 624 can thus be confidently identified in its turn with entries in the Charles I and Gonzaga inventories. Recently F. Hartt has plausibly associated three further surviving pictures with these three (two more at Hampton Court—*Jupiter and Juno entering Heaven* (302) and *Chiron and Achilles* (266)—and one in a private collection) together with six more which are lost but which can be deduced from drawings or descriptions. The resulting series of a dozen pictures would make up a homogeneous scheme of decoration for a room of medium size.[1]

Hitherto catalogued as Giulio Romano. The fact that in no. 624 the heads of all three of the main figures are shown in nearly complete profile may indicate some desire of the artist's to emulate the style of an antique frieze. But it has been achieved at the cost of such distortion as also to suggest some incompetence.[2] It is significant in this context that both the central and the left-hand figure are shown with the heads at more natural angles and also more skilfully foreshortened in the *modello* at Chatsworth (see DRAWING below). This seems in itself an indication of studio participation in the execution of no. 624.[3]

It has been pointed out that the infant Jupiter in no. 624 recurs in Tintoretto's *Venus, Mars and Vulcan* (Munich) and in a *Madonna* formerly at Bridgewater House.[4] It seems likely that all derive from an antique prototype, perhaps via Michelangelo's lost *Sleeping Cupid* which was at Mantua in the sixteenth century.

DRAWING: Chatsworth 99 (*Hartt, op. cit.,* no. 303). Modello for no. 624. Pen and bistre wash, 0·332 × 0·549 (edges trimmed to an octagon). Reproduced Hartt, fig. 456.

ENGRAVING: By Patas in the *Galerie du Palais Royal,* vol. 1 (1786).

PROVENANCE: 1627 Mantua inventory, no. 301: *un' historia di done che parechiano una cuna in campo di paesi, ornamento nero, opera di Giulio Romano.*[5] In Van der Doort's inventory (*c.* 1639) of Charles I's collection: *A Mantua peece done by Julio Romano 12 Item . . . Cupidd lyeing along uppon a wicker banck and Some 4 figures by and 8 naked nimphs more a farr of Sitting at the water Side Intire litle figurs . . . hight 3 f 6—breadth 5 f 9.*[6] It has not yet come to light how no. 624 left the royal collection and entered France. It does not figure in the Commonwealth inventory of 1649[7] nor is it in the 1653 inventory of Cardinal Mazarin's pictures. In the Orléans collection by 1727 when catalogued as having formerly belonged to 'L'Abbé de Camps'.[8] Exhibited for sale with some other ex-Orléans pictures at the Lyceum, London, 26th December *et seq.,* 1798 (230) (not sold)[9] and again at the same place 14th February, 1800 (48). No. 32 (as from the Orléans collection) in the Lapeyrière sale catalogue, Paris, April 1825[10] where bought Delahante.[9] No. 25 ('from the Orléans Gallery') Chevalier Sebastian Erard sale, Christie's, 22nd June, 1833, bought 'Rodd',[9] evidently on behalf of Lord Northwick, as stated in the catalogue of his sale, 24th May, 1838, no. 112 (bought in). Northwick sale, sixth day, 3rd August, 1859, no. 578, where purchased.

REPRODUCTION: *Illustrations, Italian Schools,* 1937, p. 313.

REFERENCES: (1) Frederick Hartt: *Giulio Romano,* 1958, I, pp. 211–17. The author suggests that the cycle may have been connected with the birth of Francesco III Gonzaga in 1533 and have been intended for one or both of two small rooms set aside for the Duchess in the Castello. (2) It is unlikely that this factor is materially affected by the retouching. (3) In his volume of illustrations F. Hartt (*loc. cit.,* pls. 454–465) seems to differentiate between the other surviving paintings in the series (which he heads 'Giulio and assistant') and no. 624 (which has no heading and is therefore presumably intended to be regarded as autograph). But he makes no such distinction in the text. (4) See J. Wilde: *Eine Studie Michelangelos nach der Antike in Mitteilungen des kunsthistorischen Institutes in Florenz,* IV, 1932, pp. 41 ff. Also C. De Tolnay: *The Youth of Michelangelo,* 1947 (second edition) pp. 201–3. (5) Alessandro Luzio: *La Galleria dei Gonzaga . . .,* 1913, p. 114. (6) Published by Oliver Millar, *Walpole*

Society, vol. XXXVII, p. 19. (7) Information kindly communicated by Oliver Millar. (8) Du Bois de Saint Gelais: *Description des Tableaux du Palais Royal*, 1727, p. 275. (9) MS. note in the Gallery copy. (10) Date and owner's name in a MS. note in the Gallery copy.

GIULIO ROMANO and GIOVANFRANCESCO PENNI

225 S. MARY MAGDALENE BORNE BY ANGELS

Fresco secco, transferred, and mounted on canvas in the nineteenth century. Cleaned and remounted on rigid (Sundeala) support, 1969. False top corners and false strip along base removed then. Dimensions now *c.* 65 (1·651) high × *c.* 93 (2·362) (arched top).

Unretouched area of damage, extreme right. A few sizable losses of original paint and many small ones where nails had been punched. In other areas paint quite well preserved.

Stated in the National Gallery catalogue of 1854 (by Wornum) to have come from the church of SS. Trinità de' Monti, Rome. Therefore identifiable with one of the lunette frescoes in the Massimi chapel mentioned by Vasari, who says that the vault, lunettes, stucco and other ornaments, together with the altarpiece of the chapel, were by Giulio Romano assisted by Gianfrancesco Penni. Later on, Vasari specifies the lunettes as four frescoes of S. Mary Magdalene.[1]

In default of contemporary documentation it may be supposed that Vasari, writing only some thirty years after the event, is more probably right than wrong in saying that the frescoes were the work of Giulio Romano and Penni. In its general arrangement and in the facial types of some of the angels no. 225 may be compared with the celestial group in Giulio's *Stoning of Stephen* (Genoa, S. Stefano).[2]

A small picture (Florence, Pitti, no. 346) of the subject, attributed to Taddeo Zuccari, may derive in part from no. 225.

ENGRAVING: L.D. (reproduced H. Zerner: *Ecole de Fontainebleau*, 1969 as L.D.73)

PROVENANCE: Massimi chapel of SS. Trinità de' Monti, Rome (see above). Removed before 1834[3] and probably after 1818.[4] Mrs Jameson (1850) refers to it in the possession of M. Joly de Bammeville.[5] The 1854 National Gallery catalogue says 'formerly in the possession of M. Joly de Bammeville'. Presented by Lord Overstone, 1852.

REPRODUCTION: Negative in the Gallery's possession.

REFERENCES: (1) Vasari/Milanesi V, 620–1. The relevant passage is the same in the 1550 edition. Vasari's account seems to have been the basis of later descriptions of the paintings in the chapel—e.g. Titi (*Studio di Pittura . . . nelle Chiese di Roma*, 1674, p. 410). (2) The elaborate modern monograph on Giulio Romano (by F. Hartt, 1958) overlooks no. 225. In the 1929 Gallery catalogue it appears under 'Pictures withdrawn from exhibition', but in some of the earlier editions it is dealt with in some detail. (3) 2nd Italian edition, of that year, of Melchiorri's *Guida Metodica di Roma, e suoi contorni*. Reference from J. Simon. Carl Bunsen (*Beschreibung der Stadt Rom*, III, 1838, pp. 599–600) also speaks of the frescoes as 'zu Grunde gegangen'. (4) The second edition, 1818, of Michelangelo Prunetti's *Saggio Pittorico . . . delle . . . Pitture . . . in Roma*, p. 147, mentions the lunettes at the Trinità de' Monti. This is not absolutely certain evidence that they were still there as such guide books, particularly second editions, were sometimes out of date in certain respects. (5) Mrs. Jameson: *Sacred and Legendary Art*, 2nd ed., 1850, p. 221.

ITALIAN School

643 (a) THE ATTACK ON CARTAGENA
    (b) THE CONTINENCE OF SCIPIO

644 (a) THE RAPE OF THE SABINES
    (b) THE RECONCILIATION OF ROMANS AND
        SABINES

Four pictures framed as two. All transferred from panel to canvas.[1] Painted area of each $14 \times 60\frac{1}{4}$ ($0\cdot356 \times 1\cdot53$). No. 643 cleaned, 1966. Some obvious losses of paint in all four, but the discoloured state of the varnish precludes a more detailed account of the condition.

It may be considered one of the minor curiosities of the history of art that these four pictures, with two others of the same series, were included in such celebrated collections as those of the Emperor Rudolf II, Queen Christina and Orléans under an attribution as improbable as Giulio Romano. An alternative attribution, made in earlier editions of the National Gallery catalogues and elsewhere, to one of his school, Rinaldo Mantovano, has likewise no justification. An attribution to Andrea Schiavone was made at least as early as the eighteenth century and has been periodically revived.[2] No. 643 (b) (*The Continence of Scipio*) has indeed at first sight something in common with Schiavone. But the other three have much less. Nevertheless the same hand seems to have been responsible for the execution of all four, and as his abilities appear to have been modest some degree of eclecticism is the more easily explained. The fountain, left centre in no. 644 (a) (*The Rape of the Sabines*), with Neptune and a dolphin, is rather difficult to imagine prior to Giambologna's at Bologna which was not finished until about 1566. The buildings shown in the background of the same picture appear for the most part to be vague reminiscences of Roman ones. Some minor eclectic painter active probably around the third quarter of the sixteenth century is as near an attribution as seems prudent.[3]

The other two pictures which accompanied these four up to the dispersal of the relevant portion of the Orléans collection in 1802 were a *Coriolanus* and a *Scipio rewarding the Soldiers*. The former was last recorded in the Morrison collection, Basildon Park. The latter was sold in 1970.[4] The titles of the pictures in the series are traditional, and may not be correct.

A *Triumph* (no. 28 of the Vienna gallery) is claimed in the gallery catalogue to have belonged originally to the series. Three further similar pictures are at Leningrad.[5]

The Orléans catalogue of 1727 refers to Livy as the literary source.[6]

ENGRAVINGS: By Nicolas Tardieu (643 a and b; 643 b appears in reverse) and Philippe Simonneau (644 a and b) in the *Cabinet Crozat*, 1729, pls. 54, 57,

52 and 53. Another series, by Couché fils and others, appeared in the first volume (1786) of the *Galerie du Palais Royal*.

PROVENANCE: The four pictures comprising nos. 643 and 644, together with the other two already mentioned, were undoubtedly in the collection of the Emperor Rudolf II at Prague and passed, after the Sack of 1648, to Sweden and figured successively in the Queen Christina, Odescalchi and Orléans collections. Nevertheless the early inventories are very imperfect. The Marquis du Fresne's inventory of 1652 of Queen Christina's collection, for instance, lists, under the heading 'de Prague': *94. 5 longs tableaux tous de mesme façon et grandeur, avec des personnages romains, des batailles et des villes sur des fonds de bois* and later, still under 'Prague', *267 . . . un long tableau representant des romains, sur du bois.*[7] The 1621 Prague inventory seems only to contain two relevant entries though it would be possible that several of the panels may have been mounted together: *149. Eine fürneme Taffel darauff Trojanische Historien, von Julio Romano. 150. Die ersten Romaner geschichten, als Raptis de Sabini und desgleichen Historien, vom Julio Romano.*[8] All six appear in the 1689 inventory of Queen Christina's collection at Rome: *47. Sei quadri in tavola bislonghi rappresentanti il Ratto ed Istoria dei Sabinesi, di mano di Giulio Romano, longhi palmi sei e alti palmi uno e mezzo per ciosenno . . . .*[9] Also in the 1721 Christina inventory.[10] In the 1727 Orléans catalogue.[11] Passed with the other Orléans pictures to England[12] and exhibited for sale with some of them at Bryan's, 88 Pall Mall, 26th December, 1798 *et seq.* (nos. 125, 127, 131, 134, 136, 138) (where retained for the Duke of Bridgewater,[13] one of the syndicate which had bought the Orléans collection). Anonymous sale (by Peter Coxe, Burrell and Foster), 13th May, 1802 (nos. 49–54). This is the last record of all six together. Nos. 643 and 644 figured as lots 15, 16, 67 and 68 in the Jeremiah Harman sale, 17–18th May, 1844 (bought Nieuwenhuys).[13] Previously, what were apparently nos. 644a and 643b, but without the other two, had appeared as lots 116 and 117, Ph. Panné sale, 27th March, (2nd day), 1819.[14] All four bought with the Beaucousin collection, 1860. No. 643 exh. Stockholm (Queen Christina), 1966 (1203, 1204).

REPRODUCTION: *Illustrations, Italian Schools*, 1937, p. 310.

REFERENCES: (1) A note on the back of one of the companion pictures—the *Coriolanus* (formerly Morrison collection, Basildon Park) is recorded to the effect that all six pictures were transferred from wood to canvas by Hacquin in 1774. The 1786 Orléans catalogue gives them as still on wood, but can be shown to be wrong in this respect in other instances (e.g. no. 1 of this Gallery). (2) Mariette in the *Cabinet Crozat* (1729, I, 19) mentions a Schiavone attribution and also opines from marks then visible which he interpreted as made by locks that the series had formed part of cupboard doors. (3) Certain details such as the women's hair dressing would accord best with a dating in the 1550's (notes in the Gallery archives by Stella Mary Pearce). (4) The *Scipio* was last recorded at auction in London—anonymous sale, Sotheby's, 15th July, 1970, lot 72 (as 'Circle of Giuseppe Porta'). (5) Reproduced in *Zeitschrift für bildende Kunst*, 1913, pp. 269, 271. (6) Evidently XXVI, 42 and 50 (nos. 643 a and b) and I, 9 and 13 (nos. 644 a and b). (7) Olof Granberg: *La Galerie de Tableaux de la Reine Christine de Suède*, 1897, appendix II, pp. XXX and XXXVIII. (8) Olof Granberg: *Kejsar Rudolf II's Konstkammare . . .*, 1902, Bilaga I, p. IX. (9) Granberg 1897, appendix III, p. LXI. (10) Granberg, 1897 appendix IV, pp. XCIV–V, nos. 21, 22, 25, 26, 29, 31. (11) By Du Bois de Saint Gelais, pp. 279 ff. (12) For the vicissitudes of the Orléans collection see Buchanan: *Memoirs* I, (1924), pp. 9–220. (13) MS. notes in the copy of the catalogue in the Gallery library. (14) Note in the Gallery copy of the catalogue says bought Rubens. Graves (*Art Sales*, III, 1901, p. 82) says bought 'Hubent'. There may be some confusion with the Geo. Hibbert sale (13th June, 1829) where another picture from the series, but not one of our four, was lot 51 (*Coriolanus*). This, or the last of the six—*Scipio giving Rewards*—was lot 5), Earl of Mulgrave sale, 12th May, 1832.

1052 PORTRAIT OF A YOUNG MAN

Panel,[1] 25¾ × 19⅜ (0·645 × 0·492).

Good condition. Slightly damaged by cracking. *Pentimento* of the sitter's right shoulder under the fur collar. A lower neck line is also visible under the top rim of the shirt.

In the Northwick and Sarah Solly collections as Raphael; since entering the Gallery, as 'Milanese School' which may be correct but need not be. Morelli thought it German or Flemish[2] and Jacobsen suggested Bartolommeo Veneto.[3] The latter attribution was taken up by Berenson but only momentarily (1936 *Lists*). The costume would accord with a dating a year or two on either side of 1518.[4]

VERSION: On the Berlin market in 1933.[5]

PROVENANCE: No. 100 in the catalogue of the Northwick collection, Thirlestaine House, Cheltenham, 1858 (*Hours in Lord Northwick's Picture Galleries*, p. 22, 'Portrait of the Duke of Urbino by Raphael').[6] Lot 1587, Northwick sale, 19th August, 1859, bought Colnaghi.[7] Bequeathed by Miss Sarah Solly, 1879.[8]

REPRODUCTION: *Illustrations, Italian Schools*, 1937, p. 233.

REFERENCES: (1) Walnut, according to information in the Gallery archives. (2) *Munich and Dresden*, 1893, p. 279. (3) *Repertorium für Kunstwissenschaft*, 1901, p. 358. (4) Notes by Stella Mary Pearce in the Gallery archives. (5) Noted by E. K. Waterhouse. He described it as 'inferior'. (6) Bequeathed as this to the Gallery. (7) Marked copy of the sale catalogue in the Gallery library. (8) Miss Solly's will (1873) specifies the picture as having belonged to her father, Edward Solly. There is no confirmation of this, and in the case of another picture (now no. 1053, de Witte) of which the same was stated some doubt was expressed at the time of Miss Solly's death by her executor (letter in the Gallery library).

2510 PORTRAIT OF A YOUNG MAN

Panel, 10½ × 8½ (0·266 × 0·215).

Face and hair pretty well preserved, the rest less so.

In earlier editions of the catalogue as Umbrian School, with an alternative attribution to the Bolognese and a doubtful identification of the sitter with Raphael. In Salting's MS. notes what seems to be this picture appears as 'portrait of a young man' by Timoteo Viti with erased attributions to Lo Spagna and Bissolo. It is most unlikely that there is any reliable authority for the sitter's being Raphael. The work appears to be from one of the provincial Italian Schools early in the sixteenth century.

PROVENANCE: Salting Bequest, 1910.

REPRODUCTION: *Illustrations, Italian Schools*, 1937, p. 369.

3117 A MAN AND HIS WIFE

25¾ × 29 (0·654 × 0·736).

Much damaged.[1]

The extent of the damage is such that no attempt at a precise attribution in the circumstances is justifiable.[2] In the less damaged areas the handling seems coarse and undistinguished.

The costume is perhaps provincial (or at any rate not Venetian), around the mid 1540's.[3]

PROVENANCE: No. 464 in the 1841 catalogue of the Costabili collection, Ferrara. In the possession of Layard by 1869 when lent by him to South Kensington, no. 24 (as from the Costabili collection). Layard Bequest, 1916.

REPRODUCTION: *Illustrations, Italian Schools*, 1937, p. 385.

REFERENCES: (1) The possibility that the paint was transferred from panel could not be entirely excluded. (2) Nevertheless many have been made. The 1841 Costabili catalogue had Paolo Veronese, Layard's MSS. (in the Gallery archives) favour Garofalo while recording a tentative attribution by Morelli to 'Crespi' and another (with query) to Dosso Dossi. Mündler (diary in the Gallery archives) had suggested Torbido, Berenson (1907 only) Giulio Campi, and Lafenestre and Richtenberger (*Venise*, n.d., p. 307) Lotto. After this rich harvest of increasingly improbable suggestions the Gallery catalogue of 1920 suggested merely 'Veronese School, late XV century', emended in the 1929 edition to 'XVI century'. A note in the Gallery archives quotes a suggestion by R. Longhi of 'Cremonese School'. (3) Notes in the Gallery archives by Stella Mary Pearce.

3119   A JESSE-TREE

Parchment or paper, painted area $8\frac{3}{4} \times 5\frac{1}{2}$ (0·222 × 0·14).
Good condition.
Most of the decorative passages are picked out in gold.

Since it entered Layard's possession in the nineteenth century it has always been called 'Giulio Clovio' or 'attributed to Giulio Clovio', but no serious justification for the attribution has ever been advanced. In point of fact the marked mannerisms of the style of no. 3119 cannot be paralleled in Giulio Clovio's signed or documented works. A suggestion of Girolamo Genga, made by Philip Pouncey,[1] has a great deal to commend it, though no documented miniatures by this artist are known.

PROVENANCE: Purchased, 1866, by Layard from Grüner of Dresden.[2] Exh. Leeds, 1868 (596)[3] (lent Layard) and South Kensington, 1869 (34) (lent Layard). Sir A. H. Layard Bequest, 1916.

REPRODUCTION: *Illustrations, Italian Schools*, 1937, p. 101.

REFERENCES: (1) Oral communication. (2) *L'Arte*, 1912, p. 452. Also Layard papers in the Gallery archives. (3) Earlier editions of the catalogue inexplicably give the exhibition number at Leeds as 107 (which was 'Morone, The Holy Family, lent by Sir G. Islay Campbell, Bart.').

3125   THE HOLY FAMILY

Panel, $19\frac{1}{2} \times 15\frac{1}{8}$ (0·495 × 0·384).
Much darkened. Such of the paint as is visible appears in good state.

One of a number of strange pictures of which what seems to be a group of five were assembled in an article by F. Zeri.[1] In this he characterized the hand as combining Northern and Sodomesque elements and christened it *Master of the Stockholm Pietà*. Leaving the other pictures out of consideration the present writer would agree with Zeri to the extent that no. 3125, which was attributed to Sodoma, on Morelli's authority, when in Layard's possession, seems a hybrid combining Italianate and non-Italianate elements and that the Italianate ones seem close to Sodoma. But he is less convinced that the others are necessarily Northern and would consider an alternative possibility that they might be Spanish. Until such time as a similar picture appears with a signature or other documentation the problem of the authorship is unlikely to be solved.

PROVENANCE: Manfrin collection, Venice (label on the back), from which bought by Sir A. H. Layard in 1880.[2] Layard Bequest, 1916.

REPRODUCTION: *Illustrations, Italian Schools*, 1937, p. 175.

REFERENCES: (1) *Burlington Magazine*, vol. 92, 1950, pp. 108 ff. The other four pictures are the Stockholm *Pietà* and Madonnas at Bergamo and formerly in the Crespi collection and on the Rome art market. (2) Layard MSS. in the Gallery archives. Layard's note and the label leave no doubt of the Manfrin provenance but owing to the brevity of the entries in the Manfrin catalogues and the uncertainty of the attribution of no. 3125 it cannot be identified with certainty.

3817 PORTRAIT OF A LADY WITH A DOG

Panel,[1] 33 × 27¾ (0·838 × 0·705).

Paint very worn in places, particularly in the hair which is much restored, and in the ear.[2] Further damage through horizontal cracks in the panel. Cleaned 1960.

Formerly as Sofonisba Anguisciola, which is improbable. Alternative suggestions have included one of her sisters or Lavinia Fontana. A rather more probable candidate is a male painter, Bartolomeo Passarotti, a number of whose portraits are very much of this type. Finer points of style criticism, however, are applicable only with difficulty owing to the damage suffered by no. 3817. For the same reason detailed analysis of the hair style and costume is unwise, though the general fashion is clearly that of a fairly late period in the sixteenth century.

PROVENANCE: Presented by Sir Henry Howorth, through the N.A.-C.F., 1923.

REPRODUCTION: *Illustrations, Italian Schools*, 1937, p. 12.

REFERENCES: (1) Not canvas, as the 1925 and 1929 catalogues have it. (2) The pearls on top of the head are original. Those at the side are hypothetical, and probably incorrect, restoration.

ITALIAN SCHOOL (?),
sixteenth–seventeenth century

5448 THE VISITATION

45 × 86 (1·14 × 2·18).

Retouched towards the edges, and many *pentimenti*, particularly on the figure of S. Zacharias. The Virgin's blue robe cracked. Once ascribed to Murillo,[1] and in earlier editions of the National Gallery catalogue doubtfully as French. A realist painter of Lombardy at the turn of the sixteenth–seventeenth centuries seems more probable.[2]

PROVENANCE: From Lord Boston's collection, Hedsor, Bucks.[3] His sale, Christie's, 6th March, 1942 (64), where bought Leger. Purchased, Martin Colnaghi Fund, from Colnaghi's, 1944.

REPRODUCTION: *Illustrations, French School*, 1950, pl. 59.

REFERENCES: (1) Letter from Lord Boston in the Gallery archives. (2) Oral suggestion by Michael Levey. (3) An *Annunciation* by 'Morellio' is mentioned at Hedsor by Thomas Langley, *The History and Antiquities of the Hundred of Desborough*, 1797, p. 278.

ITALIAN School (?)
period uncertain

6357   BUST OF A BEARDED MAN

White marble, height *c.* 25″ (0·635).
Inscribed on the back:

> LEONARDVS
>
> RINALDIVS
>
> A   VICTORIA   F
>
> MDXXXXVI

A modern bronze bust corresponding almost exactly with the present one, and bearing the same inscription, was in the art market in Florence, *c.* 1960.[1] The fact that the inscribed date (1546) would make it much the earliest known bust by Alessandro Vittoria, together with the consideration that prolonged research has failed to confirm the existence of a Leonardo Rinaldi at this date suggests that the present bust dates from post-Renaissance times.[2]

PROVENANCE: In the possession of W. P. Gibson from *c.* 1946 until his death in 1960.[1] Presented by the N.A.-C.F., 1964, in memory of W. P. Gibson, Keeper of the National Gallery, 1939–60.

REPRODUCTION: A negative in the Gallery's possession.

REFERENCES: (1) Photograph in the Gallery archives. (2) Information kindly supplied by Sir John Pope-Hennessy and R. Lightbown.

BERNARDINO LANINO
apprenticed 1528, died between 12th June, 1581 and 25th April, 1583[1]

He was a member of a Vercelli family of painters. Lomazzo, writing of Lanino as a contemporary (1584) refers to Gaudenzio Ferrari as 'suo precettore'.[2] A quantity of his pictures survive in Piedmont and Lombardy. His art perpetuates Gaudenzio's version of the Luini tradition.

REFERENCES: (1) For these dates cf. A. M. Brizio: *La Pittura in Piemonte*, 1942, p. 229. (2) *Trattato* . . ., 1584, p. 372. Lanino's name is said to be linked with Gaudenzio's as early as 1530 (Venturi: *Storia* . . . IX, II, 875).

700 ALTARPIECE: MADONNA AND CHILD WITH S. MARY MAGDALENE, A SAINTED POPE, S. JOSEPH(?) AND S. PAUL

Panel, arched top, 81 × 52½ (2·057 × 1·327).

Some damage, partly caused by vertical cracking in the wood, but general condition seems fairly good.

In the middle distance Christ appears (as a gardener) to S. Mary Magdalene. In the background a figure seems to be preaching to some others.

Signed on the *cartellino* bottom left:

Bernardinus
Effigiabat 1543

The paper in S. Paul's hand reads:

Justificati /
ex fide / ergo
/ ad ——

The figure who wears the papal tiara was identified in earlier editions of the catalogue as S. Gregory, and in an eighteenth-century document (discussed below) as S. Ambrose (who was never pope). In fact, his identity is not established (his halo is almost concealed by the tiara but may just be discerned at the sides).

On 29th November, 1540 Lanino was commissioned to paint an *ancona* for the chapel belonging to Francesco de Strata in the church of S. Paolo at Vercelli.[1] The contract does not specify the subject, but this is given in detail in an unpublished record of 1759[2]:

> *Memorie sopra la fondazione, progressi ed interessi del convento di San Paolo dei Predicatori della Città di Vercelli, compillato [sic] dal Padre Fra Luigi Galateri di Savigliano 1759, p. 399—Altare di S. Maria Maddalena: Fu eretto verosimilmente circa la metà del 500 dalla famiglia Strata . . . Consiste in un quadro di legno finente in cima in un semicircolo con cornice e cimasa azurrate e dorate; in mezzo vi è dipinta la Vergine Maria col Suo Divin Figlio in braccio, alla destra S. Maria Maddalena e S. Ambrogio arcivescovo; a sinistra S. Paolo con un altro Santo dietro; sotto si legge: Bernardinus effigiebat anno 1543—Nella gradinata che forma uno zoccolo al quadro, vi sono sei piccoli scudi, in cui vi è effigiata la conversione e vita della Santa.*

The specification of the semicircular top and of the saints, and above all the quotation of the form of the signature and date leave no doubt that the picture in question corresponded with no. 700.[3] As the latter is clearly autograph and as no such picture now exists in the church of S. Paolo at Vercelli it may be assumed that the two are identical. The predella mentioned in the document of 1759 is missing.

The inscription on the paper held by S. Paul is evidently the beginning of the fifth chapter of his Epistle to the Romans: *Justificati ergo ex fide, pacem habeamus ad Deum*. . . . The illegible and abbreviated word after 'ad' may therefore be 'Romanos'.

The group of the Madonna and Child recurs in another Lanino altarpiece, from S. Maria delle Grazie at Novara, now in the Brera, Milan. In this work the other figures are different.[4]

DRAWING: Barber Institute, Birmingham University. Cartoon for the upper half of the figures of the Madonna and Child, S. Mary Magdalene and the male saint between the latter and the Virgin. Attributed in the Barber Institute catalogue (1952) to Gaudenzio Ferrari. In view of Lanino's close relations with Gaudenzio such an attribution need not be incompatible with the assumption that the cartoon was used by Lanino for no. 700. The male saint in the cartoon wears a mitre instead of a tiara; otherwise, apart from some simplification in the draperies, it corresponds closely with the painting.

VERSION: Vercelli, Istituto di S. Maria Maddalena. Apparently an old copy.[5]

PROVENANCE: From the altar of S. Maria Maddalena at the church of S. Paolo, Vercelli, where mentioned as late as 1759 (see above). Presumably removed when the church was secularized in 1802.[6] In 1836 in the possession of one G. D. Maggi, a print-seller in Turin.[7] Purchased from G. H. Phillips, London, 1863.

REPRODUCTION: *Illustrations, Italian Schools*, 1937, p. 182.

REFERENCES: (1) Document summarized by A. M. Brizio: *La Pittura in Piemonte*, 1942, p. 228. (2) Kindly communicated by Vittorio Viale in a letter of 25th August, 1947 to Martin Davies, who had initiated the enquiry. In another letter Viale gave the full text of the 1540 contact. (3) The wrong identification of the tiaraed figure with S. Ambrose, the inclusion, in the quotation of the inscription, of the word 'anno' and the spelling 'effigiebat' for 'effigiabat' are clearly slips and of no significance. Right and left in the document are evidently calculated from the Madonna's point of view. (4) Various other heads in no. 700 seem to recur in other works by Lanino, but in view of the obvious limitations of his repertory there seems no point in cataloguing them. (5) Reproduced A. M. Brizio: *Vercelli* (*Catalogo delle Cose d'Arte e di Antichità d'Italia*), 1935, p. 178. (6) A. M. Brizio, *op. cit.* (1935), p. 131. (7) Further archival communication from Vittorio Viale.

BERNARDINO LICINIO
born not later than 1491, still alive 1549

One of a family of artists. Ridolfi,[1] following Vasari, confused the issue by stating that the name Licinio was also borne by the painter Pordenone and that the family as a whole came from Friuli. This mistake was still current in the nineteenth century, but it has since been established[2] that Pordenone's name was not Licinio and that the latter family came, not from the Friuli, but from the village of Poscante (Bergamo). The Licinio family was well established at Murano and at Venice by the end of the fifteenth century, and it is at the latter city that Bernardino is first recorded, in 1511, in a contemporary document as a painter. He is referred to, still at Venice, in subsequent documents, the last being dated 1549. He presumably died some time between then and 1565 since he is not referred to in his brother Zuan Baptista's will of that date.[3] The latter died in 1568, aged 77. This gives the date of his birth as 1491 and, since he was apparently younger than Bernardino, also the *terminus ad quem* for the birth of the latter.[4]

A sufficient number of pictures signed by Bernardino Licinio survives to permit of an estimate of his work which emerges as that of a minor Giorgionesque, following the Giorgione/early Titian tradition in portraiture, and in religious painting predominantly that of Palma Vecchio.

REFERENCES: (1) *Maraviglie*, ed. Hadeln, vol. 1 (1914), pp. 112 ff. (2) By Vincenzo Joppi (*Contributo Terzo alla Storia dell' Arte nel Friuli . . .*, 1892, p. 29) and by G. Ludwig in the Prussian *Jahrbuch*, 1903, *Beiheft*, pp. 44 ff. (3) See Ludwig, *op. cit.*, p. 55. (4) Ludwig, *loc. cit.*

1309 PORTRAIT OF STEFANO NANI

36 × 30⅓ (0·91 × 0·77).

The present discoloured varnish makes a reliable estimate of the condition difficult. Nevertheless it seems in good state.

Inscribed and signed: STEPHANVS | NANI.ABAVRO | XVII. MDXXVIII | .LYCINIVS.P.

The figure XVII in the inscription presumably refers to the sitter's age. According to Frizzoni no member of the Venetian patrician family of Nani bore the christian name Stefano and he suggested in consequence that the inscription meant that the sitter came from the village of Auro in the province of Brescia or alternatively that it was a case of a derivation from the old Venetian name of Orio.[1] Gustav Ludwig found documents showing that Stefano Nani held the post of *Scrivan delle Rason vecchie* in the year 1542 and that he was also *Scrivan* of the *Scuola della Trinità*.[2]

VERSION: Rome, Accademia dei Lincei (from Palazzo Corsini).[3]

PROVENANCE: This or an identical copy was in the Algarotti collection in the eighteenth century.[4] Otherwise first recorded in the Manchester exhibition of 1857 (no. 171, 'Pordenone', lent F. Perkins). George Perkins sale, 14th June, 1890 (43), as Pordenone, where bought for the Gallery.

REPRODUCTION: *Illustrations, Italian Schools*, 1937, p. 185.

REFERENCES: (1) Frizzoni in *Archivio Storico dell' Arte*, 1895, p. 98. Berenson (*Lists*, 1936) gives the sitter's name as Stefano Nani Doria. (2) G. Ludwig in Prussian *Jahrbuch*, 1903, *Beiheft*, p. 56. (3) Berenson, *loc. cit.*, lists this as autograph. (4) *Catalogue des Tableaux . . . de la Galerie du feu Comte Algarotti à Venise*, n.d. The collection was formed by Count Francesco Algarotti and continued by his brother, Bonomo. The latter died in 1776. On page XIX of the catalogue, under the heading 'REGILIO *Jean Antoine* dit *Licinius* & plus communement le *Pordenon*' is a description of a picture exactly corresponding with no. 1309 down to the inscription and the dimensions. It is possible that this may have belonged to Algarotti as early as 1743, since he mentions a 'Pordenone' in a letter of 17th June of that year (published by Posse in the Prussian *Jahrbuch*, 1931, *Beiheft*, p. 42), and this picture does not seem to have been bought by the Saxon king, unlike others discussed in the same context.

3075 MADONNA AND CHILD WITH SS. JOSEPH AND A
      FEMALE MARTYR

C. 27 wide (0·68). Original panel 19⅛ high (0·48) to which narrow
strips of later wood have been added, top and bottom.

Extensively retouched, particularly in the flesh areas. Nevertheless,
the statement in earlier editions of the National Gallery catalogue that
it is 'completely repainted' is a great exaggeration.

As 'Venetian School' in the editions of 1920 onwards. Attributed to
Licinio when in Layard's possession and by Crowe and Cavalcaselle.[1]
Closely related in style to other pictures of the same type, such as
those in the Uffizi,[2] the Piccinelli collection, Bergamo and (formerly)
in the Crespi collection, Milan (Madonna and Child with SS. Joseph,
infant John the Baptist and Anthony of Padua—A. Venturi's catalogue
p. 156). None of these pictures is signed but all are acceptable as
Licinio's.

PROVENANCE: Tanara collection, Verona, from which purchased before 1869
by Sir A. H. Layard.[3] Exh. South Kensington Museum, 1869 (52) (lent Layard).
Layard Bequest, 1916.

REPRODUCTION: *Illustrations, Italian Schools*, 1937, p. 374.

REFERENCES: (1) *Painting in North Italy*, 1912 ed., vol. III, p. 190, note (as
'Venice, Lady Layard'). An ephemeral attribution to Girolamo da Santa Croce
is referred to in earlier editions of the National Gallery catalogue. (2) Reproduced by Venturi, *Storia*, IX, III, p. 479. (3) Layard MSS. in the Gallery
archives.

BERNARDINO LOSCHI
active 1500, died 1540

In a document of 1501 he is referred to as 'M.° Bernardino di M.°
Giacomo Loschi di Parma ora abitante in Carpi'.[1] A triptych at S.
Felice sul Panaro (Modena) is signed 'Bernardinus Luscus Parmensis
Carpi incola Pictor Ill. D. D. Aliberti Pii Carpi 1500'.[2] He is also men-
tioned as court painter to Alberto Pio in documents up to 1522.

REFERENCES: (1) G. Campori: *Gli Artisti Italiani e Stranieri negli Stati
Estensi*, 1855, p. 295. (2) Thieme-Becker, under Loschi, Bernardino.

Ascribed to BERNARDINO LOSCHI

3940 PORTRAIT SAID TO BE OF ALBERTO PIO

Panel, *c.* 23 × 19½ (0·584 × 0·495).

Outside the original panel, of which the dimensions are given above,
there is a band of later wood covered with gilding which impinges *c.* ⅛″
on to the original panel all round.

Repaint stippled on in innumerable small areas but most of the main outlines are probably not significantly changed.

Earlier editions of the catalogue give the inscription on the upper hem of the black tunic as: ALBERTUS PIUS CARPENSIS MDXII. It is now almost illegible and it cannot be guaranteed that it is original. On the dome of the temple on the left are remains of the letters ΔΙΟΝΥΣΩ. The corresponding one on the right, more fragmentary still, seems intended to read ΦΟΙΒΩ. The inscription on the open book in the sitter's hand, damaged like the others, is the Aeneid VI, 724–47—the opening of the prophecy of the future glory of Rome, made by Anchises to his son in the underworld.[1]

In the J. C. Robinson collection as Pintoricchio. An attribution to Peruzzi, first made by J. P. Richter, but subsequently changed by him to 'Lombard School',[2] was tentatively retained in the 1929 catalogue. The clue to the correct attribution would depend to some extent on the authenticity or otherwise of the inscription giving the sitter's name as Alberto Pio and the date 1512.

Alberto Pio, lord of Carpi, was born in 1475 and aimed at making his small court a centre of Humanism,[3] he himself being an accomplished scholar. In the event he spent most of his life outside his own domains and died in exile in 1531. Though the features in no. 3940 do not resemble those in two medals inscribed 'ALBERTVS PIVS DESABAVDIA CARPICOMES' they are not incompatible with those shown in a fresco in the Cappella Pio in the *castello* at Carpi,[4] and seem to agree fairly well with those in a bust which in 1929 still belonged to Principe Pio.[5]

The type of portrait to which no. 3940 belongs, with the sitter shown at half length in front of a parapet flanked by pilasters with a landscape visible between them, was a Florentine development of the opening years of the sixteenth century.[6] By about 1512 it might be expected to have percolated down to the level of the artist of no. 3940. The sitter's costume and hair-style accord well with this date and are in fact a curious combination of Italian and German fashions at that period.[7] As Alberto Pio was acting as the Emperor's ambassador in the years 1511–12 the costume may be regarded as a significant indication of the correctness of the identification. It therefore seems to the present writer more probable than not that the existing inscription, even if not entirely authentic, yet reproduces an authentic one. Alberto Pio, though mainly resident in Rome at this time, seems also to have spent some time at Carpi in the year 1512.

The provincial style of no. 3940 would in any case be more compatible with a Carpian origin than a Roman one, and in point of fact an altarpiece of 1515 at Modena (Galleria Estense), signed by Bernardino Loschi, is sufficiently close in style to no. 3940 to suggest him as author without further ado.[8] Since Loschi was court painter to Alberto Pio at Carpi the argument might therefore be turned at this point by saying that if this attribution is allowed[9] that would in the circumstances be a further indication of the correctness of the identification of the sitter.

The presence in the background of no. 3940 of the Muses, together with a number of fauns, Silenus on his ass, and a fountain, presumably the Castalian Spring, is evidently connected in some way with the Humanist interests of the sitter. Stella Mary Pearce has demonstrated that the symmetrical arrangement of the two temples derives from theatrical scenery.[10] Whether the whole of the background was therefore intended to commemorate some specific theatrical entertainment written by the sitter or performed in his honour is one of several unsolved problems.[11]

PROVENANCE: Sir J. C. Robinson collection (as Pintoricchio). Bought Mond, 1890.[12] Exh. R.A., 1895 (140) (lent Mond). Ludwig Mond Bequest, 1924.

REPRODUCTION: *Illustrations, Italian Schools*, 1937, p. 274.

REFERENCES: (1) This inscription deciphered by E. K. Waterhouse. J. P. Richter (Mond catalogue, II, 1910, p. 471) claimed that the text was intended to represent printing, not manuscript, and went on to see in this an allusion to Alberto's interest in the Aldine press. (2) Mond catalogue, II, 1910, pp. 468–9. Peruzzi had engaged in architectural work for Alberto at Carpi. (3) For this and other biographical data see Tiraboschi: *Biblioteca Modenese*, IV, 1783, pp. 156 ff. (4) For the medals see Hill: *Corpus* nos. 1184 and 1185. The Cappella Pio fresco is reproduced by Litta, and also by Pietro Foresti in *Bollettino d'Arte*, 1912, p. 320. (5) The photograph of this in the Gallery archives was kindly supplied by Principe Pio. There is, however, some doubt whether the sitter is the right Alberto Pio, as there were several of that name. The portrait statue on Alberto's tomb (Louvre) shows him too much later in life to be significant in this context. It may be noted à propos no. 3940 that a good likeness would hardly be to be expected in the circumstances as Alberto seems to have spent very little time at Carpi and Loschi was clearly a very inferior painter. (6) The probable prototype is the *Mona Lisa*, which presumably had the side columns originally since they feature in some of the old copies. (7) Notes by Stella Mary Pearce. (8) The attribution to Loschi was originally suggested by Adolfo Venturi (in a footnote in a review by Frizzoni in *Archivio Storico dell' Arte*, 1898, p. 77. Venturi claimed to have found a monogram BL interlaced. Frizzoni himself later (*L'Arte*, VII, 1904, p. 270) suggested an artist in the territory of the Pio. (9) Among other features which the Modena picture and no. 3940 have in common are the peculiar large dark eyes and a certain tendency for fingers to be depicted in a horizontal position. (10) Among several comparable instances pointed out by her in an unpublished paper kindly put at the disposal of the present writer one particularly relevant to no. 3940 is an illustration of MONS PARNASSUS by Hans von Kulmbach published in Conrad Celtes' *Petri Tritonii Melopoeia Augustae vindelicorum* of 1507. This shows, left and right in the background, small circular temples inscribed as of Minerva and Diana whose figures surmount their domes. In front are the Muses, Silenus, Bacchus and other figures; also a fountain. (11) Another is the identity of the reclining man—apparently in armour—seen dictating to one of the Muses on the right. Also, the relevance of the passage from the Aeneid in the sitter's hand. If this was a pious hope in the resurgence of Carpi from the ravages of war to heights comparable with ancient Rome it would be an extreme instance of local patriotism. The left part of the background of no. 3940 is so rubbed as to be barely legible in parts. Among other details is a figure on a car, presumably Bacchus, in front of Silenus. The figure with sword and shield is evidently Minerva who is almost as far down stage as the Muses. Richter (Mond catalogue) interprets the background as 'an allegory of the expulsion of anarchy'. Richter (*loc. cit.*) further uses the oddity of the fact that the sitter's name is inscribed on no. 3940 but not the name of the artist to support his theory that it was painted for Paolo Giovio's gallery. (12) Richter, Mond catalogue *loc. cit.*

LORENZO LOTTO
born *c.* 1480, still alive September, 1556

The approximate date of his birth is deduced from his will of 1546, in which he describes himself as 'circha' 66 years old. He was apparently from Venice, but led a nomadic life and was active also at Treviso and Bergamo and in various cities of the Marches, particularly Recanati, Jesi, Ancona and Loreto. In 1509 he was in Rome. In 1554 he became an oblate of the Santa Casa at Loreto.

Lotto was influenced at the beginning by Giovanni Bellini, among others, but evolved an individual style at an early stage. There are many signed and dated works.

699 THE PHYSICIAN, GIOVANNI AGOSTINO DELLA TORRE, AND HIS SON, NICCOLÒ

$33\frac{1}{4} \times 26\frac{3}{4}$ (0·844 × 0·68).

The main figure, though thinly painted, is still fairly well preserved. For the condition of the younger figure, in the background, see below. Cleaned 1965.

Signed (on the arm of the chair, bottom right):

L.LOTVS.P. | 1515

The scroll held by the foreground figure in his right hand is inscribed:

Medicorum Esculapio | *Joanni Augustino Ber* | *gomatj*

The letter on the table behind is inscribed:

Dno Nicolao de la tur | *re nobili bergom . . .* | *. . . amicosingmo* | *Bg.mj*

The book held by the main figure inscribed: *Galienus.*

The restoration of 1965 showed that the signature and the date had been at least 'refreshed', though as the date accords with the age of the sitters and with the fashions, as well as with Lotto's development as painter, it may merely augment or replace an authentic original. No. 699 has been changed by restoration on at least three occasions. Some time before 1812, when Zancon's engraving was published, the right hand figure was repainted to include a large circular hat.[1] This is mentioned in the Lechi catalogue of 1824. After the picture entered Morelli's possession in 1859 this figure was again repainted (by the Milanese restorer, Molteni) whose work included replacing the round hat with a smaller one, worn on the back of the head. Most of this repaint was removed in 1965, revealing the remains of the original, with a small hat low down over the right eye. Other arbitrary changes in the costume and background were also removed at this time.

Morelli, to whom the picture belonged at one time, first suggested that the figure on the right (Niccolò) was added later.[2] He deduced, on the flimsiest evidence, that Lotto was in Venice in the year (1515) when no. 699 was painted, and by reiterating the statement made by Zancon (*op. cit.*) to the effect that Giovanni Agostino della Torre was a professor in the university of Padua, he concluded that Lotto called at Padua on his return from Venice to Bergamo in 1515, painted the portrait of Giovanni Agostino there and then took the picture to Bergamo where he added the figure of Niccolò. This theory was supported by Berenson.[3] There is, however, no justification for assuming Lotto's presence in Venice in 1515,[4] and it is certain that Giovanni Agostino della Torre was not then at the university of Padua.[5] In point of fact there can be little doubt that the artist and both sitters were all at Bergamo in the year 1515. Nevertheless this need not refute Morelli's theory that the figure of Niccolò was added later. The placing of the figures in relation to the surround forcibly suggests this, while the occurrence of an after-thought need not also presuppose a lengthy time-lag.[6] Niccolò della Torre was the son of Giovanni Agostino.[7] The latter died in 1535 at the age of 81.[8]

DRAWINGS: Tietze and Tietze-Conrat[9] connect a head of a bearded man in the Uffizi (no. 1876F) with no. 699. Though there seems some similarity of features there is no need to assume either that the Uffizi drawing represents Niccolò della Torre or that it is a study for no. 699. Berenson, indeed (*op. cit.*, 1955, p. 221) dates the drawing some ten years after the painting.

ENGRAVING: Zancon (*loc. cit*), 1812.

PROVENANCE: In 1812 in the possession of General Teodoro Lechi of Brescia (Zancon, *op. cit.*). According to Morelli[10] Lechi had bought it in that year from the della Torre family at Bergamo. No. 31 in the Lechi catalogue of 1824. No. 44 in the Lechi catalogue of 1837. Sold by Lechi, 31st May, 1847,[11] to Count Festetits, Vienna. No. 142 in the sale of the latter's collection, Vienna, 11th April, 1859, where bought by Morelli,[12] from whom purchased, 1862.

REPRODUCTION: *Illustrations, Italian Schools*, 1937, p. 200.

REFERENCES: (1) *Galleria Inedita*, 1812, tavola XIV. Morelli suggested (MS. quoted by Frizzoni in *Archivio Storico dell' Arte*, 1896, p. 24) that this was due to a seventeenth-century restoration. For detailed descriptions of the vicissitudes of the various restorations see Cecil Gould: *Lorenzo Lotto and the Double Portrait*, in *Saggi e Memorie di Storia dell'Arte*, 5, 1966, pp. 45 ff. See also R. Bassi-Rathgeb in *L'Arte*, January–June, 1959. According to this scholar the picture was restored by one Speri of Brescia after Lechi bought it. (2) *Munich and Dresden*, 1893, p. 51, note 1. (3) Monograph of 1895, p. 138. Italian edition of 1955, p. 53. (4) Berenson (*op. cit.*, 1955, p. 52) admitted that Morelli's evidence for Lotto's stay in Venice in 1515 was inadmissible. (5) Frizzoni (*Archivio Storico dell' Arte*, 1896, p. 23, note 2) stated that no Giovanni Agostino da Bergamo figured in the registers of the university of Padua. Furthermore, the university was closed in 1509 as a result of the war and no professor of medicine was nominated until 1518. (6) Banti (*Lotto*, 1953, p. 71) rejects the theory of Niccolò's being an after-thought *consentendo all'unità di tempo per tutto il dipinto.* (7) Frizzoni, *loc. cit.* Zancon, *loc. cit.*, had referred to them as brothers. (8) Frizzoni, *loc. cit.* (9) *Drawings of the Venetian Painters*, 1944, p. 185. (10) MS. quoted by Frizzoni, *loc. cit.* (11) Information supplied by Conte Fausto Lechi, 1950. (12) *Loc. cit.*

1047 FAMILY GROUP

45¼ × 55 (1·149 × 1·397).

On the whole in reliable condition. A certain amount of local retouching. Signed: .L.Lotto. This signature does not appear in the (nineteenth century) engravings of the picture (see ENGRAVINGS below), but it gives no indication of being a forgery.

No. 1047 has been associated with the following entry in Lotto's account book: *A dì 23 settembre del 47 die dar el sopradito misser Zuane de la Volta mio patron di casa per un quadro de picture, con el suo retrato de naturale et la dona con doi fioli tutu insema cioè n. 4—qual quadro era iudicato e per bontà e per colori finissimi con el coperto suo sul timpano duc. 50.*[1]

The specification merely of a man and his wife and two children would not of itself be sufficient to link document and picture. But the inclusion in the document of the date—1547—constitutes a further indication, since the costumes in no. 1047 certainly date from about then (cf. for example, closely comparable female costumes in the frescoes of music-making ladies and gentlemen painted by Niccolò dell' Abate between 1547 and 1552 in the university at Bologna).[2] These considerations, combined with the fact that no other portrait group by Lotto of a married couple and two children is known, would render the identification of the subject of no. 1047 with the family of Giovanni della Volta a plausible possibility.

ENGRAVINGS: 1. By Ricciani. No. 112 in *Choix de Gravures à l'Eau Forte . . . de la Galerie de Lucien Bonaparte*, 1812 (does not reproduce the signature on the painting). 2. By Cristofani, in Rosini: *Storia della Pittura Italiana*, epoca terza (1845), pl. CXXXVI (there stated to be in England). As in no. 1 the signature is omitted.

PROVENANCE: No. 170 ('Carlo Lotto—His Own Family') in the original catalogue (1812) of the Lucien Bonaparte collection.[3] No. 171 (again under this heading), Lucien Bonaparte sale, 6th February *et seq.*, 1815. Lot 160, Lucien Bonaparte sale, 14th May *et seq.*, 1816. Lot 31 ('Portrait of the Artist with his Wife and Children') in the sale of 'Edward Solly, esq., Deceased', 8th May, 1847, as from Lucien Bonaparte's collection.[4] Presumably bought in. Bequeathed by Miss Sarah Solly, 1879.

REPRODUCTION: *Illustrations, Italian Schools*, 1937, p. 201.

REFERENCES: (1) Extracts from Lotto's account book were published in *Le Gallerie Nazionali Italiane*, I (1894), pp. 115–224. Part of the entry quoted here is given on p. 126 of that publication, but it is given in fuller detail in Berenson's monograph on Lotto, 1955, p. 165 (Italian edition). Recently (1969) the book has been fully published, ed. P. Zampetti. The entry in question is on p. 98 of this edition. (2) Reproduced in Venturi: *Storia . . . IX*, vi, pp. 600–1. Berenson (*loc. cit.*) specifically says that it was the costumes in no. 1047 which caused him to revise his earlier dating of the picture to 1523 (1895 edition of his monograph, p. 194). (3) Printed in W. Buchanan's *Memoirs of Painting*, vol. II (1824), pp. 288–94. (4) The signature—'L. Lotto'—is mentioned on this occasion as also in an undated 'Descriptive catalogue of the Collection of Italian Pictures of the Raffaelle Period of the late Edward Solly, Esq.' in which no. 1047 figures as no. XIII.

1105 THE PROTHONOTARY APOSTOLIC, GIOVANNI GIULIANO

37 × 28⅛ (0·94 × 0·714).[1]

Good condition in general. Some retouching, notably round the sitter's right eye.

The two letters in front of the sitter are both inscribed:
Al Rdo monsig Juliano proton . . . aptico | dgmo S. . . . | a Padua | al borgo dogni santj[2]

G. F. Hill[3] drew attention to a portrait medal in the Museo Civico at Brescia inscribed IOANNES. IVLIANVS. PROTONOTARIVS. APOSTOLICVS which clearly represents the same sitter. He also quoted passages in Sanudo's diary relative to the sitter, viz.:

1504. Zuan Zulian, Son of Ser Marco, mentioned as *cubicolario del Papa*.

1517. The prothonotary Zuan Zulian benefited under the will of Pietro Grimani.

1518. He entertained Antonio Pucci on his way to Rome.[4]

No. 1105 has been generally attributed to Lotto[5] except by Longhi, who proposed Moretto as author instead.[6] This attribution has found little support[7] and is unacceptable on stylistic grounds—no. 1105, although differing in conception from the run of Lotto's portraits, shows many features of handling closely comparable with signed works.[8]

The *Catholic Encyclopaedia* (1911) gives the following definition of a Prothonotary Apostolic: 'member of the highest college of prelates in the Roman Curia, . . . also . . . the honorary prelates on whom the pope has conferred this title and its special privileges'.

PROVENANCE: Purchased from M. Guggenheim, Venice, 1881.

REPRODUCTION: *Illustrations, Italian Schools*, 1937, p. 200.

REFERENCES: (1) Dimensions of outside of stretcher. The original canvas turn-over still exists and is roughly painted. (2) The elaborate abbreviations cannot be printed, but the three words mainly affected are clearly 'protonotario', 'apostolico' and 'degnissimo'. It has been suggested that the illegible words are 'se ascriva' (for 'si indirizzi'). This would make good sense, though at the cost of twisting the letters somewhat. (3) *Burlington Magazine*, vol. 29 (1916), p. 245. (4) Hill quoted two more entries from Sanudo—one of 1519 referring to a Zuan Zulian, canonico Cenedese, and one of 1528, mentioning a 'prelate Zulian'—but pointed out that it could not be established that they referred to the prothonotary. (5) E.g. by Berenson (monographs of 1895 and 1955), Borenius (edition of Crowe and Cavalcaselle's *Painting in North Italy*, vol. iii (1912), p. 428) and A. Venturi (*Storia* IX, iv, p. 43). (6) In *Pinacotheca*, 1928-9, p. 270. Reasserted in *Viatico* . . ., p. 62. (7) The attribution is supported, unsurprisingly, in Banti and Boschetto: *Lotto*, 1953, p. 107. (8) Cf., for example, the landscape with that in no. 1047 of this Gallery. It may be added that if no. 1105 were by Moretto it would have to be an early work, as Longhi admitted. The (very slight) indications afforded by the costume, however (notes by Stella Mary Pearce in the Gallery archives), would tend to favour a date not before the 1530's. Berenson (*Lotto*, 1955) dates no. 1105 *c.* 1519/20.

2281 VIRGIN AND CHILD, WITH SS. JEROME AND ANTHONY OF PADUA

Canvas,[1] $35\frac{1}{4} \times 29\frac{1}{4}$ (0·895 × 0·743).
Much worn and restored.

The signature has clearly been tampered with. In its present state it reads: (?)*Lo* (or *u*)*renti–* (the letter after the *i* may be *u* and *s* run together) *Lotto | 1521*. It seems probable that *some* signature was always on the picture—perhaps of the form *Laurentius Lotus*, which is that used on another version (Costa di Mezzate, see below)—but in their present state both signature and date are unreliable.

The present inferior appearance of no. 2281 seems partly due to its bad condition. Another version, almost identical, but superior in quality is in the Museum of Fine Arts, Boston, Mass. (from the R. M. Dawkins collection).

A picture dated 1522 (Contesse Giuseppina and Maria Edvige Camozzi, Costa di Mezzate)[2] of slightly smaller dimensions (0·74 × 0·68) repeats the Virgin and Child group of no. 2281, but substitutes SS. John the Baptist and Catherine of Alexandria and also omits the landscape background.

VERSIONS: Costa di Mezzate and Boston, Mass. (see above).

PROVENANCE: Catalogued by Berenson (*Lotto*, 1895, p. 187) as in the possession of Mrs. Martin Colnaghi. Exh. R.A., 1908 (28), lent Martin Colnaghi, by whom bequeathed, 1908.

REPRODUCTION: *Illustrations, Italian Schools*, 1937, p. 202.

REFERENCES: (1) Catalogued since entering the Gallery as on panel, but it is on canvas now and there is no record of its having been transferred. Before entering the Gallery it was catalogued as on canvas in the R.A. winter exhibition, 1908. The vertical crack through the Child's body suggests at first that the picture had originally been on panel, but other factors indicate the opposite. (2) No. 47 in the Lotto exhibition, Venice, 1953, in the catalogue of which reproduced.

4256 A LADY AS LUCRETIA

$37\frac{3}{4} \times 43\frac{1}{2}$ (0·959 × 1·105).

Canvas, probably transferred from panel, and probably somewhat cut down.

The orange parts of the dress and the background damaged and retouched. Otherwise quite well preserved. Cleaned 1964–5.

Inscribed on the paper: NEC VLLA IMPVDICA LV | CRETIÆ EXEMPLO VIVET.[1] (Livy, I, 58). Attributed in the nineteenth century to Giorgione. The Lotto attribution, which cannot be doubted, was first made by Crowe and Cavalcaselle.[2] Entitled 'Lucretia' in the 1929 catalogue and elsewhere.[3] The practice of allegorical or 'fancy' portraiture was more common in the seventeenth and eighteenth centuries than in the sixteenth. In one sixteenth-century prototype—Bronzino's *Andrea Doria as Neptune* (Milan, Brera)—the sitter assumed the dress, or undress, of the mythological character in question. In another— no. 24 of this Gallery—a lady in her ordinary clothes is shown with the attributes of S. Agatha. In no. 4256 the lady, for the moment, is identifying herself with Lucretia (represented in the drawing in her left hand) in order to assert her virtue, and points to the inscription on the table to emphasize her sentiment.[4] The costume in no. 4256 unequivocally indicates a date around the year 1530.[5] In view of this, and of the Pesaro provenance, the sitter was probably Lucrezia Valier, who married Benedetto Francesco Giuseppe di Gerolamo Pesaro in 1533.[6] The picture as a whole is pre-eminently of the type which has been claimed, and justifiably, as an influence on the young Caravaggio.[7]

VERSION: Old copy mentioned by Crowe and Cavalcaselle in the Liechtenstein collection (Crowe and Cavalcaselle, *loc. cit.*).

DRAWINGS: Venturi[8] drew attention to a female head formerly in the Oppenheimer collection. Facially it resembles the sitter of no. 4256 but the costume is different and no support seems to have been found for the attribution of it to Lotto. The same applies to a drawing published by Suida.[9]

PROVENANCE: Identifiable with no. 39 in the inventory of Palazzo Pesaro, Venice, October, 1797—*Giorgione, bella copia, Donna con ritratto di Lucrezia in mano 2·9 × 3·3*—and with the 'Portrait of a woman (h. l) holding in her left hand a drawing of Lucretia stabbing herself by Giorgione' mentioned in a letter of 20th November, 1828 from James Irvine in Venice, who had recently bought it from the Abate Celotti.[10] Lent (as Giorgione) to B.I., 1854 (46) by Sir James Carnegie (Lord Southesk) of Kinnaird Castle, Brechin, from whom bought, 1855, by R. S. Holford.[11] Exh. R.A., 1887 (124) as Lotto (lent R. S. Holford), Grafton Galleries ('Fair Women'), 1894 (9) (lent Captain G. L. Holford), New Gallery (Venetian Art), 1894–5 (218) (lent Captain G. L. Holford), Grosvenor Gallery, 1913–14 (48) (lent Sir G. L. Holford). Lot 68, Sir G. L. Holford sale, Christie's, 15th July, 1927, where purchased with the aid of gifts from the Benson family and from the N.A.-C.F. Exh. National Gallery (N.A.-C.F. exhibition), 1945–6 (17).

REPRODUCTION: *Illustrations, Italian Schools*, 1937, p. 201.

REFERENCES: (1) The *o* of *exemplo* seems originally to have been an *m*. (2) *North Italy*, vol. II (1871), pp. 159–60 and 532 '. . . displays the well-known smorphia and affectation of Lotto'. Banti and Boschetto (*Lotto*, 1953, p. 83) are wrong in ascribing a Cariani attribution to Crowe and Cavalcaselle. (3) E.g. in the catalogue by R. F. Benson of the Holford collection. (4) 'The lady doth protest too much, methinks' as Hamlet's mother remarked. Though there is not, so far as is known, any evidence that no. 4256 was painted to counteract the impugning of the sitter's virtue attention may be drawn to a comparable allegorical portrait of the seventeenth century—Van Dyck's *Lady Venetia Digby as Prudence* (Windsor). Lady Venetia was notoriously imprudent. (5) Berenson (*Lotto*, 1955, p. 133): 'non è anteriore al 1529/30'. A detailed analysis of the costume by Stella Mary Pearce is in the Gallery archives. (6) M. Jaffé: *Burlington Magazine*, 1971, pp. 696 ff. (7) See W. Friedländer: *Caravaggio Studies*, 1955, pp. 44 ff. (8) *Storia* IX, iv, pp. 87–8. (9) *Pantheon*, 1928, p. 531. (10) Jaffé *op. cit.* (11) Date of purchase from Christie's sale catalogue, 15th July, 1927 (68).

GIAN FRANCESCO DE' MAINERI
recorded from 1489 to 1506

Always referred to in contemporary documents as a native of Parma and signed his pictures as such. The documents show that he was employed at the Este court at Ferrara and by the Gongaza at Mantua. A letter of 1504 describes him as a miniaturist and painter in connection with an undertaking by him to finish an altarpiece begun by Ercole de' Roberti. A signed *Holy Family* (of which many replicas exist) was formerly in the Testa collection, Ferrara. A head of the Baptist, also signed, is in the Brera. These works reveal appreciable influence of Ercole de' Roberti and rather less of Mantegna.

Literature: In addition to the references given in the article in Thieme-Becker see Luzio: *La Galleria dei Gonzaga . . .*, 1913, pp. 196–7.

See COSTA and (?) MAINERI, No. 1119.

Damiano MAZZA
active 1573

Mentioned by Ridolfi[1] as a follower of Titian and as a native of Padua. A document quoted by Hadeln[2] records payment to him in 1573 for an altarpiece in the church at Noale (Veneto). This picture is still in position and is in a markedly Titianesque style. Pictures mentioned by Ridolfi as Mazza's which are still identifiable are a *Coronation of the Virgin* in the church of the Ospedale di SS. Giovanni e Paolo in Venice and, perhaps, no. 32 below.

REFERENCES: (1) Ridolfi/Hadeln, I, pp. 223–4. (2) Article in *Zeitschrift für bildende Kunst*, 1913, pp. 249–54.

Ascribed to Damiano MAZZA

32 THE RAPE OF GANYMEDE

Octagon enlarged to rectangle.[1] The eight sides of the original octagon are each about 28″ (0·71) long. The rectangle measures $69\frac{3}{4} \times 73\frac{1}{2}$ (1·77 × 1·866). Cleaned 1955.

Good condition in general. There has been a vertical tear running down from half way along the under side of the eagle's left wing. In the 1929 catalogue as 'School of Titian'. The attribution to Damiano Mazza, first made, tentatively, by Crowe and Cavalcaselle,[2] and later, more emphatically, by Hadeln,[3] depends on identifying no. 32 with a ceiling painting mentioned by Ridolfi[4] as having been in a pavilion at Casa Assonica, Padua, and as the work of Damiano Mazza. Ridolfi describes it as representing Ganymede carried off by the eagle and as of such high quality as to be mistaken for a Titian. No. 32 was in Palazzo Colonna in Rome during the eighteenth century and may therefore be identified with a *Rape of Ganymede* specified by Mariette[5] as the work of Titian, as having been engraved by G. Audran and as having entered the Colonna possession through the marriage of the 'connétable . . . avec l'héritière de la maison Salviati'. The Audran engraving in question is after no. 32. The marriage was evidently that between Fabrizio Colonna and Caterina Salviati which took place, according to Litta, in 1717. No. 32 can thus be identified with the

'Ganimede di Titiano' mentioned as belonging to Duca Salviati at Rome in a guide book of 1664.[6] Even if Ridolfi's information is correct (and the date of his work—1648—is far from constituting first-rate documentation in regard to Mazza) it would be necessary to find a connection between the Ganymede ceiling at Padua before 1648 which was by Damiano Mazza but could be mistaken for a Titian and the first certain mention of no. 32—at Rome as 'Titian' before 1664. The fact that no. 32, though strongly Titianesque (comparable in design with the Salute ceiling decorations from S. Spirito and in format with the *Historia* of the Biblioteca Marciana) was clearly not painted by him, that it was evidently intended for a ceiling and that Ridolfi's use of the past tense ('vedevasi') suggests that the Assonica picture was no longer *in situ* at the time when he wrote, renders an assumption of identity very tempting. A further link, though an imperfect one, exists in a remark in Mündler's note-book[7] that a picture seen by him at Padua in 1856 was a replica of no. 32 and that the owner attributed it to Damiano Mazza. While it is possible that the owner's attribution was due not to a geniune local tradition but to speculative identification with Ridolfi's account the present writer is led to conclude that the attribution of no. 32 to Mazza, though not demonstrated, is yet a plausible possibility. Whether or not the design is due in some or any degree to Titian cannot be determined.

The Ganymede legend is given in different forms by different classical writers, but one of the chief variables—whether or not the eagle was Jupiter himself in disguise—is irrelevant to no. 32 or to other well-known *cinquecento* representations of the subject, such as Correggio's or Michelangelo's.

VERSION: Sketch copy at Windsor (6741). A painted copy, anonymous sale, Christie's, 17th February, 1961 (76), later chez Kisters, Kreuzlingen.

ENGRAVINGS: By G. Audran (octagonal) and Dom. Cunego (1770) (rectangular).

PROVENANCE: Mentioned by Mariette as in Palazzo Colonna, Rome (see above). No. 120 ('opera celebre di Titiano') in the Colonna catalogue of 1783. A MS. note (? early nineteenth century) against this entry in a copy of the latter catalogue in the possession of E. K. Waterhouse reads 'venduto a Gio. de Rossi' who may therefore have been an intermediary for Alexander Day who exhibited the picture, with others, in London in 1800–1.[8] Bought by Angerstein, May, 1801.[9] Purchased with the Angerstein collection, 1824.

REPRODUCTION: *Illustrations, Italian Schools*, 1937, p. 358.

REFERENCES: (1) Ramdohr (*Ueber Mahlerei . . . in Rom*, II, 1787, p. 72) accuses Carlo Maratti of having made the sky too blue during a restoration, but there is no evidence that the enlargement was also due to him. (2) *Titian*, vol. II (1877), p. 459. An attribution to Tintoretto is made in J. B. S. Holborn: *Tintoretto*, 1903, pp. 34–5. (3) *Zeitschrift für bildende Kunst*, 1913, p. 252. Also E. Tietze-Conrat in *Art Bulletin*, 1945, p. 271. (4) Ridolfi/Hadeln, I, p. 224. Francesco Assonica was a friend of Titian's and possessed pictures by him. See Vasari/Milanesi, VII, 456, and Cicogna: *Inscrizioni . . .*, iii, 152. (5) *Abecedario*, V, p. 321. (6) Bellori (?): *Nota delli Musei, Librerie, Galerie . . . di Roma*, 1664, p. 49. (7) In the Gallery archives. (8) W. Buchanan: *Memoirs*, II (1824), p. 4. (9) Farington Diary, 7th May, 1801 (vol. 1, p. 308).

Lodovico MAZZOLINO
active 1504–1524

Ferrarese School. Vasari says he was a pupil of Costa, but the context does not inspire confidence and in any case Costa seems to have spent little of his working life in Ferrara where Mazzolino's early work was executed. There are several signed and dated works and others only dated. From elements in Ercole Roberti and Costa, modified, apparently, by influence from Dosso, Mazzolino evolved a style chiefly adapted to religious paintings on a small scale. Active mainly at Ferrara, where he was employed by the Este. In 1524 he was working at Bologna. The fundamental modern reference work is an article by Adolfo Venturi in *Archivio Storico dell'Arte*, 1890, p. 447.

82 MADONNA AND CHILD WITH SS. JOSEPH, ELIZABETH, FRANCIS AND THE INFANT JOHN THE BAPTIST

Panel, arched top,[1] $20\frac{7}{8} \times 15\frac{1}{2}$ (0·529 × 0·393).
Good condition. Cleaned 1959.
Pentimenti in the architectural background suggest that an earlier idea was for two arches (with a round window between) supported by three twisted columns.

The presence of the monkey on the left may explain a remark in the J. Humble sale catalogue (11th April, 1812): *Probably painted to oblige a particular religious order, as there is a Satyrical allusion in it to the Monkish dissensions of that day.* Inasmuch as the pun would not work in Italian some other interpretation of the symbolism of the monkey would have to be sought, and in fact the general meaning seems fairly clear. There is abundant evidence of the monkey's standing in Christian iconography as a symbol of evil[2] and the fact that he is here shown taking fright at the lamb, which is a common symbol of the Passion, would indicate that he foresees the subjugation of evil through the Passion of Christ.

PROVENANCE: Stated in the MS. inventory (in the Gallery archives) of the Holwell Carr collection to have come from the Palazzo Durazzo, Genoa.[3] J. Humble sale, Christie's, 11th April, 1812 (58) where bought Holwell Carr, who lent it to the British Institution, 1823 (147). Holwell Carr Bequest, 1831.

REPRODUCTION: *Illustrations, Italian Schools*, 1937, p. 226.

REFERENCES: (1) Later wood has been added at the top to make up a rectangle. (2) See H. W. Janson: *Apes and Ape Lore*, 1952. (3) In the 1929 catalogue the picture is stated to have come from the Lercari Palace, Genoa, to have been imported by Wilson in 1806 and sold by Coxe in 1807. In fact this information seems really to apply to no. 169 of this Gallery.

169 THE TRINITY WITH THE MADONNA, SS. JOSEPH AND NICHOLAS OF TOLENTINO AND ANGELS

Panel, $31\frac{3}{4} \times 24\frac{1}{4}$ (0·803 × 0·606).
Apparently in good condition.

PROVENANCE: According to the 1847 catalogue (by Wornum) of the National Gallery from the Lecari Palace, Genoa (this apparently a mistake for Lercari), and therefore presumably identical with a picture imported from Italy by A. Wilson and sold in 1807 by Peter Coxe (*27. Mazzolino di Ferrara. The Holy Family with St Francis. From the Lecari Palace . . .*).[1] Purchased from William Beckford, 1839.

REPRODUCTION: *Illustrations, Italian Schools*, 1937, p. 225.

REFERENCE: (1) Buchanan: *Memoirs*, II (1824), p. 200. The incorrect identification of S. Nicholas of Tolentino with S. Francis apparently explains why some of the provenance of no. 169 (i.e. Lercari, Wilson and Coxe) is wrongly included in that of Mazzolino no. 82 in the National Gallery catalogue of 1929.

641 CHRIST AND THE WOMAN TAKEN IN ADULTERY

Panel, arched top, $18\frac{1}{8} \times 12\frac{1}{8}$ (0·46 × 0·307).

Somewhat worn, and made up in places. Spotty remains of old varnish. On the step on the right is the date—15xxii (apparently: the last figure is dim).

An inscription on the back reads: *No. 270. DEL / MAZZOLINO / From the Aldobrandini Palace Rome / and / Fonthill Abbey*.

PROVENANCE: Aldobrandini Palace from before 1603.[1] William Beckford, Fonthill (no. 71 on the 7th day—15th October—in proposed sale of 1822 which did not take place), no. 178 on 25th day—11th October—of sale of 1823, bought 'Smith',[2] evidently in fact bought in on this occasion as it appears as lot 41 'from the Aldobrandini Palace' in the Beckford sale, 20, Lansdown Crescent, Bath, 3rd day, 26th July, 1848. Exh. B.I., 1849 (136), lent Thomas Stokes: catalogued as 'The Reproof' by Mazzolino di Ferrara. Thomas Stokes sale, 7th July, 1853 (56, specified as ex-Aldobrandini and ex-Beckford, bought Smith).[3] Purchased with the Beaucousin collection, 1860.

REPRODUCTION: *Illustrations, Italian Schools*, 1937, p. 226.

REFERENCES: (1) 1603 inventory, no. 270 (*Palatino*, 1964, p. 208). 1626 inventory, no. 136 (*Arte Antica e Moderna*, 1960, p. 433). 1682 inventory, no. 477 (*Arte Antica e Moderna*, 1963, p. 175). Also undated inventory (before 1665), no. 270 (*Palatino*, 1964, p. 208). (2) According to Redford: *Art Sales*, vol. 2 (1888), p. 239. (3) Redford, p. 240.

1495 CHRIST DISPUTING WITH THE DOCTORS

Panel, $12\frac{1}{4} \times 8\frac{3}{4}$ (0·31 × 0·227).

Good condition.

The Hebrew inscription is stated to read 'The house which Solomon built unto the Lord'.

Mazzolino painted this subject on many occasions but the other versions differ in design. The most important is a full-size altarpiece at Berlin, dated 1524, which has some similarities in arrangement to no. 1495. There is a further, smaller, version at Berlin of which replicas are stated to have been in the Northbrook collection and in the Capitoline Museum, Rome. Another is in the Doria collection, Rome, and others are referred to in the Dawson Turner sale (14th May, 1852, lot 53)[1] in the collection, in 1890, of the Marchese Fransoni, Florence[2] and in the hands of F. Bonnemaison in 1811.[3] Drawings of this subject attributed to Mazzolino are in the British Museum and the Albertina.

PROVENANCE: Stated[4] to have come from the Bardini collection, Florence. Purchased from Agnew, 1897.

REPRODUCTION: *Illustrations, Italian Schools*, 1937, p. 225.

REFERENCES: (1) Reproduced in Dawson Turner's *Outlines in Lithography*, 1840, p. 49. (2) See Adolfo Venturi in *Archivio Storico dell' Arte*, 1890, p. 462. (3) See the Penrice Letters, p. 18. (4) In the 1920 edition of the National Gallery catalogue.

3114 THE NATIVITY

Panel, $15\frac{1}{2} \times 13\frac{1}{2}$ (0·394 × 0·343).

A good deal of the foliage of the central tree and of the area between the Virgin and the shepherd (including the ox) is repainted, evidently as a result of serious damage to the panel. Retouching also in most of the flesh areas.

The style differs appreciably from that of the mature (and more mannered) Mazzolino, and the assumption that the picture is an early work (which is reasonable) is strengthened by similarities between certain parts of the landscape and corresponding features in a triptych at Berlin which is dated 1509 and is unmistakably by Mazzolino. On the back is the Costabili brand C.G.B.C. (in two places) and the number 129.

PROVENANCE: Costabili collection, Ferrara.[1] Bought by Layard[2] who lent it to the South Kensington Museum, 1869 (11). Layard Bequest, 1916.

REPRODUCTION: *Illustrations, Italian Schools*, 1937, p. 224.

REFERENCES: (1) Laderchi: *Descrizione* . . ., I (1838), no. 90. (2) No. 51 in his MS. note-book in the Gallery archives.

ALTOBELLO MELONE
active 1516–18

School of Cremona. A fresco of the *Flight into Egypt* in Cremona cathedral is signed Altobellus de Melonibus and dated 1517. Two other frescoes in the same series are also signed, and a further one bears the same date (1517) The contracts (of 1516 and 1518) for these frescoes were published by Federico Sacchi.[1] The frescoes are also mentioned by Vasari[2] who further speaks of a chapel frescoed by Altobello at S. Agostino, Cremona and a painting in the Corte Vecchia, Milan.[3] The Anonimo Morelliano refers to Altobello as 'discepolo de Armanin'.[4] The style of the Cremona frescoes leaves little or no doubt that the Anonimo meant Romanino.[5] The influence of Boccaccio Boccaccino is also apparent.

Of the few panel pictures reasonably attributable to Altobello no. 753 of this Gallery is probably the most important.

REFERENCES: (1) *Notizie Pittoriche Cremonesi*, 1872, pp. 182–6. As Cremona used the Florentine date system the date—13th March, 1517—of the second contract would be 1518 n.s. (2) Vasari/Milanesi VI, p. 459. (3) Vasari/Milanesi VI, p. 492. L. Grassi (*Proporzioni*, III, 1950, pp. 143 ff.) attributes the S. Agostino frescoes to Pietro da Cemmo. The Milan painting no longer exists. (4) Ed. Frimmel, 1888, p. 44. (5) For some discussion, detailed, but controversial, of the Altobello/Romanino relationship, see Ferdinando Bologna in *Burlington Magazine*, 97, 1955, pp. 240–50.

753 THE WALK TO EMMAUS

Panel, painted area *c.* $57\frac{1}{4} \times 56\frac{3}{4}$ ($1 \cdot 455 \times 1 \cdot 442$).

The panel extends about another 2″ on either side.

Condition fair. Somewhat damaged by past flaking, most noticeably in the cloak of the figure on the spectator's right. Cleaned 1973, to reveal that the cloaks of both disciples, and the feet of the right hand one had been overpainted in the nineteenth century. This overpaint was then removed.

Christ is shown as a pilgrim with hat, staff and shell.[1] In the background He is shown again, this time between the other two, approaching the village of Emmaus. The biblical source for the episode is Luke xxiv, 13–35.

The attribution of no. 753 to Altobello Melone cannot be demonstrated before the mid-seventeenth century,[2] but making allowance for the difference of medium it accords well in style with Altobello's frescoes in Cremona cathedral, particularly with the *Flight into Egypt* which is a signed work.[3]

VERSION: An old copy on canvas was in 1950 at Locko Park, Derbyshire. Later at Bob Jones University.

PROVENANCE: From the Carmelite church of S. Bartolomeo at Cremona where first mentioned in 1627.[4] Giuseppe Aglio (1794) specifies that since the suppression of the church it had entered the Fraganeschi collection[5]; a label bearing the name Fraganeschi is still visible on the back of the picture.[6] The Fraganeschi collection was housed at Villa Rocca, Cremona.[7] Seen in 1856 by Otto Mündler in the possession of Conte Castelbarco at Milan,[8] from whom purchased 1864.[9]

REPRODUCTION: *Illustrations, Italian Schools*, 1937, p. 228 (before cleaning: photograph after cleaning in article by the present writer, *Burlington Magazine*, 1974.)

REFERENCES: (1) Stella Mary Pearce, in notes in the Gallery archives, draws attention to analogies between Christ's pilgrim dress in no. 753 and those in the Marziale *Supper at Emmaus* of 1507 (Berlin). As Marziale had spent some time at Cremona there may be some positive connection here. (2) F. Baldinucci: *Notizie dei Professori* . . . 1846 ed., II, pp. 68–9. (3) Ferdinando Bologna (*Burlington Magazine*, 97, 1955, p. 249) places no. 753 'at the beginning of [Altobello's] last phase' (whenever that may be) 'if, for no other reason, because of the close analogy between the gestures of the hands' in it and in the Cremona *Last Supper*. (4) See Federico Sacchi: *Notizie Pittoriche Cremonesi*, 1872, pp. 132–3. The document in question is a letter of 24th June, 1627 from Cardinal Pietro Campori, bishop of Cremona, to the Padre Generale of the Carmelites informing him that he had recently had an 'immagine, chiamata dei SS. Pellegrini . . . tavola antica' in the church of S. Bartolomeo removed temporarily from the church in order to be copied. The painter's name is not specified, but from subsequent descriptions such as Baldinucci's (*loc. cit.*) or Zaist's (*Notizie Istoriche de' Pittori Cremonesi*, 1774, I, p. 61) it seems clear that the picture was no. 753. As the copy which the Cardinal had had made is specified as on *canvas* it may be identical with the Locko picture (see Version below) which is also on canvas. The latter in any case may be the picture referred to at Locko by Waagen (*Galleries and Cabinets* . . ., 1857, p. 497) . . . 'Vincenzo Catena.— To this master I attribute a capital picture of very original conception, of Christ with the disciples at Emmaus. S. James is here represented as aged. The figures two-thirds life-size'. (5) *Le Pitture e le Sculture della Città di Cremona*, pp. 183–4. (6) The label reads 'Di Altobello Melone del 1530 assai bello e conservato Fraganeschi'. The date, 1530, may be an allusion to the statement of Orlandi (*Abecedario Pittorico*, 1763, p. 52) that Altobello 'fioriva circa il 1530'. (7) Sacchi, *op. cit.* p. X. (8) Mündler's note-books in the Gallery archives. (9) It was not exhibited until the end of 1866, having in the meantime been restored by Molteni at Milan (Sacchi, *loc. cit.*). In the meantime, also, the death had occurred of the Director, Sir Charles Eastlake, at Pisa on 24th December, 1865. For details of Molteni's restoration, see article by the present writer, *Burlington Magazine*, 1974.

MICHELANGELO
1475–1564

Michelangelo Buonarroti. Florentine school, but gradually worked more and more in Rome, in the direct employ of successive popes. His early works were primarily in sculpture and for the last twenty-odd years of his life he was active chiefly as architect. His principal paintings are three great works in fresco—two in the Sistine chapel and one in the Pauline chapel of the Vatican. The 'official' biography published by Condivi during Michelangelo's lifetime (1553) and the one in the second edition (1568) of Vasari consitute a large corpus of mainly reliable information.

Writing from the point of view of a contemporary Vasari considered Michelangelo the greatest artist both of modern times and Antiquity, and planned his monumental history to lead up to him as its apex. Posterity did not fully endorse this verdict, and during the seventeenth and eighteenth centuries Michelangelo's reputation declined, as Reynolds pointed out in the Fifth Discourse (1772). During the past century the tide has turned again.

The vast Michelangelo literature is summarized in Steinmann and Wittkower's *Michelangelo—Bibliographie* (1927); later bibliographies in successive volumes of C. de Tolnay's monograph (1943–).

790 THE ENTOMBMENT (unfinished)

Panel, painted surface $63\frac{2}{3} \times 59$ (1·61 × 1·49).[1]

A good deal of local damage, probably caused by neglect in the past. The head, bare shoulders and exposed arm and leg of the bearer on the spectator's left of Christ are the best preserved passages. Cleaned 1968–9.

The moment depicted is the halt before the Entombment.

In previous editions of the National Gallery catalogue the beardless

figure who supports Christ's body on the spectator's right has been
said to be S. Mary Magdalene. But the breadth of the shoulders and
the height are those of a man, also the function depicted—manual
labour. Therefore S. John. And the woman squatting, bottom left,
therefore S. Mary Magdalene, not Mary Salome, and finally the bearer
on the spectator's left Nicodemus, not S. John. The bald man supporting
Christ's body from the back is unchanged as S. Joseph of Arimathaea,
and the outlined figure, kneeling facing inwards on the right (clearer in
the Siena sketch copy, for which see below) unchanged as the Virgin
Mary. The female behind her on the extreme right either Mary Salome
or Mary the sister of Martha.

Ascribed to Michelangelo as early as 1697, and acceptable as his work
to the present writer, as well as to a number of others, but not all.[2] The
restoration of 1968–9 emphasized disparities in both the style and the
technique. While the bearer on the spectator's left is in accord with
Michelangelo's style in the early years of the sixteenth century, his
counterpart on the spectator's right, and the female on the extreme
right, show a style which first appears in the concluding stages of work
on the Sistine ceiling (finished 1512). The technical disparities do not
entirely coincide with the stylistic ones. The flesh of the bearer on the
spectator's left, and the face and neck of the woman squatting below
him, are in a smooth technique without visible brush strokes. All the
rest is more broadly painted. As all the top paint has now been shown to
be oil (the smooth parts had formerly been thought to be in tempera)
and as Christ's body, for example, though painted in the broader
manner, proves to be no less finished than the flesh of the bearer on the
spectator's left, the most probable explanation of the disparities
(assuming that Michelangelo was responsible for the whole of the painting) would be that there was an interval between the execution of different
parts of it. To the present writer, who first put forward this thesis, it
still seems the most likely. Thus, the squatting woman on the left and
the bearer above her would have been designed and partly painted
before the interruption, and the two figures on the spectator's right of
Christ designed and painted after it. Christ's body was probably
designed and laid in before the interruption, but painted after it.[3]

As regards specific dating of the first phase of the work, a strong case
can now be made out for an unusually precise one—between the 14th
January and the 17th April, 1506. During this time Michelangelo was
impatiently awaiting the arrival in Rome of marble from Carrara for the
first stage of his project for the tomb of Pope Julius II. On the earlier
date the Läocöon had been discovered. Attention has recently been
drawn to the demonstrable effect which this sculpture exercised on the
Entombment, and, in particular, on features which have been identified
as dating from the first phase of it, and which must therefore have been
executed after the discovery.[4] The modish costume of the squatting
Mary Magdalene would accord with this date, being similar to that in
Costa's *Court of Isabella d'Este* (Louvre) which was commissioned in
November, 1504.[5] The upper terminus—17th April, 1506—is that of

Michelangelo's precipitate flight from Rome to Florence, which would probably have necessitated his leaving behind in Rome any work of any size which he might have started there. And if, as seems very plausible, the picture was originally intended as the altarpiece for the interior of the *tempietto* which Michelangelo had planned as part of his first project for the Julian tomb, he is unlikely to have started work on it after he left Rome.[6]

No such precision is possible when trying to define the second period of work on the Entombment.

It has been suggested (in the 1929 catalogue and elsewhere) that no. 790 derives from Mantegna's engraving of the same subject and also from Rogier van der Weyden's painting (Uffizi). While it is reasonable to suppose that Michelangelo may have been acquainted with both these works, and while it may be conceded that no. 790 displays features which can be paralleled in both, the resemblance is not great in either case.

COPY: Sketch copy (drawing), 23·1 × 20·5 cm. Siena, Biblioteca Comunale, ref. no. of album S.I.4. Published and discussed by the present writer in the *Burlington Magazine*, vol. 93 (1951), p. 281.

DRAWINGS: 1. Louvre (Berenson 1742). Study, autograph or copy, for the squatting Magdalen, nude and holding the Crown of Thorns and the Nails. Verso contains the word 'Alessandro' in Michelangelo's hand.

2. Louvre (Berenson 1589 verso). Published by Wilde as a study for 'S. John' (i.e. the left hand bearer, really Nicodemus). More probably Michelangelo's design for the real S. John (the right hand bearer) at the time of the first phase of work on no. 790.[7]

3. Cleveland, Ohio (Berenson 1599A verso). Neck, shoulders and forearm of a man pulling. Has been associated with the left hand bearer in no. 790, but not enough of the pose is shown to establish the connection.

PROVENANCE: Identifiable by a label on the back (*fleur-de-lis* with the number 468) with a picture in an inventory of 7th May, 1697 of Farnese possessions which had remained in Rome (*Un quadretto in tavola in qualche parte guasto e non finito con Nro Sig. re morto S. Gio. Tre Marie et un Apostolo, si dice esser di Michel'Angelo, N. 468*). An almost identical entry, but without the number, is in the 1693 inventory (extract in the Gallery archives). In the Fesch collection in Rome in the nineteenth century.[8] At some stage in the dispersal of the collection it seems to have been detached as part of the dregs and thus to have been picked up in Rome, by July, 1846, by the British painter, Robert Macpherson,[9] from whom purchased, 1868.

REPRODUCTION: *Illustrations, Italian Schools*, 1937, p. 229.

REFERENCES: (1) The Siena sketch copy (see COPY) suggests that some trimming may have taken place, particularly at the base. (2) The chart of attributions may be given as follows: A (for Michelangelo) Berenson (*Lists*, 1936 and 1963), A. Venturi (*Storia* . . ., IX, I and *Michelangelo* in the edition *Valori Plastici*, n.d.), Toesca (article on Michelangelo in *Enciclopedia Italiana*, 1935), Fiocco (articles in *La Critica d'Arte*, August, 1937 and *Le Arti*, October, 1941), Holmes (*Burlington Magazine*, vol. II (1907), p. 235, Bertini (*Michelangelo fino alla Sistina*, 2nd ed., 1945) and J. Wilde (verbal communication). B. (Michelangelo's design, executed by one of his followers) Symonds (*The Life of Michelangelo Buonarroti*, 1893), Knapp (*Klassiker der Kunst* volume, 1907: in a monograph (1923) the same author seems inclined to credit Michelangelo with the execution also), Thode (*Michelangelo und das Ende der Renaissance*, vol. 3, 1912) and

Woelfflin (*Die Jugendwerke des Michelangelo*, 1891). C (against Michelangelo) J. C. Robinson (Bandinelli—letter to *The Times* newspaper, 1st September, 1881), C. de Tolnay ('Antonio Mini or another of Michelangelo's *garzoni*'— *The Youth of Michelangelo*, 1943), F. Antal (Battista Franco—review in *Zeitschrift für Kunstgeschichte*, vol. 1, 1932) and A. E. Popp (pupil of Michelangelo referred to as 'Carlone'—in *Belvedere*, vol. 8, 1925). S. J. Freedberg (*Painting of the High Renaissance in Rome and Florence*, 1961, p. 257) suggests that Michelangelo started no. 790 after the Doni tondo but left it unfinished when he left Florence. The so-called 'Manchester Master' (see no. 809) then took over, but after continuing for a time realized his incompetence to complete the work and left it in its present state. This singular theory prompts the reflection that merely to take over a work left unfinished by Michelangelo—let alone subsequently to abandon it still unfinished—would postulate a degree of boldness on the part of the 'Manchester Master' of which the quality of the pictures assigned to him by Professor Freedberg and others would give no inkling. (3) See 'Michelangelo's *Entombment of Christ*—Some New Hypotheses and Some New Facts' by Michael Levey, Cecil Gould, Joyce Plesters and Helmut Ruhemann. Published by the National Gallery, n.d. (1970). (4) Alastair Smart: *Michelangelo: The Taddeo Taddei Madonna, and the National Gallery Entombment* in Journal of the Royal Society of Arts, October, 1967, pp. 835 ff. (5) Notes on the costumes by Stella Mary Pearce. She also dates the hair length of the left hand bearer mid way between the relatively short length of Michelangelo's *Proculus* of 1494–5, the *Bacchus* of 1496 onwards or the *David* of 1501–3 on the one hand and the Sistine *ignudi* of 1508–12 on the other. (6) Michael Levey in the publication cited in reference 3. (7) See article by the present writer in *Burlington Magazine*, 1974, p. 31. (8) So stated in the *Kunstblatt*, Stuttgart and Tübingen, 1846, p. 196, at which time the Fesch sale was still in progress. There is a further reference in the *Bulletin des Arts* dated 10th August, 1846. No. 790 does not figure in the Fesch sale catalogue. A MS. entry in the Medici inventory of 1553 ('Nella prima stanza della Guarda roba secreta') (Carta 30, recto) includes the entry 'Quadretto pittoui la nra donna cō Christo deposto di Croce di disegno di Michelaglo no finito' suggests, on the strength of the last two words, identity with no. 790, but was more probably a painted copy after a well known drawing by Michelangelo. (9) For the date cf. *Tübinger Kunstblatt*, *loc. cit.* The details of the discovery conflict in the different sources. The *Tübinger Kunstblatt*, the most reliable because the earliest in time, refers to no. 790 as part of the Ausschuss' of the Fesch collection which was bought by a picture dealer who sold it to Macpherson. Later (*Deutsches Kunstblatt*, 1855, p. 84) it is stated that the picture was found in the hands of a carpenter who was going to make a table from it, and later still (*The Early Life of Clement Burlison ... written about 1897*) that Macpherson found it doing duty as part of a street barrow. Redford (*Art Sales*, I (1888), p. xix) says that a great many of the Fesch pictures which had been in the basement of Palazzo Falconieri, where the Cardinal lived, had been removed to Villa Paolina and that in 1845 some of these, if not all, were sold (including no. 790) by the Principe di Musignano to 'D. Vito Enei' (Enea Vito), a Roman dealer. Some more details of these accounts are given in an article by the present writer (*Burlington Magazine*, 93 (1951), p. 281). Michael Levey points out (oral communication) that Macpherson's ownership of the picture in Rome is mentioned in the Postscript (by M. O. W. Oliphant) to Gerardine Macpherson's *Memoirs of the Life of Anna Jameson*, 1878, p. xiv.

Ascribed to MICHELANGELO

809 MADONNA AND CHILD WITH S. JOHN AND ANGELS
(UNFINISHED) (THE 'MANCHESTER MADONNA')

Panel, $41\frac{1}{2} \times 30\frac{1}{4}$ (1·05 × 0·76). The technique is mainly tempera (see *Burlington Magazine*, 106 (1964), pp. 546 ff).

General condition good. Some local damage and repaint in Christ's right arm, in a small portion of the Madonna's left hand and in a strip extending down for about three inches from just to the left of Christ's right elbow. Also in the Madonna's shoulder-knot, in the jewel on her forehead and in the part of her head-dress immediately above it. Cleaned 1964. Inventory number 677 (evidently Borghese) bottom left.

In the 1929 catalogue as Michelangelo.

The attribution to Michelangelo dates, in all probability, from at least as early as the end of the seventeenth century, but this in itself is inconclusive as documentation, and the stylistic considerations are complicated and ambiguous. The problem centres round the existence of a number of curious pictures which have been associated with no. 809 in recent years. The key one of these is a circular Madonna and Child in the Vienna Academy. Another Madonna (New York, ex-Contini) seems clearly by the same hand as the Vienna picture, as does a third, though with rather less certainty, in a private collection at Baden. More recently two further pictures—a Madonna in a Florentine collection and a Pietà in the Galleria Nazionale, Rome—have been added to the group, and still others may be expected to accrue.[1] These five pictures are clearly not by Michelangelo himself, but incorporate Michelangelesque features. As they bear some resemblance to no. 809 but are greatly inferior to it the question arises whether the latter is the masterpiece of the anonymous painter of the other five or whether Michelangelo himself was directly involved to some extent in its production but not in that of the others. If it were autograph it would have to be very early, and since there is no means of judging Michelangelo's handling of paint in a panel picture at this stage of his career the question cannot be settled.[2]

PROVENANCE: Almost certainly identifiable with a picture in the Villa Borghese, Rome by the end of the seventeenth century (Domenico Montelatici: *Villa Borghese fuori di Porta Pinciana*, Rome, 1700, p. 210: 'dipinto dal Buonaroti, benche non del tutto terminato, in cui vien figurata Maria Vergine con Giesù bambino, e. S. Giouanni Battista in mezzo à quattro Angioli'). What was certainly the same picture is recorded in the Borghese inventories of 1725 and 1765 (identical words): 'Un quadro in Tavola con la Madonna, Gesù Cristo e S. Giovanni con quattro altre figure, cioè due dipinte e due disegnate, dentro una Cornice di legno negra, venata di bianco di pmi 5½ × 4½ incirca'.[3] This picture seems to have left the Villa Borghese by 1790.[4] Probably picked up by Alexander Day during the upheavals following the Napoleonic invasion of Italy (C. F. von Rumohr: *Italienische Forschungen*, 1831, vol. 3, p. 96: 'Wir besitzen einige malerische Versuche des Michelangelo, welche in die Jahre 1500 bis 1506 fallen: das Rund *a tempera* in der florentinischen Gallerie (1503); das (wohl ältere) schönere, halbbeendigte Gemälde *a tempera*, sonst im Besitze der Madame Day zu Rom, jetzt in England.')[5] Alexander Day sale, Pantechnicon, 21st June, 1833 (31), bought Seguier. Purchased by H. Bonar.[6] Offered to the Gallery (as Ghirlandajo) by Mrs. Bonar in 1844. Exh. (by Mrs. Bonar) B.I., 1847 (59—as Ghirlandajo). Sold, 1849, by Colnaghi for Mrs. Bonar to H. Labouchère (afterwards Lord Taunton)[7] who exh. it (as Michelangelo)[8] at Manchester in 1857 (100 in provisional catalogue, 107 in definitive catalogue) and B.I., 1859 (15). Exh. by his executors, R.A., 1870 (151) and purchased from them, 1870.

REPRODUCTION: *Illustrations, Italian Schools*, 1937, p. 230.

REFERENCES: (1) The first three pictures in this group (together with one at Dublin which is unconnected) were reproduced and discussed by Fiocco in *Le Arti*, October–November, 1941, pp. 5–10, who attributed all of them to Michelangelo. R. Longhi (same journal, December, 1941) proposed instead an anonymous painter for the group, including no. 809. The last two pictures were published and discussed by F. Zeri (*Paragone*, July, 1953, pp. 15–27). The argument used by the latter writer against Michelangelo's authorship of no. 809—that it incorporates motives used by Michelangelo at different stages of his career—is a recurrent fallacy. More recently S. J. Freedberg associated himself with these writers in classing no. 809 in the 'Master of the Manchester Madonna' group (*Painting of the High Renaissance in Rome and Florence*, 1961, p. 256). (2) Of the various alternative names put forward from time to time as author of no. 809 mention may be made of 'Antonio Mini'. This attribution was made by A. E. Popp ('Garzoni Michelangelos' in *Belvedere*, vol. 8, 1925) on the strength of supposed stylistic resemblances to a group of Michelangelesque drawings attributed to Mini largely on her own authority. No documented paintings by Mini are known. Berenson ('Andrea de Michelangiolo e Antonio Mini' in *L'Arte*, 1935) refuted this theory but it was later revived by Tolnay ('The Youth of Michelangelo', 2nd ed., 1947, p. 236). (3) Paola Della Pergola: 'La Madonna di Manchester nella Galleria Borghese' in *Paragone*, March, 1954, pp. 47–8. The number painted on the picture (677) does not figure in the 1693 inventory of pictures then in Palazzo Borghese. Presumably it was already in Villa Borghese. (4) Della Pergola, *loc. cit.* (5) Day was active in Italy at this time and several of the pictures acquired by him then entered the National Gallery later. The present writer is grateful to Johannes Wilde for drawing his attention to the passage in Rumohr. (6) Charles Blanc: 'La Vierge de Manchester, tableau de Michel-Ange' in *Gazette des Beaux-Arts*, 1859, I, p. 216: 'depuis trente ans environ, la vierge de Michelange était en Angleterre'. A note, recorded as having been in the Gallery's archives, reported that Bonar had bought the picture in Italy on the advice of Camuccini but the picture's presence at the Day sale in 1833 would seem to refute this. (7) Evidence of Morris Moore before the Select Committee on the National Gallery (p. 696 of the 1853 Report, where, however, the date of Mrs. Bonar's offer is wrongly given as 1845). (8) The reattribution to Michelangelo seems to have been due to Waagen (*Treasures . . .*, vol. II, 1854, p. 417). The statement made there that no. 809 is circular (repeated in Berenson's *Lists*, 1936 ed.) was corrected in the Supplement of 1857.

After MICHELANGELO

1868   LEDA AND THE SWAN

$41\frac{1}{2} \times 55\frac{1}{2}$ ($1 \cdot 05 \times 1 \cdot 35$).

The picture has suffered very severely and is half ruined.

The design appears to derive from an antique motive known from copies after sarcophagus reliefs and gems,[1] and the pose is similar to that of Michelangelo's marble 'Night' (Medici Chapel, Florence).[2] Condivi says that Michelangelo painted for the Duke of Ferrara (Alfonso I d'Este) a picture in tempera representing the coition of Leda and the Swan. He adds that he (Michelangelo) ultimately gave it to a pupil who took it to France where it was bought by the King. The picture has long since disappeared but it is generally assumed that no. 1868 is an old copy of it. The theory that it is by Rosso may be correct but the evidence is inconclusive.[3] Even if the provenance from Fontainebleau were established (see below) it can hardly be Michelangelo's original. Cassiano dal Pozzo on his visit to Fontainebleau in 1625 speaks of a Leda there by Rosso after a drawing by Michelangelo[4] (there is some contemporary evidence that Rosso may have made such a copy).[3] He makes no mention of an original by Michelangelo which he could hardly have failed to do had one been there. At the end of the seventeenth century it was said (by de Piles[5] and Florent le Comte)[6] and was afterwards widely repeated that the original had been burnt on grounds of indecency by Des Noyers who was *Surintendant* from 1638 to 1643. Mariette quotes this story but refutes it by saying that he had himself seen the picture (which he assumed to be Michelangelo's original but which could equally well have been no. 1868 or another copy) and that it had later passed to England.[7] In the Sir Joshua Reynolds sale a picture which may have been no. 1868 is stated in the catalogue to be Michelangelo's original and to have come from the French royal collection and that of Earl Spencer. A receipt exists at Althorp for £70 paid by the Hon. John Spencer for a Leda by Michelangelo to the representatives of a Dr. Hickman, dated 18th July, 1736 and countersigned by George Knapton, then curator of paintings at Althorp. This picture (with no. 651 of this Gallery) was included among some mortgaged by the Hon. John Spencer in 1742.[8] These dates are sufficiently close to Mariette's not to exclude the possibility that his picture and the Althorp one were the same, but all positive evidence seems lacking. To sum up. It is unlikely that Michelangelo's original was still in existence by 1625. A copy of it may or may not have been burnt between 1638 and 1643. No. 1868 may in fact have come from Fontainebleau and be the work of Rosso. But inasmuch as the provenance cannot be checked more closely and there may well have been other copies of Michelangelo's picture in eighteenth-century France and elsewhere this point cannot be established.

When no. 1868 was presented to the National Gallery by the then Duke of Northumberland in 1838 he stated that it was not suitable for public exhibition[9] and presumably for this reason it does not figure in National Gallery catalogues until 1915.

VERSIONS: Museo Correr, Venice, Dresden and Schlossmuseum, Berlin.[10] A cartoon of the same subject, attributed to Michelangelo, is in the Diploma Gallery of the Royal Academy. A marble copy by Ammanati is in the Bargello, Florence. A variant by Etty appeared at Christie's, 18th November, 1966 (166) and 22nd March, 1968 (5). A pen and ink drawing by Géricault is in the museum at Orléans.

ENGRAVINGS: Michelangelo's design, engraved by Cornelius Bos and by Etienne Delaune.

PROVENANCE: Presented by the Duke of Northumberland, 1838. As stated above perhaps identical with lot no. 87 in the fourth day's sale (17th March, 1795) of the Sir Joshua Reynolds sale catalogue. Redford states that at the Reynolds sale the picture was bought by the executors of Lord Berwick and it is usually assumed that it passed from the Berwick family to the Northumberland family some time between 1795 and 1838, but there seems no evidence on this point.[11]

REPRODUCTION: *Illustrations, Italian Schools*, 1937, p. 231.

REFERENCES: (1) See A. Michaelis: *Michelangelos Leda und ihr antikes Vorbild* in *Strassburger Festgruss an Anton Springer*, 1885 and, for the subject in general, J. Wilde: *The Genesis of Michelangelo's Leda* in the Fritz Saxl memorial volume (1957) pp. 270 ff. (2) For the thematic relationship of the two cf. Edgar Wind: *Pagan Mysteries in the Renaissance* (1958), pp. 129 ff. (3) See Maurice Roy: *La Léda de Michel-Ange*, 1923. (4) See E. Müntz: *Le Château de Fontainebleau au XVIIe siècle* in *Mémoires de la Société de l'histoire de Paris*, vol. XII, 1885, pp. 268-9. (5) *Abrégé de la Vie des Peintres*, 2nd ed. (1715), pp. 213–14. (6) *Cabinet des Singularitez*..., 1669, vol. II, pp. 34–5. (7) *Abecedario*, vol. I (1746), p. 224. (8) Documents at Althorp. The Reynolds sale catalogue adds that the picture had been bought by the Hon. John Spencer in 1746. This may be a misprint for 1736. (9) Letter in the Gallery archives. (10) For reproductions of the other versions see Tolnay: *The Medici Chapel* (1948), plates 279–85. (11) George Redford: *Art Sales*, vol. II (1888), p. 240.

Paintings after Drawings by MICHELANGELO

Although Michelangelo himself painted no more than a handful of easel pictures during the whole of his long career there is abundant contemporary evidence (mainly in Vasari) that pictures were painted from his designs by other artists during his lifetime. The extent to which Michelangelo was personally involved in this practice varied. In the case of Sebastiano del Piombo, Michelangelo executed the cartoon for the *Pietà* (Viterbo)[1] and at other times merely provided drawings or sketches for the principal figures. Sometimes, as in the case of Pontormo's *Venus and Cupid*,[2] the Sebastiano *Pietà* already mentioned or the cartoons and drawings given to Antonio Mini,[3] Vasari records that Michelangelo made the cartoons with the express intention of specific artists' making pictures from them. At others Vasari merely states that certain artists made pictures from existing drawings by Michelangelo— e.g. Francesco Salviati, who, he says, did a painting of the *Fall of Phaeton* from Michelangelo's drawing,[4] Marcello Venusti who executed two *Annunciations* in this way[5] as well as 'una infinità' of small pictures,[6] and Giulio Clovio who painted a version of Michelangelo's Ganymede drawing.[7] The inventory of Clovio's goods at his death supplements Vasari in this respect since it contains a number of pictures specified as after Michelangelo.[8]

The most important of the pictures in this category—Sebastiano's *Raising of Lazarus*—is catalogued separately under that artist's name since it was the result of a collaboration between two artists and not a mere copy. Since it is in the latter category that the three pictures included in the following section belong it should be borne in mind that the identity of the executant is as difficult to determine as usual in such circumstances and that no attempt has in fact been made to settle the matter. For the same reason discussion of the date, style and iconography of Michelangelo's original has been curtailed, since it does not directly concern the paintings.[9]

REFERENCES: (1) Vasari/Milanesi V, 568. (2) *Op. cit.*, VI, 277. (3) *Op. cit.*, VII, 202. (4) *Op. cit.*, VII, 17. (5) *Op. cit.*, VII, 271–2. (6) *Op. cit.*, VII, 575. (7) *Op. cit.*, VII, 567. (8) Printed in Steinmann and Wittkower: *Michelangelo-Bibliographie*, p. 433. (9) In connection with the subject of this note in general cf. J. Wilde: *Cartonetti by Michelangelo* in *Burlington Magazine*, 101 (1959), pp. 370 ff.

8 'THE DREAM' ('IL SOGNO')

Slate, $25\frac{3}{4} \times 22$ (0·653 × 0·558).

In general well preserved. Some damage and repaint in the left leg of the principal figure.

Michelangelo's presentation drawing is in the Seilern collection (ex-Weimar). The name *Il Sogno* is used by Vasari for it (1568).[1] The scenes in the background clearly represent deadly sins but no contemporary explanation of the allegory has survived.[2] Some of the figures in the design recur in the painting of the *Battle of Montemurlo* (Florence, Pitti) by Battista Franco who has been suggested as executant of no. 8.[3] It may be noted, however, that Giulio Clovio is known to have executed painted versions of this design.[4] Several others are recorded, notably in the Barberini Palace, Rome in the mid-seventeenth century,[5] in the Kunsthistorisches Museum, Vienna (no. 101 in Frimmel's catalogue of 1898, from the Leopold William collection, in Paris 1809–15) and in the Uffizi (attributed to Allori, on the back of a portrait formerly said to represent Bianca Capello).

The main figure repeats the pose of Lazarus in no. 1 (Sebastiano del Piombo)—a figure for whose design Michelangelo was also responsible.

PROVENANCE: Bequeathed by the Rev. Holwell Carr, 1831.[6]

REPRODUCTION: *Illustrations, Italian Schools*, 1937, p. 231.

REFERENCES: (1) Vasari/Milanesi V, 431. (2) Beatrizet's engraving, inscribed 'MICHAEL ANGELVS INVEN' (Passavant: *Le Peintre-Graveur*, VI, 1864, p. 119, no. 112; reproduced by Tolnay: *Michelangelo: The Final Period*, 1960, p. 306) constitutes early documentation, if any were needed, of Michelangelo's authorship of the design. It includes various phallic details which are also just visible in reproductions of the Seilern drawing but not in no. 8. Tolnay (*op. cit.*, pp. 181–2) also summarizes the various interpretations of the iconography in general. (3) E.g. by Alessandro Marabottini: *Il Sogno di Michelangelo in una copia sconosciuta* in *Scritti . . . in onore di Lionello Venturi*, I, 1956, pp. 347–58, supported by W. R. Rearick: *Battista Franco and the Grimani Chapel* in *Saggi e Memorie di Storia dell' Arte*, 2 (Fondazione Giorgio Cini), 1959, p. 138 and Tolnay (*op. cit.*, p. 182). (4) Two figures in the inventory taken at the time of his death and reproduced by Steinmann and Wittkower: *Michelangelo-Bibliographie*, p. 433. (5) The 1631 inventory (printed by J. A. F. Orbaan: *Documenti sul Barocco in Roma*, 1920, p. 501) has *un quadro antico di chiaro oscuro, di mano di Michael Angelo Buonarota, di diverse figure ignude, alto palmi 3 e largo 5 . . . dipinto in tavola*. See also reference 6 below. (6) Said in Holwell Carr's (MS.) inventory and the National Gallery catalogue of 1832 to have come from the Barberini Palace. But this is probably only speculative identification of the picture with the one described there in Tetius: *Aedes Barberinae ad Quirinalem*, 1642, p. 158 which was presumably the same as the one in the 1631 inventory (see reference 5) and thus apparently of different proportions. In any case the earlier history of no. 8 is unknown. A picture answering to its description was lot 52 in an anonymous sale, Christie's, 26th May, 1810. This was probably lot 80 in the Udney sale, 18th May, 1804 (as Venusti and as from 'Cardinal Aldobrandini of Florence'). Later it re-appeared as lot 41, 9th March, 1811, Troward sale and 30th April, 1825 (92) (Du Roveray sale) (bought in).

1194   THE PURIFICATION OF THE TEMPLE

Wood, 24 × 15¾ (0·60 × 0·40).

Very good state. The Borghese number 391 inscribed on the face, bottom left.

Traditionally and generally attributed to Marcello Venusti (active 1548, died not before 1579) who, according to Vasari, executed numerous painted copies on a small scale of drawings and also frescoes (e.g., the Last Judgment) by Michelangelo. He may in fact be responsible for the execution of no. 1194, but there is no contemporary documentation.

No presentation drawing by Michelangelo is known in respect of this design. But there is a small sketch in the Ashmolean (Parker 328) and three (more detailed) sketches in the British Museum (1860—6-16-2/1, 2 and 3) of which the largest (1860—6-16-2/3) contains all the figures (but not the architectural background) in no. 1194. The figures in this drawing (as in the others) are naked. Otherwise they correspond fairly closely. The twisted columns in the background of no. 1194 are similar to those in the Raphael cartoon of the Healing of the Lame Man and derive ultimately from the six presented by Constantine to St Peter's. These were universally believed in the later Middle Ages to have come from Solomon's temple, and as such passed into the iconography of the Renaissance. Later in the sixteenth century and in the seventeenth they were often carried out in architecture, notably by Bernini in his baldacchino at S. Peter's.

This design may well have influenced El Greco in his different representations of the subject, one of which is no. 1457 of this Gallery.

PROVENANCE: In the Villa Borghese by 1650.[1] No. 391 in the 1693 inventory (printed in *Arte Antica e Moderna*, 1964, p. 456, modern serial no. 275) where the execution is ascribed to 'Luca Cangiassi'. During the French occupation acquired, according to Passavant,[2] by the *commissaire* Reboul from whom, after a 'long time' bought by Woodburn.[3] Presumably sold by him to Lawrence, since reacquired at the sale of the latter's collection (15th May, 1830, lot 122). Seen at Woodburn's by Passavant, 1833. Hamilton Palace sale, fourth day (24th June, 1882, lot 402),[4] bought Mainwaring. Lot 911 at seventh day's sale (13th June, 1885) of Christopher Beckett Denison collection, bought Agnew, from whom purchased, 1885.

REPRODUCTION: *Illustrations, Italian Schools*, 1937, p. 379.

REFERENCES: (1) Manilli: *Villa Borghese*, 1650, p. 113: *Christo, che scaccia i negoziāti dal Tempio . . . di Marcello Venusti*. Also noted (in the Palazzo Borghese) by Ramdohr (*Ueber Mahlerei und Bildhauerarbeit in Rom*. 1787, vol. I, p. 296). (2) *Tour of a German Artist in England*, 1836, vol. I, pp. 247–8. (3) A label formerly on the back of no. 1194 read: *Vender à M. Woodburn les* (?)

vendeures Chassés du Temple de Marcello Venusti provenant de la galerie Borghese inscrit au catalogue sous le No. 67 de la quarter Stanza. E de S.A. (4) Label on back.

1227   THE HOLY FAMILY ('IL SILENZIO')

Wood, 17 × 11¼ (0·431 × 0·285).

Good state.

Hitherto catalogued as by Marcello Venusti who may in fact be responsible for the execution. One of many painted copies after a presentation drawing in red chalk by Michelangelo once in Sir Thomas Lawrence's collection and now in that of the Duke of Portland.[1] The design was engraved in 1561 by Bonasone, inscribed as being Michelangelo's. The painted copy at Leipzig is signed by Marcello Venusti and dated 1563 and the majority of the others listed here under 'versions' have been attributed either to him or to Sebastiano del Piombo.

K. Langedijk (*Nederlands Kunsthistorisch Jaarboek*, 1964) identifies the figure on the left with Harpocrates. He would have to be rather the Giovannino with the attributes of Harpocrates (wolf's skin and finger to the lips).

VERSIONS: The more accessible are in the galleries of Leipzig, Vienna, Oxford (Ashmolean), Schleissheim, Leningrad, Rome (Corsini), Wiesbaden, Dresden and Liverpool, also in the collections of the Duke of Northumberland, the Marquess of Lansdowne and the Marquess of Bristol.

ENGRAVING: The original drawing engraved by Bonasone (see above).

PROVENANCE: From Hamilton Palace—no. 380 in fourth day of sale (24th June, 1882).[2] Bought Agnew for Lord Windsor from whom purchased (again through Agnew) 1887.[3]

REPRODUCTION: *Illustrations, Italian Schools*, 1937, p. 379.

REFERENCES: (1) See Cecil Gould: *Some Addenda to Michelangelo Studies*, *Burlington Magazine*, 1951, 279 ff. (2) Label on back of panel. (3) In the catalogue of the Hamilton Palace sale (which wrongly describes the picture as including S. Elizabeth instead of S. Joseph) stated to be from the Borghese Gallery, but there seems no other evidence for this. Brought to England, according to Redford (*Art Sales*, II, p. 259) by Woodburn in whose possession seen by Passavant (1833).

MORETTO DA BRESCIA
c. 1498–1554

His name was Alessandro Bonvicino. He is described as 'Alexander dictus Moretus' as early as 1529. In a document of December, 1553 he is referred to as 'Alexander Morettus q. D. Petri de Bonvicinis pictor civis et habitator Brixie'. Vasari (1550 and 1568) calls him simply 'Alessandro Moretto'.

The approximate date of his birth is deduced from his tax return of 1548 in which he declares himself 'di età di anni circa cinquanta'.

The legend that Moretto was Titian's pupil was first printed by

Ridolfi, but may have no other foundation than the strong influence of
Titian which his work shows.

Active throughout his career at Breşcia and in the neighbourhood,
principally as the painter of altarpieces and other religious pictures.
His portraits, though relatively few, are also of importance. The
existence of an active studio can be deduced both from the enormous
quantity of his output and from its uneven quality.

299   PORTRAIT OF A YOUNG MAN

$44\frac{3}{4} \times 37$ (1·136 × 0·939).

Paint on the whole very well preserved. Some small local losses due to
flaking. The original turnover of the canvas is preserved. Cleaned 1973.

On the sitter's cap the inscription: ἸΟΎ ΛΊΑИ/ΠΟΘῶ[1]. On the table a
pair of gloves, a seal, some coins and an object, perhaps an ink-well, in
the form of a hollow metal foot wearing a sandal.[2]

In the finished picture there is an anomaly in the pose. The sitter
rests his right arm on a cushion on the table, and his left on a chair-arm,
but his legs are in a standing, not a seated pose. X-ray photographs show
that there were open books in front of the sitter, evidently on a table, at
which he would have been shown seated.

Said, in earlier editions of the catalogue, to have been attributed to
Moroni when in the Lechi collection, but already as Moretto in 1856
when seen by Mündler (see PROVENANCE below) and consistently as
such since entering the Gallery. An attribution to Lotto[3] cannot be
sustained, though his influence is undoubted. In style and handling no.
299 shows essential affinities with Moretto's altarpiece of S. Nicholas of
Bari of 1539 (Brescia, Pinacoteca Tosio e Martinengo).

Catalogued on entering the Gallery as 'an Italian nobleman of the
Sciarra Martinengo Cesaresco family'. The first word of the Greek
inscription on the sitter's cap was read as του, the inscription translated
as 'I am exceedingly desirous of it' and related to Conte Sciarra's
known desire to avenge the murder of his father, Conte Giorgio.

A certain W. Fred. Dickes pointed out[4] that the first word was not του
but ιου and went on to propose an alternative reading of the inscription
as a reference to one Giulia Pozzo.[5] Since, as he satisfied himself, a lady
of this name did in fact exist he concluded that no. 299 represented her
husband, one Giacomo Gromo di Ternengo. This identification was
accepted in editions of the Gallery catalogue from 1898 to 1911. From
1912 a return was made to Conte Sciarra Martinengo Cesaresco.

The far-fetched nature of the Gromo di Ternengo identification does
not inspire confidence in its correctness, while the existence of an old
copy of no. 299 at Palazzo Martinengo, Salò (Garda) constitutes some
indication that the sitter was in fact connected with that family.[6] It
would not be impossible that he is indeed Conte Sciarra Martinengo
Cesaresco as the family tradition has it and was as said at the time of
purchase, but there are certain difficulties. The sitter's costume is
datable to the period between the mid 1530's and the mid 1540's,[7] and

the style of the painting, as already indicated, is consistent with Moretto's at that period. According to Ottavio Rossi,[8] Conte Sciarra was page to Henri II of France who created him, at the age of barely eighteen, Knight of S. Michel. The date of Conte Sciarra's birth is not known. Henri II, however, succeeded to the throne in 1547 and reigned until 1559. If Rossi's information is correct, therefore, Conte Sciarra would have been born between 1529 and 1541, according to the period of Henri's reign when he was knighted. As he could not have been less than about sixteen, at the minimum, when no. 299 was painted this could not have been before about 1545 and would probably have been somewhat later, which is rather late for the costume as shown and for the style. Secondly, according to Rossi, Conte Sciarra was in France when he heard of the murder of his father at Brescia. This occurred on 26th October, 1546.[9] He returned to Brescia to avenge him, but having killed his (wrong) man was promptly exiled and returned to France. In consequence it may be doubted whether he would have been in Brescia long enough for Moretto to have painted his portrait. Though neither of these objections, in view of the relatively late date of Rossi's book, would be fatal to the Conte Sciarra identification, taken together they must at least tend to favour some caution in accepting it. The alternative identification with Conte Giorgio, the father of Conte Sciarra, seems considerably more improbable still.[10]

VERSION: Copy recorded c. 1910 in Palazzo Martinengo, Salò (see above).

PROVENANCE: Recorded by Otto Mündler in 1856[11] as in the possession of Charles Henfrey at Turin, and as formerly belonging to Conte Teodoro Lechi of Brescia. According to information from the Martinengo Cesaresco and Lechi families[12] the portrait was sold in 1843 by Contessa Marzia Martinengo to the Napoleonic general, Conte Teodoro Lechi. The latter took it with a few more of his pictures to Turin when exiled from Brescia in 1848 or 1849 and sold it to Charles Henfrey in 1854.[13] Purchased from the latter in 1858 (details of the purchase given in Lady Eastlake's *Memoirs*, II, 1895, p. 98).

REPRODUCTION: *Illustrations, Italian Schools*, 1937, p. 241.

REFERENCES: (1) The mark above the first letter in the first word consists of a short vertical stroke together with a very short horizontal one joining it half way up its left side. A similar inscription figures in a portrait of a young man by Mabuse (no. 27 of the Kassel gallery; other versions also known). (2) A comparable object, evidently an ink-well, is shown in a Moroni portrait of a scholar, Earl of Rosebery coll., exh. R.A., 1960 (72). (3) In an unsigned review in *L'Arte*, January, 1933, p. 70, section 34. (4) *The Athenaeum*, 3rd June, 1893. (5) The literal translation of the words ἰού λίαν ποθέω, spaced, as they are, as three words is 'alas, I desire too much'. If the first two words were run together the punning translation 'I desire Giulia' would be conceivable. The further punning translation 'Giulia Pozzo' would, however, involve sacrifice of the 'desire'. (6) Letters of c. 1910 in the Gallery archives, together with a photograph of the copy. (7) Notes by Stella Mary Pearce in the Gallery archives. (8) *Elogi Historici di Bresciani Illustri*, 1620, pp. 355–9. (9) P. Guerrini: *Una Celebre Famiglia Lombarda, I Conti di Martinengo*, 1930, pp. 416–19. In this work Conte Giorgio II, the father of Conte Sciarra, is misprinted Giorgio III. (10) Suggested by Pietro da Ponte: *L'Opera del Moretto*, 1898, p. 95. Supported by Guerrini, *loc. cit.* Guerrini reproduces (p. XXVIII) an engraving inscribed as representing Conte Giorgio, signed Andreas de Abbiatis and apparently dated 1530. He claims that this was Paolo Maria de Abbiatis and that the design was inspired by no. 299. In fact the engraving is very feeble and the likeness non-committal. Considerations of costume and style, however, would exclude Conte Giorgio for no. 299 as he would have been too old, being born in 1501. (11) Notes in the Gallery archives. (12) Letters in the Gallery archives. As they were written long after the events in question their accuracy cannot be guaranteed. (13) It should be noted, however, that no. 299 does not figure in the printed Lechi catalogue of 1852.

625   ALTARPIECE: MADONNA AND CHILD WITH S. BER-NARDINO AND OTHER SAINTS

$140 \times 91\frac{1}{2}$ (3·55 × 2·32).

Relatively free of repaint for a picture of its size and age except along the joins in the canvas which are much repainted. The arrangement of these joins is highly unusual. The lower half of the picture, consisting of the five male saints, is on two pieces of canvas joined horizontally just above the little finger of S. Francis' right hand and half way up the crook surmounting S. Nicholas' crozier. The upper half is in five pieces, of which the largest frames the figures of the Madonna and Child and SS. Catherine and Clare. This piece extends to the edge of the picture on the right-hand side but not on any other. At its base it is separated from the top of the upper piece of the lower half of the picture by a horizontal strip some $8\frac{1}{2}''$ high. To the left of this and of the piece containing the celestial figures a vertical strip some 5″ wide extends to the top of the picture. To the right of it at the top a further horizontal strip some 4″ high, divided into two unequal pieces, runs along the top of the piece containing the celestial figures as far as the right edge of the picture. The two pieces of canvas comprising this strip are of herring-bone weave (arranged vertically in the smaller, right-hand section, horizontally in the other). The other pieces of canvas are twill. It could be deduced that the upper and lower halves of the picture were painted separately— presumably as a matter of convenience owing to the great size of the work. When the time came to join them it would have been found that a mistake had been made and that the upper half was slightly too small, necessitating enlargement by means of strips. It would also be possible that the canvas was cut in two when the picture left the church. Cleaned 1968–9.

Pentimento in S. Nicholas' mitre. X-ray photographs show that he was originally sloping his crozier over his right shoulder.

Of the saints shown S. Jerome is identifiable by his lion, S. Joseph by his flowering staff, S. Bernardino by the monogram IHS and by the three mitres at his feet, S. Francis by the stigmata, S. Nicholas of Bari by the three golden spheres in his left hand, S. Catherine of Alexandria by the crown in her left hand and S. Clare by the monstrance beside her.

The three mitres at S. Bernardino's feet are inscribed:

VRB / INI, SI / ENE and FERRA / RIAE.

This is in allusion to the bishoprics which he refused. His book is inscribed:

PATER / MANI / FESTA / VI NO / MEN / TVVM / HOMI / NI / BVS (John xvii, 6).

The original destination is not known. The presence of no less than three Franciscan saints—Bernardino, Clare and Francis himself—would indicate a Franciscan church and the prominence of S. Bernardino very possibly one dedicated to him. For this reason the provenance given in the Northwick sale catalogue, namely the Brescian church of SS. Faustino e Giovita, which in the sixteenth century was a Benedictine house, is improbable. There is no church in Brescia dedicated to S. Bernardino, and a destination within Brescia would in any case have been surprising, owing to the singular fact that all five male saints shown repeat the design of saints in three other altarpieces by Moretto in or from Brescian churches. The S. Jerome recurs in the altarpiece with SS. Margaret and Francis in the church of S. Francesco: the SS. Joseph, Francis and Nicholas are repeated in the *Coronation of the Virgin* in the church of SS. Nazzaro e Celso.[1] The central figure in no. 625, S. Bernardino, is an adaptation (to fit a standing posture and different attributes) of the *S. Anthony of Padua Enthroned* (Brescia, Pinacoteca Tosio e Martinengo, from the church of S. Maria delle Grazie). In no. 625 some studio assistance is likely, though Moretto's own touch is unmistakable in many areas. Nevertheless it gives the appearance of a routine work compared with the greater brilliance of the other three altarpieces. For this reason the present writer would regard it not as experimental for them but as partly repetitious; therefore later in date. The fact, as revealed by the X-rays, that S. Nicholas in no. 625 was originally shown sloping his crozier over his right shoulder as he does in the SS. Nazzaro e Celso altarpiece is a further pointer in this direction. The S. Margaret altar is dated 1530.[2]

PROVENANCE: Said (in the National Gallery Report dated 2nd April, 1860, appendix 2, no. III) to have been taken from Brescia to Cremona towards the end of the eighteenth century by 'Monsignor Germani', to have passed at his death to 'Dr. Faccioli of Verona'[3] and to have been sold by the latter in 1852 to Lord Northwick. The Brescian provenance, specified in 'Hours in Lord Northwick's Picture Galleries', 1858, p. 12 and in the Northwick sale catalogue as the church of SS. Faustino e Giovita, is not confirmed, and is doubtful for the reasons already given.[4] No. 1087 in the Northwick sale, 11th day, 11th August, 1859, where purchased.

REPRODUCTION: *Illustrations, Italian Schools*, 1937, p. 242.

REFERENCES: (1) It would be interesting, though not easy, to ascertain whether the corresponding figures are of identical dimensions in all cases. The dimensions of the *S. Margaret* and *Coronation* altars are given by Gombosi (*Moretto da Brescia*, 1943, pp. 95 and 98) as 2·5 × 2·04 m. and 2·88 × 1·98 m. respectively. No. 625 measures 3·55 × 2·32 m. but contains more figures than either of the other two pictures. (2) Antonio Morassi (*Catalogo delle Cose d'Arte e di Antichità d'Italia, Brescia*, 1939, p. 457) says of the *Coronation* 'fu eseguito nel 1534'. No evidence is vouchsafed for this statement which may only derive from a vague remark of Stefano Fenaroli's (*Dizionario degli Artisti Bresciani*, 1877, p. 45). Stella Mary Pearce, in notes in the Gallery archives, favours a date in the second half of the 'twenties for no. 625. (3) This was presumably the reason for Crowe and Cavalcaselle's statement (*History of Painting in North Italy*, 1912 ed., III, pp. 298–9) that no. 625 'seems to have been completed for a Veronese church'.

(4) In addition it may be noted that none of the eighteenth- and nineteenth-century printed guide books mentions no. 625 in the church. The latter, however, was rebuilt from 1622 onwards. It would be possible that pictures were removed on that occasion and not replaced.

1025 PORTRAIT OF A GENTLEMAN

$79\frac{1}{4} \times 36\frac{1}{4}$ (2·01 × 0·92).

Condition very fair. *Pentimento* in the outline of the sitter's face against the arch. Cleaned 1970–1.

Dated ·M·D·XXVI.

With the exception of a portrait of a monk of 1519 (Verona, Museo Civico) no. 1025 is the only surviving dated portrait by Moretto.[1] In the history of art its importance is still greater. Vasari says (Vasari/ Milanesi, VII, p. 445) that the practice of full-length portaiture which was already common by the time of writing his second edition (in the 1560's) originated with Titian. It is true that Titian did more to develop it than any other painter, and that it was principally his example which conditioned the main stream of later development in the genre, such as Van Dyck's in the seventeenth century and the British School in the eighteenth. Vasari specifies as prototype Titian's portrait of Diego di Mendozza of 1541. In fact the earliest Titian full-length portrait in existence is the *Charles V with a dog* (Prado) of not before 1532 and this is merely a free copy of one by Jakob Seisenegger.[2] No. 1025 is in line with a type of portraiture practised by Titian from a still earlier period, but happens to antedate by at least six years his first known life size full-length portrait.[3]

The sitter wears the badge of S. Christopher in his hat. As the picture comes from the Fenaroli of Brescia in which family that of Avogadro merged in the eighteenth century there would be a possibility that the sitter was Gerolamo II Avogadro, since he died in 1534 and seems to have been the only male member of the family at the date in question.[4]

The attribution to Moretto does not seem to have been questioned and could hardly be.

PROVENANCE: Recorded by Rumohr (before 1832) in the possession of Conte Fenaroli at Brescia,[5] where it remained until 1876 or shortly before. Purchased, 1876, from Giuseppe Baslini of Milan.[6]

REPRODUCTION: *Illustrations, Italian Schools*, 1937, p. 243.

REFERENCES: (1) A portrait of a man, dated 1533 (Genoa, Brignole-Sale) is sometimes attributed to Moretto, but more often doubted. (2) See G. Glück in *Festschrift Julius Schlosser*, 1927, pp. 224–42. (3) The point concerns the *aristocratic* type of full-length portrait which Titian was to develop. Naturally there had been full-length portraits before, whether in groups (Mantegna's *Gonzaga Family* at Mantua or Melozzo da Forlì's *Sixtus IV* in the Vatican) donor portraits in altarpieces or some single ones—equestrian portraits such as Simone Martini's *Guidoriccio* at Siena or the Uccello and Castagno grisailles in the Duomo at Florence, Castagno's series of famous men and women from the Volta di Legnaia or Carpaccio's *Young Man in Armour* (Thyssen-Bornemisza collection, Lugano). Northern examples had included Van Eyck's double portrait of the Arnolfini (no. 186 of this Gallery), Cranach's *Herzog Heinrich der Fromme* and *Herzogin Katharina* (Dresden, latter dated 1514) and Strigel's *Conrad Rehlingen* (Munich, dated 1517). (4) Genealogical tree in the Gallery archives, kindly supplied by Conte Fausto Lechi of Brescia. Chizzola and Carboni (*Le Pitture ... di Brescia*, 1760, p. 177) specify *Due Ritratti al naturale in piedi, del Moretto* in Palazzo Avogadri; also one by Moroni. No. 1025 (Moretto) and nos. 1022 and 1023 (Moroni) all came from the Fenaroli collection and therefore probably previously the Avogadri, so they may be the three in question, as a Moretto-Moroni confusion would not be impossible. (5) *Drey Reisen nach Italien*, p. 323. Gombosi (*Moretto da Brescia*, 1943, p. 105) says no. 1025 was in the Erizzo-Maffei collection at Brescia. He does not quote his evidence and his statement is unlikely. (6) National Gallery Report for 1876 says 'formerly in the Casa Fenaroli at Brescia'. It can only have been a short time with Baslini since Stefano Fenaroli in his *Dizionario degli Artisti Bresciani*, published in 1877, gives it as still in Casa Fenaroli (p. 42). Nos. 1022, 1023 and 1024 (Moroni) were purchased at the same time from Baslini, likewise as ex-Fenaroli. Frizzoni (*Arte Italiana del Rinascimento*, 1891, p. 342) and 'P.d.P.' (Pietro da Ponte) (*L'Opera del Moretto*, 1898, p. 96) state that the Fenaroli-Baslini part of the transaction took place in 1876.

1165 ALTARPIECE: MADONNA AND CHILD WITH SS. HIPPOLYTUS AND CATHERINE OF ALEXANDRIA

The original canvas is rectangular and measures $91\frac{1}{2} \times 55\frac{1}{2}$ ($2\cdot323 \times 1\cdot409$). The painted area has an arched top. Strips on each side about $1''$ wide are unpainted, as are the spandrels of the arched top. As the top of the arch stops about $1\frac{1}{4}''$ short of the top of the canvas the dimensions of the painted area are therefore c. $90\frac{1}{4} \times 53\frac{1}{2}$ ($2\cdot292 \times 1\cdot358$).

Very worn. S. Catherine's face and hands are perhaps the worst in this respect, but wearing is apparent in most areas.

The stone is inscribed:

M̄ĒBRIS DISSOLV

(the V somewhat truncated by the edge of the stone)

VOLVERVNT
NE VINCVLIS
DIVEL^{L}E^{R}ĒTVR
ÆTERNIS

Cartellini under the saints read (left): s (?) (only traces remain) HIPPOLYTVS, (right) S. AECATERINA.

The inscription on the stone evidently alludes to the martyrdom of the two saints portrayed. S. Catherine was tortured on a wheel and beheaded. S. Hippolytus, the gaoler of S. Lawrence (who converted him), was dragged by wild horses.

Said to have been commissioned by Canonico Conte Tomaso Caprioli (see PROVENANCE below) who died in 1538. The indications afforded by the costume would suggest that it was in fact painted a few years later than that.[1] Stylistic factors also seem to the present writer to favour a relatively advanced date in Moretto's career as instanced, among other ways, by the 'shot' colours of S. Catherine's cloak—greyish purple with blue high lights. The high altar (*Madonna and Saints*) of the church of S. Giovanni Evangelista at Brescia is a Moretto altarpiece of similar type.[2] The latter picture is signed 'Alixander Brix'.[3] This form also occurs on a lunette of the *Coronation of the Virgin* in the same church and both these pictures were used as starting point for reconstructing an *œuvre* for a hypothetical 'Alessandro Bresciano' who should be distinct from Moretto. This theory, originally put forward by Morelli,[4] was developed by Nicodemi[5] who included no. 1165 in this group. But it has not found favour and has no positive evidence to support it.

Philip Pouncey (notes in the Gallery archives) suggests that the Virgin's pose derives from a Mantegna engraving (Bartsch XIII, 232, 8).

PROVENANCE: Identifiable in an unpublished inventory dating from between 1780 and 1790 of pictures belonging to Conte Faustino Lechi of Brescia (under Moretto)[6]: *S. Ippolito e. S. Caterina; in gloria la Madonna col Bambino. Ai piedi dei due Santi vi è un cartello coi nomi; 'Divus . . .' e in mezzo, sopra una lapide, sta scritto un altro detto. Pala d'altare su tela (braccia 6 × 3)—Comperata dall' Abate Caprioli; era nella sua chiesa di Flero'.* Flero is hamlet some 5 km. south of Brescia. The church, or chapel, in question was secularized around the beginning of the twentieth century and part of the fabric incorporated into a private house. Only the apse is said to survive. On 21st April, 1802, no. 1165 was sold, with 191 other items from Palazzo Lechi, to an Englishman, Richard Vickris Pryor.[7] No. 1165 is identifiable as lot 18 in the sale at Christie's, 1st May, 1821 of Italian pictures 'purchased by a person of distinguished taste at Rome, on the first invasion of Italy by the French armies'. In the sale catalogue S. Hippolytus is wrongly called S. George. Nevertheless the presence in the same sale of six other pictures, one of which (no. 20) is specified as from the Lechi collection and the other five (nos. 12, 13, 16, 17 and 19) identifiable in the 1780–90 Lechi inventory leaves no doubt of the identity. In the copy of the sale catalogue in the National Gallery library no. 1165 is stated to have been bought by 'Peacock'. No. XVII in the 'Descriptive Catalogue' (n.d.) of Italian pictures belonging to 'the late Edward Solly, Esq.'; lot 20 in the latter's sale, 8th May, 1847, where bought Coningham.[8] Lot 53, William Coningham sale, 9th June, 1849 (as 'The Assumption of the Virgin' from 'Mr. Solly's collection') where bought Palgrave.[8] Exh. by 'Fras. Palgrave, Jun.' Manchester, 1857 (no. 253 in provisional cat., no. 232 in definitive cat.) and presented by him, 1884.

REPRODUCTION: *Illustrations, Italian Schools*, 1937, p. 242.

REFERENCES: (1) Notes by Stella Mary Pearce in the Gallery archives. (2) Gombosi (*Moretto da Brescia* 1943, p. 95) dates this picture 'um 1521–24' though calling no. 1165 ('spätere vierziger Jahre' (p. 106)). Morassi (*Catalogo delle Cose d'Arte . . . Brescia*, 1939, p. 302) has 'del periodo tardo' for the S. Giovanni Evangelista picture also—more probably, in the present writer's view. (3) So Gombosi, *loc. cit.* Morassi (*loc. cit.*) omits mention of the signature. (4) *Die Galerie zu Berlin*, 1893, p. 112, n. 2. (5) *Girolamo Romanino*, 1925, pp. 124 and 126. (6) Extract from inventory together with the topographical information given here was kindly supplied by Conte Fausto Lechi to whom the present writer's grateful thanks are due. (7) Further information supplied by Conte Fausto Lechi. (8) Marked copy of the sale catalogue in the Gallery library.

3094   MADONNA AND CHILD WITH SAINTS

Panel, $17\frac{5}{8} \times 24\frac{3}{4}$ (0·448 × 0·629).

Fairly extensive local damage, caused by repeated flaking; but surface quality remains in a number of places, particularly in the draperies.

In the 1920 edition of the catalogue the saints were identified as SS. Dominic and Francis. In the 1929 edition they appeared as SS. Dominic and Anthony of Padua. The latter seems indeed the correct identification of the saint on the spectator's right in no. 3094 but the one on the left, with the star on his breast, seems intended as S. Nicholas of Tolentino.

Acceptable as a very early work of Moretto, more primitive in style than the *Last Supper* (Brescia, S. Giovanni Evangelista) which was commissioned in 1521. In some ways more nearly comparable with the *Coronation of the Virgin* in the same church which is undated but must be somewhat earlier.[1]

VERSION: Morelli[2] mentions 'a charming little Madonna in tempera' by Calisto Piazza da Lodi in the Paul Delaroff collection, which was a 'copy of an early work by Moretto belonging to Sir Henry Layard'. This picture did not figure in the Paul Delaroff sale catalogue (Paris 23rd–24th April, 1914) but may have been the picture sold, according to Gombosi,[3] in New York (Spinola sale) in 1928.

PROVENANCE: Bought from Count Averoldi of Brescia by Morelli for Layard[4] before 1868 when lent by the latter to Leeds (79).[5] Exh. South Kensington Museum, 1869 (27, '. . . Moretto . . . Virgin and Child with SS. Francis and Dominic'), lent Layard. Sir A. H. Layard Bequest, 1916.

REPRODUCTION: *Illustrations, Italian Schools*, 1937, p. 245.

REFERENCES: (1) This picture was for a time attributed to an hypothetical 'Alessandro Bresciano'. See entry for no. 1165. (2) *Italian Painters*, London, 1892, p. 287, n. 7. (3) *Moretto da Brescia*, 1943, p. 106. (4) Layard MSS. in the Gallery library. (5) The 1920 catalogue gives the date of Layard's purchase as 'January, 1865'.

3095 PORTRAIT OF A MEMBER OF THE AVEROLDI FAMILY (?)

$40\frac{1}{2} \times 35\frac{3}{16}$ (1·29 × 0·894).

The clothes are in fair condition; the face and hands somewhat worn, the sky more so.[1]

The praying attitude suggests a fragment. It has something of the appearance of a donor's portrait in an altarpiece, but the direction of the eyes—looking towards the spectator would be unusual in this context. An old copy (see VERSION below) shows a table on the right with a crucifix on it and a prayer-book open at the Psalms: also a pillar behind the sitter. In this copy the sitter gives the impression of being seated at the table, and if that were the case it is likely that no. 3095 was already in its present state at the time when the copy was made and that the additions were inventions of the copyist's and a misunderstanding. For in no. 3095 the attitude is not that of a seated man: he is evidently kneeling on his left knee. His right knee comes forward and the cloak falls over it. X-ray photographs of no. 3095 show no trace of table, crucifix, prayer-book or pillar.

Gombosi[2] catalogues no. 3095 as a late Moretto ('um 1550'). By this tiⅿe the dividing line between Moretto and Moroni would have been very thin (see entry for no. 2093, ascribed to Moroni).[3] The slight indications afforded by the costume accord with this period.[4]

A label on the back says 'Ettore Averoldi 1865' and this is apparently the only authority for the identification of the sitter as given in the catalogues from 1920 to 1929. This label is evidently the work of Layard, recording the date of his purchase of the picture. In his MS. catalogue, however, he says merely 'a member of the Averoldi family'. In view of the provenance of the picture this would be not improbable. The copy of the picture already mentioned (see also VERSION below) is said to bear a fragmentary name 'orus' (for 'Christophorus').

VERSION: Reproduced by Gombosi (*Moretto da Brescia*, 1943, pl. 110, discussed by him p. 105). Evidently the same picture was lot 84, anonymous sale, Sotheby's, 19th November, 1952 (photograph in the Gallery archives).

PROVENANCE: Bought by Morelli for Layard from Count Averoldi, December, 1864–January, 1865.[5] Exh. South Kensington, 1869 (lent Layard) (15). Layard Bequest, 1916.

REPRODUCTION: *Illustrations, Italian Schools*, 1937, p. 243.

REFERENCES: (1) A note in Layard's MS. catalogue says 'restored by Molteni'. (2) *Moretto da Brescia*, 1943, p. 105. (3) Layard (correspondence with Morelli of which a copy is in the Gallery archives) quotes the Duc d'Aumale as attributing no. 3095 to Moroni. This does not appear to have been followed. Brognoli (*Nuova Guida di Brescia*, 1826, p. 201) mentions works by Moretto in Averoldi possession. (4) Notes in the Gallery archives by Stella Mary Pearce. (5) Layard papers in the Gallery archives.

3096   CHRIST BLESSING S. JOHN THE BAPTIST

$25\frac{3}{4} \times 37$ (0·653 × 0·93).

Thinly painted and somewhat retouched in places, but in general well preserved.

Gombosi[1] drew attention to the fragmentary character of the picture and suggested the somewhat smaller *Christ in the Wilderness* (New York, Metropolitan Museum) as another fragment from the same picture. In no. 3096 it is not only the unusual shape and type which suggest a fragment: the relatively summary treatment of the figures would be more appropriate to background than to foreground. The type and shape of the hypothetical parent picture could not be determined. No. 3096 could have been cut either from the background of a large upright altarpiece, such as the *Nativity* (Brescia, Pinacoteca Tosio e Martinengo)[2] or from an oblong picture, such as the *Elia Dormente* (Brescia, Duomo Vecchio).[3] A third possibility is illustrated by a strange picture by Moroni which shows the half length figure of a praying donor in the foreground and S. John baptizing Christ in the background.[4] The type and scale of these background figures are comparable with those of no. 3096.

The attribution to Moretto has not been challenged and is acceptable.

PROVENANCE: Bought at Brescia by Morelli for Layard[5] not later then 1869, when exh. South Kensington (39), lent Layard. Sir A. H. Layard Bequest, 1916.

REPRODUCTION: *Illustrations, Italian Schools*, 1937, p. 245.

REFERENCES: (1) György Gombosi: *Moretto da Brescia*, 1943, p. 106. (2) Gombosi *op. cit.*, no. 72, pl. 87. (3) Gombosi *op. cit.*, no. 33, pl. 97. (4) Genoa, Basevi collection (ex-Morlani). Exh. *Pittori della Realtà*, Milan, 1953 (18), also repr. Venturi, *Storia* IX, IV, 1, p. 229, fig. 193. (5) Layard MSS. in the Gallery library. Brognoli's Guide to Brescia (1826) mentions (p. 218) 'un bel San Giovanni nel deserto del Moretto' in the collection of Rodolfo Vantini.

GIOVAN BATTISTA MORONI
active 1546–7, died 1578

In contracts of 1564 and 1577[1] he is referred to as 'd'Albino', which is some 12 km. north east of Bergamo. Occasionally Moroni himself adds the name of the town of Albino after his signature. His training would have been in Brescia, as Ridolfi (1648) refers to him as the pupil of Moretto. This apprenticeship is confirmed by a document of 1549 in which 'Zuan Battista fiol di mistro Francesco d'Albin' is linked with Moretto, both being at Brescia.[2] That this person was in fact Moroni is made clear by reference to the 1564 contract, already mentioned, in which the painter is alluded to as 'Gi. Battista Morone pittore d'Albino' but signs 'Gio. Batt.a filiolo d. m.r Franc.o Morone'.

An *Annunciation* (Trento, S. Chiara), attributable to Moroni, is dated 1546.[3] A portrait in the John G. Johnson collection, Philadelphia is signed with the initials G.B.M. and dated 1547.

In the later 1540's and earlier 1550's Moroni seems to have moved backwards and forwards to some extent between Brescia and Albino. The presence in churches at Trento of pictures attributable to him suggests one or more visits there. There is no indication of his presence at Brescia after Moretto's death in 1554. Thereafter Moroni's activities centre on the Bergamo area.

In all his work Moroni showed himself a close follower of Moretto. In portraiture, always acknowledged to be his principal field, he developed considerably the Morettesque type. In religious painting Moroni was frequently a mere pasticheur of Moretto (see entry of no. 2093 below).

REFERENCES: (1) The 1564 contract is printed by Davide Cugini (*Moroni Pittore*, 1939, pp. 52–3) from the original. The 1577 one is from F. M. Tassi: *Vite de' Pittori Scultori e Architetti Bergamaschi*, 1793, I, pp. 169–70. Cugini (*loc. cit.*) says the original of this can no longer be found. (2) Document printed in *Archivio Storico Lombardo*, 1915, pp. 179–80, and by G. Gombosi: *Moretto da Brescia*, 1943, p. 88. (3) Cugini, *op. cit.*, pp. 37 and 312.

697 PORTRAIT OF A MAN ('THE TAILOR')

$38\frac{1}{2} \times 29\frac{1}{2}$ (0·97 × 0·74).

Many old retouchings in the background on the spectator's right. Otherwise very good state. Cleaned 1968.

The cleaning revealed that the picture had earlier been smaller all round.

The clothes worn by the sitter are neither those of the artisan nor of the nobility.[1] They are those of the middle class.[2] The essentials of the costume are very similar to those worn by the boys in the *Cuccina Family before the Madonna* of Veronese (Dresden), datable to 1571.[3] This constitutes some indication of the period of origin of no. 697. A. Venturi had already discussed it in the context of Moroni's late works.[4]

Described in the seventeenth century by Marco Boschini[5]:

> *Me despiase che quà no' porta el caso*
> *De nominar de la Casa Grimana*
> *La Galaria de i quadri, che sorana*
> *La saria a molte, co' se fesse el sazo.*
> *Tutavia quel Moron, quel Bergamasco,*
> *Per esser gran pitor, brauo, e valente,*
> *El vogio nominar seguramente,*
> *Che de bona monea l'hà pien el tasco.*
> *Ghè de i retrati: ma in particular*
> *Quel d'vn Sartor, sì belo, e sì ben fato,*
> *Che'l parla più de qual se sia Auocato;*
> *L'hà in man la forfe, e vù el vedè a tagiar.*

The mention of the shears (*forfe*), together with the Grimani provenance of no. 697, leaves no doubt about the identification. Though not supported by earlier documentation, the attribution to Moroni cannot be questioned.

PROVENANCE: In Casa Grimani at Venice from before 1660 (see above). Said to have passed from there, around 1845, to a painter called Schiavone from whom the collector, Antonio Piccinelli di Seriate, tried unsuccessfully to buy it.[6] Subsequently (?1846)[6] Schiavone sold it to Federigo Frizzoni de Salis of Bergamo, from whom purchased, 1862.

REPRODUCTION: *Illustrations, Italian Schools*, 1937, p. 248.

REFERENCES: (1) As was claimed by J. P. Richter in a note in the Gallery archives—'the costume is that of a nobleman'. (2) Notes by Stella Mary Pearce in the Gallery archives. Cf. another sixteenth-century portrait of a tailor—by Mazzola Bedoli (Naples no. 120). (3) R. Gallo in *Emporium*, 1939, p. 148. (4) A Venturi, *Storia . . .*, IX, IV, I, p. 250. Also G. Lendorff: *Giovanni Battista Moroni*, 1939, p. 141. (5) *La Carta del Navegar Pitoresco*, 1660, p. 327. In a pamphlet in the Gallery library—'*Pitture e Scolture nel Palazzo di Casa Grimani S. Maria Formosa* (n.d., printing and paper of the later eighteenth or earlier nineteenth century)—there is no mention of no. 697. (6) MS. note by Piccinelli in a volume of Tassi's *Vite dei pittori . . .*, published by R. Bassi-Rathgeb in *Bergomum*, no. 1, 1955.

742 PORTRAIT OF A MAN HOLDING A LETTER

Original canvas *c.* 32 × *c.* 25½ (*c.* 0·813 × *c.* 0·648). Made up to 35 × 28½ (0·889 × 0·724) with further surrounding canvas of different weave.

Good condition.

The inscription on the letter is imperfectly legible. The first line apparently reads: *Al Mag? Sig.‾ Juli-*. The second line, presumably giving the surname, is totally illegible. The isolated word below, probably indicating the town to which the letter was to be sent, begins, apparently, with an R, followed by five more letters.[1]

Entitled 'A Lawyer' in earlier editions of the catalogue, but the costume shown would not specifically indicate this, while the document in the sitter's right hand is not necessarily a legal one.[2] The attribution to Moroni, as a late work,[3] is uncontested.

PROVENANCE: No. 90 ('*Portrait d'homme à barbe. Costume noir, fraise et manchettes blanches. Il est appuyé sur une table, tenant une lettre, qui indique probablement le nom du personnage qui s'est fait représenter. Toile. Haut., 81; larg., 65 cent.*') in the Comte de Pourtalès-Gorgier sale, Paris, January–February, 1865. Bought after the sale, in May 1865, from Charles Edmond de Pourtalès.[4]

REPRODUCTION: *Illustrations, Italian Schools*, 1937, p. 247.

REFERENCES: (1) Rovetta (some 35 km. north west of Bergamo) or Rovato (some 15 km. west of Brescia) would be possibilities. (2) Burckhardt (*Beiträge zur Kunstgeschichte von Italien*, 2nd ed., 1911, p. 336) seems, strangely, to be referring to no. 742 in the following passage: '*Sodann hat Moroni den einzigen, und höchst lächerlichen Wichtigthuer der ganzen italienischen Porträtkunst verewigen dürfen oder müssen (National Gallery): wie es scheint einen Verhörrichter im Augenblick des hochmütigsten, insolentesten Sieges über irgend ein schuldiges oder unschuldiges Opfer; in der Provinz war dies Bild, wie es scheint, noch innerhalb des Respektes möglich, während es in Venedig den vollsten Hohn würde erregt haben, trotz erstaunlicher Behandlung.* (3) Notes on the costume by Stella Mary Pearce in the Gallery archives favour a date in the early 1570's. (4) Annual Report for 1865, p. 4.

1022 PORTRAIT OF A GENTLEMAN

$79\frac{5}{8} \times 41\frac{3}{4}$ (2·022 × 1·06).

Good condition. Cleaned, 1969.

The fashionable costume accords well with that shown in datable portraits of the mid and later 1550's, such as the Moroni portrait of a man in the Ambrosiana of 1554.[1] As the picture comes from the Fenaroli of Brescia, in which family that of Avogadro merged in the eighteenth century, the sitter could be either Pietro Avogadro (who made a will in 1565) or Faustino Avogadro (who made a will in 1557) since they were the only males of the family who would have been adult in the 1550's. They were the sons of Gerolamo II Avogadro, who may be the sitter of no. 1025 (Moretto). Both were soldiers.[2]

The metal brace worn by the sitter from his left knee to his left foot is apparently an attempt to counter the condition known as 'drop-foot'.[3]

PROVENANCE: Avogadro-Fenaroli family of Brescia (see above), from whom purchased, c. 1876, by Giuseppe Baslini of Milan.[4] Bought, together with nos. 1023, 1024 and 1025, from Baslini, 1876.

REPRODUCTION: *Illustrations, Italian Schools*, 1937, p. 252.

REFERENCES: (1) Notes in the Gallery archives by Stella Mary Pearce. (2)

Information kindly supplied by Conte Fausto Lechi of Brescia. See also reference no. 4 in the entry for no. 1025. (3) Letter in the Gallery archives from the Librarian of the Royal College of Surgeons in England. This diagnosis was made à propos no. 1022 by three members of the college independently. The condition of drop-foot is defined as due to a 'loss of function (without deformity) in the muscles of the ankle caused by inflammation or disease of the nerves controlling the muscles'. (4) See entry for no. 1025. Morelli (*Munich and Dresden*, p. 65, n. 4) refers to no. 1022's having been wrongly attributed by Mündler to Moretto when in Casa Fenaroli.

1023   PORTRAIT OF A LADY

$60\frac{7}{8} \times 42$ ($1\cdot547 \times 1\cdot067$).

Good condition.

Suggested in earlier editions of the catalogue that the sitter may have been the wife of the sitter of no. 1022. The two pictures did indeed come from the same family, and the costume in no. 1023 accords with the fashions of the same period, namely the mid or later 1550's.[1] Nevertheless, the two portraits can hardly have been intended as pendants, being different in dimensions, and with poses not complementary.

PROVENANCE: Avogadro-Fenaroli family of Brescia (see entry for no. 1025, Moretto) from whom purchased, *c.* 1876, by Giuseppe Baslini of Milan. Bought, together with nos. 1022, 1024 and 1025, from Baslini, 1876.

REPRODUCTION: *Illustrations, Italian Schools*, 1937, p. 249.

REFERENCES: (1) Notes by Stella Mary Pearce in the Gallery archives. She draws attention in particular to similarities of costume to portraits by Sofonisba Anguisciola.

1024   CANON LUDOVICO DI TERZI

$39\frac{1}{2} \times 32$ ($1\cdot002 \times 0\cdot813$).

Very good condition. Not lined until 1960, very unusually for a sixteenth-century picture.

The letter in his hand inscribed:

> Al Molto R.^{do} M Lud.^{co} di Terzi
> Can.^{co} di ᴵᴮgomo Dig.^o et Proth.^o
> ap.^{co} Sig.^r mio osser.^{mo}
> ᴵᴮgomo

VERSION: Sarasota, Ringling Museum, no. 107.

PROVENANCE: Perhaps the picture mentioned by Ridolfi (à propos Moroni portraits): *Tre de' quadri si conservano in Bergamo, l'uno appresso dell' Archidiacono Terzi . . .*[1] Described by Brognoli (1826) in the Fenaroli collection, Brescia.[2] Purchased, ca. 1876, from the Avogadro-Fenaroli family of Brescia (see entry for no. 1025, Moretto and no. 1022, Moroni) by Giuseppe Baslini of Milan, from whom bought, 1876, with nos. 1022, 1023 and 1025.

REPRODUCTION: *Illustrations, Italian Schools*, 1937, p. 250.

REFERENCES: (1) Ridolfi/Hadeln, I, 148. (2) Paolo Brognoli: *Nuova Guida per la Città di Brescia*, p. 207.

1316 PORTRAIT OF A GENTLEMAN

73 × 39¼ (1·854 × 0·997).

Good general condition. Some damage in the painted masonry, right. Cleaned, 1969.

Called Titian in the nineteenth century and accepted as such by Waagen.[1] First identified as a fine and characteristic work of Moroni by Sir Charles Eastlake.[2] The costume shown, which was evidently intended to be worn under armour, accords best with a date in the mid 1550's.[3]

PROVENANCE: First recorded at Longford Castle in the 1853 catalogue of that collection (no. 133). Purchased, together with nos. 1314 and 1315, from the fifth Earl of Radnor, 1890, with the aid of gifts from Lord Rothschild, Sir E. Guinness, Bt. (Lord Iveagh) and Charles Cotes.

REPRODUCTION: Illustrations, Italian Schools, 1937, p. 249.

REFERENCES: (1) Treasures . . ., III, 1854, p. 140. Also Galleries and Cabinets . . ., 1857, p. 360, where still as Titian. (2) Note in his handwriting—'Moroni, vy. fine'—against the entry 'Titian. 133. Full-length portrait' in his copy, now in the Gallery library, of the 1953 catalogue of pictures at Longford Castle. (3) Notes by Stella Mary Pearce in the Gallery archives.

2094 PORTRAIT OF A GENTLEMAN

39 × 31½ (0·99 × 0·8).

Good condition under discoloured varnish.

The writing on the letter appears to be illegible.

Berenson's inclusion of no. 2094 under Sofonisba Anguisciola as well as under Moroni was presumably a slip.[1] Clearly an autograph Moroni, datable from the costume around the end of the 1560's.[2] The name 'Il Cavaliere' or 'Il Gentile Cavaliere', used in earlier editions of the Gallery catalogue, was evidently a fanciful Victorian invention which had been dropped as early as the time of the New Gallery exhibition (1894–5), only to be revived later.

VERSIONS: A copy of the whole design said to have been in the Bassi sale, Milan, 9th November, 1898 (34).[3] A version of the head and shoulders only was lent by Goudstikker to the Italian exhibition, Amsterdam, 1934 (251), where stated to be ex-Decourcelles, Paris and ex-Nemes (sold Lucerne, Fischer, 22 vi. 1963, 1202).

PROVENANCE: In the John Samuel collection by 1868 when lent by him to Leeds (249). Also to the R.A., 1870 (64). The John Samuel collection passed by inheritance to Miss Lucy and Miss Louisa Cohen by whom lent to the New Gallery, 1894–5 (180) and by whom bequeathed, 1906.

REPRODUCTION: Illustrations, Italian Schools, 1947, p. 252.

REFERENCES: (1) Lists, 1932 edition. In the 1936 edition under Moroni only. (2) Notes by Stella Mary Pearce in the Gallery archives. She points out that the costume appears French rather than Italian, though a stylish North Italian of this period might affect it. (3) Earlier editions of the Gallery catalogue. Also G. Lendorff: Giovanni Battista Moroni, 1939, p. 140.

3123 CHASTITY

$60\frac{3}{8} \times 34\frac{1}{4}$ ($1\cdot533 \times 0\cdot87$).

Badly damaged by abrasion in some areas; worst in her head, neck and left breast. In other areas the paint is fairly well preserved. Cleaned 1969.

Inscribed:

> CASTITAS
> INFAMIAE NVBE
> OBSCVRATA
> EMERGIT

As Moroni in the first catalogue (1920) after it entered the Gallery. Demoted to 'School of Moroni' in the editions of 1925 and 1929. Nevertheless it is extremely close in style to no. 1023 (Moroni) of this Gallery, and in quality in some respects superior to it. There is therefore no reason to doubt that it is fundamentally autograph, as, indeed, it is consistently shown in Berenson's *Lists*. No. 1023 is datable by the smart costume to the mid or later 1550's. The hair-style in no. 3123 seems that of a decade or more earlier[1]—perhaps a deliberate archaism attributable to the extreme oddity, for Moroni, of the subject.

Ripa (1645)[2] mentions the sieve as symbol of Chastity. This doubtless derives from the story told by Valerius Maximus and other classical writers of the Vestal Virgin Tuccia who carried a sieve of water from the Tiber to the temple to prove her innocence. In the circumstances it is hardly possible to settle the academic question whether the subject of no. 3123 is *The Vestal Tuccia* or *Chastity in general, symbolized by the Vestal Tuccia*. Cf. Follower of Mantegna, no. 1125.[A]

PROVENANCE: Manfrin collection, Venice (labels on the back)—no. 134 in the 1856 catalogue, no. 4 in the 1872 catalogue, on both occasions as the Vestal Tuccia by Lattanzio Gambara.[3] Purchased from the Manfrin collection by Sir A. H. Layard, October 1880.[4] Layard Bequest, 1916.

REPRODUCTION: *Illustrations, Italian Schools*, 1937, p. 253.

REFERENCES: (1) Notes by Stella Mary Pearce in the Gallery archives. (2) *Iconologia*, p. 86. (3) Cristiani: *Della Vita ... di Lattanzio Gambara*, 1807, p. 31, mentions a fresco of this subject by Lattanzio. (4) Layard MS. in the Gallery archives.

3124 LEONARDO SALVAGNO (?)

Painted area irregular, *c*. $38\frac{3}{4} \times 28\frac{1}{8}$ ($0\cdot985 \times 0\cdot714$).

The face very much worn.

Inscribed at the top LEONARDVS SALVANEVS. This does not look original and below it can be seen the remains of other letters—perhaps 'Hieronamo', as suggested in earlier editions of the Gallery catalogue.

The book inscribed:

> AC CIVITATIS
> BERGOMI
> PRIVILEGIA

Judging principally from the handling of the ruffs presumably the remains of a Moroni, datable from the costume probably to the early 1570's.[1]

PROVENANCE: Thieni collection, Vicenza, from which bought by Layard[2] apparently in 1865 and certainly before 1869 when lent by him to South Kensington (5). Layard Bequest, 1916.

REPRODUCTION: *Illustrations, Italian Schools*, 1937, p. 250.

REFERENCES: (1) Notes in the Gallery archives by Stella Mary Pearce. (2) Layard MSS. in the Gallery archives.

3128 PORTRAIT OF A MAN

Original canvas $16\frac{3}{4} \times 14\frac{3}{4}$ (0·426 × 0·375).
A strip about 1″ wide had been added at the top.
Good condition.[1] Cleaned 1959.
The attribution to Moroni cannot be questioned.

PROVENANCE: Bought by Morelli from Mündler for Sir A. H. Layard[2] before 1869 when lent by the latter to South Kensington (28). Layard Bequest, 1916.

REPRODUCTION: *Illustrations, Italian Schools*, 1937, p. 251.

REFERENCES: (1) The statement by Gertrud Lendorff (*Giovanni Battista Moroni*, 1939, p. 147, no. 85) that the picture is 'fortemente danneggiato' is entirely untrue. (2) Layard MSS. in the Gallery archives.

3129 PORTRAIT SAID TO REPRESENT A COUNT LUPI

Original canvas $18\frac{1}{2} \times 15\frac{5}{8}$ (0·47 × 0·397). A strip about $1\frac{1}{4}$ wide has been added at the top.[1]
Good condition in general. A few odd retouches, notably down parts of the outline of the face and tunic on the spectator's right.
Inscribed:

DVM SPIRITVS
HOS REGET ARTVS [Virgil: *Aeneid*, iv, 336]

Underneath the centre of this quotation there is a decorative flourish which is flanked by the word ANNOR (on the left) and XXX (on the right). These letters, together with two further decorative flourishes on either side, are in lighter paint than the motto and the centre flourish and also much less carefully formed. It is therefore questionable whether they are original, and perhaps most probable that they were added somewhat later, possibly on behalf of the sitter in lieu of a date.
The attribution to Moroni is acceptable. The costume shown accords best with a date around 1560.[2]

PROVENANCE: Purchased from Count Lupi of Bergamo, as representing one of his ancestors, by Sir A. H. Layard,[3] before 1868, when exh. by him, Leeds (278)., Exh. South Kensington, 1869 (44) (lent Layard). Layard Bequest, 1916.

REPRODUCTION: *Illustrations, Italian Schools*, 1937, p. 251.

REFERENCES: (1) A note in the Gallery archives says that the strip was added by Molteni, Milan, 1865, who also 'rectified the trunk of this young man'. (2) Notes in the Gallery archives by Stella Mary Pearce. Davide Cugini (*Moroni Pittore*, 1939, p. 317) dates no. 3129 to 1558, while G. Lendorff (*Giovanni Battista Moroni*, 1939, p. 69) places it around 1560. (3) Layard MSS. in the Gallery archives.

Ascribed to G. B. MORONI

2090 AN ANGEL

Panel, thinned to *c.* 0·002 m. and remounted on another panel, 59½ × 21 (1·51 × 0·533).

The main loss of paint is on a vertical line running from top to bottom about a third of the picture's width from the left. This includes the angel's eyes and also much of his nose and forehead. In other areas the paint is well preserved.

Inscribed: COELORVM (most of the O and of the E are restoration but enough remains of the original letters to ensure, in the context, that that was what the letters originally were). Cleaned 1957. For commentary and PROVENANCE see under no. 2093.

VERSION: A small picture, corresponding in most details, was lot 106A, Miss Grizel Davies sale, Sotheby's, 21st June, 1950 as 'C. Piazza'. Another was lot 150, anonymous sale, Sotheby's, 16th January, 1963.

2091 AN ANGEL

Panel, thinned to *c.* 0·002 m. and remounted on another panel. 59½ × 21 (1·51 × 0·533).

A vertical line of damage about a third of the picture's width from the left avoids the important portions of the angel and passes between the V and the E of the inscription. The original edge of the picture on the right is missing: the original paint stops in a wavy line which cuts off the tips of the angel's fingers. In other areas the paint is well preserved.

Inscribed: AVE REGINA.

Cleaned 1957.

VERSION: Lot 150, anonymous sale, Sotheby's, 16th January, 1963.

For commentary and PROVENANCE see under no. 2093.

2092 S. JOSEPH

Panel, thinned to *c.* 0·002 m. and remounted on another panel, 59½ × 21 (1·51 × 0·533).

A vertical line of damage about a third of the picture's width from the right includes the nails of the two middle fingers of the saint's left hand and the toe of his left foot. Isolated patches of damage elsewhere including the saint's left eye and most of his mouth. The original edge stops short of the present edge on the left-hand side.

Inscribed: S. IOSEPH

Cleaned 1958.

For commentary and PROVENANCE see under no. 2093.

2093 S. JEROME

Panel, thinned to *c.* 0·002 m. and remounted on another panel, 59½ × 21 (1·51 × 0·533).

The most damaged of the four. A vertical line of damage about a third of the picture's width from the right runs from top to bottom but there are also many shorter vertical damages, throughout most of the saint's draperies but missing, for the most part, his face and hands.

The inscription would have read: S. HIERONIMVS.

Of this most of the first I is missing together with much of the N, all of the second I, most of the M and isolated parts of other letters. Enough remains, however, to leave no doubt of the original form.

Cleaned 1958.

With nos. 2090, 2091 and 2092 in the 1929 catalogue as Moretto. It has apparently not been indicated hitherto that nos. 2090–3 were originally two double-sided panels. The joins in the wood and the subsequent trimming sustained by one of the panels leaves no doubt of this. No. 2093 was on the back of no. 2090 and no. 2092 on the back of no. 2091. The arrangement would have been that when the panels were shut the two angels faced each other, with the inscription *Ave Regina Coelorum* reading across the bases of both. When open, there must have been, to judge from the inscription already mentioned, a representation of the Virgin in the centre, flanked by S. Joseph on the spectator's left and S. Jerome on the right. The fact that the two saints are appreciably more damaged than the angels suggests that the triptych was normally kept open. A triptych of similar type in the Brera (no. 92) shows in the centre the Assumption of the Virgin. The right wing has S. Clare and S. Catherine of Alexandria. The left, S. Paul and S. Jerome. The Brera triptych is from the church of S. Bernardino in Gardone Valtrompia, and it is significant that the figure of S. Jerome in its left wing repeats (in reverse and on a smaller scale—the panel is 1·03 in height) the S. Jerome of no. 2093. The Brera triptych is attributed to Moretto, but Gombosi listed it as Moroni and postulated a lost Moretto *Assumption* as prototype for the central panel.[1] The repetition of the figure of S. Jerome in a work variously attributed to Moretto and to Moroni is nevertheless irrelevant to the question of the attribution of nos. 2090–3 as between these two painters. Not only did Moroni borrow motives from Moretto[2]: Moretto and his studio not infrequently repeated his own—e.g. in no. 625 of this Gallery. It is rather in the quality of the execution and in the colouring that the clue to the attribution of nos. 2090–3 should be sought. The handling seems too coarse for Moretto himself, and if the responsibility were his it would have to be concluded that the execution had devolved entirely on his studio. Since, however, the style accords best with that of Moretto's late period[3] and since at that time Moroni was his pupil, and presumably his best pupil, participation by the latter would in any case be possible and even likely. The cool range of the colours used is a further pointer in the direction of Moroni.

PROVENANCE: Stated in the catalogue of the exhibition of Venetian Art, New Gallery, London, 1894–5, to have been in the collection of 'Prof. G. Morelli'. Subsequently acquired by John Samuel and passed to his nieces, Anna Louisa and Lucy Cohen, by whom lent to the exhibition (nos. 56, 57, 64, 65). Nos. 16, 17, 18 and 79 in the catalogue (1895) of the John Samuel collection, where stated to have been exhibited R.A., 1870. This is incorrect, but nos. 2090 and 2091 only were lent by John Samuel to the R.A., 1871 (293 and 295). Bequeathed by the Misses Cohen, 1906.

REPRODUCTION: *Illustrations, Italian Schools*, 1937, p. 244.

REFERENCES: (1) G. Gombosi: *Moretto da Brescia*, 1943, pp. 66 and 119. (2) Moroni's *Assunta* (Brera), for example, is a mere paraphrase of Moretto's (Brescia, Duomo Vecchio), while the *Fathers of the Church* (Trento, S. Maria Maggiore), formerly attributed to Moretto, but more probably by Moroni, is a conflation of two separate Moretto altarpieces—at Frankfurt a.M. and in the Brera. (3) Gombosi, *op. cit.*, p. 106, 'Entstehungszeit: Vierziger Jahre'.

NICCOLÒ DELL' ABATE
c. 1509-12–1571

Two contemporary sources, Lancellotto and Forciroli, disagree about the date of his birth, the former saying he was aged thirty-five in 1547 and forty in 1552, the latter that he was born in 1509. Forciroli's information, however, being derived from relations of the painter, is perhaps more likely to be correct. He was born at Modena. The fact that Lancellotto refers to him as 'Niccolò degli Abati' and to his father as 'Giovàn degli Abati', combined with the fact that the picture of S. Geminiano (Modena, Galleria Estense) is inscribed 'Abati Nic.' would seem to constitute evidence against the assumption, long held, that he was only called 'dell' Abate' because he was the assistant of Primaticcio who held, in France, the office of 'Abbé de S. Martin', since this refers to a later stage in Niccolò's life.

He was working in Bologna from 1547 or 1548 and is recorded at Fontainebleau in 1552 where he spent the rest of his life, engaged, with Primaticcio, on decorative work which has not survived. Of existing works, the decorations detached from the Beccherie at Modena and an altarpiece at Dresden are vouched for by Vasari as Niccolò's. A few other surviving paintings have been reliably attributed to his Italian period.

His style, so far as it is possible to judge it, seems to have been formed on elements derived from Dosso Dossi (as regards landscape, which appears to have been his speciality) and from Parmigianino (for figures).

5283 THE STORY OF ARISTAEUS

74½ × 93½ (1·88 × 2·36). Probably cut slightly on the right.

Good condition for a picture of its size and age. The paint in general has worn thin and been made up in places (particularly in the sky). Cleaned 1954–5.

The attribution to Niccolò probably dates from at least as early as the first half of the nineteenth century (see PROVENANCE below) and the same attribution for the similar picture in the Louvre (see below) is of the eighteenth century. At least one attempt, however (by Gamba),[1] has been made to attribute the latter to Primaticcio. No. 5283 has all the characteristics of the School of Fontainebleau, in which Primaticcio and Niccolò dell' Abate, often in partnership, were the dominant painters. While the traditional attribution to the latter would seem probable (since the landscape is the main element and Niccolò is known from the Fontainebleau records to have been a landscape specialist) it is desirable to emphasize that the evidence is very incomplete.[2]

Virgil (Georgics IV, 315–558) describes how a shepherd called Aristaeus, distressed by the sudden death of his bees, called on his mother, Cyrene, for help and was referred by her to the sea-god, Proteus. The latter explained that Aristaeus was being punished by Orpheus, whose wife, Eurydice, being chased by Aristaeus, overlooked in her flight the presence of a serpent which thereupon bit her to death. Her nymphs then gave themselves to lamentation, and Orpheus sought the comfort of his lyre (prior to seeking Eurydice in the Infernal Regions).

In no. 5283 Orpheus is clearly recognizable charming wild animals in the middle distance. In the right foreground three nymphs appear unaware of the attempt on the virtue of Eurydice, who is shown stepping on the serpent (centre) and dead (towards the right). The god, extreme right, is presumably Proteus and the figures above him presumably Aristaeus consulting Cyrene.

A picture likewise attributed to Niccolò dell' Abate (Louvre, formerly Orléans, Bridgewater and Sutherland collections) representing the Rape of Proserpine is so similar to no. 5283 as to suggest it may have been painted as companion to it. Nevertheless the Louvre picture is appreciably narrower (1·96 × 2·18) than no. 5283 (which itself seems to have been cut slightly on the right) and also rather higher. It not only gives no indication of ever having been cut or added to but has demonstrably not been since the eighteenth century.[3] If no. 5283 had been one merely of a pair of pictures it would be most natural to suppose that the other was identical in size and that its subject was the conclusion of the story (whereby Aristaeus, having sacrificed cattle to the nymphs, is ultimately rewarded by finding bees swarming in the carcasses). If, on the other hand, no. 5283 was intended as one of a series of Rapes it would accord well with the subject of the Louvre picture, and if there were a sufficient number of such pictures it is possible to imagine that not all need have been identical in size and shape.[4]

PROVENANCE: Very possibly the picture to which, in a letter dated 30th August, 1827, the dealer, W. Buchanan drew the attention of J. G. von Dillis, director of the Munich Gallery, as a possible purchase by the latter institution[5]: *Nicolo del' Abatte—A Grand Landscape by this Master, equal to Titian's*

Landscapes—with the Korey Euridice beautifully treated—size of the picture about 8 feet—the price £1,000. Almost certainly in an anonymous sale, Christie's, 16th April, 1831: *Niccolo del ABATI Orpheus and Eurydice. A grand and extensive landscape, with a City on the Sea Shore, and elegant Figures in the foreground, illustrating the Story of Orpheus and Eurydice* (bought in at 55 guineas). The same picture was lot 14, the Hon. W. B. Grey sale, Christie's, 15th June, 1836 (bought Lister). It should be noted that the Talbot collection, from which no. 5283 came, is said to have been formed by T. M. Talbot, who died in 1813.[6] Purchased at the Margam Castle sale (Miss E. C. Talbot, Christie's, 29th October, 1941, lot 356) on behalf of the National Art-Collections Fund, by whom presented, 1941. Exh. N.A.-C.F. Exhibition (in honour of Sir Robert Witt), National Gallery, 1964 (3), Exhibition of Cleaned Pictures, National Gallery, 1947 (39).

REPRODUCTION: *16th-century Italian Schools*, plates, 1964, p. 150.

REFERENCES: (1) Quoted in the catalogue of the *Exposition de l'Art Italien*, Paris, 1935 (p. 147). (2) Anthony Blunt (*Art and Architecture in France 1500–1700*, 1953, p. 82 n. 78) tentatively identifies no. 5283 and the Louvre picture with two of a set of four for which Niccolò was paid in 1557 but gives no reason for this identification. (3) The engraving in the *Galerie du Palais-Royal* published in 1786 shows it with the same proportions as now. In the 1727 Orléans catalogue (by Du Bois de Saint Gelais) the dimensions are given as 'haut de six pieds, large de six pieds huit pouces' (p. 355). (4) E.g., the series of portraits painted by Lawrence for the Waterloo Chamber at Windsor Castle vary considerably in size and shape. Erika Langmuir (*Burlington Magazine*, 1970, pp. 107, proposes as literary source for no. 5283 Poliziano's *Orfeo*, supplemented by 'an anonymous manuscript . . . of an amplification of Poliziano's drama'. (5) Copy in the Gallery archives. (6) Note in the catalogue of the sale at Christie's, 29th October, 1941. This would not exclude the possibility of no. 5283's being the picture mentioned by Buchanan or the one in the Christie sale of 1831. Buchanan, in another part of the letter already quoted, admits that he was not himself the owner of the pictures he was offering and the name of the owner at the Christie sale was not revealed. Alternatively the picture could have been added to the Talbot collection after the death of T. M. Talbot. The Margam Castle collection is not mentioned by Passavant or by Waagen.

NORTH ITALIAN School

640   THE ADORATION OF THE MAGI

Panel, arched top, $17\frac{3}{8} \times 12\frac{5}{8}$ (0.442×0.321).

Bottom right, an inventory number 206 painted.

Basic condition seems fairly reliable under the present discoloured varnish.

Catalogued from 1861 to 1912 as Dosso Dossi. Subsequently as 'Ferrarese School, early XVI century'. Some derivation from the early Correggio *Epiphany* is the Brera has been claimed[1] and alternative attributions made to Battista Dossi[2] and to Girolamo da Carpi.[3] The latter has had some support[4]; and faced with the Modena picture of the same subject (Galleria Estense no. 190), plausibly attributed to Girolamo, it is perhaps possible to see an embryonic stage of it in the snouty faces and the landscape of no. 640. Nevertheless the difference in quality and confidence between the two, and similarly between no. 640 and

Girolamo's altar at S. Martino, Bologna (dated 1532 on the frame) is such that many untraced intermediate stages would have to be assumed.[5]

PROVENANCE: Purchased with the Edmond Beaucousin collection, Paris, 1860.

REPRODUCTION: *Illustrations, Italian Schools*, 1937, p. 132.

REFERENCES: (1) By W. C. Zwanziger: *Dosso Dossi*, 1911, p. 112. The resemblance is fairly general. A comparable general resemblance could be pointed out between no. 640 and a drawing by Giulio Campi in the British Museum (1941–11–8–14). (2) Jacobsen in *Repertorium für Kunstwissenschaft*, XXIV, 1901, p. 347. (3) By Zwanziger, *loc. cit.* (4) E.g. from H. Mendelsohn (*Dosso Dossi*, 1914, p. 191), A. Serafin (*Girolamo da Carpi*, 1915, pp. 42–3), R. Longhi (orally, 1939) and F. Antal (*Art Bulletin*, June, 1948, p. 81). (5) Against the attribution to the young Girolamo da Carpi is the view of Stella Mary Pearce (notes in the Gallery archives) that the Madonna's hairdressing style would accord best with a dating in the early 1550's.

692 S. HUGH

Panel, painted area $16\frac{1}{4} \times 12\frac{5}{8}$ (0·413 × 0·32). This is delimited by a narrow surrounding red band.

Inscribed:

8 VG

Considerably damaged by vertical splits in the panel. The white habit, being relatively free of folds, gives an impression in the present state of the picture of having been intended merely as underpainting. If that were the case the halo, inscription and crozier might well be later additions and the habit perhaps not intended to be white and therefore not Carthusian. But no evidence to confirm this hypothesis has yet come to light.

Bequeathed as Masaccio,[1] then temporarily attributed to Mansueti.[2] Catalogued from 1864 as Lodovico da Parma, a personality of the utmost obscurity whose artistic output is not defined. Some influence from the later portraits of Giovanni Bellini seems clear, but no convincing specific attribution has yet been made.

Originally identified in the Gallery catalogues with S. Hugh of Grenoble. In later editions S. Hugh of Lincoln was added as alternative. As both were canonized bishops entitled to wear the Carthusian habit no decision seems possible.

PROVENANCE: Bequeathed by Lt.-General Sir W. Moore, 1862.

REPRODUCTION: *Illustrations, Italian Schools*, 1937, p. 191.

REFERENCES: (1) National Gallery minutes of December meeting, 1862. (2) National Gallery Report for 1863.

2511 PORTRAIT OF A MUSICIAN

Panel, $26\frac{1}{4} \times 21\frac{7}{8}$ (0·667 × 0·559).
Condition fair. Rather thinly painted, and worn in places.
Not specifically attributed when in Salting's collection. Ascribed

since entering the Gallery to Giulio Campi.[1] Claude Phillips[2] suggested
a Northern hand, tentatively specifying Joos van Cleve. Linked by P.
Hendy[3] with a female portrait in the Philadelphia Museum (Wilstach
collection, no. 48, where successively attributed to Bronzino and
Giulio Campi) which had recently been attributed to O. Sirén to
Parmigianino. None of these suggestions seems satisfying in the case of
no. 2511.

PROVENANCE: In the possession of George Salting by 1894, when lent by him
to the New Gallery Venetian Exhibition (85).[4] On loan to the National Gallery,
1902. Salting Bequest, 1910.[5]

REPRODUCTION: *Illustrations, Italian Schools*, 1937, p. 71.

REFERENCES: (1) Perhaps the picture listed in Salting's possession by Berenson
in his 1907 *Lists* (North Italian Painters). But Salting also owned another
portrait of a musician, also lent by him (as Giulio Campi) to the New Gallery
Venetian exhibition of 1894 (265). (2) *Burlington Magazine*, 17, 1910, p. 22. (3)
Burlington Magazine, 50, 1927, p. 168. (4) Wrongly stated in the exhibition
catalogue (where it is unattributed) to be on canvas. (5) Various brands are on
the back—a coronet above the letters S.G (?); the letters A/N.C enclosed within
a heart-shaped form, surmounted by a cross. Also a complicated heraldic seal.

3945 PORTRAIT OF A MAN IN A LARGE BLACK HAT
Panel, painted area $23\frac{7}{8} \times 19\frac{3}{8}$ (0·607 × 0·492).
A number of small local damages due to past flaking.
Pentimenti in the outlines of the shoulders, of the hat and of the
hand.
As Savoldo in earlier editions of the catalogue, and accepted as such by
Berenson, among others. Savoldo's style as portraitist is not precisely
defined,[1] but it can hardly be claimed that no. 3945 bears any significant
resemblance to the most authentic example of it—the donor in the
Hampton Court *Nativity*.[2] An alternative attribution to Basaiti has been
suggested tentatively by Creighton Gilbert.[3] It is true that the portrait
of a man at the Accademia Carrara, Bergamo (no. 563, from the Morelli
collection), signed by Basaiti and dated 1521, has obvious features in
common with no. 3945,[4] but the present writer is not convinced that one
hand was responsible for both, though this would be a possibility.

VERSION: A later variant, including more body below the hand and no black
tie was in the present century in the possession of St Clair Baddeley of Painswick.
A copy, presumably replacing the original, is recorded at Burghley.

PROVENANCE: Stated in the Mond catalogue[5] as having been bought by Dr.
Mond in 1888 and as having been in the possession of the Marquess of Exeter at
Burghley House, also as having been identified as Baldassare Castiglione.[6]
Therefore identifiable with the 'Count Balthazar Castiglione, in black dress and
cap, 24 in. by 19½ in.', attributed to Pordenone, which was lot 279 in the Marquess of Exeter sale, Christie's, 9th June, 1888. In the copy of the sale catalogue
in the Gallery library this lot is marked as purchased by Mond.[7] Mond Bequest.
1924.

REPRODUCTION: *Illustrations, Italian Schools*, 1937, p. 325.

REFERENCES: (1) Cf. Creighton Gilbert: *Ritrattistica Apocrifa Savoldesca* in
Arte Veneta, 1949, p. 103. (2) Signed and dated 1527. The so-called *Gaston de*

Foix in the Louvre and the Contini-Bonacossi *Flautist* are also signed, but are in a different genre. It may be pointed out that a strong element of portraiture seems present in many of Savoldo's representations of saints, particularly elderly male ones. (3) Private communication in the Gallery archives. Gilbert also mentioned the attribution in a published work—*Alvise e Compagni* in *Scritti di Storia dell'Arte in Onore di Lionello Venturi*, I. 1956, pp. 294–5, n. 7. (4) Gilbert also adduces the donor in the Correr Basaiti *Madonna* as comparison. The costume in no. 3945, according to notes by Stella Mary Pearce in the Gallery archives, accords best with a date *c*. 1520–5. (5) By J. P. Richter, vol. II, 1910, p. vi. (6) Richter, *op. cit.*, p. 392. He catalogues the picture as 'North Italian School'. He seems to overestimate the extent of the repaint, but restoration may have taken place after he wrote and before the picture entered the Gallery. The present writer has not succeeded in identifying no. 3945 among the earlier records of pictures at Burghley. (7) The 1925 and 1929 catalogues are therefore wrong in including J. C. Robinson among former owners. The mistake evidently comes from misreading Richter (*op. cit.*, p. vi). His system of punctuation in fact indicates Robinson not as the former owner but as the originator of the Savoldo attribution.

4033   PORTRAIT OF A LADY IN A PLUMED HAT

Apparently painted on paper, mounted on canvas, $17\frac{5}{8} \times 13\frac{3}{8}$ (0·448 × 0·34).

The face seems in fair state. Rather thin and retouched elsewhere.

In the 1929 catalogue as Flemish School, though an earlier attribution to 'Salviati' is recorded there. The costume and style alike indicate an Italian, and probably specifically North Italian, origin. Antal's suggestion of Niccolò dell' Abate is not acceptable.[1] The costume accords best with a date in the second half of the 1560's or early 1570's.[2] By this period Niccolò had long been in France.

PROVENANCE: The 1929 catalogue identifies it, no doubt correctly, with lot 109, anonymous sale, Christie's, 21st February, 1903 ('M. Ridolfo, bt. Kennedy') and lot 165, anonymous sale, Christie's 9th April, 1910 ('M. Ridolfo, bt. Carfax'). Claude Phillips Bequest, 1924.

REPRODUCTION: *Illustrations, Continental Schools (excluding Italian)*, 1937, p. 124.

REFERENCES: (1) *Burlington Magazine*, vol. 59, 1931, p. 226. (2) Notes in the Gallery archives by Stella Mary Pearce.

LELIO ORSI

c. 1511–1587

The inscription (composed by his son) on his grave at Novellara records that he died on 3rd May, 1587 at the age of 76, that he was great in architecture, greater in painting and greatest of all as draughtsman.

Since 1890, when Thode first attributed to Orsi an existing set of frescoes, a considerable amount of research has brought to light contemporary documents confirming the existence of a painter of this name (he is not mentioned either by Vasari or Baldinucci, and such seventeenth- and eighteenth-century accounts of his work as there are are of no great authority in view of their date). The documents in question record his activity as a painter at Reggio nell' Emilia in 1536 and 1544. From 1546 to 1552 he was apparently at Novellara, in 1553 at Venice and by December, 1554 in Rome. He was back at Novellara by 1559 and seems to have spent there most of the remaining years of his life.

In spite of this relative plenty of authentic biographical information no contemporary document has yet been discovered attributing to Orsi an existing painting. A single drawing (the *Madonna della Ghiara*) is said to be signed and dated 1569.[1] The form of the draperies in this work bears some relation to those in a group of small religious pictures which constitute the core of those currently attributed to Orsi and of which the best are two at Modena (*Martyrdom of S. Catherine* and *Dead Christ with Charity and Justice*), two at Naples (*S. George* and *Sacrifice of Isaac*) and no. 1466 below. These pictures, which are clearly the work of a single artist, show an individual combination of Correggesque, Michelangelesque and Northern elements. The fact that extremely beautiful drawings exist which are connected with several of them would, if Orsi were indeed the author, bear out the statement on his tomb.

In view, therefore, of the fact that twentieth-century scholarship has built up an *œuvre* for Orsi on foundations if possible more tenuous than those of Giorgione's, the results, although plausible, should perhaps be taken with some reserve.

The best summary (and bibliography) of the Orsi problem is contained in the Catalogue (by Roberto Salvini and Alberto Mario Chiodi) of the exhibition at Reggio Emilia in 1950.

REFERENCES: (1) See pp. xii and 136 of the Reggio catalogue referred to in the text.

Ascribed to LELIO ORSI

1466   THE WALK TO EMMAUS

$28 \times 22\frac{1}{2}$ (0·7 × 0·56).[1]

General condition appears fairly good. A little worn and retouched in places.

The attribution to Orsi has been general since the time when the picture was in the Scarpa Gallery (see PROVENANCE).

The attitude and physical type of Christ and of the figure on the (spectator's) left of him are very similar to that of figures on the right of Michelangelo's *Crucifixion of S. Peter* (Vatican, Cappella Paolina), and almost certainly derive from them. The latter work was finished in 1550 which would thus constitute in any case a *terminus post quem* for dating no. 1466.[2]

DRAWINGS: Wadsworth Atheneum, Hartford, Connecticut (accession no.

1938, 257, Summer Collection). Crayon, heightened with white, on brown paper, 13⅛ × 10⅝. Fine finished drawing for the three figures, without the landscape. Another (attributed to Orsi) Louvre no. 6686, and yet another in the possession (in 1955) of Mr. and Mrs. Charles Muskavitch, Auburn, Calif. A drawing in the Palazzo Rosso (no. 572) ,Genoa, is of inferior quality and doubtful authenticity.

PROVENANCE: Scarpa Gallery, Motta di Livenza (no. 17 in the catalogue of 1874),[3] lot 32[4] at the sale (Milan) of the Scarpa Gallery, 1895, where purchased (through Colnaghi).[5]

REPRODUCTION: *Illustrations, Italian Schools*, 1937, p. 260.

REFERENCES: (1) Binding covers about ¼″ of the picture nearest the edge all round. The canvas has been re-lined with one closely resembling the original in grain and colour. (2) It should be noted that one of the Orsi documents is a letter of 1559 to a friend in Rome in which he asks for drawings of the Cappella Paolina. (3) Printed in *Archivio Veneto*, VIII, 1874. (4) Damaged label on the back. (5) Adolfo Venturi (*Storia . . .*, vol. IX, part VI, p. 634) speaks also of a *Crucifixion* by Orsi in the National Gallery from the Scarpa gallery. Such a picture was indeed lot 31 at the Scarpa sale but it was not bought by the National Gallery.

L'ORTOLANO
born not later than 1487, still active 1524

Ferrarese School. His name was Giovanni Battista Benvenuti. A shadowy figure, not mentioned by Vasari. His existence as a painter in Ferrara is recorded in three documents dating from 1512, 1520 and 1524 respectively (the last date also figures on a picture of S. Margaret, at Copenhagen, generally attributed to L'Ortolano). There are no signed or documented works, though no. 669 below was attributed to him as early as 1621. This and a group of stylistically associable pictures show a style close to Garofalo's but distinct from any known phase of it. Though the border-line between L'Ortolano's and Garofalo's *œuvres* in their entirety can hardly be precisely defined, since a number of pictures exist which might be attributed to either, a distinction between specific works of the two painters was already being drawn, as Venturi points out,[1] as early as 1586.

REFERENCES: (1) Venturi: *Storia*, IX, IV, p. 320.

669 ALTARPIECE: SS. SEBASTIAN, ROCH AND DEMETRIUS

Panel, transferred to canvas, arched top, 90¾ × 61 (2·304 × 1·549).

On the whole well preserved for a transferred picture, despite a number of obvious losses and retouchings. Cleaned 1972.

The identity of the saint on the right is indicated by the *cartellino* at his feet which reads .s. DEMET/RIVS. This saint was proconsul of Achaia and was stabbed to death with a lance by order of the emperor Maximinianus on account of his extensive conversions of heathen. The general arrangement of the figures combined with the type of still life on the ground and its position in the foreground suggests a derivation from Raphael's S. Cecilia altarpiece at Bologna. The latter work was finished not later than 1516, and the costume of no. 669 also favours a date around that time.[1]

From the church of S. Maria at Bondeno, near Ferrara, where attributed to L'Ortolano from 1621 onwards.[2] The chief dissenters have been Morelli[3] and Frizzoni[4] who preferred an attribution to Garofalo. Nevertheless the touch is more vigorous than Garofalo's and the forms rather more primitive. In spite of the lack of contemporary evidence for identifying L'Ortolano's style there seems no legitimate reason to doubt the traditional attribution in this case, which is indeed older (1621) than any other L'Ortolano attribution.

COPY: One still at S. Maria di Bondeno. Another, Christie's, 14th February, 1930 (96), from the Barker sale, 1879, exh. Leeds, 1868 (26). Later re-sold as lot 167, Phillips, Son & Neale, 21st August, 1972. Figure of S. Demetrius only, with a different background. This or a similar picture appeared at Sotheby's, 7th December, 1960 (49) (now P. Ganz, New York).

PROVENANCE: Guarini (op. cit.), 1621, mentions it in the church of S. Maria di Bondeno, near Ferrara,[5] where it was still to be seen in 1844.[6] Also mentioned by Scannelli: Il Microcosmo della Pittura, 1657, p. 319. In October, 1855, in the possession of Ubaldo Sgherbi, a dealer at Ferrara,[7] who sold it (to England, he thought) by August, 1856.[8] By July, 1857 in the possession of Alexander Barker in London[9] who exh. it, B.I., 1858 (19). Purchased from Barker, 1861.

REPRODUCTION: Illustrations, Italian Schools, 1937, p. 260.

REFERENCES: (1) Costume notes by Stella Mary Pearce in the Gallery archives. (2) Guarini: Compendio . . ., p. 448. (3) Italian Painters, Borghese and Doria-Pamfili Galleries . . .(1892), p. 207. (4) Arte Italiana del Rinascimento, 1891, pp. 285 ff. (5) Guarini, it is true, describes it as un S. Sebastiano tra un S. Domenico, ed un S. Rocco di mano dell' Ortolano, but the Domenico is clearly an error or misprint for Demetrio as the later history of the picture leaves no doubt of its identity. (6) Boschini's footnote to Baruffaldi (Vite . . ., vol. 1, p. 179) published in that year. (7) Mündler's diary, in the Gallery archives. (8) Mündler, op. cit. (9) Mündler, op. cit.

PALMA GIOVANE
1544–1628

His name was Iacopo Palma, the son of Antonio Palma and the great-nephew of Palma Vecchio.[1] The date of his birth is from Ridolfi whose accuracy does not seem to have been questioned in this instance. Patronized in youth, according to Borghini, by Guidobaldo, Duke of Urbino, who sent him to study in Rome. He may still have been in Rome in 1568.[2] Boschini, in his notes on Titian in the introduction to the Ricche Minere (1674), says Palma told him he had had some instruction from Titian, whose last Pietà he completed.

Active for nearly all his long life in Venice, engaged on a multitude of commissions, mainly religious and historical, including work on the redecoration of the Doge's Palace following the fires of 1574 and 1577. His important series of paintings at the Oratorio dei Crociferi, Venice, is documented as of 1583–96. His vast practice included commissions for pictures to be sent to widely different parts of Italy and also abroad (e.g. to the Emperor Rudolph II and King Sigismund III of Poland).[3]

Palma Giovane was left the dominant personality in Venetian painting on the death of Tintoretto in 1594.

REFERENCES: (1) Borghini, *Il Riposo*, 1584, p. 559. For the relationships in the Palma family see G. Ludwig in the Prussian *Jahrbuch*, 1901, pp. 184–9. (2) Drawing inscribed 'Mateo da leze pitor in Roma nel 1568 quale (?) morto poi nel . . . compagno di giacomo palma', repr. in *A Selection from the Collection of Drawings formed by C. Fairfax Murray*, n.d., pl. 74. For details of Palma Giovani's sojourn in Rome see G. Gronau: *Documenti Artistici Urbinati*, 1936, *passim*. (3) Ridolfi/Hadeln, II, pp. 189–95.

1866 MARS AND VENUS

$51\frac{1}{2} \times 65\frac{1}{4}$ ($1 \cdot 309 \times 1 \cdot 656$).

Thick engraved varnish at present. The canvas has been torn in several places; otherwise the paint seems fairly well preserved.

In the 1929 catalogue as 'Ascribed to Palma Giovane'. The attribution to Palma Giovane dates, in all probability, from as early as the mid-seventeenth century (see PROVENANCE below). No reasonable doubt concerning its basic correctness need be entertained, in view of the obvious resemblance between no. 1866 and a *Venus and Cupid* at Cassel which is a signed work of Palma Giovane. There may, however, be studio assistance.

Mythological pictures by Palma Giovane are rare. Ridolfi mentions in his catalogue of this painter's works only one representation of *Mars and Venus*—which he says was painted for Cavaliere Marino, the poet.[1] It is, however, doubtful for two reasons whether no. 1866 can be identical with the Marino picture. First, because the poet himself describes the picture as 'Venere in atto di disuelarsi a Marte',[2] which is not an accurate description of no. 1866, since the action in question is there shown as already complete. Secondly, Venus' hair-dressing, which is fashionable, would accord best with a dating probably in the late 1580's.[3] which is somewhat early if the picture was painted for Marino (born 1569). Alternatively, Ridolfi mentions 'alcune Veneri di giocondissimo colorito' among the pictures painted by Palma Giovane for the Emperor Rudolph II.[4] But though no. 1866 would have accorded admirably with that monarch's taste there is no positive evidence for assuming his implication.[5]

PROVENANCE: Almost certainly the picture seen by Richard Symonds in the possession of the Earl of Northumberland in 1652: 'Palma Giovene. A Venus whole body on a bed, and Mars a fat red knave which she pulls down and Cupid pulls off his buskins'.[6] The latter picture was clearly the one recorded in Symon Stone's (unpublished) list of pictures at Petworth (1671) ('a large piece done by young Palmer of Mars Venus and Cupid'). No. 1866 was presented (as by Tintoretto) in 1838 by the Duke of Northumberland, together

with no. 1868 (*Leda*, after Michelangelo). As the donor stated at the time that
the pictures were not suitable for public exhibition[7] they hung for many years
in the Director's office[8] and no. 1866 was not catalogued until 1929.

REPRODUCTION: *Illustrations, Italian Schools*, 1937, p. 263.

REFERENCES: (1) Ridolfi/Hadeln, II, p. 202. (2) *La Galeria del Cavalier
Marino*, 1620, p. 13. It appears that Marino later presented his picture to
Giovan Carlo Doria and then tried to persuade Palma to do him a replica
on a small scale (see Hadeln, *op. cit.*, p. 202, note 2). (3) Notes by Stella
Mary Pearce in the Gallery archives. (4) Ridolfi/Hadeln, II. p. 194. (5) There
is no record of a *Mars and Venus* by the younger Palma in the 1621 inventory
of Rudolph's pictures (published by Olof Granberg; *Kejsar Rudolf II's
Konstkammare . . .*, 1902, Bilaga 1). (6) C. H. Collins Baker in *Burlington
Magazine*, vol. 21, 1912, p. 235. (7) Letter in the Gallery archives. (8) Collins
Baker, *loc. cit.*

PALMA VECCHIO
active 1510, died 1528

He was from Serinalta (Bergamo) but already domiciled in Venice
(where he lived for most of the rest of his life and where he died) when
first mentioned in documents (1510).[1] The date usually given for his
birth (1480) rests on no other evidence than Vasari's statement that he
was 48 years old at his death. His name was originally Iacomo Negreti.
He had adopted the name Palma as early as 1513.[2]

There is no reliable information on Palma's apprenticeship and the
documentation of works attributable to him is extremely unsatisfactory.
Three surviving pictures (Chantilly, Ottawa and Berlin) bear Palma
signatures but the authenticity of the signatures has been questioned in
all three cases, and the Berlin picture, in particular, is merely a copy of
one by Carpaccio. Of documented works, what is probably part of a
Sposalizio which was reported to be finished in 1522 was in the
Giovanelli collection (Venice), but it is only a small fragment and is
much restored. An *Adoration of the Kings* (Milan, Brera) is certainly
identical with one commissioned of Palma in 1525 but its appearance
suggests that it was largely executed by Palma's pupils after his death
three years later. A portrait of Francesco Querini (Venice, Querini
Stampalia collection) is beyond reasonable doubt identical with one
specified in an inventory of Palma's goods, but it is unfinished.[3] Of
eight pictures attributed to Palma by the *Anonimo Morelliano* (Marcantonio Michiel) four have been plausibly identified with existing
pictures (at Dresden,[4] Alnwick,[5] Brunswick[6] and Leningrad[7]) but the
identification is in no case beyond dispute. Finally, Vasari speaks,
among other pictures, of the important altarpiece of S. Barbara at S.
Maria Formosa, Venice, but the date of his work and his general
vagueness on Palma does not render this good authority. Nevertheless,
the S. Barbara (which is also mentioned as Palma's by Sansovino) shows
a highly individual style which is certainly not that of any other known
painter and which can be easily recognized in a number of other
pictures—mainly religious scenes and portraits of voluptuous blonde

women. The attribution of pictures of this kind to Palma is thus precarious in an academic sense only, and in fact is never doubted. His *œuvre*, though resting on foundations as apparently insecure as those of the city of Venice itself, is yet in the main equally firm.[8] But the extreme scarcity of reliable information precludes any rigid chronology, and thus the definition of the early and of the latest work of Palma is of the greatest difficulty. His putative early works have frequently been confused with Catena's putative late ones and his own putative late ones with Bonifazio's putative early ones.

REFERENCES: (1) The date 1500 occurring with a 'Palma' signature on the Chantilly picture (see below) is not usually accepted as genuine. (2) It could be questioned whether 'Iacomo de Antonio de Negreti depentor' and 'Jacomo Palma depentor' were really the same person. However a comparison of the family connections of 'Jacobus pictor quondam ser Antonii Nigreti' (document of 1523, reproduced by Ludwig in the Prussian *Jahrbuch*, 1903, *Beiheft*, pp. 66–7) and of 'Iacobus Palma pictor qm. ser Antonij' (Palma's will, reproduced by Ludwig, *op. cit.*, pp. 70–1) leaves no doubt on this matter. Furthermore, Molmenti (in *Emporium*, June, 1903, quoted by Venturi, *Storia*, IX, iii, pp. 387–8) states that the 'Jacomo de Antonio de Negreti' and 'Jacomo Palma' signatures are written in identical handwriting (facsimiles in further article by Ludwig, Prussian *Jahrbuch*, vol. 22 (1901), p. 185). (3) A companion portrait of Francesco's wife, little more than a lay-in, is not specified in the inventory. The attempts made by Ludwig (*loc. cit.*) to identify other pictures mentioned in the inventory can hardly be upheld. (4) 'Three Sisters' (repr. Gombosi, *Klassiker der Kunst, Palma*, p. 63). (5) Portrait of a Lady (repr. Gombosi, p. 84). (6) Adam and Eve (repr. Gombosi, p. 31). (7) Christ and the Adulteress (repr. Gombosi, p. 2). (8) These words were written in the 1950's.

636 PORTRAIT OF A POET, PROBABLY ARIOSTO

33 × 25 (0·83 × 0·63).
Transferred from panel to canvas by Paul Kiewert, Paris, 1857.[1]
Remounted on panel, 1916.

Much restored. The best preserved passages are the white shirt and the red silk of the sleeves.

The identification of the sitter with Lodovico Ariosto (1474–1533), made in the early editions of the National Gallery catalogue but long abandoned, may well be correct for the following reasons[2]:

1. The costume of no. 636 accords most easily with a date around 1515–16.[3] Ariosto would then have been 41 or 42 years old which is not inconsistent with the appearance of the sitter.

2. The most authentic likeness of Ariosto—the wood-cut by Titian in the edition of 1532 of the *Orlando Furioso*—is in profile and certainly dates from some years after no. 636. Nevertheless, it shows some basic similarity of feature—the high forehead with hair receding at the top, very long nose with high bridge, short upper lip and straggling beard.

3. What appears to be the original of numerous painted portraits of Ariosto—a portrait attributed to Titian (Casa Oriani, Ferrara)[4]—though less well authenticated than Titian's engraving, yet probably represents him. Being only in semi-profile a comparison with no. 636 is easier and

some degree of resemblance seems undeniable. In particular, it shows, like no. 636, a slight squint.[5]

4. The sitter of no. 636, with a book in his hand and laurels behind, seems intended not merely as a poet but to some extent also as the type of poet. Owing to Ariosto's pre-eminent fame it is questionable whether any other poet would have been painted in this guise at this time—precisely the period, if the indications afforded by the costume are correctly interpreted, of the initial publication of the *Orlando Furioso* (1516), the success of which was 'instantaneous and universal'.[6]

A near-contemporary description of Ariosto's features refers to his hair as black and wavy ('i capelli neri e crespi'),[7] whereas the hair in no. 636 is brown. Some or all of this effect, however, may be due to the repaint, and this should also be borne in mind when considering Ariosto's description of himself as bald for some time before the year 1517.[8] In any case, baldness is a relative term: Ariosto is not shown as entirely bald in Titian's wood-cut published in 1532. Consideration of these various factors leads to a conclusion that the identification of no. 636 with Ariosto is a plausible possibility though it cannot be demonstrated with certainty.

No. 636 appears in the National Gallery catalogues from 1861 to 1888 as 'Portrait of Ariosto, by Titian'. From 1889 to 1901 it figures as 'Portrait of a Poet, by Palma'. In the 1906 edition it makes a fleeting appearance as 'Portrait of a Poet, by Titian' and from 1911 to 1929 again as 'Portrait of a Poet, by Palma'. The attribution to Palma, now general and unquestionable, seems first to have been published by Reiset.[9]

VERSION: The same copy (called Rossetti) was lot 61, anon. sale, Christie's, 2nd June, 1967, and lot 80, anon. sale, Christie's, 27th July, 1967. It, or another, was lot 176, anon. sale, Christie's, 21st December, 1967.

PROVENANCE: In the Tomline collection[10] probably after 1850 (the year of Waagen's visit: he does not mention the picture).[11] In Paris by 1857 (when it was transferred to canvas). Purchased with the Beaucousin collection, 1860. Earlier provenance obscure. The assumption, made in the 1929 catalogue and elsewhere, that it was successively in the Renieri and Vianoli collections at Venice[12] rests on identifying it with each of two pictures recorded respectively by Ridolfi (1648) and Fontanini (1736) but which are not necessarily even identical with each other. Ridolfi says that Titian *fece il di lui* (Ariosto) *ritratto in maestosa maniera con veste di velluto nero foderato di pelle di lupi ceruieri apparendogli nel semo con gentil sprezzatura le crespe della camiscia. Hor trouasi in Venetia appresso del Signor Nicolò Renieri degno Pittore, ornato di molte riguardeuoli conditioni.*[13] It will be seen that the specification of a black velvet robe lined with lynx fur is not an adequate description of the gorgeous colours of the dress in no. 636—regardless of whether or not the basic material of the robe in the picture could justly be called black velvet or the fur lynx. Fontanini says simply *già molti anni io vidi l'Ariosto dipinto da Tiziano presso i signori Vianoli in Venezia a San Canciano.*[14] It is thus apparent that the Vianoli picture is not necessarily identical with the Renieri—in which collection, incidentally, there seems to be no other mention of it.[15]

REPRODUCTION: *Illustrations, Italian Schools*, 1937, p. 264.

REFERENCES: (1) Tracing from inscription made at the time. (2) No. 636 has not figured as Ariosto in the National Gallery catalogues since the edition of

1888. The purchase in 1904 of the Darnley Titian (no. 1944) as 'Ariosto'—an impossible identification—confused the issue and may have had something to do with no. 636 being catalogued again as Titian in the 1906 edition only (the first in which no. 1944 appeared). Cook (*Giorgione*, p. 82) refers to an article in the *Magazine of Art*, 1893, in which no. 636 is considered to be 'the portrait of Prospero Colonna, Liberator of Italy, painted by Giorgione in the year 1500'. (3) Notes in the Gallery archives by Stella Mary Pearce. (4) Published by Georg Gronau (*Burlington Magazine*, LXIII, 1933, pp. 194–203). Gronau dismisses the identification of no. 636 with Ariosto, partly because earlier champions of it had based their case on an assumption of identity with a picture mentioned by Ridolfi as by Titian. This latter hypothesis is in fact improbable owing to the lack of close correspondence in the dress (see below under PROVENANCE). (5) Pointed out by Giuseppe Agnelli: *I Ritratti dell' Ariosto* (*Rassegna d'Arte*, 1922, pp. 82–98). The author accepts the identification of no. 636 with Ariosto. A Titian portrait in the Indianapolis Museum, said to be of Ariosto, also has a squint. (6) J. Shield Nicholson: *Life and Genius of Ariosto* (1914), p. 58. Regarding the dating of no. 636, Gombosi (*Klassiker der Kunst, Palma Vecchio*, 1937, p. 65) suggests 'about 1515'. (7) From the biography attached to one of the editions of the *Orlando Furioso* of 1558. The status of this biography is discussed by Agnelli, *loc. cit*. (8) *Satira*, II, lines, 217 ff . . . *il capo calvo da un tempo* . . . (9) *Une Visite aux Musées de Londres en 1876* in *Gazette des Beaux-Arts*, 1877, vol. XV, p. 452. Reprinted 1887, p. 126. Crowe and Cavalcaselle (*Titian*, vol. 1, 1877, pp. 200–1) had suggested Pellegrino da San Daniele or Dosso Dossi. (10) Tomline provenance from a note in the Gallery archives. (11) Waagen on the Tomline collection is pp. 439–43 of vol. III of *Treasures of Art in Great Britain* (1854). (12) Not Vianoti as the 1929 catalogue would have it. (13) Ridolfi/Hadeln, I, p. 162. (14) Quoted by Agnelli, *loc. cit*. (15) Hadeln, *loc. cit*., note 2. Sir Charles Eastlake (MS. note-book in the Gallery's archives, entry for 1858, the fifth book for that year) refers to it in the Beaucousin collection: 'it is said that the portrait has always been in the family from which it was purchased (at a high price)'.

3939 A BLONDE WOMAN

Wood. Original panel 30½ × 25¼ (0·77 × 0·64). To this a strip 1″ high has been added along the top. On the right the priming extends to the edge of the wood. On the left and at the bottom it stops short of it, but paint (whether original or later) extends beyond it in these places to the edges.

Very fair condition. The repaint, most extensive in the shadow side of the face and adjoining hair, is for the most part easily recognizable. Called 'Flora' in earlier editions of the National Gallery catalogue, partly, no doubt, because of the flowers held in her right hand, and probably also because of the resemblance, often pointed out, to Titian's famous picture called by this name (Uffizi). Though not capable of proof, in default of contemporary written references to the picture, it is likely enough that some such intention existed, since the summary treatment of the features in no. 3939 precludes an assumption of precise portraiture.

In type and handling alike pre-eminently characteristic of Palma. Despite the extremely unsatisfactory state of the documentation in general (see the biographical notice of him) the attribution to him cannot be questioned. The omission of no. 3939 in the 1957 edition of

Berenson's *Lists* (Venetian School) was presumably a mistake, as it figures in earlier editions.

Comparison of the hair style shown here with similar features in contemporary Venetian painting—particularly dated works of Lotto—suggests a date around 1520.[1]

VERSIONS: 1. Formerly Duke of Northumberland, Syon (sold Sotheby's, 26th March, 1952 (109)).[2] 2. Anonymous sale, Sotheby's 12th December, 1934 (62). 3. Spahn (*Palma Vecchio*, 1932, p. 126) mentions another (with a pearl necklace) sold at Cologne, 1904.

PROVENANCE: William Delafield sale, Christie's, 30th April, 1870 (53) (as Paris Bordone) where bought Becci.[3] Bought Mond, 1889,[4] (just before this, Richter had tried to interest the National Gallery in the purchase—Richter/Morelli correspondence, 1960, pp. 555–6). Lent by Mond to R.A., 1892 (119), Grafton Galleries ('Fair Women'), 1894, no. 8 and 'Venetian Art', New Gallery, 1894–5, no. 210. Mond Bequest, 1924.

REPRODUCTION: *Illustrations, Italian Schools*, 1937, p. 264.

REFERENCES: (1) Notes by S. M. Pearce in the Gallery archives. (2) Presumably the picture referred to by J. P. Richter (Mond catalogue, 1910, vol. 1, p. 136) as being labelled 'Sir Peter Lely, after Titian', from which (and on no other evidence) Richter deduced that the original (i.e. no. 3939) had belonged to Charles I. A picture in the inventory of Charles II (no. 318) is not no. 3939 but the 'Sibyl' at Hampton Court which repeats the design of a picture (ex-Queen Christina and Orléans, engraved in the 1786 catalogue of the latter) erroneously identified by Gronau (*Gazette des Beaux-Arts*, 1895, p. 435) with no. 3939. (3) Richter, *op. cit.*, p. x. In the National Gallery copy of the Delafield sale catalogue the buyer's name is spelt 'Beggie'. (4) Richter, *loc. cit.*

Ascribed to PALMA VECCHIO

3079   S. GEORGE AND A FEMALE SAINT

Canvas (transferred from panel),[1] $40\frac{1}{2} \times 28\frac{3}{4}$ (1·02 × 0·73).

Much damaged and heavily repainted.[2]

The wingless soldier is identified as S. George by the remains of the dragon on the ground beside him. But there is no reason to suppose, as has been done hitherto, that the lady is his Princess. No. 3079 is in all probability the fragment of a *Sacra Conversazione*. The Madonna and Child would have been farther to the left and the female figure would have been intended as another saint. There is a complete picture precisely of this type by Palma in the Munich Gallery (no. 1108 in the 1911 catalogue of the Alte Pinakothek). The attribution to Palma does not seem to have been questioned, but the condition of the picture is too bad to permit of certainty.[3]

PROVENANCE: Layard's MS. states 'from the Grimani family at Venice, purchased from the dealer, Richetti'. Lent by Sir Austen Layard to South Kensington, 1869 (no. 6). Layard Bequest, 1916.

REPRODUCTION: *Illustrations, Italian Schools*, 1937, p. 265.

REFERENCES: (1) In 1880, by Professor Botti, according to Layard (no. 7 in his MS. catalogue in the Gallery archives). The transfer was done very unevenly.

If the picture is held up to a strong light some areas are seen to be translucent, others opaque. Evidently the support and priming were entirely removed in some places but not in others. X-ray photographs also show this effect. (2) An old Alinari photograph (no. 13,604) shows differences in the picture's appearance and was probably taken before the restoration by Cavenaghi which took place soon after September, 1896 (letter from Lady Layard in the Gallery archives). (3) Ludwig's statement (Prussian *Jahrbuch*, XXIV, 1903, *Beiheft*, p. 78) that no. 3079 is identical with one which figures in Palma's inventory is ruled out by the fact that the latter picture was specified as on canvas whereas no. 3079 was originally on panel.

Marco PALMEZZANO
1458/63–1539

From Forlì, and active there. In a document of 1483 he is described as over twenty and under twenty-five, and this is more probably correct than an inscription on his self-portrait of 1536 (Forlì Pinacoteca) which is interpreted to mean that he was then eighty. Luca Pacioli (1494) says that Palmezzano was the pupil of Melozzo da Forlì, and it is presumably an allusion to this that some of Palmezzano's earlier works are signed 'Marcus de Melotius'. There are many signed and dated works of religious subject. He appears to have been much influenced by Giovanni Bellini and other Venetians.

The monograph by C. Grigioni (1956) contains a detailed bibliography and documentation.

596   THE DEAD CHRIST IN THE TOMB, WITH THE VIRGIN MARY AND SAINTS

Panel, $38\frac{3}{4} \times 66$ (0·985 × 1·676).

The two top corners are new (see below).

A good deal of local damage and retouching—particularly along the lines of the horizontal splits in the panel.

The two male saints at the extremities are identifiable with S. Valeriano (on the spectator's left), with the blue and white standard of Forlì, and (spectator's right) San Mercuriale, first bishop of Forlì, with the red and white banner of the Guelphs.[1]

No. 596 was painted as lunette to crown an altarpiece of Christ administering the sacrament to the Apostles. This was in the Duomo at Forlì and is now in the Pinacoteca there; it is signed by Palmezzano and documented as finished in 1506.[2] Both the main panel and no. 596 are mentioned by Vasari, though wrongly ascribed to 'Rondanino'.[3]

The main panel is stated to measure 2·2 × 2·15.[4] Some 0·474 ($18\frac{5}{8}$″) has therefore been cut from no. 596 at the sides—0·237 ($9\frac{3}{8}$″) on each side, if it was cut symmetrically, as the present made up corners suggest. If the lunette was a perfect semicircle it would have been 1·075 ($42\frac{5}{16}$″) high, so that no more than 0·09 ($3\frac{1}{2}$″) would have been cut in the upright dimension.

The arrangement of the figures is somewhat unusual, since S. John and the Maries appear to be actually *in* the tomb.[5]

PROVENANCE: From the high altar of the Duomo at Forlì. Later moved to the chapel of S. Valeriano which had been rebuilt in 1821 and was demolished in 1840.[6] Then taken to the bishop's residence where it is said to have been used as a kitchen table.[7] Bought, cut down and restored by the painter, Girolamo Reggiani, and sold by him to the Roman dealer, Enea Vito, in 1851.[8] It subsequently changed hands again in Rome.[8] Reggiani probably added to the false signature 'Marchus de Melotius' which he believed to be that of Melozzo da Forlì[9] and which was removed when the picture entered the Gallery. Purchased from Gismondi of Rome, 1858.

REPRODUCTION: *Illustrations, Italian Schools*, 1937, p. 267.

REFERENCES: (1) Identification first (apparently) published in *Alcune Memorie intorno il pittore Marco Melozzo da Forlì*, 1843, by 'G.R.P.' (G. Reggiani pittore), p. 16. He describes the picture as a work of Melozzo da Forlì. (2) Egidio Calzini: *Marco Palmezzano e le sue Opere* in *Archivio Storico dell' Arte* VII, 1894, p. 345, n. 1. He also reproduces the main panel. (3) Vasari/Milanesi VI, 323 . . . *andava immitando l'opere di Rondanino da Ravenna, pittore più eccelente di Marco, il quale aveva poco innanzi messo allo altar maggiore di detto duomo una bellissima tavola dipintovi dentro Cristo che communica gli Apostoli, ed in un mezzo tondo sopra un Cristo morto, e nella predella di detta tavola storie di figure piccole de' fatti di Sant' Elena* . . . Elsewhere (Vasari/Milanesi V, 253) Vasari gives the name as Rondinello. The main panel, but not no. 596, is also mentioned by Marchesi: *Vitae Virorum Illustrium Foroliviensium*, 1726, p. 257 and in a *Guida* (Tipografia Casali) to Forlì of 1838, p. 10. (4) *Guida di Forlì*, 1893, p. 83. (5) Some of this effect may be due to the painter's not being able to organize the space differently: Christ is in any case differentiated from the other figures by sitting on a support which is distinct from the tomb and higher. (6) 'G.C.' (Giovanni Casali): *Intorno a Marco Palmezani*, 1844, p. 13, n. 2. (7) Egidio Calzini, *op. cit.*, p. 346, n. 3. Another and more illustrious picture now in this Gallery—no. 790 Michelangelo—is also said to have suffered a similar indignity, and likewise passed through the hands of Enea Vito. (8) Calzini, *loc. cit.* (9) Letter from Sir Charles Eastlake in the Gallery archives. Crowe and Cavalcaselle (*History of Painting in Italy*, vol. V, 1914, p. 52) give the form of the false signature as 'Marchus Melozii'.

PARMIGIANINO
1503–1540

His name was Girolamo Francesco Maria Mazzola, called 'Il Parmigianino'. A surviving baptismal entry gives the date of his birth as 11th January, 1503.[1] His youth was spent mainly in Parma. From about 1524 to 1527 he was in Rome; then, until 1531, mainly in Bologna. Thereafter in Parma again until shortly before his death, which took place at Casalmaggiore. His surviving works consist almost exclusively of religious paintings and portraits.

He was clearly precocious and originally trained, according to Vasari, by his two uncles, who, after the early death of his father, brought him up. His art was formed under the influence of Correggio, Raphael and Michelangelo. From these three dissimilar masters of the High Renaissance Parmigianino evolved an original Mannerism of the greatest elegance. His work had considerable local influence and his example was also followed in the French school of the sixteenth century.

Parmigianino has been the subject of four separate monographs published since the First War: by L. Fröhlich-Bum (1921), Giovanni Copertini (1932). A. O. Quintavalle (n.d., 1948) and Sydney J. Freedberg (1950). See also A. E. Popham on the *Drawings* (1953 and 1971).

REFERENCES: (1) Milanesi (edition of Vasari, vol. V, p. 218) assumes that by modern reckoning the date would be 1504. Had Parmigianino been born in Florence instead of Parma such would indeed have been the case. But according to a letter (in the Gallery archives) from Dr. Ettore Falconi of the Archivio di Stato, Parma, the system in force in Parma at the time was the same as the modern one and the date in consequence 1503.

33 ALTARPIECE: THE MADONNA AND CHILD WITH SS. JOHN THE BAPTIST AND JEROME

Poplar (arched top), 135 × 58½ (3·43 × 1·49).[1]

Considerably damaged by flaking, probably as early as the seventeenth century.[2] In areas which have been relatively free from this (such as the Baptist's right arm, all the upper part of the Child's body and the Madonna's red robe) the paint is in good condition and most of the surface quality intact.

Called in earlier editions of the catalogue 'The Vision of S. Jerome', but there is no evidence either for such a title's having been applied to this picture earlier than the beginning of the nineteenth century or for S. Jerome's ever having had such a vision.[3]

In his first edition (1550) Vasari says[4]:

> *Destosi allora vn pensiero al Signor Lorenzo Cibo, inuaghito della maniera sua, & venutone Partigiano [sic] di fargli fare qualche opera: & gli fece metter mano in vna tauola per San Saluatore del Lauro, da mettersi a vna cappella vicino alla porta. In questa figurò Francesco vna Nostra donna in aria che legge, con vn fanciullo fra le gambe. Et in terra con straordinaria & bella attitudine ginochioni cō vn piè, fece vn San Giouanni, che torcendo il torso, accenna CHRISTO fanciullo, & in terra a giacere in iscorto San Girolamo in penitenza, che dorme. La quale opera quasi a fine ridusse di tal profezzione, che se la fortuna non lo impediua, egli ne sarebbe stato lodatissimo; & ampiamente remunerato. Ma venne la ruina del sacco di Roma, nel MDXXVII. La quale non solo fu cagione che alle arti per vn tempo si diede bando, ma ancora, che la vita a molti artefici fosse tolta. Et mancò poco che Francesco non la perdesse ancor egli: & cio fu, che su'l principio del sacco, era egli si intento alla frenesia del lauorare, che quando i soldati entrauano per le case, & gia nella sua erano alcuni Tedeschi entrati, egli per romore che facessero, nō si mosse mai dal lauoro. Perilche giunti sopra, & vedutolo lauorare, stupiti di quella opera, che faceua, lo lasciarono seguitare.*

The account in the second edition (1568) differs in a number of details[5]:

> *Sentendo la fama di costui il signor Lorenzo Cibo, capitano della guardia del papa e bellissimo uomo, si fece ritrarre da Francesco; il quale si può dire che non lo ritraesse, ma lo facesse di carne e vivo. Essendogli*

poi dato a fare per madonna Maria Bufolina da città di Castello una tavola, che dovea porsi in San Savatore del Lauro in una cappella vicina alla porta, fece in essa Francesco una Nostra Donna in aria che legge, ed ha un fanciullo fra le gambe; ed in terra con straordinaria e bella attitudine ginocchioni con un piè fece un San Giovanni, che torcendo il torso accenna Cristo fanciullo, ed in terra a giacere in iscorto è un San Girolamo in penitenza che dorme. Ma quest' opera non gli lasciò condurre a perfezione la rovina ed il sacco di Roma del 1527; la quale non solo fu cagione. . . .

Vasari then gives the same story of the Imperial soldiery surprising Parmigianino at work and leaving him unmolested. Vasari concludes the account in his second edition with the words:

e così inviatolo verso la patria, si rimase egli [Parmigianino's uncle] *per alcuni giorni in Roma, dove dipositò la tavola fatta per madonna Maria Bufolina ne' frati della Pace; nel refettorio de' quali essendo stata molti anni, fu poi da messer Giulio Bufolini condotta nella lor chiesa a Città di Castello.*

The main discrepancy between the two editions concerns the patron— Lorenzo Cibo in the first, Maria Bufolina of Città di Castello in the second. As Biondo (1549)[6] mentions a Madonna by Parmigianino as then in the church of the Pace in Rome (only referred to by Vasari in his second edition) and as there is ample evidence that no. 33 belonged to the Bufalini family at Perugia in the eighteenth century[7] the second edition is likely to be the more accurate in this respect. In any case, the provenance of no. 33 can leave no doubt that it is the picture Vasari meant.[8]

The eclecticism of Parmigianino is well shown in no. 33. The pose of the Madonna and of the Child is evidently Michelangelesque in origin, that of the Baptist ultimately Leonardesque, though the motive was variously adapted by Raphael and by Correggio. The latter was probably the chief source for the pose of S. Jerome.

DRAWINGS: The following groups of drawings are for the whole composition:

1. (*a*) British Museum 1882–8–12–488. Pen and wash drawing which is certainly an early idea for the composition of no. 33. The motive of the circular form round the Madonna (composed of the arched top of the picture combined with the crescent moon) has not yet been introduced by the other main feature of the design of no. 33—the legs appearing above the Baptist's outstretched right arm—is already present in the drawing. The legs in question in the latter are similar to those in the painting but are those of the Virgin (who is standing), not the Child. The conception of the Baptist in this drawing is more or less the same as in the painting but the S. Jerome is different, being shown seated. In general, the drawings show that Parmigianino evidently experienced considerable difficulty in evolving a pose for the S. Jerome which should blend with the group of the Baptist and the Madonna and Child already fixed at an early stage.

(*b*) The *verso* of this drawing has a less detailed variant in red chalk. S. John here appears to be seated and S. Jerome is hardly indicated at all.

2. Parma (reproduced by Copertini, I, pl. XLV). Pen. Clearly from a later

stage than no. 1 (a) above, all these figures being shown essentially as in the painting. But in this sketch the upper and lower halves of the picture are shown side by side—the Madonna and Child appearing to the right of the sleeping S. Jerome.

The following groups of drawings are for the Virgin and Child alone:

3. (a) Chantilly, Musée Condé. Pen, ink and wash (repr. Popham, pl. XXX). Two studies of the Madonna seated with the Child. In the left-hand sketch the figures are seated on a marble plinth (Rosaspina 438–40). These studies clearly represent a very early stage indeed—so much so that were it not for the drawings on the *verso* (see no. 8 below) which certainly connect with the painting, one might assume that they were intended for a different purpose.

(b) Ashmolean Museum, Oxford (Parker 441, ex-John Ford collection). Pen and wash. The Virgin and Child are arranged similarly to no. 1 above, but as the Virgin is seated it probably represents a later stage.

(c) A copy in aquatint of a very similar drawing (in reverse) is in the Rosaspina album in the British Museum (no. 206), the original stated to belong, in Rosaspina's time, to Antonio Armano.

(d) Further copies of similar drawings are in the Rosaspina album (no. 553), at Leningrad (reproduced) by Fröhlich-Bum, fig. 10) Windsor (Popham and Wilde, 651) and reproduced by C. Mentz[9] from the collection of Henry Reveley.

(e) Three drawings of a standing Madonna with the Child (British Museum Cracherode Ff. 1. 94, Frankfurt, Städelsches Kunstinstitut no. 4255 and Louvre 6379) seem to represent early ideas.

(f) A further drawing (of the Madonna clasping the Child, Rosaspina 196–7) is only doubtfully connected.

4. (a) In a damaged sketch at Naples (1–C–145–70) the Madonna's pose comes near to that of the painting, but the Child's arms are different.

(b) A more advanced stage still is represented by drawings, probably copies, in the Albertina[10] and at Wilton House.[11] by Rosaspina (467–9) and by engravings by M. Corneille (of a drawing in the Jabach collection) and by Vorsterman. In these the group of the Madonna and Child has assumed most of the characteristics of the painting.

(c) A further drawing also representing an advanced stage of development is in the *Ecole des Beaux-Arts*, Paris (Popham XXXIII). The Virgin's head and neck are not shown: the lower part of the Child's body is as in the picture.

The following groups of drawings are for the S. Jerome:

5. (a) British Museum 1905–11–10–32. Pen, ink and wash. From an early stage in the evolution and similar to the S. Jerome in no. 1 (a) above. In this drawing S. Jerome is burying his head in his hands.

(b) A brush drawing (Louvre 6971) shows a recumbent S. Jerome, perhaps an early idea for the final form.

(c) Three further sketches of S. Jerome (British Museum, Payne Knight, pp. 2, 131) are claimed by Freedberg[12] to belong to the series but are not necessarily connected.

6 (a) Louvre 6423. Red chalk. Attitude approaching that in the painting.

(b) Rosaspina album (448–50). Copy after a drawing from a more advanced stage still. S. Jerome is shown almost as in the painting except for the position of the arms.

(c) Uffizi 13611F, pen and ink. Sheet of sketches of which one of S. Jerome's right hand is almost exactly as in the painting.

The following miscellaneous drawings have also been connected with no. 33:

7. Ashmolean Museum, Oxford (Parker 442) (ex-Joseph Rignault collection), black and white chalk. The Virgin naked except for heavy drapery covering her left leg. Her pose is as in the picture; *verso* has slight sketches of legs and a study for the Child.

8. Chantilly, Musée Condé (*verso* of 3 (a) above). Two studies for S. John and one for S. Jerome on the same sheet. Right-hand figure of Baptist in similar pose to painting. S. Jerome quite different.

9. Frankfurt. Städelsches Kunstinstitut 13,772. Damaged drawing showing the upper parts of the two saints' bodies, the Baptist's again similar to the final version, S. Jerome's totally different.

10. British Museum 1860–6–16–23. Head of the Baptist, evidently copied from the painting.

ENGRAVING: By Bonasone (Bartsch 62).

VERSIONS: 1. Palazzo Mancini, Città di Castello. Actual size. According to Magherini Graziani (*loc. cit.*) by Cav. Bernardino Gagliardi (1609–60). Mentioned by G. Mancini (1832)[13] the then owner. Presumably distinct from the copy (? destroyed in the earthquake of 1789) which was substituted by the Bufalini in the church of S. Agostino at Città di Castello when they removed the original (see PROVENANCE).

2. Sir Philip Miles sale (Leigh Court gallery). Christie's, 28th June, 1884 (46). 1' 4" × 1'.

3. Duke of Westminster sale, Christie's, 4th July, 1924 (24). Mentioned by Waagen (*Treasures* . . ., II, p. 170). Engraved as no. 135 in the 1821 catalogue of the Grosvenor Gallery.

4. John Samuel collection (p. 15 in the 1895 catalogue). Broader format through displacement of S. Jerome farther to right. Partial copies in the Palazzo Tadini, Lovere and (of the Baptist) in a Crucifixion by G. B. Pacetti ('Sguazzino') in S. Fortunato, Città di Castello.[14] In the British Museum there is an engraving of the Baptist's head by Francesco Novelli (1764–1836) inscribed as from a picture belonging to Filippo Mattei Baldini of Pergola. A painted pastiche in the Museo Correr, Venice, is attributed to Francesco da Santacroce (no. 75).

PROVENANCE: Painted in Rome in 1527. For the somewhat conflicting evidence for the circumstances, see above. L. Scaramuccia (*Le Finezze dei Penelli Italiani*, 1674) and Certini's MS. (first half of the eighteenth century)[15] mention no. 33 as in the church of S. Agostino at Città di Castello. Affò (1784) says that in his day it had already been withdrawn (in a somewhat damaged state) by the Bufalini to the *palazzo* to prevent further deterioration, its place being taken in S. Agostino by a copy.[16] A nineteenth-century source gives the date of this removal as 1772.[17] Later (probably in 1789)[18] it was sold by the Bufalini to James Durno, an English painter[19] living in Italy and by him, in Rome, to the 1st Marquess of Abercorn.[20] Durno's death, in Rome in 1795 (together with a reference, of 9th December, 1795, in the Farington diary)[21] gives that year as *terminus ad quem* for the latter transaction which may, indeed, have occurred as early as 1792.[22] Sold by Lord Abercorn, before 9th May, 1809, to a dealer called Harris.[23] Between then and 1819 its seems to have belonged to Hart Davis.[24] Lent, 1819, to the British Institution by G. Watson Taylor (1), at whose sale, 14th June (second day) 1823 (61) bought by Holwell Carr for the British Institution, where exhibited again in 1824 (2). Presented by the Directors of the British Institution, 1826.

REPRODUCTION: *Illustrations, Italian Schools*, 1937, p. 271.

REFERENCES: (1) Measurements by P. M. R. Pouncey. (2) A MS. (Uffizi, Miscellanee MSS., vol. 1, no. 60, inserto 26) quoted by Magherini Graziani (*L'Arte a Città di Castello*, 1897) says of no. 33: *dal mezo in giù in molti luoghi scrostata et guasta*. Professor C. Fasola, writing from the Uffizi in 1939 (letter in the Gallery archives) dates this document to the mid-seventeenth century. See also above under PROVENANCE. (3) There is, however, a passage in the Golden Legend which describes S. Jerome sleeping in the desert. A possible explanation would be that the combination of the Baptist and S. Jerome might have suggested a vision that S. Augustine is apocryphally said to have had of those two saints (see no. 3946, Signorelli, of this Gallery). Though no. 33 came from a church dedicated to S. Augustine (at Città di Castello) there are discrepancies. (4) P. 847. (5) Vasari/Milanesi V, pp. 224 ff. (6) Michel Angelo Biondo: *Della Nobilissima Pittura* (Venice, 1549), p. 19. (7) A MS. account (*Chiese e Conventi Tifernati* by Alessandro Certini) is to the effect that Nicolò di Pietro Bufolini, the uncle of Giulio and a colonel on duty in Rome during the Sack, acquired no. 33 at that time from the marauding soldiery. The exact date of this MS. is uncertain, but works published by this author appeared during the second quarter of the eighteenth century. The relevant extract is published on p. 182 of *L'Arte a Città di Castello*, by G. Magherini Graziani (1897). The latter gives (p. 34) the then location of the MS. as *Archivio della Canonica di San Florido* (Città di Castello). A further extract quoted by him says that the frame of the picture at that time was adorned with the Bufalini arms quartered with those of Vitelleschi di Corneto. (8) A minor discrepancy is that Vasari says the Madonna is reading, whereas in no. 33, though there is a book on her lap, neither she nor the Child are reading it. L. Fröhlich-Bum (*Parmigianino*, 1921, p. 22) dismisses the identification on the ground that no. 33 is not unfinished. Vasari's words are equivocal on this subject but could be interpreted to mean that as the Sack of Rome occurred when Parmigianino had nearly but not quite finished the picture he was thereby denied the réclame of a first public showing. (9) *Imitations of Ancient and Modern Drawings*, 1798. (10) S.L. 59. (11) Reproduced by Strong: *Reproductions . . . of Drawings . . . at Wilton House*, 1900. (12) *Parmigianino*, 1950, p. 176. (13) *Istruzione Storico-Pittorica per visitare le Chiese e Palazzi di Città di Castello*, 1832, vol. 1, p. 269. (14) The latter according to Mancini, *op. cit.*, vol. I, p. 186. (15) Quoted by Magherini Graziani, *op. cit.*, p. 182. (16) *Vita del graziosissimo Pittore Francesco Mazzola*, p. 59. This statement disproves one by Magherini Graziani (*loc. cit.*) that the Bufalini family withdrew the picture from the church as a result of the earthquake of 1789. (17) *Memorie Ecclesiastiche di Città di Castello raccolte da M.G.M.A.V. di Città di Castello*, vol. 4, Città di Castello, 1843, p. 240 f. (18) Magherini Graziani (*loc. cit.*) mentions a document of 1833 referring to a sale in 1789 to James Durno of various pictures from Città di Castello including one from the Bufalini family. It seems probable that the latter was no. 33. (19) Mancini, *op. cit.*, p. 60 mentions the sale to Durno. (20) W. Buchanan: *Memoirs of Painting*, 1824, I, p. 72. (21) 'More, the landscape painter, was concerned with an Italian in picture dealing; and had a concern in the picture of Parmigianino bought by the Marquess of Abercorn for 1500 guineas.' Inasmuch as Buchanan (reference no. 20, above) says Lord Abercorn bought no. 33 from Durno in Rome the part played by More in the transaction is not clear. There is also a mysterious reference in the Farington diary, 9th March, 1795: 'Champernowne I called on and went with him and Simpson the picture dealer to see a large Parmigiano which belongs to Mr. Christie's father.' A 'large Parmigiano' in England at this precise time certainly reads like a reference to no. 33. Nevertheless the style 'Mr. Christie's father' seems inapplicable either to James Durno or to the Marquess of Abercorn and since the other evidence shows fairly conclusively that no. 33 belonged to one or other of the latter at this time it was presumably a question of another large picture attributed to Parmigianino. (22) A transcript, in the Gallery archives, of a letter in Italian (headed 'from Hume, 31st July, 1792') reads as follows: *Un Cavaliere Inglese ha fatto ultimamente l'acquisto d'un bellissimo quadro di Parmigiano, è stato pochi anni fa un pezzo d'altare in un convento d'una città non molto lontana di Perugia, il quale è stato rovinato da un terremoto, ma felicitatamente il quadro non ha sofferto; rappresenta la Vergine col Bambino sopra, e giù il San Giovanni a mezzo inginocchiato, che mostra col dito il Salvatore in lontananza. Dorme il San Giuseppe. Questo è opera bellissima e ben conservata, e mi fa ricordare dei capi d'opera d'Italia.* It seems not impossible that the 'Cavaliere Inglese' should be Lord Abercorn, or that S. Jerome should be described in error as S. Joseph or even that no. 33, after judicious restoration at the hands of Durno, should give the impression of being 'ben conservata'. (23) The Farington diary entry for that date (vol. V, p. 157). On 26th June, 1808 William Beckford claimed in a letter that the Marquess of Abercorn had offered it to him for £3,000, through Benjamin

West, which was more than Beckford was prepared to pay (letter in Boyd Alexander's *Life at Fonthill, 1807–1822* (1957), p. 72). (**24**) Mrs. Jameson: *A Handbook to the Public Galleries of Art in and near London* (1842), part 1, p. 61.

GIOVANFRANCESCO PENNI
1496(?)–*c*. 1528

According to Vasari he was a Florentine, who, with Giulio Romano, was accorded special favours by Raphael, lodging in his house and being treated as his son. Vasari adds that Raphael made them his heirs. His rôle was evidently that of assistant to Raphael and executant of his designs. His own artistic personality is still very imperfectly defined. Vasari concludes by saying 'visse Giovanfrancesco anni quaranta, e l'opere sue furono circa al 1528'. This is generally interpreted to mean that he died at the age of forty about 1528. There is, however, some evidence that he may have been born in 1496 (Vasari/Milanesi IV, 643, n. 2).

See 225 GIULIO Romano and Giovanfrancesco PENNI.

BALDASSARE PERUZZI
1481–1536

He was from Siena but active in maturity mainly in Rome, in the service, among other patrons, of Agostino Chigi and successive popes. Panel pictures by him are rare. He occupied himself mainly with frescoes and architecture and with various forms of draughtsmanship, particularly perspective, for which he was famous and which he applied with preeminent success to theatrical scenery. He was also notably interested in recording the antiquities of Rome and elsewhere.

167　THE ADORATION OF THE MAGI

Pen and ink and brown wash on paper tinted brown. The original paper has been incorporated into a rectangle measuring $44\frac{1}{4} \times 42\frac{1}{8}$ (1.125×1.07). The original paper is of very uneven outline at the top and sides and some reduction has certainly occurred there. At the sides the figures, where truncated by the cutting or fraying of the original paper, have been completed on the paper of the later surrounding rectangle. There are also a number of repairs on the original paper area.

Signed: BAL· SENEN·/F

In his first edition (1550) Vasari describes no. 167 as follows:

> *Et ancora fece al Conte Gio. Batista sopradetto* [Bentivogli] *vn disegno d'vna Natiuità co' magi di chiaro oscuro, cosa marauigliosissima a vedere i caualli, i carriaggi, le corti di tre Re con tanta grazia da Baldassare imaginate; nella quale fece muraglie di tempii & inuenzioni di casamēti nella capanna bellissima; la quale opera fece poi colorire il Conte a GIROLAMO TREVIGI, che molto fu lodata.*

The sense of this passage remained unchanged in the second edition (1568).[1]

Datable to the period 1522–3 when Peruzzi is recorded in Bologna, which is the context of Vasari's account.

The horse on the right, and its groom, probably derive from the antique group on the Quirinal.

The painted copy by Girolamo da Treviso, mentioned by Vasari, may be no. 218 of this Gallery.

VERSIONS: No. 218 of this Gallery. Another, not traced since the nineteenth century, was dated 1576.[2] A pen and ink copy with variations, signed by Hans Bol and Frederik Vermuelen, is in the Dresden Print Room.[3]

ENGRAVING: By Agostino Carraci, 1579 (Bartsch vol. 18, no. 11). This includes a number of features not occurring in no. 167, notably four more angels, together with *putti* and cherubs' heads, in the upper corners, and the star in front of the arch. Another engraving by Cesare Roberti.

PROVENANCE: Despite gaps in the pedigree evidently the work described by Vasari (1550) and by Pietro Lamo (1560)[4] in the possession of the Bentivoglio family in Bologna. Zani (1820)[5] published information from Carlo Bianconi to the effect that it had remained in the Bentivoglio family's possession until 1759 when it was bought by 'Mr. Danton' for the King of England. In fact 'Mr. Danton' was evidently Richard Dalton, who wrote to Lord Bute from Florence on 17th November, 1758[6] saying that the Bentivoglio family were selling the Peruzzi drawing described by Vasari and engraved by Agostino Carracci. Dalton was buying for both Lord Bute and the Prince of Wales, but it has not yet emerged how no. 167 entered the possession of Lord Vernon, by whom presented, 1839.[7]

REPRODUCTION: *Illustrations, Italian Schools*, 1937, p. 273.

REFERENCES: (1) Vasari/Milanesi IV, 597. (2) Michelangelo Gualandi: *L'Adorazione dei Magi, Pittura del XVI Secolo*, 1853. (3) Reproduced *Old Master Drawings*, VII (1932–3), pl. 17. Philip Pouncey, in notes in the Gallery archives, drew attention to the recurrence of the group of God the Father and angels in Bartolomeo Cesi's work of the same subject in S. Procolo, Bologna (repr. *Critica d'Arte*, IV, 1939, after p. 57) and to reminiscences of the lower part in Alfonso Lombardi's relief in the predella of the Arca di S. Domenico, Bologna (1533); also to three cognate compositions by Peruzzi: a drawing at Sigmaringen (repr. Frizzoni: *L'Arte Italiana*, 1891, 217), an unlocated painting of which a photograph is in the Gallery archives (A. C. Cooper, no. 12301) and a drawing in the Uffizi (no. 589, attr. Genga). (4) *Graticola di Bologna*, 1560, ed. of 1844, p. 35. (5) Pietro Zani: *Enciclopedia Metodica Critico-Ragionata . . .*, part II, vol. V, 1820, p. 202. He adds that the drawing is supposed to have been lost at sea on the way to England. (6) MS., apparently unpublished, in the Bute papers kindly communicated by Basil Skinner of the Scottish National Portrait Gallery. (7) Probably not identical with an *Adoration of the Magi*, attributed to Peruzzi in the Truchsessian Gallery (no. 537 in the 1804 catalogue, no. 222, 3rd day's sale, 29th March, 1806).

CALISTO PIAZZA DA LODI
Active 1514,[1] died probably 1562[2]

He was a member of a family of Lodi artists known as Piazza or de' Toccagni. On signed pictures located outside Lodi he signs Calistus (or Chalistus or Calixtus) Laudensis. On works in Lodi he signs

Calistus de Platea. Active up to 1529 apparently mainly in Brescia, there-after mainly at Lodi.[3] A number of signed altarpieces survive which show him to have been a follower of Romanino.

REFERENCES: (1) Chizzola (*Le Pitture di Brescia*, 1760, p. 141) mentions a work no longer extant, apparently dated as of that year. (2) For the date of death see Luigi Cremascoli: *L'Incoronata di Lodi*, 1956, p. 20, quoting a MS. by P. C. Cernuscolo. Also M. Gualandi: *Memorie Originali Italiane*, I, 1840, p. 175. (3) Thieme-Becker (article Piazza, Calisto) have an inexplicable reference to a fresco in the Escorial painted by Calisto in 1539. At this date the Escorial did not exist.

Ascribed to CALISTO PIAZZA DA LODI

2096   PORTRAIT OF A MAN

Panel, $29\frac{3}{4} \times 23$ (0.756×0.589).
General condition fair despite some obvious old damages.

Hitherto catalogued as Romanino or 'ascribed to Romanino',[1] though an earlier attribution to Calisto da Lodi is recorded by H. Cook.[2] The modelling of the head seems too weak for Romanino and the handling too crude, and although both he and Calisto da Lodi are ill-defined as portraitists no. 2096 seems to accord better with donors and other individually treated heads in authentic altarpieces by the latter than with comparable heads, such as that of the donor in the Salò altarpiece of S. Anthony, by the former.

The costume shown would accord best with a dating around 1528–9.[3]

PROVENANCE: An inscription recorded as formerly on the back said 'Ettore Averoldi Brescia 1865'.[4] Exh. New Gallery, London, 1893–4, no. 169 (lent by the Misses Cohen). No. 22 ('Romanino') in the 1895 catalogue of the John Samuel collection, dedicated to his memory by his nieces, the Misses Cohen, by whom bequeathed, 1906.

REPRODUCTION: *Illustrations, Italian Schools*, 1937, p. 312.

REFERENCES: (1) The Romanino attribution is accepted by Berenson (*Lists*, various editions excluding the last, of 1968), Venturi (*Storia . . .*, IX, III, p. 856) and Nicodemi (*Gerolamo Romanino*, 1925, p. 198). (2) In *L'Arte*, 1907, p. 152. (3) Notes by Stella Mary Pearce in the Gallery archives. In this connection mention may be made of an attribution to L'Ortolano (reported by M. L. Ferrari: *Il Romanino*, 1961, p. 309, as originating in R. Longhi). L'Ortolano's existence is not documented after 1524. For the rest the present writer can see no similarity of execution between no. 2096 and no. 669. The latter is the least badly authenticated work of L'Ortolano. F. Heinemann (*Giovanni Bellini e I Belliniani*, I, 1962, p. 277, no. V. 405) apparently proposes an attribution of no. 2096 to Morando. (4) Therefore perhaps identical with the portrait by Romanino of Ghirardo Averoldi mentioned in the Averoldi collection by Brognoli, *Nuova Guida . . . di Brescia*, 1826, p. 201.

PONTORMO

1494–1557

His name was Jacopo Carucci, called 'da Pontormo' from the Tuscan village (near Empoli) where he was born. His father, according to

Vasari, was also a painter and had been a pupil of Domenico Ghirlandaio. During his childhood Pontormo was brought to Florence, in the neighbourhood of which he continued to work for the rest of his life. Vasari says he was successively the pupil of Leonardo da Vinci, Albertinelli, Piero di Cosimo and Andrea del Sarto. The various difficulties (which are complicated) in the way of reconciling Vasari's account of Pontormo's apprenticeship with the known movements of these four masters are put in detail in the first appendix to F. M. Clapp's monograph (1916).

His work was mainly of religious subjects though he also painted a number of portraits. His highly individual, neurotic style was formed on that of Andrea del Sarto. He subsequently reacted in different ways to Dürer's engravings and to Michelangelo.

1131 JOSEPH IN EGYPT

Panel, painted surface $38 \times 43\frac{1}{8}$ (0·96 × 1·09).

The original panel is $44\frac{3}{4}$ (1·14) wide, there being narrow vertical strips on each side of the painted area. Along the base another strip of wood seems to have been added later. Before the picture was last cleaned (in 1940) a signature (·JACOMO DA PONTORMO·) spanned the join between the original panel and this addition. What now remains (on the original panel only) consists of four symbols not previously visible (O and i followed by two indecipherable letters or figures) and then the top half of the inscription as visible before the cleaning. Although the existing inscription is certainly old it is most unlikely to be a genuine signature.[1]

Fair condition.

Four separate episodes are combined. On the left Joseph (who is dressed throughout in a brown tunic and mauve cloak) addresses Pharaoh and indicates an old man kneeling on his left.[2] Right foreground, Joseph on a car, with his arm round one of his sons, listens to a man reading a document (presumably the spokesman of the mob who are clamouring—evidently for bread—in the centre, the bulk of whom are being restrained by two men). Right middle distance, Joseph leads one of his sons up the stairs, at the top of which the other is welcomed by a woman. Right background, Joseph presents his sons to the dying Jacob (Genesis xlvii (from verse 13) and xlviii).[3]

It seems likely that Joseph in this picture is presented as a forerunner or type of Christ. One of the Pontormos (likewise of Joseph) in this series from Panshanger (see below) is inscribed 'Salvator Mundi'.

No. 1131 is one of a series of pictures (of which nos. 1218 and 1219 of this Gallery are others) executed, according to Vasari,[4] by Andrea del Sarto, Pontormo, Granacci and Bacchiacca for Pier Francesco Borgherini, a Florentine gentleman. Three others by Pontormo, identifiable as from the same series, were in the Cowper collection at Panshanger[5] and those by Andrea del Sarto, Granacci and Bacchiacca divided between the Pitti and Uffizi Galleries (Florence), the Borghese

(Rome) and the National Gallery. The Pontormos from Panshanger were originally intended, according to Vasari, to be let into *cassoni*. No. 1131 also may have constituted part of the furnishing but Vasari seems to distinguish it from the other Pontormos.

It is likely that so complicated a programme took several years to execute, but there is no very precise evidence for dating. In his life of Sarto Vasari mentions a marriage bed in connection with the Borgherini decorations and in his biography of Pontormo puts a speech into the mouth of Borgherini's wife in which she says that the whole programme had been ordered by her father-in-law in honour of their marriage. This took place in 1515[6] and the decorations would in the circumstances be unlikely to date from much before then. On the other hand it is improbable that no. 1131, at least, was painted much later since Vasari identifies the youth shown in it seated, with a basket, on the steps as Bronzino. The latter was born in 1503 and appears still a child.[7] As he would have been twelve at the time of the Borgherini wedding a dating of no. 1131 as soon as possible after 1515 would therefore be reasonable.[8] The costumes also accord best with a dating as near to 1515 as possible.[9]

Vasari's description (Milanesi edition, vol. VI. pp. 261–2) shows the esteem in which no. 1131 was held in the sixteenth century:

> *Ma chi vuol veder quanto egli facesse di meglio nella sua vita, per considerare l'ingegno e la virtù di Iacopo nella vivacità delle teste, nel compartimento delle figure, nella varietà dell' attitudini e nella bellezza dell' invenzione, guardi in questa camera del Borgherini, gentiluomo di Firenze, all' entrare della porta nel canto a man manca, un' istoria assai grande pur di figure piccole; nella quale è quando Iosef in Egitto, quasi re e principe, riceve Iacob suo padre con tutti i suoi fratelli, e figlioli di esso Iacob, con amorevolezze incredibili: fra le quali figure ritrasse, a piedi della storia, a sedere sopra certe scale, Bronzino allora fanciullo e suo discepolo, con una sporta; che è una figura viva e bella a maraviglia. E se questa storia fusse nella sua grandezza (come è piccola) o in tavola grande o in muro, io ardirei di dire che non fusse possible vedere altra pittura fatta con tanta grazia, perfezione e bontà, con quanta fu questa condotta da Iacopo: onde meritamente è stimata da tutti gli artefici la più bella pittura che il Puntormo facesse mai; nè è maraviglia che il Borgherino la tenesse quanto faceva in pregio, nè che fusse ricerco da grandi uomini di venderla per donarla a grandissimi signori e principi.*

The gabled gateway in the background of no. 1131, which is markedly Northern in appearance, is apparently borrowed, with variations, from Lucas van Leyden's engraving (dated 1510) of *Ecce Homo* (Bartsch 71). The scroll held by the kneeling man, bottom right, is inscribed but appears indecipherable.[10]

COPY: Louvre (no. 1725, where attributed Andrea del Sarto), pen and ink.[11] A derivative by Breenbergh in the Barber Institute, Birmingham.

DRAWINGS: Uffizi 6537F (Berenson 2040). Red chalk, 23·5 × 11·5 cm. Study

for drapery over extended right arm. Berenson suggests for the figure on the
extreme left of no. 1130 but Clapp (*Pontormo*, 1916, p. 159) doubts this.

Uffizi 6581F (Berenson 2081). Red chalk 17 × 13 cm. Head of an old man.
Connected by Berenson with several heads in no. 1131 and with the S. Michele
Visdomini altarpiece (see note no. 7). J. Cox Rearick (*The Drawings of Pontormo*,
1964, text, pp. 155–6) associates three further drawings with no. 1131, and in
Master Drawings, 8, no. 4, 1970, p. 367 adds a fourth.

PROVENANCE: Pier Francesco Borgherini; later (according to Milanesi, in
vol. VI, p. 262 of his edition of Vasari) in possession of Giovan Gherardo de'
Rossi. Very possibly no. 157 in the Aldobrandini inventories of 1603 and before
1665 (printed in *Palatino*, 1964, N. 7–8, p. 162). Noted by Waagen[12] in the
collection of the Duke of Hamilton (by whom exh. R.A., 1873, 194).[13] Purchased,
Clarke Fund, Hamilton Palace sale, 1st July, 1882 (766). Cleaned Pictures
Exhibition, National Gallery, 1947 (36).

REPRODUCTION: *Illustrations, Italian Schools*, 1937, p. 287.

REFERENCES: (1) For three reasons: so full a signature would be unique in
Pontormo's work, the letters themselves are of wretched quality and there
seems to be no authority for the form of the christian name (in contemporary
documents printed in the appendix to Clapp's monograph Pontormo's name is
referred to variously as Jacopo, Jachopo, Giacopo, Jacobo or Jacopino, but
never Jacomo). (2) The exact significance of this group is not clear. Pouncey
(draft catalogue entry in the Gallery archives) assumed that the elderly couple
and the youth were Egyptians for whom Joseph is pleading before Pharaoh.
But no such episode occurs in Genesis xlvii, where Joseph negotiates with the
Egyptians independently of Pharaoh. Alternatively the old man in blue on his
knees could be Jacob being presented, on arrival in Egypt, by Joseph to Pharaoh.
Vasari's description (quoted in the text of this entry) indeed mentions such a
scene but seems to be confusing Joseph with Pharaoh and Jacob's family with
the crowd of Egyptians. (3) An interpretation on these lines was first published
by J.-P. Richter in *The Academy*, 1882, p. 211. Rachel Wischnitzer goes into
the question in greater detail in *Gazette des Beaux-Arts*, March, 1953, pp.
145–66. (4) Vasari's references to the subject are scattered through his biogra-
phies of Andrea del Sarto, Granacci, Pontormo, Baccio d'Agnolo, Aristotile da
San Gallo and Perugino. There are further references in Borghini: *Il Riposo*
(1584), pp. 420, 447 and 482. (5) The Panshanger Pontormos passed by
inheritance to Lady Salmond in 1952. (6) Litta, under Acciaiuoli, to which
family Pier Francesco Borgherini's bride, Margherita, belonged. (7) This much,
at least, may justifiably be inferred and Vasari, indeed, describes Bronzino in
this connection as a child ('fanciullo'). Attempts which have been made by
several scholars to define more precisely the age of the youth are mere hypotheses. (8) Pontormo's altarpiece at S. Michele Visdomini, Florence is dated
1518 and has features in common with no. 1131, notably the heads of SS.
James and John which are of similar type to the dying Jacob in no. 1131 and to
several of the Egyptians in the centre. The source in all cases was probably the
Laöcoön. (9) Stella Mary Pearce, in notes in the Gallery archives, points out
that the clothes are clearly fashionable, that the men wear small hats and that
already by 1518–19 men's hats were at their largest. (10) Clapp (*Pontormo*, 1916,
p. 157) endeavoured to read it, but his version does not seem to the present
writer to bear any close correspondence with the characters, and in any case
does not make sense. (11) According to Clapp, *op. cit.*, p. 159. (12) *Treasures . . .*,
III (1854), p. 299 (as Bacchiacca). Possibly identifiable with 'Andrea dell
[sic] Sarto Part of the life of Joseph' which was lot 69 in 'Mr. Denestry' sale,
17th April (2nd day), 1766. (13) The present writer has been unable to identify
no. 1131 with any entry in the numerous (MS.) Hamilton inventories of the
seventeenth, eighteenth and nineteenth centuries. The possible Aldobrandini
identification suggested by John Shearman.

3941   A DISCUSSION

Wood, transferred to canvas, $13\frac{7}{8} \times 9\frac{2}{5}$ (0.35×0.23). Considerably rubbed, and restored in many places.

The subject was identified by Andrew Pigler as 'Herod and the Three Magi'.[1] To support his thesis he reproduced a drawing by Pieter de Witte which clearly does represent such a subject.[2] While this theme may in fact be applicable to no. 3941 a considerable element of doubt must remain. None of the figures is shown with the attributes of a king and there are no further accessories which might establish the identification.

The attribution of no. 3941 to Pontormo has been general[3] except for the National Gallery catalogue of 1929 where it is attributed to Francesco Rossi (Salviati) and J. C. Rearick (*The Drawings of Pontormo*, 1964, pp. 374 and 394) who ascribes it to Cavalori.The loss of a great deal of surface quality makes it difficult to pronounce with confidence, but certain features, particularly the contours of the drapery over the right knee of the figure on the left, together with his right leg, are characteristic of Pontormo.

VERSION: Musée Magnin, Dijon (formerly colls. Gaddi, the Rev. Sanford, Lord Methuen and Brunner).[4] Perhaps no. 38 (Sarto) in the 1847 Sanford Catalogue.

PROVENANCE: Conte Enrico Costa, Florence; bought 1892 by Ludwig Mond.[5] Mond Bequest. 1924.

REPRODUCTION: *Illustrations, Italian Schools*, 1937, p. 316.

REFERENCES: (1) *Art Bulletin*, XXI (1939), p. 230. The text is Matthew ii, 7 where Herod asks the Magi to inform him when they have found the Child. (2) All the figures are shown crowned, and an episode in the background clearly shows the procession of the Magi guided by the star. The location of the drawing was not known to the author of the *Art Bulletin* article at the time of its publication. (3) E.g. Berenson (*Lists*, 1932 and 1936), Clapp (*Pontormo*, 1916, p. 156) and Richter (Mond catalogue, vol. II, pp. 449–50). (4) Label on the back of it, according to a letter from Maurice Magnin in the Gallery archives. (5) Richter's Mond catalogue, II, p. vii.

GIOVANNI ANTONIO PORDENONE
Married 1504, died 1539

In a fresco at Valeriano of 1506 (his earliest surviving dated work) he signs Zuane Antonius de Sacchis, subsequently generally known as Giovanni Antonio da Pordenone, from his home town in the Friuli. His father, Angelo de Lodesanis, was from the neighbourhood of Brescia (Corticelle). The old date given as that of his birth (1484) depended merely on Vasari's statement that he died in 1540 at the age of 56.[1] When it was found that he died in fact in 1539 the birth date was accordingly shifted to 1483. In any case there is no more reliable evidence for it. Vasari, and following him Ridolfi, is likewise responsible for the mistake, long prevailing, that Pordenone's surname was Licinio.[2]

Active as a painter of religious frescoes and altarpieces over a wide area of northern Italy. A journey to Rome—of which Vasari makes no mention—is usually assumed, and may have occurred. But the evidence for it is confined to the existence of a fresco reasonably attributed to Pordenone at Alviano in Umbria (some fifty miles north of Rome). Reminiscences of the Roman work of Raphael and of Michelangelo are adduced as supporting evidence. The journey has been hypothetically dated 'around 1515'[3] and 1516.[4]

Pordenone died at Ferrara. Vasari emphasizes his attempt to set up as a rival to Titian.

REFERENCES: (1) Milanesi ed., vol. V, pp. 118 and 121. (2) This myth was exploded by Vincenzo Joppi (*Contributo Terzo alla Storia dell' Arte nel Friuli . . .*, 1892, p. 29). Hadeln (Ridolfi/Hadeln, I, p. 113, note 3) suggests a misreading of an inscription on an engraving after Pordenone by Fabio Licinio as source of the error. (3) W. Arslan, article on Pordenone in Thieme-Becker. (4) Fiocco, *Pordenone*, 1939, p. 46.

4038   S. BONAVENTURE

Panel, octagonal, each side c. 11¾ (0·299) (variable), overall measurements of painted area 28¾ × 27⅞ (0·721 × 0·708).

The red of his mantle in reasonably good state. His lawn sleeves, hood, face and hands heavily retouched, also the shadow of his Cardinal's hat. The tail of his mitre on the spectator's right seems originally to have extended in front of (or behind) his hood. For commentary and provenance see under no. 4039.

4039   S. LOUIS OF TOULOUSE

Panel, octagonal, each side c. 11¾ (0·299) (variable). Overall measurements of painted area 28¼ × 27⅞ (0·718 × 0·708).

Similar state to no. 4038, but less retouched. The area behind his head (with the crudely painted and architecturally meaningless mouldings) is suspect.

This and no. 4038 are stated in the catalogue of the Francis Capel-Cure sale (1905) to have come from a ceiling in the Scuola di S. Francesco ai Frari at Venice, on the strength of which they were connected by C. Jocelyn Ffoulkes[1] with part of a series of nine pictures by Pordenone described by Boschini (1664) as in that building[2] (the four Evangelists and SS. Bonaventure, Louis, Bernardino and Anthony of Padua in separate compartments round a central full length, apparently on a smaller scale, of S. Francis receiving the stigmata). The central panel is missing. The four Evangelists and SS. Bernardino and Anthony were subsequently located at Budapest[3] and since they are clearly part of the same series as nos. 4038 and 4039 no doubt can be entertained of the provenance of all from the Scuola di S. Francesco, despite gaps in the pedigree. The perspective of the background in the four Evangelist pictures (which are square) indicates that they would have been in the corners of the ceiling, the four Franciscan saints (which are octagonal) at the sides.[4]

A. M. Zanetti, in his *Descrizione* (1733)[5] says that the paintings had decorated the ceiling of a ground floor room at the Scuola but that at the time of writing they were in an upper room. In the same writer's *Della Pittura Veneziana* (1771)[6] the reason is given for the removal— the pictures were deteriorating in their original site. Nos. 4038 and 4039 are characteristic works of Pordenone's late style and closely comparable with the Beato Lorenzo Giustiniani altarpiece (Venice, Accademia), commissioned in 1532. It is therefore reasonable to assume a similar date of origin, and Ridolfi in fact mentions the two works in the same sentence (Ridolfi/Hadeln, I, p. 125).

PROVENANCE: With no. 4038, from the Scuola di S. Francesco ai Frari, Venice (see above). The Scuola was suppressed probably at the end of the eighteenth century. In 1778 nos. 4038 and 4039 and the other seven pictures of the series were handed over to 'Giuseppe Rocchi Vicario per il Signor Francesco Nardi Guardian Grande'.[7] Said to have been bought in Venice probably around the middle of the nineteenth century by Edward Cheney,[8] from whom they passed to Francis Capel-Cure.[9] His sale, Christie's, 6th May, 1905 (58).[10] Sir Claude Phillips Bequest, 1924.

REPRODUCTION: *Illustrations, Italian Schools*, 1937, p. 288.

REFERENCES: (1) In *L'Arte*, VIII (1905), pp. 284–5. (2) *Le Minere . . .*, S. Polo, p. 305, also in *Le Ricche Minere* (1674), S. Polo 47. Ridolfi (Ridolfi/ Hadeln, I, 125) when referring to what is clearly the same series, speaks in error of the Doctors of the Church in addition to the four Evangelists. (3) See A. Pigler in the Budapest *Jahrbuch*, 1931, pp. 118–30. (4) Earlier descriptions of the shapes of the panels are sometimes contradictory. Zanetti (*Descrizione*, p. 300) speaks of them as 'parte ottagoni e parte rotondi' and in the Capel-Cure catalogue (and by Ffoulkes) the National Gallery pictures are referred to as 'hexagonal'. As regards the disposition on the ceiling, the four Evangelists are shown with transverse beams behind their heads, thus forming corners which would have been intended to blend with the corners of the room. SS. Anthony, Bernardino and Bonaventure are shown merely with flat mouldings behind them. S. Louis of Toulouse was probably originally shown likewise, the attempt at a transverse beam behind his head being probably later repaint. A diagrammatic reconstruction was published by Juergen Schulz ('Vasari at Venice', *Burlington Magazine*, 103, 1961, p. 508. See also the same writer's *Venetian Painted Ceilings of the Renaissance*, 1968, p. 83. (5) p. 300. (6) p. 219. (7) Ffoulkes, *loc. cit.* (8) Ffoulkes, *loc. cit.* The Budapest pictures were bought in Venice in the '20's of the nineteenth century (Pigler, *loc. cit.*). (9) The sale catalogue is headed 'Collection . . . formed by Edward Cheney, Esq . . . the property of Francis Capel-Cure, Esq'. (10) In the National Gallery copy of the sale catalogue the purchaser is stated to be Carfax; apparently Phillips bought them soon after.

Ascribed to PORDENONE

2146 PORTRAIT OF A LADY

Panel, painted area $20\frac{1}{4} \times 16\frac{3}{8}$ (0·514 × 0·416).

Many small retouchings on face and hands. Bosom, bodice and the pink bow in better condition.

Purchased with the Galvagna collection as 'the Painter's Daughter, by Palma Vecchio'. Lent to Dublin in 1857 and still there when mentioned in the 1925 catalogue. First catalogued, 1929, as 'Italo-Flemish School, *c.* 1540'. The date is inadmissible on account of the costume which is closely comparable with that shown in various Italian works of around 1515.[1] The attribution to Pordenone was made by Berenson.[2] No. 2146 seems indeed to show some general affinities of type (at least in respect of the treatment of the hands and of the draperies) with the female saints in Pordenone's early *Madonna and Saints* (Venice, Accademia, from Collalto), which is dated 1511; also with the Madonna della Misericordia (Pordenone, Duomo) which was commissioned in 1515, and, perhaps, with certain figures in the vault frescoes in the church of S. Odorico, Villanova (commissioned 1514). The attribution therefore seems a plausible possibility to the present writer, though in default of an authentic early Pordenone portrait the evidence is too vague to permit of certainty.[3]

PROVENANCE: Bought, 1855, with the Galvagna collection, Venice.

REPRODUCTION: *Illustrations, Italian Schools*, 1937, p. 179.

REFERENCES: (1) Notes by Stella Mary Pearce in the Gallery archives. (2) *Lists*, 1936. (3) An attribution, apparently oral, by R. Longhi to 'Lotto in a Palmesque phase' (note in the Gallery archives) seems much less probable to the present writer.

GIULIO CESARE PROCACCINI
1574–1625

From Bologna, but settled at an early age in Milan.[1] He was a member of a family of artists and originally worked as a sculptor. His earliest datable works as painter are of 1604–5.[2] As early as 1619 Borsieri[3] remarked on the formative influence of Parmigianino on G. C. Procaccini's painting.

REFERENCES: (1) For documentation of biographical data see Nikolaus Pevsner: *Giulio Cesare Procaccini* in *Rivista d'Arte*, XI, 1929, pp. 321 ff. Also Adriana Arfelli in *Arte Antica e Moderna*, 8, 1959. (2) A *Pietà* (Milan, S. Maria presso S. Celso) has a (modern) label on the frame with the date 1604. The *Martyrdom of SS. Nazaro & Celso* in the same church has a similar label with the date 1607. The 1605 commission was for the Cappella del Broletto (three pictures now in the Castello Sforzesco, Milan). (3) Quoted by Pevsner, *op. cit.*, p. 323.

Ascribed to GIULIO CESARE PROCACCINI
219 THE DEAD CHRIST SUPPORTED BY ANGELS

Panel, $24\frac{1}{2} \times 18\frac{3}{8}$ (0·622 × 0·467).[1]

Condition fairly good. Some evident but not large retouchings in the angels' faces and in Christ's body and loin cloth. An extra eye and eyebrow, just visible to the spectator's left of the angel on the right are probably an earlier position of the latter.

Catalogued as Sodoma until 1861. Not catalogued during the period 1862–90 when on loan to the South Kensington Museum (Victoria and Albert Museum). Thereafter as Lombard School. There is a picture of the same subject and similar arrangement in the Siena gallery[2] attributed to Sodoma, but the hand is different and the picture is clearly earlier in style than no. 219. The present attribution to Giulio Cesare Procaccini has not been made before and is tentative. The 'malerisch' handling of Christ's loin cloth would to some extent accord with that of Giulio Cesare Procaccini (cf. the Brera *Magdalen*, among other instances). At the same time, the *cinquecento* type of design and strong influence of Parmigianino would suggest an earlier work than the earliest datable ones—e.g. the altarpiece, likewise of the *Pietà*, in S. Maria presso S. Celso, Milan.

PROVENANCE: Presented by Sir Walter Calverley Trevelyan, Bart., 1849, who had bought it at Città di Castello in 1837.[3]

REPRODUCTION: *Illustrations, Italian Schools*, 1937, p. 191.

REFERENCES: (1) A strip at the top about 1″ high seems a later addition. (2) No. 361. Photograph Anderson 21188. (3) Inscription on the back.

SCIPIONE PULZONE
Active 1569, died 1598[1]

The words 'da Gaeta' which appear after his name in several contemporary references give the town of his birth. Active throughout his maturity in Rome apart from some visits to Naples and Florence. Borghini, writing within Pulzone's lifetime (1584),[2] stresses that his name had been made as a fashionable portraitist and that for that reason he wished to prove himself in the field of religious painting also. A number of such pictures in fact survive, executed in a style which conspicuously eschews the extravagances of design and draughtsmanship then current among the Mannerist painters in Rome.

REFERENCES: (1) Date of death from an archive quoted in Thieme-Becker under Pulzone. Baglione, who says he died at thirty-eight, is certainly wrong, though the sense of his statement—that Pulzone died prematurely—is sound. (2) Raffaello Borghini: *Il Riposo*, 1584, p. 578.

1048 PORTRAIT OF A CARDINAL

Tin-plated copper, painted area $37\frac{1}{8} \times 28\frac{1}{4}$ (0·943 × 0·718). Good condition.

A smaller version (head and shoulders only but otherwise almost identical) in the Galleria Nazionale, Rome (ex-Corsini) is traditionally identified as Cardinal Savelli. No. 1048 is first recorded in the National Gallery minutes (1879) under this identification but it was not included in the printed catalogues. Until the edition of 1906 as 'Italian School, 16th century, Portrait of a Cardinal'.[1] Subsequently attributed to Pulzone.[2] This seems correct.[3]

VERSION: Rome, Galleria Nazionale, Palazzo Barberini.[4]

PROVENANCE: Purchased from W. Campbell Spence, Florence, 1879.[5]

REPRODUCTION: *Illustrations, Italian Schools*, 1937, p. 294.

REFERENCES: (1) Egerton Beck (*Burlington Magazine*, VII, 1905, p. 287) casts doubt on the sitter's being a cardinal on the ground that the *mozzetta* is not exactly crimson but purplish. (2) F. M. Clapp (*Pontormo*, 1916, pp. 214–15) mentions unspecifically an attribution to Pontormo and, together with the Corsini picture, 'another portrait of the same personage . . . in Chantilly'. The two Pulzone male portraits at Chantilly (nos. 59 and 60 in Gruyer's catalogue of 1899) seem in fact to have no connection with the sitter of no. 1048. The Galleria Nazionale, Rome catalogue (by N. di Carpegna, 1955 ed., p. 52) goes further by referring to the Chantilly picture as an 'altra replica' of the Corsini one. Litta (Savelli di Roma in British Museum copy) illustrates what is apparently the Corsini picture as representing Cardinal Giacomo Savelli, who died in 1587. There was also a Silvio Savelli who was made cardinal in 1596 and died in 1599. (3) Venturi (*Storia* IX, VII, p. 766) is clearly wrong in considering no. 1048 an early work. (4) Reproduced in di Carpegna's Palazzo Barberini catalogue, 1955, fig. 55. (5) Stated on unspecified authority to have been at Arezzo previously.

RAPHAEL
1483–1520

His christian name was Raffaello, the patronymic Santi, or de' Santi (Sante). On such of his pictures as are signed (e.g. no. 3943 of this Gallery) he normally uses a latinized form of his christian name and of his native city of Urbino—Raphael Urbinas. His father, the painter Giovanni Santi, died in 1494. Pietro Perugino, traditionally said (first, apparently, by Simone Fornari, 1549–50)[1] to have been Raphael's master, divided his time at this period mainly between Florence and Perugia. Until he settled in Rome at about the age of twenty-five Raphael's own life was nomadic over a considerable area of Umbria and Tuscany, but the main outlines of his movements are indicated by the location of his commissioned works. First of these was an altar commissioned in 1500 for S. Agostino at Città di Castello (fragments survive at Naples and Brescia). A further altarpiece for Città di Castello (now no. 3943 of this Gallery) was dedicated in 1503. The *Coronation of the Virgin* (Vatican) comes from the church of S. Francesco at Perugia and is datable *c.* 1503. A third altarpiece from Città di Castello, the *Sposalizio* (Milan, Brera) is dated 1504. A fresco in S. Severo at Perugia bears the date 1505. An altarpiece of the Madonna and Child enthroned with saints (now no. 1171 of this Gallery, the *Ansidei Madonna*) is dated 1505 (?) and comes from Perugia, as does a similar but undated altarpiece (main panels in the Metropolitan Museum, New York, but the central portion of the predella now no. 2919 of this

Gallery). A further work for Perugia, the *Entombment* (main panel Rome Borghese) is dated 1507. There is little doubt that before this date Raphael had been to Florence (there is some, but not impeccable, evidence for a visit in 1504) but the number and duration of his visits there is uncertain. The traditional estimate of Raphael's 'Florentine period' ('circa 1504–1508') is indeed impossible to verify, and in the sense of continuous residence is demonstrably false. In surviving contemporary documents Raphael is in fact only recorded at Florence on one occasion—in an autograph letter to his uncle, Simone Ciarla, of April, 1508[2]—and six months before that he was certainly in Urbino.[3] Judging from Vasari's account and from the strong Florentine influence (particularly Leonardo's) in those of Raphael's pictures which are datable to the years *c*. 1504–8 it is nevertheless likely enough that he spent an appreciable amount of time in Florence at this period.

Raphael had settled in Rome before October, 1509, perhaps as early as September, 1508 if a letter of that month to Francesco Francia is genuine (it is only known in the form published by Malvasia in 1678 and is in a questionable literary style).[4] In Rome Raphael worked for a number of private patrons—particularly the Sienese banker, Agostino Chigi. But from the beginning he would have been mainly occupied at the Vatican, where, after the accession of Leo X in 1513, papal demands on his time increased almost to the point of monopoly. On Bramante's death in 1514 Raphael was appointed architect in charge of continuing the rebuilding of S. Peter's, and by the end of his life he seems to have been entrusted with the planning and execution of all papal enterprises in the arts, whether pictorial, decorative, architectural, archaeological or theatrical. To undertake commitments so extensive and so various a staff of assistants was necessary.

The fame of Raphael, which in extent and duration has probably surpassed that of every other European painter of modern times, would have been assisted in the early stages by his collaboration—a new development in Italian art—with the engraver, Marcantonio Raimondi.

REFERENCES: (1) Quoted in Vincenzo Golzio: *Raffaello nei Documenti . . .*, 1936, p. 195. (2) Golzio, *op. cit.*, pp. 18–19. (3) Golzio, *op. cit.*, pp. 16–18. (4) Golzio, *op. cit.*, pp. 19–22.

27 POPE JULIUS II

Panel, $42\frac{1}{2} \times 31\frac{3}{4}$ (1·08 × 0·87).
Very good condition. Cleaned 1970.
Bottom left, the inventory number, 118 (Borghese: see below).
The cleaning of 1970 clarified traces of papal crossed keys and tiaras (more clearly visible in X-ray photographs), arranged in a diagonal pattern, and half showing through the green curtain behind the sitter. They evidently constitute pentimental remains of an earlier idea, consisting, according to microscopical and chemical examination, of golden yellow keys and tiaras, the latter probably with white or silver ribbons, on an ivory or pale pink ground. These could have been intended

either as embroideries or as part of a woven curtain.[1] Spots of bright blue (azurite) pigment identified by further microscopical examination in the background of the picture, near the right edge and just above the pope's left wrist, could have been one of the colours of the earlier curtain. Alternatively, they could indicate that at one stage the curtain was intended to be shown looped up to reveal blue sky, as in the Raphaelesque portrait of Giuliano de' Medici (New York, Metropolitan Museum). Dark lines still visible in the green curtain a little higher up than this area (the most conspicuous curving upwards from the tassel on the spectator's right of the chair towards the top right hand corner of the picture, another in a loop underneath the first) could be read as remains of such folds.

Hitherto catalogued as an early copy[2] of what was considered by his contemporaries to be one of the most celebrated and epoch-making of Raphael's portraits. The pentimenti described above, as revealed by the 1970 cleaning, together with further research into the picture's pedigree undertaken at the same time, leave virtually no doubt that it is the original. The latter, according to an entry of September, 1513 by the Venetian diarist, Marin Sanudo, had at that period been recently set up in the church of S. Maria del Popolo, in Rome. Vasari (1550 and 1568) mentioned the picture, which was then purloined from the church in 1591 by the nephew of the then pope, Cardinal Sfondrati, who incorporated it into his private collection. Between the years 1595 and 1608 Cardinal Sfondrati was offering his collection for sale.[3]

The inventory number, 118, on no. 27 identifies it with a picture in the inventory of 1693 of pictures in Palazzo Borghese in Rome.[4] There is some evidence that the numbered items in that inventory had belonged to Cardinal Scipione Borghese, who, in 1608, had bought *en bloc* virtually the whole of Cardinal Sfondrati's collection, numbering 71 pictures.

Datable 1511-12, as Julius II wore a beard in that period only.[5] Though there were numerous examples dating from before Raphael's time of representations in various media (illuminated manuscripts, frescoes and reliefs) of notabilities enthroned, seen obliquely and usually with attendant figures,[6] the present picture appears to be the prototype of what became virtually a formula—the three-quarter length, single figure of a pope seated in an arm chair and seen from an angle. From no. 27 descended such famous examples as Sebastiano del Piombo's *Clement VII* and Titian's *Paul III* (both Naples), Velázquez' *Innocent X* (Rome, Doria) and innumerable others, in painting and photography, down to modern times.

VERSIONS: Uffizi, Florence and Pitti (the former probably a studio version of no. 27, the latter probably a copy by Titian). What is claimed as the cartoon in Palazzo Corsini, Florence. Many old copies exist.

DRAWING: Chatsworth (Fischel: *Raphaels Zeichnungen* V, 257). Red chalk study for the head.

PROVENANCE: Certainly identifiable, through the painted inventory number, 118, with the picture of that number in the 1693 inventory of pictures in Palazzo

Borghese in Campo Marzio, Rome, and thus presumably identical with the picture which was in S. Maria del Popolo from 1513 to 1591, in the possession of Cardinal Sfondrati from 1591 to 1608, and in Borghese possession from then on (see above). Probably left Borghese possession between 1794 and 1797.[7] In the Angerstein collection by the time of the catalogue of 1823.[8] Bought with the Angerstein collection, 1824.[9]

REPRODUCTION: Booklet by the present writer, 1970 (see reference 3).

REFERENCES: (1) Microscopical and chemical examination by Joyce Plesters. The objects as revealed by the X-rays consisted of five separate groups of papal crossed keys rising diagonally from just above the pope's left hand to the top edge of the picture at the point above his head. Another pair is to the left of the left hand knob of the chair. There was a papal tiara between the top of the pope's head and the top of the knob on the left, and another tiara above this one, diagonally to the left. Perhaps others towards the top right of the picture. Above the pope's right forearm (enclosing a pair of crossed keys) was a form suggestive of a folded letter or handkerchief, and against the right hand edge of the picture were two semi-circular forms. In a letter in the Gallery archives Donald King drew attention to the orphrey of the cope of Pope Gregory IX in Raphael's fresco of the Decretals in the Stanza della Segnatura. This includes the Della Rovere oak and a papal umbrella, but the present writer is unable to read either of these symbols into the X-ray prints of no. 27. (2) Originally catalogued, after entering the Gallery in 1824, as Raphael, but this was soon abandoned. (3) For further details see the present writer's booklet: *Raphael's Portrait of Pope Julius II, the Re-Emergence of the Original*, n.d. (1970). Also the present writer's article in *Apollo*, September, 1970, p. 187. (4) Published by Paola Della Pergola: *Arte Antica e Moderna*, 1964, pp. 219 ff and 451 ff, and 1965, pp. 202 ff. (5) Julius returned to Rome bearded in June, 1511. For the removal of the beard in March 1512 see A. Luzio: *Isabella d'Este di fronte a Giulio II*, 1912, pp. 109–110. (6) K. Oberhuber in *Burlington Magazine*, 1971, pp. 124 ff. discusses this and other relevant points in detail. See also K. Schwager: *Über Jean Fouquet in Italien, und sein verlorenes Porträt Papst Eugens IV* in *Argo, Festschrift für Kurt Badt*, 1970, pp. 206 ff. (7) C. Gould, *op. cit.* (8) Where wrongly stated to be on canvas. (9) Early editions of the National Gallery catalogue include the Falconieri and Lancellotti palaces in the provenance, but no evidence for this is to hand. An old label on the back of the picture has the number 110.

168   S. CATHERINE OF ALEXANDRIA

Panel, $28\frac{3}{16} \times 21\frac{3}{4}$ (0·715 × 0·557).

Very well preserved for an early *cinquecento* picture.[1]

Bottom right, in white paint, an inventory number, 136 (Borghese: see below).

Cleaned 1967.

The marked stylistic affinities with the *Entombment* (Rome, Villa Borghese) which is dated 1507 postulate a similar date of origin, probably at the end of Raphael's "Florentine period".

VERSION: In the nineteenth century in the Trubetzkoy collection, St Petersburg.[2]

DRAWINGS: Louvre (Fischel 207). Cartoon in grey chalk, punched for transfer. The dress differs in some respects from what is shown in the painting. The cartoon includes a knot of drapery on the saint's right shoulder (there is no trace of this either visible in no. 168 or in X-ray photographs of it). This feature seems to have been associated with classical dress. Similar shoulder knots occur in other paintings by Raphael and his circle, notably in two of the antique heroes (Publius Scipio and Quintus Cincinnatus) in the Cambio frescoes at Perugia, and in the Muse with a lyre, on Apollo's left, in Raphael's *Parnassus* fresco.[3] The mantle in the cartoon falls in relatively simple folds round the saint's right hip, whereas in the painting the folds are more complex. The slate-grey over-dress in the painting likewise breaks into elaborately crinkled folds as it meets the line of the mantle where it is drawn across her thighs. In the cartoon these folds are simple. Finally, the draperies above the saint's right elbow show marked folds in the cartoon and not in the painting.

Oxford, Ashmolean no. 536 (Fischel no. 205). Three sketches for the pose (one perhaps from a male model) and a study for the neck. In the most developed of these sketches the saint appears to be holding the martyr's palm in her left hand. This was already discarded by the cartoon stage. This study, though dating from an early stage in the evolution of the design, nevertheless already shows it truncated above the knees, as in the painting. The fact that in another drawing (Fischel no. 206) which reflects a later stage the figure is shown at full length suggested to Fischel that Raphael was anxious to work out the full implications of the pose even though not intending to use it in its entirety. The *verso* of the Ashmolean sheet has a developed study for the face and five sketches of *putti*.

Chatsworth (Fischel no. 206). According to Fischel a copy of a lost drawing. On the left is the finished pose of the saint at full length as already mentioned.

PROVENANCE: Mentioned by Manilli (1650) in Villa Borghese, Rome.[4] Subsequently recorded in Palazzo Borghese.[5] As a result of the Napoleonic invasion of Italy it was acquired by Alexander Day who offered it for sale in London in 1800–01.[6] Offered again, by Buchanan, in 1808.[7] Later in the possession of Lord Northwick,[8] by whom exh. B.I., 1816 (5). By 1824 in the possession of William Beckford,[8] from whom purchased, 1839.

REPRODUCTION: *Illustrations, Italian Schools*, 1937, p. 295.

REFERENCES: (1) Crowe and Cavalcaselle (*Raphael*, I, 1882, p. 341, note) point out that the traces of gold on the band across the bosom may once have been a signature. As they also opine that 'the surface is injured by a most unfortunate cleaning' the student of picture-cleaning as a psychological study may be interested to compare this with Passavant's view—'ce ravissant tableau est, en général, parfaitement conservé' (1860 ed., II, p. 56. German ed. of 1839, II, p. 71). The picture was not cleaned since it entered the Gallery in 1839 until 1967. (2) Passavant: *Raphael d'Urbin*, II, 1860, p. 57. (3) Notes by Stella Mary Pearce. In connection with the classical origin, later suppressed, of part of the costume, cf. Fischel's remark (*Raphael*, 1948, I, p. 65) that S. Catherine's attitude in no. 168 'comes from Classical sculpture, presumably from a sarcophagus with figures of the Muses'. A derivation from Michelangelo's S. Matthew has also been mentioned in this connection. (4) P. 112 'sopra la porta, il quadro di S. Caterina Martire, è di Raffaelle'. (5) E.g. by P. Rossini, 1693 (*Il Mercurio Errante*, I, p. 40) and Ramdohr (1787) (*Ueber Mahlerei . . .*, I, p. 293). In the 1693 Borghese inventory, no. 164 (internal number 136) (P. Della Pergola, *Arte Antica e Moderna*, 1964, p. 227. No. 168 is conceivably identical with an 'imagine in figura di Caterina santa' which Di Rafaello da Urbino' which Pietro Aretino mentioned in a letter of August, 1550 to Agostino d'Adda as destined for the Queen of France (communication from Michael Levey). (6) W. Buchanan: *Memoirs . . .*, II, 1824, p. 7, no. 22. Paola Della Pergola (*Per la Storia della Galleria Borghese* in *Critica d'Arte*, 1957, pp. 135–42) identifies no. 168 with 'una Santina, in tavola, di Raffaele' which was included in a list of Borghese pictures sold to 'Sig.r Durand' before 9th April, 1801. She also tentatively suggests it entered the Borghese collection in the first place with Lucrezia d'Este's things, but there seems to be no specific mention of it in the 1592 inventory subsequently published by her (*Arte Antica e Moderna*, no. 7, 1959). (7) No. 2 'from the Villa Aldobrandini' in his catalogue published in that year. In 1769 the Aldobrandini inheritance had passed to the Borghese family. (8) Buchanan, *Memoirs, loc. cit.*

213   AN ALLEGORY ('VISION OF A KNIGHT')

Panel. Painted area $6\frac{3}{4}$ (0·171) square. Outside this there are the remains of a narrow gold border.

Bottom left, in dark paint, the inventory number 69 (Borghese: see below).

Slightly worn in places and a good deal of engrained old varnish visible, but in general very well preserved.[1]

For COMMENTARY and PROVENANCE see below.

213A   AN ALLEGORY

Cartoon for no. 213.
Paper measures $7\frac{3}{16} \times 8\frac{7}{16}$ (0·182 × 0·214).
Bottom right, in ink, the number, 83.

Pen and ink, punched for transfer. Some obvious damage and discoloration in the head of the figure on the spectator's right. It is noticeable that the shading on the left of the skirt of the figure on the left breaks off without an outline as though against a ruler or other superimposed object.

The contrast in clothing of the two female figures—severe in the case of the one on the spectator's left, delicate in the one on his right—and of the objects which each holds out towards the sleeping figure—sword and book on the one side, flowers on the other—has suggested to some critics that the subject is a version of the opposition of *Virtus* and *Voluptas*[2] and therefore of the *Hercules at the Cross Roads* theme. The contrast in the landscape background to the two figures—mountainous on the left, valley landscape on the right—has also been adduced in this context. A derivation from a woodcut of the *Hercules at the Cross Roads* subject in Sebastian Brant's *Stultifera Navis* (Bâle, 1497) was suggested by R. De Maulde La Clavière.[3] This woodcut is square, like no. 213, and the armed figure is likewise shown asleep. Otherwise there is no correspondence in a pictorial sense. Against any orthodox interpretation on these lines it can be objected that the sleeping youth in no. 213 has none of the attributes of Hercules (club and lion-skin) and also that he is shown as a delicate, essentially un-Herculean figure. Furthermore, despite the severity of the appearance of the figure with sword and book and the undoubted element of contrast with the other female figure, the latter is of modest bearing, her clothes are not *décolleté* and she is in general far from conveying an impression of *Voluptas* (this effect is more marked in the painting: in the cartoon the bosom is rather less modest). There would therefore be a possibility of a different interpretation, with the female figures representing complementary attributes rather than antagonistic ones. The first, at least, of these objections would be obviated by assuming that no. 213 illustrated a special instance of or derivation from the Hercules theme, as was proposed and elaborated by E. Panofsky.[4] He assumed a pictorial connection between the sleeping figures in no. 213 and in Brant's woodcut, deriving the latter in its turn from a sleeping *Paris* in the mediaeval iconography of the *Judgement of Paris*. He then demonstrated that the dialogue between *Virtus* and *Voluptas* inserted by Jacob Locher into his Latin version of Brant's *Stultifera Navis* incorporated phrases from passages in the *Punica* of Silius Italicus and stated that the latter book was so well known in Renaissance Italy that anyone reading Locher would recognize the connection with Silius. As the passage in the latter specifically referred to the choice of the young Scipio Africanus (which the corresponding passage in Locher did not) Panofsky adduced that as the subject of no. 213.

Though the appearance of the young knight in no. 213 is far more consonant with a young Scipio[5] than with Hercules, and though Panofsky's interpretation may well in fact be correct it should be pointed out that there are various discrepancies with Silius' account. According to him, for example (*Punica* XV), *Virtus* wore a snow-white robe and he makes no mention of the flowers held by the one figure in no. 213 or the book and sword of the other. Above all, he describes the glance of *Voluptas* as 'wanton' (*lasciva*).[6]

A picture of the *Three Graces* (Chantilly, Musée Condé) is the same size as no. 213 and like it was first recorded in Borghese possession in 1650.[7] Like no. 213 again it is stylistically acceptable and accepted as a very early Raphael, comparable with the Louvre *S. Michael* and possibly dating from before Raphael's apprenticeship to Perugino. An alternative dating nearer 1504 has also been proposed.

DRAWINGS: 1. No. 213A of this Gallery (Fischel no. 40). Generally accepted as Raphael's cartoon for the picture. A comparable punched cartoon for a small picture is the *Annunciation* in the Louvre (Fischel 28), accepted as Raphael's cartoon for part of the predella of the Vatican *Coronation of the Virgin*. No. 213A differs in some minor details from no. 213—namely in the neck-line, simpler in the painting than in the drawing, of the left-hand figure, and in the substitution in the painting of three horsemen in the background for the bridge in the cartoon.

2. Weimar, Museum. Drawing of youths in contemporary costume posed exactly as the two female figures in no. 213, even to the sword and book held by the left-hand one.[8] Two autograph drawings at Oxford (Fischel nos. 18 and 19) also show youths in tights, this time posing for angels in the Vatican *Coronation of the Virgin*. In a third drawing (Lille, Fischel 15) a youth in tights poses for the Virgin Mary in the same picture and another for the Christ. The Weimar drawing appears too weak, at least in its present state, to be attributable to Raphael. If it is not the remains of such a drawing it could be a copy of one.[9]

PROVENANCE: Manilli (1650) mentions no. 213 in Villa Borghese, Rome. 1693 inventory.[10] Ramdohr (1787) describes it as in Palazzo Borghese.[11] Acquired by William Young Ottley in Rome, December, 1798[12] and offered by him for sale in London from 1799 to 1811.[13] Passavant (1833)[14] saw both no. 213 and no. 213A (apparently the earliest mention of the existence of the latter) in the possession of Lady Sykes in London, and later (1839) stated that she had obtained no. 213 from the estate of Sir Thomas Lawrence.[15] The 1847 National Gallery catalogue says that no. 213 (and presumably also no. 213A) were subsequently in the possession of the Rev. Thomas Egerton, from whom purchased, 1847. No. 213A was exh. R.A., 1960 (549).

REPRODUCTION: *Illustrations, Italian Schools*, 1937, p. 296.

REFERENCES: (1) The French edition of Passavant (*Raphael d'Urbin*, II, 1860, p. 17) says no. 213 is signed 'RAPH. VRBI. INV'. The element of invention in fact seems not to have been Raphael's in this case but Passavant's French translator's. (2) First specifically, apparently, by R. De Maulde La Clavière (*Gazette des Beaux-Arts*, 1897, vol. I, pp. 21–6). Passavant (*Rafael von Urbino*, I, 1839, p. 69) had already characterized the two females as standing for noble aspirations and the pleasures of life respectively. (3) *Loc. cit.* (4) *Hercules am Scheidewege*, 1930, *passim*. (5) Cf. in this context the Scipio figure in Perugino's fresco in the Cambio at Perugia. (6) It is precisely the maidenly, unwanton appearance of the right-hand figure in no. 213 which seems the main objection to Panofsky's theory. Even in certain contemporary illustrations, undoubtedly of the *Hercules* theme, which he illustrates, such as Niccolò Soggi's (?) from Berlin, the *Voluptas* figure is more wanton in appearance. Panofsky himself was apparently aware of this difficulty and attempted to overcome it (p. 83) by postulating that the two figures in no. 213 stood for ethical principles which in this case were not entirely irreconcilable. An interpretation on these lines was sketched briefly by E. Wind (*Burlington Magazine*, 1950, pp. 350–1) and subsequently elaborated by him (*Pagan Mysteries in the Renaissance*, 1958, pp. 78 ff.). According to him, the book, sword and flower 'signify the three powers in the soul of man: Intelligence, Strength and Sensibility'. The first two are spiritual, the third sensual, which is why they appear in the proportion of two to one. Wind notes that this Platonic scheme of the tripartite life is referred to by Macrobius in his *Dream of Scipio* and he claims to see 'a similar division, but with different accents' in the Chantilly *Three Graces*. Panofsky went on to deduce a Sienese origin for the two pictures on the strength of the Borghese provenance and of an assumed derivation of the *Three Graces* picture from the famous antique sculpture at Siena. He finally associated the commission of both pictures with the confirmation of one Scipione di Tommaso Borghese who was born in 1493. It was this part of Panofsky's thesis which was used as starting-point in an essay in destructive criticism by Klaus, Graf von Baudissin (Prussian *Jahrbuch*, LVII, 1936, pp. 88–97). The latter pointed out, *inter alia*, that the Chantilly picture need not derive directly from the Siena group and that much of the Borghese collection was acquired in the seventeenth century. For other interpretations see R. Eisler, *Revue archéologique*, 1930; Kurt Forster, *Art Quarterly*, 1972 (p. 425) and M. E. van Lohuizen-Mulder: *Rafaels Encomium van Scipio Africanus Maior*, 1973 (dissertation, Utrecht university). (7) Manilli: *Villa Borghese*, p. 111. (8) Photograph in the Gallery archives. Attention seems first to have been drawn to this drawing by C. Ruland in 'The Works of Raphael . . . at Windsor Castle', 1876, p. 144. (9) Crowe and Cavalcaselle (*Raphael*, I, 1882, p. 201, note) refer to a further drawing in the Accademia, Venice. (10) Manilli, *op. cit.*, p. 111: *Gli altre trè sono similmente di Raffaelle: cioè, vn Soldato, che giace dormendo alla campagna.* For the 1693 inventory see *Arte Antica e Moderna*, 1964, p. 458. (11) *Ueber Mahlerei und Bildhauerarbeit in Rom*, I, 292 . . . *ein bewaffneter Ritter der in einer Landschaft schläft, und von zwei Heiligen bewacht wird . . . aus der ersten Manier Raphaels.* (12) Sale catalogue in the library of the Victoria and Albert Museum (press-mark G4). (13) No. 27 ('from the Borghese Palace') in the Ottley sale, Christie's, 16th May, 1801. Lot 21 in an anonymous sale, evidently Ottley, 118 Pall Mall (dated in MS. 'January, 1801' in the copy of which a photostat is in the Gallery library). Lot 88 in the Ottley sale, 25th May, 1811. Passavant (*Tour of a German Artist in England*, 1836, p. 248, note) says no. 213 was one of the pictures which passed through the French *commissaire*, Reboul, and later belonged to Woodburn. This seems incorrect in view of the 1798 Ottley catalogue. (14) *Kunstreise durch England und Belgien . . .*, pp. 104–5. (15) *Rafael von Urbino*, II, 1839, p. 26. In the English translation (1836) of Passavant's *Kunstreise* (*Tour of a German Artist in England*, I, p. 232) there is a translator's footnote against the mention of no. 213 'Purchased of Mr. Ottley for four hundred and seventy pounds'. Nothing is said there of a Lawrence provenance.

The two statements could in theory be reconciled by assuming that it was Lawrence, and not Lady Sykes, who bought the picture from Ottley at this price. A priced copy, in the Gallery library, of the 1811 Ottley catalogue has the sum of 390 guineas against no. 213 (lot 88). It may have been bought in at that price.

744 MADONNA AND CHILD WITH THE INFANT BAPTIST
('THE ALDOBRANDINI MADONNA' OR 'THE GARVAGH MADONNA')

Panel, $15\frac{1}{4} \times 12\frac{7}{8}$ (0·387 × 0·327).
Cleaned 1971. This disclosed that a narrow strip across the base had originally been included in the design, then cancelled and finally overpainted at a later date. This overpaint now removed and with it the misgivings sometimes expressed about the picture's quality.[1] Damage otherwise confined to many small spots.

Sketches for no. 744 are contained in the so-called Pink Sketch-book (see DRAWINGS below). This also contains designs associable with the Madonnas *Mackintosh* (no. 2069 of this Gallery), *Bridgewater* (Duke of Sutherland), *Loreto* (J. Paul Getty Museum), *Alba* (Washington) and *della Sedia* (Florence, Pitti).[2] It may therefore be deduced that all these works were in some stage of evolution more or less concurrently, and since the Pink Sketch-book also contains a study for the *School of Athens* this is likely to have been during Raphael's early years in Rome. Greater precision than this in dating the individual pictures would be difficult to achieve, but it may be indicated that the sketches show that the evolution of the *Aldobrandini/Garvagh* and *Mackintosh* Madonnas (nos. 744 and 2069), which share the basic characteristic of the pose—with the Madonna's face frontal but with her legs sideways on to the spectator—was particularly closely related.

DRAWINGS: Fischel no. 352 (Lille, Musée Wicar) has sketches for the Madonna and both children in no. 744 as well as a sketch for the Child in the Loreto Madonna. Fischel nos. 346, 347, 348 and 349 (Lille, Musée Wicar, and British Museum) have various sketches for the Madonna and Child which have points in common with both no. 744 and with no. 2069 (the *Mackintosh* Madonna) and may be regarded as embryonic stages from which both finally emerged.

VERSIONS: Various old copies are listed by Passavant (1838 edition, II, p. 132). Another was presented to the National Gallery of Scotland in 1936. A version attributed to Sassoferrato is in the Louvre (no. 1493), another was in the Fausti sale, Milan, 1913 (40 bis). Others have passed through the London sale rooms in the 1960's. A sketch copy is in the Whitworth Art Gallery, Manchester. There is an etched variant (in reverse) by Passerotti.

PROVENANCE: Described in some detail by Ramdohr (1787)[3] as being in the apartments of Prince Aldobrandini in Palazzo Borghese, Rome. In 1769 an arrangement had been reached whereby the Aldobrandini fortune and title should be held by the second son of the head of the Borghese family. One of the other pictures described by Ramdohr in Prince Aldobrandini's apartments (now no. 18, Luini, of this Gallery) (see 'The Earlier Italian Schools' by Martin Davies) was demonstrably part of the Aldobrandini heritage which had passed to the Pamfili family as a result of Olimpia Aldobrandini's marriage in 1647 to Camillo Pamfili. Before that, however, in 1638, Olimpia had married Paolo Borghese, and it might therefore be possible that no. 744 was identical with the

'Vergine, con Christo, e San Giouannino . . . di Raffaelle' mentioned by
Manilli in his *Villa Borghese* (1650, p. 112). In any case it was probably one of the
several Raphael Madonnas which had passed into Aldobrandini possession with
the collection of Lucrezia d'Este, who died in 1598.[4] Acquired by Alexander
Day as a result of the Napoleonic invasion of Italy and exhibited by him for sale,
first in 1800–1, no. 10 ('from the Aldobrandini Cabinet').[5] Later (1816) at the
Royal Mews Gallery.[6] Sold by Day in 1818[7] to Lord Garvagh, by whom lent
to the B.I., 1819 (64) and 1845 (6) and from whom purchased, 1865.

REPRODUCTION: *Illustrations, Italian Schools*, 1937, p. 297.

REFERENCES: (1) E.g. Fischel (*Raphael*, 1948, p. 128). In the same place he
postulates a derivation, incomprehensible to the present writer, from the Christ
Child in no. 744 of a Rubens then with an Amsterdam dealer. (2) Of the six
pictures in question it may be noted that in two with a well-preserved landscape background, namely no. 744 and the *Alba* Madonna, the landscape in each
has the same bluish-green tonality and that this seems the dominant tone of
both pictures as a whole. (3) *Ueber Mahlerei und Bildhauerarbeit in Rom*, I,
pp. 306 and 309. (4) The 1592 inventory of Lucrezia d'Este's works of art which
later passed to the Aldobrandini contains the following: '1. Una Madonna
di mano di *Raffaello d'Urbino*. N.1./2. Un quadro di una Madonna qual'è in
mezzo al reliquario di man di *Raffaello d'Urbino*. N.1./76. Uno di una Madonna
N.S. di mano di *Raffaello* schiapata con cornice di legno dorato. N.2./112. Uno
di Una Madonna di *Raffaello* cornisato di noce all'antica. N.1./114. Uno di una
Madonna di *Raffaello* cornisato di noce. N.1' (published by Paola Della Pergola
in *Arte Antica e Moderna*, no. 7, 1959; she gives the date of Lucrezia's death as
1596, but Litta has 1598 and is more probably right). G. Gronau (*Documenti
Artistici Urbinati*, 1936, pp. 50 and 250) identifies no. 744 with a 'Madonna di
Raffaello ch'è antica di casa nostra' which Duke Francesco Maria of Urbino
was trying to reclaim after Lucrezia's death, but the description is too imprecise
to establish the matter. (5) Buchanan: *Memoirs . . .*, II, p. 5. (6) Note by E. K.
Waterhouse. (7) Note in the Gallery's MS. catalogue.

1171   ALTARPIECE: MADONNA AND CHILD WITH S. JOHN
THE BAPTIST AND S. NICHOLAS OF BARI ('THE
ANSIDEI MADONNA')

The panel measures *c.* 94 × 61½ (2·388 × 1·562) (arched top).

Painted area *c.* 82½ × 58½ (2·096 × 1·486).

Exceptionally good condition for a picture of its size and age. The only
damages worth mentioning are where paint has flaked along the vertical
cracks in the wood—e.g. in the canopy of the throne and in the vault on
either side of it, in the (spectator's) right side of the Madonna's dress
and under S. Nicholas' left wrist.

Cleaned 1956.

The frieze above the throne inscribed:

· SALVE · MATER · CHRISTI.

The hem of the Madonna's mantle by her left hand has characters
which have been interpreted as a date—either MDV or MDVI or
MDVII according to whether or not one or both of the two strokes
which follow the V, and which are appreciably shorter than it and the
M and the D, are intended to be included or are merely decorative. In
this connection it must be stressed that in his earlier work Raphael
followed Perugino's practice in frequently ornamenting the edges of

robes with lettering which is normally cabalistic in appearance and purely decorative in intent. Nevertheless occasionally Raphael undoubtedly incorporated a genuine inscription in this way and sometimes combined it with meaningless characters. In the small *Holy Family* in the Prado, for example, the hem of the Madonna's dress at the neck line bears the letters 'Raphael Vrbinas, MD·VII'. The so-called *Niccolini-Cowper* Madonna (Washington), moreover, has the letters 'MDVIII·R·V·PIN' which can only indicate a date, together with Raphael's initials, appended to a series of meaningless hieroglyphs. Finally, the *Madonna of the Meadow* (Vienna) has the letters 'M·D·V' very deliberately written in the middle of a series of meaningless characters round the Madonna's neck line, followed, on the far side of an ornament, by a stroke perhaps intended as a I. In the case of no. 1171, though it might not be prudent to state dogmatically either that the letters in question were intended as a date, or, if they were, which of the three possible readings is correct, the present writer would record conclusions which he regards as personal. First, bearing in mind Raphael's practice in the other pictures mentioned, it seems to him probable that the critical letters were in fact intended as a date. Secondly, excluding art-historical considerations and having regard merely to the mixture of real and decorative elements in the inscription, the present writer would conclude that the last two small strokes are decorative in intent and would read the date as MDV.

From external sources there is no precise evidence for dating the work. Vasari (1568), describing it, says: '*Dopo queste opere . . . ritornò Raffaello a Perugia, dove fece nella chiesa de' frati de' Servi in una tavola alla cappella degli Ansidei, una Nostra Donna, San Giovanni Battista e San Nicola*' and immediately goes on to speak of the S. Severo fresco, which bears the date 1505. Taking only comparable monumental altarpieces by Raphael into account it is at least clear that no. 1171 is considerably more advanced than no. 3943 of this Gallery, which was dedicated in 1503, and appreciably less so than the *Madonna del Baldacchino* (Florence, Pitti) of about 1508. As in the case of the S. Antonio altar, of which part of the predella is no. 2919 of this Gallery, it has been suggested that the mixture of Umbrian and Tuscan elements which has been traced in no. 1171 postulates that Raphael started it before his first visit to Florence, probably in 1504, and completed it on his return. Such may indeed have been the case, but one of the so-called Florentine elements in no. 1171—the Baptist's stance—does not constitute unequivocal evidence in this respect. A resemblance has been noted between it and the same saint in the Verrocchio/Credi altar in Pistoia cathedral. It is, however, possible that such a resemblance is coincidental, or the connection indirect, since the Baptist in no. 1171 is similar to the S. Joseph (in reverse) in Raphael's own altarpiece of the *Sposalizio* (Milan, Brera) which is dated 1504, conceivably before Raphael's first visit to Florence. The architectural setting in no. 1171 is undoubtedly connected in some way with that in Perugino's altarpiece of the Madonna and Child with S. Anne and other saints (Marseilles).

The juxtaposition of the Infant Christ and the adult Baptist is not uncommon in altarpieces. Other examples in this Gallery are nos. 750 (Venetian School), 1119 (Costa and (?) Maineri) and 804 (Marziale).[1]

According to Passavant (1839)[2] the predella of no. 1171 consisted of three scenes of which two were so badly damaged at the time when the main panel left Italy that they were left behind. The third—of the Baptist preaching—is apparently the picture later in the Marquess of Lansdowne's collection at Bowood. Passavant referred to the subject of the whole predella as being scenes from the life of the Baptist, but older sources give the subject of the other two panels as a shipwreck and the Marriage of the Virgin.[3]

VERSION: Perugia, S. Fiorenzo. Copy by N. Monti.

DRAWINGS: Crowe and Cavalcaselle (Raphael, I, 1882, pp. 226–7, notes) mention drawings at Frankfurt, Lille, Oxford and in the British Museum (Fischel nos. 52, 50, 51 and 46) in connection with no. 1171. But the connection is not direct. Fischel says of his no. 53 (Vienna, Albertina)—Madonna with a pomegranate—that it 'gehört eng mit der Madonna Ansidei zusammen'.

PROVENANCE: Ansidei family chapel (of S. Nicholas of Bari) in the church of S. Fiorenzo, Perugia, Baldassare Orsini (1784) already speaks of the original as in England, a copy by Nicola Monti replacing it in the chapel.[4] Details of the transaction were published by Passavant (first in 1833)[5] and by George Scharf.[6] From these accounts it seems that the sale was negotiated in 1764 by Gavin Hamilton for Lord Robert Spencer who later gave the picture to his brother, the 4th Duke of Marlborough. Purchased from the 8th Duke, Blenheim Palace, with a special Parliamentary Grant, 1885.

REPRODUCTION: Illustrations, Italian Schools, 1937, p. 298.

REFERENCES: (1) Instances of these figures recurring in different compartments of the same polyptych are also numerous—e.g. in this Gallery nos. 629 (Costa), 788 (Crivelli), 1103 (Fiorenzo di Lorenzo) and 530 (Gregorio Schiavone). In no. 777 (Morando) the Baptist is not yet adult but nevertheless appears much older than the Christ Child. No. 33 (Parmigianino) includes both the adult Baptist and the infant Christ but only as part of a vision. No. 1450 (Sebastiano del Piombo) has both in the foreground. (2) Rafael von Urbino, II, p. 44. (3) L. Manzoni: La Madonna degli Ansidei in Bollettino della Regia Deputazione di Storia Patria per l'Umbria, V, 1899, pp. 627–45. An element of uncertainty must remain, however, as the three subjects are not all specified in the same document. (4) Guida . . . di Perugia, 1784, p. 197. A document of 1776 quoted by L. Manzoni (loc. cit.) mentions the altarpiece as already gone. (5) Kunstreise durch England und Belgien, p. 174. (6) 1862 Blenheim Palace catalogue, p. 40.

2069   MADONNA AND CHILD ('THE MACKINTOSH MADONNA')

Canvas, transferred from panel between 1729 and 1786,[1] painted area $31 \times 25\frac{1}{4}$ (0·788 × 0·642).

As early as the eighteenth century reported as being damaged.[2] Now so damaged and restored, and so dimmed by old varnish, that the original surface quality is nowhere perceptible. X-ray photographs indicate total loss of paint in vertical strips down the centre of the picture particularly in the lower half. Also, notably, in another vertical strip just to the spectator's left of the Child's shoulder. These were perhaps caused by movement in the panel and may have contributed to the decision to transfer it to canvas.[3] In other areas the X-ray photographs reveal forms which are obscured by damage but which follow the general lines of the composition as at present visible to the naked eye.

It follows from the extent of the damage that it is no longer possible to state with confidence merely on visual evidence that no. 2069 is, or was, Raphael's original. Nevertheless this seems likely. Despite its ruin it conveys to most critics an indefinable air of authority which is lacking in the copies. In the oldest extant critique, furthermore, namely that contained in the 'Crozat Gallery' of 1729, though it is stated that certain people have deduced from the appearance of the Virgin's head that the work might be by Timoteo Viti rather than by Raphael himself, there was yet no suggestion that it was a copy. Known as the 'Mackintosh Madonna' or the 'Madonna of the Tower' (visible in the left background). This tower figures in the engraving in the 1786 Orléans catalogue but not in that in the 'Crozat Gallery' of 1729. As the picture had been transferred to canvas in between these two dates it would be possible that the tower was an invention perpetrated at the time of the transfer. Nevertheless this would not absolutely follow, since the Crozat engraving is clearly of somewhat inferior quality and might be inaccurate to that extent.

The preliminary sketches (see DRAWINGS below) show that the evolution of the design of no. 2069 was intimately associated with that of no. 744. Both pictures are datable to the early years of Raphael's Roman period (see the entry for no. 744). Another sketch (Fischel no. 368) links the evolution of no. 2069 with that of the *Sistine* Madonna and of the *Madonna di Foligno*.

VERSIONS: As early as 1518 Domenico Alfani had used the design of no. 2069 for the Madonna and Child group in his *Madonna with SS. Gregory and Nicholas* (no. 364 in the Perugia gallery; the date is on the frame). Versions by or attributed to Sassoferrato are no. 174 and no. 175 of the Borghese gallery and (in the nineteenth century) in the Leuchtenberg collection (engraved by H. Anschütz) and lent by Mark Phillips to the Manchester exhibition of 1857 (no. 357 in the definitive catalogue). A number of other old copies are recorded. The group of the Madonna and Child in Ingres' *Vow of Louis XIII* (Montauban) is to some extent a pastiche of no. 2069.[4] Also at Montauban is a copy of no. 2069, attributed Ingres.

DRAWINGS: British Museum 1894-7-21-1. Cartoon for the picture. Charcoal on paper, pricked for transfer, $27\frac{7}{8} \times 19$ (0·708 × 0·482). Berenson denied the attribution of this cartoon to Raphael and therefore the connection with no. 2069.[5] To justify the latter deduction he indicated differences between cartoon and painting in the oval of the Madonna's face, in the form of both her hands and in her left sleeve. Since both the Madonna's hands in no. 2069 are largely repaint no more need be said on that point. The far greater elaboration of the sleeve in the painting seems a valid objection, though the prick marks in the cartoon are said to correspond with the painting.[6] In any case comparable, if less extreme, discrepancies seem to occur in connection with two further panel paintings for which Raphael's cartoons survive, namely the S. Catherine (painting is no. 168 of this Gallery, cartoon is in the Louvre) and 'La Belle Jardinière' (painting in the Louvre, cartoon at Holkham Hall). In both these works there are differences in the draperies in the paintings as compared with the cartoons. Fischel accepted the British Museum cartoon as being that for no. 2069,[7] and this would seem justified.

Further drawings (Fischel nos. 346-7-8-9 at Lille (Musée Wicar) and British

Museum) have sketches of the Madonna and Child associable with both no. 2069 and no. 744 (the '*Aldobrandini* Madonna'). These sketches may be regarded as embryonic stages from which both emerged. A further study already mentioned (Fischel no. 368, Frankfurt) and to some extent also Fischel no. 369 (Chatsworth) appear to link no. 2169 with the *Sistine* and *Foligno* Madonnas.

ENGRAVINGS: By Jean Charles Flipart—no. 22 in the 'Crozat Gallery', 1729, and by J. Bouilliard—in the 1786 catalogue of the Orléans collection (*Galerie du Palais Royal*, vol. 1, IVe tableau de Raphael). Both these prints are in reverse. A further engraving, by P. W. Tomkins, dated 1808, was published in Tresham and Ottley's *British Gallery of Pictures*, 1818.

PROVENANCE: The 'Crozat Gallery', 1729, p. 11 says that the Regent Orléans had it from 'M. Dorat' who had it from the Sieur Beauchamp'.[8] The Rogers sale catalogue (1856) says purchased from the Orléans gallery by 'Mr. Hibbert'; therefore identical with lot 74 'Raffaello da Urbino—The Madonna and Infant Christ' in the sale at Bryan's Gallery, London, 26th December, 1798 of Italian pictures from the Orléans coll. (purchaser's name given as 'Mr. Hibbert' in the copy in the Gallery Library) and perhaps with a 'Raphael. Virgin and Child [from the] Orléans collection' which was lot 67 in the combined sale of Sir Simon Clarke and George Hibbert, Christie's, 14–15th May, 1802. In the possession of Henry Hope by 1808 (when engraved as such by Tomkins). Probably lot 67 ('Raffaelle. The Virgin and Infant Christ. From the Orléans collection'), Henry Hope sale, Christie's, 29th June, 1816, at which sale, according again to the Rogers sale catalogue, purchased by Samuel Rogers. Lot 727 at the Rogers sale, 6th day, 3rd May, 1856, at which bought by R. J. Mackintosh (according to a printed list of purchasers).[9] Lent by Mackintosh to Manchester, 1857 (140 in the provisional catalogue, 133 in the definitive catalogue) and by Miss Mackintosh to the R.A., 1902 (82). Presented by Miss Eva Mackintosh, 1906.

REPRODUCTION: *Illustrations, Italian Schools*, 1937, p. 297.

REFERENCES: (1) The *Recueil d'Estampes* ('Crozat Gallery'), I, 1729, pl. 22 has it as 'sur bois', while the Orléans catalogue of 1786 says 'sur toile'. (2) 'Crozat Gallery', I, 1729, p. 11 'quoyque le temps ait endommagé ce tableau . . .'. Also the Orléans catalogue, I, 1786, under the engraving of the picture, 'ce tableau a beaucoup souffert, particulièrement dans le Ciel'. (3) Fischel (*Raphael*, 1948, I, p. 129) attributes the ruin of no. 2069 to a fire, but there is no record of such a fire. (4) Though Ingres would never have seen no. 2069, one of the Sassoferrato copies reached the Borghese gallery in 1818—two years before Ingres left Rome. He probably also knew the Flipart and Bouilliard engravings. (5) *Study and Criticism of Italian Art*, second series, pp. 39–47 of the 1910 edition. (6) Pouncey and Gere: *Italian Drawings . . . Raphael and his Circle*, 1962, p. 23. (7) *Raphaels Zeichnungen*, VIII, no. 362–3. (8) Du Bois de Saint Gelais in the 1727 Orléans catalogue, p. 433, mentions no. 2069 but gives no further details. Mrs. Jameson (. . . *Private Galleries . . . in London*, 1844, p. 399) says that the picture had been in the Orléans collection since 1721. Her information on the picture was repeated in the Rogers sale catalogue. (9) In earlier editions of the National Gallery catalogue and in a MS. note in one of the copies of the sale catalogue in the Gallery library the purchaser's name is given as Gritten, who may therefore have been buying for Mackintosh.

2919   THE PROCESSION TO CALVARY

Panel, $9\frac{1}{2} \times 33\frac{1}{2}$ (0·241 × 0·851).

Somewhat worn in many areas. Christ's crown of thorns seems to have been obliterated.

Painted as the central panel of the predella of the altarpiece for the nuns of S. Anthony of Padua at Perugia. Vasari (1568; IV, p. 324) describes the altarpiece as follows:

Gli fu anco fatto dipignere nella medesima città dalle donne di santo Antonio da Padoa in vna tauola la Nostra Donna & in grembo a q̃lla, si come piacque a quelle semplici, & venerande donne, Giesu Christo vestito; & da i lati di essa Madonna san Piero, san Paulo, santa Cecilia, & santa Chaterina. Alle qual' due sante vergini fece le piu belle, & dolci arie di teste, & le piu varie acconciature da capo, il che fu cosa rara in que' tempi, che si possino vedere. E sopra questa tauola in vn mezzo tondo dipinse vn Dio Padre bellissimo, e nella predella dell' altare tre storie di figure piccole, Christo quando fa orazione nell' orto; quando porta la Croce, doue sono bellissime mouenze di soldati, che lo strascinano; & quando è morto in grembo alla madre. Opera certo mirabile, deuota, e tenuta da quelle donne in gran venerazione, e da tutti i pittori molto lodata.

The three predella panels described by Vasari, together with two smaller ones of single saints,[1] were sold by the nuns to Queen Christina of Sweden in 1663[2] and later passed with her pictures to the Orléans collection. The main panel of the altar and its lunette followed, being sold by the nuns in 1677–8 to Antonio Bigazzini of Perugia. The latter are now in the Metropolitan Museum, New York. The predella panels remained together until the dispersal of the Orléans collection at the end of the eighteenth century. The *Agony* is now at New York (Metropolitan) the *Pietà* at Boston, Mass. (Isabella Stewart Gardner Museum.) The two single saints are at Dulwich.

The mixture of Umbrian and Florentine elements in the main panel of the parent altarpiece of no. 2919 has suggested that Raphael began that portion of it before his first visit to Florence—probably in 1504—and completed it on his return. The altarpiece would in any case be datable to this period, and for this reason the resemblance, not otherwise great enough to justify comment, between the Madonna group in no. 2919 and in Perugino's portion of the *Deposition* (Florence, Accademia) may be noted (whatever it may signify) since Perugino is documented as executing it between August, 1505 and January, 1506.[3] The execution of no. 2919 seems to the present writer to be basically autograph.[4] The headgear of some of the men is intended to be Jewish.[5]

VERSION: Old copy, in 1950 in the possession of Arthur Pollen (then lot 38, anonymous sale, Sotheby's, 10th July, 1963). As it is in reverse and the colours different it may have been made from an engraving. The proportions also are different, more sky being shown at the top and more ground at the bottom.[6] Crowe and Cavalcaselle (*Raphael*, I, 1882, p. 240, note) mention a copy in Palazzo Panciatichi, Florence. A pen drawing in the Uffizi (Fischel: *Versuch einer Kritik . . .*, 1898, no. 77) shows the whole composition.

ENGRAVINGS: By Nicolas de Larmessin (in reverse) in the *Crozat Gallery* (1729) and by Couché fils and Liénard in vol. 1 of the Orléans catalogue (1786). In both cases more sky is shown at the top.

PROVENANCE: S. Antonio, Perugia. Sold in 1663 to Queen Christina of

Sweden, at Rome. No. 143 in the 1689 inventory of her pictures (which were then sold to Don Livio Odescalchi), no. 257 in that of 1721 (when they were bought by the Regent Orléans).[7] Described on pages 437–8 of the 1727 catalogue (by Du Bois de Saint Gelais) of the Orléans collection. Lot 88 in the sale at Bryan's Gallery, London, 26th December, 1798 of Italian pictures from the Orléans collection, where, in the copy in the Gallery library, the buyer's name is given as 'Mr. Hibbert'.[8] Therefore probably lot 44 in the sale, Christie's, 14th May, 1802, of the combined collection of Sir Simon Clarke and George Hibbert, where bought Woodburn.[9] In the Miles collection, Leigh Court, by 1822 (no. 21 in the printed catalogue, by John Young, of that year).[10] Exh. R.A., 1870 (59) (lent Sir William Miles). Lot 54, Sir Philip Miles sale, Christie's, 28th June, 1884, where bought Agnew. Exh. New Gallery, London, 1893–4, no. 242 and R.A. 1902, no. 14 (lent Lord Windsor in both cases). Purchased from the first Earl of Plymouth (Lord Windsor), Temple West Fund, 1913. Exh. Stockholm (Queen Christina), 1966, I, 176.

REPRODUCTION: *Illustrations, Italian Schools*, 1937, p. 300.

REFERENCES: (1) The *Crozat Gallery*, 1729, p. 12 mentions a S. Francis and a S. Anthony as existing with the three main predella panels in the Orléans collection. They were evidently too slight to be mentioned by Vasari. The sale document of 1663 (see reference 2 below) also refers to 'cinque quadretti di divotione'. A. Venturi (*Studi dal Vero*, 1927, p. 201) claims a third saint (another S. Francis, now at Dresden) as belonging to the series. (2) *Giornale d'Erudizione Artistica di Perugia*, 1874, pp. 304–15. (3) Bombe: *Perugino (Klassiker der Kunst)*, 1914, p. 247. The Deposition altarpiece had been left unfinished by Filippino Lippi at his death in April, 1505. A derivation of the Christ in no. 2919 from Joos van Ghent's Urbino *Eucharist* was postulated by Fischel (*Raphael*, 1948, p. 46). (4) Gronau (*Klassiker der Kunst* volume on Raphael, 1923 ed., p. 224) endorses the suggestion of J. P. Richter (*Art Journal*, March, 1902) that the execution of the predella was by Eusebio da San Giorgio. (5) Notes on the costumes by Stella Mary Pearce. (6) Referred to by Harold Nicolson in *The Spectator*, 2nd August, 1946, p. 114. (7) Olof Granberg: *La Galerie . . . de la Reine Christine . . .*, 1897, appendix III, p. LXXIII and appendix IV, p. CVII. (8) For the complicated deals attending the export of the Orléans collection from France see W. Buchanan: *Memoirs of Painting*, I, 1824, pp. 1–216. (9) 'Raphael . . . Christ bearing the Cross . . . An early picture of this great master . . . admired in the Orléans coll. . . . ' Buyer's name at this sale kindly communicated by Messrs. Christie. (10) Where wrongly stated as having been bought at the Orléans sale in February, 1800. There is no such picture in the Orléans sale of 14th February, 1800 and such a provenance in any case conflicts with the other evidence.

3943 ALTARPIECE: THE CRUCIFIED CHRIST WITH THE VIRGIN MARY, SAINTS AND ANGELS

Panel, arched top. Painted area 110½ × 65 (2·807 × 1·65).

Vertical joins and splits in the wood (one of which passes through Christ's face and chest) have led to flaking in those areas on several occasions. Otherwise the condition seems basically good. Cleaned 1966–7.

Signed, at the bottom of the cross: RAPHAEL/VRBIN/AS/P

Above the cross the inscription: ·I·N·R·I·

Painted for the altar of the Gavari family in the church of S. Domenico at Città di Castello where it remained until 1818. Vasari (1568) says of this painting: *se n'andò . . . a Città di Castello; dove fece una tavola . . . in San Domenico . . . d'un Crucifisso; la quale, se non vi fusse il suo nome scritto, nessuno la crederebbe opera di Raffaello, ma sì bene di Pietro* [Perugino]. This still seems a fair comment: almost every element in no. 3943 conforms with the Peruginesque repertory.

The inscription still existing in S. Domenico above the Gavari altar reads:

HOC·OPVS·FIERI·FECIT·DNICVS/THOME·DEGAVARIS·MDIII[1]

The presence in this context of S. Jerome (recognizable by the stone in his right hand) is sufficiently unusual to presuppose some special reason for his inclusion,[2] while the fact that two predella panels (at Lisbon and Raleigh, formerly in the collection of Mrs. Derek Fitzgerald, from the Cook collection) whose provenance cannot be traced back to source both represent scenes from the legend of S. Jerome[3] is the most cogent of several reasons for assuming that they came from this altar.[4]

DRAWINGS: Vienna, Albertina. Fischel IV, no. 185. Sheet containing three pen studies apparently connected with the Virgin in no. 3943 and one with the Christ. Variously adjudged as preparatory to no. 3943 and as a later variant of it. Oxford, Ashmolean 509. Silver point study of a kneeling youth. Claimed by K. T. Parker (*Old Master Drawings*, XIV (1939–40), pp. 37–8 and in his catalogue (1956) of Ashmolean drawings, vol. II, p. 259) to be for the Magdalen in no. 3943. See also Fischel: *Raphaels Zeichnungen*, I, pl. 4.
Ottawa, National Gallery of Canada. Silver point study of a standing saint. Published by A. E. Popham (*Old Master Drawings*, XIV (1939–40), pp. 50–1) who quoted an opinion of Fischel that it 'might represent an alternative conception of St John for the Mond Crucifixion'.

VERSION: Città di Castello, Pinacoteca. Old copy made in 1818 to replace the original.

PROVENANCE: Gavari altar in S. Domenico, Città di Castello. Sold from the church in 1818 to Cardinal Fesch.[5] He kept it first in Paris but brought it to Rome in 1823.[6] No. 479–500 in the fourth part of the Fesch sale, Rome, 1845, bought by the Principe di Canino.[7] In 1847 Lord Ward (later Earl of Dudley) bought from the Principe di Canino all the otherwise unsold Fesch pictures.[8] Lent by Lord Ward to Manchester, 1857 (159 in the provisional catalogue, 123 in the definitive catalogue), R.A., 1871 (307) and 1892 (151). Dudley sale, 25th June, 1892 (81) where bought Richter for Ludwig Mond. Mond Bequest, 1924.

REPRODUCTION: *Illustrations, Italian Schools*, 1937, p. 299.

REFERENCES: (1) Photograph of the altar with the copy of the painting specially inserted was published by Wolfgang Schöne: *Raphael*, 1958, p. 48. (2) S. Jerome had also figured in two Peruginesque *Crucifixions*—Uffizi no. 3254 and Accademia, Florence no. 78 (Bombe, *Klassiker der Kunst* Perugino, 1914, pl. 22 and 45). (3) Full details are given by Tancred Borenius in the catalogue of the Cook collection, vol. I, 1913, pp. 73–5. (4) J. P. Richter (*The Mond Collection*, 1910, II, 527) alleges that there would not have been space for a predella. Nevertheless the photograph published by W. Schöne (*loc. cit.*) indicates the contrary, even if, as he says, there may have been some difference between the width of the original frame and that of the copy. (5) Details of the sale in G. Magherini Graziani: *L'Arte a Città di Castello*, 1897, pp. 242–3. (6) Quatremère de Quincy (tr. Francesco Longhena) *Istoria . . . di Raffaello Sanzio . . .*, 1829, p. 15, n. 1. (7) Marked copy of the sale catalogue in the Gallery library. (8) *Kunstblatt*, 5th August, 1847, p. 152.

After RAPHAEL

661   THE SISTINE MADONNA

Drawn in pencil on 24 pieces of paper, stuck together and mounted on canvas.

$101\frac{1}{2} \times 80$ $(2 \cdot 578 \times 2 \cdot 032)$.

The paper is now discoloured, and in places stained.

A tracing by Jakob Schlesinger, from the altarpiece at Dresden. Jakob Schlesinger (1792–1855), painter and restorer of pictures, was active at Dresden during the years 1820–1823. He subsequently worked at Berlin as instructor at the Academy and restorer at the Museum. According to the National Gallery MS. catalogue the present tracing was made in the year 1822.

PROVENANCE: Sold, 1855–6, by Schlesinger's son, apparently to Messrs. P. & D. Colnaghi, Scott & Co.,[1] by whom presented, 1860.

REPRODUCTION: Negative in the Gallery's possession.

REFERENCE: (1) Letters from the younger Schlesinger in the Gallery archives. They were forwarded by Messrs. Colnaghi but bear no address.

929   MADONNA AND CHILD

Panel, painted area $34\frac{1}{4} \times 24\frac{1}{8}$ $(0 \cdot 87 \times 0 \cdot 613)$.

Very good condition.

An old and close copy, very possibly dating from the sixteenth century,[1] of the 'Bridgewater Madonna' in the Sutherland collection (on loan to the National Gallery of Scotland). In no. 929 the Child has a wisp of drapery which does not figure in the original, either in its present state or in eighteenth-century engravings after it.[2]

PROVENANCE: A label on the back reads 'Ce Tableau appartient à M. le Prince Charles. Purchased in May 1722' (the word 'purchased' crossed out and 'Paris' written by the side of it, perhaps in another hand) 'Copied from the original inscription 8th April, 1852, Augusta E. Bentley'. The writing on the original label in question, farther down on the back of the picture, is now very difficult to read, but the date, 1722, is still clear.[3] Perhaps lot 56 ('Raffaelle . . . The Virgin and Child') Earl of Carysfort sale. Christie's, 14th June, 1828.[4] Noted in the Wynn Ellis collection by Waagen.[5] Wynn Ellis Bequest, 1876.

REPRODUCTION: *Illustrations, Italian Schools*, 1937, p. 301.

REFERENCES: (1) Waagen (II, p. 293) suggested Innocenzo da Imola as executant. (2) By Nicolas de Larmessin in the 'Crozat Gallery' and by A. L. Romanet in the Orléans catalogue. (3) The inscription as given in the 1929 catalogue is only a paraphrase. (4) Suggested by Tancred Borenius (catalogue of the pictures at Elton Hall, 1924, pp. xlii and 114). He says that 'Ellis', whom he identifies with Wynn Ellis, by whom no. 929 was bequeathed to the Gallery, is given as purchaser in the sale catalogue. Of the two copies in the Gallery library this is true for one. The other (which has 'Agnew' against this lot) may be wrong. (5) *Loc. cit.*

Derivative of RAPHAEL

4031   A FEMALE SAINT

Panel, $37\frac{3}{4} \times 29\frac{1}{2}$ $(0 \cdot 959 \times 0 \cdot 743)$.

Very fair condition.

In the 1929 catalogue as Dosso Dossi. The conception appears to derive basically from the Roman works of Raphael with certain reminiscences of Giulio Romano, Parmigianino and Dosso. Hence an attribution to Girolamo da Carpi,[1] an eclectic of precisely that kind, was understandable. Nevertheless various factors suggest that the picture does not date from the Renaissance.[2] The panel, in the first place, is apparently mahogany, sliced, as appears from an X-ray photograph, in such a way as to expose old worm holes. These were filled in before painting started. The technique revealed by the X-rays, moreover, is entirely foreign to Renaissance practice as are certain features of the costume and hair style.[3] Finally, a cleaning test shows that the flesh was not painted in flesh colour but yellowish. This last factor is a strong indication that the picture may have been painted specifically to look like an Old Master. The existence of another version (see VERSIONS below) would not be incompatible with the possibility that no. 4031 may be a copy, or part copy, of something.

VERSION: Another version, perhaps rather better, was reported in 1950 at Downton Castle (Boughton-Knight collection). It was lot 96 in an anonymous sale, Sotheby's, 11th July, 1962.

PROVENANCE: No. 144 (Giulio Romano) in the Lady Beryl Gilbert sale, Christie's, 8th February, 1918 as from Revesby Abbey, Boston, Lincs. This collection had come from J. Banks Stanhope in the mid-nineteenth century.[4] Sir Claude Phillips Bequest, 1924.

REPRODUCTION: *Illustrations, Italian Schools*, 1937, p. 126.

REFERENCES: (1) R. Longhi in *Ampliamenti nell' Officina Ferrarese*, 1940, p. 37, supported by F. Antal in *Art Bulletin*, 1948, p. 81, n. 4. (2) This had already been suggested by E. K. Waterhouse (notes in the Gallery archives). (3) Notes by Stella Mary Pearce in the Gallery archives. (4) Note by E. K. Waterhouse in the Gallery copy of the sale catalogue.

GEROLAMO ROMANINO
Born *c.* 1484–7, still alive 1559

Brescian School. The uncertainty concerning the date of his birth springs from the fact that in documents dated 1517, 1534 and 1548 his age is given as 33, 47 and 62 respectively. The date—1566—usually given for his death comes from a very late source.[1] A portrait at Innsbruck inscribed with the date 1562 is included by Berenson (1936) in his attributions to Romanino.

On pictures, such as the early Venice *Pietà* or the Salò altar of S. Antonio, which are signed, Romanino uses a latinized form—Hieronimus Romanus or Rumanus. In contemporary documents he is referred to sometimes as Hieronimo di Ruma or Jeronimo Romani but sometimes also in the diminutive form, Romanin or Romanino, which has become universal since.

His earliest surviving dated work (*Pietà*, now in the Accademia,

Venice) is of 1510 and comes from the church of S. Lorenzo at Brescia. By April, 1513, Romanino was in Padua and seems already to have been there at least long enough to have painted some organ shutters.[2] In 1519–20 he was working at Cremona, in 1524 at Asola and in 1531–2 at Trento. The total of his travels in northern Italy was probably very extensive, but his residence was at Brescia, of which city he was invited to become a municipal councillor in 1559. The great extent of Romanino's output was already remarked by Vasari.[3] It is mainly of religious subjects but some portraits have been attributed to him (see entry for no. 2096, ascribed to Calisto Piazza da Lodi).

REFERENCES: (1) Federico Nicoli Cristiani: *Brevi Notizie intorno a' più' celebri Pittori Bresciani*, being an appendix to his *Vita . . . di Lattanzio Gambara*, 1807, p. 180. (2) N. Baldoria in *Archivio Storico dell' Arte*, 1891, pp. 59–60 (G. Nicodemi in his monograph on Romanino, 1925, p. 17, n. 1, falsely gives the date of the issue as 1892) quotes in full a contract between Romanino and the monks of S. Giustina, Padua of 30th April, 1513—'et ritrouandosse magistro Hieronymo da bressa depentor qui nel monasterio . . . etiam ha facto le portelle del organo'. (3) Vasari/Milanesi VI, 504 '. . . Jeronimo Romanino ha fatte . . . infinite opere'.

297 ALTARPIECE: THE NATIVITY WITH SS.
ALESSANDRO OF BRESCIA, JEROME,
GAUDIOSO AND FILIPPO BENIZZI

Five panels.   Centre c. $102\frac{1}{2} \times 45\frac{1}{2}$ ($2\cdot608 \times 1\cdot156$) (arched top)
Lower wings each $62\frac{1}{2} \times 25\frac{1}{2}$ ($1\cdot588 \times 0\cdot648$)
Upper wings each $29\frac{1}{4} \times 25\frac{1}{2}$ ($0\cdot743 \times 0\cdot648$).

The two full-length saints somewhat more damaged than the other three panels, but on the whole the work is remarkably well-preserved for its size and age. S. Alessandro panel cleaned 1965. The four others cleaned 1968, revealing that the original ox had been overpainted in the nineteenth century (see Reference 12).

Of the four saints in the side panels S. Jerome is readily identifiable by his lion, crucifix and stone. The other full-length saint is specified by all the early writers (see below) as S. Alessandro, to whom the church from which the altarpiece came was dedicated. The other two are identifiable as S. Gaudioso (in bishop's robes) who was buried in the church and S. Filippo Benizzi (wearing a black habit), the fifth general of the Servites to whom it belonged.

Painted as the high altarpiece of the church of S. Alessandro, Brescia, where it is first recorded in detail by Ridolfi (1648).[1] Ridolfi and all later writers specify it as a work of Romanino. Ridolfi also mentions a *S. John and the Magdalen lamenting the dead Christ* at the top of the altarpiece and an *Annunciation* and *Adoration of the Kings* on the shutters. (Averoldo (1700)[2] specifies that the three figures in the *Lamentation* were half-length and that the *venuta* and *offerta* of the Magi were on the inside of the shutters and were in gouache. He does not mention the *Annunciation* which was evidently on the outside of the shutters, as was later specified by Chizzola (1760)[3] who also mentions that the shutter paintings were on canvas. It has been suggested that the *Adoration* shutters now in SS. Nazaro e Celso, Brescia were part of the shutters of no. 297. What claimed to be the *Pietà* was seen at Brescia by Mündler in 1858 in the house of the abate Antonio Averoldi.

Averoldo (1700)[4] mentions a tradition that the altarpiece was painted in rivalry with Titian's at another Brescian church, namely SS. Nazaro e Celso, and this story, for what it is worth, should be considered in conjunction with a statement by Cozzando (1694) to the effect that no. 297, or part of its then frame, bore the date 1525.[5] If the latter statement is true (there is no other evidence for it, but from a stylistic point of view there would be nothing against it) the former is plausible enough, as Titian's altarpiece is dated 1522, is likewise in five compartments of similar proportions and would have constituted, when it was set up at Brescia, an obvious challenge to the local painters.

Some heads, most of them in profile, crudely drawn on the back of the S. Jerome and S. Alessandro panels, have been published.[6]

DRAWING: Oxford, Ashmolean Museum. Virgin adoring the Child. Exh. R.A., Diploma Gallery, 1953 (93), in the catalogue of which related vaguely to no. 297, though attributed to Moretto. The resemblance is indeed only general, and lacks in particular the motive of the Child kicking with His right leg.[7]

PROVENANCE: From the church of S. Alessandro, Brescia (see above). The church was remodelled in 1785.[8] Its inmates, the Servites, were turned out in 1797.[9] Either occasion might have caused the removal of no. 297[10] but it is not in fact recorded again until Brognoli mentions it in the Averoldi collection at Brescia (1826).[11] Brognoli makes no mention of the *Pietà* or shutters but the former was seen by Mündler in 1858 in the house, at Brescia, of the abate Antonio Averoldi.[12] Purchased from the Conti Angelo and Gherardo Averoldi, 1857. S. Alessandro panel exh. Brescia (*Romanino*), 1965 (27).

REPRODUCTION: *Illustrations, Italian Schools*, 1937, p. 311 (before cleaning).

REFERENCES: (1) Ridolfi/Hadeln, I, p. 269. Ridolfi refers to S. Gaudioso as 'S. Gaudentio' and to S. Filippo Benizzi as 'Beato Felice Seruita'. An earlier reference still—by Ottavio Rossi, in *Elogi historici di Bresciani illustri*, 1620, pp. 502-4—speaks merely of the S. Alessandro altar as one of Romanino's best works. (2) Giul' Anton Averoldo: *Le Scelte Pitture di Brescia . . .*, 1700, pp. 147-8. (3) Luigi Chizzola: *Le Pitture e Sculture di Brescia . . .*, 1760, p. 120. (4) *Loc. cit.* (5) Leonardo Cozzando: *Vago e Curioso Ristretto profano e sagro dell'Historia Bresciana*, 1694, p. 120 '. . . . sù la quale anco è notato l'anno della sua facitura MDXXV'. (6) Martin Davies: *Paintings and Drawings on the Backs of National Gallery Pictures*, 1946, plates, 2, 3, 4 and 5. (7) For discussion of this motive see the entry for no. 2907, Brescian School. This drawing is stated in the Report of the National Art-Collections Fund, 1956, to have been acquired by the Ashmolean Museum, Oxford. It does not figure in K. T. Parker's catalogue published in that year. (8) Paolo Brognoli: *Nuova Guida per la Città di Brescia*, 1826, p. 112. (9) Brognoli, *loc. cit.* (10) G. Nicodemi: *Gerolamo Romanino*, 1925, pp. 19 and 198, claims that the Averoldi acquired the pictures in 1785, but does not give his evidence. (11) *Op. cit.*, p. 201 . . . 'del Romanino vi è l'antica tavola che era a sant' Alessandro divisa in cinque quadri'. (12) Mündler's notebooks in the Gallery archives. The brief paragraphs on the collection of the Ab. Antonio Averoldi given in Federico Odorici's *Guida di Brescia*, 1853, p. 179, do not specifically mention the *Pietà*. M. L. Ferrari (*Il Romanino*, 1961, facing pl. 48) has further bibliography and a false reference to the New Gallery

Exhibition of 1895. For details of nineteenth-century overpainting see article by the present writer, *Burlington Magazine*, 1974.

Ascribed to ROMANINO

3093   PEGASUS AND THE MUSES

Panel, 15 × 45½ (0·381 × 1·156).
The wood has suffered some bruising and denting, with corresponding loss of paint in those areas.

A photograph of the damaged remains of a coat of arms, roughly painted on the back of the panel, has been published.[1] Across this are traces of an inscription read in earlier editions of the catalogue as 'Girolo Romanino Bresciano V., 1546' but now barely legible for the most part, though the date is still fairly clear. The singular circumstance that this date accords well with the style of the costumes shown[2] suggests that the inscription may record some authentic tradition, irrespective of when it was written. Though there are no documented works of Romanino of this type—i.e. small furniture pictures—it might be expected that routine productions of his studio intended for such a purpose might look like this.[3]

The fact that the female figures in the foreground are nine in number and that some of them are shown playing musical instruments and some of the others singing leaves little doubt that they are intended for the Muses. The presence of Pegasus clinches the matter. He is shown kicking with his hoof, as a result of which the fountain of Hippocrene gushed, as can be seen, from the rock. The five small figures in the middle distance are presumably some of the nine daughters of Pierus who engaged in a singing contest with the Muses on this occasion.[4]

The form of Pegasus' body as shown here appears to be derived from the bronze horses of S. Mark's, Venice.

PROVENANCE: Given by Morelli to A. H. Layard[5] before 1869 when lent by Layard to the South Kensington Museum (no. 30). Layard Bequest, 1916.

REPRODUCTION: *Illustrations, Italian Schools*, 1937, p. 312.

REFERENCES: (1) Martin Davies: *Paintings and Drawings on the backs of National Gallery Pictures*, 1946, p. xi, pl. 34. The writer comments that 'there seems no reason for supposing the back to be later than the front'. (2) Notes by Stella Mary Pearce in the Gallery archives. In these a dating around 1543–5 had been proposed independently. (3) Layard (notebook in the Gallery archives) suggested that the picture had formed part of a *cassone*. Stella Mary Pearce reports two further panels of very similar type in the museum at Bourges. The attribution of no. 3093 to Romanino was included in Berenson's lists of 1907 but omitted in later editions. G. Nicodemi (monograph of 1925, p. 198) admits the Romanino attribution. Maria Luisa Ferrari (*Il Romanino*, 1961, p. 309) suggests Marcello Fogolino, who might indeed be an alternative. (4) Ovid (*Metamorphoses V*) has one version of the story. (5) Layard MS. in the Gallery archives.

Pier Francesco SACCHI
Born *c.* 1485, died 1528

He was from Pavia, as emerges from the form of signature on several of his paintings ('de Papia') but already settled in Genoa by 1501 when apprenticed 'etatis annorum sexdecim in circa'[1] to the painter Pantaleo Berengerio. Few paintings—and they exclusively of religious subject—can be confidently attributed to him.

REFERENCE:(1) For this and other documents cf. Federigo Alizeri: *Notizie dei Professori del Disegno in Liguria*, vol. III, Pittura, 1874 ed., pp. 142 ff.

3944   S. PAUL WRITING

Panel,[1] $41\frac{3}{4} \times 32\frac{1}{4}$ (1·06 × 0·819).

Some damage from splitting (vertically), particularly in the saint's blue tunic. His head and hands are in fair state.

The words written by the saint are in Greek but make use of old and fancy characters and abbreviations. The passage as given in a modern Greek Testament (retaining the line-divisions of the original) is as follows:

'Η ἀγάπη μακρ
οθυμεῖ, χρηστεύεται·
ἡ ἀγάπη οὐ ζηλοῖ·
ἡ ἀγάπη οὐ περ
περεύε [ται,] . . .

(I Corinthians xiii, 4. *Charity suffereth long, and is kind; charity envieth not; charity vaunteth not itself, is not puffed up*).

As Ghirlandaio at the time it was bought for Dr. Mond. Published as Sacchi in J. P. Richter's catalogue of the Mond collection (1910). In the following year Gustavo Frizzoni[2] said that the Sacchi attribution was due to him. To support it he drew attention to the *Four Doctors of the Church* (Louvre) which is signed by Sacchi and dated 1516. This picture is indeed so similar to no. 3944 in so many respects as to justify the attribution of the latter without further ado.[3]

PROVENANCE: In 1857 in the possession of Domenico Odone, Genoa, where recorded by Eastlake and Mündler, whose descriptions are sufficiently detailed to identify it despite a subsequent gap in the pedigree.[4] Eastlake mentions no attribution; Mündler has 'style of Giovenone?'. Bought by Ludwig Mond in London, 1893.[5] Mond Bequest, 1924.

REPRODUCTION: *Illustrations, Italian Schools*, 1937, p. 317.

REFERENCES: (1) Poplar, according to a letter from B. J. Rendle of the Forest Products Research Laboratory. (2) *Rassegna d'Arte*, March, 1911, p. 45. (3) Martin Davies, in notes in the Gallery archives, postulates some connection between no. 3944 and Gaudenzio Ferrari's version of the subject for S. Maria delle Grazie, Milan (now Louvre), which is considerably later (dated 1543). (4) Eastlake, 31st August, 1857: *St Paul writing—wood—2 f 7 w. 3 f 5 h sitting profile at a table & desk—his sword leaning against it, a crucifix before him . . . he holds a pen in his rt hand & with the left steadies the paper before him with a stiletto or grattoir, an inscription appar. Greek (perhaps the beginning of one of the epistles) written in the book before him.* Mündler's entry of the same date is less detailed. These passages are in notebooks in the Gallery archives. **(5)** Richter, Mond catalogue, vol. II, p. v.

Francesco SALVIATI
Born 1510, died 1563

His christian name sometimes in the form Cecchino. His surname was de' Rossi. He took the name Salviati from a Cardinal of that name who was an early patron. Active in maturity alternately in Rome and Florence (with visits to Venice in 1539–41 and France in 1554–5) in the various capacities of painter of frescoes, altarpieces and portraits and designer of tapestries and miscellaneous objects of art. Vasari, as a close friend, devotes a particularly detailed biography to him in which he emphasizes his increasingly neurotic behaviour.

Follower of Francesco SALVIATI

652   CHARITY

Panel, painted are $9\frac{1}{8} \times 7$ (0·245 × 0·178). The original panel has been let into another one.

Pretty good condition.

Hitherto as Francesco Salviati. Though obviously dependent on his famous and considerably larger picture of the same subject in the Uffizi the forms and handling alike are much tamer. H. Voss (1920)[1] referred to no. 652 as a replica of a picture in the Durazzo Pallavicini gallery, Genoa which he ascribed to Francesco Brina. This attribution found some support[2] but some of the comparable works have alternatively been ascribed to another Salviati follower, Michele di Ridolfo.[3]

VERSIONS: One said by H. Voss (*loc. cit.*) to be in the Durazzo Pallavicini Gallery, Genoa. Another in the Muzeum Narodowe, Warsaw.[4]

PROVENANCE: Said (in the National Gallery Report for 1860) to have been in the Fesch collection. Purchased with the Beaucousin collection, Paris, 1860.

REPRODUCTION: *Illustrations, Italian Schools*, 1937, p. 316.

REFERENCES: **(1)** *Die Malerei der Spätrenaissance in Rom und Florenz*, I, p. 194. **(2)** E.g. from W. Stechow in Thieme-Becker (article on Francesco Salviati). **(3)** E.g. the *Holy Family* in the Museo Bandini, Fiesole (from the Florence Accademia, no. 185). Also the small panels of Lucretia and Leda in the Galleria Borghese, Rome (53 and 54). **(4)** Published by Maria Mrozińska in the museum's bulletin for 1956.

Giuseppe SALVIATI
Active 1535, still alive 1573

His name was Giuseppe Porta. He took the name Salviati from his master, Francesco Salviati, who himself had adopted it from his patron,

Cardinal Salviati. According to Vasari, he came from Castelnuovo della Garfagnana[1] (east of Carrara) and was taken in 1535, 'giovanetto', to Rome, where he became Francesco Salviati's pupil. Accompanying the latter on his visit to Venice, in 1539,[2] he was encouraged by his reception there and decided to settle. He returned to Rome in 1565[3] for a short time to finish, according to Vasari, a painting started by Francesco Salviati in the Sala Regia of the Vatican. The last evidence of his existence is in a letter of 27th November, 1573.[4] His book on the Ionic capital was published in 1552.

Ridolfi records that Salviati lived so long in Venice that he was considered Venetian,[5] and it is significant in this context that no. 3942 of this Gallery should have been attributed formerly to Zelotti. The frescoes on the exterior of Venetian buildings, on which Salviati's fame primarily rested during his life time, have not survived. The key works for reconstructing his *œuvre* are the three *tondi* in the *Libreria* at Venice, which are documented as of 1556-7,[6] together with a number of pictures mentioned by Vasari[7] as in Venetian churches and still identifiable. Though the precise chronology of these is difficult to establish, the general tendency, as was to be expected, is of a Central Italian art gradually becoming more Venetian. In certain works Giuseppe Salviati approaches fairly close in style, at least superficially, to Paolo Veronese.

REFERENCES: (1) Vasari/Milanesi, VII, pp. 45-7. Ridolfi (Ridolfi/Hadeln, I, p. 241) also records a signature in the form 'Ioseph Garfagninus'. (2) The date is deduced from Vasari's statement (VII, 17-18) that Francesco Salviati went to Venice shortly before the marriage of Duke Cosimo, which occurred in June, 1539. (3) Date from payment published by R. Lanciani: *Storia degli Scavi di Roma*, III, p. 228. (4) Cf. B. Gonzati: *La Basilica di S. Antonio di Padova*, 1852-3, vol. I, p. CI, Doc. XCIII. (5) *Op. cit.*, p. 240. (6) Cf. Laura Pittoni: *La Libreria di S. Marco*, 1903, pp. 111 ff, and *Archivalische Beiträge aus dem Nachlass G. Ludwigs*, 1911, pp. 142-5. (7) *Loc. cit.*

3942 JUSTICE

Original canvas *c.* $34\frac{1}{4} \times 41\frac{1}{4}$ (0·87 × 1·048). Canvas subsequently added round the curved part brings the over-all measurements to $35\frac{1}{2} \times 49\frac{1}{4}$ (0·902 × 1·251). This later canvas includes the horns of the crescent moon and most of the left hand lion. As the crescent moon is not normally associated with Justice it may have been added for merely decorative reasons—to blend with the semi-circular shape of the painting. The additions seem to be crudely painted but at what date cannot be determined.

The paint on most of the original canvas is thin and there are numerous retouchings, particularly on the left.

In the Cavendish Bentinck sale, in 1891, as by Zelotti, but subsequently convincingly identified by J. P. Richter[1] with a picture from the *Zecca* (Mint) at Venice which had been sent to Milan in 1808— 'Porta Giuseppe. La Giustizia sedente fra due Leoni . . . mezza figura in tela, e mezzo tondo, altezza 2-8. pied. venez. larghezza 3-7. pied.

venez.'[2] (i.e. $36\frac{1}{4} \times 49''$).[3] Evidently the picture was among those looted at the time of the Napoleonic régime which were never restored to their place of origin. Various paintings 'in mezza luna' are specified by Boschini (1664) as in the *Zecca*, but not this one.[4] The coat of arms shown is that of a branch of the Contarini family.[5] The *Zecca* was rebuilt for the most part between 1537 and 1545.[6] The officials known as *Provveditori in Zecca* held office at this time for one year. A Tommaso Contarini was elected *Provveditore* in October, 1542 and a Paolo Contarini in October, 1558. These are presumably identical with the Tommaso and Paolo Contarini whose dates were 1506–60 and 1532–87 respectively, both of whom bore the form of the Contarini arms shown in no. 3942.[7] The latter could have been commissioned, therefore, either in 1542–3 or in 1558–9. Stylistically the attribution to Giuseppe Salviati is unexceptionable. The figure is comparable with the *Libreria* decorations of 1556–7 and with the S. Francesco della Vigna altarpiece of the Madonna and Child with SS. Bernard and Anthony Abbot (the latter vouched for as Giuseppe Salviati's by Vasari in effect, though his description of it is vague).

PROVENANCE: Almost certainly painted for the *Zecca* at Venice and sent to Milan with other Napoleonic loot in 1808 (see above). No. 759 in the G. A. F. Cavendish Bentinck sale, Christie's, 13th July, 1891,[8] where bought Richter for Mond. Ludwig Mond Bequest, 1924.

REPRODUCTION: *Illustrations, Italian Schools*, 1937, p. 289.

REFERENCES: (1) Mond catalogue, vol. 1 (1910), pp. 178–85. Berenson (*Lists*, 1957) maintains the Zelotti attribution. (2) Richter, *loc. cit.*, quotes the documents *in extenso*. The extract given here is from two of them. (3) Richter's calculation. (4) *Le Minere* . . ., pp. 84–6. (5) Rietstap (*Armorial Général*, vol. 1, 1884, p. 456) lists it as no. 4 of the various forms of the Contarini arms, of which the basic one was the diagonal blue and gold strips as shown in the second and third quarterings here. (6) G. Lorenzetti: *Venezia e il suo Estuario*, 1956, p. 155. (7) This information kindly supplied by Dr. Ferruccio Zago of the Archivio di Stato, Venice. A third Contarini, Federico, held office for three months only in 1543. The pictures mentioned by Boschini (*loc. cit.*) as in the *Zecca* range from Bonifazio to Domenico Tintoretto and would therefore have been put there at different times. (8) 'Zelotti, 759 Justice, with a shield bearing the arms of the Contarini family.'

ANDREA DEL SARTO
1486–1530

Andrea d'Agnolo, called 'del Sarto' from his father's trade as tailor. Vasari, who wrongly gives the date of his birth as 1478,[1] specifies his apprenticeship to Piero di Cosimo (among others) and his partnership at an early stage of his life with Franciabigio. Admitted in December, 1508 to the *Arte de' Medici e Speziali*. He spent most of his life in Florence but in 1518–19 was in France in the service of François I whose displeasure, according to Vasari, he subsequently incurred by not returning to France after leave of absence in Florence.

Most of his surviving works, apart from some portraits, are of religious subject.

REFERENCE: (1) The documents in question are given in Ingeborg Frænckel: *Andrea del Sarto*, 1935, pp. 130–3. Paolo Pino's inclusion of Sarto among living artists (*Dialogo di Pittura*, 1548, p. 24) is evidently a mistake. Another mistake, long current, was that his family name was Vannucci (or Vannucchi).

17 MADONNA AND CHILD WITH SS. ELIZABETH AND JOHN THE BAPTIST

Panel, $41\frac{3}{4} \times 32$ (1·06 × 0·81).

Fairly widespread local damage, partly due to past blistering. The Madonna's face seem to have been less subject to this than other parts and to be in fair state. A number of *pentimenti* are visible to the naked eye, and others in an infra-red photograph. Dark lines visible in the flesh areas and elsewhere are evidently part of the under-drawing.

The attribution of no. 17 to Sarto himself has hitherto found little support,[1] with the notable exception of Berenson (1936 *Lists*). The problem is complicated by the existence of another composition, represented by versions almost identical with each other at Leningrad and Windsor, both inscribed as by Sarto. These pictures repeat the group shown in no. 17 and include an extra figure, S. Catherine, on the right. To knit the composition together the gaze of the Christ Child is altered, so that He seems to be looking back towards S. Catherine. In these pictures too the toes of the Madonna's right foot are shown, whereas in no. 17 she wears a shoe.

It is outside the scope of the present entry to consider the authenticity or otherwise of either the Leningrad or the Windsor picture, but two factors may be indicated concerning their relation to no. 17. First, of the many *pentimenti* in no. 17 two in particular are significant. Both are visible to the naked eye but are clearer in an infra-red photograph. The two middle fingers of the Madonna's left hand were originally touching, and not as now with a space between them. The first finger and the big finger were not changed but the little finger and the one above it were higher up than at present. Again, the thumb and all the fingers of S. Elizabeth's right hand were originally higher up (dark lines very clearly visible as well as ordinary *pentimenti*) but as the position of her arm does not seem to have been altered, the angle of the hand (as a whole) to it would have been somewhat less. In both these respects it is the final form of no. 17, and not the original one, which corresponds with the equivalent feature in the Leningrad and Windsor pictures. Secondly, the draperies of S. Elizabeth's skirt assume a somewhat characterless form in the Leningrad and Windsor pictures. In no. 17 these draperies are quite different, very much more monumental and more typical of Sarto.

The latter consideration leads the present writer to conclude that a great deal of no. 17 is likely to be Sarto's autograph work; the former, that it is probably earlier than the Leningrad and Windsor pictures. The

Leningrad version was variously dated by Berenson 'probably no later than 1515' and '1519'.[2]

VERSIONS: For the Leningrad and Windsor pictures see above. A photograph in the Gallery archives of what was evidently a copy of no. 17 is marked as from the collection of 'Canon Hirscher in Freiberg i. B., Rinecker Sale, Cologne, 1888'.

PROVENANCE: Recorded by Ramdohr (1787)[3] and by Vasi (1797)[4] in the Villa Aldobrandini, Rome and therefore probably identical with a Sarto which is listed in the Aldobrandini inventories of 1603 and later.[5] Purchased in Rome, 1805, through Camuccini, for Buchanan by Irvine who stated that it had come from the Villa Aldobrandini.[6] Selected on arrival in England by the Rev. Holwell Carr who had already purchased from Champernowne and Buchanan a sixth share in this and other pictures to be imported.[7] Exh. B.I., 1816 (3), lent Holwell Carr. Holwell Carr Bequest, 1831.

REPRODUCTION: *Illustrations, Italian Schools*, 1937, p. 318.

REFERENCES: (1) Waagen (*Treasures of Art* . . ., I, 1854, p. 322) attributed it to Puligo, Jacobsen (*Repertorium für Kunstwissenschaft*, XXIV, 1901, p. 368) tentatively to Bugiardini. Recently Puligo has again been suggested (if that is the word), as though independently, by S. J. Freedberg (*Painting of the High Renaissance in Rome and Florence*, 1961, p. 497). This writer postulates a cartoon by Sarto as basis and accepts the Leningrad picture as autograph. It may be remarked that Puligo is an obvious waste-paper basket for Sarto, but as long as the main collection of the work of both remains in Palazzo Pitti, where most pictures are discoloured and difficult to see, it is difficult to imagine any substantial progress in clarification. (2) The 1519 dating (1909, 1932 and 1936 *Lists*) was presumably on the assumption that it was painted in France. In the first edition of his *Florentine Drawings* (1903, I, p. 291) he had said 'probably no later than 1515' and this was unchanged in the second edition (I, p. 290). In the same work (1938 edition, no. 2376, vol. 2, p. 308, repr. vol. 3, fig. 927) he catalogued a drawing in the British Museum as a copy by Puligo of the S. Catherine in the Leningrad picture. (3) *Ueber Mahlerei und Bildhauerarbeit in Rom* . . ., II, p. 182. '. . . angeblich von A. del Sarto'. (4) *Itinéraire Instructif de Rome* . . ., p. 268. (5) Printed in *Palatino*, 1964, p. 206, no. 233, *Arte Antica e Moderna*, 1960, p. 432, no. 112 and *Arte Antica e Moderna*, 1963, p. 78, no. 380. (6) Buchanan: *Memoirs*, II (1824), pp. 162–3. (7) Buchanan, *loc. cit.* The *Farington Diary* (vol. VIII, p. 100, entry for 24th November, 1816) tells a story (discreditable to Holwell Carr) about the purchase of what may have been no. 17.

690 PORTRAIT OF A YOUNG MAN

Signed, top left, with the artist's monogram.

$28\frac{1}{2} \times 22\frac{1}{2}$ (0·72 × 0·57).

Basic condition fair for a picture of the period painted on fine linen.[1] Cleaned 1971, revealing that the sitter's hands were meant to be somewhat truncated on the left of the picture, and a corresponding strip on the right revealed.

Originally catalogued (from 1864) as 'His Own Portrait' and with the object in the sitter's hands identified as a book. In the 1889 edition the book is queried and the suggestion made that the object is really modelling-clay and the sitter in consequence a sculptor. The object has also been identified as a stone, whether for sculpting or for use in building. From 1901 as 'Portrait of a Sculptor'. Though the pose and the direction of the eyes do suggest a self-portrait the features are far more handsome and finely chiselled than those of the figure on the right of the SS. Annunziata *Magi*, vouched for by Vasari as a self-portrait of Andrea and probably the basis of the woodcut portrait in Vasari's edition of 1568.[2] The object in the sitter's hands is damaged and now scarcely legible, but if the Uffizi drawing 661 *recto* (see DRAWINGS below) is in fact a preliminary study for no. 690 it does seem as though intended for a book.

Clearly close in style to the *Madonna delle Arpie* which is dated 1517.[3]

DRAWINGS: Di Pietro reproduces four studies (in the Uffizi) as being for no. 690.[4]

PROVENANCE: Cavaliere Niccolò Puccini of Pistoia, from whose estate bought, 1862, by Sir Charles Eastlake for the Gallery.[5] Reiset[6] claims it was once in the collection of the Marchese Campana, but this was in fact a different picture seen, in 1856, by Eastlake in the Campana collection in Rome and described by him as on panel and measuring 2' 10½" × 1' 3½".[7]

REPRODUCTION: *Illustrations, Italian Schools*, 1937, p. 319.

REFERENCES: (1) Already lined when seen by Eastlake in the Puccini collection in 1862. This and his statement at the time that it was 'painted on the finest linen' would at least give no support to a theory that it was ever on panel, even though not disproving it. Apparently cleaned by Pinti just before entering the Gallery. (2) It may be worth mentioning in this context that the present writer has long wondered if the sitter of no. 690 may be the same as that of a portrait of an engraver of precious stones (Louvre, no. 1241, attributed to Pontormo). Jacobsen (*Repertorium für Kunstwissenschaft*, XXIV, 1901, p. 368) makes further suggestions of this kind. (3) Stella Mary Pearce, in notes in the Gallery archives, favours a slightly later date for no. 690—about 1521–3. (4) Filippo di Pietro: *Disegni di Andrea del Sarto negli Uffizi*, 1910, pp. 26 and 30. (5) Luigi Biadi (*Supplemento*, of 1832, p. 16 to his *Notizie d'Andrea del Sarto* of 1829) notes no. 690 as 'Ritratto d'Andrea del Sarto, operato da se medesimo' in the Puccini collection at Pistoia. (6) *Une Visite à la Galerie Nationale de Londres* (1887), p. 157. (7) Eastlake MS. in the Gallery archives.

GIAN GIROLAMO SAVOLDO
active 1508, still alive 1548

Referred to in contemporary documents as of or from Brescia and signs as such on certain paintings (e.g. no. 3092 of this Gallery), but first recorded at Florence, in 1508.[1] Thereafter apparently mainly resident at Venice,[2] though a period at Milan can be deduced, probably between 1532 and 1535.[3] The date of his death has not come to light, but Aretino refers to him in a letter of 1548 as being then in his decrepitude.[4]

Of datable paintings, an inscription on the *SS. Anthony and Paul the Hermit* (Venice, Accademia) has been unconvincingly claimed as reading 1510.[5] A male portrait in the Brera with a disputed date on the parapet has been unconvincingly attributed to Savoldo. In 1521 Savoldo is documented as finishing the altarpiece of the Madonna and Saints in the church of S. Niccolò at Treviso, which had been commissioned of Fra' Marco Pensaben and already partly executed. The Hampton Court

Nativity with Donors is signed and dated 1527. Dates are also recorded on altarpieces at S. Maria in Organo, Verona (1533) and S. Giobbe, Venice (1540).

Paolo Pino, who said he was his pupil, emphasizes that Savoldo painted few pictures[6] and Vasari that he did not work on a large scale.[7] In addition, it seems he was in the habit of repeating his own compositions with some degree of modification or variation. Savoldo's relation to Giorgione and to Northern art, and, later on, Caravaggio's relation to him are questions which arise from a study of his art.

REFERENCES: (1) *'die secunda decembris 1508. Johannes Jeronimus Jacopi domini Pieri de Savoldis de Brescia pictor ad presens in civitate Florentie volens venire ad magistratum dicte artis et poni et scribi in Matricula . . .'* (from the *Libro di Matricola dell' Arte dei Medici*, published by Giusta Nicco Fasola, *Lineamenti del Savoldo* in *L'Arte*, 1940, p. 58, n. 1). (2) For documentation cf. Venturi, *Storia . . .*, IX, III, pp. 745–8 and G. Ludwig in Prussian *Jahrbuch* 1905, *Beiheft* pp. 117–23. (3) The main evidence is Paolo Pino's statement (*Dialogo di Pittura*, 1548, p. 5V) *'un tempo fù prouiggionato dall' ultimo Duca di Melano* [sic]'. For deductions from this and from Vasari, particularly with regard to the date, cf. Creighton E. Gilbert: *Milan and Savoldo* in *Art Bulletin*, 1945, pp. 124 ff. (4) *Lettere*, V (1609), p. 64. (5) See Creighton E. Gilbert, *loc. cit.* (6) *Loc. cit.* (7) Vasari/Milanesi VI, p. 507.

1031   S. MARY MAGDALENE APPROACHING THE SEPULCHRE

Painted area $34 \times 31\frac{1}{4}$ (0·864 × 0·79). All round this area is a band *c.* $\frac{3}{4}''$ wide, now painted dark but evidently originally the turn-over, as nail-marks are visible along it. Cleaned 1960.

Paint rather thin, abraded and made up in places, and unevenly cleaned in the past, but general condition fairly good.

Several other versions exist (see VERSIONS below). Of these, that at Berlin is signed by Savoldo. No. 1031 is not signed but the Savoldo attribution is unexceptionable. The Berlin picture omits the small vase and is called merely 'A Venetian Woman', but its presence in the other versions, including no. 1031, seems sufficient to identify the figure with the Magdalen. It is as of this subject that Rossi (1620) and Ridolfi (1648) refer to what was probably no. 1031 (see PROVENANCE below). The biblical source would have been John xx, 1: *The first day of the week cometh Mary Magdalene early, when it was yet dark, unto the sepulchre, and seeth the stone taken away from the sepulchre.* In the accounts given in all the other three Gospels S. Mary Magdalene was not alone on this occasion.

The landscape background recalls the view of Venice from one of the nearer islands but has not been precisely identified.

VERSIONS: At Berlin (see above), Contini-Bonacossi collection, Florence (ex-Giovanelli, Venice) and formerly Warwick Castle.[1] None of these three is precisely like any of the others or precisely like no. 1031. The variable factors are the type of landscape on the left (or, in the Berlin version, its absence), form of the architecture on the right, form and surround of the vase (or, in the Berlin version, its absence) and above all the system of folds of the draperies and their colour.

PROVENANCE: Perhaps the picture which belonged before 1620 to Lorenzo Averoldo of Brescia, described by Ottavio Rossi in his *Elogi* . . . *di Bresciani Illustri*, published in that year (p. 502) as '*una bellissima Maddalena coperta da un pan bianco*', since this is the only known version with whitish draperies; all the others are gold or brown.[2] Ridolfi adds, à propos the Averoldo picture, that many copies had been made of it.[3] Recorded by Chizzola and Carboni (*Le Pitture* . . . *di Brescia*, 1760, p. 180) in Palazzo Avogadri, Brescia. Later in the eighteenth century the Avogadri family merged into that of Fenaroli, in whose possession no. 1031 was noted by Odorici (1853),[4] from which sold in 1877[5] to the Milanese dealer, Baslini, from whom purchased 1878.

REPRODUCTION: *Illustrations, Italian Schools*, 1937, p. 324.

REFERENCES: (1) The Warwick Castle picture is traditionally attributed to Agostino Carracci. (2) Creighton Gilbert in a private communication, kindly volunteered, mentions a copy of the head only, also with gold or brown draperies, at an auction at Louisville, Kentucky in 1951. He also refers to Delogu's suggestion that Savoldo's Magdalen is 'quoted' by Veronese in his small *Deposition* in the Louvre. (3) Ridolfi/Hadeln I, 271–2. If no. 1031 is identifiable with the Averoldo picture it would exclude an alternative identification, tentatively advanced in earlier editions of the catalogue, with Ridolfi's further mention of '*Madama d'Ardier, Ambasciatrice Francese, haueua . . . vna delle Maddalene dette*' (i.e. one of the copies of the Averoldo picture). (4) *Guida di Brescia*, p. 193: '*Maddalena di Tiziano. Videro alcuni in questo vago dipinto una zingara: ma non pare; tutto per quella vece mi suaderebbe a riconoscervi la peccatrice del Vangelo*'. Crowe and Cavalcaselle (*Titian*, II, 1877, p. 438) while attributing it themselves to Savoldo, mention the Titian attribution which prevailed under Fenaroli ownership. Chizzola and Carboni (*loc. cit.*) also have the Titian attribution—'*una Maddalena involta in un panno, dipinta da Tiziano*'. Information on the merging of the Avogadro and Fenaroli families is in letters from Conte Fausto Lechi in the Gallery archives. Conte Lechi adds that he could find no trace of an Averoldo-Avogadro marriage and he therefore doubts whether no. 1031 is the picture mentioned by Rossi and Ridolfi. Oliver Millar (*Walpole Society*, vol. 37, 1958–60, published 1960, p. 231, note to page 44 (11)) suggests that no. 1031 may be identical with a 'lamenting Stooping woeman' by 'Breciano' in Charles I's collection. The dimensions tally approximately but it would be very unlikely that such a picture should find its way back to Brescia *after* having been in Charles' possession. (5) Letter in the Gallery archives of 16th September, 1877 from Baslini—'*in questi giorni ho acquistato dal Conte Fenaroli di Brescia un ritratto di donna del Savoldo, mezza figura velata*'.

3092   S. JEROME

Canvas,[1] $47\frac{1}{3} \times 62\frac{1}{2}$ (1·204 × 1·588).

The lower half of the saint's red robe appears to be in fair state. Much of the rest of the picture is rather abraded. An X-ray photograph of the saint's head shows that he was originally clean-shaven and apparently also short-haired. Cleaned 1971.

Signed, on the rock under the book:

> *jouānes jeron*
> *imus de brisio*
> *de sauoldis*
> *faciebat*[2]

The outline of the church on the left in the background, and its large size in relation to the houses in front of it, suggests that it may be inspired by SS. Giovanni e Paolo (S. Zanipolo) at Venice. A comparable view occurs in the background of the Savoldo altarpiece in the Brera.[3] Savoldo is reported in 1532 as living near S. Zanipolo.[4]

The saint is shown without his lion or his cardinal's hat, but the stone in his right hand, together with his action in kneeling to a crucifix, constitute sufficient means of identification.

DRAWINGS: Louvre, Paris. Chalk drawing of the head of the saint.[5] Creighton Gilbert[6] acutely notes that whereas the outline of the saint's hair in no. 3092, where it falls limply to the nape, corresponds with the Louvre drawing this was not always the case. Old photographs of the painting—such as Alinari no. 13606, taken when it was still in Layard's house at Venice—show the ends of the saint's hair curling upwards from the nape. Gilbert assumed that the painting may have been altered deliberately, in order to make it correspond with the drawing. This may have been the case, but as the infra-red photograph of this area shows the hair virtually as it now is and does not show the curls, the latter may themselves have been repaint.[7]

Three more drawings, British Museum and Albertina, were attributed by L. Fröhlich-Bum[8] to Savoldo and brought into some connection with no. 3092. The attribution of them to Savoldo was rejected by the Tietzes[9] and by C. Gilbert.[10]

PROVENANCE: Recorded in 1855, and again in 1858, by Mündler as in the possession of Bruschetti, the proprietor of the Albergo Reale at Milan who also dealt in pictures.[11] Bought in Milan from Bruschetti's heirs by Sir A. H. Layard[12]—in 1864, according to A. Venturi, who also stated that it had been in the 'famiglia Delfico'.[13] The alleged Manfrin provenance, given by Crowe and Cavalcaselle,[14] is unlikely or false, since the picture does not figure in the Manfrin lists of 1851 when the collection was still intact.[15] Possibly identical with Ridolfi's mention (1648) of '*Madama d'Ardier, Ambasciatrice Francese, haueua vn San Girolamo orante nel deserto*' by Savoldo.[16] This is not quite so inconclusive as it would be in the case of many other painters, since Savoldo is known to have painted relatively little, and no other S. Jerome in the desert by him is known (but see reference 7 of the present entry). Exh. Leeds, 1868 (91), South Kensington, 1869 (8) and R.A., 1870 (16), in all cases lent Layard. Layard Bequest, 1916.

REPRODUCTION: *Illustrations, Italian Schools*, 1937, p. 324.

REFERENCES: (1) Wrongly said in earlier editions of the catalogue to be on wood. (2) The third letter of the first word of the signature misread as *h* and the penultimate letter of the same word as *i* in earlier editions of the catalogue. The third letter for the first word also seems to be *u* in the forms of signature used by Savoldo in the Brera altarpiece and in the so-called Gaston de Foix in the Louvre. Though there are some losses of paint in the area of the inscription they do not materially affect the letters. (3) Cf. also the view of Venice, including the Doge's Palace, but evidently not attempting complete accuracy, in the background of the Savoldo *Rest on the Flight* (Aldrighetto Castelbarco Albani collection, Milan; exh. Giorgione exhibition, Venice, 1955 (109)); also the background of no. 1031 of this Gallery. (4) '*Gioanne Jeronimo da Bressa pictore dignissimo sta in Venetia in calle dala Testa apresso a Santo Gioanne et Paulo*' (Ludwig: Prussian *Jahrbuch*, 1905, Beiheft p. 121). (5) Reproduced Hadeln: *Venezianische Zeichnungen der Hochrenaissance*, 1925, pl. 20. (6) *Savoldo's Drawings put to Use* in *Gazette des Beaux-Arts*, vol. 41 (1953), p. 5. (7) Gilbert's general thesis in the article quoted in reference 6 is that the surviving drawings by Savoldo of single heads were made in connection with variants in his existing pictures, being an intermediate stage between the first and second painted versions, and intended to clarify the more divergent features in the later version. He then deduces as a tentative possibility that the difference between the former state of the saint's hair in no. 3092 and in the Louvre drawing may mean that the latter was preparatory not to the former but to a later version which no longer survives. This conclusion was reached before the infra-red photograph was taken. The X-ray of the clean-shaven and apparently short-haired saint in no. 3092 supports Gilbert's theory to the extent of showing that the Louvre drawing came after no. 3092, and not before it. (8) Vienna *Jahrbuch*, N.F. II (1928), p. 190. (9) Hans Tietze and E. Tietze-Conrat: *The Drawings of the Venetian Painters*, 1944, pp. 247–8. (10) *Loc. cit.* (11) Mündler's diaries in the Gallery archives. (12) Layard papers in the Gallery archives. (13) A. Venturi: *La Formazione della Galleria Layard a Venezia* in *L'Arte*, XV (1912), p. 452. (14) *North Italian Painters*, III (1912), p. 319, note. (15) Manfrin MS. lists in the Gallery archives. (16) Ridolfi/Hadeln I (1914), p. 272. The objection of Crowe and Cavalcaselle (*loc. cit.*) to this identification on the grounds that the picture must have returned to Paris since Félibien mentions it need not be valid as Félibien seems to be quoting Ridolfi. Even if it had gone to Paris it could have been brought back to Italy again later.

Andrea SCHIAVONE
active 1540(?), died 1563

His name was Andrea Meldolla, called 'Schiavone' because he came from Zara on the Dalmation coast.[1] Vasari says he himself commissioned a picture from him in the year 1540. It is not known where Schiavone was in that year and Vasari does not specify where the incident occurred,[2] but as Vasari was not in Venice until the following year, and as Schiavone spent at least the last part of his working career there it has sometimes been assumed that Vasari meant 1541.[3]

Facts concerning Schiavone and documented works by him are alike extremely scanty. His etching of the *Rape of Helen* is dated 1547 and a letter to him from Pietro Aretino dates from the following year, as does a reference in Paolo Pino's *Dialogo di Pittura*.[4] Between 1556 and 1560 he received payment for work at the *Libreria*, Venice[5] (an important commission; the painters involved are said to have been chosen by Titian). In 1563 he died.[6] Lomazzo says (apparently) that he was the pupil of Parmigianino.[7] Vasari's statement that the majority of Schiavone's work was done for private patrons explains the extreme difficulty of identifying it from the early sources. Works in the two Venetian churches specified by Vasari are still in position[8] but are clearly not characteristic. The key paintings are the three *tondi* for the *Libreria*,[9] and starting from them and the signed etchings it is possible to identify a considerable number of extant paintings in a style in which the blending of elements derived from Titian and from Parmigianino occasionally approaches close to Tintoretto.[10]

REFERENCES: (1) This is proved by his will in which he describes himself as 'Io Andrea pittor fiol del condam miser Simon Meldola' (on the back is written 'Ser Andreas Meldola de Hiadra pictor'). The documents in question were published by G. Ludwig in the Prussian *Jahrbuch*, vol. XXIV, 1903,

Beiheft, p. 88. In a further document of 1563 the painter is described as 'Andreas Sclabonus dictus Medola' (document published by E. Harzen in *Deutsches Kunstblatt*, 1853, pp. 327–9, also (less well) by A. Venturi, *Storia . . .*, IX, IV, I, pp. 691–2). These documents contribute to disproving the theory, now abandoned but widely held in the nineteenth century, that Andrea Medola or Meldolla, whose signature appears on some etchings, was distinct from Andrea Schiavone (see particularly Harzen, *loc. cit.*). Further confusion came from Ridolfi's statement that Schiavone came from Sebenico, that he was born in 1522 and died at the age of 60. This led Moschini (*Guida per la Città di Venezia*, vol. II, 1815, p. 628) to identify him with a certain Andrea di Nicolò da Curzola, also called Andrea da Sebenico. To conform with Ridolfi, Moschini alleged that the latter artist died in 1582, but in fact he was still alive in 1591 (Hadeln's edition of Ridolfi, I, p. 247, note 1). (2) Contrary to what is stated by L. Fröhlich-Bum—article on Meldolla, Andrea in Thieme–Becker, where she alleges that Vasari specified Venice as the locale. The relevant passage in Vasari is vol. VI of the Milanesi edition, pp. 596–7. (3) See W. Kallab: *Vasaristudien*, 1908, p. 69. Against this assumption it should be pointed out that Vasari does not give the date in figures but in words ('L'anno mille cinquecento e quaranta'). (4) April, 1548. Published in vol. IV, p. 222, of the Paris edition (1608) of Aretino's letters. Fröhlich-Bum (*loc. cit.*) refers to this letter as 'nicht datiert'. The reference to the 1548 edition of Pino's *Dialogo* is pp. 18v and 19r. (5) Documents in *Archivalische Beiträge aus dem Nachlass G. Ludwigs*, 1911, pp. 144–5. (6) Ludwig in the Prussian *Jahrbuch*, *loc. cit.* (7) Index of the 1584 edition of the *Trattato*: 'Andrea Schiauone, copioso pittore, discepolo del Mazzolino'. (8) Viz. S. Sebastiano and the Carmine. The *Presentation in the Temple* at the latter church, attributed to Schiavone by Vasari, has frequently been attributed to Tintoretto. (9) The documents published by Ludwig speak of 'tondi' without specifying which ones. This omission however was made good by Ridolfi—'i tre primi tondi verso il campanile'. (10) The fundamental modern work on Schiavone is an article by L. Fröhlich-Bum in the Vienna *Jahrbuch*, vol. 31, 1913–14, pp. 137 ff.

Ascribed to ANDREA SCHIAVONE

1883   A MYTHOLOGICAL FIGURE

$7\frac{3}{8}$ (0·187) square.
Worn, and made up in places.

For provenance and commentary see under no. 1884.

ENGRAVING: The design (in a more upright format) engraved by Antonio Belemo as after Parmigianino. An etched version of this, by R. Ford, is dated 1822.

1884   TWO MYTHOLOGICAL FIGURES

$7\frac{3}{8}$ (0·187) square.
Worn, and made up in places.

Nos. 1883 and 1884 are characteristic of a type of mythological picture of which a fair number of examples survive. The attribution of such pictures to Schiavone is general, but cannot be shown to extend back to the sixteenth century. Some similar paintings at Vienna—such as the *Curius Dentatus*, *Scipio Africanus*, *Birth and Education of Jupiter*, *Apollo and Daphne* and *Apollo and Cupid*, are catalogued as the work of Schiavone in the Leopold William inventory of 1659 and engraved as his in the *Theatrum Pictorium* of the next year.[1] Some of these pictures are very close in type to nos. 1883 and 1884. Earlier still are some drawings in the Andrea Vendramin sketch-book of 1627 where a number of mythological scenes are marked as 'di Andrea Schiavon'.[2] Finally, the female figure in no. 1884 repeats almost exactly the attitude of Psyche in the ex-Chatsworth *Marriage of Cupid and Psyche*, which of all the Schiavone mythologies comes closest in style to the documented allegories of the *Libreria* ceiling (see biographical notes on Schiavone). The present writer has therefore no doubt that nos. 1883 and 1884 are either by or after Andrea Schiavone, though the present condition precludes a decision between these alternatives.

No precision seems justified as regards the subject of the two pictures. No. 1883 was tentatively identified in earlier editions of the National Gallery catalogue as 'Apollo killing the Python', and the male figure in no. 1884 characterized as 'old'.

PROVENANCE: With no. 1883 probably in the Algarotti collection in the eighteenth century.[3] In the Baron V. Denon collection, 1826.[4] Later Beaucousin collection, with which purchased, 1860.[5] Lent to Dublin in the same year and not catalogued until 1915.

REPRODUCTION: *Illustrations, Italian Schools*, 1937, p. 326.

REFERENCES: (1) The Hampton Court *Judgment of Midas*, whose pedigree may extend back to the Reynst collection in the seventeenth century, is probably in the same category (see D. Mahon: *Notes on the 'Dutch Gift' to Charles II*, part III, in *Burlington Magazine*, vol. 92, 1950, p. 13). (2) E.g. pages 57–60 of Borenius' edition of the book. See also his article in the *Burlington Magazine*, vol. 60 (1932), p. 140. (3) P. XXII of the catalogue—'Schiavone, André . . ., Apollon dans un bois qui tire de l'arc. Le pendant. Un vieillard qui tient une jeune fille embrassée. Sur bois, hauts 6½ pouc. 1. 6½ pouc. (Ce dernier tableau a été mis en estampe par A. M. Zanetti)'. The present writer has not traced Zanetti's print. If the reference is indeed to nos. 1883 and 1884 the catalogue is in error in describing the pictures as on wood as they are not only now on canvas but appear always to have been. (4) Pp. 19–20 of the volume headed 'Tableaux' of the Denon catalogue—'Schiavone (André) . . . des sujets de la Fable . . . largeur des deux autres 7 pouces et demi.—H. 6 pouces et demi'. The fact that a third picture—of Diana and Callisto—is grouped with these two in the Denon catalogue and that a picture of the same subject and size (with a 'pendant' of Solomon and the Queen of Sheba) also figured in the Algarotti catalogue is some confirmation that the Denon pictures had been in the Algarotti collection. (5) As 'formerly in the collection of Baron Denon' (National Gallery Report, 1860).

SEBASTIANO DEL PIOMBO
born *c.* 1485, died 1547

His name was Sebastiano Luciani,[1] called Sebastiano Veneziano in Rome, and Fra Sebastiano del Piombo after his appointment to that office in 1531. The date of his birth is deduced only from Vasari's statement that he died in 1547 at the age of 62, but as Vasari had known Sebastiano personally this is unlikely to be substantially inaccurate. Apprenticed first, according to Vasari, to the aged Giovanni Bellini in Venice, then to Giorgione, on whose style he modelled his own. The *Anonimo Morelliano* says that Sebastiano finished one of Giorgione's pictures.[2]

In 1511 Sebastiano went from Venice to Rome at the invitation of Agostino Chigi, for whom, on arrival, he painted some frescoes at the Villa Farnesina. With the exception of a visit to Venice in 1528–9 he remained in Rome for the rest of his life and abandoned his Venetian style in favour of a Roman one.

Some time after his arrival in Rome Sebastiano made the acquaintance of Michelangelo who made considerable efforts to help him in his art. Vasari[3] implies that this was a deliberate move on Michelangelo's part; that he had resented the denigration of his powers as colourist which had been spread by the Raphael faction and that he sought to discredit the latter, without openly participating, by giving Sebastiano some of his drawings to paint from. Whatever Michelangelo's motives in fact may have been there is no reason to doubt Vasari's statement that he supplied a 'piccolo disegno' for the decoration of the Borgherini chapel in S. Pietro in Montorio,[4] while in the commission for an altarpiece for Cardinal Giulio de' Medici to send to his diocese at Narbonne the rivalry between Michelangelo and Sebastiano, on the one hand, and Raphael, on the other, became direct and undoubted. Michelangelo assisted Sebastiano with his altarpiece, while Raphael was engaged on an alternative for the same commission. Sebastiano's contribution is now no. 1 of this Gallery.

After Raphael's death in 1520 Sebastiano was regarded as the leading painter in Rome. But in 1531 he was appointed to the lucrative office of the *Piombo* (keeper of the papal seal) and thereafter painted very little. Vasari stresses that his greatest talent lay in the field of portraiture.

REFERENCES: (1) Cf. G. Ludwig in the Prussian *Jahrbuch*, XXIV (1903), *Beiheft*, p. 110. (2) Usually identified with the *Three Philosophers* at Vienna. (3) Ed. Milanesi, V, pp. 566–71. (4) For the most recent and informed discussion of this subject, cf. Johannes Wilde: *Italian Drawings in the Department of Prints and Drawings in the British Museum, Michelangelo and his Studio*, 1953, pp. 27–31. Cf. also reference no. 14 in the entry for no. 1 of this Gallery.

1   THE RAISING OF LAZARUS

Canvas, transferred from panel, *c.* 150 × 114 (3·81 × 2·89).[1]

Said to have been restored by Benjamin West 'whose hand is especially apparent in the right leg of Lazarus, above and below the knee'.[2] Considerably damaged by flaking. Re-mounted on board, 1966. Cleaned 1967.

Signed, lower left: SEBASTIANVS. VENETVS. FACIE|BAT

The account given by S. John (chapter 11) is accurately followed, though with some compression. S. Mary Magdalene is shown in the foreground kneeling to Christ and some Jews in the background murmuring. The first episode took place slightly before the miracle, the second immediately after it. The figure behind Lazarus, being the only other prominent woman, must therefore be Martha. Round Christ are grouped the apostles.

Vasari gives the following account of the circumstances in which the picture was commissioned and executed[3]:

> *Dopo, facendo Raffaello per lo cardinale de' Medici, per mandarla in Francia, quella tavola, che dopo la morte sua fu posta all' altare principale di San Piero a Montorio, dentrovi la Trasfigurazione di Cristo; Sebastiano in quel medesimo tempo fece anch' egli in un' altra tavola della medesima grandezza, quasi a concorrenza di Raffaello, un Lazzaro quatriduano, e la sua resurrezione; la quale fu contraffatta e dipinta con diligenza grandissima, sotto ordine e disegno in alcune parti di Michelangelo. Le quali tavole finite, furono amendue publicamente in concistoro poste in paragone, e l'una e l'altra lodata infinitamente; e benchè le cose di Raffaello per l'estrema grazia e bellezza loro non avessero pari, furono nondimeno anche le fatiche di Sebastiano universalmente lodate da ognuno. L'una di queste mandò Giulio cardinale de' Medici in Francia a Nerbona al suo vescovado, e l'altra fu posta nella Cancelleria, dove stette infino a che fu portata a San Piero a Montorio, con l'ornamento che vi lavorò Giovan Barile. Mediante quest' opera avendo fatto gran servitù col cardinale, meritò Sebastiano d'esserne onoratamente rimunerato nel pontificato di quello* (i.e. Clement VII).

Contemporary documentation—mainly the letters of Leonardo Sellajo to Michelangelo—gives many details of the progress of the work The chronicle of events is as follows.

The commission would have been given to Sebastiano not later than some time in the year 1516.[4] On 19th January, 1517 Leonardo Sellajo told Michelangelo that Sebastiano had had money to buy the wood, also that Raphael was trying hard to prevent his undertaking the job, not wishing to stand the comparison.[5] By 26th September, 1517 Sebastiano had already started painting and was reported to be making good progress.[6] In January, 1518 Michelangelo returned to Rome on a short visit, during which he saw the picture.[7] On 2nd July, 1518 Sebastiano explained the delay in continuing; he did not wish Raphael to see his work since he had still not started his own. Sebastiano reaffirmed on this occasion his eagerness to continue and said he thought he would bring no discredit on Michelangelo.[8] By 1st May, 1519 the picture is described as finished,[9] on 10th December it is said to be 'vernicato' and on 29th December, 1519 Sebastiano reported that it had been exhibited 'in pallazo' with success.[11] The picture was again exhibited from 12th April, 1520, together with the *Transfiguration* of Raphael, who had died six days before.[12]

Regarding the problem of the collaboration of Michelangelo and Sebastiano, the latter's statement, in his letter of 2nd July, 1518, that he thought he would not bring shame on Michelangelo is significant but not conclusive. Probably the reference is to that. But as Sebastiano was known to have been Michelangelo's protégé any work by the former would be liable to be interpreted as reflecting to some extent on the latter. As Vasari had known both Michelangelo and Sebastiano well there is no reason to doubt the substance of his statement that the picture was executed 'sotto ordine e disegno in alcune parti' of Michelangelo himself.[13] The words 'ordine' and 'disegno', however, may be interpreted in varying ways, while 'alcune parti' is an elastic term. The problem therefore concerns the extent and the nature of Michelangelo's participation.

The degree of supervision by him was certainly slight: he would only have seen the picture on one occasion during work on it—in January, 1518, some months after Sebastiano had begun painting. Evidence of his assistance centres round the existence of three preparatory studies (one at Bayonne, two in London—see DRAWINGS below) for the figure of Lazarus and for two of his attendants. These drawings had for some time been generally attributed to Sebastiano until Johannes Wilde reattributed them, with convincing arguments, to Michelangelo, as part of his fundamental reassessment of aspects of the latter's style as draughtsman.[14] He postulated the existence of drawings by Michelangelo, no longer surviving, for the figure of Christ in no. 1 (one of the British Museum drawings, no. 16, contains also sketches of a left foot corresponding with that of Christ in the painting) and pointed out that the Christ in no. 1 is an epitome of the God the Father in the first four scenes on the Sistine ceiling, just as the figure of Lazarus is a second Adam. As Sebastiano also used the Lazarus design in his fresco of the prophet on the left half of the arch above the Borgherini chapel in S. Pietro in Montorio, Rome—a work which dates from the autumn of 1516[15]—the drawings would date from before then. The figure of Lazarus in no. 1, and, to a lesser extent, the attendant behind him, corresponds closely with the later of the two British Museum drawings (no. 17), but the attendant on the spectator's right in the foreground of no. 1 is closer to the earlier one (no. 16). Michelangelo subsequently re-used the design for Lazarus, in its final form, for that of the main figure in his composition known as 'The Dream' (see no. 8 of this Gallery). The other subordinate figures in no. 1, as well as the landscape, would have been of Sebastiano's invention, as is shown by the Frankfurt drawing for Martha (see DRAWINGS below).

VERSION: Narbonne, Cathedral (Basilique Saint-Just), chapel of S. Martin. Painting of c. 1750 by Carle Vanloo, replacing the original.[16] A small copy, attributed Géricault, on loan to Stuttgart Museum, 1967.

DRAWINGS: A. Attributable to Sebastiano.

Frankfurt, Staedel Institute. Study in black chalk for Martha (Berenson, Florentine Drawings, 1938, II, p. 320, no. 2479B). Corresponds closely with the painting except for the position of the fingers of both hands, which are less raised in the drawing. Those of her left hand show many pentimenti and seem to have caused difficulty to the artist. For this reason and on account of the figures behind Martha in the drawing (apparently some apostles who were later placed farther to the left) Berenson's suggestion that it is after the painting and not a study for it is unacceptable.

B. *Attributable to Michelangelo.*

1. Bayonne, Musée Bonnat, no. 682 (Berenson no. 2474C). Two studies in red chalk representing an early stage, one for Lazarus alone, the other accompanied by one of the attendants.

2. British Museum, London (Wilde no. 16, Berenson no. 2483). Red chalk study for Lazarus and two attendants. Also sketches of a left foot, perhaps Christ's.

3. British Museum, London (Wilde no. 17, Berenson no. 2484). Red chalk study for Lazarus and two attendants. (For an attempt to deny the attribution of these drawings to Michelangelo, cf. S. Freedberg, *Art Bulletin*, 1963, pp. 253 ff. Also L. Dussler (1959).)

ENGRAVING: By R. De Launay (in reverse), in vol. 1 of the *Galerie du Palais Royal* (1786–1808).

PROVENANCE: Sent from Rome to Narbonne Cathedral some time after 12th April, 1520. Bought or begged by the Regent Orléans from the Chapter of Narbonne some time before his death in 1723 and perhaps after 1715.[17] Page 448 ff of the 1727 catalogue (by Du Bois de Saint Gelais) of the Orléans collection in the Palais Royal. No. 241, Orléans sale, Lyceum, London, 26th December ff, 1798 where bought Angerstein.[18] No. 1 in the Angerstein catalogue of 1823. Bought with the Angerstein collection, 1824.

REPRODUCTION: *Illustrations, Italian Schools*, 1937, p. 281.

REFERENCES: (1) In the Orléans catalogue of 1727 stated to be on panel. Said to have been transferred to canvas by Hacquin in 1771 (so the National Gallery Board minutes of 27th June, 1880, though the Orléans catalogue of 1786–1808 speaks of it as still on wood: the initials E.B.H. and date 1771 are recorded as inscribed on the back). Though subsequent examination (at the Gallery in 1929) suggested that the picture may merely have been relined on that occasion and found no confirmation that the support had originally been wood there can be no doubt about this. Not only does the 1727 Orléans catalogue specify it: a contemporary document (19th January, 1517, see below) reports Sebastiano as having money to buy wood for the picture. The matter was clinched by the discovery of fragments of wood during the cleaning of the 1960's. (2) Note in the MS. catalogue in the Gallery archives. (3) Vasari/Milanesi, V, 570–1. Note 1 on page 571 summarizes the events arising from the contemporary dispute concerning the valuation of no. 1. (4) Johannes Wilde: *Italian Drawings in the . . . British Museum, Michelangelo and his Studio*, 1953, p. 30. The deduction rests on the assumption that Michelangelo was sponsoring the undertaking and the fact that he left Rome on the 31st December, 1516 (Frey: *Die Briefe des Michelangelo Buonarroti*, 1907, p. 101). (5) Leonardo Sellajo to Michelangelo (Karl Frey: *Sammlung Ausgewählter Briefe an Michelangelo Buonarroti*, 1899, pp. 58–9): . . . *vi schrissi, chome Bastiano aveva tolto a fare quella tauola, avuti danari per fare e* [*el*] *legname. Ora mi pare, che Rafaello metta sotosopra el mondo, perche lui nonlla faca per non uenire a paraghonj.* (6) Frey: *Sammlung . . .*, p. 79, Leonardo Sellajo to Michelangelo: *Bastiano . . . a chomincata la tavola e fa miracholj, dj modo che ora maj si puo dire, abbia vinto.* (7) For this visit of Michelangelo to Rome, cf. Frey: *Die Briefe . . .*, p. 102. For his having seen the progress of the work cf. Sebastiano's letter to him of 29th December, 1519 (Steinmann and Wittkower: *Michelangelo Bibliographie*, 1927, p. 441 and pl. V): *basta che hauete uisto l'opera principiata.* Though no date is specified for this event it could only have been in January, 1518. (8) Frey: *Briefe an . . .*, p. 104: *Credo, che Leonardo* [*Sellajo*] *ui habi dicto el tutto circha le cosse mie come vanno et circha la tardita del opera mia, non sia fornita. L'o intertenuta tanto, che non uoglio, che Rafaello ueda la mia, in sino lui non ha fornita la sua . . . et al presente non atendo ad altro, che ognj modo me la espediro prestissimo, addesso che sun fora de suspecione, et credo non ui faro uergogna. Ancora Rafaelo non ha principiata la sua.* A letter of 20th July, 1518 (Domenico da Terranuova to Michelangelo, Frey, *Briefe an . . .*, p. 106) reports an intrigue of Raphael's to try to get Sebastiano's picture framed not in Rome but in France. (9) Frey, *Briefe an . . .*, p. 143: *Bastiano vi si rachomanda e a finito, di modo che ognuno resta balordo, e fra pochi giorni andra alla chapella.* (10) Frey, *Briefe an . . .*, p. 148. (11) Letter given in Steinmann/Wittkower, *loc. cit.* An extract from the diary of Marcantonio Michiel (given in E. A. Cicogna: *Intorno la Vita e le Opere di Marcantonio Michiel*, 1861, p. 46) says: *Non tacerò questo che la terza domenica dell' Advento* [according to A. Cappelli: *Cronologia, Cronografia e Calendario Perpetuo*, 1930, p. 103, this fell on 11th December that year] *m. Sebastiano pictore messe una sua Tavola, ch'egli havea fatto per la Cattedrale di Narbona, et era la resuretione di Lazaro, la pose in palazo, così rechiedendo il Papa in l'antisala, ove la fu veduta con grande sua laude et di tutti, et del Papa.* (12) Milanesi: *Les Correspondants de Michel-Ange*, I, 1890, p. 6. (13) Cf. also Lodovico Dolce: *Dialogo della Pittura* (1557; ed. of 1735, pp. 102 and 104) where he makes Pietro Aretino record Raphael's expressed pleasure in taking on the Michelangelo–Sebastiano partnership. (14) Professor Wilde's work is incorporated partly in his catalogue (1953) of the drawings of Michelangelo and his studio in the British Museum and partly in some lectures which he delivered at the University of London in May, 1947. The present writer was present on those occasions. At the time of writing the lectures have not been published, but the text of the portion relevant to no. 1 was most kindly supplied by Professor Wilde and is now in the Gallery archives. (15) Leonardo Sellajo to Michelangelo, 22nd November, 1516 (Frey, *Briefe an . . .*, p. 51): *. . . Bastiano a fatto que dua profeti.* (16) Pierre Caillard: *Narbonne et Ses Environs*, n.d., pp. 23–4. (17) Caillard, *loc. cit.* This says the picture was given to the Regent, but Milanesi (edition of Vasari, V, pp. 570–1, note 2) says 24,000 francs were paid for it. Mariette (*Abecedario*, IV, p. 403) says 'M. le duc d'Orléans, régent, eut fait l'acquisition du tableau . . .'. The second edition of de Piles' *Abrégé de la Vie des Peintres* was published in 1715 and speaks of the picture as still at Narbonne. It is described at Narbonne in the *Voyage de Bachaumont et de Chapelle* (1656) (ed. of 1878, Anger, at the end of a volume opening with the *Mémorie de Grammont*, p. 433). The date of the arrival of no. 1 at Narbonne and of its departure have not so far been revealed, despite some research carried out on behalf of the present writer in the *Archives du Départment de l'Aude* by Monsieur V. Chomel, through the kind offices of Monsieur Robert Mesuret. Even the location of the picture within the Cathedral during the two centuries it was there is not entirely clear. Louis Narbonne (*La Cathédrale Saint-Just de Narbonne*, 1901, p. 97) says it was 'placé d'abord' in the absidal chapel of St Michel where it was replaced by a *Fall of the Rebel Angels* by Antoine Rivalz which is still there (the engraving of it, by Barthélemy Rivalz, is dated 1728— see R. Mesuret: *Les Miniaturistes du Capitole*, 1956, p. 77). The copy of no. 1 by Carle Vanloo which arrived at Narbonne some time after its departure was placed in the chapel of St Martin. It is sometimes said (e.g. by R. Mesuret in *Gazette des Beaux-Arts*, 1957, p. 330) that no. 1 was at one time over the high altar. The present writer could find no confirmation of this. According to Louis Narbonne (*op. cit.*, pp. 102–10) a new high altar had been consecrated in 1510, which was ornamented principally with sculpture. This was replaced by another high altar in 1694–5 which still exists. For the Regent's methods, cf. *Bulletin . . . de l'Histoire de l'Art français*, 1876, p. 41. (18) Marked copy of the sale catalogue in the Gallery library. Angerstein's purchase also recorded in the Farington Diary, I, pp. 258–9. For the intermediary history of the Orléans collection see the entries for no. 270 Titian or 1326 Veronese. Sir Thomas Lawrence said he was 'instrumental in urging Mr. Angerstein to buy' no. 1 (letter printed on pp. 416–18 of vol. II (1831) of D. E. Williams' *Life and Correspondence of . . . Lawrence*.)

24 A LADY AS S. AGATHA

Painted area $36\frac{3}{8} \times 29\frac{5}{8}$ (0·924 × 0·753).

Flesh areas worn, and made up in places. Green dress in good state. Cleaned 1970.

Signed, bottom right:

.F. SEBASTIANV(S)
.VEN.
.FACIEBAT
..ROMÆ.

Inventory no. 60 (or perhaps 160) painted, bottom left (probably Borghese; see below).

The letter 'F' before the name 'Sebastianus' in the signature shows that the picture was painted in or after the year 1531, when Sebastiano was appointed to the office of the *Piombo* which carried the style 'Frate'. After this time he painted very little. The Hermitage *Christ Bearing the Cross* also has this form of signature, and both pictures would be among Sebastiano's latest works. The martyr's palm, the halo, the pincers and the breasts in the dish identify the character portrayed by the sitter as S. Agatha. This was presumably the lady's christian name (cf. entry for no. 4256, Lotto).

PROVENANCE: No. 56 ('St Appolonia'), B.I., 1828 (lent Holwell Carr), where stated to be 'from the Borghese collection'. The Rev. W. Holwell Carr Bequest, 1831.[1]

REPRODUCTION: *Illustrations, Italian Schools*, 1931, p. 282.

REFERENCES: (1) In a MS. list, in the Gallery archives, of the Holwell Carr pictures called (also as ex-Borghese) 'Giulia Gonzaga'—which was a portrait mentioned by Vasari—under which name it got into the National Gallery catalogues. In view of the attributes of S. Agatha this is most improbable. The Borghese inventories have not, as yet, yielded confirmation of a Borghese provenance. The figure is probably 160—which is missing in the 1693 Borghese inventory.

1450 MADONNA AND CHILD WITH SS. JOSEPH AND JOHN THE BAPTIST AND A DONOR

Panel, $38\frac{1}{2} \times 42$ (0·978 × 1·067).

Some losses of paint, particularly in the Child's forehead, left cheek and right leg, in the donor's robes and in the area of background round S. Joseph's head. Paint in other areas reasonably well preserved. Cleaned 1958.

Berenson,[1] seeing a likeness between the donor in no. 1450 and a study at Chatsworth for one of the apostles in Sebastiano's fresco of the Transfiguration in the Borgherini chapel of S. Pietro in Montorio, Rome, postulated that both represent Pierfrancesco Borgherini. Though some degree of resemblance between the two faces seems admissible to the present writer it is difficult to decide such matters, and in any case no authenticated portrait of Pierfrancesco is known. A further

suggestion by Berenson is equally inconclusive. Leonardo Sellajo, in
a letter to Michelangelo of 1st March, 1517, quoted Sebastiano as saying that with the help of a cartoon by Michelangelo he would be able to
paint a picture which should satisfy Pierfrancesco Borgherini.[2] Berenson
connected no. 1450 with this incident. Though this period would be
acceptable on stylistic grounds as an approximate date of origin for
no. 1450 the episode adumbrated in the letter in question seems too
hypothetical for further consideration here.[3] Even the assumption
inherent in Berenson's theory—that no. 1450 is based on a cartoon, or
at least a design, by Michelangelo—cannot be demonstrated (this
hypothesis had been advanced long before—see reference 10). A quick
sketch, attributed to Sebastiano, but possibly by Michelangelo, has
been connected with no. 1450, but with insufficient reason, in the
present writer's view (see DRAWING below). Though strong influence
of Michelangelo has always, and justifiably, been recognized in no. 1450
there is no precise prototype among his works.[4]

DRAWING: Berenson no. 2489 (successively Heseltine and Koenigs collections).
Study in red chalk for a Madonna and Child. Berenson as Sebastiano. Before
that as Michelangelo.[5] Connected by D'Achiardi,[6] Fischel[7] and Pallucchini[8]
with no. 1450, but the connection seems inconclusive. One of the chief characteristics of no. 1450—the sheltering gesture of the Madonna's right arm—is
lacking in the drawing, where her right arm is raised, as in Sebastiano's
Madonna del Velo (Naples). Though the attitude of the Child in the drawing
seems similar to no. 1450 it is not certain whether the former incorporates a
notable peculiarity of the latter—the fact that the Child straddles His mother's
knee (this motive also occurs, though applied differently, in Michelangelo's
Medici Madonna). No sign in the drawing of SS. John or Joseph.

PROVENANCE: Probably 'una tavola della B. Vergine col Bambino, ed un
Santo, di Fra Sebastiano del Piombo' described by C. G. Ratti (*Instruzione di
Quanto può vedersi . . . in Genova*, 1780, p. 265) as in 'Palazzo pur Brignole
abitato dal Sig. Carlo Cambiaso'. Purchased, 1807–8, 'du sénateur Cambiaso
à Gênes' by J. B. P. Le Brun.[9] In the possession of Sir Thomas Baring, 2nd
Bart. (1772–1848), by 1816, when exh. by him, B.I., no. 7, 'from the Collection
of the Senateur Cambiaso, at Genoa'.[10] Exh. B.I., 1840, no. 63, lent Baring,
by whom sold to William Coningham, 1843.[11] No. 61 in the latter's sale,
Christie's, 9th June, 1849, where bought Thomas Baring[12] (grandson of the
2nd baronet: in 1866 he succeeded his father, who had been created Baron
Northbrook in the same year, and was himself created Earl of Northbrook in
1876). Exh Manchester, 1857 (no. 213 in the provisional catalogue, no. 161
in the definitive catalogue, lent T. Baring), R.A., 1870 (130) and 1894 (113)
lent by the Earl of Northbrook,[13] from whom purchased, 1895.

REPRODUCTION: *Illustrations, Italian Schools*, 1937, p. 280.

REFERENCES: (1) *Florentine Drawings . . .*, 1938, II, pp. 319–20. (2) Letter
printed by Karl Frey: *Sammlung Ausgewählter Briefe an Michelagniolo Buonarroti*, 1899, p. 63. (3) In particular, the wording of the letter of 1st March, 1517,
is too vague to presuppose a connection, as postulated by D'Achiardi (*Sebastiano
del Piombo*, 1908, pp. 149–50, note 1) with a letter of 22nd April, 1525, in
which Sebastiano tells Michelangelo to tell apparently Pierfrancesco that his
picture will be ready in two days (Milanesi: *Les Correspondants de Michel-Ange*,
1890, p. 32). (4) The general inspiration is undoubtedly the Sistine ceiling. The
attitude of the Child in no. 1450 is reminiscent of that of the *putto* supporting
the book for Daniel. The latter's projecting left arm and hand has itself something in common with the Madonna's right in no. 1450. (5) Cf., e.g. *Original*

Drawings by Old Masters of the Italian School (Heseltine collection), privately printed, 1913, no. 6. (**6**) *Sebastiano del Piombo*, 1908, p. 149, note 1. (**7**) In *Old Master Drawings*, XIV (1939–40), p. 31. The author says Berenson is wrong in giving an Oppenheimer provenance for the drawing. (**8**) *Sebastian Viniziano*, 1944, p. 52. (**9**) See his *Recueil de Gravures* . . ., 1809, pp. 37–9. Outline engraving of no. 1450 as his no. 21. (**10**) The exh. cat. says 'Holy Family with St Francis (sic), composition and drawing, Michael Angelo . . .' W. Buchanan (*Memoirs of Painting* . . ., II, 1824, pp. 251–3) says that the finest of the Le Brun pictures, including no. 1450, were purchased by Baring. (**11**) *A Descriptive Catalogue of the Collection of . . . the Earl of Northbrook*, 1889, p. 151. (**12**) Marked copy of the sale catalogue in the Gallery library. (**13**) In the 1870 exh. cat. the owner's name is given as 'Thomas Baring, Esq., M.P.', but he had been Baron Northbrook since 1866.

2493 THE DAUGHTER OF HERODIAS

Panel, $21\frac{5}{8} \times 17\frac{1}{2}$ (0·55 × 0·445).

Dated, bottom right; 1510. Fairly extensive damage, probably due to past flaking. Cleaned 1971.

One of the key works of Sebastiano's early (Venetian) period. Very close in style to a *Magdalen* of almost the same dimensions (Washington, Kress collection, ex-Cook collection) and to the high altarpiece of the church of S. Giovanni Cristosomo, Venice. The latter work is described by Vasari (1568)[1] as Sebastiano's and is datable 1510–11.[2]

PROVENANCE: In the possession of George Salting by October, 1900,[3] by whom lent 1902–10. Salting Bequest, 1910.

REPRODUCTION: *Illustrations, Italian Schools*, 1937, p. 282.

REFERENCES: (**1**) In his first edition (1550) Vasari had attributed the picture to Giorgione. The reference to it in the second edition corrects his earlier statement and tries to excuse it. (**2**) For the documents see Rodolfo Gallo in *Arte Veneta*, 1953, p. 152. (**3**) MS. list, in the Gallery archives, of that date, of Salting's pictures, in which it figures.

SODOMA
1477–1549

His name was Giovanni Antonio Bazzi (formerly, and incorrectly, referred to as 'Razzi'). From about 1512 he is regularly referred to in documents as 'Giovanni Antonio detto il Sodoma' and he uses the word 'Sodoma' himself in his signature.[1] For this reason, and in view of the undoubted esteem which he enjoyed in his lifetime, Vasari's story that the name was given to him because of his way of life has long been questioned.

He was from Vercelli, where he was apprenticed to Martino Spanzotti for seven years from 1490. By the opening years of the sixteenth century he had moved to Siena where he remained, on and off, for the rest of his life. He was in Rome in 1508 and probably again later. He also paid several visits to Florence, and (in the years 1539–45) was at Volterra, Pisa and Lucca. As painter of religious panels and frescoes he was very prolific.

REFERENCE: (1) Documents published by Robert H. Hobart Cust: *Giovanni Antonio Bazzi* . . ., 1906, pp. 256–340. This work also gives, *inter alia*, the evidence for the date of Sodoma's birth.

1144 MADONNA AND CHILD WITH SS. PETER, CATHERINE OF SIENA AND A CARTHUSIAN DONOR

Panel,[1] $19\frac{1}{4} \times 14\frac{7}{8}$ (0·49 × 0·378).
Good condition in general.

Always considered an autograph work hitherto, but the forms and handling alike are noticeably weaker than in the Spina altar (Pisa, Museo Civico) which is documented as of 1542, is of comparable type and evidently of the same period. In consequence some studio intervention in no. 1144 would be possible.

PROVENANCE: Said by Giovanni Rosini (1845), the then owner, to have been painted for the sacristy of the Certosa at Pisa.[2] Still in Rosini's possession in 1856 and 1857, when noted by Eastlake and Mündler.[3] Purchased from Charles Fairfax Murray, Florence, 1883.[4]

REPRODUCTION: *Illustrations, Italian Schools*, 1937, p. 335.

REFERENCES: (1) Poplar, according to a letter from B. J. Rendle of the Forest Products Research Laboratory. (2) *Storia della Pittura Italiana*, V (1845), p. 49. Apparently not mentioned, however, in the published Certosa inventories (A. Manghi: *La Certosa di Pisa*, 1911). (3) Diary and notebook in the Gallery's possession. (4) An entry in the Gallery's MS. catalogue, made at the time when the picture entered the Gallery, specifies it as having been in the Rosini collection at Pisa. The dimensions of the Rosini picture as given by Mündler also correspond.

3947 S. JEROME IN PENITENCE

Panel,[1] $55\frac{1}{2} \times 44$ (1·41 × 1·118).
Numerous vertical splits and joins in the wood have led to extensive flaking. The saint's left arm and hand and the landscape background particularly affected in this respect. In other places, as in the high-lit portions of the saint's flesh, appreciable areas are still well preserved. Cleaned 1972.

The attribution to Sodoma himself can hardly be questioned, despite the unsatisfactory condition. Of comparable works, no. 3947 bears some general resemblance of type to the Pisa *Sacrifice of Isaac*, documented as of 1542; also, in some respects, to the Naples *Resurrection* which is signed and dated 1535; therefore, like these pictures, probably a late work. Another Sodoma of S. Jerome, comparable with no. 3947 in style but of a different design, was reproduced by Cust (1906)[2] as in the collection of 'Mr. J. R. Saunders' of London.

PROVENANCE: Noted by Otto Mündler in May, 1858 at the Monte di Pietà Rome[3] from which later bought by Morelli who in 1890 sold it to Ludwig Mond.[4] Exh. R.A., 1891 (110) and New Gallery, 1893–4 (201) (lent Mond). Mond Bequest, 1924.

REPRODUCTION: *Illustrations, Italian Schools*, 1937, p. 336.

REFERENCES: (1) Identified as poplar by the Forest Products Research Laboratory. (2) *Giovanni Antonio Bazzi* . . ., p. 359. (3) Mündler's notebooks in the Gallery archives. (4) J. P. Richter's catalogue of the Mond Collection, vol. II (1910), p. 373.

Ascribed to SODOMA

1337 HEAD OF CHRIST CROWNED WITH THORNS BEARING HIS CROSS[1]

Panel,[2] $15\frac{1}{4} \times 12\frac{1}{2}$ (0·387 × 0·317).
A number of small losses of paint.

Despite the odd proportions, and despite assertions in earlier editions of the catalogue, it does not seem to have been cut, since at top and bottom the paint does not quite extend to the edges, and at the left it goes over them.

In former editions of the catalogue as 'Sodoma'. This attribution was accepted in Cust's monograph and by Berenson (*Lists*, 1932 and 1936) but though the picture is to some extent of Sodoma's type the touch does not seem to be his.

PROVENANCE: From the Habich collection, Cassel, from which lent for a time to the Cassel Gallery.[3] Purchased from Dr. Habich, 1891.

REFERENCES: (1) Identified as such, correctly, when lent to the Cassel Gallery but not subsequently. (2) Earlier editions of the catalogue, in which almost every statement concerning no. 1337 is wrong, have 'Canvas'. A letter in the Gallery archives from B. J. Rendle of the Forest Products Research Laboratory describes it as European whitewood or white deal. (3) O. Eisenmann: *Führer durch die Kgl. Gemäldegalerie zu Cassel*, 5th ed., p. 26.

246 MADONNA AND CHILD

Panel, $31\frac{3}{8} \times 25\frac{5}{8}$ (0·797 × 0·651).

The blue of the sky stops about $1\frac{1}{2}''$ from the top. Above this is a strip of light paint or priming over which the Madonna's halo has been continued. A good deal of local damage. At the time of writing (1961) much discoloured by varnish and dirt.

In the Joly de Bammeville sale as Pacchiarotto and catalogued as such after entering the Gallery until 1877. From 1878 as Pacchia. The confusion of these names was general until the mid-nineteenth century.[1] The attribution to Pacchia was admitted by Berenson (*Lists*) and A. Venturi.[2] Though it may be correct, the picture in its present state is hardly attributable, while the fact that the design corresponds with that of a (slightly smaller) picture attributed to Sodoma (see VERSION below) is a relevant factor.

VERSION: Published by R. H. H. Cust (*Giovanni Antonio Bazzi*, 1906, two plates, before and after restoration, facing p. 65, catalogued on p. 359). Then in the collection of J. P. Richter; exh. R.A., 1904 (39), lent Mrs. Richter.

PROVENANCE: Lot 40 in the E. Joly de Bammeville sale, 12th June, 1854, where purchased.

REPRODUCTION: *Illustrations, Italian Schools*, 1937, p. 261.

REFERENCES: (1) Milanesi (Vasari/Milanesi VI, p. 428) investigates the sources of the confusion which he was the first to unravel. No. 246 had been re-attributed to Pacchia as early as 1866 (Crowe and Cavalcaselle, vol. III of the edition of that year, p. 383, n. 3). (2) *Storia . . .*, IX, V, p. 354.

Follower of SODOMA

4647 THE NATIVITY WITH THE INFANT BAPTIST AND SHEPHERDS

Panel,[1] $47\frac{1}{8} \times 38$ (1·197 × 0·965).

Disfigured in places by uneven cleaning but paint in general well preserved.[2]

Right background, the annunciation to the shepherds. Centre background, the approach of the Magi.

A similar picture in the Siena gallery (no. 356) is catalogued as 'School of Sodoma'.[3] Both seem too feeble to be attributable to Sodoma himself at any stage of his career, and also do not suggest a student working to his design. They seem rather the work of a relatively unaccomplished *pasticheur* of various elements in Sodoma's repertory.[4] C. Brandi, in the 1933 Siena catalogue, suggested Giomo del Sodoma for the Siena picture, but admitted that his style was ill-defined.[5]

PROVENANCE: A letter in the Gallery archives of 18th June, 1903 addressed to Robert H. H. Cust from Ernest Hartland of Hardwick Court, Chepstow, says, à propos no. 4647, 'I bought it at Florence in 1875 from Mr. Jarves the writer on art who resided for many years in Florence and was collecting for the Metropolitan New York Museum. I have his authority for its having been in a private chapel at St Sepolchro at Arezzo'. 'Mr. Jarves' was evidently James Jackson Jarves, part of whose collection is now at New Haven, Conn. 'St Sepolchro at Arezzo' is presumably Borgo S. Sepolcro. Presented by the widow of Ernest Hartland in accordance with his wish, 1932.

REPRODUCTION: *Illustrations, Italian Schools*, 1937, p. 336.

REFERENCES: (1) Identified as poplar by the Royal Botanic Gardens, Kew. (2) Ernest Hartland's letter of 1903 (see Provenance above) contains the information that he had witnessed the cleaning of no. 4647 and that 'some high lights on the edge of the Virgin's robe had I think been put on about 250 years afterwards which had turned black which had to be carefully removed'. (3) A variant of this picture was offered to the Gallery in 1939 by L. Kaart, Estonia. (4) An obvious quarry which may well have been drawn on in both cases is Sodoma's altarpiece of the *Adoration of the Magi* (Siena, S. Agostino). This dates from before 1536 when it was the subject of a legal award. (5) C. Brandi: *La Regia Pinacoteca di Siena*, 1933, p. 292. Berenson (*Lists*, 1936) includes no. 4647 among Sodoma's works.

For SODOMA see also the entry for no. 1128 (Signorelli: *The Circumcision*) in *The Earlier Italian Schools* by Martin Davies.

Giovanni Antonio SOGLIANI
1492–1544

Pupil of Lorenzo di Credi in Florence, with whom, according to Vasari, he remained twenty-four years. What are presumably his early works are strongly influenced by Credi. Later he reacted as strongly to Fra Bartolommeo and also to the work of Albertinelli, Andrea del Sarto and, occasionally, Raphael. He was engaged for some years on paintings for Pisa cathedral. His altarpiece of the *Martyrdom of S. Arcadius* (Florence, S. Lorenzo) is signed and dated 1521 and his *Miracle of S. Dominic* (Florence, S. Marco) initialed and dated 1536.

645 MADONNA AND CHILD

Panel, $6\frac{4}{5} \times 4\frac{1}{10}$ (0·17 × 0·1).
Good condition.

Originally catalogued as Albertinelli. The attribution to Sogliani, which is acceptable, seems first to have been made, tentatively, by Crowe and Cavalcaselle.[1] Morelli[2] and Emil Jacobsen[3] also suggested it, as though independently, and it was accepted by Berenson.[4]

PROVENANCE: Beaucousin collection, Paris, with which purchased, 1860.

REPRODUCTION: *Illustrations, Italian Schools*, 1937, p. 337.

REFERENCES: (1) *History of Painting in Italy*, 1866, vol. III, pp. 492 and 516. (2) Orally to J. P. Richter in 1883 (note in the Gallery archives). (3) In *Repertorium für Kunstwissenschaft*, vol. XXIV (1901), p. 339. (4) *Lists*, 1932, and 1936.

Jacopo TINTORETTO
1518–1594

The date of his birth is deduced from the certificate of his death in May, 1594, which gives his age as 75 years and 8 months.[1] The family name was Robusti. Jacopo took the nickname, Tintoretto, from his father's profession of dyer (*tintore*).

Tintoretto's apprenticeship has been much disputed. Ridolfi speaks of an apprenticeship of ten days under Titian.[2] Bonifazio, Schiavone and Bordon have also been suggested as his master. Tintoretto's contemporary, Raffaello Borghini, does not discuss the question of apprenticeship, but apparently states[3] (his account is a little confused) that he modelled his draughtsmanship principally on Michelangelo's (some of whose sculptures he certainly knew in casts or models) and his colouring on Titian's.[4] The only occasion when Tintoretto is recorded as having left Venice was in 1580 when he was at Mantua. There is no documentary evidence either for or against his having visited Rome, and such a visit has often been postulated.[5]

There is great difficulty in identifying Tintoretto's early work. The earliest surviving dated picture indisputably his work is the *Last Supper* of 1547 at S. Marcuola, Venice. A picture of Apollo and Marsyas (Wadsworth Atheneum, Hartford, ex-Bromley-Davenport) is generally identified with one of a pair painted for Pietro Aretino in 1545, and a large *Sacra Conversazione*, signed 'IACHOBUS' and dated 1540 is an acceptable attribution.[6] From 1547 on there are a considerable number of datable works.

Though the greater part of Tintoretto's vast output consisted of religious paintings, many portraits and a number of mythologies, allegories and histories also survive. He was evidently able and willing to modify his style considerably in accordance with the nature of the commission, and Ridolfi and Boschini report instances of deliberate imitation by Tintoretto of the styles of Schiavone[7] and of Veronese.[8] Ridolfi[9] and Boschini[10] also give details of his technical procedure, particularly in respect of his use of small, draped models. Tintoretto's son, Domenico, assisted him in his later works and carried on the studio after his death. Another son, Marco, and a daughter, Marietta, were also painters.

REFERENCES: (1) F. Galanti: *Il Tintoretto* (discorso letto il 8 agosto, 1875 nella R. Accademia in Venezia). 1876, pp. 76 f. (2) Ridolfi/Hadeln, II, p. 13. (3) Raffaello Borghini: *Il Riposo* . . ., 1584, p. 551. (4) It may have been this statement, together with Paolo Pino's hypothesis (not specifically referring to Tintoretto) of the perfection to be expected from a combination of Michelangelo's draughtsmanship and Titian's colouring (*Dialogo della Pittura*, 1548, p. 24) which was the basis of Ridolfi's famous story of Tintoretto's writing on the wall of his studio 'il disegno di Michel Angelo e'l colorito di Titiano'. (5) For this, see in particular Simon H. Levie: *Daniele da Volterra e Tintoretto* in *Arte Veneta*, 1953, pp. 168–70. (6) Formerly with Leger, London. Reproduced and discussed by R. Pallucchini, *La Giovinezza del Tintoretto*, 1950, p. 74. (7) Marco Boschini, *Le Ricche Minere* . . ., 1674, Sestier di Canareggio, pp. 11–12. (8) Ridolfi, *op. cit.*, p. 38. (9) Ridolfi, *op. cit.*, p. 15. (10) Boschini, *op. cit.*, preface ('Breve Instruzione').

16 S. GEORGE AND THE DRAGON

62 × 39½ (1·575 × 1·003) (arched top).

The lower half of the picture, though somewhat worn and retouched, is in generally good condition. The upper half is more thinly painted and more worn. Of several *pentimenti* mention may be made of the flap (painted on top of the grass) half way along the upper outline of the princess' fluttering cloak. Cleaned 1963.

The latest cleaning disclosed that the canvas within the spandrels was originally painted black. At a later date false clouds had been painted over these areas. The canvas in the spandrels is continuous.

The historical S. George suffered martyrdom under the Emperor Diocletian, but there is no surviving authority earlier than the twelfth century for his fight with the dragon,[1] which was subsequently popularized by inclusion in the Golden Legend.

Several features of the iconography of no. 16 are unusual. In Renaissance representations of S. George and the dragon the princess is most usually shown either on her knees in prayer or else running away. In the present picture Tintoretto has combined the two actions: the princess has suddenly dropped to her knees during flight. The form of the dragon's victim and the figure in the clouds are still more unusual in representations of this subject. According to the Golden Legend, the dragon ate a daily diet of human victims whose mangled limbs are frequently included, but hardly ever their intact corpses (though another instance is the Signorelli in the Rijksmuseum, Amsterdam). As to the celestial personage, no such feature is normal in Renaissance representations of S. George and the dragon, though an angel is shown in a picture by Sodoma (Washington, Kress collection, ex-Cook collection).[2] The figure in no. 16 has no wings and seems intended as God the Father, while the attitude of the dragon's victim recalls that of the crucified Christ. The relatively small scale of the picture, together with its type, would suggest that it was commissioned by a private patron and he, in consequence, may be presumed to have specified some personal interpretation of the S. George legend.[3]

The attribution of no. 16 to Tintoretto cannot be questioned, but the unusualness of its type and scale in his œuvre is, again, an obstacle in the way of precise dating. It has been considered an early work,[4] but the type of landscape shown does not bear this out.

In the landscape background of the Adam and Eve (Venice, Accademia, from the Scuola della Trinità), which is datable 1550–3,[5] there is an early attempt at the concealed or 'magical' lighting which reached an extreme form in the SS. Mary of Egypt and Mary Magdalene of the mid-1580's (Scuola di S. Rocco). The lighting of the trunks of the three trees in the middle distance in no. 16, and of the trunk and branches of the windswept tree to the spectator's right of them, is much more advanced than in the Adam and Eve. As it occurs in a comparable form in the great Crucifixion of S. Rocco, which is dated 1565, the present writer would tend to favour a dating for no. 16 not earlier than the 1560's.

DRAWING: Paris, Louvre (no. 5382). Charcoal drawing (Tietze: Venetian Drawings, 1738). Study (without the drapery) for the corpse, centre. The figure's left hand, roughly indicated, is truncated by the edge of the sheet. A more carefully drawn detail (corresponding with the form as shown in no. 16) is sketched underneath.[6]

VERSION: A picture of this subject at Leningrad (no. 134 in the Hermitage catalogue of 1891) has been attributed to Tintoretto but seems (on photographic evidence only) no more than a pastiche of various Tintorettesque elements. The upright format, the city walls and to some extent the general disposition seem to derive from no. 16, but the mangled body of the dragon's victim is based on that of the slave in the Miracle of St Mark.

PROVENANCE: In the possession of the Rev. W. Holwell Carr in 1821, when exhibited by him at the British Institution (46). Before that, said to have belonged to 'R. Westall'— presumably Richard Westall, R.A.[7] On account of the correspondence of the dimensions, almost certainly identical with a picture sold at Prestage's, London, 2nd February, 1764,[8] where stated to have come from 'the Cornaro Family', and identified with one mentioned by Ridolfi (1648) in the possession of 'Signor Pietro Corraro Senatore'[9] and by Boschini (1660) as in 'Casa Corer'.[10] Corraro and Correr are variants of the same name, but Cornaro is distinct, and assuming that the references are to the same picture it could be deduced either that it passed from one family to another or that the names were confused. Holwell Carr bequest, 1831.

REPRODUCTION: *Illustrations, Italian Schools*, 1937, p. 350.

REFERENCES: (**1**) Von Taube von der Issen: *Die Darstellung des Heiligen Georg in der italienischen Kunst*, 1910, p. 4. (**2**) Von Taube von der Issen, *op. cit.*, p. 57, also cites an instance in an Avignon fresco. (**3**) What may well have been no. 16 is first recorded in the possession of Pietro Corraro in the seventeenth century (see PROVENANCE). According to Litta, however, no member of the Corraro family during Tintoretto's working career bore the christian name of Giorgio. (**4**) E.g. Berenson (*Lists*, 1936) 'giovanile', von der Bercken (1942) 'um 1548–58', Tietze (1948) 'from the 1550's'. (**5**) Gustav Ludwig in *Italienische Forschungen*, vol. IV (1911), pp. 136 ff. (**6**) The drawing was roughly (and wrongly) labelled 'study for a Prometheus' by A. L. Mayer (*Burlington Magazine*, vol. XLIII, 1923, p. 34). (**7**) *Essays and Criticisms by Thomas Griffiths Wainewright . . . collected . . . by W. Carew Hazlitt*, London, 1880, p. 179: 'formerly in the hands of R. Westall, Esq., where I once saw it' (this reference kindly communicated by Frank Simpson). In the MS. list in the Gallery archives of the Holwell Carr pictures no. 16 is one of the very few without indication of previous ownership. (**8**) Lot 143 in the general catalogue, lot 31 in the catalogue of the first day's sale: 'St George killing the dragon, a fine picture particularly mentioned by Boschini, p. 329, and by Ridolfi, vol. 2, p. 45, by Giacomo Tintoretto . . . 5,3 × 3,3'. (**9**) Ridolfi/Hadeln, II, p. 54: 'Trouasi il Signor Pietro Corraro Senatore vn gratiossisimo pensiero di San Giorgio, che vccide il Drago, con la figliuola del Rè, che impaurita sen fugge, e vi appaiono alcuni corpi de' morti di rarissima forma.' It may be noted that in no. 16 there is only *one* corpse, not several, and that although the princess appears to be running away she is in fact on her knees. These discrepancies need not rule out the identification, however. (**10**) *La Carta del Navegar Pitoresco*, p. 329: '. . . L'è vn San Zorzi a caualo brauo, e forte, | che de ficon và con lanza in resta, | E amazza el Drago, e la Rezina resta | Libera dal spauento, e da la morte. | Questo a Casa Corer fè corer tuti.' Boschini specifies that this picture is on a relatively small scale.

1130 CHRIST WASHING HIS DISCIPLES' FEET

79 × 160¾ (2·006 × 4·083).

Considerably damaged. The area where the local damage is most extensive is in the figure on the left (with the torch), the lower part of whose body seems to fade out. Before the restoration of 1956 this area was covered with a small table of later date and the floor entirely overpainted in a biscuit colour with the lines of the tiles 'corrected' so as to be parallel with the lower edge of the picture. The cat and the projecting flap of the skirt of the apostle on the right (wiping his feet) were originally painted on top of the floor, no doubt as an afterthought, and soon wore thin. Only the base and some of the outline of the cat and a little of the outline of this flap are original paint. The figure of Christ is fairly well preserved and is the least damaged major portion of the picture. Cleaned 1956.

A comparable arrangement of the floor tiles to that revealed by the restoration of 1956 also occurs in Tintoretto's *Last Supper* at S. Polo, Venice, where the horizontals meet the lower edge of the picture at a still sharper angle. It is probable that Tintoretto was trying, in this respect, to follow the precepts of Serlio who gives a scientific demonstration of this principle (*Il Secondo Libro di Prospettiva*, 1618 ed., pp. 42V, 43R). Tintoretto was certainly acquainted with this book, since the architectural background of the Escorial *Foot-washing* is a fairly literal reproduction of Serlio's illustration 'Della Scena Tragica'.

Almost certainly from the church of SS. Gervasio e Protasio (S. Trovaso), Venice. Since its history before the year 1882 is unknown this point cannot be established with complete certainty, but the strong circumstantial evidence is as follows:

1. In the *Riposo* Borghini mentions a *Foot-washing* and a *Last Supper* by Tintoretto in the Capella del Sacramento in the church of S. Trovaso.[1] As the *Riposo* was published within Tintoretto's lifetime (1584) this is good evidence of authenticity.

2. In the Cappella del Sacramento at S. Trovaso there is now to be seen (on the right) a *Last Supper*, clearly by Tintoretto, and (on the left) a *Foot-washing*, clearly not by him. The two pictures line the lateral walls of the chapel and on account of their size and shape were obviously designed for it. They are of the same size as each other and also (with the exception of a narrow strip along the top) as no. 1130.[2] Since the latter is acceptable stylistically as Tintoretto's and corresponds in design (as well as in size) with the picture now in S. Trovaso it may be concluded that that picture is a copy painted to replace it.

The church of S. Trovaso was burnt down in September, 1583 and rebuilt.[3] But the Cappella del Sacramento which adjoins the extremity of the left transept is clearly in an earlier style of architecture than the body of the existing church. The distinctive architectural style of the chapel includes both sides of the arch separating it from the transept. On the base of the left pilaster of this arch, on the side nearest the transept, is inscribed the date, MDLVI.[4] It may therefore be deduced that the structure of the chapel escaped the fire, and its date would give some indication of that of the paintings. Though no greater precision is possible in this matter, it may be pointed out that a date not long after 1556 would be stylistically acceptable for no. 1130, the handling of which is hardly more summary than that of the *Miracle of the Paralytic* (church of S. Rocco, Venice) which is documented as dating from 1559.

The date when no. 1130 would have left S. Trovaso is a more difficult problem. No reliance can be placed on the wording of descriptions of the two paintings in the guide books, since the authors in many cases reproduced information derived from earlier writers years after it was out of date and in any case could not be relied on to distinguish an original Tintoretto from an old copy.[5] Even the engraving published in Louisa's *Il Gran Teatro delle Pitture e Prospettive di Venezia* (1720) could have been taken from the copy.[6] For this reason the attitude of so thorough a connoisseur of Tintoretto as Ridolfi is the more important. In Venetian churches where there are two paintings by Tintoretto which are obviously a pair he is normally at pains to describe both— e.g. S. Marcuola (*Foot-washing* and *Last Supper*), S. Giorgio Maggiore

(*Last Supper* and *Manna*), Madonna dell' Orto (*Golden Calf* and *Last Judgement*) or S. Cassiano (*Crucifixion* and *Christ in Limbo*). But at S. Trovaso, while describing the *Last Supper* in some detail, he makes no mention of a *Foot-washing*.[7] If this was not an oversight on his part it would follow either that no *Foot-washing* was there when he wrote or else that there was one which he did not consider to be by Tintoretto. In either case there would thus be a possibility that no. 1130 was no longer in S. Trovaso in the mid-seventeenth century. The further possibility that it was removed because of damage sustained in the fire of 1583 is, however, apparently excluded by microscopic examination of the paint.[8]

In the design of no. 1130 may be traced the germ of that of one of Tintoretto's latest works—the *Last Supper* of S. Giorgio Maggiore.

ENGRAVING: By Andrea Zucchi in Louisa's *Il Gran Teatro delle Pitture e Prospettive di Venezia* (1720), no. 45 (see above).

VERSIONS: Venice, S. Trovaso. Copy replacing no. 1130. The other pictures of this subject by Tintoretto are of different designs, viz.: 1. Escorial (almost certainly from S. Marcuola and Charles I's collection). A large-scale copy of this was lot 43 in the Delahante sale (Phillips, 2nd June, 1814). It was unsold on that occasion but bought on the next day by Sir Matthew White Ridley, who presented it to St Nicholas church, Newcastle-upon-Tyne, in 1815, where it remained until recently.[9] A variant of the Escorial picture was in the collection of Lord Farnham, Cavan, Ireland (reproduced in von der Bercken: *Tintoretto* 1942, pl. 28).[10] 2. Wilton, since at least 1731.[11] 3. Venice, S. Moisé. 4. Venice' S. Stefano. A picture in the Sir Joshua Reynolds sale, 1795 (4th day, lot 90) claimed to be from 'St Emacora' (i.e. S. Marcuola), but need not have been of the same design.

PROVENANCE: From Hamilton Palace. No. 353 at the sale, 24th June, 1882, where purchased, Clarke Fund (see also above).

REPRODUCTION: *Illustrations, Italian Schools*, 1937, p. 349.

REFERENCES: (1) P. 554 (à propos Tintoretto): *In San Geruaso, e Protaso . . . nella Cappella del Sacramēto . . . vi sono due quadri, nell' uno quando Christo laua i piedi agli Apostoli, e nell' altro quando cena con quelli.* (2) The present writer measured the length of the S. Trovaso *Foot-washing* copy and made it 160″ (4·064)—which is virtually the same as no. 1130. He was unable to measure its height, but it is clearly slightly greater than in the case of no. 1130, having an extra strip along the top. The S. Trovaso *Last Supper* is given in the catalogue of the Tintoretto exhibition (Venice, 1937, no. 27) as 2·21 × 4·13. (3) Giulio Lorenzetti: *Venezia* (1926, p. 515). (4) Lorenzetti, *op. cit.*, p. 516 (1956 ed., p. 540), gives the date of the chapel as 1566. This is presumably a misprint, but it was followed by Mayer (*Burlington Magazine*, December, 1936, p. 282). (5) Even Lorenzetti (*op. cit.*, p. 516) does not make the distinction entirely clear. (6) In Louisa's engraving (which is truncated on the left) the figure on the right is shown wearing a kind of turban and his right sleeve falls to the wrist with much interruption in the folds. In both these respects the engraving is nearer to the copy now in S. Trovaso than to no. 1130. The most striking difference between the latter and the engraving is the figure in the left background—in the engraving it is a man (presumably Judas) going out, in no. 1130 a woman coming in. The latter is original paint and painted on the same canvas as the rest of the picture (contrary to what is stated by Mayer, *loc. cit.*). This area of the copy now in S. Trovaso is entirely dark and that picture also appears to contain no cat. (7) Ridolfi/Hadeln, II, p. 39. (8) An examination of samples of paint disclosed undiscoloured madder and copper resinate (both of which brown readily on exposure to heat) and also reveal no blistering, bubbling or charring of the paint. See the National Gallery Report, July, 1956–June, 1958. (9) The copy in the National Gallery library of the Delahante sale catalogue belonged to Lord Colborne (brother of Sir Matthew White Ridley) who annotated it with this information regarding the sale. The date of presentation to St Nicholas, Newcastle, is from the church authorities there. A photograph of the Newcastle picture is in the Gallery archives. (10) Misprinted by von der Bercken, *op. cit.*, p. 109, as 'Lord Lee of Farnham' and by Tietze (*Tintoretto*, 1948, p. 350) as 'Lord Lee of Fareham'. (11) For the Wilton picture see Tancred Borenius, *Burlington Magazine*, vol. 61 (1932), p. 103.

1313 THE ORIGIN OF THE MILKY WAY

$58\frac{1}{4} \times 65$ ($1 \cdot 48 \times 1 \cdot 65$).

Some retouching in the sky and clouds and in the flesh of Juno, Jupiter, the infant Hercules and the two *putti* on the left. The coloured draperies, eagle, peacocks and *putto* bottom right are in fairly good state. Cleaned 1972.

A horizontal line of repaint (clearer in X-ray and infra-red photographs than to the naked eye) covering losses of original paint some seven or eight inches above the base (cutting across Juno's right ankle and the nose of the *putto* in the bottom left hand corner) suggests that the picture had at one time been folded at this point and pressed down. This may indicate that a sizeable piece has been cut from the base,[1] since if a picture is folded horizonatally in one place only it would be natural to do so not towards the base but across the centre (as in fact was done when Titian's *Venus and Adonis*, now in the Prado, was sent to Philip II in London—see Crowe and Cavalcaselle: *Titian*, II, 1881, pp. 238 and 509). In point of fact the existing line of repaint corresponds approximately with the centre of the height of the composition as shown in a drawing at Venice inscribed 'Do. Tintoretto' (see DRAWINGS below) of which the upper part reproduces the design of no. 1313 but which also includes a recumbent figure of a woman and flowers at the base.

The full composition is also reproduced in a less accurate sketch copy by Jacob Hoefnagel (Berlin) and in a painted copy (private collection, Munich, in 1929). The fact that Jacob Hoefnagel was court painter to the Emperor Rudolph II from 1602 suggested to Erna Mandowsky[2] that his drawing might be copied from a picture thus described in the 1621 inventory of the Emperor's collection at Prague: '295. Wie die Natur in den Wolken getragen wirdt, undter Ir das fruchtbare Erdtreich, ein schön Stück, von Tentoret'[3] and that this in its turn could be identified with one of the four pictures which Ridolfi specified as painted by Tintoretto for Rudolph II: 'Giove . . . che arreca al seno di Giunone Bacco fanciullo . . .'.[4] The wording of the entry in the 1621 inventory is repeated (with the omission of the artist's name) in a later inventory (after 15th February, 1637) of the Prague pictures,[5] but the picture in question had either left Prague before 1648, when the bulk of the pictures were looted by the Swedish troops, or else was not included in the booty, since it does not seem to figure in the summary inventory (1652) of Queen Christina's collection and is certainly not in the more detailed inventories of 1689 and 1721.

As the pedigree of no. 1131 cannot be traced farther back than the collection of the Marquis de Seignelay, who died in 1690, it cannot be established with certainty that it is identical with the picture in the Prague inventories or that the latter was identical with the one described by Ridolfi. Nevertheless the various factors already mentioned seem to the present writer to render both assumptions probable. No. 1313 is comparable in design and type with Tintoretto's paintings in the *Anticollegio* of the Doge's Palace, dating from shortly before 1578. Juno's hair style is also consonant with Tintoretto's practice at that time.[6] Rudolph became emperor in 1576.

Entitled 'L'Alaitement d'Hercule' in the Orléans collection and 'Juno and the Infant Hercules; or, The Origin of the Milky Way' when exhibited at Manchester in 1857. Hyginus (*Poeticon Astronomicon* II, XLIII) quotes various legends accounting for the Milky Way. The probable source for no. 1313, first indicated by Mandowsky (*loc. cit.*), was the *Geoponica*, a Byzantine botanical text-book of which Italian translations had been published at Venice in 1542 and 1549. In chapter XX of book XI of this work (*Historia del Giglio*) it is related how Jupiter, wishing to immortalize the infant Hercules (whose mother was the mortal, Alcmene) held him to the breasts of the sleeping Juno. The milk continued to flow after the child, sated, had stopped drinking, the milk which spilt upwards becoming the Milky Way, the downward stream giving birth to lilies. The latter are clearly visible in the Venice and Berlin drawings and in the painted copy, the recumbent figure next them being identified by Mandowsky with the Earth. Mandowsky also indicated Tintoretto's patron, the learned doctor, Tommaso Rangoni, as the painter's probable adviser for the story, since it is depicted, in a simplified form, on the reverse of his medal.[7] Of the objects held by the *putti* the bow, arrows and torch are common erotic symbols. The net is used by Ripa (*Iconologia*, 1645, pp. 281 and 287) in connection with Deceit which would also fit the present context as regards Jupiter's intention (Juno would not have consented had she been awake), though it is apparent that Hercules' energy has had the effect of awakening his unwitting foster-mother.

A comparable picture by Rubens (Prado, no. 1168) is from a different version of the legend. There is only one stream of milk, and Juno is fully awake, and directing it towards the child. The latter is more probably the infant Mercury.

VERSION: Small painted copy (29¼ × 21″), already mentioned, with the addition of recumbent female figure and flowers at the base, with Ludwig F. Fuchs, Munich, 1929 (photograph in the Gallery archives).

DRAWINGS: Sketch copies, already discussed, in the Accademia, Venice, and Kupferstichkabinett, Berlin. The Venice drawing was first published (by Loeser, *Rassegna d'Arte*, III, p. 177) as Domenico Tintoretto and as a preliminary study for no. 1313. The attribution of no. 1313 to Domenico need not be considered seriously, while even the signature ('Do. Tintoretto') on the drawing is doubted by Tietze and Tietze-Conrat (*Drawings of the Venetian Painters*, 1944, p. 268, no. A 1552). The latter authors consider the drawing a copy after no. 1313, perhaps dating from the seventeenth century. The Berlin drawing is stated (in the 1921 catalogue, by Max J. Friedländer, of the Kupferstichkabinett) to be signed 'Ja Hoefnagel'.

ENGRAVING: By P. R. De Launay, jeune (in reverse) in *Galerie du Palais Royal*, vol. 2 (1808).

PROVENANCE: Probably painted for the Emperor Rudolph II (see above). Marked in the 1727 Palais Royal catalogue (by Du Bois De Saint Gelais) as coming from 'M. de Seignelay'—i.e. the Marquis de Seignelay, who died in 1690.[8] Lot 238, Orléans sale, Lyceum, London, 26th December ff, 1798, when bought in by Bryan.[9] In the possession of the Earl of Darnley by 1828, when lent by him to the B.I. (112).[10] No. 298 in the definitive catalogue of the Manchester exhibition, 1857 (lent Lord Darnley). Purchased from the Earl of Darnley, 1890.

REPRODUCTION: *Illustrations, Italian Schools*, 1937, p. 348.

REFERENCES: (1) In the 1727 catalogue of the Palais Royal the dimensions of no. 1313 were already the same as now—'haut de 4 pieds huit pouces, large de cinq pieds un pouce'. This is the same as in the Palais Royal catalogue (vol. 2) of 1808 which contains an engraving showing the picture in its present form. (2) In the *Burlington Magazine*, vol. 72 (1938), pp. 88–93. (3) The 1621 Prague inventory is reproduced as 'Bilaga 1' in 'Kejsar Rudolf II's Konstkammare' by Olof Granberg (1902). The descriptions of pictures in this inventory are generally vague or inaccurate and for this reason the curious wording used in the present instance does not necessarily constitute evidence against the identification. (4) Ridolfi/Hadeln, II, p. 50. Ridolfi's confusion of the infants Hercules and Bacchus would be only a slight error and one for which Mandowsky (*op. cit.*, footnote 3) has an explanation. Hadeln (*loc. cit.*, footnote 3) identifies the picture mentioned by Ridolfi with the 'Jupiter und Semele im plitz, von Tentoreto' which is no. 172 in the 1621 Prague inventory. This is inadmissible, as the latter picture is clearly identical with the 'Jupiter und Semelle in Bley' (therefore presumably a cartoon) which is no. 277 in the later Prague inventory (after 15th February, 1637—see reference 5 below). (5) The later inventory reproduced as appendix 1 to 'La Galerie de Tableaux de la Reine Christine de Suède' by Olof Granberg (1897). For the dating of it see p. XV of the 1938 catalogue of the Gemäldegalerie of the Kunsthistorisches Museum, Vienna. (6) Notes by Stella Mary Pearce in the Gallery archives. (7) It was suggested by E. Newton (*Tintoretto*, 1952, p. 169) that no. 1313 was actually painted for Rangoni. The latter is thought to have died in 1577 (Tiraboschi, *Storia della Letteratura Italiana*, vol. VII, 1809 edition, p. 653, also Rodolfo Gallo: *Contributi su Jacopo Sansovino*, in *Saggi e Memorie di Storia dell' Arte*, Fondazione Giorgio Cini, 1957, p. 105). If, therefore, the suggested dating of no. 1313 to precisely that period is justified, as well as the assumption of the Prague provenance, it might be possible to sustain the hypothesis that no. 1313 was intended for Rangoni, but that he died and so it became the nucleus of four pictures painted for Rudolph. Nevertheless, the type of no. 1313 seems to fit it better for a princely destination than for a doctor's household. (8) C. Stryienski (*La Galerie du Régent*, 1913, p. 154) indicates no. 1313 as in the first Orléans inventory of 1724. (9) Annotated copy of the catalogue in the Gallery library has 'Mr. Bryan' against this entry. The same information is given by Buchanan (*Memoirs*, I, 1824, p. 132). The date 1792 given as that of Bryan's purchase in the Gallery catalogues of 1915–29 is a mistake. (10) Passavant (*Tour of a German Artist in England*, vol. II (1836), p. 197) specifically connects the picture in the Orléans sale with that in the Darnley collection.

4004 PORTRAIT OF VINCENZO MOROSINI

$33\frac{1}{4} \times 20\frac{3}{8}$ (0·845 × 0·515).

Good condition in general. The face rubbed in parts and retouched. The outline of the face on the spectator's right is 'worried' and there are traces of *pentimenti*. It is possible that the outline of the forehead may have been modified slightly by repaint.

The identity of the sitter is established by comparison with the portrait which figures in the *Resurrection* on the altar of the Morosini funerary chapel in S. Giorgio Maggiore, Venice, and with an inscribed portrait in the Doge's Palace.[1] The pose of no. 4004 corresponds so closely with that of the portrait in the *Resurrection* that it may either have been intended as a study for it or else have been used subsequently for that purpose. The Doge's Palace portrait is dated 1580, and the *Resurrection* documented as *c.* 1585.[2] As the sitter's age in no. 4004 appears similar to that in the other two portraits it may be assumed to be a fairly late work of Tintoretto. Vincenzo Morosini (1511–88), Senator of the Republic, was Prefect of Bergamo in 1555 and *Savio di Terrafirma*. In 1578 he was appointed *Procurator di San Marco de Citra* and in 1584 President of the University of Padua.

The sitter is shown wearing the *Stola d'Oro* over his right shoulder,[3] which was the privilege of the Knighthood of that name. At a later date the head of the Morosini family for the time being was a knight of the *Stola d'Oro* by hereditary right.[4] In the case of Vincenzo it would have been conferred in recognition of special services.

PROVENANCE: Purchased, 1922, by Messrs. Agnew from Count Contini, Via Nomentana, Rome.[5] Purchased by the N.A.-C.F. from Agnew, and presented in commemoration of the Fund's Coming of Age and of the National Gallery Centenary, 1924. Exh. National Gallery (N.A.-C.F. Exhibition), 1945–6 (2).

REPRODUCTION: *Illustrations, Italian Schools*, 1937, p. 349.

REFERENCES: (1) Both these portraits are reproduced by D. S. MacColl: *Tintoretto's 'Vincenzo Morosini'* (*Burlington Magazine*, XLIV, 1924, pp. 226–71). The whole picture of the *Resurrection* is reproduced as pl. 227 in Von der Bercken's *Tintoretto* (1942). A further (uninscribed) portrait was reproduced as plate 54 in the catalogue of *'Quattrocento Pitture Inedite'*, Venice, 1947. According to Stringa (edition of 1604 of Sansovino's *Venetia, Città Nobilissima* . . ., p. 167) the S. Giorgio altarpiece was started by Tintoretto and finished by his son. A portrait by Jacopo Tintoretto in the Accademia, Venice, identified as representing Battista Morosini, is of similar type and proportions to no. 4004, though slightly larger (repr. Von der Bercken, *op. cit.*, pl. 342). The latter portrait, unlike no. 4004, does not connect with the S. Giorgio altarpiece. (2) Cigogna: *Inscrizioni Veneziane*, IV (1834), p. 350, note 253. (3) According to P. Hélyot (*Histoire des Ordres Monastiques*, vol. 8, 1719, p. 362) the stole should be worn over the *left* shoulder. In the Doge's Palace portrait of Vincenzo Morosini this is the case. But in Tintoretto's portraits in general the rule seems by no means rigid, the stole tending to be worn over whichever shoulder is nearer the spectator in the portrait. The pattern of the embroidery, too, was not fixed. (4) Tentori: . . . *Storia . . . di Venezia*, vol. II (1785), p. 363, says the hereditary honour was instigated in favour of Lorenzo Morosini, brother of the Doge Francesco Morosini (died 1694). (5) Information supplied by Messrs. Agnew.

Ascribed to JACOPO TINTORETTO

1476 JUPITER AND SEMELE

Panel, $9 \times 25\frac{3}{4}$ (0·22 × 0·654). Painted area slightly less.

Good condition in general. Some slight losses from flaking. Some retouching on Semele's body.

Hitherto as Andrea Schiavone. The Tintoretto attribution was first published by E. K. Waterhouse,[1] who pointed out the affinities with six *cassoni* panels at Vienna.[2] The latter, which were themselves formerly attributed to Schiavone, are undoubtedly very similar to no. 1476 both in design and handling, and of the two attributions that to Tintoretto (as an early work) seems the more probable to the present writer.

PROVENANCE: In the collection of Frederic Leighton (later Lord Leighton of Stretton, P.R.A.) by 1876, when exh. by him, R.A. (189) (as Schiavone). Lord Leighton sale, Christie's, 3rd day, 14th July, 1896 (362) (as Schiavone), where purchased.

REPRODUCTION: *Illustrations, Italian Schools*, 1937, p. 327.

REFERENCES: (1) In *Burlington Magazine*, vol. 50 (1927), p. 344. The Tintoretto attribution was confirmed by Berenson (*Lists*, 1957) and by Pallucchini (*Arte Veneta*, 1951, p. 111). (2) Repr. Pallucchini: *La Giovinezza del Tintoretto*, 1950, pls. 101–6.

Style of TINTORETTO

2147 PORTRAIT OF A CARDINAL

$25\frac{1}{4} \times 21$ (0·641 × 0·533).

A line of damage, perhaps caused by a fold, extends nearly vertically up the canvas, a third of the way from the right. The discolouration of the varnish precludes a more detailed estimate of the condition or the authorship.

Lent to Dublin immediately after entering the Gallery and not catalogued until the edition of 1925.

PROVENANCE: Galvagna coll., Venice. Bought, 1855.

REPRODUCTION: *Illustrations, Italian Schools*, 1937, p. 351.

After TINTORETTO

2900 THE MIRACLE OF ST MARK

$16 \times 23\frac{1}{2}$ (0·406 × 0·597).

Slightly damaged in places by cracking, some of which is bituminous. Sketch copy, apparently dating from the first half of the nineteenth century, of the large picture in the Accademia, Venice. The suggestion, made in earlier editions of the National Gallery catalogue, that it might be the work of Etty would not be impossible, but there is no positive evidence.

REPRODUCTION: Negative in the possession of the Gallery.

PROVENANCE: Lady Lindsay Bequest, 1912.

Follower of TINTORETTO

2161 PORTRAIT OF A LADY

$38\frac{3}{4} \times 31\frac{3}{4}$ (0·984 × 0·807).

Much discoloured by old varnish and engrained dirt. Basic condition of the figure probably sound.

In the 1929 catalogue as 'Veronese School, XVI century'. Purchased as 'Portrait of Pellegrina Morosini, wife of Bartolommeo Capello . . . by Pordenone'.[1] Pellegrina married Bartolommeo in 1544, their children Vettore and Bianca, being born in 1547 and 1548 respectively. The costume shown in no. 2161 is datable around the middle of the century and would therefore not refute such an identification; but while the provenance from the Capello family would lend it some support it would be necessary to produce further supporting evidence, which is not forthcoming, to confirm it.

Lent in 1857 to Dublin and not catalogued until 1915, when it appears as 'Pellegrina Morosoni [sic], ascribed to Pordenone'. The Pordenone attribution need not be seriously considered. The connection with a certain type of Tintorettesque portrait was first pointed out by J. Wilde who had isolated a group of pictures of this type.[2]

PROVENANCE: Purchased, Venice, 1855, from the heirs of the Signori Capello.

REPRODUCTION: *Illustrations, Italian Schools*, 1937, p. 386.

REFERENCES: (1) National Gallery Report, 1856, p. 28. (2) Cf. his article: 'Wiedergefundene Gemälde aus der Sammlung des Erzherzogs Leopold Wilhelm', Vienna *Jahrbuch*, 1930, pp. 253 ff.

TITIAN (TIZIANO VECELLIO)
active before 1511, died 1576

The form of signature used in his letters is variously Titiano, Tiziano, Tizian, Tician or Ticiano, Vecellio. On such of his pictures as are signed he uses the latinized form, Titianus or Ticianus. The form Titian was already usual in England as early as the seventeenth century. Exceptional forms of what purports to be his signature—'Tician da Cadore'[1] in connection with the Padua frescoes of 1511 or 'Titianus Cadorinus' on the Ancona *Madonna* of 1520—accord with Dolce's statement (1557) that he came from Cadore (Pieve di Cadore, in the Dolomites).

The date of his birth has been the subject of controversy, and cannot be established exactly. The earliest sources, all of which date from the last years of Titian's life, when he was certainly very old, are contradictory, and show that confusion on the subject already existed. Thus, in 1561 Garcia Hernandez had referred to Titian as already over 80, and the same correspondent, writing in 1564 to Philip II of Spain, says that 'according to people who have known him for many years' Titian was 'about 90'—therefore born about 1474.[2] In 1567 Thomas de Cornoça, writing likewise to Philip II, refers to Titian as being 85 years old—therefore born in 1482.[3] Vasari, writing in 1566-7, says that Titian was born in 1480.[4] Soon after Titian's death, Borghini (1584) says that Titian died in 1576, aged 98 or 99—therefore born in 1477 or 1478.[5] In 1622 Tizianello, a collateral descendant of the painter, dedicated an anonymous biography which stated that Titian was born in 1477.[6] This date was followed by Ridolfi.[7] The sense of the context of all three of the earliest of these statements—the two Spaniards' and Vasari's—is that Titian's activity at the time was remarkable for so old a man, from which it may be deduced that Titian's age was already becoming legendary in the 1560's. This aspect colours still more the famous statement by Titian himself in a 'begging letter' of 1571 to Philip of Spain in which he claims to be 95—therefore born in 1476. Paradoxically, the discovery, in 1955, of what purported to be the register of Titian's death in August, 1576, at the age of 103 tilts the balance if anything against the maximum age rather than for it. For this information must have come from Titian's family or his household, and like his letter of 1571 it would have constituted the 'official' figure. The fact that the official figure should thus have increased by three years within the space of five is sufficient in itself to discredit its reliability. It would be permissible to deduce from these conflicting statements that towards the end of his life Titian either did not know his own age exactly or else that he did but exaggerated it.[8] In either case it is clearly impossible, in view of the uncertainty prevailing at so early a date, to come to a firm conclusion now.

The limits for Titian's birth as given in the written sources—ranging from 1473 to 1482 or later—might in theory be narrowed by the existence of a painting datable to a very early period, but in fact this aspect is equally vague, since no precisely datable painting by Titian survives prior to the frescoes of 1511 in the Scuola del Santo at Padua. Dolce[9] says that Titian joined Giorgione in working on the frescoes (now destroyed) of the Fondaco dei Tedeschi, for his share in which Giorgione was paid in 1508. A picture of Tobias and the Angel (Accademia, Venice from Santa Caterina) is problematically linked with a confused reference by Vasari to one painted by Titian in 1507. Vasari also gives a date—1508—to Titian's wood-cuts of the *Triumph of Faith*. The picture at Antwerp of Jacopo Pesaro presented to S. Peter by the Borgia Pope, Alexander VI, is in a different category. The event commemorated—the appointment of Jacopo Pesaro as commander of the papal galleys—occurred in 1501, which is thus the earliest possible date for the picture. But its upper limit need not necessarily be fixed, as has been claimed, by the lack of allusion in the picture to the victory which took place in 1502, or even by the fact of Alexander's death which occurred in 1503.

Of Titian's apprenticeship, Dolce[10] reports that he was sent at the age of nine to Venice to study painting where he was taught first by the Zuccati, who were mosaicists, then in succession by Gentile and Giovanni Bellini of each of whom he tired and finally attached himself to Giorgione. This account, as the earliest and as dating from well within Titian's lifetime, is probably basically reliable, but it should be borne in mind that the star of the Bellini had set to a great extent by the time when Dolce wrote, whereas Giorgione's was still high. In consequence of this it would have done Titian credit to have preferred the latter. As to the evidence of the surviving paintings, the present uncertainty, among the smaller religious pictures and those of secular subjects, which are late works of Giorgione and which early ones of Titian may be regarded as some indication, at least, that in these fields Titian approached Giorgione closely. But in Titian's major religious works of the earlier period the influence of Giorgione is slighter than that of Giovanni Bellini. The transition, in particular, from Bellini's altarpiece of 1513 in the church of S. Giovanni Crisostomo, Venice, to Titian's *Assunta* of 1516–18 is intelligible, at least as regards technique, without presupposing the influence of Giorgione.

The completion of the *Assunta*, though the records of its reception are fragmentary, would have established Titian's reputation as the greatest of Venetian painters, and from then to the end of his life, more than half a century later, his career was a series of spectacular successes, and correspondingly well documented. His activity was not confined to leading commissions within the Republic. His services, whether as portraitist or as painter of mythologies or religious subjects, were competed for by the chief princely families outside the Veneto—the Este (see no. 35 below), the Gonzaga, the Farnese, the Della Rovere and even the French king, François I. The Farnese patronage led to Titian's visit to Rome in 1545. More important still were his relations with the Habsburgs. In 1533 Charles V created him Count Palatine and Knight of the Golden Spur. The Imperial favour thus shown was continued by Charles' successor as King of Spain, Philip II, for whom Titian worked almost exclusively during his last years.

During the seventeenth century Titian's influence, particularly in respect of his development of the 'tonal' method of painting, was to be dominant. Palma Giovane's statement to Boschini that Titian finished his later pictures 'more with his fingers than his brush'[11] constitutes important contemporary evidence of his practice. A tradition was reported by Ridolfi[12] to the effect that Titian was in the habit of touching up students' copies of his originals which then passed as his own work. In addition, he frequently repeated his own designs, often after long intervals of time. The existence of an undoubtedly genuine Titian, therefore, does not necessarily exclude the possibility of his participation in other versions or variants. The high market value of his work at all times since his death provided an inducement to forgery, and in the case of certain early seventeenth-century painters, pre-eminently Padovanino, the border-line between follower and forger becomes obscured. At least one picture possibly in the latter category—no. 3 of this Gallery—is probably identical with one which was in the collection of Charles I as a Titian.

REFERENCES: (1) Reproduced by Bernardo Gonzati: *La Basilica di S. Antonio di Padova*, vol. 1 (1852), p. CXLIII. (2) Hernandez' letters are reproduced in Crowe and Cavalcaselle: *Titian*, vol. II (1877), pp. 522, 534–5. (3) Quoted by Gronau in his reply to Herbert Cook. This correspondence, which started with Cook's attempt to date Titian's birth as late as about 1489, is reprinted in an appendix to the later editions of Cook's *Giorgione*. An equally polemical attempt to revert to the traditional dating was made by F. J. Mather, Jr., in the *Art Bulletin*, 1938, pp. 13–25. (4) At the beginning of his biography of Titian, Milanesi ed., vol. VII, p. 426. On page 459 of the same volume Vasari lists Titian's works 'infino alla sua età di circa settantasei anni'. Elsewhere (pp. 427–8) Vasari seems to imply that Titian was only 18 when he started painting in Giorgione's manner in the year 1507, but this seems no more than an embroidery of Dolce's account. (5) *Il Riposo*, 1584, p. 529. (6) Ed. of 1819, p. II. (7) Ridolfi/Hadeln, I, p. 152. (8) The first obituary notice in the issue of *The Times* newspaper of Friday, 6th January, 1956 is a modern illustration of a comparable principle. The subject was Mlle. Jeanne Bourgeois, known as Mistinguett. (9) *Dialogo della Pittura* (1557). Ed. of 1735, p. 284. (10) *Op. cit.* (11) Marco Boschini: preface to *Le Ricche Minere . . .* (1674). (12) *Op. cit.*, p. 227.

4 THE HOLY FAMILY AND A SHEPHERD

Original (fine grain) canvas ca. $39 \times 54\frac{3}{4}$ ($0 \cdot 99 \times 1 \cdot 37$). The first lining canvas projects slightly beyond this all round and has been roughly painted. The original canvas has probably been cut on all four sides— slightly at the bottom and on the left, more at the top and most of all on the right (see VERSIONS below).

Somewhat worn in places, but in general well preserved for a picture of its type and period. Cleaned 1954.

Doubt has been expressed on occasion concerning Titian's authorship of this picture[1] and such is the lack of definition of the painter's early work that some doubt is likely to remain. Nevertheless the most plausible of the alternative candidates proposed is the young Paris Bordon,[2] and the stylistic indications which have been claimed as favouring him are scantier and less convincing than those in favour of Titian.[3] In connection with the latter's claim, several *Holy Family's* both full length and half length have been associated with no. 4,[4] but some of them are not above question as Titian and they are not entirely homogeneous as a group. The most convincing stylistic analogy for the attribution of no. 4 to Titian seems to the present writer to lie in the altarpiece of S. Mark and four other saints (Venice, S. Maria della Salute). This is an undoubted early Titian and shows similarities of disposition, draperies and physiognomical type alike.[5] The fact, not hitherto published, that the Titian attribution for no. 4 dates back at least to the seventeenth century is a further factor (see PROVENANCE).

Described in the 1929 catalogue as 'unfinished', but despite the sketchy treatment of the ass' head there seems no justification for this statement.

VERSIONS: A copy was lot 157, Christie's, 30th April, 1954. A free copy, lot 9. Christie's, 31st October, 1958. A sketch copy inscribed 'Pallazo Borghese nella Vigna' shows more space round the figures than now exists in no. 4 and indicates that the latter has been cut—fairly considerably on the right, rather less at the top and less still on the left and at the bottom. This sketch, apparently of the seventeenth century, seems to have been in the Dolgoroukoff collection, Moscow, in 1907.[6] An old copy, with an extra strip along the top, in the crossing of the Val-de-Grâce, Paris.

PROVENANCE: Identifiable on the strength of the sketch copy (see VERSIONS) with an entry in the Borghese inventory of 1693 ('nell'Appartamento Terreno che gode il Sig.r Principe di Rossano')—kindly communicated by Paola Della Pergola: '. . . un quadro grande in tela, la Madonna, e il Bambino e San Giuseppe, un Pastore in ginocchioni No. 334 cornice dorato di Titiano'.[7] Bought in Italy by W. Y. Ottley, 1797–9.[8] Lot 15 ('Palace Borghese') in anonymous (Ottley) sale, 118 Pall Mall, London (January, 1801). W. Y. Ottley sale, Christie's, 16th May, 1801. Lot 45 (again as ex-Borghese), W. Champion sale, 23rd–24th March, 1810, where bought by the Rev. Holwell Carr,[9] by whom bequeathed, 1831.

REPRODUCTION: *Illustrations, Italian Schools*, 1937, p. 352.

REFERENCES: (1) E.g. by Crowe and Cavalcaselle (*Titian*, vol. II (1877), p. 428), Fischel (*Klassiker der Kunst* volume on Titian, 5th edition, p. 305, note to pl. 21), and Tietze (*Tizian*, 1936, Tafelband, pp. 293–4). The latter refers to further sceptics. The Titian attribution has been upheld by Gronau (*Titian*, English edition, 1904, p. 31), Berenson (*Lists*, 1936, p. 491), A. Venturi (*Storia* . . .. IX, III, p. 199) and Suida (*Tiziano*, 1933, p. 26). (2) Proposed by K. Oettinger (*Magyar Müvészet*, 1931) and apparently supported by Tietze (*loc. cit.*). (3) The case for Bordon's authorship of no. 4 rests primarily on the signed early altarpiece in the Galleria Tadini at Lovere (repr. in Venturi, *Storia* . . ., IX, III, p. 1002) which probably dates from the '20's of the sixteenth century (see Bailo and Biscaro: *Paris Bordon*, 1900, pp. 132–3). If, as seems likely, the *Nativity* by Giovanni da Asola (Duomo, Asola, reproduced and discussed by Fiocco, *Bollettino d'Arte*, anno V (1925–6), vol. 1, pp. 198 and 201) derives from no. 4 it would more or less exclude Bordon's authorship of the latter without more ado, as the Asola picture dates from as early as 1518. A picture comparable with it is no. 1377 of this Gallery. (4) Suida (*op. cit.*, pp. 25–6) associates no. 4 with the Prado, Bache, Dresden, Vienna and Louvre half-length *Holy Family's* (his plates XLI, LXXV, LXXXII, LXXXIII, LXXXIV) and with the Bridgewater House full-length *Holy Family* (his plate LXXIX). (5) The Salute picture is usually (and probably correctly) associated with relief from the plague of 1510. This would also be a possible date (i.e. within a few years from 1510) for no. 4. (6) Reproduced (as Anthony Van Dyck and wrongly labelled as at Chatsworth) and discussed by Frizzoni, *Rassegna d'Arte*, VII (1907), pp. 154–5. (7) Probably the first of the two pictures described by Ramdohr (*Ueber Mahlerei und Bildhauerarbeit in Rom* . . ., vol. 1, 1787, p. 299) as in Palazzo Borghese: *zwei heilige Familien von Tizian. Auf der einen betet ein Hirte den Christ an . . . Das Kind ist in einem angenehmen Halbschatten gehalten; auch ist der Hirte sehr wahr und gut gestellet.* (8) W. Buchanan: *Memoirs*, II, pp. 21 and 27. Preface to anonymous (Ottley) sale catalogue has 'purchased . . . at Rome . . . 1799, 1800'. (9) Redford: *Art Sales*, vol. II (1888), p. 256. Redford's misprint of Champion as 'Campion' was followed in the National Gallery catalogues of 1915–29.

35 BACCHUS AND ARIADNE

69 × 75 (1·75 × 1·9).

Signed on an urn, left foreground, TICIANVS F.

The picture has suffered in the past from blistering and from relining. The most damaged area is the sky, which is covered with innumerable small retouchings. Bacchus' neck and the middle of his cloak are in similar state. Other retouchings, though less numerous, in the flesh and draperies of the other figures. The following areas well preserved: most of the foreground, the cheetahs, the distant landscape and the trees. Cleaned 1967–9. Since then, slightly more of the painted area has been revealed by the frame.

As regards the textual source, Lomazzo[1] mentions no. 35 with other Renaissance representations of Triumphs and then quotes classical writers who cited the return of Bacchus from India as the prototype of the practice of Triumphs in general. Lomazzo proceeds to quote in translation a passage from Catullus[2] as constituting material suitable for illustration in such circumstances. He does not specifically associate this passage with Titian, but Ridolfi appends the names Ovid ('Met. li. 8') and Philostratus, as well as Catullus, as marginal notes to his description of no. 35.[3] This is the earliest recorded opinion that more than one classical writer was drawn on for the subject and this seems in fact to have been the case. The passage of Catullus quoted by Lomazzo specifies in Bacchus' train figures variously waving thyrsi, rending and throwing a mangled heifer's limbs, girt with writhing snakes, thronged round the mysteries borne in dark caskets, beating cymbals and tambourines and playing horns and pipes. The accurate portrayal of all these features in no. 35, with the exception of the pipe player who is not shown, confirms Ridolfi's specification of Catullus as a source. But the meeting of Bacchus and Ariadne does not occur there, and for this the main source seems to have been Ovid; not the *Metamorphoses* as mentioned by Ridolfi, but the *Ars Amatoria*.[4] Here (I, 525–66) Ariadne is described wandering distractedly along the shore, barefoot and clad in an ungirt tunic. She is surprised by Bacchus' train of satyrs and bacchantes and the drunken Silenus on his ass. She is frightened and attempts to flee, but the god himself reassures her. He leaps from his car towards her, promising her marriage and a place among the stars as a constellation. In this passage Bacchus' car is stated to have been drawn by tigers. The cheetahs shown instead in no. 35 introduce the third writer mentioned by Ridolfi, namely Philostratus, who, in the *Imagines*,[5] had specified the πάρδαλις[6] as particularly associated with Bacchus. The detailed programme for no. 35 was probably sent to Titian by Alfonso d'Este himself.[7] Since the sources drawn on were so well known, a conflation of them in the written programme would not in any case have been surprising.[8]

The historical events concerning the commissioning of no. 35 may be summarized as follows. A picture called *The Feast of the Gods*, now at Washington, is signed by Giovanni Bellini and dated 1514. Two Bacchanals by Titian, now in the Prado, and no. 35 are of approximately the same dimensions as Bellini's picture[9] and all four came from the studio of Alfonso d'Este in the *Castello* at Ferrara. Titian was in contact with Alfonso from 1516 and repainted part of Bellini's picture, which was certainly the earliest of the four. Although it cannot be established with certainty when he started no. 35[10] (which was apparently the second of his three) it can be proved that most of the work on it was done, after considerable delay, between the summer of 1522 and the spring of 1523. The documents for the crucial stages of its execution consist of two letters to Duke Alfonso from his agent in Venice, Giacomo Tebaldi (text published by G. Gronau, Vienna *Jahrbuch*, 1928, p. 246).

In the first of them, dated 'the last day of August, 1522', Tebaldi says he had been to Titian's studio on the preceding day and had seen the canvas which then contained ten[11] figures, the chariot and the animals drawing it.[12] At this time little more than the lay-in can have been done as Tebaldi specifies that Titian expects to be able to paint the figures in the existing attitudes—i.e. without further changes. He adds that a few details—heads and landscape—apparently not yet even sketched in, remained to be done, but that this would not take long. Titian's own estimate is that by October the canvas should be ready to transport to Ferrara where he could finish it in ten or fifteen days. Apparently Titian then shelved the work again as in the second letter in question, dated 14th October, 1522,[13] Tebaldi reports to Alfonso that he has that day rebuked Titian for the delay. Titian's defense was that he had had to change two women,[14] but that he should nevertheless be able to transport the canvas to Ferrara by the end of the month and finish it there. Tebaldi adds that he thinks Titian may keep his promise, saying that he is at work in the Doge's Palace in the mornings, but that for the rest of the day he is exclusively occupied with the *Bacchus and Ariadne*. Nevertheless it was not until 30th January, 1523 that the picture was sent to Ferrara,[15] and even then Titian did not accompany it, being on a visit to Mantua. A letter of 3rd February, 1523 from Federico Gonzaga to Alfonso d'Este[16] says that the bearer was Titian, who therefore presumably arrived at Ferrara soon afterwards. No more is heard of progress on no. 35, but as Alfonso was already very angry at the delay[17] it is inconceivable that having at last lured Titian to Ferrara he would let him go without completing the picture. As, according to Titian's own words to Tebaldi, there would then have been only ten or fifteen days work still to do and as he would have had no other commitments at Ferrara it can be assumed (even if, as is probable, Titian's estimate was deliberately optimistic) that no. 35 would have been finished some time in the spring of 1523. It must in any case have been finished before August, as by then Titian was back in Venice.[18]

VERSIONS: Various old copies exist, notably at Bergamo,[19] Accademia di S. Luca (Rome),[20] Schloss Celle and Alnwick.[21] Also Palace Hotel, St Moritz and Geneva Museum. A sketch copy, signed 'D. Wilkie' and dated 1820, was lot 83 in an anonymous sale, Christie's, 21st March, 1952 (later Lord Plunket). A copy of the figure of Bacchus, attributed 'A. Carracci', was no. 45 in the Northwick catalogue of 1858 (later Earl of Crawford). Farington (*Diary*, 15th January, 1811) mentions a 'large' copy in enamel by Henry Bone (sold Christie's, lot 123, 20th February, 1973). Crude pastiches of most of the principal figures are included in Turner's picture of the same title (Tate Gallery, no. 525).

DRAWINGS: In an article in the *Gazette des Beaux-Arts*, 1908, I, p. 135, Emil Jacobsen published a drawing in the Uffizi (Saltarelli collection, no. 7383) which he claimed as preliminary studies for no. 35 and for the Andrian Bacchanal (Prado). Nevertheless Hadeln, in his book on Titian's drawings (1924) excluded this one, and Fischel (*Klassiker der Kunst* volume on Titian, p. 307) speaks of it as copied from the paintings, which it pretty obviously is.

ENGRAVINGS: By G. A. Podestà[22] and by Joseph Juster.[23]

PROVENANCE: Mentioned by Lomazzo (1584)[24] as at Ferrara. Appropriated in 1598 and sent to Rome by the Papal Legate, Cardinal Pietro Aldobrandini,[25] when the state of Ferrara passed to the Papacy. Included in Cardinal Pietro Aldobrandini's inventory of 1603 and in those of 1626, 1682 and an undated one (before 1665). Recorded in 1638 as in the Villa Aldobrandini, Rome,[26] and subsequently (as in the same place) by (?) Bellori (1664),[27] Scaramuccia (1674),[28] Rossini (1693)[29] and in *Roma Antica e Moderna* (1765).[30] During this period the ownership had varied with the dynastic changes.[31] The heir of Cardinal Pietro Aldobrandini (d. 1621) appears to have been Cardinal Ippolito Aldobrandini (son of Pietro's sister, Olimpia, who had married another Aldobrandini, Gianfrancesco) on whom, according to Litta, all the riches of the Aldobrandini family had devolved. Cardinal Ippolito, the last surviving Aldobrandini male of the main branch, died in 1638, entailing the estate and leaving as heir his niece, also called Olimpia (daughter of Ippolito's brother, Giorgio) and then her second son (by her second marriage—to Camillo Pamfili) who had to take the name Aldobrandini. When this line too became extinct (in 1760) most of the Pamfili property passed to the Doria Landi while the Aldobrandini inheritance became the subject of a law suit between the Colonna and Borghese families, won by the latter in 1769. The judgment on that occasion was that the Aldobrandini fortune and title should be held by the second son of the head of the Borghese family. The confusion presumably prevailing over the inheritance between the years 1760 and 1769 may account for Volkmann's statement (published in 1770 but presumably referring to some time before)[32] that no. 35 was at the time of writing in the Palazzo Pamfili (i.e. Palazzo Doria). Contrary to what is often stated no. 35 appears never to have hung in the Palazzo Barberini.[33] It was back in the Villa Aldobrandini by 1787[34] and sold from there, probably in 1797 and certainly before May, 1803, when it was in the hands of Alexander Day. Day seems to have been in partnership with the brothers Camuccini.[35] Bought by Irvine for Buchanan, Rome, May, 1806,[36] who had it sent to England and sold it to Lord Kinnaird, 1806 or 1807.[37] Sold to Basely by Delahante, who had apparently purchased it privately before the Kinnaird sale (5th March, 1813).[38] In the possession of the jeweller, Thomas Hamlet, by 1816, who lent it in that year both to the R.A. for copying[39] and to the B.I. (11). Purchased from Hamlet, 1826.

REPRODUCTION: *Illustrations, Italian Schools*, 1937, p. 356.

REFERENCES: (1) *Trattato*, 1584, p. 393. (2) *Carmina*, LXIV, lines 257-65. (3) Ridolfi/Hadeln, I, pp. 141-2. Ridolfi adds that Theseus' ship is visible in the distance. This area (on the spectator's extreme left) is more distinct since the recent cleaning. The engravings of Podestà and Juster show a ship distinctly. Wind (*Burlington Magazine* 92, 1950, p. 85) denies that the ship is Theseus' on the grounds that the sails are white. However, the scale is so small that with 'dark Spanish purple' sails against the dark blue sea and the sky the ship would have been almost invisible. (4) This fact was pointed out by Graves H. Thompson ('The Literary Sources of Titian's *Bacchus and Ariadne*' in *The Classical Journal*, March 1956, pp. 259-64) who demonstrated this work as more applicable to no. 35 than is a passage in the *Fasti* (III, 459-516) which had been adduced by E. Wind. The distinction, stressed in the *Fasti* account, between Bacchus' first and second meetings with Ariadne is not drawn in the *Ars Amatoria* version. Wind's argument is contained in his book *Bellini's Feast of the Gods* (1948) which, together with John

Walker's *Bellini and Titian at Ferrara* (1956) is in other respects essential to any study of the series of pictures from Ferrara of which no. 35 was one. See also the present writer's booklet (*The Studio of Alfonso d'Este and Titian's Bacchus and Ariadne*, n.d. 1969) and Charles Hope in *Burlington Magazine*, 1971, pp. 641 ff and 712 ff. (5) *Imagines*, I, 15 and 19. (6) Translatable as leopard or panther. A letter of 15th November, 1956 to *The Times* newspaper demonstrated that the creatures shown in no. 35 are in fact cheetahs rather than leopards. (7) See correspondence printed in Crowe and Cavalcaselle: *Titian*, I, (1877) pp. 181–3. These letters do not specifically refer to no. 35 but are suggestive as regards the probable system adopted. (8) Anyone, Alfonso himself or another, who was able to draw on Catullus, Philostratus and the *Ars Amatoria* may be presumed also to have been well acquainted with the *Fasti* and the *Metamorphoses* and perhaps to have worded the programme for no. 35 in a way which presupposed such knowledge. *Fasti III* 515–16 and *Metamorphoses VIII* 176–82, for instance, describe the jewels in Ariadne's crown turning into stars, the *Fasti* specifying them as nine. Though there are in fact only eight stars in no. 35 the other accounts do not specify a number at all. (9) *Feast of the Gods* 1·7 × 1·88, Prado Bacchanals 1·75 × 1·93 and 1·72 × 1·75, no. 35 1·75 × 1·9. (10) Wind (*op. cit.*) suggests that the *Bacchus and Ariadne* was designed first of Titian's three bacchanals. But the evidence he adduces is inconclusive. (11) In the picture in its present state there are in fact eleven figures—six in the foreground (Ariadne, Bacchus, baby faun, bacchante with cymbals, athlete with snakes and faun flourishing bullock's leg) and five in the background (bacchante with tambourine, boy blowing horn, man supporting Silenus, Silenus himself and man bearing cask). If the picture was only a lay-in at the time when Tebaldi saw it the two heads next to Silenus' may not have been differentiated (in Podestà's engraving there is in fact only one in this area, making only ten figures in all; though this is presumably no more than a whim of the engraver's). (12) This letter is paraphrased (but not directly quoted) in an article by G. Campori: *Tiziano e gli Estensi* (*Nuova Antologia*, 1st series, vol. 27, 1874). Crowe and Cavalcaselle and most other writers re-quote from Campori without noticing that he made a mistake in his reading of the document, reading the word 'dece' as 'due', and stating in consequence that apart from the car drawn by animals the picture contained only two figures, the rest not even started. Venturi (*Storia*, IX, iii, 116) quotes the particular sentence accurately but does not reproduce the document *in extenso*. This, however, was done by Gronau (*loc. cit.*). (13) This document is referred to by Venturi (*op. cit.*, pp. 117 and 118) who wrongly gives its location as Mantua instead of Modena. (14) No confirmation of this statement has been forthcoming from the X-ray photographs specially taken in this connection. (15) A bill of that date for carriage is quoted by Crowe and Cavalcaselle (*op. cit.*, p. 258). (16) Crowe and Cavalcaselle, *op. cit.*, p. 281. (17) It emerges from Tebaldi's first letter that Titian was apprehensive of the possibility even of physical violence as a punishment from Alfonso for his excessive procrastination. (18) Letter of 11th August, 1523 from the Gonzaga envoy in Venice (Crowe and Cavalcaselle, *op. cit.*, p. 282). (19) No. 423 in catalogue of 1930, attributed Padovanino. (20) No. 231, attributed N. Poussin. (21) Attributed N. Poussin. Other copies are listed by John Walker: *Bellini and Titian at Ferrara*, 1957, pp. 119–21. (22) Bartsch, XX, p. 172, no. 6. Podestà was active in Rome in the mid-seventeenth century. (23) In *Pitture Scelte . . . da Carla Caterina Patina*, Cologne, 1691, p. 179. (24) *Loc. cit.* (25) Details are given in a contemporary memorandum published by Adolfo Venturi (*La R. Galleria Estense in Modena*, 1882, p. 113). The removal of no. 35 to Rome by Cardinal Aldobrandini was little more than theft. Only five pictures were concerned—the four Bellini/Titian Bacchanals and one by Dosso (see entry for no. 5279 of this Gallery). The memorandum describes no. 35 as *una pittura in quadro di mano di Tiziano dove era dipinto Lacoonte*. Such indeed is how the figure of the satyr towards the right might appear at first sight or, as here, in retrospect (since the picture had already gone when the memorandum was written). Although Titian had probably not seen the *Laöcoön* group when he painted no. 35 it is equally probable that its general appearance was known to him. At the same time the resemblance may be partly fortuitous, since the distinctive feature—the serpents writhing round the naked figure—occurs in Catullus. (26) Gasp. Celio: *Memoria fatta dell' habito di Christo*, Naples, 1638, p. 138: *Quella di Bacco che scende dal Carro è di Titiano*— as in the *Casino del Signor Principe Aldobrandini nel Monte detto Magnanapoli*. The Villa Aldobrandini at Rome is sometimes referred to in seventeenth- and eighteenth-century guide-books as above, sometimes as *Giardino Aldobrandini* and sometimes as *Villa Aldobrandini sopra al Quirinale*, but there is no doubt that all refer to the same building. No. 35 appears as no. 203 in the Aldobrandini inventories of 1605 and before 1665 (*Palatino*, 1964, p. 203) and as no. 100 in the 1626 inventory (*Arte Antica e Moderna*, 1960, p. 432) and as no. 314 in 1682 inventory (*Arte Antica e Moderna*, 1963, p. 74). (27) *Nota delli Musei, Librerie, Galerie . . . e Pittura ne' Palazzi, nelle Case . . . di Roma*, p. 6. (28) *Le Finezze*, p. 12. (29) *Il Mercurio Errante*, p. 108. (30) Vol. II, pp. 607–8. The writers referred to above (references 26 to the present one) are merely those who specify the location and at the same time use words which leave no doubt that the picture in question is no. 35. Other writers of the seventeenth and eighteenth centuries are not referred to if references are vaguer—for example Ridolfi (*Maraviglie*) having described no. 35 (p. 142), later gives its location (p. 178) simply as *da gli heredi del Signor Cardinale Aldobrandino*. It may be pointed out in this pace that Vasari, though describing the other Bacchanals at Ferrara, does not speak of no. 35. (31) The information concerning the fortunes for the family, summarized here, is derived from Litta: *Famiglie Celebri* and from the *Enciclopedia Italiana*. (32) *Historisch-Kritische Nachrichten von Italien*, II, p. 297. (33) Nikodemus Tessin (*Studieresor*, 1687–8, ed. Sirén, 1914, p. 168) mentions *vier zimblich grosse Bachanalien vom Titiano* as in Palazzo Barberini and this was repeated by Carla Caterina Patina (*Pitture Scelte*, Cologne, 1691, p. 179) and by various eighteenth-century writers, while Milanesi (ed. of Vasari, VII, p. 434, note 1) and earlier editions of the National Gallery catalogue include the Barberini in the pedigree of no. 35. The grounds for assuming that the pictures in question were copies are (a) the four original Bacchanals have never been together since the second quarter of the seventeenth century. Two were in Spain by 1638 (see W. N. Sainsbury: *Original Unpublished Papers, Illustrative of . . . Rubens*, 1859, p. 353), (b) both Rossini (*Il Mercurio Errante*, 8th ed., 1760, p. 93) and the *Roma Antica e Moderna* (1765, II, p. 283) mention four Titian Bacchanals in Palazzo Barberini and *also* (pp. 271 and II, 607, respectively) no. 35 as at the Villa Aldobrandini, (c) Orbaan (*Documenti sul Barocco in Roma*, 1920, p. 512) quotes a Barberini inventory of 1631 which says clearly that there was at that time in Palazzo Barberini a copy of what is certainly no. 35, there stated as belonging to the Aldobrandini: *un quadro d'un baccanario, con un satiretto, che tira la testa di un vitello, copiato dal Maltese da un di Titiano, che hanno li Signori Altobrandini*, width *c.* 6 Roman *palmi.* (34) Ramdohr: *Ueber Mahlerei . . . in Rom*, II, p. 181. The sojourn (in itself a little mysterious) of no. 35 in Palazzo Doria seems at first to be rendered questionable by a curious statement of Ramdohr's (*op. cit.*, p. 163) à propos the Villa Aldobrandini that *diese Villa gehört nicht dem Hause Doria, wie H. Dr. Volkmann schreibt, sondern dem Hause Borghese*. Unfortunately the reference to Volkmann's book given in this connection by Ramdohr (viz. vol. II, p. 233) is wrong (page 233 of that work is about something quite different) and it is difficult to be sure to which of Volkmann's remarks Ramdohr is referring. In his description of the Villa Aldobrandini (p. 825) Volkmann does not mention the owner. In his description of Palazzo Pamfili (i.e. Doria) on p. 295 (where he locates the *Bacchus and Ariadne*) he gives the owner of the building as *Prinz Doria aus Genua*—which is correct. Although Volkmann's statement that no. 35 hung in Palazzo Doria some time before 1770 is unsupported (for the reference of Titi: *Descrizione*, 1763, p. 320—*alcuni di Tiziano*— and of Chiusole: *Itinerario*, 1782, p. 265—*bei quadri di Tiziano*—to pictures in Palazzo Doria are too vague to constitute evidence either for or against) there seems no adequate reason to doubt it (the picture had, incidentally, very likely

hung there earlier, as the building had been bought by Cardinal Pietro Aldobrandini in 1601). It may be relevant to add in this connection that a further
Aldobrandini picture (no. 18, Luini of this Gallery) was recorded in Palazzo
Doria in 1759 and 1763, and Bottari (ed. of Vasari, vol. 3, 1760, p. 379, note 1)
says he believes the Bellini Bacchanal (which Ramdohr, *op. cit.*—1787—p. 182,
recorded in the Villa Aldobrandini and which had come with no. 35 from
Ferrara) was then in Palazzo Pamfili (Doria). (35) Buchanan: *Memoirs*, vol. II
(1824), pp. 135–6, 142–3 and 153. The evidence for the year 1797 as the date
of the sale comes from Waagen's statement (*Galleries and Cabinets of Art* . . .,
1857, p. 467) that the Bellini *Bacchanal*, still at that time the companion of
no. 35, was bought in that year by Camuccini. (36) Buchanan, *op. cit.*, II, p. 173.
(37) Whitley: *Art in England*, 1800–1820 (1928), p. 212, says the picture had
been brought to England in 1806. But Buchanan (*op. cit.*, p. 174) says it was
detained in Italy 'for a considerable time' after its purchase in May, 1806, and
the Farington Diary (vol. IV, p. 115) describes it, implying a novelty, under
the heading 'April 7th, 1807'. (38) In the copy in the Gallery library of the
1813 Kinnaird sale catalogue no. 35 (lot 88) together with two other pictures
(now nos. 62 and 194 of this Gallery) is stated to have been sold 'by private
contract' to Delahante or Lafontaine. But a letter of 7th July, 1813 from
Delahante himself to Penrice (*Penrice Letters*, pp. 30–1) strongly implies that
the purchaser was Delahante and not Lafontaine. (39) Whitley: *op. cit.*, p. 254.

224 THE TRIBUTE MONEY

Ca. 43×40 ($1 \cdot 09 \times 1 \cdot 015$).

The original canvas is of irregular shape at the base, being longer on
the right than on the left. There is therefore visible on the left (narrow-
ing towards the centre) some of a strip (about six inches wide) of later
canvas, most of which was folded over the stretcher when the picture
was cleaned in 1937. Judging by Martino Rota's engraving (see
ENGRAVINGS below) this strip roughly corresponds in extent with part
of the original canvas which would have been cut off.

Some cutting at one or both sides is also possible.[1]

Signed on the pilaster, right:—TITIANVS | .F.

The paint of the signature, examined under a microscope, gives every
indication of being original.

Good condition on the whole. The edges are much abraded and the
paint in Christ's blue mantle deteriorated.

X-ray photographs reveal *pentimenti* in all three hands and, more
particularly, in Christ's head, which was originally farther to the
(spectator's) left and somewhat inclined. The fundamental nature of the
last-named change, in particular, is a good indication that no. 224 is not
a copy.

The textual sources of the incident are Matthew xxii, 17–22, Mark xii
14–17 and Luke xx, 22–25.

No. 224 was purchased from the Soult collection. A note—'se lo
llevó el mariscal Soult'—against an entry—'*Christo nuestro Senor*, de
medio cuerpo, y un fariseo que le muestra la moneda de César, de mano
de *Tiziano*'—in an inventory of pictures transferred by Philip II to the
Escorial in 1574[2] therefore identifies it with that picture. The fact that
no. 224 was engraved by Martino Rota who appears not to have been in
Venice after 1568[3] suggests that it was painted not later than then. For

two reasons it is therefore almost certainly identifiable with the picture of the Tribute Money which Titian told Philip II in a letter of 26th October, 1568 that he had recently finished and despatched to him.[4] It follows from this (and from the genuine signature) that no. 224 was sent out by Titian from his studio as his own work, and suggestions of an independent painter—such as Paris Bordon[5]—as author are therefore inadmissible. The extent of the studio assistance (the existence of which in no. 224 has long been recognized) cannot be authoritatively defined. The feature which is least characteristic of the late Titian is the relative lack of an all-over tone, but some of this may be due to subsequent modifications in the paint—particularly as regards the blue in Christ's mantle. Most of the execution seems to the present writer acceptable as late Titian with the exception of the head of the questioner, his white sleeve, and (in its present state) of Christ's blue mantle. The design of no. 224 evidently served as model for Van Dyck's picture of the same subject (Genoa, Palazzo Bianco)—perhaps via Cornelis Galle's engraving (see below).

VERSIONS: Sedelmeyer sale, Paris, 3rd–5th June, 1907, lot 188—variant (the secondary questioner—extreme left in no. 224—is transferred to the right of the picture and his hat to the chief questioner). A copy combining features of the latter picture and of no. 224 was lot 129, anonymous sale, Christie's, 6th May, 1938. Others recorded at Wentworth Woodhouse and in the Duque de Infantados collection, Madrid.

ENGRAVINGS: By Martino Rota (see above)—Christ's nimbus much enlarged. Another engraving, by Cornelis Galle, is in reverse and with an extra figure on the side of Christ to which His finger points (as in the Sedelmeyer picture though not corresponding with it in other respects).

PROVENANCE: Sent, before 26th October, 1568 from Titian in Venice to Philip II in Spain and given by the latter, in 1574, to the Escorial (see above). Described as in the Escorial sacristy by de los Santos (1657)[6] and Ximenez (1764).[7] One of six pictures from the Spanish royal collections given, c. 1810, by Joseph Bonaparte to Maréchal Soult.[8] No. 132 in the sale of the latter's collection, Paris, 19th–22nd May, 1852, where purchased through Woodburn. Exhibition of Cleaned Pictures, National Gallery, 1947, no. 35.

REPRODUCTION: *Illustrations, Italian Schools*, 1937, p. 357.

REFERENCES: (1) Dimensions given in the Philip II inventory of 1574 as '4½ pies × 4'—i.e. roughly 49 × 44″. (2) Printed by Fr. Julián Zarco Cuevas: *Inventario de las . . . pinturas . . . donados por Felipe II al Monasterio de El Escorial (1571–98)*, p. 139. For the date of this part of the inventory see p. 16. (3) Entry in Thieme-Becker. (4) Letter printed by Crowe and Cavalcaselle: *Titian*, vol. II (1877), p. 537. (5) As made in the 1929 catalogue. (6) P. 129 in the English edition of 1760. (7) P. 307 of his *Descripción . . . del Escorial*. (8) Unpublished list of which copy in the possession of the Duke of Wellington.

270 'NOLI ME TANGERE'

42¾ × 35¾ (1·09 × 0·91).

The sky extensively worn and restored. Some wearing also in Christ's body, particularly in the upper part. Titian's use of copper resinate in much of the foliage has resulted in its changing colour from green to brown. Otherwise reasonably good condition.

Cleaned 1957.

X-ray photographs disclose changes made during the painting and others made at a later date. Originally the background consisted of a tree in the middle which was much smaller than the existing one and inclined in the opposite direction. The line of its foliage was subsequently changed by Titian into that of part of the central cloud. The ridge and buildings were on the left, not on the right.[1] Christ was shown striding away from the Magdalen, not taking a step towards her. He may also have been wearing a gardener's hat. At some time after the picture left Titian's hands and before Nicolas Tardieu's engraving was made (published in 1742, see ENGRAVINGS below) the upper portion of the Magdalen's skirt was painted over, and corresponding modifications made to her bodice. Between the date of Tardieu's engraving and that of F. Trier (immediately pre-Revolution, but not published until 1808) a further addition was made in the form of a sapling on the right of the large tree, following the line of Titian's original tree as disclosed by the X-rays. Both these additions were removed in the 1957 restoration.

Catalogued as by Titian since the seventeenth century and accepted as such by the majority of modern writers. G. M. Richter suggested a work of Giorgione subsequently worked on by Titian,[2] and the publication of some X-rays[3] was at first thought to support this theory. Both figures in their present form are clearly recognizable as Titian's, and the landscape, though very Giorgionesque in type, is no more so than in pictures such as the Capitoline *Baptism* or the Sutherland *Three Ages*, whose attribution to Titian is not in doubt. In view of the fact, moreover, that one of its principal features—the group of buildings—recurs in two further pictures in the same category—the *Sacred and Profane Love*[4] and the background of the Dresden *Venus*[5]—there would seem to the present writer to be no necessity to assume Giorgione's participation.

VERSIONS: 1. Lot 128 in the Hugh A. J. Munro sale, Christie's, 1st June, 1878, where catalogued as 'small replica of the picture bequeathed to the National Gallery by the poet Rogers'. 2. By W. Etty. Exh. Fine Art and Industrial Exhibition, York, 1866 (514)—'copy of the Rogers Titian in the National Gallery'. 3. Cracow, Czartoryski Museum. G. M. Richter (*Giorgio da Castelfranco*, 1937, p. 225) specifies a Hanfstaengl photograph, no. 24,503. 4. Copy (in reverse) of figures, in the English College, Valladolid (photograph in the Gallery archives).

ENGRAVINGS: 1. By Nicolas Tardieu (in reverse). No. 143 in *Recueil d'Estampes*, 1742. 2. By F. Trier (in reverse). No. 17 (Titian) in vol. II of *Galerie du Palais Royal* (1808). 3. By W. Ensom (Crowe and Cavalcaselle: *Titian*, 1877, vol. 1, p. 210, note).

PROVENANCE: Stated in the *Recueil d'Estampes d'après les Plus Beaux Tableaux . . . en France*, 1742 (vol. II, p. 59) that no. 270—which is engraved in that work—had been in the collection of Christoforo and Francesco Muselli at Verona, that it had been acquired by the Marquis de Seignelay (who died in 1690) who had sent agents[6] to Italy to buy it, that it had then belonged to 'M. Bertin' and that at the time of writing it was in the Orléans collection. It is therefore identifiable with Ridolfi's mention (1648) of Titian's *Maddalena con Christo nell' horto* (as belonging to Christoforo and Francesco Muselli)[7] and with a picture catalogued in the Muselli collection in 1662, despite the fact that in the latter the Magdalen is said to have one hand on her bosom.[8] Pierre-Vincent Bertin, the owner after Seignelay, died in 1711.[9] Catalogued on page 477 of Du Bois de Saint Gelais' *Description des Tableaux du Palais Royal* (1727). The Italian pictures in the Orléans collection were sold in 1792 to the Belgian banker, Walkuers, who sold them to Laborde de Méréville, who fled with them to England[10] where they were bought by Jeremiah Harman who made them over to a syndicate consisting of the Duke of Bridgewater and Lords Carlisle and Gower.[11] A sale was arranged by Bryan who exhibited them in 1798. No. 270 seems to have been lot 119 in the sale at 88 Pall Mall, 26th December, 1798, which in an annotated copy of the sale catalogue in the National Gallery library is marked as bought by Lord Gower.[12] A few of the pictures bought on this occasion by the latter and by the Duke of Bedford reappeared in an anonymous sale (by Coxe, Burrell and Foster), 12th–13th May, 1802. In this sale no. 270 was lot 55 (2nd day). Lot 91 ('from the Orléans Gallery') Arthur Champernowne sale, 2nd day, 30th June, 1820, where bought Rogers.[13] Samuel Rogers bequest, 1856.

REPRODUCTION: *Illustrations, Italian Schools*, 1937, p. 352.

REFERENCES: (1) For a discussion of the implications of the X-ray photographs see Cecil Gould in the *Burlington Magazine*, 1958, pp. 44–8. (2) *Burlington Magazine*, vol. 65 (1934), pp. 4–16. Also his letter (*Burlington Magazine*, vol. 66, p. 46). Richter's view was supported by Tietze (*Tizian*, 1936, Tafelband, p. 293). (3) In *From the National Gallery Laboratory* by F. I. G. Rawlins (1940). (4) G. M. Richter (*Giorgio da Castelfranco*, 1937, p. 263) suggests that these buildings are 'a recollection of the Rocca di Asola'. But the photograph of the Rocca which he reproduces does not bear out this statement. If a specific source had to be postulated it seems to the present writer a possibility that it might be not in any Italian building but in Dürer's engravings or woodcuts. A suggestion has been made (in a pamphlet by Cav. Tarelli of Ancona in the Gallery archives) that the background of no. 270 may represent the Porta Capodimonte at Ancona. In connection with possible further borrowings by Titian in no. 270 attention may be drawn to a suggestion by J. Wilde (note in the Gallery archives) that the figure of Christ in its final form is based on that of a Giorgionesque Venus known from an engraving by Marcantonio Raimondi (Richter, *op. cit.*, pl. LXI, bottom right, reproduces this). Richter (*op. cit.*, p. 225) also mentions 'interesting points of contact' with Fra Bartolommeo's picture of the same subject (Louvre). Kenneth Clark (*Landscape into Art*, 1949, p. 60, note 1) postulates an Antique derivation for the first form of Christ's pose. (5) Generally identified with the picture stated by the Anonimo Morelliano to have been started by Giorgione 'ma lo paese et Cupidine forono finiti da Titiano'. The buildings occur again in the background of a Titianesque *putto* (Vienna Academy 466)—see K. Oettinger in Vienna *Jahrbuch*, 1944, pp. 113 ff. (6) 'Sieurs Forest et Alvarès'. Alvarese is also mentioned in this connection by Bartolommeo dal Pozzo: *Vite de' Pittori . . . Veronesi*, 1718, p. 94. (7) Ridolfi/ Hadeln, I, p. 198. (8) Muselli catalogue quoted by G. Campori: *Raccolta di Cataloghi*, 1870, p. 178: *Christo NS che in forma d'Ortolano apparisce alla Maddalena ed ella genuflessa in atto d'adoratione posa una mano sopra un vase, e l'altra tiene al petto, in un bellissimo paese, figure di un braccio, di Titiano e in altezza quasi 2 ba e 1½ per l'altra parte.* (9) E. Bonnaffé: *Dictionnaire des Amateurs Français*, 1884, p. 21. (10) Preface to vol. 1 of the *Galerie du Palais Royal* (1808, but with title-page of 1786). Also Charles Blanc: *Le Trésor de la Curiosité*, 1858, vol. II, pp. 148–59, and W. Buchanan: *Memoirs*, vol. 1 (1824), pp. 9–220. (11) Passavant: *Tour of a German Artist in England*, vol. II (1836), p. 179. (12) Passavant adds the name 'Rogers' against the picture—evidently as meaning the owner in his day, not the purchaser at the Orléans sale. (13) Buyer's name from notes in the Gallery archives communicated by a relation of A. Champernowne. Redford (II, p. 257) and Buchanan (*loc. cit.*) mention the identity of the Champernowne with the Orléans one.

635 MADONNA AND CHILD WITH SS. JOHN THE BAP-
     TIST AND CATHERINE OF ALEXANDRIA

$39\frac{5}{8} \times 56$ ($1 \cdot 01 \times 1 \cdot 42$).

Somewhat rubbed in places, particularly in the sky, but condition in general considerably better than with the average Titian. Strips about two inches wide on the left and about an inch wide along the bottom are extensively repainted. It is possible that these are additions of canvas replacing frayed pieces of similar size. But as the weave of the canvas in these areas does not noticeably differ from that of the bulk of the picture it is more probable that the painter himself found he had insufficient space at the left and at the bottom and therefore utilized part of the turn-over of the canvas. Microscopic examination shows that S. Catherine's yellow dress has a pink under-painting.

Cleaned 1955.

In the 1861 and 1862 editions of the National Gallery catalogue it is stated that no. 635 is signed and dated 'TICIANUS, 1533'. In editions from 1863 to 1925 inclusive it is said to be 'signed TICIAN'. Before the cleaning of 1955 there was an inventory inscription 'No. 78 Di. Titio' painted at the bottom right corner. This was not old but might have been copied from the back of the original canvas. It was claimed to be an Escorial mark at the time when the picture was bought for the Gallery. In the restoration of 1955 it was covered up. No trace of a signature was found on that occasion and the one variously quoted in the early catalogues is unlikely to have been genuine.

S. Catherine is shown without an attribute but is identifiable by her type.

Two separate attempts have been made to associate no. 635 with contemporary documents but both are inconclusive. Frizzoni[1] identified it with a picture seen by the Anonimo Morelliano in the house of Andrea Odoni in Venice in 1532: *El quadro della nostra donna nel paese, cun el Christo fanziuollo et S. Giovan fanziullo, et S(anta) . . . fu de mano de Titiano*.[2] It is more likely, however, that Odoni's picture was one from the Reynst collection which was part of the Dutch gift to Charles II since the latter also included the Lotto portrait of Odoni himself which is mentioned by the Anonimo in the same context.[3] The fact that the Anonimo does not identify the female saint is a further pointer in this direction since the identity of this figure in the Reynst picture, though called 'St Elizabeth' in the Charles II inventory, might perhaps (to judge from the engraving) give rise to uncertainty. An alternative theory proposes identification of no. 635 with the 'Nostra donna con St Catherina'[4] on which Titian was working in February, 1530 for the Gonzaga and which is probably identical with the 'Madonna, con il bambino in braccio et S. Catterina' of the 1627 Mantua inventory.[5] However, the costumes in no. 635 accord best with a date in the second half of the 1530's.[6]

VERSIONS: A number of copies exist dating from various periods, none of note. More interesting are the variants. One of these, acceptable as from Titian's studio, is in the Pitti gallery, Florence. In this, the Madonna's dress is red, and there is no angel in the sky. It also shows a later moment in the episode. Whereas in no. 635 S. John is offering the Madonna a fruit complete with flower and leaf, in the Pitti variant the Madonna has taken the fruit and handed it to the Child, while S. John has now taken up a kneeling position on the right hand side of the picture and has been joined by the lamb. As in no. 635 there is still a flower between the thumb and first finger of the Madonna's right hand, but as a result of the changes it is now a growing flower which she is plucking and no longer one attached to the fruit. In a further development of this theme (picture in an anonymous sale, Christie's, 29th May, 1952, lot 129) the Child has now jettisoned the fruit and S. John leads on the lamb from the right, instead of kneeling. A version of the latter picture in a late Titianesque idiom was in the collection of the late Dr. Seymour Maynard in London; another (attributed to Schiavone and with the addition of S. Joseph) is at Vienna (no. 149 in the 1938 catalogue). A picture from the Reynst collection now at Hampton Court (no. 112) shows the Madonna as in the Pitti version, but the Child is different, S. John and S. Catherine are omitted and Tobias and the angel have replaced the shepherds in the right background. A distant derivative, showing the Child holding the fruit as in the intermediate versions but with two kneeling clerics instead of S. John and S. Catherine was in the F. E. Sidney sale (Christie's, 10th December, 1937, lot 64) and shown at Agnew's, London, summer 1939.[7] For a copy or variant belonging in 1720 to the Duc de Noailles in Paris see below under PROVENANCE.

DRAWING: Folio 12 of Van Dyck's Italian sketch-book (British Museum). Apparently after S. John.

ENGRAVINGS: 1. By K. Audran (*A Paris de l'Imprimerie de Herman Weyen* . . .) (in reverse). See reference 12 below. 2. By F. Joubert in the Coesvelt catalogue of 1836.

PROVENANCE: Referred to by Mündler in a note dating from 1856 as being then in the Beaucousin collection in Paris and formerly in the Coesvelt collection.[8] It is therefore identifiable with the picture engraved as plate 16 in the catalogue (printed in 1836) of the collection of W. G. Coesvelt, London, which figured as lots 15 and 47 respectively in the Coesvelt sales, Christie's, 2nd June, 1837 and 13th June, 1840 (bought in on the first occasion and perhaps also on the second).[9] In all three of these catalogues stated to have come from the sacristy of the Escorial and therefore fairly certainly identifiable with a picture included in a batch of forty-one sent in 1656 by Velázquez to the Escorial by order of Philip IV: *Otro del mesmo artífice* [i.e. Titian] *de un Deposorio de Santa Caterina. Está Nuestra Señora sentada en un pays; el Niño echado en su regaço; la Santa arrodillada haciéndole caricias; San Ioan Baptista niño, que trae una fruta á la Vírgen que alarga la mano para tomarla . . . Las figuras menores que el natural. Tiene de alto tres piés y medio, de largo casi cinco.*[10] The same picture was described by Francisco de los Santos and by Andres Ximenez in their works on the Escorial.[11] The date (1764) of the latter work (in which the picture is still specified as in the Escorial sacristy) would seem to preclude the identification proposed by Crowe and Cavalcaselle with a picture in the collection of the Duc de Noailles in Paris in 1720.[12] According to Velázquez' memoir the picture seems to have been one of those presented to Philip IV by the Duke de Medina de las Torres on his return to Spain from Italy. Therefore very possibly identical with the *Madonna vestita di turchino col Putto, che sta' con le braccia alte giocando con una donna in ginocchio, che l'abbraccia con S. Giovanno putto a banda dritta, al quale la Madonna porge un fiore . . . di Titiano* which appears in the inventory of 1603 of Cardinal Pietro Aldobrandini (where it is marked as presented to Cardinal Ludovisi in 1621) and which figures in the Ludovisi inventory of 1633 (44).[13] Alternatively it could have reached Spain on the return of Medina de las Torres' predecessor, the Conde de Monterrey, who brought with him the two Titian bacchanals (now in the Prado, but also ex-Aldobrandini and ex-Ludovisi). Purchased with the Beaucousin collection, 1860.

REPRODUCTION: *Illustrations, Italian Schools*, 1937, p. 353.

REFERENCES: (1) Edition of the *Anonimo Morelliano*, 1884, p. 159. (2) For the text of the Anonimo see also Frimmel's edition, 1888, p. 84. (3) See Denis Mahon: *Notes on the 'Dutch Gift' to Charles II, III*, in *Burlington Magazine*, vol. 92 (1950), p. 15. The entry in the Charles II inventory reads: 166. *Titiano. Our Saior. with his feete on a Cusheon the B. Virgin St John and St Elizabeth*. This picture is now lost. (4) See Crowe and Cavalcaselle: *Titian*, vol. 1 (1877), p. 446. (5) See Luzio: *La Galleria dei Gonzaga*, 1913, p. 115, no. 315. (6) Notes by Stella Mary Pearce on the costumes in no. 635 in the Gallery archives. If the Gonzaga picture still exists it is possibly identical with the *Vierge au Lapin* now in the Louvre. This was one of the pictures sold in December, 1665 by the Duc de Richelieu to Louis XIV (see Claude Ferraton: *La Collection du Duc de Richelieu au Musée du Louvre* in *Gazette des Beaux-Arts*, vol. 35 (1949), p. 437). (7) The list of variants could be extended. For example, a Poussin drawing formerly in the Tancred Borenius collection was from a version with S. John on the right and a sleeping hound on the left. Mündler, in his notebook (in the Gallery archives) described a picture in the Patrizi collection, Rome, in 1856: 'School of Titian, a marriage of St Catherine, similar to one in Palazzo Pitti, and to the other, once the property of Mr. Coesvelt, now of Mr. Beaucousin in Paris'. (8) See preceding reference for text of Mündler's note. (9) Mentioned as in the Coesvelt collection by Passavant (*Tour of a German Artist in England*, vol. 1 (1836), p. 185). In the Coesvelt catalogue of 1836 it is stated that the collection was 'principally made in countries subjected to the revolutionary disasters which have overwhelmed the South of Europe'. The provenance of no. 635 from the Escorial is therefore not surprising. Some account of the artistic losses of the Escorial at the time of the Napoleonic invasion is given in Fr. Damian Bermejo: *Descripción artistica del Real Monasterio de S. Lorenzo del Escorial despues de la Invasion de los Franceses* (1820). (10) See *Mémoire de Velazquez sur 41 Tableaux envoyés par Philippe IV à l'Escurial*. Edited by Baron Ch. Davillier, 1874, pp. 50–3. (11) The first edition of Santos' book was published in 1657. (12) Crowe and Cavalcaselle: *Titian*. I (1887), p. 208. The source of the information is Mariette: *Abecedario*, vol. V, p. 307, who identifies the Noailles picture with K. Audran's engraving. Whether in fact this engraving was made from no. 635 or from the Noailles version (assuming that the two were not identical) cannot be determined. Ximenez' statement is, however, not necessarily conclusive, as he drew heavily on his predecessors. (13) *Palatino*, 1964, p. 159, no. 78. Also K. Garas, *Burlington Magazine*, 1967, p. 343, no. 44. H. Wethey (*The Paintings of Titian*, I, 1969, p. 104) states that the picture was in the collection of Alfonso I d'Este. But there is no real evidence of this. There is likewise no evidence for his assertion that the blue pigments were originally glazed.

1944 PORTRAIT OF A MAN

32 × 26 (0·812 × 0·663).

The face somewhat rubbed in places.[1] The main area of the blue sleeve well preserved. The tighter portion of the sleeve (adjoining the sitter's hand) damaged by a network of pin pricks, evidently made in an attempt to treat flaking paint. The parapet extensively restored.

Cleaned 1949.

Inscribed on the parapet: T (with remains of a triangular dot before it) .V. (the dots on either side are triangular). Before the 1949 restoration the inscription read 'TITIANVS. 'IV.' on the left and '.v.' on the right. The v on the right was clearly original, having been painted 'wet in wet'. But of the letters on the left only the T in the 'IV monogram was in the same technique. The letters TITIANVS and the v of the 'IV monogram seem to have been added when the underlying paint was not only dry but already cracked. During the 1949 restoration these letters were not removed but were covered up to match the general tone of the parapet. Whoever amplified the original inscription seems to have thought that the letters 'TV' stood for 'Titiano Vecellio' or 'Titianus Vecellius'. Though this form was frequently used by Titian as a signature on documents he very rarely included the word 'Vecellio', even in an abbreviated form, when signing a picture. Nevertheless, examples do occur, as in the Uffizi portrait of Lodovico Beccadelli, which is signed '. . . Titianus Vecellius . . .' or in the Prado *Entombment*, which is signed 'Titianus Vecellius Aeques Caes'. An abbreviated form, perhaps only an inscription, occurs on the Dresden *Lavinia with a Feather Fan*— 'Lavinia Tit. V. F. AB. EO. P'. It should be borne in mind that the letter V also occurs in inscriptions on the parapet of portraits not by Titian—e.g. in the Berlin Giorgione, which has 'V V', or a portrait formerly in a private collection at Boston (Mass.), attributed to Cariani, which has 'V'.[2] Nevertheless the assumption that the letters T V, on no. 1944 as on no. 5385 of this Gallery, were in fact intended by Titian as a signature seems to the present writer more probable than not.

At the time of its entry into the Gallery no. 1944 was catalogued tentatively as representing Ariosto, whose name had been associated with it (or with another version) at least as early as the seventeenth century. In fact, the features shown bear no resemblance to those in authentic portraits of the poet (see the entry for no. 636, Palma Vecchio). An attempt, first made by J. P. Richter[3] and subsequently supported by others,[4] to identify no. 1944 with a portrait, mentioned by Vasari,[5] of a member of the Barbarigo family is hypothetical and inconclusive. The pose of no. 1944, on the other hand, and the angle of the eyes strongly suggest a self-portrait. Rembrandt's self-portrait of 1640 (now no. 672 of this Gallery) and his etched self-portrait of 1639 may in fact owe something to no. 1944 as may Van Dyck's self-portrait with a sunflower.[6]

There is no authenticated portrait of Titian as a young man or even as a middle-aged one, but those of him in old age show one feature, namely a prognathous bone structure—a huge chin and correspondingly underhung lower lip—which would be relatively unaffected by the symptoms of ageing and which is also present in no. 1944.[7] The costume shown in no. 1944 is similar to that shown in a famous portrait of which several versions are known—e.g. at Leningrad (inscribed 'Dominicus') and in, or formerly in, the collection of the Duke of Grafton.[8] These pictures show the same kind of ruffled shirt as in no. 1944, appearing over the top of a tunic cut on similar lines and with similar enormous sleeves. As both these versions are dated 1512 that would constitute some indication of the date of no. 1944.

Sometimes attributed to Giorgione in the past,[9] but without justification.

VERSION: An old copy, ex-Manfrin collection, in the collection of the Earl of Rosebery at Mentmore. Three other copies are mentioned by Crowe and Cavalcaselle.[10]

ENGRAVINGS: The design engraved by R. van Persijn (in reverse) and De Larmessin (see PROVENANCE below).

PROVENANCE: Perhaps from the collection of Alphonso Lopez and conceivably from that of Sir Anthony Van Dyck. The chief evidence for the Lopez provenance is the Persijn engraving which is inscribed as having been taken from a drawing made by Sandrart in Amsterdam from the original in the possession of Alphonso Lopez.[11] The engraving corresponds closely with no. 1944 (in reverse) except for the legend on the parapet which reads 'TITIANVS. U.' The Lopez painting was due to be sold, with others belonging to him, probably in Paris in mid-December, 1641. A letter, written apparently in November, 1641, asks the addressee, François Langlois, to remind Van Dyck of the Lopez sale, and specifically mentions the excellence of the Titian 'Ariosto'.[12] Van Dyck in fact died (in London) on 9th December, 1641,[13] but an inventory of pictures which had belonged to him, dated 1644, includes an 'Ariosto Poeta' among the Titian's.[14] It is therefore possible that shortly before his death Van Dyck had sent instructions to Paris for the purchase of the picture. But even if the one in his inventory was identical with the Lopez picture (which cannot be proved) it cannot be established with certainty that either was identical with no. 1944 and not a copy.[15] In the possession of the Earl of Darnley before 1824, when lent by him to the British Institution (34). Also lent by Lord Darnley to Manchester, 1857 (236),[16] and to the R.A., 1876 (125) and 1895 (109). Sold to Sir G. Donaldson, 1904, from whom purchased, 1904, with substantial contributions from Lord Iveagh, Mr. Waldorf Astor, Mr. Pierpont Morgan, Mr. Alfred Beit, Lady Wantage, Lord Burton and a grant from H.M. Government.

REPRODUCTION: *Illustrations, Italian Schools*, 1937, p. 354.

REFERENCES: (1) During the restoration of 1949 it was found that the moustaches and beard had been reinforced by later repaint which had changed their outlines and which was therefore removed. (2) Reproduced in Berenson's *Lists* (1957), pl. 732. Cf. *Theatrum Pictorium*, pl. 185 as Palma Vecchio (no V on parapet). (3) *Art Journal*, 1895, p. 90. (4) E.g. H. Cook (*Giorgione*, 1907, pp. 68–73) and Suida (*Tiziano*, 1933, p. 31). (5) Vasari/Milanesi, vol. VII, p. 428. (6) Collection of the Duke of Westminster. For the question of Van Dyck's ownership of no. 1944 see below and Jenny Müller-Rostock in *Zeitschrift für bildende Kunst*, 1922, pp. 22 ff. (7) For the Titian self-portraits see Gronau in the Prussian *Jahrbuch*, 1907, p. 46. (8) The Leningrad version is reproduced and discussed by J. Wilde in the Vienna *Jahrbuch*, 1933, pp. 113–36. The Grafton picture is reproduced as pl. 904 of Berenson's *Lists* (1957). (9) E.g. by Cook, *op. cit.* Also Roger Fry: *Burlington Magazine*, VI, 1904–5, pp. 136 ff. Earlier attributions to Sebastiano del Piombo are recorded by Pallucchini in his monograph on that painter, 1944, p. 185. (10) *Titian*, vol. I, p. 201. (11) Sandrart's drawing is probably the one now in the Lugt collection, The Hague. Like the Mentmore painting it has no inscription on the balustrade but the latter is restored in this place and it is not possible to assert that it never bore an inscription. In the Willem Six sale, Amsterdam, 12th May, 1734, lot 154 was 'Het Pourtrait van L. Ariosto, door Sandrart'. (12) This letter was first published by Bottari (*Raccolta di Lettere . . .*, 1764, vol. IV, p. 303). It is also printed with a commentary in Hofstede de Groot's *Die Urkunden über Rembrandt* (1906, pp. 116–18). Though the letter is signed Jacopo Stella it was stated by Mariette, who owned the original, that it was really by Claude Vignon. In either case it would have been written in Paris, and since the writer states in it that he has just inspected the Lopez pictures it would follow that the Lopez sale took place in Paris. It could hardly have occurred in Amsterdam as stated by Müller-Rostock (*op. cit.*) as the writer asks the addressee to give various messages for him in Holland when he next went there. The letter is undated but must have been written some time in November as the writer of it assumes that Van Dyck, who returned from Paris to London during that month, might still be *en route*. See E. W. Moes in *Oud Holland*, 1894, XII, p. 238. (13) From a pocket-book MS. of Nicassius Roussel, who was at Van Dyck's funeral (notice printed in W. H. Carpenter's *Pictorial Notices . . . of . . . Van Dyck* (1844, p. 44)). De Groot (*op. cit.*, p. 118) is therefore wrong in saying Van Dyck died on 11th December. (14) Müller-Rostock (*loc. cit.*) who published the inventory assumed that it really dated from the 1630's and that in consequence Lopez had acquired the picture after it had belonged to Van Dyck. W. Stechow (*Art Quarterly*, 1942, p. 143) pointed out that there was no reason to suspect the date 1644. (15) G. M. Richter (*Giorgio da Castelfranco*, 1937, p. 225) states that Sandrart copied the painting when it was in the Reynst collection at Amsterdam, and Hoogewerff and van Regteren Altena allege (*Arnoldus Buchelius 'Res Pictoriae'*, 1928, p. 99) that it was in the Van Uffelen collection before that of Lopez. The present writer could find no authority for either of these statements. Hoogewerff and van Regteren Altena (*loc. cit.*) are not justified in suggesting an identification of no. 1944 with a picture seen in the Reynst collection by Buchell. The latter was almost certainly Lotto's Odoni portrait which the authors also mention in this context (see Denis Mahon: *Notes on the Dutch Gift to Charles II*, III in *Burlington Magazine*, vol. 92, 1950, p. 15). (16) In provisional catalogue. No. 257 in definitive catalogue.

3948 MADONNA AND CHILD

$29\frac{3}{4} \times 24\frac{7}{8}$ (0·756 × 0·632).

Cleaned 1962, revealing basic condition as very good. In the 1929 catalogue as 'Mother and Child', but the type of composition is that of a Madonna and Child.

Usually now accepted and acceptable as a work of Titian's extreme old age—probably varying, as he frequently did at this period, one of his own earlier designs (see VERSIONS below). Closely comparable in handling with (and in quality rather superior to) the *Madonna and Child with SS. Tiziano and Francis and a Donor* (Titian himself) in the chapel of S. Tiziano in the Chiesa Arcipretale at Pieve di Cadore. The latter picture is mentioned as Titian's by Vasari.

VERSIONS: A picture sold at Sotheby's on 15th December, 1954 (lot 43) appeared to derive from a version of the same design but in a Titianesque idiom of an earlier phase. An old copy was lot 117, Christie's, 6th February, 1953. Another was exported in 1943.[1] A version with S. Joseph and the infant S. John was published as Titian's by Hadeln (*Burlington Magazine*, vol. LIII, 1928, pp. 55–6) but the attribution has found no support.[2] A photograph of a much damaged version of the central group with male figures on each side was in the library of Gustav Glück.[3] A modern version, by Vanessa Bell, was shown in London in 1939 (Storran Gallery).

ENGRAVING: By 'Petrus de Jode Iunior' (in reverse). Probably dates from before 1634, when the elder de Jode died. A French inscription suggests painting was then in France.[4]

PROVENANCE: Seen by Waagen, 1850–1,[5] in the collection of Lord Ward

(1st Earl of Dudley), by whom exh., Dublin, 1854 (101) and R.A., 1871 (331). Earl of Dudley sale, 25th June, 1892 (89) where bought Mond by whom exh. R.A., 1894 (110) and Grosvenor Gallery, 1913–14 (47). Mond Bequest, 1924.

REPRODUCTION: *Illustrations, Italian Schools*, 1937, p. 351.

REFERENCES: (1) Photographs in the Gallery archives. (2) Hadeln, in his article introduces as analogy the name of Cézanne, who, to judge from the photograph reproduced, would be as acceptable as Titian as author of the picture. (3) Photograph now in the Gallery archives. (4) Information from Christopher White, (5) *Treasures* . . ., vol. II (1854), p. 235.

4452 THE VENDRAMIN FAMILY

$81 \times 118\frac{1}{2}$ (2·06 × 3·01).

Some compression has occurred on the left during painting—an earlier version of the young bearded man's head is visible through the blue of the sky. The outline of the calf of a leg is visible through the red velvet robe of the left central figure. Infra-red photography discloses further underpainting in this figure which is not visible to the naked eye, namely the calf and thigh of the figure's other leg (his left) resting on the step, together with various scribbles for draperies. *Pentimenti* in the outlines of all three principal figures. X-ray photographs disclose further *pentimenti* in the head of the boy on the extreme left. Cleaned 1973–4.

Condition unequal. Most of the sky is very worn and extensively re-touched. Also the fur lining of the left sleeve of the kneeling central figure. The following areas are well preserved: the faces of all three adults, the red velvet robe and right hand of the left central figure, the piece of red velvet over the right arm of the kneeling central figure, the little boy with red stockings on the right (including the head of the dog he holds), the ewer and candlestick above the altar. Of the faces of the other children the two on the extreme right are in reliable state except for the small shadowed areas which are retouched. The face of the central boy in the group on the left is retouched in the nostril and round the eyes. The paint in the face of the boy on the extreme left is 'frizzled' and also retouched.

The cleaning of 1973–4 showed that the striped silk on the altar, the green doublet of the little boy with the dog and the grey doublet of the boy on the extreme left had all been overpainted in dark colours long after the picture was finished. There was also much repaint on the sleeve of the boy on the extreme right. All this repaint was removed. The cleaning also left little or no doubt that the picture had been cut down on both sides and at the base.

The persistent (and exaggerated) allegations that no. 4452 was a ruined picture seem to stem from a remark made by Reynolds in a letter to Lord Upper Ossory. Reynolds says that 'to painters' eyes' no. 4452 and 'the picture of Van Dyck at Wilton' were 'hardly worth the name of good copies' since cleaning.[1] It is likely that Benjamin West knew Reynolds' opinion and was influenced by it, since he too links Van Dyck's Wilton *Pembroke Family* (presumably the one Reynolds meant) with no. 4452 as being pictures ruined by cleaning.[2] Something of these rumours reappeared when the picture was acquired by the Gallery in 1929, but they were answered in a letter from Lionello Venturi asserting that the condition was remarkably good.[3]

The cross shown on the altar is a reliquary of the True Cross. It had been presented in 1360 by pilgrims to the Patriarch of Constantinople who had made it over to Philippe de Maizières, *Cancelliere* of the Kingdom of Cyprus, who had presented it, on 23rd December, 1369, to Andrea Vendramin, *Guardiano* of the Scuola di S. Giovanni Evangelista, Venice, on behalf of his confraternity.[4] It has been preserved in the Scuola, or in the church, ever since and is still recognizable as that shown in no. 4452 and, among other pictures, in Gentile Bellini's *Miracle of the Cross* (Venice, Accademia).[5] The last-named picture illustrates the most memorable connection of the cross with the Vendramin family— namely the occasion when the cross fell into a canal but remained miraculously suspended above the water until Andrea Vendramin was privileged to jump in and save it.[6] This fact, and the following entry in part of an inventory made in March, 1569, of the collection of Gabriel Vendramin, leave no doubt of the subject of no. 4452: *un quadro grando nel qual li retrazo le crose miracolose con ser Andrea Vendramin con sette fioli et mesier Gabriel Vendramin con suo adornamento d'oro fatto de man de sier Titian.*[7] The early date of this inventory (i.e. within Titian's life-time) together with its reliable character (this part of it was apparently drawn up by Tintoretto and by Titian's son, Orazio)[8] constitute excellent documentation of Titian's authorship of no. 4452.

Pouncey (*loc. cit.*) has suggested plausibly that no. 4452 may have been commissioned by the Vendramin family for a dual purpose. They would have wished in the first place to commemorate the prowess of an ancestor in rescuing the sacred relic. But the cross in addition had safeguarded the family's commercial interests on an earlier occasion, and for that reason they may well have wished, by means of the picture, to invoke continued protection.

Usually dated too late. Crowe and Cavalcaselle put it around 1560[9] and when Gronau discovered the correct identification he let himself be unduly influenced by the fact that Gabriel Vendramin died in 1552 and proposed a date around 1550.[10] Further research in the Archivio di Stato at Venice has, however, established not only that Gabriel's eldest nephew, Leonardo, predeceased him, dying in October, 1547, but that Andrea died earlier still, in January of that year.[11] Andrea's seven sons were: Leonardo (or Lunardo), born 1523, died 1547, Luca, born 1528, Francesco, born 1529, Bortolomeo, born 1530, Giovanni, born 1532, Filippo, born 1534 and Federico, born 1535. In addition to these seven sons Andrea Vendramin was the father of six daughters.[12]

As regards the identification of the figures in the picture, the man standing left centre in the red velvet robe is nearest Andrea's sons and also indicates them with his right hand. The deduction from this would be that he was Andrea. But as the latter is now thought to have been three years older than his brother Gabriel it may be that Andrea is the man kneeling, centre, and Gabriel (the collector of works of art) the man standing on the spectator's left of him. Andrea's eldest son, Leonardo (five years older than the next son) is clearly the bearded figure on the left. Of the remaining six sons the three kneeling in the left foreground are certainly older than the three on the right, so whatever the order within the groups the left would consist of the second, third and fourth sons (Luca, Francesco, Bortolomeo) and the right the three youngest (Giovanni, Filippo and Federico). Andrea Vendramin's death in January, 1547 gives a *terminus ad quem* for at least the start of the picture. But even this is too late, as Andrea's second, third and fourth sons are all shown beardless, and the eldest of these three, Luca, being born in March, 1528, would then have been nearly nineteen. The fashion for wearing beards was so general in the 'forties of the sixteenth century that it can be assumed that a youth would do so as soon as he could, and it is therefore most unlikely that Luca was more than about fifteen when the picture was started.[13] The latest date for it on these grounds is therefore about 1543. From a stylistic point of view this date is also about the earliest possible. The *Ecce Homo* (Vienna) which is dated (i.e. finished) as of that year is usually regarded as marking a new phase of Titian's style, and one to which no. 4452 belongs. The two pictures have in fact elements both of design and handling in common which would support the assumption of a similar date of origin. On two grounds, therefore, it is reasonable to suppose that no. 4452 would have been started around the year 1543. As with other of Titian's works there may well have been a delay of some years before it was completed.

VERSIONS: Old copy at Hampton Court by Symon Stone. Another, from the Lady Lucas collection, belonged to Lt.-Col. Pepys-Cockerell in 1929 (photograph in the Gallery archives). A third was at Northwick Park (no. 71 in Borenius' catalogue of 1921). A fourth was in the Neeld collection. A copy made by Gainsborough from an engraving was lot 575 in the Samuel Rogers sale, 2nd May, 1856. A sketch copy (drawing) is at Alnwick (photograph in the Gallery archives).

ENGRAVING: By Bernard Baron, London, 1732 (in reverse, with dedication to the then owner, the 6th Duke of Somerset).

PROVENANCE: Vendramin family, Venice (see above). Apparently remained in Venice until at least 1636[14] and entered the collection in England of Sir Anthony Van Dyck some time between then and his death in 1641.[15] Purchased by the 10th Earl of Northumberland from Van Dyck's executors in the year ending 17th January, 1645-6.[16] In the possession of the Earls and Dukes of Northumberland (and, from 1682 to 1750, of the Dukes of Somerset) in various residences—Suffolk House (1652), Northumberland House (1671, and 1750-1873), Petworth (1671-1750, or earlier), 2 Grosvenor Place, London (1873-c. 1900) and Alnwick Castle (c. 1900-29)[17]—until 1929, when purchased from the 8th Duke, with the aid of a special Grant and of contributions from Samuel Courtauld, Sir Joseph Duveen, the N.A.-C.F. and the Phillips fund. Exh. B.I., 1818 (86) and 1846 (109), R.A., 1873 (146) and 1930 (168),[18] National Gallery (N.A.-C.F. Exhibition), 1945-6 (15).

REPRODUCTION: *Illustrations, Italian Schools*, 1937, p. 355.

REFERENCES: (1) Letter printed in Leslie and Taylor's *Life of Sir Joshua Reynolds*, II, p. 495. (2) Farington Diary, vol. VIII, p. 179. Reynolds and West were not to be the last Presidents of the Royal Academy to utter such sentiments on this topic. (3) Letter to *The Times* newspaper, 1st August, 1929. Waagen (*Treasures*, I, 393) speaks lugubriously of 'this masterpiece' having 'suffered not a little injury' but merely instances 'the right hand of the old man and one hand of the boy on the left'. (4) Giacomo de Mezi: *Miracoli della Croce Santissima della Scuola de San Giovanni Evangelista*, Venice, 1590. See also Philip Pouncey: *The Miraculous Cross in Titian's Vendramin Family*, in *Journal of the Warburg Institute*, vol. II (1939), p. 191. (5) G. M. Urbani de Gheltof: *Guida Storico-Artistica della Scuola di S. Giovanni Evangelista*, Venice, 1895. (6) An account of the event is given by Francesco Sansovino: *Venetia Città Nobilissima . . .*, 1581, p. 100. (7) Printed by Aldo Ravà: *Il 'Camerino delle Antigaglie' di Gabriele Vendramin* in *Nuovo Archivio Veneto*, Nuova serie, tomo XXXIX (1920), p. 117. Attention was drawn to this article by Georg Gronau (*Apollo*, II, 1925, pp. 126 f) who first connected the picture with this entry. Previously it has been known as 'The Cornaro Family'. (8) Ravà, *op. cit.*, p. 181. (9) *Titian*, vol. II (1877), p. 303. (10) *Op. cit.* (11) The following biographical information is from documents (kindly communicated by the Director) in the Archivio di Stato at Venice. Andrea in fact died on 31st January, 1546—i.e. 1547, new style. (12) Documents in the Archivio di Stato, Venice already quoted. (13) This point can be neatly illustrated by studying Moretto's *Feast in the House of Simon* of 1544 (Venice, S. Maria della Pietà). In this picture one of the two young and stylish serving men on the left has a young beard, the other has one just sprouting. (14) Almost certainly identical with a picture mentioned in a letter of 9th September, 1636 from Lord Arundel's son Maltravers as being for sale in Venice (printed in *English Travellers Abroad, 1604–1667* by J. W. Stoye (1952), p. 124): *I have heard that there is a picture of Titian at Venice to bee sould for five or 6 hundred duccatts. I desire that you would enquire diligently after it, and if you like it to give earneste for it, for it is for the King, although his name must not be used. As I heare it hath some 4 or 5 figures in it, drawen after the life of some of the Nobilitye of Vennice.* (15) Recognizable as the first item in an inventory (at Vienna) of Van Dyck's collection: *Tre senatori di Venezia con loro figlioli in un quadro di Titiano* (see Jenny Müller-Rostock in *Zeitschrift für bildende Kunst*, 1922, pp. 22–4). (16) Entry in a document in the Alnwick archives published by Oliver Millar (*Burlington Magazine*, vol. XCVII, August, 1955, p. 255): (year ending 17th January, 1645–6) *for 2 pictures for his Lop. one called the Senators the other the Andromida CCli.* This corrects the date (1656) given for the purchase in the R.A. catalogue (winter exhibition), 1873, which has been widely followed. There can be no doubt of the identity. The picture was already known as 'The Senators'—an unpublished indenture (owned by the Craigie family of Sydney, Australia—photographs in the Gallery library) of 1650 concerning Van Dyck's estate refers to it in those words. See also Richard Symonds' statement 'the great picture of Titian Senators of Venice' when he saw it in the Earl of Northumberland's house in 1652 (*Walpole Society*, 1930, p. 113). A further document in the Alnwick archives (Northumberland MSS. W II 2) of 1656 regularized the sale, ten years before, of the two Titian's from Van Dyck's estate. The present writer is grateful to Oliver Millar for drawing his attention to this. (17) Information received from the Duke of Northumberland at the time of purchase. (18) Also figures as no. 64 in the catalogue of the Burlington Fine Arts Club exhibition of Titian, 1914, but was not in fact exhibited.

5385 PORTRAIT OF A LADY ('LA SCHIAVONA')

47 × 38 (1·18 × 0·97).

Much abraded, particularly in the face. The highlights of the braid in the head-dress, some of the white drapery and the marble relief in fair state. Cleaned 1959–60.

Inscribed on the parapet: .T. .V.

Of these letters the black strokes and the dots flanking them are of a different texture of paint from the surrounding grey and in places they cover cracks. They are therefore not original. But the paint of the two lighter strokes—part of the vertical of the T and the right arm of the V— gives every sign of being genuine—they were probably intended as the lighter faces of a *trompe-l'œil* 'incised' inscription. It may therefore be concluded that the existing letters T and V (which are recorded as early as 1641—see PROVENANCE below) are the remains of original initials. It seems to the present writer more probable than not that these letters stand for 'Titianus Vecellius', but see the entry for no. 1944, where the same letters occur, for an expression of some reserve. At some stage in the picture's history it seems that clumsy attempts were made to expand the 'T V' into 'TITIANVS'. The two existing letters are very deliberately spaced, dividing the lower portion of the parapet into three approximately equal lengths. The harmony of these intervals would however be broken if the existing T were used either as the first or as the third letter of 'TITIANVS'. Judging by the remains of further letters still visible it looks as though both these possibilities were tried. The space (in which there are faint traces of further letters) between the existing letters T and V would be sufficient to contain the intermediate letters I, T, I, A and N, but the final S after the V would then bring the whole word too far to the right. If, on the other hand, the existing T were used as the third letter there would be too much space between it and the V to account for the three letters I, A and N. Realization of this seems to have led to an alternative 'improvement'. There are traces not only of another T and an I before the existing T but also of an upright after the existing V. This latter fact suggests that the form 'TIT VEC', which would have solved the problem of symmetry, may have been toyed with at some stage. Consideration of these various factors leads the present writer to conclude that there is no valid reason for supposing that the original inscription ever consisted of more than the letters T and V, probably flanked by dots.[1]

The extensive changes made on the right hand side of the picture are visible to the naked eye where the red of the drapery shows through the grey of the marble. Evidently the raised portion of the parapet with the relief was an afterthought. The lady's left arm would thus have hung down like her right (Sir Charles Holmes thought that her left hand originally rested on a skull, but X-ray photographs give no confirmation of this).[2] The raising of the parapet on the right, which introduced a greater degree of asymmetry into the design, would have left a blank space which was filled by a painted marble relief—apparently of the same lady, but with pseudo-classical hair style and draperies instead of the fashionable ones worn in the main portrait. During the process the artist seems to have transformed some, at least, of the underlying contours of the original left sleeve into grains in the marble. X-ray photographs show an oval form partly encircling the area now occupied by the marble head in relief on the parapet. Also (top right corner) a rectangle enclosing clouds, and itself enclosed within a truncated circular form. This rectangle, with the clouds and truncated circle, later came to light, when the picture was cleaned in 1959–60. They had evidently been covered over at a very early stage and had then been revealed by an early restorer before being covered again. On the parapet, immediately to the left of the forehead and nose of the bust in relief, the remains of a large v are visible. These things were discussed at length in an article by the present writer in the *Burlington Magazine*, August, 1961. Alterations such as these are too common, particularly in Venetian painting, to justify in themselves an assumption that the picture was begun by one artist and finished by another. The type of portrait, its style and the presence of the initials T v leave no reasonable doubt of Titian's participation. The theory that the picture was started by Giorgione was evolved by Cook[3] by reviving a speculative identification of the sitter with Caterina Cornaro and then identifying the picture with a portrait of Caterina by Giorgione, recorded by Vasari as formerly in the house of Giovanni Cornaro.[4] The pedigree of no. 5385 cannot be traced back farther than shortly before the year 1640 and at this time it is already referred to as 'La Schiavona by Titian'. It is datable around the year 1511 by the costume which is precisely comparable with that in Titian's frescoes of that year in the Scuola del Santo at Padua. As Caterina Cornaro had died in 1510 at the age of fifty-six any portrait of her painted around that date and showing her, as in no. 5385, as a young woman, would constitute an imaginative exercise to which considerations of likeness would scarcely be relevant.[5] Nevertheless, the Caterina Cornaro identification is so far-fetched as to be totally unacceptable, and with it goes the main reason for assuming Giorgione's participation. The connection of no. 5385 with Titian's Padua frescoes is so close that there seems no valid reason for doubting his responsibility for the whole of it.[6]

DRAWING: Ugo Monneret de Villard (*Giorgione*, 1904) considered a drawing in the Uffizi (no. 718, rep. in Hadeln: *Zeichnungen des Tizian*, pl. 18) to be a preliminary study.

ENGRAVING: By Alessandro Sala. No. XIX in his *Collezione de' Quadri Scelti di Brescia*, 1817.

PROVENANCE: Mentioned in a letter of 17th November, 1640 (quoted by A. Venturi in his catalogue of the Crespi collection) addressed to Conte Alessandro Martinengo Colleone of Brescia, who had been outlawed in 1634. It appears from this letter that the Count had obtained the picture from a 'mercante di negri'. Described in detail in a related document of 12th August, 1641: *un quadro di pittura detto la Schiavona dal ginocchio in sù, qual tiene la mano su una testa finta in pietra di marmo bianco, et sotto improntato colle lettere T.V. che è di mano di Titiano pittore*. The picture was by this time in the hands of Contessa Giulia Olmo, the wife of Conte Alessandro. In the latter document Contessa Giulia was required to surrender the picture within three days[7] of 12th August, 1641. She had not, however, done so by the 11th November of that year[8] and presumably evaded doing so altogether since Sala's engraving of 1817 states that the picture was then in the possession of Conte Vincenzo Martinengo of Brescia. Recorded by Crowe and Cavalcaselle (*Titian*, vol. II, 1877, p. 58) as belonging to Signor Francesco Riccardi of Bergamo who was the brother-in-law of Conte Venceslao Martinengo Colleoni di Cavernago.[9] By 1900 in the Crespi Gallery, Milan.[10] Sold by Crespi, c. 1911–12, to Wildenstein, from whom bought, 1914, by Herbert Cook.[11] Exh. Burlington Fine Arts Club, 1914 (55) (lent Cook), R.A., 1930 (385) (lent Cook). Presented through the N.A-C.F. by Sir Francis Cook, Bart., 1942, in memory of his father, Sir Herbert Cook, Bart.

REPRODUCTION: *16-century Italian School plates*, 1964, pp. 226–7.

REFERENCES: (1) Francesco Malaguzzi Valeri (*Rassegna d'Arte*, 1, 1901, pp. 41–3) reads the inscription as 'TIT V' and assumes that the first two letters, though nearly effaced, were part of the original lettering. He quotes the restorer, Cavenaghi, as saying 'la scritta è contemporanea', but exactly which part of the 'scritta' is not specified. Cook (catalogue of the Cook collection, vol. III, p. 176) quotes Cavenaghi as considering only the letters T and V as original. The cleaning of 1959–60 in no way affected the letters T V. (2) Sir Charles Holmes in *Burlington Magazine*, October, 1914. (3) Herbert Cook: *Giorgione*, 1907, pp. 74–81; cf. also an extract from a monograph quoted on pp. 172–7 of vol. III of the Cook catalogue (1915). (4) Vasari/Milanesi, vol. IV, pp. 98–9. (5) The inscribed portrait of Caterina Cornaro by Gentile Bellini (Budapest) is in fact remarkably unlike the sitter in no. 5385. See also portrait by the same artist in his 'Miracle of the True Cross' (Venice, Accademia). The matter is best discussed by Gronau (*Repertorium für Kunstwissenschaft*, 1908, pp. 512–13). Giuseppe Maria Bonomi (pamphlet on no. 5385 published at Bergamo, 1886, p. 13) suggests plausibly that the title of no. 5385 was deliberately changed from 'La Schiavona' to 'Portrait of Caterina Cornaro' to mislead the Venetian authorities in the mid-seventeenth century when they were trying to confiscate the picture (see below under PROVENANCE). A portrait inscribed as of Caterina Cornaro also catalogued in the Cook collection (vol. III, p. 179) together with its replicas and the fancy portrait after Titian (Uffizi) are irrelevant in this context as being posthumous. (6) A. Venturi's attribution to Licinio has found no support and cannot be sustained (*La Galleria Crespi in Milano*, 1900, p. 133). The Giorgione attribution has been revived more recently by J. Wilde (*Festschrift Alexis Petrovics*, Budapest, 1934)—'wahrscheinlich ebenfalls eine Schöpfung Giorgiones'. G. M. Richter (*Giorgio da Castelfranco*, 1937, p. 236) maintained 'Giorgione, finished by Titian'. Holmes (*loc. cit.*) proposed that the alterations in the parapet of no. 5385 were made by Titian much later (about 1540) and Cook used this to the advantage of his theory by claiming that Titian made these changes in what he (Cook) regarded as Giorgione's work at the time when he painted the original of the fancy portrait in the Uffizi. There is however no acceptable evidence in support of this hypothesis and the present writer sees no reason to doubt that the changes were made during the course of painting the picture. (7) Thus Bonomi. Venturi, in the Crespi catalogue, gives 'giorni sei' instead of 'giorni tre' as well as other variations. (8) All this information from G. M. Bonomi, *op. cit.* (9) Bonomi, *loc. cit.* (10) Venturi, *loc. cit.* (11) Cook, *loc. cit.*

6376   AN ALLEGORY OF PRUDENCE

30 × 27 (0·762 × 0·685).

The head of the bearded man on the left has worn thin, and during the restoration of 1966 earlier positions of it, to the spectator's right of the profile as now visible, were disclosed. These have since been covered up. Otherwise the picture is in good condition. Cleaned, 1966.

The Latin inscription at the top reads:

EX PRÆTERITO PRÆSENS PRVDENTER AGIT NI
FVTVR- ACTIONĒ DETVRPET

There is some doubt about some of the letters, and about the syntax, but the general sense is evidently that the present does well to profit by the past when planning future action. The inscription is arranged in three sections, those on the right and left being set at an inclined angle, while the centre one is straight. The three sections are thus specifically associated with the respective heads underneath them in a pictorial sense, and the meanings also correspond. The words referring to the past are above the head of the old man on the left, and those referring to the present and the future above the heads of the middle-aged man in the centre and the youth on the right respectively.

Triple heads of this kind had already been used earlier in the Renaissance to associate the ideas of time, experience and prudence. A relief in the Victoria and Albert Museum, ascribed to the school of Desiderio de Settignano, shows the triple human heads only. A similar triple human head occurs in one of the illustrations (facing page y) to the *Hypnerotomachia Poliphili*, which had been published at Venice in 1499 and which would certainly have been known to Titian. The X-ray photographs of the present painting show that he may have based this part of the picture on this wood-cut: the neck of the central head seems to come down into a collar decorated on the left with leaf patterns of similar type to what appears in the wood-cut. Titian then changed his mind and painted in another triple head, this time of animals, under the first one. A wood cut of this type is reproduced on the very next page (page y) of the *Hypnerotomachia Poliphili*, and both types, human and animal, are shown as trophies or standards being carried in procession in the two succeeding illustrations (yI *verso* and yII). This confirms that the book was probably one of Titian's sources. This triple-headed beast —wolf, lion and dog—may originally have been derived from Cerberus in Greek and Roman antiquity, but it had then been associated with Serapis, one of the gods of Hellenistic Egypt, as is explained in the text of the *Hypnerotomachia* which accompanies the illustration. A book called *Hieroglyphica*, by Pierio Valeriano, published in 1556, associates the three-headed beast with prudence, like the three-headed human, and this book was probably another source known to Titian. The X-ray photographs of no. 6376 also show what seems to be a scroll curling round the three human heads.

The object of the picture is likely to have been a personal one. The head of the old man on the left resembles Titian himself in old age, as may be seen by comparing it with the self-portrait in the Prado.[1] For that reason it has been supposed that the central head represents his son, Orazio, and the youth on the right a young cousin, Marco Vecellio, who was born in 1545. Erwin Panofsky who has written copiously on the symbolism of this picture in his book *Meaning in the Visual Arts* and elsewhere,[2] suggests that by means of it Titian may have intended to commemorate legal and financial measures taken in connection with his estate. If the head on the right does indeed represent Marco Vecellio the picture would have been painted not earlier than about 1560, when Titian himself was not less than about 70 years old. Stylistically it is acceptable as a work dating from his last period.

PROVENANCE: Crozat, Paris (no. 157 in the 1740 inventory). Duc de Tallard sale, Paris, 1756, no. 84 (with fanciful identifications of the three heads as Alfonso d'Este, Pope Julius II, and the Emperor Charles V) as from the Crozat collection. In or before 1766 in the collection of the Chevalier Menabuoni (*Dictionnaire pittoresque & historique d'Hébert*, 1766, quoted in the *Livre-Journal de Lazare Duvaux*, 1873, tome 1, p. CCXCI, with the same fanciful identifications). Lucien Bonaparte sale, London, 3rd day's sale, 16th May, 1816, no. 167 (still with the same identifications). Lent by the Earl of Aberdeen to the British Institution 1828, no. 14 (same identifications) and to Edinburgh, 1883 (exhibition of Old Masters and Scottish National Portraits, no. 335).[3] Acquired by Alfred de Rothschild, not long before his death in January 1918 and bequeathed by him to Almina, Countess of Carnarvon.[5] Countess of Carnarvon sale, Christie's, 31st May, 1918 (usual identifications) (bought 'Roberts'). Acquired by Francis Howard before June, 1924 when lent by him to Messrs. Agnew's.[6] Lent by Francis Howard to the R.A. (*Holbein and other Masters*, 1950–1, no. 209). Francis Howard sale, Christie's, 25th November, 1955, no. 44 (bought Leggatt). Presented by David Koetser, 1966.

REPRODUCTION: National Gallery Report, January 1965–December 1966, pl. 3.

REFERENCES: (1) For some discussion of Titian's self-portraits see the entry for no. 1944 (Portrait of a Man). (2) E.g. *Hercules am Scheidewege*, 1930, pp. 1–35, and (with Fritz Saxl) in the *Burlington Magazine*, vol. 49, 1926, pp. 177 ff. The picture had first been published by von Hadeln in *Burlington Magazine*, vol. 45, 1924, p. 179. There is also an article in the *Gazette des Beaux-Arts*, 1966 by Madlyn Kahr. (3) *Chronique des Arts*, 1883, p. 252. (4) Private information. (5) Information from Alfred de Rothschild's will. (6) Information from von Hadeln's article, *loc. cit.*

6420   THE DEATH OF ACTAEON

$70\frac{3}{8} \times 78$ (1·788 × 1·981).

Very good condition for its age and size. A little worn in places, particularly in the female figure's flesh. The original paint is missing in an irregular area ca. 7 × 10″ just inside the lower right corner.

X-rays show that the main figure's right arm was not originally bent but more or less straight, the lower part of it, from the elbow to the hand, continuing the line of the upper part. The left arm, holding the bow, was a little higher.

The interpretation of the scene presents difficulties. The subjects of all the earlier paintings in the series of *poesie* for Philip II of Spain, of which the present picture was one of the last—*Danäe, Venus and Adonis, Perseus and Andromeda, Diana surprised by Actaeon, Callisto's Pregnancy, Rape of Europa*—are to be found in Ovid's *Metamorphoses*. In particular, the picture of *Diana surprised by Actaeon* (now Duke of Sutherland, on loan to the National Gallery of Scotland)—a scene which immediately preceded, and caused, Actaeon's death—follows Ovid's account fairly closely. Ovid then goes on to describe how Diana, not having, in her nakedness, her arrows to hand with which to punish Actaeon for intruding, splashed water on his face, and invited him to tell the world how he had seen her naked—if he could ('nunc tibi me posito visam velamine narres / sit poteris narrare, licet').[1] Whereupon he was transformed into a stag, and fled, pursued by his hounds, who caught up with him and killed him.

The main difficulty is thus that in Ovid's account Diana was not present at the scene of Actaeon's death. Secondly, Actaeon had left her naked and without her weapons only just before. Finally, the female in the present picture does not wear Diana's crescent in her hair (as the goddess does in both of Titian's previous depictions of her in the series). The illustrated catalogue of the Orléans collection (volume II, 1808) suggested for this reason that the female figure in the present picture was not Diana herself but one of her nymphs. Nevertheless, they were last seen naked also (in the *Diana surprised by Actaeon*), so some other explanation should be sought.

It would be possible that Titian, in this case, was drawing on a literary source other than Ovid, but perhaps more likely that he was deliberately altering Ovid in order to suit his, and his patron's, taste. There is no doubt that the series had a strong erotic intent, and that the depiction of Actaeon's death as described by Ovid—with no female present—would have been out of place. The further considerations that there was no need for anyone to shoot at Actaeon (as he is shown already half a stag, and already being attacked by his hounds), that (at least now) the female figure's bow has no arrow and no bow string, and that in an earlier state, as shown in the X-rays, the female figure may not have been shooting but merely holding her bow aloft may mean that she is not intended to be read as a literal presence but rather as a personification of Diana's vengeance.

This female figure evidently derives visually from an Antique source. An engraving of a cameo, inscribed 'Diana Cacciatrice' is included in Lachausse's *Le Gemme Antiche Figurate* (1700) and gives the essentials of the pose, including the leaping hound. Other similarities may be found in the so-called *Diana of Versailles* (Louvre)[2]

In a letter of the 19th June, 1559 to Philip II of Spain Titian said 'mi darò tutto a fornir . . . l'altre due poesie già incominciate, l'una di Europa sopra il Tauro, l'altra di Atheone lacerato da i cani suoi'. Titian reports progress with the *Europa* in further letters (22nd April, 1560, 2nd April, 1561 and 17th August, 1561) always linked with an *Agony in the Garden*. Both the latter pictures are announced as finished in a letter of the 26th April, 1562.[3] There is no further reference in the published correspondence to the *Death of Actaeon*, and the sense of the letters already mentioned suggests that Titian is unlikely to have resumed work on it until after April, 1562. Similarities in handling which it shows with the *Annunciation* in S. Salvador, Venice (the angel's head in that work and the head of the female in the present picture are very close; the *Annunciation* was already finished when Vasari, who speaks of it, visited Venice in 1566) could indicate that the bulk of the work may date from the mid 1560's.[4]

The next reference to a painting by Titian of this subject is in a letter of the 28th November, 1568 from Veit von Dornberg, Imperial ambassador at Venice, to the Emperor Maximilian II.[5] In this an offer is made

to the latter of paintings by Titian of Diana and Endymion, Actaeon at
the Fountain, the Death of Actaeon, the Pregnancy of Callisto, Adonis
killed by a Boar, Andromeda freed by Perseus, and Europa on the Bull.
All these are stated to be 'un palmo più largi che quello della religion,
che già si mandò a sua maestà caesarea'. In reply the Emperor expressed
his opinion that Titian was then too old to paint well.

Of these subjects, the originals of the Actaeon at the Fountain (*Diana
surprised by Actaeon*) and the Pregnancy of Callisto had been sent to
Philip II, probably at the end of 1559, and the Europa, as already stated,
was reported to Philip as finished in April, 1562. It follows that the
pictures of these subjects offered to the Emperor Maximilian cannot have
been identical with the originals done for Philip II, and were therefore
replicas. X-rays of the *Pregnancy of Callisto* (now Vienna)—generally
assumed, without proof, to be one of the series offered to Maximilian—
show the same forms as the original painted for Philip II and now in the
Sutherland collection, but the paint as visible to the naked eye shows
differences. It is therefore likely that this picture, and probably also the
others in the set offered to Maximilian, were studio replicas partly re-
worked by Titian himself. As it is unlikely that he would include an
original in a series of this kind it would be possible that the original of
the *Death of Actaeon* was no longer available. Since Philip II had been
apprized of its existence it could hardly have been sold to anyone else,
and may therefore already have gone to Spain. The fact that it does not
figure in the list of his paintings sent by Titian to Philip in 1574[6] has
contributed to the general opinion that the *Death of Actaeon* never
reached him, but this does not follow, as Titian himself says in that list
that there had been many others which he could no longer remember.
It is true, however, that no mention of such a picture has been found
in the Spanish royal collection in the seventeenth century.

The next reference to a picture of the Death of Actaeon by Titian
(though misnamed) occurs in an undated inventory thought to be of the
collection of Bartolomeo della Nave at Venice and sent by Lord Fielding,
British Ambassador in Venice, to his brother-in-law, the Marquess of
Hamilton, in the years 1636–8.[7] The entry in question reads: '9. A
Diana shooting Adonis in forme of a Hart not quite finished Pal 12 & 10
Titian'. This was evidently the picture acquired by Hamilton and
included in an inventory of pictures then belonging to him and then for
sale, dating from 1649.[8] The entry reads: 'Titian . . . 10 Une Diana
tirant avec un arc contre Adonis aussi grand que le naturel elle dans un
païsage avec des chiens, h. 12, la. 14 pa'.

It has been established that the bulk of Hamilton's Venetian pictures
were bought by the Archduke Leopold William.[9] One of many views of
the interior of his gallery at Brussels is dated 1651 and includes an
accurate representation of the present picture (the gallery interior is by
Teniers and is now no. 458 of the Musées Royaux des Beaux-Arts,
Brussels). On the other hand, a print in Teniers' collection of the Archduke Leopold William's Italian pictures, the *Theatrum Pictorium*, shows
the design of the Death of Actaeon, in reverse and in an elongated format,

revealing the whole of Diana's left leg and foot (which is truncated in the present picture and in the small representation in the gallery interior by Teniers of 1651) as well as some empty space behind her. The *Theatrum Pictorium* was published at Antwerp in 1660, but the sketches for it had been made some years previously, in some cases, at least, several years before the Archduke transferred his collection from Brussels to Vienna in 1656. In the *Theatrum Pictorium* print the dimensions of the picture of the Death of Actaeon are stated to be '9 alta. 12 lata', which are roughly the proportions as shown in the relevant print. There is no picture by Titian of a Death of Actaeon included in the inventory of 1659 of the Archduke Leopold William's Italian pictures (517 in number) made when the collection reached Vienna,[10] but one is included in the *Prodromus* (1735), or views of the Imperial collection at Vienna (to which the major part of the Archduke's collection—that which had not already been presented by him to his brother, the Emperor, in his life time—passed at his death in 1662). This also shows a long format, with space behind Diana, and is apparently identical with the picture engraved in the *Theatrum Pictorium*. In 1735 the present picture was in Paris in the Orléans collection, and therefore cannot be the same one.[11] Since it is equally difficult to identify the *Prodromus/Theatrum Pictorium* picture with the one in the Teniers gallery view of 1651, or *not* to identify the latter with the present picture, the conclusion would be that there were two separate versions in the collection of the Archduke Leopold William around the year 1650. The first would be the present picture (i.e. the original, mentioned as started by Titian in 1559) and the second, the one in the *Theatrum Pictorium* and *Prodromus*. The latter may have been identical with one of the replicas offered to the Emperor Maximilian in 1568. It would have to be assumed that the present picture had passed from the Archduke Leopold William to Queen Christina between 1651 and 1661–2 (when it is first definitely recorded in her possession, see PROVENANCE). The most likely channel would be by gift on the occasion of Christina's conversion which took place in Brussels in 1654. The possibility would have to be considered that the picture had entered the possession of the Archduke from a source other than the Della Nave/Hamilton collection. As Leopold William was the first cousin of Philip IV of Spain, as well as his viceroy in the Spanish Netherlands, another royal gift (to the former from the latter) would be by no means impossible. The fact that neither version is included in the 1659 inventory of the Archduke's collection could mean that, like the Vienna version of the *Pregnancy of Callisto*, the *Theatrum Pictorium/Prodromus Actaeon* would have been among the pictures sent by the Archduke from Brussels in 1651 to the Emperor in Vienna.[12] Its present whereabouts is not known. The present picture would have been in Christina's possession by the time of the Archduke's 1659 inventory.

PROVENANCE: Inventory of Queen Christina's collection in Palazzo Riario, Rome, 1662–3; *Una Diana inpiedi in atto di havere saettato Atteone, che lontano si vede presso da cani in un bellissimo paese figure al naturale . . . alta palmi otto e mezzo e larga palmi nove e mezzo—di Titiano.*[13] Noted in her collection in Rome by Nicodemus Tessin (1687).[14] No. 14 (Titian) in the inventory of 1689 (after Queen Christina's death).[15] Queen Christina's collection was inherited by Cardinal Dezio Azzolino (died, like Christina, in 1689), then by his nephew, Marchese Pompeo Azzolino, who sold it to Prince Livio Odescalchi, whose heir, Prince Baldassare Odescalchi-Erba sold it to Philippe, Duc d'Orléans in 1721, who took it to Paris (Palais-Royal). No. 9 (Titian) in the 1721 inventory.[16] Page 471 (*Diane et Actéon*, with dimensions and description, and provenance from 'La Reine de Suède') in the catalogue of 1727, by Du Bois de Saint-Gelais, of the Orléans pictures in the Palais-Royal, Paris. Engraved in vol. II of the illustrated catalogue. Passed with the Orléans collection to London,[17] where offered for sale at the Lyceum in the Strand from 26th December, 1798, lot 269 ('Titiano Vecel . . . Diana pursuing Acteon') marked in a copy of the sale catalogue in the National Gallery library as bought by 'Sir A. Hume' (Sir Abraham Hume). Mentioned in a letter of the 5th April, 1800 from Hume to his Italian agent, Sasso 'Compari io un gran quadro no terminato di Tiziano ma bello assai con Diana che seguita Acteone con cani e l'arco in mano . . .',[18] Exh. British Institution, 1819 (118) (lent Sir A. Hume). No. 16 in a list of pictures dated 27th February, 1834[19] settled by Sir A. Hume (1749–1838) and inherited by his grandson, Viscount Alford (1812–1851). The latter was the son of Sir Abraham's daughter, Sophia, and of the first Earl Brownlow. He was also the father of the second Earl Brownlow, who inherited from him. Exh. British Institution, 1845 (53) (lent Viscount Alford). Noted by Waagen (1854) among Earl Brownlow's pictures.[20] Exh. R.A., 1872 (73) and 1893 (121), New Gallery (Venetian Art), 1894–5 (166) and Grafton Galleries, 1910–11 (154), in all cases lent Earl Brownlow. Bought by Viscount Lascelles (later 6th Earl of Harewood), 1919. Exh. R.A., 1930 (169), 1950–1 (210) and 1960 (84), in all cases lent Earl of Harewood. Seventh Earl of Harewood sale, Christie's, 25th June, 1971 (27). Immediately afterwards bought by the J. Paul Getty Museum, Malibu, California. The export license applied for by the latter was delayed by the Reviewing Committee for a year, during which time the purchase price paid by the Getty Museum was raised by public appeal, with the aid of a special Exchequer grant and contributions from the N.A-C.F. and the Pilgrim Trust, a large anonymous donation and many corporate and individual contributions. As a result, purchased 1972.

VERSIONS: Formerly Austrian royal collection, engraved in the *Prodromus* (1735) (see above). A small copy by Teniers now at Barrington Court, Somerset.

ENGRAVING: J. Couché (Galerie du Palais-Royal, vol. II, 1808, pl. X) with bow string added and other inaccuracies, including incorrect proportions.

REPRODUCTION: *Illustrated General Catalogue*, 1973, p. 729.

REFERENCES: (1) Ovid: *Metamorphoses* III, 192. (2) Reproduced and discussed by Cecil Gould: *The Death of Actaeon and Titian's Mythologies*, Apollo, 1972, pp. 464 ff. (3) Letters printed by Crowe and Cavalcaselle: *Titian . . .*, II (1877), pp. 513 ff. (4) C. Gould, *loc. cit.* Harald Keller (*Tizians Poesie für König Philipp II von Spanien*, 1969, p. 163) states that much of the left part of no. 6420 was left unfinished by Titian and finished later by someone else. He produces no proper evidence for this quaint idea, nor is there any. (5) Printed in the Vienna *Jahrbuch*, 13 (1892), 2nd part, p. XLVII, no. 8804; also nos. 8806 (p. XLVIII) and 8808 (p. XLIX). (6) Crowe and Cavalcaselle, *op. cit.* p. 540. (7) Printed and discussed by E. K. Waterhouse: *Paintings from Venice for Seventeenth-Century England . . .* Italian Studies, VII, 1952, pp. 1 ff. (8) Printed by Klara Garas, Vienna *Jahrbuch*, 1967, p. 75. (9) Waterhouse. *loc. cit.* (10) Printed in Vienna *Jahrbuch*, I, 1883, Supplement, pp. LXXXVI ff. (11) It must be emphasized that the assumption that there were two versions of Titian's *Death of Actaeon* rests primarily on the evidence of the Prodromus engraving, reproducing, as it does, a picture in Vienna in 1735 whereas the present picture was then in Paris. The difference in ratio of height to width of the two pictures as shown in

Teniers' view of 1651 (nearly square), on the one hand, and in the *Theatrum Pictorium* and *Prodromus* engravings (oblong), on the other, is less significant as the proportions are sometimes falsified in engravings. Thus, what is certainly the present picture, as well as Titian's *Rape of Europa* (now Boston, Isabella Stewart Gardner Museum) and *Perseus and Andromeda* (now London, Wallace Collection) are engraved in the second volume of the Orléans catalogue in an oblong rather than a nearly square format, extra space being included at the sides. The fact that this was an engraver's license or inaccuracy is shown by the fact that the proportions as shown in the engravings do not correspond with the dimensions as specified in the letter-press underneath the engravings (e.g. *Perseus and Andromeda*, dimensions given as 5 pieds, 6 pouces high by 6 pieds, 2 pouces wide, but engraving measures 158 × 204, mm. *Rape of Europa*, dimensions given as 5 pieds, 6 pouces high by 6 pieds, 4 pouces wide, but engraving measures 158 × 208 mm. The *Death of Actaeon* is stated to be 5 pieds, 6 pouces high by 6 pieds 1 pouce wide, but the engraving measures 158 × 208 mm.). (12) 'allerlei kunstreiche Malereien in 18 Ballen'. See Franz Mareš: *Beiträge zur Kenntniss der Kunstbestrebungen des Erzherzogs Leopold Wilhelm*, in Vienna *Jahrbuch*, V, 1887, p. 351. (13) Stockholm, Riksarkivet, Azzolinisaml., vol. 48. Entry kindly transcribed by Hugh Brigstock. (14) *Studieresor*, ed. Sirén, 1914, p. 184. See also Beatrice Canestro Chiovenda: *Atheone Lacerato dai Cani Suoi*, *Commentari*, 1971, pp. 180 ff, who quotes a Latin poem about the picture when in Christina's collection by Michele Silos. (15) Rome, Archivio di Stato. Printed by O. Granberg: *Galerie de Tableaux de la Reine Christine de Suède*, 1897, pp. LIII ff. Also printed by Campori: Raccolta di Cataloghi . . ., 1870, ed., p. 339. (16) British Museum, Add. Mss., 20390. Printed by Granberg, *op. cit.*, pp. XCIII ff. (17) Sold by Philippe Egalité in 1792 to Walkuers of Brussels, who sold it to Laborde de Méréville, who brought it to England. (18) Copy in the National Gallery library. (19) Copy in the National Gallery archives. (20) *Treasures of Art in Great Britain*, II, p. 313.

Studio of TITIAN

34 VENUS AND ADONIS

$69\frac{3}{4} \times 73\frac{3}{4}$ (1·771 × 1·872).

The canvas, exceptionally, has not been trimmed: the original turn-over still exists.

The most damaged area is the upper left corner, where, as a result of scorching[1], the outline of the trees is distorted by repaint and most of the foliage unreliable. The area of sky between Adonis' right arm and the overhanging foliage is almost entirely repainted. Venus' white drapery is retouched from the shoulder to the knee. The lower part of her back is much rubbed due to the fact that this area was covered in the eighteenth century with draperies executed in water-colour. These had been removed by the time the picture was in the Angerstein collection.[2] Most of the sky is worn. The following areas are in reliable condition: the heads of both the principal figures, Adonis' red tunic, the red and pink drapery under Venus, the vase at her feet, Adonis' left hand and the heads of the two hounds on the right.

Cleaned 1924, when much old repaint was removed, and 1973.

Preliminary drawing with the point of the brush is visible in many places, notably in Venus' shoulder and right arm, in Adonis' right arm (together with ordinary *pentimenti* in the outlines) and in the sky.

Infra-red photography reveals further drawing of this kind in Adonis' red tunic.

Before the cleaning of 1973, catalogued as Titian, with the assumption of some studio assistance. It now seems that the master's own share in the execution is likely to have been minimal. Despite some differences in the arrangement of the quiver and bow, and in details of the costume, no. 34 is evidently a studio copy of the picture now in the Prado, which was painted for Philip II of Spain and documented as finished in 1554. Many other versions and variants of this composition are known (including smaller, oblong variants, reflecting Titian's late style, at Washington and New York).

PROVENANCE: No. 116 in the catalogue of 1783 of Palazzo Colonna, Rome. Acquired by Alexander Day in Italy after the Napoleonic invasion. Offered for sale by Day, 20 Lower Brook St., London, 1800–1, where bought, May, 1801, by Angerstein.[3] Purchased with the Angerstein collection, 1824.

REPRODUCTION: *Illustrations, Italian Schools*, 1937, p. 353.

REFERENCES: (1) See article by Sir Charles Holmes: *Burlington Magazine*, vol. XLIV (1924), pp. 16–22. Part of a further article on the subject, by A. L. Mayer (*Münchner Jahrbuch*, 1925, pp. 274–9), contains nothing of importance. (2) A MS. note (copy in the Gallery archives) made by Sir Abraham Hume reads: 'the present possessor [i.e. Prince Colonna] has thought fit to cover part of her [i.e. Venus'] back with a piece of linen, tho' there was nothing indecent in its appearance, but, I am assured, it is only in water-colours'. Dibdin (*Aedes Althorpianae*, vol. 1, 1822, pp. 13–14) repeats the story of the draping and adds the information that it had since been removed 'as far as it was possible'. There is a photograph in the Gallery archives of a picture belonging in 1922 to Dr. Ferdinand Gotti of Florence which purports to be an English copy of no. 34 made in Rome *c.* 1795. Marks across the lower half of Venus' back might be interpreted as light drapery. Adonis also seems to be wearing a small beard. (3) Buchanan: *Memoirs*, vol. II (1824), p. 14. Also Farington Diary for 7th May, 1801 (vol. I, p. 308).

After TITIAN

933 A BOY WITH A BIRD

$13\frac{3}{4} \times 19\frac{1}{4}$ (0·35 × 0·49).[1]

So far as can be seen through the present discoloured varnish the paint seems in good condition.

In the 1929 catalogue as Padovanino.

A copy (with the omission of the wings) of the figure of Cupid which occurs in the background of the later versions (e.g., at Washington and New York) of Titian's *Venus and Adonis* (see entry for no. 34). The outline of the leaves has been altered to suit the smaller format and clouds added of a type recalling an earlier phase of Titian's style than the Washington and New York versions. Such a transformation would not be inconsistent with the methods of a later *pasticheur* and need not imply that there was ever a Titian original exactly corresponding with no. 933 in size and format.[2] The handling of no. 933—so far as it is at present possible to judge it—seems to be of the seventeenth century, though the attribution to Padovanino seems too precise to justify.

PROVENANCE: Jeremiah Harman sale, 17th–18th May, 1844 (lot 65, as 'Titian') where bought Ellis.[3] Wynn Ellis Bequest, 1876.

REPRODUCTION: *Illustrations, Italian Schools*, 1937, p. 262.

REFERENCES: (1) Perhaps originally slightly larger. (2) Suida (*Belvedere*, 1932, Heft 7, pp. 164–6) published a picture in a Swiss private collection as being Titian's original of no. 933. While it is possible that Titian had also made use of this motive or a similar one in an earlier picture now lost (it may be noted that Ridolfi specifies that the Cupid added by Titian to Giorgione's *Venus* had a bird in his hand) it is not found in the earlier versions of the *Venus and Adonis*. (3) Marked copy of the sale catalogue in the Gallery library.

3949 PORTRAIT OF A MAN (? GIROLAMO FRACASTORO)

$36\frac{3}{8} \times 28\frac{1}{2}$ (0·92 × 0·724).

The remains of a strip of paper, stuck on, bottom left, read 'ottore Fracastoro'.

Very thin and disfigured by the remains of old, engrained varnish, also (on the face) by old retouches. Strips of the canvas at top and bottom have apparently been pressed down at some time. The outline of the hat was once farther out, towards the right.

Called in the 1929 catalogue 'Girolamo Fracastoro, ascribed to Francesco Torbido'. The Torbido attribution was due to J. P. Richter (catalogue of the Mond collection, 1910) but although it was supported by Berenson[1] and by A. Venturi[2] Richter later[3] admitted that it was hypothetical, apparently depending on the identification of the sitter, the fact that Vasari[4] records portraits of Fracastoro by Titian, Caroto and Torbido and that he (Richter) could not support an attribution to Titian or Caroto. Gronau[5] pointed out the improbability of the Torbido attribution and indicated the Titianesque qualities of the design of no. 3949, in particular the close resemblance to that of the portrait of Tommaso Mosti (Florence, Pitti). Richter's final view,[6] that the picture is a copy after an unidentified Titian, would seem, despite the (?) *pentimento* in the hat, the least improbable.

The identity of the sitter is a harder problem. The paper still existing on the front of the canvas may well record an old inscription formerly visible on the back of it. Nevertheless, the degree of antiquity of this legend cannot be checked, while the great fame of Fracastoro, in his life time and subsequently, may have caused his name to be hypothetically or spuriously attached to various unconnected portraits.[7] The contemporary and attested portraits of Fracastoro—the woodcut (1538) from the *Hieronymi Fracastorii Homocentrica*, and a portrait medal (in profile)[8] —show long hair and beard, and also a fur collar, as in no. 3949. A different portrait, in profile, illustrating the second edition (1574) of Fracastoro's collected works, shows him with bald head uncovered. Apart from the lack of any object in no. 3949 indicating the sitter's scientific or literary interests, there is therefore nothing against the identification of him with Fracastoro, but equally no means of establishing it.

PROVENANCE: Almost certainly identical with a picture appearing successively as nos. 86, 93 and 66 in the 1824, 1837 and 1852 catalogues respectively of the collection of Conte Teodoro Lechi of Brescia. The description is invariably 'ritratto del celebre Fracastoro' by Titian, described as half-length, bearded, wearing fur, right arm leaning on a support and as measuring 0·9 × 0·73. In a type-script (in the Gallery archives) supplied by Conte Fausto Lechi it is stated that this picture was sold in 1854 to the 'inglese Henfrey'. No. 3949 is listed in the Mond catalogue as having been bought by Ludwig Mond from 'H. Ward, Esq., London' in 1895, so the intermediary history is still obscure. Mond Bequest, 1924.

REPRODUCTION: *Illustrations, Italian Schools*, 1937, p. 359.

REFERENCES: (1) *Lists*, 1936. (2) *Storia* . . ., IX, III, p. 916. Likewise Dirce Viana: *Francesco Torbido detto Il Moro*, 1933, p. 70. (3) *Burlington Magazine*, vol. 48 (1926), p. 216. A letter on the ethics of such attributions appears in the same volume, p. 322. (4) Ed. Milanesi, VII, p. 455, and V, pp. 286 and 295. (5) *Burlington Magazine*, vol. 48 (1926), p. 144. Gronau's attribution to Titian himself (followed by Suida, *Tiziano*, pl. LXb) cannot be supported. (6) *Loc. cit.* Richter's tentative attribution to Felice Brusasorci may be noted without further comment. (7) A probable example is the portrait formerly in the Fellner collection, Budapest (reproduced in the *Klassiker der Kunst* volume on Palma Vecchio, p. 124) inscribed as representing Fracastoro and as painted by Titian. (8) Both reproduced by E. Schaeffer in the Prussian *Jahrbuch*, vol. XXXI (1910), pp. 132 and 138 (the author's identification of a portrait at Verona attributed to Titian with Fracastoro is questionable). The date of Fracastoro's birth, now apparently established as 1472 (publication of 1953 by R. Brenzoni correcting his earlier publication), would not be inconsistent with the apparent age of the sitter in no. 4939 assuming a Titian original dating from *c*. 1515–30. In a later publication ('Il Girolamo Fracastoro di Londra . . .' in 'Il Fracastoro', anno LIII, p. 5, 1960) the same author claims that no. 3949 is not identical with the Torbido portrait of Fracastoro mentioned by Vasari.

4222 THE TRINITY

$51\frac{1}{2} \times 38\frac{3}{4}$ (1·31 × 0·985).

Considerably rubbed and largely repainted. The extent of this repainting is discussed below. Superficially cleaned in 1926.

In the 1929 catalogue as Titian.

'The Trinity' was Titian's own name for the large picture of this design, now in the Prado, which was despatched from Venice to the Emperor Charles V in 1554 and has long been known as 'La Gloria'.[1] The figures of God the Father and of Christ are indistinguishable in themselves, but the one on the spectator's left must be Christ, since otherwise Christ could not be on the right hand of God the Father. Beneath them, on the spectator's left, is the Virgin, with S. John the Baptist behind her. In the foreground are (left to right) Ezekiel (on the eagle), Moses (holding the tables), Noah (holding the ark) and David (with the harp). The female figure between the last two (with her back to the spectator) may be S. Mary Magdalene. Higher up, on the spectator's right, the Emperor Charles V kneels. Behind him are the Empress, Philip II and Mary of Hungary. Below this group the portraits of (?) Pietro Aretino and of Titian himself are introduced (all these portraits are more clearly recognizable in the Prado picture). Titian also said that he had introduced into the latter the portrait of Francisco Vargas, the Emperor's ambassador.[1]

An engraving of Titian's design by Cornelis Cort[2] differs in numerous details from the Prado picture, and since these differences affect the status of no. 4222 it is desirable to tabulate them as follows:

Cort's engraving	*Prado picture*
1. God the Father has His right hand up. He wears a cloak fastened at the neck whose folds are drawn over His knees. He holds a short baton. His orb is large and has no cross.	God the Father has his right hand down. He wears a single voluminous garment. He holds a tall sceptre. His orb is small and has a cross.
2. Christ is shown in profile. His right hand is raised and holds a short baton. The fold of a cloak hangs from His right shoulder and is gathered over His right knee. His orb is large and is on His right knee. It has no cross.	Christ is shown nearly in full face. His right hand is only half raised and holds a long sceptre. No cloak is visible at His shoulders and the draperies at His right knee are probably part of His single garment. His orb is small and on His left knee. It has a cross.
3. The Virgin's veil billows out slightly behind her neck.	The Virgin's veil is gathered round her neck.
4. S. John Baptist's fur-lined cloak is over his left shoulder.	The upper part of S. John Baptist's body is naked.
5. The figure whose head is between the Baptist and the Virgin is bald.	The figure between the Baptist and the Virgin has dark hair.
6. The claws of Ezekiel's eagle rest on a scroll.	There is nothing under the claws of Ezekiel's eagle.
7. Moses is shown in profile. The lowest fold of his loin cloth hangs vertically down.	Moses is looking away from the spectator. The folds of his loin cloth are rounded at the base.
8. Noah's ark has no dove.	Noah's ark has a dove.
9. David looks over his left shoulder. The drapery round his shoulders has a fur lining. The lowest extremity of the loin cloth which falls from his left knee curls back.	David looks over his right shoulder. The drapery round his shoulders has a narrow ermine trimming but no fur lining. The folds of his loin cloth are simple at the base.
10. The head above David's is almost in profile.	The head above David's is nearly three-quarter face.
11. Titian himself wears a turban and a cloak.	Titian is bare-headed and his left arm is also bare.
12. The fingers of (?) S. Mary Magdalene's right hand appear to touch the Emperor's drapery.	The fingers of (?) S. Mary Magdalene's right hand are clear of the Emperor's drapery.

Cort's engraving	Prado picture
13. The figure on the spectator's left of Titian faces the latter. His features do not resemble those of Pietro Aretino.	The figure on the spectator's left of Titian faces the Trinity. His features resemble those of Pietro Aretino.
14. Philip II is shown in profile.	Philip II is shown three-quarter face.
15. The angel whose arm is round the Empress turns his face towards her.	The angel whose arm is round the Empress faces the Trinity.
16. Angels top right hold small branches with few leaves.	Angels top right hold biggish branches with many leaves.
17. The empty space in the centre shows even rays emanating from the Dove. At the top of the picture clouds cut sharply across the angles to frame the figures of God and Christ.	Half the empty space in the centre is filled by a large cloud from which emanate a few rays. Cherubs' heads fill the top of the picture. There appear to be no clouds there.
18. There are two small cabins in the landscape at the base.	There is only one cabin in the landscape at the base.

No. 4222, in its present state, corresponds in all respects with the exception of no. 15 with the Prado picture. But X-ray photographs show in each case different forms underneath, and these differences correspond exactly with Cort's engraving. In certain cases the earlier forms show through in the form of *pentimenti*—e.g., in the crownless orb on Christ's right knee, in the Virgin's veil or in the fingers of (?) S. Mary Magdalene's right hand.

Cornelius Cort was working for Titian in Venice from 1565 and his engraving of *The Trinity* is dated 1566. But as the Prado picture had left Venice twelve years earlier he must have worked in this case from a drawing or *modello* supplied by Titian.[3] Bearing in mind that no. 4222 originally corresponded with Cort's engraving and that it was altered later the order of events may have been any of the following:

1. Cort could have based his engraving on no. 4222 in its original state. In that case no. 4222 would have been Titian's own *modello*.[4]

2. Cort could have worked from a *modello* by Titian now lost, of which no. 4222 in its original state could have been a copy.

3. No. 4222 in its original state could have been painted from Cort's engraving.

Of these possibilities no. 1 is rendered highly improbable on account of the relative crudeness and un-Titianesque quality of the execution of the original state of no. 4222 as revealed by the X-rays. The second possibility can likewise be virtually eliminated on account of the curious fact that some of the draperies are painted on top of different colours: the green dress of (?) S. Mary Magdalene, for example, is over pink paint, and parts of David's blue drapery and of Christ's robe of the same colour are over red (distinct from the brick-colour ground). In all cases some of the top paint has worn away. These particular colours would be unusual, or even pointless, as underpainting, which in itself would be an unusual technique in a *modello* and almost inconceivable in a copy of a *modello*. It is precisely this factor which tilts the balance in favour of the third possibility—that no. 4222 was originally painted from Cort's engraving. In that case it was almost inevitable that the colours should not correspond with those in the large picture.

The sum of the evidence therefore leads the present writer to conclude that Cort's engraving was made from a sketch or *modello* supplied by Titian and now lost which would have represented an earlier stage in the evolution or would have been sufficiently vague or undefined in certain details to account for the differences between the engraving and the big picture, and that no. 4222 was originally the work of some painter (whose name, working period and nationality are now alike undiscoverable) who had access to Cort's engraving, but not to the Prado picture or to Titian's *modello*. At some stage it would have been 'corrected' by reference to the original, the forms being altered where they differed (with the exception of the angel whose arm is round the Empress, which was apparently overlooked) and some of the colours changed (they now in fact correspond more or less with those in the Prado picture). The fact that no. 4222 in its present overpainted state superficially resembles the work of Titian whereas the forms disclosed by X-ray photographs appear entirely foreign to him suggests that the transformation was effected by a clever artist who may have been activated by some dishonest intention of uttering the result as Titian's own *modello*. The appearance and style of the top paint suggest that the transformation was made probably not later than the eighteenth century. It must have been done in Spain (where, indeed, the picture is first recorded) but in view of the circumstances, and of the amount of damage sustained, the identity of the second painter involved is as impossible to discover as that of the first.[5]

ENGRAVING: Cort's engraving is discussed above.

PROVENANCE: Said to have been discovered about 1808[6] in a gambling house in Madrid by De Bourke, afterwards Danish Minister to London.[7] Brought to London by Wallis.[7] In the collection of Samuel Rogers before 1833.[8] Rogers' sale, 3rd May, 1856 (725), where bought Lord Harry Vane[9] (afterwards Duke of Cleveland) by whom exh. Manchester (*Art Treasures Exhibition*), 1857 (provisional catalogue no. 229), and R.A., 1872 (114). Cleveland sale, 8th March, 1902 (37) where bought Sir William Corry.[9] Corry sale, Claremont, Esher, 25th–28th October, 1926 (285), where bought Mears[10] for Colnaghi. Purchased from Colnaghi, December, 1926 with the aid of the Lewis Fund.

REPRODUCTION: *Burlington Magazine*, vol. L, 1927, p. 52.

REFERENCES: (1) See letter from Titian to the Emperor, dated 10th September, 1554 (reproduced by Crowe and Cavalcaselle, *Titian*, vol. II (1877), pp. 507–8). (2) Reproduced in an article by Sir Charles Holmes, *Burlington Magazine*, vol. L (1927), p. 52. (3) Alfred Stix (Vienna *Jahrbuch*, XXXI (1913–14), p. 340) quotes Titian's letter of 1565 (. . . *fatto metter in stampa di rame il disegno della pittura della Trinità*) as referring definitely to a drawing. But the word 'disegno' need only mean 'composition'. (4) This was claimed by Holmes, *loc. cit.*, and supported by Hadeln (letter of 1926 to Otto Gutekunst in the Gallery archives) and by Tietze (*Tizian*, 1936, Textband, p. 211, and in *Die Graphischen Künste*, 1938, p. 10—the latter article gives further references). Holmes' thesis was developed in ignorance of the results of the X-rays, with which it is incompatible. The same applies to one advanced by Palma Bucarelli (*Gazette des Beaux-Arts*, 1935, II, pp. 247–8). (5) A. L. Mayer suggested the name of Francisco Rizi as author of no. 4222 and quoted support from F. J. Sánchez Cantón (*Boletin de la Sociedad Española de Excursiones*, 1934, pp. 297–8). In a letter of the same year (copy in the Gallery archives) Mayer also mentioned the names of Pablo Esquert, José Antolínez, Luca Giordano and Cerezo. A. Porcella (*Revisione alla Mostra di Pittura Spagnuola* (1930), p. 9) referred to no. 4222 simply as a Spanish copy of the Prado picture. A copy of the latter is recorded as early as 1635 in the Duke of Buckingham's collection (see *Burlington Magazine*, X, 1906–7, p. 379). (6) Mrs. Jameson: *Companion to the . . . Private Galleries .٭. . in London*, 1844, p. 402. (7) This information from the Samuel Rogers' sale catalogue. (8) Passavant: *Kunstreise . . .*, p. 86. No. 4222 seems to have been offered by Yeates to Penrice in 1814 (*Letters . . . to . . . Thomas Penrice*, n.d., p. 40). (9) Marked copy of sale catalogue in the Gallery library. (10) Marked copy of the sale catalogue in the library of the Victoria and Albert Museum.

Follower of TITIAN

1123　MYTHOLOGICAL SCENE

Panel, 30 × 52 (0·762 × 1·327).[1]

A number of obviously worn passages and retouchings in the flesh and lighter portions of the sky. Draperies and landscape details fairly well preserved. Cleaned 1966.

At Hamilton Palace as Giorgione. Catalogued since entering the Gallery as 'Venetian School' except in the editions of 1901–15 where it appears as 'School of Giorgione'. Other suggestions have been 'Lattanzio Gambara, Beccaruzzi and others of their class',[2] Cariani[3] and Bonifazio.[4] Of these, the last is the only one to merit serious attention, but it is hypothetical and not entirely satisfactory. In nearly every respect no. 1123 seems to depend directly on Titian.

Called 'Venus and Adonis' in earlier editions of the National Gallery catalogue and 'Hippomenes and Atalanta' by Waagen[5] and Crowe and Cavalcaselle.[5] The incidents in the background would certainly seem to tell the story of Adonis—those on the left of the main figures being connected with his death and with Venus' lament over his body, those on the right with his birth. In the centre of the latter three episodes Myrrha is apparently being driven from the house by her father when he had discovered that she had been his paramour. On the left she seems to be turning into a tree. On the right the baby Adonis is being born from the tree. Nevertheless it is doubtful if the main figures are Venus and Adonis. The man holds an apple in his right hand, and this suggests that the couple are intended as Hippomenes and Atalanta, whose story is so closely linked by Ovid with that of Adonis that he interrupts the latter to tell it and then continues with the Adonis story again.[6] On the other hand, Cupid—who is seen in no. 1123 being despatched by Venus in the sky, top right, and about to pierce the lovers in the main scene—does not figure in Ovid's account of the Atalanta story, where Venus intervenes in person.

PROVENANCE: Hamilton Palace. No. 383 ('Giorgione') in the 4th day (24th June, 1882) of the Hamilton Palace sale, where purchased. Very possibly before that in the Lely sale.[7]

REPRODUCTION: *Illustrations, Italian Schools*, 1937, p. 375.

REFERENCES: (1) Approximate dimensions of original panel to which strips about ¼" wide have been added all round and painted over. (2) Crowe and Cavalcaselle: *Painting in North Italy*, vol. III (1912), p. 55. The authors refer to the picture as a 'small canvas' (no. 1123 is on wood) and describe it as Hippomenes and Atalanta. Nevertheless it seems that this is the picture referred to. Waagen also (*Treasures of Art in Great Britain*, vol. III (1854), p. 303) refers to 'Hippomenes and Atalanta accompanied by Cupid, in a landscape'. (3) W. Schmidt in *Repertorium für Kunstwissenschaft*, 1908, p. 117. (4) Berenson (with query) in *Lists*, 1932 and 1936. In his 1957 edition he lists it as a 'Giorgionesque painting'. (5) *Loc. cit.* (6) Metamorphoses X. (7) *Burlington Magazine*, editorial, August, 1943, p. 186, n. 12.

Imitator of TITIAN

3   A CONCERT

39 × 49¼ (0·99 × 1·25).

Flesh areas much worn and made up. Thicker paint of the green-blue and red robes better preserved. Heavily discoloured by old varnish. It is open to question whether the notes on the musical score were ever legible. In the picture's present worn state they are not.

In the 1929 catalogue as 'School of Titian'. This type of composition —elaborately dressed figures, usually shown at half length, making music—was pre-eminently associated with the Giorgionesque, the most famous example being the *Concert* in the Pitti. Among such pictures, where the attitude of the characters towards the music is apt to appear half-hearted, it would be very difficult to find a parallel for the vigorous singing, with wide open mouth, of the boy in no. 3, whose appearance in general seems somewhat foreign to the Renaissance.

The costumes shown, and the hair-style of the lady, would admit of dating in the 1540's (but not earlier) provided that considerable alterations were made later.[1] Even on these grounds however the picture would fit more easily into the idiom of the early seventeenth century when certain Giorgionesque features reappeared, and on the whole the present writer is led to regard it as a deliberate imitation of Titian dating from that period. Jacobsen, alone of earlier writers, had proposed so late a dating with his suggestion of 'early Padovanino'.[2] This seems to be on the right track, but such precision, at least in the picture's present darkened state, would be hard to justify.

VERSIONS: An inferior copy at Pommersfelden. Another (with a *trompe-l'œil* frame) was lot 142, anonymous sale, Christie's. 9th March, 1951. A variant (three or four figures instead of five) was at Brunswick in the nineteenth century.[3]

ENGRAVINGS: By H. Danckerts and (in reverse) by J. Gronsveld. See also below under PROVENANCE.

PROVENANCE: History prior to entering the Angerstein collection is uncertain.[4] It corresponds however with a picture catalogued in the collection of Charles I as from Mantua and with two engravings by H. Danckerts and J. Gronsveld.[5] The entry in Bathoe's catalogue of Charles I's collection (p. 99) is as follows: *A Mantua piece done by Titian. Imprimis. A picture of some five half figures, one whereof being a teaching, another singing, another playing upon a bandore, the fourth playing upon a flute, the fifth being a woman listening to the musick, painted upon cloth, half figures so big as the life . . . 3f.3 4f.3.* What is presumably the relevant entry in the Mantua inventory of 1627 reads: *Doi quadri . . . uno dipintovi homini che cantano di musica, mezze figure . . . di mano di Titiano.*[6] The Charles I picture was probably the 'picture of musick by Georgion' in the Commonwealth sale lists.[7] Hendrick Danckerts was active at The Hague 1645–53, in Italy 1653–7 and later in England. Johannes Gronsveld was active at Amsterdam from 1679 and died there in 1728. Though in theory there could thus be as many as three replicas of no. 3 there is nothing against the assumption that the Mantua/Charles I picture, the Danckerts picture and the Gronsveld picture were identical with each other and with it. The first part of the equation, indeed, is strongly supported, if not proved, by the fact that Danckerts' engraving is inscribed 'Ex collectione regis Magnae Brittanniae'. Purchased with the Angerstein collection, 1824.

REPRODUCTION: *Illustrations, Italian Schools*, 1937, p. 357.

REFERENCES: (1) Notes on the costumes by Stella Mary Pearce in the Gallery archives. (2) *Repertorium für Kunstwissenschaft*, XXIV (1901), p. 372. Other suggestions had been 'Schiavone or Zelotti' (Crowe and Cavalcaselle, *Titian*, vol. II, 1877, pp. 459–60), 'Florigerio' (R. Longhi, 1929, apparently verbally; a picture at Munich, claimed in the 1929 catalogue of the National Gallery as 'somewhat similar', is attributed to Florigerio) and 'copy after Titian' (Berenson, *Lists*, 1936). E. Tietze, in a letter in the Gallery archives, suggests a derivation from a fifteenth-century Ferrarese picture. (3) Crowe and Cavalcaselle, *History of Painting in North Italy*, vol III (1912), pp. 53–4. The picture was presumably no. 260 ('? Giorgione') in the Brunswick catalogue of 1849. (4) The National Gallery catalogues of 1915–29 include the statement 'perhaps from R. Strange Coll., 1771'. The evidence for this eludes the present writer. (5) Crowe and Cavalcaselle, *Titian*, II, p. 460. (6) Alessandro Luzio: *La Galleria dei Gonzaga . . .*, 1913, p. 113; also in Carlo D'Arco: *Delle Arti e Degli Artefici di Mantova*, vol. II (1857), p. 160. (7) Crowe and Cavalcaselle (*History of Painting in North Italy*, vol. III, 1912, p. 41) connect no. 3 with a 'Giorgione' in James II's collection, but the latter was in fact a picture still at Hampton Court ('Master of the Pitti Three Ages'). See, in this connection and for the entry in the Commonwealth sale lists, Denis Mahon: *Notes on the 'Dutch Gift' to Charles II, III* (*Burlington Magazine*, vol. 92, 1950, p. 14).

VENETIAN School, Sixteenth century

173 PORTRAIT OF A MAN

Stretcher measures $47 \times 38\frac{1}{2}$ ($1 \cdot 195 \times 0 \cdot 977$).

Of this, a strip just under $3''$ broad along the base is of later canvas, while strips roughly $1\frac{1}{2}''$ wide (varying) at the sides and top have been crudely overpainted at a later date.

The face appears to be in tolerable condition. The existing heavily discoloured varnish renders difficult an assessment of the state of the rest, though there is certainly an appreciable amount of damage.

In the 1929 catalogue as Jacopo Bassano. Also attributed to Francesco Bassano,[1] Domenico Tintoretto[2] and Beccaruzzi.[3] If the indications of dating—ca. 1585-95—afforded by the costume are correct,[4] this is much too late for Beccaruzzi and rather late for Jacopo Bassano. Of the remaining candidates, Domenico Tintoretto, and Francesco, Gerolamo and Leandro Bassano would all be possibilities, but the condition of the picture and relative lack of definition of the style of all but Leandro of the artists in question as portraitists precludes a decision.

PROVENANCE: From the collection of Alleyne FitzHerbert, first and last Baron St Helens (1753-1839).[5] Passed to his nephew, Henry Gally Knight, the writer on architecture, by whom presented (with no. 174), 1839.

REPRODUCTION: *Illustrations, Italian Schools*, 1937, p. 22.

REFERENCES: (1) Quoted in the 1929 catalogue. (2) By Morelli, according to J. P. Richter (note in the Gallery archives). (3) By Fiocco (quoted by Arslan: *I Bassano*, 1931, p. 345). (4) Notes by Stella Mary Pearce in the Gallery archives. (5) Letter from Henry Gally Knight in the Gallery archives.

272 A COLOSSAL DECORATIVE FIGURE

$59\frac{7}{8} \times 45\frac{5}{8}$ (1·521 × 1·159).

Apparently thinly painted—so far as can be seen through the existing varnish, some of which is almost opaque.

The turn-over of the canvas on the right is incompletely covered with paint, and gives the impression of never having been completely painted, rather than of paint which has existed and has since been rubbed off. As the figure is truncated to the right it is therefore more probable that the continuation was on a separate canvas than that an appreciable amount of the existing canvas has been cut off. In the 1929 catalogue as 'Italian School, 16th century'. Presented as by Pordenone, and accepted as such by Crowe and Cavalcaselle.[1] This type of spandrel figure, however, seems typical of a rather later fashion in the Veneto, and was not uncommon among the followers of Paolo Veronese.[2]

PROVENANCE: Stated (in the MS. catalogue in the Gallery archives) to have come 'from a church in the territory of Venice'. Presented, 1855, by Cavaliere Vallati of Rome.

REPRODUCTION: *Illustrations, Italian Schools*, 1937, p. 176.

REFERENCES: (1) *North Italian Painters*, vol. III (1912), p. 182, note 1, no. 8. (2) Cf. e.g. the frescoes at the Villa Coldogno, near Vicenza (repr. A. Venturi, *Storia* . . ., IX, IV, II, pls. 721-6).

595 PORTRAIT OF A LADY

$28\frac{3}{4} \times 22\frac{3}{4}$ (0·73 × 0·578).

Flesh and background worn. Hair and much of the dress appear to be in a better state. Cleaned 1961.

Purchased as by Zelotti. Tentatively ascribed in the 1929 catalogue to Badile. Both these names can be excluded on account of the costume which is much earlier (ca. 1516–17).[1] Berenson's tentative attribution to Palma Vecchio,[2] supported by Wilde,[3] is not open to this objection but is equally unacceptable to the present writer who is unable to recognize in no. 595 either the conception or the handling of Palma.

A smaller figure, such as Licinio,[4] would seem preferable, but a verdict is the harder to come by on account of the picture's condition.

PROVENANCE: Bought at Rome, 1858, from 'Signor Menchetti'.

REPRODUCTION: *Illustrations, Italian Schools*, 1937, p. 372.

REFERENCES: (1) Notes by Stella Mary Pearce in the Gallery archives. (2) *Lists*, 1936 and 1957 (with query). (3) MS. note (based on photographic evidence only) in the Gallery archives. (4) Oral suggestion by Michael Levey.

3108	A NAVAL BATTLE

Panel, $6\frac{3}{4} \times 15\frac{1}{4}$ (0·171 × 0·387).

Good condition.

Formerly catalogued as 'Italian School, XVI century'.

One of a series of at least four, all from the Manfrin collection.[1] A fifth panel, of identical style and type, but unknown provenance, appeared at auction in 1929.[2] All five pictures were probably painted as part of some furniture, and it is reported by Ridolfi[3] that Andrea Schiavone, to whom no. 3108 was attributed by Berenson,[4] had specialized in this work at the outset of his career. To the present writer, however, the pictures, though of a certain Schiavonesque type, seem too far from the most acceptable examples of Schiavone's secular style (such as the ex-Chatsworth *Psyche* and the Vienna mythologies—see entry for no. 1884) to justify so precise an attribution.

PROVENANCE: Manfrin collection, Venice, in the nineteenth century (see above) from which bought by Sir A. H. Layard, 1880.[5] Layard Bequest, 1916.

REPRODUCTION: *Illustrations, Italian Schools*, 1937, p. 177.

REFERENCES: (1) No. 3108 has on the back a Manfrin label on which is written 'A 31'. Also 'No. 24' painted on the wood. A Manfrin label on which was written 'A 30' was on the back of the second picture of the series—Oscar Andersen sale, Sotheby's, 16th November, 1949 (140), panel, 7 × 15½ (0·178 × 0·394) 'Scipio Africanus receiving turbaned envoys' (existence of the Manfrin label checked by the present writer at the time of the sale). The other two pictures were in the Dr. Szeben collection, Budapest, as Bonifazio and ex-Manfrin, 0·165 × 0·44 and 0·165 and 0·38 respectively. The Manfrin numbering was changed more than once. The four pictures in question are clearly identifiable as nos. 24, 35, 32 and 33 of 'Stanza Segnata A' in a MS. catalogue (in the Gallery library) of 1851 and as nos. 22, 23, 29 and 30 in the printed catalogue of 1856. In the 1872 catalogue only three of the pictures appear, one evidently having been sold. The other three are nos. 22, 23 and 24. All pictures in all cases are as Bonifazio, height specified in all cases where it is given as 0·18, width varying from 0·38 to 0·45. (2) A. G. B. Russell sale, Sotheby's, 9th May,

1929, lot 7—'Andrea Schiavone . . . Horatius on the Bridge . . . panel, 10¼ × 21⅛.' (3) Ridolfi/Hadeln, I, p. 248. (4) *Lists*, 1936 and 1957. (5) Layard's MS. catalogue in the Gallery archives.

4037 THE STORY OF CIMON AND EFIGENIA

Panel, 26¾ × 47¼ (0·67 × 1·2).

Much damaged by flaking, and extensively repainted. A sizeable piece, clearly, has been cut on the left. The shape which its inclusion would have produced suggests that the picture was designed as part of a piece of furniture.

Hitherto catalogued as 'School of Palma Vecchio' and called 'Nymphs and a Shepherd'. The story of Cimon and Efigenia occurs in the Decameron (fifth day, first story).[1] Cimon, the illiterate son of a rich Cypriot, was sent by his father to live on his country estate. Walking one day from one farm to another Cimon found a young woman asleep near a spring, two maid-servants and a man-servant asleep at her feet. Cimon stopped, resting on his staff, and gazed at her until she woke up, which she did before her servants. In no. 4037 it would have to be assumed that the other two servants and the spring were included in the portion cut off on the left. The fact that the man is shown leaning on his staff and that the woman he was gazing at has just awakened whereas the other has not, being distinctive features of the Decameron story, seem sufficient to justify the identification of the subject. A painting by Rubens (Vienna) can be vouched for as representing the same subject through being catalogued as such as early as 1635.[2]

The attribution to Palma has often been made,[3] particularly in conjunction with a picture of similar type at Frankfurt. Nevertheless J. Wilde seems correct in pointing out that the latter picture is in fact by a different hand.[4] His tentative attribution of no. 4037 to Domenico Mancini on the strength of certain stylistic affinities with the Lendinara *Madonna* signed by that artist seems to have more to commend it than the Palma attribution, but the bad condition of no. 4037 encourages caution.

PROVENANCE: Acquired by Sir Claude Phillips before June, 1907.[5] Bequeathed by him, 1924.

REPRODUCTION: *Illustrations, Italian Schools*, 1937, p. 266.

REFERENCES: (1) The identification suggested by J. Wilde (note in the Gallery archives). (2) Inventory of Duke of Buckingham's pictures (*Burlington Magazine*, vol. 10, 1906–7, p. 379). (3) E.g. by Adolfo Venturi (*Storia* IX, iii, 423), Gombosi (*Klassiker der Kunst* volume on Palma, 1937, p. 36) and Berenson (*Lists*, 1936). Also Mariacher in his monograph (1968). (4) J. Wilde: *Die Probleme um Domenico Mancini*, in Vienna *Jahrbuch* (N.F., vol. 7, 1933, pp. 104 ff). The statement in the National Gallery catalogue of 1929 that no. 4037 combines motives from the Frankfurt picture and from no. 3079 of this Gallery is hardly to be taken seriously. (5) Article by C. J. H[olmes] in *Burlington Magazine*, vol. 11, pp. 188–9. The same writer reverts to the subject in a letter to the *Burlington Magazine*, vol. 47 (1925), p. 272.

5466 LANDSCAPE WITH MYTHOLOGICAL FIGURES

$72\frac{3}{4} \times 81\frac{1}{4}$ ($1\cdot847 \times 2\cdot06$).[1]

Worn thin in many places, and damaged in particular along the horizontal join of the canvas in the centre, but in general in fairly good condition. Cleaned 1955.

For commentary and provenance see the entry for no. 5467.

REFERENCE: (1) At some time in the past notches have been cut in the canvas and stretcher at both sides, c. 8–9″ from the top and bottom.

5467 THE SONS OF BOREAS PURSUING THE HARPIES

$72\frac{3}{4} \times 80\frac{3}{4}$ ($1\cdot847 \times 2\cdot05$).[1]

Thin in places, but in general well preserved. Cleaned 1955.

In the possession of their former owner as Tintoretto, but clearly belonging to the genre known as Veneto-Flemish landscape and in particular to the type practised by Paolo Fiammingo and Ludovico Pozzoserrato.[2]

The principal surviving landscape paintings whose attribution to Fiammingo has some external support are the following:

1. A set of four *Continents* at Kirchheim (Schwaben). These are apparently to be identified with some mentioned in contemporary correspondence with Fiammingo.[3]

2. A *Rape of Proserpine* (Rome, Doria gallery) together with its pendant, *Orpheus*.[4] The *Rape of Proserpine* connects with a drawing in the Rijksmuseum, Amsterdam, which is inscribed 'Paolo Fiamengho' on the back.

The principal surviving landscapes justifiably attributable to Pozzoserrato are the following:

1. A *Tower of Babel* at Kirchheim. Bears monogram.[5]

2. A *Fall of Phaeton* at Hanover (Kestner Museum). Bears monogram.[6]

3. Six pictures at the *Monte di Pietà* at Treviso. Attribution due to Ridolfi.[7]

Nos. 5466–7 are extremely similar in design to a landscape engraving of Aesop's fable of the raven and the scorpion, which is inscribed as by Raphael Sadeler after 'Lodovico Pozzo',[8] and in colour (particularly in respect of the greyish tone of the foliage) to the Kirchheim *Babel* and the Treviso pictures.[9] The chief difficulty comes from the existence of comparable features in the Kirchheim series—which includes three further sets of four landscapes with figures[10]—in which both Fiammingo and Pozzoserrato participated, but which display considerable homogeneity of landscape style. Starting with the four *Continents*, documented as Fiammingo, all seventeen pictures of this kind at Kirchheim would seem attributable to Fiammingo and studio. Starting with the *Babel*, which has Pozzoserrato's monogram, the reverse is the case. It is clear from this that the styles of Fiammingo and Pozzoserrato were very close, at least at one period, and at Kirchheim some collaboration between the two seems *prima facie* a probability. Ridolfi stated that Fiammingo excelled in foreground landscape and Pozzoserrato in distant landscape.[11] In the 1959 catalogue the present writer attributed nos. 5466/7 to Pozzoserrato. He now feels such precision to be premature. The distinction between Fiammingo and Pozzoserrato, and the possibility of their collaboration, requires further investigation. There was also at least one other painter of this type—Pietro Mera (*Arte Veneta*, XVIII, 1964, pp. 172–3). A picture apparently by the same hand as nos. 5466–7 is the *Diane chasseresse* at Nancy (no. 128 in the 1909 catalogue, attributed to Tintoretto), since then variously ascribed to Sustris and to Fiammingo.

Regarding the subject of the pictures, the air-borne monsters in no. 5467 are readily recognizable as harpies, and the bearded man on the ground, right, with upraised hand who seems to derive from the figure of Homer in Raphael's *Parnassus*, is clearly intended to be blind. He is therefore identifiable with Phineus who had been smitten by Zeus with blindness and a lingering old age and to have his food defiled by the harpies. The story is given in book II of the *Argonautica* of Apollonius Rhodius (which would have been well known in sixteenth-century Venice after the Aldine edition of 1521), where Zetes and Calais, the sons of Boreas, who were winged, chased the harpies away from Phineus and would have killed them but for the intervention of Iris. If this account is in fact the source for no. 5467 it has been followed with some licence. The depiction of the same figure (in this case the two sons of Boreas) more than once within the same picture is not unusual in Mannerist works, but whereas in the *Argonautica* Iris plays a restraining rôle here she seems rather to be encouraging the harpy hunt. A further unexplained peculiarity is the monster at the top, centre, who seems to have a combination of wings and human arms and legs (as the sons of Boreas did) but also a head like a bird's and the tail of a harpy. If no. 5467 were regarded as no more than a fantasy on the Phineus theme it might be legitimate to consider its pendant, no. 5466, as a fantasy on the Circe story, a version of which also figures in the *Argonautica* (book IV). The exact theme of no. 5466 would be difficult to define, but the most striking element is that three, at least, of the main figures are monsters—the woman, centre, whose body tails into the head half of a serpent, and the creatures, of unspecific sex, upper left and lower left, who have the heads respectively of an indeterminate monster and of a pig. The figures in Circe's train in the *Argonautica* are described as not resembling wild beasts or men but with a medley of limbs, compounded of various ones. This would be a fair description of the figures shown in no. 5466. Nevertheless the main feature of the Circe episode in the *Argonautica*—the purification by Circe of Jason and Medea—is certainly not the theme of no. 5466, while the erotic nature of the activity shown in the picture, together with the presence of the recumbent man on the right and other details, do not figure in Apollonius Rhodius' account. Either, therefore, no.

5466 is an illustration of a different story, as yet unidentified, or it is a fantasy loosely based on the Circe story.

PROVENANCE: Bought, together with no. 5466 (as Tintoretto) by Frederick Cavendish Bentinck in October, 1892 from A. Marcato of Venice who said he had purchased them 'a good many years before . . . they had originally been part of the decoration of one of the rooms in the Palazzo Vendramin & were removed from the Palazzo many years before when certain alterations were carried out'.[12] Bought from F. C. Bentinck, 1944.

REPRODUCTION: Negatives in the possession of the Gallery.

REFERENCES: (1) At some time in the past notches have been cut in canvas and stretcher at both sides, c. 8–9″ from the top and bottom. (2) An attribution in *Arte Veneta* (1947, p. 148) to Rottenhammer need not be considered seriously. For Fiammingo see Ridolfi/Hadeln, II, pp. 81–3. Ridolfi refers to him as 'Paolo Franceschi' or 'Paolo Fiamingo' and confirms that he was Flemish. Not identical, as formerly supposed, with a painter called Paolo de' Freschi, but very possibly identical with one Pauwels Franck who was a master in the Antwerp guild of St Luke in 1561. The death certificate (20th December, 1596) of 'Paolo Fiamengo pittor' gives his age as 50. As this would make him a master at the early age of 15 either the Franck-Fiammingo identification or, more probably, the statement of age at death, is likely to be wrong (Ridolfi gives the date of his birth as 1540). Surviving documented works include a painting in the *Sala del Gran Consiglio* of the Doge's Palace and a signed *Pietà* at Munich (no. 1159 in the 1904 edition of the catalogue of the Alte Pinakothek). Also four pictures at Kirchheim discussed in this entry. For Pozzoserrato see the article by L. Menegazzi (*Saggi e Memorie di Storia dell'Arte*, I, 1957, pp. 165 ff). (3) The documentation is given in detail in G. Lill: *Hans Fugger und die Kunst*, 1908, pp. 140–4, where also one of the *Continents* is reproduced (fig. 26, pl. XIX). (4) Nos. 174 and 175 in the catalogue by E. Sestieri (1942). The *Proserpine* and its drawing reproduced in the *Münchner Jahrbuch*, 1924, pp. 136–7. (5) Reproduced by R. A. Peltzer in the *Münchner Jahrbuch*, 1924, p. 146. (6) Reproduced by Peltzer, *op. cit.*, p. 150. (7) Ridolfi/ Hadeln, II, 94. A detail of one of them reproduced by Coletti in *Dedalo*, anno VI, 1925–6, vol. II, p. 406. (8) Reproduced C. Sterling in *Old Master Drawings*, December, 1931, pp. 44–8. (9) The present writer was able to study the Kirchheim and Treviso pictures *in situ* but knows the Hanover one only in reproduction. (10) Three pictures of one series are reproduced by Peltzer, *op. cit.*, pp. 133, 134 and 135, where they are attributed to Fiammingo. Two of another series on pp. 130–1, likewise as Fiammingo. The last series, the four seasons, not reproduced. (11) Ridolfi/Hadeln, II, p. 93: 'Paolo fiamingo . . . che preualeva nelle cose vicine. Ludouico però più dilettaua nelle lontane.' Ridolfi's further description of the type of landscape favoured by Pozzoserrato, an evidently romantic genre, with extensive views, mountains, ruins and water, fits nos. 5466–7 well. (12) Memorandum by F. C. Bentinck in the Gallery archives. Various *palazzi* in Venice have borne the title 'Palazzo Vendramin'. Of these the most famous—Palazzo Vendramin-Calergi, which was the scene of Wagner's death in 1883—had been bought by the Duchesse de Berry in 1844. The sale of her pictures (Hôtel Drouot, Paris, 19th April, *et seq.* 1865) did not include nos. 5466–7.

(?) VENETIAN SCHOOL, Sixteenth century

2903   A CONCERT

Canvas, transferred from panel, $35\frac{3}{4} \times 48\frac{1}{2}$ (0·9 × 1·23).

Considerably damaged. The largest area of repaint is the curved portion of the lyre, centre. Obvious repaint also in all three faces, and elsewhere.

Variously attributed to Lotto,[1] 'early Pordenone',[2] Palma and Bonifazio.[3] As 'School of Palma Vecchio' in the 1929 catalogue. Although the debt to Palma is obvious—in particular to such a picture as his *Three Sisters* at Dresden[4]—he is no more acceptable as author than the other three.[5] In point of fact no. 2903 seems to be by the same hand as a female portrait shown at the Giorgione exhibition in Venice in 1955 (no. 125)[6] and there attributed to a Friulan painter. Both pictures show some similarity of type and handling to certain pictures attributed to Licinio but no attested Licinio so summary in treatment is known to the present writer.

PROVENANCE: In St Petersburg in the year 1868.[7] Exh. R.A., 1872 (67) (lent by Sir Coutts Lindsay) and 1888 (124) (lent by Lady Lindsay)—both times as 'The Painter's Daughters' by Palma Vecchio. Lady Lindsay Bequest, 1912.

REPRODUCTION: *Illustrations, Italian Schools*, 1937, p. 266.

REFERENCES: (1) K. Oettinger in *Belvedere*, 1930 (ii), pp. 10 ff. The author of this article claimed that a drawing in the Oppenheimer collection was a study for no. 2903. The drawing in question was sold as Previtali at the Oppenheimer sale (10th, 13th, 14th July, 1936, lot 154). (2) Apparently oral communication from 'Dr. Kurth, Berlin' recorded in the Gallery archives. (3) Berenson (*Lists*, 1936 and 1957) as begun by Palma and finished by Bonifazio. (4) The costumes shown in no. 2903 would accord best with a date around 1523–4 (notes by S. M. Pearce in the Gallery archives). If the Dresden Palma is identical, as is usually assumed, with the picture seen by Michiel in 1525 it must naturally have been painted before then. (5) The theory of 'early Pordenone' is automatically excluded by the dating of the costumes to the 'twenties. (6) Ex-collections, Manfrin, Malmesbury, Barker and C. Butler. Anonymous sale, Sotheby's 10th November, 1954 (72). (7) Label on the back saying (in Russian) that it had been transferred from wood to canvas in St Petersburg in 1868.

3107 SOLOMON AND THE QUEEN OF SHEBA

31 × 73 (0·788 × 1·854).
Thin in many places, and some repaint.

The figures on the spectator's left, around Solomon, though relatively solid, yet seem for the most part painted on top of the architecture and pavement. The figures on the spectator's right are sketched quickly on top of the background and appear unfinished. It is therefore questionable whether any figures were originally intended and very probable that the main object of the picture was an essay in assembling different types of pseudo-classical building, perhaps influenced by the illustrations of architectural books, such as Serlio's, and possibly done with a view to theatrical scenery.

In any case no. 3107 is an oddity and correspondingly difficult, or impossible, to attribute. In the 1929 catalogue as 'Venetian School, XV–XVI century'. Suggestions have included Bonifazio, Schiavone, Bordon, Christoph Schwarz,[1] 'Jacopo Stella',[2] Paolo Farinati[3] and Lambert Sustris.[4] The latter has received the most support and, among known painters, appears the least improbable.[5] The type of architectural background bears some resemblance to that in two large pictures (*Annunciation* and *Marriage of the Virgin*) in the Accademia at Venice attributed to G. P. Silvio.

PROVENANCE: Bought by Sir A. H. Layard in Madrid in 1872, Ascribed by him to Bonifazio. Layard Bequest, 1916.

REPRODUCTION: *Illustrations, Italian Schools*, 1937, p. 376.

REFERENCES: (1) These four attributions cited by A. Venturi (*L'Arte*, 1912, p. 456). (2) Quoted in a note in the Gallery archives as the opinion of W. Suida and L. Venturi. (3) Recorded in the 1929 catalogue. (4) Opinions recorded in the Gallery archives of R. A. Peltzer, Gamba and Berenson. In the 1957 edition of the latter's *Lists* no. 3107 is included as Sustris. (5) The *Baptism* (Caen), the only signed work of Lambert Sustris, was undergoing prolonged restoration at the time when the present entry was being written and was not available for inspection.

PAOLO VERONESE
born probably 1528, died 1588

His name was Paolo Caliari, called 'Veronese' from his native city of Verona. The date of his birth is deduced from the register of his death on 19th April, 1588, which gives his age as sixty. This agrees with a further register, of 1529, whereby the age of 'Paulo', son of Gabriel di Piero (which was indeed the name of the painter's father) is given as one year. Ridolfi's statement that Veronese was born in 1530 (corrected from 1532 in the original edition) may be due to his assuming that a bust on the painter's grave which gives his age as fifty-eight was made at the time of death rather than two years before it. A further inventory at Verona, of 16th April, 1541, of Gabriel di Piero's family refers to 'Paulo' as already 'depentor' but gives his age as ten years and that of other members of the family also as different from what is stated in the earlier document, which in Paolo's case at least is likely to be the more accurate. A final entry, of 2nd May, 1541, gives 'Paulus' as aged fourteen and as the 'discipulus seu garzonus' of the painter Antonio Badile.[1] No parentage is specified but this also probably refers to Paolo Veronese. Vasari calls him the pupil of Caroto,[2] but Ridolfi,[3] and also Borghini,[4] of 'Antonio Badile suo Zio'. Veronese married Badile's daughter in 1566.[5]

Of Veronese's earliest works, a damaged altarpiece (Verona, Museo, from S. Fermo Maggiore) has been identified with the first work listed by Ridolfi and provisionally dated 1548 or soon after, as being the year when the chapel from which it came was built. A *Christ in the Temple* (Prado) bears marks which can be read as the date—1548. One of the frescoes from the Villa Soranza, near Castelfranco, bears the date 1551. These are vouched for by Vasari (1568) as the work of Veronese and Zelotti.[6] An altarpiece of the *Temptation of S. Anthony* (Caen, from Mantua cathedral) is documented as finished before March, 1553. Veronese had settled in Venice certainly by the beginning of the year

1555 and perhaps as early as 1553 (the carved decoration of the ceiling of the *Sala del Consiglio de' Dieci* in the Doge's Palace, for which Veronese supplied some of the paintings, contains the Donato arms, presumably referring to the Doge, Francesco Donato, who died in that year). In 1555 Veronese completed the first items in the decoration of the church of S. Sebastiano, which occupied him, on and off, for the next fifteen years and which constitutes the most important of his earlier works. Soon afterwards his contribution (1556–7) to the decoration of the ceiling of Sansovino's *Libreria* was adjudged the best of the seven painters' who participated. From then until the end of his life Veronese shared with Tintoretto (Titian being by this time very old) the status of the leading painter in Venice and was his rival for the most important commissions. In 1573 Veronese was arraigned before the Inquisition in connection with the large *Feast* now in the Venice Accademia.

Ridolfi's statement that Veronese 'riueriua Titiano come padre dell'Arte, & apprezzaua molto il viuace ingegno del Tintoretto'[7] seems a fair general comment on his art. In addition, Domenico Brusasorci, Parmigianino, Moretto and Giulio Romano all appear to have contributed something to his formation. Ridolfi says that Veronese visited Rome with Girolamo Grimani, who is known to have gone there in 1555, 1560 and 1566.[8]

Relatively few of Veronese's surviving paintings are dated or are reliably datable, and attempts at precision in reconstructing the chronology have met with formidable obstacles. Though his artistic beginnings are still obscure in some ways, it is clear that as soon as Veronese reached maturity as an artist he evolved not one style but several, corresponding roughly with the nature of the undertaking, whether altarpiece, ceiling, feast subject or mythology. Thereafter he continued to work concurrently in these several styles, within each of which he developed relatively little. Similarities between two of Veronese's pictures, therefore, by no means necessarily imply a similar date of origin, nor dissimilarities a dissimilar one. The *Consecration of St Nicholas*, for example, which is no. 26 of this Gallery and which dates from 1562, has more in common as regards both space composition and design with a very late work in the same category—the *Miracle of S. Pantalone* of 1587 (Venice, church of S. Pantalone)—than it has with a coeval painting in a different one—the *Marriage at Cana* (Louvre: 1562–3).[9] Phenomena to some extent comparable may be observed within the *œuvre* of Tintoretto, though less extreme in degree, while the more highly organized state of the studio which assisted Veronese in his vast output of vast pictures renders the connoisseurship of his work almost as difficult as its chronology.

A number of surviving paintings are signed as being by the 'heirs of Paolo Veronese'.[10] By this was evidently meant Paolo's brother, Benedetto, and his sons, Carlo and Gabriel, whose collaboration is explained in a letter to Giacomo Contarini[11] and who carried on Paolo's studio after his death. In addition, imitations of Veronese, with or without dishonest intent, started at an early date. The Paduan painter,

Alessandro Varotari ('il Padovanino') (1588–1648) is particularly associated with this activity. For Veronese's crucial rôle in eighteenth-century Venetian painting cf. *passim* Michael Levey: *Painting in Eighteenth-Century Venice* (1959).

For notes on Veronese's technical procedure see the introduction to Boschini's *Ricche Minere* (1674), and his *Carta del Navegar Pitoresco* (1660).

REFERENCES: (1) For the relevant documents connected with the date of Veronese's birth cf. Ridolfi/Hadeln, I, pp. 297, note 1, and 349, note 1, and P. Caliari: *Paolo Veronese*, 1888, pp. 9, note 2, 12, notes 1 and 3, 164, note 4. (2) Ed. Milanesi, V, p. 290, and VI, p. 370. (3) Ridolfi/Hadeln, I, 298. (4) *Il Riposo*, 1584, p. 561, where the form 'Baillo' of the surname is used. (5) Caliari, *op. cit.*, p. 70, note 1. (6) Vasari/Milanesi, VI, p. 370. The fragment with the date (Venice, Seminario) also bears a signature, 'paulus f'. (7) Ridolfi/Hadeln, I, p. 349. (8) Ridolfi/Hadeln, I, p. 310, note 3. (9) Among other examples may be cited the *Feast in the House of Levi* (Venice, Accademia) which is the type of great feast-subject and the *Trinity with SS. Peter and Paul* (Vicenza, Museo, from S. Croce) which is a small upright altar. Both of these appear largely autograph, the former broadly but carefully painted, the latter hastily. The differences between them in general appearance are extreme. Both are dated 1573. Two other works of the same year—the *Adoration of the Kings* (no. 268 of this Gallery) and the *Madonna of the Roses* (Venice, Accademia)—would owe some of their differences from the others to studio assistance. Conversely, Veronese's ceiling style, in particular, developed remarkably little over the years—cf. the similarity between the S. Sebastiano ceilings of the mid-'fifties and the 'Venice Enthroned' of the *Sala del Maggior Consiglio* of the Doge's Palace dating from more than twenty years later. (10) Examples are two of the decorations in the *Sala del Maggior Consiglio* of the Doge's Palace (scenes from the career of Pope Alexander III), an *Adoration of the Shepherds* (Venice, Accademia), two *Baptisms* (Venice, Redentore and New York, cathedral of S. John the Divine) (for the latter picture cf. W. Suida in *Art Quarterly*, VIII, 1945, pp. 175–87) an *Annunciation* (Reggio Emilia, Museo Civico) and a *Last Supper* (Naples, S. Martino). (11) Printed in Caliari, *op. cit.*, pp. 177–8.

26 THE CONSECRATION OF S. NICHOLAS

Original canvas *c.* $111\frac{1}{4} \times 67\frac{1}{4}$ (2.825×1.708). Narrow strips have been added at the sides and base. The original canvas is missing at the upper corners in triangles whose sides measure *c.* 10" (0.254) from the corners in both directions.[1] Cleaned 1964.

Always rather summarily painted and now somewhat rubbed and made up, particularly in the sky.

On the death of the Archbishop of Myra in Lycia it was revealed to one of the provincial bishops assembled to elect a successor that a young priest named Nicholas had been divinely chosen and would present himself at the cathedral on the morrow. The prophesy was precisely fulfilled, the newcomer being consecrated Archbishop of Myra on the spot. In 1087 his remains were translated to Bari.

On 30th March, 1562, Paolo Veronese received the balance of payment[2] due to him in respect of work commissioned on 27th December, apparently of the previous year,[3] and specified as consisting of three altarpieces for the altars of SS. Nicholas, Anthony and Jerome in the monastery church of S. Benedetto Po, near Mantua. The three altars were described soon afterwards by Vasari[4] as being the best pictures in the church, and by Borghini, and again, in greater detail, by Giovanni Cadioli (1763).[5]

Three altarpieces answering to this description are still in position at S. Benedetto, all clearly copies after Veronese. As the S. Nicholas altarpiece corresponds exactly with no. 26 and the SS. Anthony and Paul with a painting formerly in the Walter P. Chrysler collection[6] it can be assumed that the pictures existing in the church are copies put up to replace the originals. Confirmation of provenance from S. Benedetto in respect of no. 26, together with a reference to the original of the S. Jerome altarpiece, comes from an entry in the A. Delahante sale catalogue at Phillips, 2nd or 3rd June,[7] 1814, lot 41: 'Veronese: St Jerome . . . together with the Communion of St Jerome, now in the British Institution, to which it was a companion in the church of the Monastery of St Benedict, Mantua.' The latter picture, despite the apparent discrepancy in the subject, was certainly no. 26 (see PROVENANCE below). The former was later accidentally destroyed by fire at Yates' Galleries in 1836.[8]

Though there is no indication of when no. 26 would have left S. Benedetto, and therefore no continuity in its history, the fact that it is stylistically acceptable as an original Veronese, together with the existence of the copy *in situ*, can leave no reasonable doubt concerning the provenance. The altarpiece of the Madonna and SS. Anthony and Paul was removed from Mantua during the Napoleonic occupation,[9] but as both no. 26 and the altarpiece of the Madonna and S. Jerome were apparently imported into England by Delahante early in the nineteenth century they had evidently become separated from it, possibly some time before.[10]

PROVENANCE: Erroneously stated in all relevant editions of the National Gallery catalogue (i.e. from 1830 to 1929) to have come from the church of S. Niccolò dei Frari at Venice. The mistake was due to speculative identification of no. 26 with old references to a Veronese of the same subject at S. Niccolò, now in the Accademia, Venice. The provenance which is almost certainly correct, namely S. Benedetto Po, has been discussed above. Said to have been imported into England by Alexis Delahante and sold by him to the British Institution in 1811.[11] Exh. 1812, 1816 (87), 1821 (106) and 1824 (160), B.I., by the Governors of which presented, 1826. Cleaned Pictures Exhibition, National Gallery, 1947 (41).

VERSION: Old copy at S. Benedetto Po (see above). Some small copies also known.

REPRODUCTION: *Illustrations, Italian Schools*, 1937, p. 380.

REFERENCES: (1) It is probable that this shape was dictated by the original frame. The copy of the Madonna with S. Jerome, still at S. Benedetto, has the upper corners cut and there are indications of the same thing in the published photograph of the Madonna with SS. Anthony and Paul (see text below). (2) The document recording payment published by P. Caliari: *Paolo Veronese*, 1888, pp. 52–3. (3) The reference in the payment document to the original agreement says of it 'sub die vigesima septima m̄s decembris anni proxime decursi milli quingentesimi sexaḡemi primi iuxta stijllum notariorum, non autem secūdum comunem, usum modo loquendi'. The usage then common in Mantua began the year on 25th December and by this system '27th December, 1561' would be 27th December, 1560, N.S. The notary's use of the words 'proxime decursi' however seems as though the passage can only mean that the 'stijllus notariorum' in this case means 1561 when it says 1561. The resulting deduction, that the three altarpieces were all executed within three months, takes some believing. (4) 1568. Ed. Milanesi, VI, pp. 490–1. (5) Borghini—*Il Riposo* 1584, p. 561; Cadioli: *Descrizione . . . di Mantova*, p. 128. (6) For discussion and photographs of this picture cf. Lionello Venturi: *Un' opera inedita di Paolo Veronese* in *Commentari*, January, 1950, pp. 39–40. See also the 1956 catalogue of the Chrysler collection exhibited at Portland, Oregon. The *Inventario degli Oggetti d'Arte d'Italia*, VI, *Provincia di Mantova*, 1935, p. 148, mistakenly refers to the copy as representing the Virgin and Child 'e in basso S. Benedetto e altri santi'. In fact there can be no doubt either from this copy or from the photograph published by Venturi of the presumed original that the saints are Anthony and Paul the Hermit, as Cadioli had specified. (7) Of two copies of the catalogue in the National Gallery library (both printed) one has '2nd June', the other '3rd June'. (8) Whitley: *Art in England, 1821–1837*, 1930, p. 313. In the meantime the picture had figured in the Beckford sale, 26th day, 14th October, 1823, lot 269, and in a final Delahante sale, 29th June, 1830, lot 81. (9) Lionello Venturi, *op. cit.*, quotes from a contemporary inventory the entry relating to this picture. (10) The *Inventario*, already mentioned, attempts to use the superior quality noted by Cadioli à propos no. 26 as opposed to the other two altarpieces to suggest that the originals of the latter had already been removed by this time and replaced by copies. This is possible, but the fact that later on no. 26 appears to accompany the original of the S. Jerome altarpiece, the original of the SS. Anthony and Paul having got separated, would render it improbable. If all three altarpieces had, as it seems, been painted within the space of three months there would have been unevenness in quality in any case. (11) The earliest specific source for the Delahante provenance of no. 26 seems to be Thomas Uwins' evidence in 1850 before the Select Committee on the National Gallery (pp. 7–8 of the printed Minutes of Evidence). He also gave evidence before the 1853 Committee in the same sense. Some more details were given subsequently by Thomas Smith (*Recollections of the British Institution*, 1860, pp. 63–4). Nevertheless, two much earlier references, though vague, are certainly to no. 26, namely Delahante's letter to Penrice of 7th July, 1813 (pp. 28–30 of the printed *Letters . . . to . . . Thomas Penrice*): 'P. Veronese—the companion of the one sold to the Institution' (referring to the Madonna with S. Jerome, discussed above) and a reference, already quoted, in the Delahante sale catalogue of 2nd June, 1814.

268 ADORATION OF THE KINGS

140 × 126 (3·55 × 3·2).[1]

Widespread abrasion due to having been stored off the stretcher in the last century (see PROVENANCE). Nevertheless this is local and not general and the affected areas are nowhere large in extent. In the remaining areas the paint is well preserved.

Cleaned 1957.

Dated (on the lowest step, bottom right): M.D.LXXIII.[2]

From the church of S. Silvestro, Venice, where first noted by Sansovino (1581).[3] Three other large pictures by Veronese are also dated 1573, namely the *Feast in the House of Levi* (Venice, Accademia, from

SS. Giovanni e Paolo) ('20th April'), *Madonna del Rosario* (Venice, Accademia, from S. Pietro Martire, Murano) ('December') and *Trinity with SS. Peter and Paul* (Vicenza, Museo, from S. Croce). It is therefore not surprising that studio assistance has long been recognized in no. 268. Most of the handling lacks the brilliance of Veronese's own touch, but the design is evidently his and the tone remarkably unified and characteristic of him.

The present writer would incline to the view that Veronese, having designed the picture in the smallest detail, left most of the execution to his studio but finally spent some time working over parts of it himself. His own touch is unmistakable in the Madonna and Child and in the foremost king. He probably touched up other areas.[4]

DRAWINGS: 1. Haarlem, Teyler's Stichting, B 65. Reproduced, Hadeln: *Venezianische Zeichnungen der Spätrenaissance*, 1926, pl. 32. The figures at the bottom of the sheet are clearly preparatory studies for the Madonna and kings in no. 268. The king in the (vertical) centre of the sheet, however, is seen not from the side, as are both the first and second kings in no. 268, but from the back, his page stretching his right arm (holding the train) almost to the ground. Both these features occur in another version of the subject by Veronese—at S. Corona, Vicenza. Since the altar for which it was painted was constructed between 1572 and 1581 it is possible that Veronese was working on the two versions simultaneously. Nevertheless the upper sketches on the Haarlem sheet, to which the king in question belongs, appear very amorphous and belonging to a primitive stage in the conception. If, as seems likely, the lower sketches represent a later stage, an alternative and perhaps more probable explanation is that the Vicenza picture was painted after no. 268 and that in it Veronese returned as regards the first king to a motive he had toyed with for no. 268 and then abandoned.[5] 2. Formerly Koenigs collection (ex-Wauters). Reproduced Tietze and Tietze-Conrat: *Drawings of the Venetian Painters . . .*, 1944, pl. CLX, 3. Study for the king in the red robe (the second king).[6]

ENGRAVING: Etching by Carlo Sacchi, dated 9th March, 1649.

VERSIONS: Copy on reduced scale (1·6 × 1·4) Madrid, Prado (489). Another, with variations, S. Pierre des Minimes, Clermont-Ferrand (signed Guillaume Rome [apparently] Brionde, 1637). A partial copy with variations was lot 21, anonymous sale, Sotheby's 23rd February, 1955. Another partial copy was engraved by Sim. Gribelin (1712) as from a painting at Windsor (still in the collection of H.M. The Queen; in 1957 on loan to Somerset House). A copy probably by Francesco Minorello was noted by Mündler in Palazzo Pisani at Este in the mid-nineteenth century.[7] What claimed to be the *modello* is catalogued as in the collection of Giovanni Vianelli, Canon of Chioggia (1790 cat., p. 113). A small eighteenth-century copy, Wagner Museum, Würzburg (F 73). Other small copies known.

PROVENANCE: From, and clearly painted for, S. Silvestro, Venice (see above). The interior of the church was completely remodelled in 1836–43[8] and as a result no. 268, together with other works of art, was taken down in the year 1837 and removed to an adjoining room where it was folded twice, horizontally.[9] When the remodelling of the church was finished it was found that the larger pictures no longer fitted. No. 268 was bought in August, 1855, by the dealer Toffoli from whom purchased in November of the same year.

REPRODUCTION: *Illustrations, Italian Schools*, 1937, p. 380.

REFERENCES: (1) Approximate measurements only. It is difficult to determine exactly where the original painted area stops. (2) G. A. Moschini (*Guida per*

Venezia, 1815, II, part I, 154) misreads the date as 1571. A. Quadri (*Otto Giorni a Venezia*, I, 1821, 273) follows him in this. (3) Also mentioned by seventeenth-and eighteenth-century writers on Venice and Veronese such as Ridolfi, Boschini, Barri and Zanetti. (4) A note in the Gallery archives records Richter as following Morelli in identifying Bassanesque elements in no. 268. While it can be excluded that either Jacopo Bassano or any of his sons can have participated in the execution of the picture (as was suggested in the 1929 catalogue), certain features in it do seem to indicate some *rapprochement* between the styles of Veronese and Jacopo Bassano. (5) For dates of the construction of the S. Corona altar see E. Arslan: *Vicenza, I, Le Chiese*, 1956, p. 67 (with bibliography). (6) Two more drawings vaguely deriving from no. 268 are at Düsseldorf (Budde 104, as Andrea Sacchi) and the Albertina (Stix-Bum 105). See also: R. Cocke: *An Early Drawing by Paolo Veronese*, *Burlington Magazine*, 1971, p. 726, n. 6. Also a drawing at Windsor (Popham & Wilde, 1016). (7) Mündler's note-books in the Gallery archives. (8) G. Lorenzetti: *Venezia e il suo Estuario*, 1956, p. 603. (9) National Gallery Report, 1856, p. 27.

294 THE FAMILY OF DARIUS BEFORE ALEXANDER

93 × 187 (2·362 × 4·749).

Unusually good condition for a picture of its size and age.[1] Slight wearing in the sky and in a few other areas. The horizontal line of the seam of the canvas repainted in parts. *Pentimenti* notably on the left, where the two small horses and their groom are lightly painted on top of the pillars, also in the shoulder and upper arm of the halbadier, extreme left. Cleaned 1958.

Quick preliminary sketching in grey with the point of the brush is visible in many of the architectural features, and in the neighbourhood of the balustrade seen through the arch on the left. Traces of it above the half pillars of the colonnade suggest that Veronese had toyed with the idea of a broken entablature. Later restorers in fact fulfilled this, both right and left of the central monument, at the sacrifice of perspective. These restorations were removed in the 1958 cleaning. The architectural features of the central monument or fountain were modified several times. In its present form there is clearly meant to be an appreciable amount of space separating it both from the colonnade in the background and from the balustrade in the foreground. In the angle of the existing colonnade, however, on the spectator's right, it is still possible to trace mouldings which correspond exactly in type and height with the double entablature of the central monument. Between this area and the latter (behind the figures of Alexander and his *entourage*) there are also traces of a single entablature at the lower of the two levels. Evidently the original background to the figures on this side was the stone wall now seen only in the central monument. Further indications that the whole idea of the colonnade, with its greater splendour, was an afterthought come from the presence, as revealed by infra-red photography, of several large-scale heads in the area of sky to the spectator's right of the central monument and from traces of a large pyramidal shape in the sky and balustrade to the left of it.

Always recognized as a superb original. Any studio assistance there may have been would have been the minimum.

Though called by Ridolfi 'la Costanza di Alessandro' there can be little doubt, despite Veronese's usual embroidery of the story in the interests of decoration, that the episode illustrated is the mistake in identifying Alexander after the Battle of Issus. This story is told by Arrian,[2] Quintus Curtius Rufus,[3] Diodorus Siculus[4] and Valerius Maximus.[5] Their accounts differ slightly in details, the common elements being that when, after the battle, Alexander and his bosom friend, Hephaestion, visited Darius' family, the mother of Darius, misled by Hephaestion's greater height, offered him the obeisance due to the victorious monarch. When her mistake was pointed out Alexander magnanimously alleviated her confusion by saying of Hephaestion that he too was Alexander. In no. 294 the most prominent figure, in crimson, would naturally be taken for Alexander. Whether for this reason he is really Hephaestion would, in the circumstances, be an arguable point.[6]

First mentioned by Ridolfi, 1648,[7] as 'in Casa Pisana'. Boschini soon afterwards (1674) specifies the setting as 'Casa Pisana nelle Procuratie di S. Marco'.[8] D'Argenville (1762)[9] prints a story to the effect that Veronese had painted the picture in one of the Pisani country houses as a return for hospitality received. Cigogna (1834) specifies that the country house in question was the Palazzo Pisani at Este[10] where indeed a copy of no. 294 was seen by Mündler in 1857.[11] It has sometimes been assumed[12] that no. 294 was painted for Francesco Pisani who had commissioned of Paolo Veronese in 1555 the *Transfiguration* for the Duomo at Montagnana. This would provide a *terminus ad quem* for dating no. 294 as Francesco died in 1567.[13] Nevertheless no evidence has been published in favour of this assumption and the indications afforded by the various costumes in no. 294 suggest a later dating, perhaps towards the end of the 'seventies.[14] The fact that the colonnade in no. 294 seems to be the same as one in the much-damaged fresco of *S. Sebastian before Diocletian* (Venice, S. Sebastiano)[15] which may date from the later 1550's, would not in itself be sufficient evidence for assuming a similar date of origin for the two paintings.

Although much uncertainty remains concerning the date and the circumstances of the execution of no. 294 it need not be doubted that it was painted for the Pisani family—presumably the S. Polo branch since it came from their *palazzo*. It may incorporate portraits of them[16]

ENGRAVING: By N. R. Cochin in C. C. Patina: *Pitture Scelte*, 1691.

VERSIONS: Full scale seventeenth-century copy by Francesco Minorello recorded by Mündler in Palazzo Pisani at Este in 1857.[17] Subsequent to the purchase of no. 294 by the National Gallery the former owner decided to have this copy brought to Venice to replace the original in Palazzo Pisani a S. Polo.[18] Small copies at Cassel and in the following sales: Sir Allan Adair, 8th December, 1950 (169), Anonymous, 18th February, 1953 (attr. F. Guardi), and Anonymous, 16th July, 1954. A copy said to be 'at least two hundred years old' was in 1926 in the collection of Francis Carey Lea, Philadephia. Many owners have claimed at different times to possess the 'sketch' for the picture, among them the Président de Brosses (*Lettres Familières*, 1931 ed., I, 206). Tiepolo's fresco (1743) of the same subject at the Villa Cordellina, Montecchio Maggiore, is a distant derivative. Algarotti later (1751) said he had wished to commission

Tiepolo to copy no. 294.[19] Other small copies are known, and a copy drawing published as an original study (Orliac: *Véronèse*, 1939, p. 146).

PROVENANCE: Purchased, 1857, from Conte Vettor Pisani, Venice.

REFERENCES: (**1**) C. A. Levi (*Le Collezioni Veneziane* . . ., 1900, pp. CCXLVII–CCXLVIII) refers to a restoration by Lattanzio Querena, about the year 1800, who was rumoured to have repainted one of the figures. (**2**) *Anabasis of Alexander* II, 12. (**3**) *History of Alexander the Great*, III, 12. (**4**) *History*, XVII, 37. (**5**) *Factorum et Dictorum* . . ., IV, 7. See also J. P. Richter in *Burlington Magazine*, LXII, 1933, pp. 181 ff. (**6**) Goethe seems to have thought so (*Italienische Reise*, 8th October, 1786). The action of the man on the spectator's right, pointing to himself with his right hand, and the laurel decoration on his armour, would make more sense as Alexander than as Hephaestion. The present writer is grateful to Mr. Philipp P. Fehl for drawing his attention to this aspect of the problem. (**7**) Ridolfi/Hadeln, I, pp. 337–8. (**8**) *Le Ricche Minere* . . ., Breve Instruzione, 56 f. Scannelli (*Il Microcosmo della Pittura*, 1657, p. 248) and Martinioni's edition of Sansovino (1663, p. 375) had also mentioned the picture. (**9**) *Abrégé de la Vie des* . . . *Peintres*, 1762, I, 262 ff. (**10**) *Inscrizioni* . . ., IV, 235. (**11**) Mündler's notes in the Gallery archives. (**12**) E.g. in Bruno Brunelli and Adolfo Callegari: *Ville del Brenta e degli Euganei*, 1931, p. 337. (**13**) Pietro Caliari: *Paolo Veronese*, 1888, p. 25, note 1. (**14**) Notes on the costumes by Stella Mary Pearce in the Gallery archives. (**15**) Reproduced Fiocco: *Paolo Veronese*, 1928, p. 58, fig. 42, and Rodolfo Pallucchini: *Veronese* (in series *I Grandi Artisti Italiani*), 3rd ed., 1953, pl. 25. (**16**) It is possible that research among the genealogy of the Pisani family might identify the patron and thereby narrow the dating of the picture. The detailed article by R. Gallo ('I Pisani ed i Palazzi di S. Stefano e di Stra' in *Archivio Veneto*, vol. XXXIV–XXXV, 1944, published 1945) does not cover this. The same writer, however, in a personal (oral) communication, suggests that the patron may have been Vettor Pisani (b. 1528). (**17**) Mündler's notes in the Gallery archives. (**18**) C. A. Levi: *Le Collezioni Veneziane* . . ., 1900, pp. CCXLVI–CCXLVIII. (**19**) Cf. Bottari-Ticozzi, *Raccolta di Lettere*, VII, 1822, 390–1. A Tiepolo 'modèle' of the subject (p. xxvi of the French ed. of the Algarotti catalogue, n.d. but after 1776) was perhaps for the Cordellina fresco. A sketch by Tiepolo after the head of the bearded man on the spectator's left of the central figure in red is in the National Gallery of Victoria, Melbourne.

931   S. MARY MAGDALENE LAYING ASIDE HER JEWELS
$46\frac{1}{4} \times 64\frac{3}{8}$ ($1\cdot175 \times 1\cdot635$).

Much damaged. The canvas plainly shows through in places, notably in the white drapery covering the shoulders of the bearded man with the red cap (his right hand to his chest) towards the spectator's right. The faces of the two men on his left (on the spectator's extreme right) crudely daubed with old repaint. Likewise most of the flutings of the pillar on the spectator's right. Little remains of the Magdalen's left hand; her face also much damaged. The following areas in reasonably good state: Christ's face and clothes, the face of the young man on His left, the face and cloak of the woman on His right, the drapery over the Magdalen's knee, and the cloak of the woman on her left (who draws her attention to Christ).

Pentimento in the head of the man on the spectator's right (with his right hand on his cloak). His beard was originally larger, and covered more of his neck.

Partly cleaned, 1936.

Called by its present title since entering the Gallery. Before that as

'Christ and the Woman in Adultery'. Though emphasis is evidently laid on the unfastened necklace the alternative title might perhaps be correct.

Catalogued as Veronese from the time when it entered the Gallery until the edition of 1920, when it appeared as 'after Veronese'. As such also in the 1929 catalogue. The unusual *pentimento*, already indicated, would more or less exclude the hypothesis that the picture is a copy, irrespective of other considerations. Of these, it may be noted that it shows the influence both of the Parmigianino circle[1] and of the early Tintoretto.[2] In addition, it contains many points of contact with acknowledged works of Veronese.[3] On the strength of the latter the present writer accepts it as a Veronese and on the strength of the former as a very early work, associable with the *Anointing of David* (Vienna)[4] and perhaps also with the original of the *Raising of Lazarus* (copy in the Uffizi)[5] and *Presentation in the Temple* (Dresden).[6]

PROVENANCE: Sir Gregory Page Turner (see below), but not in his sale (Phillips, 19–20th April, 1815). Lent by William Smith, M.P., B.I., 1823 (130) as 'The Woman in Adultery' by Veronese. Anonymous sale (Smith), Christie's, 16th May, 1829 (69) ('P. Veronese—The Woman taken in Adultery . . . formerly in the collection of Sir Gregory P. Turner, Bart. of Blackheath', bought Ellis. In a MS. list of the Wynn Ellis pictures as 'Woman taken in Adultery'.[7] Noted by Waagen in Wynn Ellis' possession (still as 'Woman taken in Adultery').[8] Wynn Ellis Bequest, 1876. Cleaned Pictures Exhibition, National Gallery, 1947, no. 40.

REPRODUCTION: *Illustrations, Italian Schools*, 1937, p. 385.

REFERENCES: (1) Among other points may be noted the figure of the Magdalen, inspired by works such as Parmigianino's etching of the Virgin Annunciate (repr. Copertini: *Il Parmigianino*, II, 1932, pl. CXIV). Also the curved colonnade in the background which was a normal feature of the Parmigianinesque repertory (cf. the background of his *Marriage of S. Catherine* at Bardi or the *Circumcision*, repr. Copertini, *op. cit.*, pl. CXLV, also a drawing by Bedoli in the Albertina, repr. Fröhlich-Bum: *Parmigianino . . .*, 1921, fig. 136). Above all, the girl in profile (in the background, slightly to the spectator's right of the centre) is of a standard Parmigianinesque type. (2) The system of composition used—with excessive crowding together of the figures and plenty of space round them—though exemplified in the Parmigianino circle, seems closer in no. 931 to Tintoretto's practice in pictures such as the *Miracle of S. Mark* of 1548. (3) For example, the system of draperies used in no. 931 is similar to that in the Montagnana *Transfiguration* among others, while the design as a whole may be considered a foretaste of the Louvre *Supper at Emmaus*. Also, the Parmigianinesque profile of the girl, already indicated, recurs in an almost exactly similar form in Veronese's allegory of *Peace* (Rome, Capitoline). (4) Repr. Fiocco: *Paolo Veronese*, 1928, pl. XI. Formerly attributed to Zelotti and to Farinati. The male figure advancing on the spectator's left of the picture is extraordinarily like several in no. 931. (5) Repr. F. H. Meissner: *Veronese* (Künstler-Monographien series), 1897, pl. 43. Stella Mary Pearce, in notes in the Gallery archives, points out the extreme oddity and inconsistency of nearly all the costumes in no. 931, which in her opinion are entirely contrary to Veronese's normal practice. (6) Repr. Fiocco, *op. cit.*, pl. IX. For discussion of the early Veronese see Michael Levey, *Burlington Magazine*, March, 1960. (7) MS. in the Gallery library. (8) Waagen: *Treasures . . .*, II, 1854, p. 293.

1041 THE VISION OF S. HELENA

$77\frac{3}{4} \times 45\frac{1}{2}$ (1·975 × 1·156).

A good deal of wearing and repaint in the sky, in the cross and in the *putti*. The arm of the cross which points in the direction of the saint's head was originally inclined downwards at a steeper angle. The top left arm of it seems to have been painted out. S. Helena's face and most of her dress seem to be in good state. *Pentimento* in her right hand. Cleaned 1960.

The identification of the subject with S. Helena is universal and probably correct, but the iconography is unusual. Earlier Venetian representations of S. Helena, such as Cima's at S. Giovanni in Bragora, Venice or Palma Vecchio's (Milan, Brera) had shown S. Helena standing under the cross. Veronese was apparently pleased with the form of presentation as here since he repeated it—his S. Helena in the Vatican gallery, though quite different in design from no. 1041, likewise shows the saint seated and asleep, a *putto* near her holding a cross. Though S. Helena is said to have received divine guidance in her quest for the cross,[1] the essential requisite concerned the exact place in which to dig in order to find it, and to this end the vision shown both in no. 1041 and in the Vatican picture would be useless. Some of the unsuitability of the presentation to the subject may spring from the fact that the design was not Veronese's own and that it was never intended for S. Helena. The immediate source was evidently an engraving, ascribed to a follower of Marcantonio Raimondi, in which the female figure is shown in exactly the same attitude as in no. 1041, even the line of the window and some of the folds of the dress being the same. The apparition in the sky is different, consisting of one adult angel instead of two *putti*, and with a relatively smaller cross. The presence of an animal (called by Bartsch and Passavant a dog, but conceivably intended for a lamb)[2] lying curled up asleep at the saint's feet shows that the subject of the engraving can hardly be S. Helena. It may be an allegory or just possibly a representation of S. Agnes.

The engraving in its turn derives from Parmigianino. If he ever did a painting or other finished work of art of it, it has long since disappeared, but the essentials are preserved in a drawing by him in the Uffizi.[3] This consists of a female figure who corresponds closely (in reverse) with the one in the engraving and who is shown in a similar relation to the window. The seat she sits on (under which is the animal again) is inscribed 'Danae', which may well be a later addition. On the same sheet are some architectural studies, which may be unconnected, and two flying angels, one of whom is clearly the source (again in reverse) of the angel in the engraving. It is these angels in Parmigianino's drawing which lead back to the earliest stage in the progression, since they are copied, with minor and inessential variations, from two who support the Almighty in Raphael's *Moses and the Burning Bush* (Vatican, ceiling of the Stanza d'Eliodoro). Parmigianino's female figure has the same position relative to the angels as Raphael's Moses and was clearly inspired by that figure —the essentials of the pose are similar, hand (with Raphael both of them) to head and one leg raised—though the connection, being looser, could hardly be demonstrated if the angels in the two works corresponded less closely than they do. Though the function of Parmigianino's drawing is uncertain it is clear that in adapting Raphael's motives he changed the subject, that his own subject (whatever it was) may or may not have been changed in adaptation by the anonymous engraver, and that the latter's subject in its turn was changed by Veronese when he took over the design.

Even without these iconographic peculiarities it is clear that no. 1041 is exceptional in Veronese's *œuvre*, and although for that reason the attribution to him may legitimately be questioned it remains acceptable to the present writer. The fact that Veronese reacted as a young man to the Central Italian influences with which he would have come in contact at Mantua but seems already to have become impervious to them by the time of his visit to Rome might favour a relatively early dating for no. 1041, as being based on a Central Italian idea. Its colouring and technique, too, have much in common with the Vicenza *Madonna and Child with S. Peter and a female Saint* which is undated but certainly fairly early.

It has been claimed that no. 1041 is identical with a picture of the same subject described by Ridolfi as having been in Casa Contarini at Padua.[4] It is true that Ridolfi says that the cross in that picture was supported by two small angels—which would apply to no. 1041 and not to the Vatican picture, which has only one. Nevertheless no positive evidence to support the identification has come to light, nor any certain identification of the remaining pictures described by Ridolfi in the same context.

ENGRAVING: See above. Also by the elder Vorsterman, Antwerp.

VERSIONS: A derivative in fresco (with the cross arranged differently and supported by three *putti*) was formerly in the Villa Guarnieri at Romanziol (reproduced by A. Moschetti: *I Danni ai Monumenti e alle Opere d'Arte delle Venezie nella Guerra Mondiale*, 1932, fig. 334, where attributed to Veronese). An old copy at Goodwood is labelled 'Passignano'. Among references to pictures by Veronese of this subject are 'St Helena, held to be Paulo Verrona's' in the posthumous inventory of Rubens' collection[5] and two 'inventions de la Croix par Sainte Hélène' recorded by the Président de Brosses at Rome in the 'Palais des Ursins' and the 'Palais Santa Croce'.[6] A 'St Helena with the Cross from P. Veronese' by C. Jarvis was lot 65 in the latter's sale, 11th March, 1739–40.

PROVENANCE: Stated (in the catalogue of the W. Comyns sale, 1815) to have been the property of the 1st Duke of Marlborough, who died in 1722. Included in the sale (6th June, 1803, lot 60) of pictures formerly the property of the Duke's son-in-law, Francis, 2nd Earl of Godolphin, to whom it had presumably passed by inheritance.[7] Bought on this occasion by 'Mr. Comyns'.[8] No. 73 in the latter's sale, 6th May, 1815, where bought Ponsonby.[9] No. 109, anonymous sale (said to be 'Dorrien'),[10] 2nd March, 1816, where bought Lord Yarmouth[11] (later 3rd Marquess of Hertford) by whom exh. B.I., 1819 (30). No. 118 in the sale of the 3rd Marquess' possessions at St Dunstan's, Regent's Park, London, 9th July, 1855, where bought Emery.[12] No. 74 in the Hon. P. Ashburnham sale, 19th May, 1860, where bought 'Monro',[13] No. 144 in the H. A. J. Munro of Novar sale, 1st June, 1878, where purchased.[14]

REPRODUCTION: *Illustrations, Italian Schools*, 1937, p. 384.

REFERENCES: (1) See *Les Petits Bollandistes*, 3rd May (*Invention de la Sainte Croix*). S. Helena is said to have been about eighty years old at the time. (2) Bartsch: *Le Peintre Graveur*, XIV, no. 460: 'cette belle estampe . . . est attribuée par quelques uns à Marc-Antoine. Le dessein paroit être du Parmesan; mais il y a des auteurs qui le croient de Raphaël'. Passavant (*Le Peintre-Graveur*, VI, 1864, p. 89, no. 122) as by a pupil of Marcantonio. Another state, or other version, omits the angel and has been claimed as the origin of a Beham engraving of the Madonna (Fritz Burger: *Die Deutsche Malerei* (Handbuch für Kunstwissenschaft), I, p. 103). A drawing supposed to be a study for the engraving was bought by H. D. Gronau at the Heseltine sale, 28th May, 1935 (124). There is an engraving inscribed 'Micha. Ange. bonarotanus. Florentinus' which uses the pose; which also occurs in a painting in a retable of S. Ursula (Post: *Spanish Painting*, vol. XII, part 1, fig. 36). (3) 1971 E. There is a photograph of this drawing in the W. Gernsheim series, no. 2971. Passavant (*loc. cit.*) had already drawn attention to this drawing. (4) Ridolfi/Hadeln, I, p. 318, note 5. (5) *Catalogue of the Works of Art in the Possession of . . . Rubens*, ed. Dawson Turner, 1839, p. 4, item 22. (6) *Lettres Familières*, 1931 ed., II, pp. 447 and 468. (7) Recorded in Lord Godolphin's possession by Vertue (*Note-books*, Walpole Society, vol. III, 1933–4, p. 133). (8) Marked copy of the sale catalogue of which photostats in the Gallery library. Seen in the possession of 'Commyn's the picture cleaner in Pall Mall' by Coleridge in 1804 (*Unpublished Letters of S. T. Coleridge*, ed. E. L. Griggs, 1932, p. 317). (9) Redford, II, p. 260. (10) Graves: *Art Sales*, III, 1921, p. 302. (11) Redford, *loc. cit.* (12) Marked copy of the sale catalogue in the Wallace collection. (13) Marked copy of the sale catalogue in the Gallery library. The catalogue says that the picture was 'purchased at the sale of the Duke of Leeds' pictures by the late Marquis of Hertford'. The 'Duke of Leeds' sale' was presumably the one of 6th June, 1803, of pictures formerly belonging to the 2nd Earl of Godolphin. The current but unspecified owner was indeed presumably his great-grandson, the 6th Duke of Leeds, but Lord Hertford did not buy the picture until later. (14) In former editions of the National Gallery catalogue stated to be from a chapel at Venice. No evidence is now available for this statement. Also stated in the earlier editions that it was 'engraved by Bonasoni and others'. The present writer has been unable to confirm the existence of a Bonasone engraving.

1318 ALLEGORY OF LOVE, I

$74\frac{3}{4} \times 74\frac{3}{4}$ (1·899 × 1·899).

Thinly painted and consequently rather worn, particularly in the sky. A line of repaint along the horizontal seam of the canvas in the centre.

A number of *pentimenti*, notably in the woman's shoulders and in the head and shoulders of the man on the spectator's right.

Centre, a naked woman, seen from the back, exchanges a note with a man (left) in a doublet. Right, a bearded man, in the undergarment of a suit of armour, holds up the woman's right arm. A wingless child has his right arm round the woman's left leg. A winged putto at a clavichord, left.

The letter slipped by the woman into the right hand of the man on the spectator's left is inscribed: *Che*(?)/*uno*(?) *possede*.[1] Entitled 'Unfaithfulness' in earlier editions of the National Gallery catalogue.

Cleaned 1946.

For commentary and provenance see under no. 1326.

REFERENCE: (1) There is some doubt about some of these letters.

1324 ALLEGORY OF LOVE, II

$73\frac{1}{2} \times 74\frac{1}{4}$ ($1\cdot866 \times 1\cdot885$).[1]

Very good general state: the best preserved of the four.

Some retouching along the central horizontal seam. Many *pentimenti*, notably in the back of the left hand of the woman on the spectator's left of the two, in the left arm of the more prominent woman (next her), in the fingers of the man's left hand, in his chest and left leg, and in the *putto's* right arm, shoulders and right leg.

A man, seen from the back and dressed only in a loin cloth, lies on a piece of fallen marble cornice. A winged putto stands on his chest and chastises him with his bow. To the left, two women. The one on the extreme left, fully dressed, holds an ermine in her right hand and with her left clasps the right hand of the other woman, whose bosom is *décolleté*. In the background, a mutilated statue of a satyr and, on the right, part of a statue of Pan.

Entitled 'Scorn' in earlier editions of the National Gallery catalogue. Cleaned 1950.

For commentary and provenance see under no. 1326.

REFERENCE: (1) The binding covers some of the painted area as the turn-over is part of the top canvas.

1325 ALLEGORY OF LOVE, III

$73\frac{1}{4} \times 76\frac{1}{2}$ ($1\cdot861 \times 1\cdot943$).

The sky a good deal rubbed and retouched; much wearing down the right hand edge. Some wearing in the woman's body and in the capital of the pilaster. Otherwise generally good condition.

Pentimento round the outline of the head of the principal male figure and in his outstretched arm; also in the outline of his green sash as it crosses his left shoulder.

Right, a naked woman sleeps on a bed, a nearly empty beaker of wine on the ledge in front of it. Farther left, a man in armour raises his left arm in astonishment, while led on by a winged boy whose right hand is on the man's sword and who brandishes in his left an arrow in the direction of the woman. Another man just glimpsed, extreme left. In the vault above, a painted relief with the Continence of Scipio.[1]

Entitled 'Respect' in earlier editions of the National Gallery catalogue. Cleaned 1951.

For commentary and provenance see under no. 1326.

REFERENCE: (1) See A. Pigler: *Barockthemen* II, (1956) pp. 404–9. In the engravings by Desplaces and by Cathelin and Couché (see ENGRAVINGS below) the scene is clearer though not necessarily accurate. These show the left hand of the seated figure resting on a shield or mirror and (in Desplaces' engraving) another figure behind.

1326 ALLEGORY OF LOVE, IV

$73\frac{3}{4} \times 73\frac{1}{2}$ ($1\cdot874 \times 1\cdot867$).

General condition good. Some wearing in the sky and in the sphere on the left.

Obvious *pentimento* in the left hand and arm of the naked seated female figure.

Top left, a naked female, with a cornucopia under her right leg, holds out a garland of leaves over the head of a young woman who holds an olive branch in her left hand which is also held by the man behind her with his right. Right foreground, a dog; and a wingless child holding a gold chain.

Entitled 'Happy Union' in earlier editions of the National Gallery catalogue. Cleaned 1946.

The titles hitherto applied to nos. 1318, 1324–6 date only from the period of their entry into the Orléans collection. The general message of the allegories is not very obscure, but there is no authoritative key to it, and the attempts at detailed interpretation which have been published are partly subjective, as well as mutually incompatible.[1]

Nos. 1318, 1324, 1325 and 1326 are identifiable in the inventory made after 15th February, 1637, of the collection at Prague of the Emperor Rudolph II, who died in 1612. They do not figure in the 1621 inventory. Though there would remain nevertheless a possibility that they had been commissioned by Rudolph (with whose taste their erotic subject matter would conform) the point cannot be settled. Borghini (1584) specifies two pictures painted by Veronese for Rudolph,[2] and the 1621 inventory lists six as in his collection, of which at least two seem not to have been painted for him.[3] The existence, in Van Dyck's Italian sketchbook, of sketches apparently after nos. 1318 and 1325 (see DRAWINGS below) is not conclusive evidence that the paintings were in Italy during Van Dyck's travels there (1621–7) as a possibility would remain that the sketches were made from copies, or even from *modelli*.

First suggested in the *Recueil d'Estampes* (1742)[4] that the four pictures were executed for a ceiling. This is plausible enough, as Veronese used this kind of foreshortening in ceiling paintings such as those at S. Sebastiano, Venice and in the Doge's Palace.

Though there is no definite evidence for dating the series the costumes and hair styles shown would accord best with Veronese's practice in the mid-1570's.[5]

Though a varying degree of studio assistance is apparent in all four pictures the homogeneity of the design and of the handling and tone when seen from a distance—which, if they were in fact intended as ceiling decorations, would be the normal viewing range—point to close supervision by a controlling personality, obviously Veronese himself. For this reason glaring disparities in quality are rare, though an example are the two *putti* at the lower left corner of no. 1318, of which the one on the spectator's right is painted in the same delicate technique as the woman's back in the same picture, while the *putto* next him, on the left of all, is more coarsely modelled and different in tone. Passages of outstandingly brilliant execution, such as the woman's back in no. 1318, the more prominent of the two women in no. 1324 or the sheet on which the woman reclines in no. 1325, as well as the beaker in the foreground of the same picture, are characteristic of the highest quality of Veronese's own work. But even in the areas which would have been painted by an assistant some finishing touches by the master himself are not to be excluded.[6]

DRAWINGS: Oxford, Ashmolean Museum. Sketch copy (wash) by Delacroix of part of no. 1318 (in reverse). Van Dyck's Italian sketch-book (British Museum from Chatsworth) contains sketches apparently after nos. 1318 and 1325 on both sides of folio 36 (Cust's pagination).

ENGRAVINGS: In vol. II of the *Recueil d'Estampes* ('Crozat Cabinet') (1742) no. 1318 by Simon Vallée, no. 1324 by Benoist Audran, nos. 1325 and 1326 by Louis Desplaces. In vol. II of the *Galerie du Palais-Royal* (1808) no. 1318 by J. A. Pierron, no. 1324 by J. Couché, no. 1325 by Cathelin and Couché and no. 1326 by Beljambe and Cathelin.

PROVENANCE: Nos. 1318, 1324, 1325 and 1326 figure as nos. 453, 451, 455 (probably) and 449 in the inventory of the Rudolph II collection at Prague taken after 15th February, 1637,[7] as nos. 99, 98, 96 and 97 in the 1652 inventory of Queen Christina of Sweden's collection, as nos. 3, 1, 2 and 4 in the 1689 inventory and as nos, 73, 71, 72 and 74 in the 1721 inventory. Rudolph II's collection was looted by the Swedes at the Sack of Prague in 1648 and taken to Sweden. Many of the pictures, including nos. 1318, 1324-6, were taken by Queen Christina to Italy after her abdication in 1654, and after her death were sold (in 1721) to the Duc d'Orléans. In the 1727 catalogue (by Du Bois de Saint Gelais) of the Orléans pictures at the Palais Royal, Paris (pp. 377-80), in which building they adorned the 'Salon Octogone' (Palais Royal catalogue, II, 1808). The Italian pictures in the Orléans collection were sold in 1792 to the Belgian banker, Walkuers, who sold them to Laborde de Méréville, who fled with them to England,[8] where they were bought by Jeremiah Harman, who made them over to a syndicate consisting of the Duke of Bridgewater and Lords Carlisle and Gower.[9] A sale was arranged by Bryan who exhibited the pictures in 1798. Nos. 1318, 1324-6 were apparently lots 169, 181, 243 and 245 of the Lyceum portion of the sale (26th December, 1798), all marked 'not sold' in the copy of the sale catalogue in the Gallery library. Probably lots 26, 34, 42 and (?) 57 in the sale (by Peter Coxe, Burrell and Foster) of 'the remaining part of the Orléans collection of Italian Paintings' at Bryan's Gallery, Pall Mall, London, 14th February, 1800. In the possession of the Earl of Darnley by 1818, when lent by him to the B.I. (nos. 23, 75, 99 and 145). Exh. Manchester, 1857 (nos. 274, 273, 271 and 272 in the provisional catalogue, nos. 287, 288, 285 and 286 in the definitive catalogue), and R.A., 1877 (nos. 103, 115, 126 and 95)—on both occasions lent by the Earl of Darnley, from whom acquired: no. 1318 purchased 1890, nos. 1324 and 1326 purchased 1891. No. 1325 was presented by Lord Darnley, 1891. Cleaned Pictures Exhibition, National Gallery, 1947 (42, 43, 45 and 44). No. 1325 exh. Stockholm (Queen Christina) 1966 (I/194).

REPRODUCTIONS: *Illustrations, Italian Schools*, 1937, pp. 382-3.

REFERENCES: (1) E.g. Edgar Wind: *Pagan Mysteries in the Renaissance* (1967), appendix 8, pp. 272-5. Also A. Braham, *Burlington Magazine*, 1970, pp. 205 ff. (2) *Riposo*, p. 563. (3) An inventory made by Jacopo Strada in connection with his purchases for Albert V, duke of Bavaria, lists two Veronese's, quoting inscriptions on them ('omnia vanitas' and 'honor et virtus post mortem floret') which identify them with pictures later in the Emperor's collection and now in the Frick collection (see J. Stockbauer: *Die Kunstbestrebungen am Bayerischen Hofe, Quellenschriften für Kunstgeschichte*, VIII, 1874, p. 43). It may be noted that the 1808 Palais Royal catalogue contains a fantastic claim (vol. II, 'XIVeme

Tableau de Paul Véronese') that nos. 1318, 1324–6, are part of the decorations at Maser as described by Ridolfi. These are, in fact, frescoes. **(4)** 'Crozat Cabinet', II, p. 67. **(5)** Notes by Stella Mary Pearce in the Gallery archives. **(6)** The 1929 catalogue commits itself to the statement 'nos. 1318 and 1326 wholly by the master's hand', while the catalogue of the 1947 Exhibition of Cleaned Pictures lists nos. 1318 and 1324 as Veronese and 1325 and 1326 as 'studio of Veronese'. Though the present writer's point of view is much nearer to the latter than to the former, he regards the whole series as homogeneous to the extent of seeing both autograph and studio execution in all four, only the ratio varying. It must be stressed that the organization of Veronese's work-shop was clearly very elaborate and that we have no detailed knowledge of it. **(7)** For this date see p. XV of the 1938 catalogue of the Kunsthistorisches Museum, Vienna. The relevant inventories are printed in Olof Granberg: *La Galerië de Tableaux de la Reine Christine de Suède*, 1897. **(8)** See preface to vol. 1 of the *Galerie du Palais-Royal* (1808), also Charles Blanc: *Le Trésor de la Curiosité*, 1858, vol. II, pp. 148–59, and W. Buchanan: *Memoirs*, I (1824), pp. 9–220. **(9)** Passavant: *Tour of a German Artist in England*, II (1836), p. 179.

After VERONESE

97   THE RAPE OF EUROPA

Canvas on panel, $23\frac{3}{8} \times 27\frac{1}{2}$ (0·594 × 0·699).

A certain amount of repaint is visible through the present heavily discoloured varnish. Basic condition nevertheless probably quite good.

In all references from the seventeenth century onwards and including editions of the National Gallery catalogue prior to that of 1911 stated to be by Veronese and regarded as the sketch or *modello* for the large picture in the Doge's Palace, Venice. The coarseness of the execution, however, leaves no doubt that it is in fact a copy, differing from the original in various ways—it is in reverse, there are three, instead of four, attendant maidens, a *putto* holds the head of the white bull behind which is an extra bull and there are two, instead of three, flying *putti*. Minor variations include the presence of the drapery in the foreground, the lack of a dog and a different arrangement of the trees and distant figures.

These arbitrary variations and the relatively small size of no. 97 would leave a possibility that it may have been painted with fraudulent intent to 'manufacture' a preliminary sketch for the big picture.[1]

ENGRAVING: By R. De Launay (in reverse), 'XVIIeme tableau de Paul Calliari' in vol. II (1808) of 'Galerie du Palais-Royal'.

PROVENANCE: Probably no. 657 ('Europa auff einem Weissen oxen') in the inventory (after 15th February, 1637)[2] of the Emperor Rudolph II's collection. No. 12 in the 1689 Queen Christina inventory. No. 5 in the 1721 inventory. Page 369 in 1727 catalogue (by Du Bois de Saint Gelais) of the Orléans pictures in the Palais Royal. Probably lot 47 in the Orléans sale, by Bryan, 88 Pall Mall, London, 26th December, 1798,[3] where bought 'Mr. Willet'.[4] Lot 107, John Willett sale, by Peter Coxe, London, 2nd June, 1813, where bought Holwell Carr,[5] by whom exh., B.I., 1818 (91). The Rev. W. Holwell Carr Bequest, 1831. Exh. Stockholm (Queen Christina) 1966 (I/198).

REPRODUCTION: Negative in the possession of the Gallery.

REFERENCES: (1) Various other versions of the Doge's Palace picture exist, notably large-scale variants in the Capitoline and at Dresden. No. 97 is, however, even farther from these than from the Venice picture. (2) For this date see p. XV of the 1938 catalogue of the Kunsthistorisches Museum, Vienna. The relevant inventories are printed in Olof Granberg: *La Galerie de Tableaux de la Reine Christine de Suède*, 1897. (3) For details of the vicissitudes of the Orléans collection see the entries for nos. 270 (Titian) of 1326 (Veronese). (4) Marked copy of the sale catalogue in the Gallery library. (5) Mark (in pencil but probably contemporary) in copy of the sale catalogue in the Gallery library.

FRANCESCO and BERNARDINO ZAGANELLI
both active from 1499; Francesco died 1531-2, Bernardino 1509 or soon after[1]

On the joint works signed by both and dated 1499, 1504 and 1509 they state that they are brothers and from Cotignola. As Francesco's name precedes Bernardino's he was probably the elder. The sequence of the joint works, and Francesco's when alone after Bernardino's death, seems essentially a unity, the main stylistic sources being, apparently, Palmezzano, Costa and Francia.

REFERENCE: (1) Cf. for biographical data Corrado Ricci in *Rassegna d'Arte*, April, 1904, pp. 49 ff. Also A. Paolucci: *L'Ultimo tempo di Francesco Zaganelli* in *Paragone*, 193, 1966, pp. 39–73, and Renato Roli in *Arte Antica e Moderna*, 1965, pp. 223 ff.

BERNARDINO ZAGANELLI

1092   S. SEBASTIAN

Pancl, arched top. A band of dark paint *c.* $\frac{3}{4}''$ wide surrounds the painted area. The latter measure $47 \times 17\frac{3}{8}$ ($1 \cdot 194 \times 0 \cdot 442$).
Fair condition despite many small old retouchings.
Signed on the *cartellino*:

$$B\ \Lambda\Lambda RD^I N\hat{V}$$
$$COT_I G\overset{\circ}{L}A$$
$$\cdot P \cdot$$

Believed to be the only existing work signed by Bernardino Zaganelli alone (i.e. without his brother). If, as seems likely, no. 1092 is identical with a panel from an altarpiece formerly in the Carmine at Pavia (see PROVENANCE below) it would have been executed around 1505–6, according to documents referred to by Ffoulkes and Maiocchi.[1] From another document it emerges that the S. Sebastian was the centre panel of the lower row.[2]

PROVENANCE: Probably part of the altarpiece commissioned by the foreign students of the University of Pavia for their chapel in the Carmine.[1] The S.

Sebastian panel in that work is specifically mentioned by Malaspina (1819),[3] Lanzi (1822)[4] and Laderchi (1856),[5] all of whom add that it is signed. What was certainly no. 1092 was mentioned by Crowe and Cavalcaselle (1871) as belonging at that time to Frizzoni at Bellagio and as 'perhaps' from the Carmine altar.[6] Purchased by Sir William Boxall from Baslini of Milan, and by the National Gallery from F. Sacchi in London, 1880.[7]

REPRODUCTION: *Illustrations, Italian Schools*, 1937, p. 390.

REFERENCES: (1) *Vincenzo Foppa*, 1909, p. 192. (2) Crowe and Cavalcaselle: *History of Painting in North Italy*, vol. II, 1912, p. 313, no. 1. (3) *Guida di Pavia*, p. 62. (4) *Storia Pittorica . . .*, vol. 5, p. 28. (5) *La Pittura Ferrarese . . .*, p. 59. (6) Crowe and Cavalcaselle, *op. cit.*, first edition (1871), I, p. 601. The authors' reserve on the question of the provenance of no. 1092 may be due to vagueness, since they add that the Carmine altar was 'dismembered at the close of the eighteenth century', which was not the case. It may also be observed that a footnote in Milanesi's Vasari (vol. V, 1880, p. 256, n. 2) speaks of the Carmine altar as though it were still *in situ*. (7) National Gallery Report for 1880.

FRANCESCO ZAGANELLI

3892 ALTARPIECE. THE BAPTISM OF CHRIST

Panel, painted area *c.* 79 × 75 (2·007 × 1·905).

Somewhat worn and retouched in places; also damaged to some extent by flaking and cracking and by worm, but in general fairly well preserved for a picture of its size and age.

Signed on the *cartellino*, bottom left:

·xħs·   ·1514·
frãcischus choti
gnolensis·   ·F·

The scroll wound round the left arm of the cherub above Christ reads:

·HIC· / ·EST · FILIVS· / MEVS · DIL^{E}CTVS·

The Baptist's scroll is inscribed:

·ECCE· / AGNVS· / ·DEI·

For commentary and PROVENANCE see under 3892A.

3892A THE DEAD CHRIST WITH ANGELS

Lunette, painted area *c.* 39⅝ (0·981) (centre) × 79¾ (2·025).

The lunette to no. 3892.

Some obvious blemishes on Christ's flesh and along a horizontal crack in the panel some two-thirds of the way up. Otherwise quite good condition.

The cherub in the air above Christ in no. 3892 is similar to one in Francesco Zaganelli's *Immaculate Conception and Saints* (Forlì, Pinacoteca) who holds a scroll, and is likewise wingless. It will be noted both that the angels in no. 3892A supporting the dead Christ and the pair on the left of no. 3892 are also wingless.[1] The two female figures on the left of no. 3892 were identified in the 1929 catalogue as the Virigin and S. Anne. The latter might alternatively be S. Elizabeth. Either of them, and the Virgin also, would be highly unusual in a Baptism.

PROVENANCE: From the Laderchi chapel at S. Domenico, Faenza; removed at the end of the eighteenth century when the chapel was being restored and taken to the Laderchi house, from which sold. In Rome, 1847.[2] Probably bought soon afterwards by the Erskine family of Linlathen, Forfarshire, from whom it was— eventually acquired by the Gallery, since Waagen (1854) says of the Erskine collection 'good Italian pictures purchased in Rome by the advice of M. Colombo'.[3] Mentioned as in the Erskine collection in the 1912 edition of Crowe and Cavalcaselle.[4] D. C. E. Erskine sale, Sotheby's 5th December, 1922 (92 and 93) (bought in).[5] Purchased from the executors of D. Erskine, 1924.

ENGRAVING: Arundel Society portfolio, 1910.

REPRODUCTION: *Illustrations, Italian Schools*, 1937, p. 391.

REFERENCES: (1) Even the Angel Gabriel in Francesco Zaganelli's *Annunciation* (formerly Berlin) appears to be wingless. (2) All this information from Conte Camillo Laderchi: *La Pittura Ferrarese*, 1856, p. 59. The altarpiece had been referred to by Lanzi (*Storia Pittorica della Italia*, V, 1822, p. 27). Laderchi mentions the signature but misreads the date as 1515. (3) Waagen III, p. 315. (4) Crowe and Cavalcaselle, *North Italy*, II, p. 310, n. 3. (5) The 1929 catalogue incorrectly gives the year of the sale as 1924 and does not give the month or day at all.

FEDERICO ZUCCARI
1504(?)–1609

The (considerably) younger brother of Taddeo. From the Urbino area (S. Angelo in Vado) but brought up partly in Rome, where he was active for much of his maturity though working at different times at Venice, Florence and elsewhere in Italy. He also visited Holland and England (drawing in the British Museum of Queen Elizabeth I dated from London, May, 1575) and Spain (1585–8). He was largely responsible for the foundation, in 1593, of the Accademia di S. Luca in Rome.

Pasticheur of FEDERICO ZUCCARI

1241 THE CONVERSION OF THE MAGDALEN

Panel,[1] $11\frac{3}{4} \times 23$ (0·298 × 0·584).

In general in good condition. Some small damages and retouching in horizontal lines—particularly in the architecture seen through the central arch—caused by cracking in the panel.

The legendary, extra-biblical subject is rare but is comparable with that of no. 931 (Veronese) of this Gallery.

In the 1929 catalogue and earlier editions as Pedro Campaña. A similar picture in the Borghese Gallery (see VERSIONS below) has been variously attributed to Federico Zuccari (as early as 1682), Carletto

Caliari and painters in the neighbourhood of Lavinia Fontana and Marten de Vos. In 1955 Paola Della Pergola who had already drawn attention to the general similarity of the Borghese version to the *Marriage at Cana* and other works by Luca Longhi published Philip Pouncey's discovery[2] that the figures in the foreground on the right and the kneeling man on the left derive directly from a design of the same subject as no. 1241 by Federico Zuccari. This was a fresco in the Grimani chapel of S. Francesco della Vigna at Venice which Vasari describes[3] and which was datable to the early 1560's. It has perished, but its pendant, the *Resurrection of Lazarus*, survives and facilitates the identification of the design of the lost *Magdalen* in an engraving and drawings.[4] The fact that no. 1241 is therefore a pastiche of a Federico Zuccari fresco complicates the problem of the identity of the painter rather than simplifies it. As regards the Ravenna *Marriage at Cana*, already mentioned, which is signed by Luca Longhi and his son, Francesco, and dated 1581, the first difficulty is in comparing a large fresco with a small panel. Nevertheless, both no. 1241 and the Borghese version share one peculiarity with the Ravenna fresco; all three incorporate a number of heads which are clearly portraits and which are so arranged that the eyes look out at the spectator. But even here there are complications. The costumes and hair styles of the 'portrait figures' in no. 1241 accord best with a dating around the 1570's while the corresponding figures, or at least the men, in the Borghese version, who are not the same persons, seem rather later—perhaps in the 1580's or '90's. Furthermore, the clothes of the little boy talking to the little girl, top right in no. 1241, seem somewhat later still. They would be normal in the opening years of the seventeenth century, whereas the corresponding child in the Borghese picture is dressed differently and in an earlier style. Finally, the hair style of the bearded man in no. 1241 (looking at the spectator from above the outstretched right arm of the woman gesticulating to the Magdalen) would be usual in a much earlier period—the 1520's.[5] Whatever may be the explanation of these highly abnormal features of the costume they at least suggest that Luca Longhi, who died in 1580, is unlikely as executant of either no. 1241 or the Borghese picture. His son and imitator, Francesco, who lived until *c.* 1620, might be a possibility, though a hypothetical one.

A further point of obscurity is how the name Campaña first became attached to no. 1241. It seems to have been published first by Lanzi[6] who says that the picture which is now no. 1241 was painted by Campaña for the 'Patriarca Grimani' who had brought him to Venice. The latter part of the statement does not accord with the scanty biographical information available on Campaña from more reliable sources. But the fact that no. 1241 is based on a fresco in a chapel belonging to the Grimani family may well have been realized by Lanzi, and this might explain part of his statement, though it would not account for the introduction of a painter at once so rare and so improbable in the present context.

VERSION: Rome, Villa Borghese (see above). W. Rearick also draws attention to a comparable picture of Christ Preaching in the Temple, Museo dell' Opera del Duomo, Milan, attributed to Tintoretto.[7]

PROVENANCE: No. 29 ('Compana') in the 1822 catalogue of the Philip John Miles collection, Leigh Court,[8] most of which had been formed by Richard Hart Davis. Buchanan (1824)[9] says that the Hart Davis picture (i.e. no. 1241) had been in the Vitturi collection at Venice and that this collection had been bought c. 1774–6 by Thomas Moore Slade who sent it to England. Lanzi (1822 edition)[10] adds that the Slade picture had been painted by 'Pier Campanna' for the 'Patriarca Grimani' who had bequeathed it to a friend. Sir Philip Miles sale, Christie's, 28th June, 1884 (8) where bought Richter,[11] from whom purchased, 1888.

REPRODUCTION: *Illustrations, Continental Schools*, 1937, p. 42.

REFERENCES: (1) Pear wood, according to a letter in the Gallery archives from B. J. Rendle of the Forest Products Research Laboratory. (2) Paola Della Pergola in *Bollettino d'Arte*, anno XXXIX, 1954, pp. 135 ff. and anno XL (1955), pp. 83–4. (3) Vasari/Milanesi VI, 586–7. (4) Paola Della Pergola *op. cit.* Cf. also W. R. Rearick: *Battista Franco and the Grimani Chapel* in *Saggi e Memorie di Storia dell'Arte*, 2, 1959, pp. 122–37. (5) Notes by Stella Mary Pearce in the Gallery archives. She points out further that some of the non-portrait figures are in biblical or oriental fancy dress which probably derives from the Zuccari fresco though this may have been modified to some extent in the engraving. (6) *Storia Pittorica della Italia*, 1822 ed., vol. II, pp. 83–4: 'Pier Campanna . . . a Venezia fu condotto dal Patriarca Grimani, a cui dipinse varj ritratti e la rinomata Maddalena condotta da S. Marta al tempio a udire la predica di G. C. Questro quadro, dal Patriarca lasciato ad un suo amico, dopo molt' anni è passato al Sig. Slade in Inghilterra'. (7) Rearick, *op. cit.*, p. 135, n. 116. (8) With line engraving. The catalogue entry says that the painter has introduced 'the Portraits of Solyman the Magnificent, Francis the First, Charles the Fifth, Cardinal Bembo, Titian, Giorgione, Bellini, and Henry the Eighth; Anna Boleyn and Queen Elizabeth when a little girl'. (9) *Memoirs of Painting*, I, 1824, pp. 320–34. (10) *Loc. cit.* (11) Marked copy in the Gallery library of the sale catalogue.

INDEX OF PICTURES WHOSE ATTRIBUTIONS HAVE BEEN CHANGED FROM THE EDITIONS OF 1959 AND 1962

Former attribution	No. of picture	Present attribution
BRESCIAN SCHOOL	930	Ascribed to BERNARDINO DA ASOLA
BRESCIAN SCHOOL	2907	Ascribed to BERNARDINO DA ASOLA
Ascribed to CARIANI	41	Ascribed to BERNARDINO DA ASOLA
FRENCH SCHOOL (?), seventeenth century	5448	ITALIAN SCHOOL (?), sixteenth–seventeenth century
Ascribed to NICCOLÒ DELL'ABATE	5283	NICCOLÒ DELL' ABATE
Ascribed to POZZOSERRATO	5466	VENETIAN SCHOOL
Ascribed to POZZOSERRATO	5467	VENETIAN SCHOOL
After RAPHAEL	27	RAPHAEL
TITIAN	34	STUDIO OF TITIAN
VENETIAN SCHOOL	1377	Ascribed to BERNARDINO DA ASOLA

SUBJECT INDEX

A. Saints

S. Agatha:
Sebastiano del Piombo, no. 24

S. Alessandro:
Romanino, no. 297

S. Andrew:
Gaudenzio Ferrari, no. 3925

S. Anne:
Bronzino, no. 5280 (?)

S. Anthony Abbot
Giorgione, no. 6307

S. Anthony of Padua:
Garofalo, no. 671
Lotto, no. 2281
Moretto, no. 3094

S. Augustine:
Garofalo, no. 81

S. Bernardino:
Moretto, no. 625

S. Bonaventure:
Pordenone, no. 4038

S. Catherine of Alexandria:
Bonifazio, no. 1202
Style of Bonifazio, no. 3536
Garofalo, no. 81
Garofalo, no. 3118
Moretto, no. 625
Moretto, no. 1165
Raphael, no. 168
Titian, no. 635

S. Catherine of Siena:
Brescianino, no. 4028
Ferrarese School, no. 3102
Sodoma, no. 1144

S. Clare:
Garofalo, no. 671
Moretto, no. 625

S. Demetrius:
L'Ortolano, no. 669

S. Dominic:
Ferrarese School, no. 3102

S. Elizabeth:
Bronzino, no. 5280 (?)
Garofalo, no. 170
Mazzolino, no. 82
Andrea del Sarto, no. 17
Style of Bonifazio, no. 3536

S. Francis:
Garofalo, no. 170 (?)
Garofalo, no. 671
Mazzolino, no. 82
Moretto, no. 625

S. Gaudioso:
Romanino, no. 297

S. George:
Ascribed to Palma Vecchio, no. 3079
Giorgione, no. 6307
Tintoretto, no. 16

S. Helena:
Veronese, no. 1041

S. Hippolytus:
Moretto, no. 1165

S. Hugh:
North Italian School, no. 692

S. James the Greater:
Bonifazio, no. 1202
Girolamo da Treviso, no. 623

S. Jerome: Bonifazio, no. 1202
Catena, no. 694
Lotto, no. 2281
Moretto, no. 625
Ascribed to Moroni, no. 2093
Parmigianino, no. 33
Raphael, no. 3943
Romanino, no. 297
Savoldo, no. 3092
Sodoma, no. 3947

S. John the Baptist:
Baroccio, no. 29
Fra Bartolommeo, no. 3914
Ascribed to Fra Bartolommeo, no. 1694
Bonifazio, no. 1202
Style of Bonifazio, no. 3536
Ascribed to Catena, no. 3540
Brescianino, no. 4028
Bronzino, no. 5280
Costa, no. 629
Costa and (?) Maineri, no. 1119
Garofalo, no. 170
Mazzolino, no. 82
Ascribed to Michelangelo, no. 809
After drawing by Michelangelo, no. 1227

B. Old Testament Scenes and Characters

Moses, Story of:
  Follower of Costa, nos. 3103, 3104
Sheba, Queen of:
  (?) Venetian School, sixteenth
    century, no. 3107

Solomon:
  (?) Venetian School, sixteenth
    century, no. 3107
Tower of Babel:
  Leandro Bassano, no. 60

C. NEW TESTAMENT SCENES AND CHARACTERS
(N.B. Madonna and Child groups not included, nor either
separately except in episodes from the Gospels)

Adoration of the Magi:
  Dosso Dossi, no. 3924
  Giorgione, no. 1160
  Ascribed to Girolamo da Treviso,
    no. 218
  North Italian School, no. 640
  Peruzzi, no. 167
  Veronese, no. 268
Adoration of the Shepherds:
  Follower of the Bassano, no. 1858
  Ascribed to Bernardino da Asola,
    no. 1377
Agony in the Garden:
  After Correggio, no. 76
  Garofalo, no. 642
Annunciation:
  Gaudenzio Ferrari, no. 3068
Baptism:
  Francesco Zaganelli, no. 3892
Calvary, Procession to:
  Ridolfo Ghirlandaio, no. 1143
  Raphael, no. 2919
  Ascribed to Sodoma, no. 1337
    (Christ alone)
Christ disputing with the doctors:
  Mazzolino, no. 1495
Christ taking leave of His Mother:
  Correggio, no. 4255
Christ washing His Disciples' Feet:
  Tintoretto, no. 1130
Crucifixion:
  Raphael, no. 3943
Dives and Lazarus:
  After Bonifazio, no. 3106
Ecce Homo:
  Correggio, no. 15
  After Correggio, no. 96

Good Samaritan:
  Jacopo Bassano, no. 277
Nativity:
  Fra Bartolommeo, no. 3914
  Costa, no. 3105
  Mazzolino, no. 3114
  Follower of Sodoma, no. 4647
'Noli Me Tangere':
  Titian, no. 270
Pietà, Entombment, Dead Christ:
  Dosso Dossi, no. 4032
  Michelangelo, no. 790
  Palmezzano, no. 596
  Ascribed to G. C. Procaccini, no.
    219
  Francesco Zaganelli, no. 3892A
Purification of the Temple:
  After drawing by Michelangelo, no.
    1194
  Jacopo Bassano, no. 228
Raising of Lazarus:
  Sebastiano del Piombo, no. 1
Resurrection:
  Gaudenzio Ferrari, no. 1465
Salome:
  Sebastiano del Piombo, no. 2493
Tribute Money:
  Titian, no. 224
Visitation:
  Italian School (?), no. 5448
Walk to Emmaus:
  Altobello Melone, no. 753
  Ascribed to Lelio Orsi, no. 1466
Woman taken in Adultery:
  Mazzolino, no. 641

D. PORTRAITS

Albani:
  Cariani, no. 2494
Alberto Pio:
  Ascribed to Bernardino Loschi, no.
    3940 (?)

Ariosto, Lodovico (?):
  Palma Vecchio, no. 636
Averoldi:
  Moretto, no. 3095 (?)

Bracci, Monsignor Mario:
Ascribed to Girolamo da Carpi, no.
20

Fiera, Battista:
Costa, no. 2083

Fracastoro, Girolamo (?):
After Titian, no. 3949

Giuliano, Giovanni:
Lotto, no. 1105

Gritti, Andrea:
Catena, no. 5751

Julius II, Pope:
Raphael, no. 27

Lupi, Conte:
Moroni, no. 3129 (?)

Martinengo, Ludovico:
Bartolommeo Veneto, no. 287

Medici, Cosimo I de':
Studio of Bronzino, no. 704

Medici, Cardinal Ippolito de':
Ascribed to Girolamo da Carpi, no.
20

Medici, Piero de':
Bronzino, no. 1323

Morosini, Vincenzo:
Tintoretto, no. 4004

Nani, Stefano:
Licinio, no. 1309

Salvagno, Leonardo (?):
Moroni, no. 3124

Savelli, Cardinal:
Pulzone, no. 1048 (?)

Savonarola, Fra Girolamo:
Florentine School (?), no. 1301

Terzi, Canon Ludovico di:
Moroni, no. 1024

Titian (?):
Titian, no. 1944

Torre, Giovanni Agostino della, and
Niccolò della:
Lotto, no. 699

Vendramin Family:
Titian, no. 4452

Volta, Giovanni della and family (?):
Lotto, no. 1047

E. PROFANE SUBJECTS (excluding portraits)

Actaeon:
Titian, no. 6420

Adonis:
Studio of Titian, no. 34
Follower of Titian, no. 1123

Alexander the Great:
Veronese, no. 294

Ariadne:
Titian, no. 35

Aristaeus:
Niccolò dell' Abate, no. 5283

Bacchanal:
Dosso Dossi, no. 5279

Bacchus:
Titian, no. 35

Boreas, sons of:
Venetian School, no. 5467

Cartagena, Attack on:
Italian School, no. 643 (a)

Chloe:
Bordon, no. 637

Cimon:
Venetian School, sixteenth century,
no. 4037

Corybantes:
Studio of Giulio Romano, no. 624

Cupid:
Bronzino, no. 651
Correggio, no. 10
Garofalo, no. 1362
Studio of Titian, no. 34
Follower of Titian, no. 1123

Curetes:
Studio of Giulio Romano, no. 624

Curtius, Marcus:
Ascribed to Bacchiacca, no. 1304

Daphnis:
Bordon, no. 637

Darius, family of:
Veronese, no. 294

Diana (?):
Titian, no. 6420

Efigenia:
Venetian School, sixteenth century,
no. 4037

Europa:
After Veronese, no. 97

Flora (?):
Palma Vecchio, no. 3939

Ganymede:
Ascribed to Damiano Mazza, no. 32

Harpies:
Venetian School, no. 5467

INDEX OF COLLECTIONS

(N.B. This index does not include all dealers or dealers' agents
or unconfirmed provenance)

NUMERICAL INDEX

LIST OF PAINTINGS ACQUIRED
SINCE 1974

JACOPO BASSANO
active about 1535; died 1592

6490   THE WAY TO CALVARY

Canvas, 57 × 52½ (145 × 133)
Purchased by private treaty from the Trustees of the Earl of
  Bradford with the aid of a contribution from the National
  Heritage Memorial Fund, 1984.

PARMIGIANINO
1503–1540

6427   THE MYSTIC MARRIAGE OF SAINT CATHERINE

Wood, 29$\frac{3}{16}$ × 22½ (74·2 × 57·2)
Purchased, 1974.

6441   PORTRAIT OF A MAN

Wood, 35¼ × 25⅛ (89·5 × 63·8)
Purchased, 1977.

PONTORMO
1494–1557

6451   JOSEPH SOLD TO POTIPHER

Wood, 24 × 20$\frac{5}{16}$ (61 × 51·6)
Purchased with the aid of the N.A.C.F. (Eugene Cremetti Fund),
  1979.

6452   PHAROAH WITH HIS BUTLER AND BAKER

Wood, 24 × 20⅜ (61 × 51·7)
Purchased with the aid of the N.A.C.F. (Eugene Cremetti Fund),
  1979.

6453   JOSEPH'S BROTHERS BEG FOR HELP

Wood, 14$\frac{5}{16}$ × 65⅛ (36·3 × 142·5)
Purchased with the aid of the N.A.C.F. (Eugene Cremetti Fund),
  1979.

RAPHAEL
1483–1520

6480 SAINT JOHN THE BAPTIST PREACHING

Wood, $9 \times 20\frac{7}{8}$ (23×53)
Purchased by private treaty, 1983.